JENSEN'S SURVEY
OF THE
NEW TESTAMENT

JENSEN'S SURVEY OF THE NEW TESTAMENT

Search and Discover

by

IRVING L. JENSEN

MOODY PRESS

CHICAGO

Grateful acknowledgment is made to The Lockman Foundation for permission to quote from *The New American Standard Bible,* © 1960, 1962, 1963, 1968, 1971, 1972, 1973, 1975, and 1977.

The use of selected references from various versions of the Bible in this publication does not necessarily imply publisher endorsement of the versions in their entirety.

Ground plan of Herod's Temple (p. 68) reproduced from *The New Bible Dictionary,* ed. J. D. Douglas (Inter-Varsity Press, London, 1962), by permission of the Universities and Colleges Christian Fellowship.

Library of Congress Cataloging in Publication Data
Jensen, Irving Lester.
    Jensen's Survey of the New Testament.

    Bibliography: p. 520.
    Includes index.
    1. Bible. N.T.—Text-books. I. Title. II. Title:
Survey of the New Testament.
BS2535.2.J46   225.6'1   80-28064
ISBN: 0-8024-4308-7

25 27 30 28 26

Printed in the United States of America

To Charlotte and our children — Donna, Karen, and Bob

ACKNOWLEDGMENTS

I have been very gratified over the reception that the companion volume, *Jensen's Survey of the Old Testament*, has had since its publication. It is my prayer that God will use this New Testament survey guide to inspire many of His children in the experiences of New Testament survey and give them priceless joys of discovering for themselves the blessed truths of His book.

Many thanks go to my wife, children, friends, students, and the Moody Press staff for all the inspiration, encouragement, and help that they shared in the production of this and other volumes. Those are the unexposed, supportive ministries always cherished and remembered by me.

Contents

Part 1

THE EVENT
The Life of Christ

Part 2

THE SEQUEL
The Church, Christ's Body

Part 3

THE MESSAGE
Christ the Savior, Sanctifier,
and Coming King

Charts

Charts in Appendix

Other Charts and Diagrams

Maps

Preface

The New Testament is the "new birthplace" of a Christian, because there is where divine power transformed his life. Spiritually, he feels at home there. There is a hunger in his heart to read and study the New Testament, because God gave that written Word not only for the believer's salvation but also for his edification — food for growing and maturing and serving. And he should want to learn the *whole* New Testament, not just selected parts of it. A sound starting point for such a study project is *survey*, which is viewing the New Testament as a full unit, section by section, and book by book. That is the approach of this study guide.

The main purpose for this New Testament survey guide is to involve the reader *personally* in a firsthand survey of the Bible text. All too often, students of New Testament survey read the sound instruction of others regarding the content of the Bible books but fail to spend time reading the Bible text for themselves. This book has been written to start the reader onto paths of study in each New Testament book, to *search and discover* for himself the great themes of each book. Throughout the chapters much help (such as outlines) is supplied on what the Bible books teach, but those suggestions are intended to confirm and amplify the reader's personal study and to encourage a pursuit into the more difficult or elusive New Testament portions. The reader is always encouraged to do his own study before dwelling long on help from others.

One specific aim of this book is to guide the student into seeing *how* the message of each New Testament book is organized structurally, because for a full understanding of the Bible text one needs to know not only *what* God said, but *how* He said it. This aim partly accounts for the appearance of so many charts throughout the book, because charts show structural organization clearly and vividly.

Students of Bible survey often overlook the application stage of their study, because in survey they do not analyze the Bible text in detail. But survey study should not rule out practical application. One of this book's purposes is to lead the reader into a time of personal reflection as he considers practical spiritual applications of the Bible book that he has just surveyed. At that stage the slogan should be *reflect and apply*. That is how all Bible study should conclude.

This survey guide also includes other important helps for study, as seen in the following descriptions of the parts of each chapter.

I. PREPARATION FOR STUDY

The opening paragraphs of each chapter prepare the reader for his survey of the Bible book assigned to that chapter. This is a crucial part of one's study, because here is where motivation and momentum, as well as direction, are gained.

II. BACKGROUND

Originally, every book of the Bible was written in a particular local setting. This section of the chapter discusses that background, much information of which is not always supplied by the text of the Bible book itself. Some important items are intentionally repeated from time to time to help impress them on the reader's mind.

III. SURVEY

The actual survey process is the main part of each chapter and should occupy most of the student's time. The basic Bible version used throughout these studies is the *New American Standard Bible*. Chapter 3 is devoted entirely to a discussion of the survey method of study. Here the reader will learn what procedures are recommended for surveying a book of the New Testament.

IV. PROMINENT SUBJECTS

Immediately following each chapter's Survey section is a discussion of prominent subjects of the Bible book. Technical subjects or problems of the Bible text are not included, because these are not part of survey study. The comments that are shared are intended to round out the student's survey and to give suggestions for further study at a later time.

V. KEY WORDS AND VERSES

Usually certain words and verses can be identified with the particular theme of each Bible book. Suggestions are made here, but the reader is urged to look for more.

VI. Applications

The questions asked here will help the student apply the teachings of the New Testament book to his own life and circumstances.

VII. Review Questions

An effective learning procedure is to review what has been studied by answering review questions. The questions given here are about the solid portions of the survey project and include the background of the New Testament book. They are not questions on the Prominent Subjects section.

VIII. Further Study

Suggestions for further study are intended for those who want to pursue various themes of the book in greater detail. This study is not part of the survey process.

IX. Outline

A brief outline of the New Testament book is included here, as a reference point for the survey project.

X. Selected Reading

Three kinds of books are cited here: general introduction, commentary, and other related sources. For the most part, the lists are of books in print, written from a conservative, evangelical viewpoint. (Exceptions are not identified as such.)

XI. Survey Chart

Near the end of each chapter is a complete survey chart for the New Testament book.

Note: After the student has completed his survey of the New Testament, he is ready to begin the analytical stage of study, which moves segment by segment through each New Testament book. Helps for analysis may be found in my Bible Self-Study Guides (Moody Press) and *The Layman's Bible Study Notebook* (Harvest House).

Introduction to the New Testament

Survey Method of Study

These three introductory chapters prepare the reader for his survey studies of the books of the New Testament. Chapter 1 views the fascinating story of how these writings came *from God to us*. Chapter 2 describes the setting of the New Testament: historical, religious, political, and physical. Then in Chapter 3 the reader is introduced to the survey method of study, in order to give him tools for his personal study of the New Testament books.

1

History of the New Testament Writings

The last words God ever wrote to man are recorded on the pages of the New Testament. The book is that momentous and precious. The purpose of this introductory chapter is to describe what the New Testament is and how it came to be, so that the reader's appreciation of its value will be enhanced. The principle applied here is, "He uses best what he values most."

I. GOD'S FINAL REVELATION

In the Old Testament God had given a partial revelation of Himself, having spoken through prophets and angels, but the full and final revelation came by His Son Jesus. "In the past God spoke to our forefathers through the prophets at many times and in various ways, but in these last days he has spoken to us by his Son" (Heb. 1:1-2a, NIV). Observe how the two eras are compared in the accompanying diagram.

After Jesus had provided purification for sins, "He sat down at the right hand of the Majesty on high," because His atoning death was finished (Heb. 1:3; cf. John 19:30). The revelation was that final. The written Word of the New Testament records the story and revelation of this Son of God.

To say that the New Testament is God's final revelation of Himself is not to say that the Old Testament is obsolete. The New Testament was never intended to replace the Old. Rather, it is the sequel to the Old Testament's origins, heir of its promises, fruit of its seed, the peak of its mountain. The ministry of Christ would be an enigma without the Old Testament. For example, it is the Old

15

Testament that explains Jesus' words, "I was sent only to the lost sheep of the house of Israel" (Matt. 15:24). The best preparation for a study of the New Testament is to become acquainted with the foundations of the Old.

REVELATION THEN AND NOW

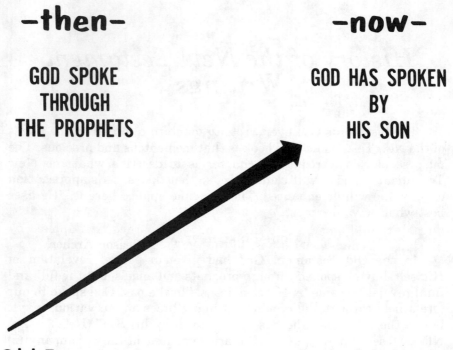

-then-   **-now-**

GOD SPOKE   GOD HAS SPOKEN
THROUGH   BY
THE PROPHETS   HIS SON

Old Testament   New Testament

As God's final revelation, the New Testament records the fulfillments of Old Testament prophecy, the last words and works of Christ on earth, the birth and growth of Christ's church, prophecies of the last times, and clear statements and interpretations of the Christian faith. Every earnest Christian wants to spend much time studying these final words of God.

II. THE NEW TESTAMENT FROM GOD TO US

There was already a "Bible" when the first New Testament books were being written. Usually that book of God was referred to as the

Scripture(s) (e.g., Matt. 21:42). We now call it the Old Testament; it was the only Bible of Jesus and the apostles. Then, a couple of decades after Christ's ascension, the Holy Spirit began to move and inspire chosen saints to write letters and historical accounts that would eventually be brought together in a volume to be known as the New Testament.

Today when we hold a copy of the English New Testament in our hands, it is fair to ask how accurately it represents the original autographs. Involved in the anwer is the history of the New Testament — from God (first century A.D.) to us (twentieth century). It is a fascinating story of miracles, involving stages of transmission, canonization, and translation. The starting point of such a history is divine revelation.

A. REVELATION

Revelation is God's communication of truth to man, without which man cannot know God. The word *revelation (apocalypsis)* means "uncovering," or "drawing away of a veil."

Before there was any Scripture, God revealed Himself to man through such media as conscience, nature (*general* revelation), and direct conversation with people (*special* revelation).[1] But there was need of a form of revelation that would be permanent, explicit, and retentive of a large volume of revealed truth. For that, God chose the written form of human language to be read, learned, and applied by all the succeeding generations. In the words of Gleason Archer,

> If there be a God, and if He is concerned for our salvation, this is the only way (apart from direct revelation from God to each individual of each successive generation) He could reliably impart this knowledge to us. It must be through a reliable written record such as the Bible purports to be.[2]

Recall the powerful words of Hebrews 1:1-3 (NIV) studied earlier: *God. . .has spoken to us by his Son.* The Son is the Living Word; the Bible is the written Word of the Son.

B. INSPIRATION

All the books of the Bible — New Testament as well as Old Testament — came into being by the Holy Spirit's direct ministry of inspiration. Two crucial questions at this point are: How did the

---

1. Read Romans 1:18-21 for an example of general revelation, and Genesis 3:8-19 for an example of special revelation.
2. Gleason L. Archer, *A Survey of Old Testament Introduction*, p. 15. Read this same source for a good discussion of the inadequacies of oral tradition as a sole transmitter of God's special revelation to man.

human authors know what God wanted them to write? and, Were their writings without error? We cannot explain the supernatural process of inspiration that brought about the original writings of the Bible. Paul refers to the process as *God-breathing*. (Read 2 Timothy 3:16, where the phrase "inspired by God" translates the Greek *theopneustia*, which literally means "God-breathed.") Peter says the Bible authors were undergirded, or carried along, by the Holy Spirit. ("Men spoke from God as they were carried along by the Holy Spirit," 2 Pet. 1:21, NIV.) These verses, along with many, others, assure us that when the Bible authors wrote, all their words expressed infallibly and without error the truths that God wanted to convey to mankind. In the original autographs, all the words were infallible in truth, and final in authority. Such accuracy applies to every part of the originals — to matters of history and science as well as to spiritual truths. If the Bible student does not believe this scriptural infallibility and inerrancy, his study of the biblical text will be haunted by confusing and destructive doubts.

As noted earlier, when the New Testament authors were writing their manuscripts, the only complete body of Scripture was the Old Testament.[3] The question may be asked, Were the New Testament writers aware that they were composing works that would eventually become part of the total Scriptures of God? This is a valid question, because not everything the authors wrote became part of the New Testament.[4] We do not know to what extent the writers sensed or discerned the God-breathing or undergirding ministry of the Spirit in their minds and hearts as they wrote. They were surely conscious that they were recording God's truth (see 1 Cor. 14:37), just as they knew they were preaching His glad tidings publicly (see Gal. 1:11,12). Regardless of the nature of their own personal perception that they were authoring *uniquely inspired* manuscripts at the time they wrote, the truth remains unshakeable, based on the Bible's own statements of its origin, that all the Scriptures were inspired, written by chosen authors who were undergirded as they wrote. Just what New Testament books were among those inspired Scriptures is the subject of our later study of canonization.

---

3. Individual New Testament books were in the process of being recognized as Scripture after their public appearances, but the timing varied from book to book. (This will be studied later under Canonization.) For example, when Paul wrote 1 Timothy (A.D. 62), the gospel according to Luke (A.D. 60) was recognized as part of Scripture. Read 1 Timothy 5:18, where Paul quotes from Deuteronomy 24:15 and Luke 10:7 under the same heading "Scripture."

4. For example, in 1 Corinthians 5:9 Paul refers to an earlier letter written to the Corinthian church. That letter was not intended by God to be a part of inspired Scripture.

C. THE ORIGINAL AUTOGRAPHS

The twenty-seven books of the New Testament were written over a period of about fifty years (c. A.D. 45-95), by eight or nine authors. All but a few words and phrases were written in Koine Greek, which was the marketplace vernacular of the first-century Mediterranean world.[5] It was written in that universal language to make it initially accessible to world readership.

The writing material of most of the autographs was paperlike papyrus. (Some autographs might have been written on animal skins, such as parchment or vellum.) Sheets of papyrus, usually about ten inches long, were attached together to make a long, rolled-up scroll, easy for reading.[6] (The paged codex, or book, did not supplement the roll until the second or third century A.D.) The Bible text was written in vertical columns with pen and ink, with no space between words, sentences, or paragraphs, and with no punctuation marks. Verse and chapter divisions were not made until centuries later.

Most of the New Testament books were letters (epistles) written to individuals (e.g., 1 Tim. 1:1-2), churches (e.g., 1 Thess. 1:1), or groups of believers (e.g., 1 Pet. 1:1-2). Luke wrote a gospel and a historical book to share with a friend Theophilus (Acts 1:1), and it is very likely that the other three gospels were written to share with individuals or churches.[7]

The present order (canon) of books in our New Testament is not the chronological order in which the books were written. Chart 1 shows a suggested chronological order of writing for the New Testament books.[8] Study the chart carefully and try to visualize the growing zeal of the saints during the last decades of the first century as the inspired writings began to circulate from city to city. Answer the following questions on the basis of the information supplied by the chart.

1. What was the first book to be written? the last? How many years transpired between the two?

2. Note when each of the gospels appeared.[9] One of the reasons the gospels were not the first books to appear was that much of the

5. At about ten places in the originals the authors recorded Aramaic words or phrases and usually gave the translation in Greek. See Mark 15:34.
6. One sheet was used for short books, such as Jude.
7. These background facts will be studied in more detail as each individual book is surveyed.
8. The dates when New Testament books were written are not part of the Bible text. Most dates, however, have been accurately determined, usually by associating the author with historical references in various books. The dates of each of the books will be studied in more detail in the survey section of this book.
9. There are differing views concerning the dates of Matthew and Mark. Some Bible students hold that Mark was the first gospel written.

A CHRONOLOGICAL ORDER OF THE WRITING OF THE NEW TESTAMENT BOOKS

CHART 1

BOOK	AUTHOR		PLACE WRITTEN	DATE A.D.	PERIODS		
					PERSONNEL	APOSTOLIC LITERATURE	CHURCHES
JAMES	James		Jerusalem	45			
GALATIANS		JOURNEY EPISTLES		48		BEGINNINGS	FOUNDING
MARK?							
1 THESS			} Corinth	52	FIRST PAULINE PERIOD		
2 THESS	Paul		}				
1 COR			Ephesus	55			
2 COR			Macedonia				
ROMANS			Corinth	56			
MATTHEW	Matthew		Jerusalem?	58	FIRST HISTORICAL RECORDS		
LUKE	Luke		Rome				
ACTS	"			61			
COLOSSIANS		PRISON EPISTLES			CENTRAL PAULINE PERIOD		
EPHESIANS	Paul		Rome	61			
PHILEMON							
PHILIPPIANS							ESTABLISHING
1 TIMOTHY		PASTORAL EPISTLES	Macedonia	62	PAUL'S LEGACY	CENTRAL	
TITUS	Paul		Corinth?	—			
2 TIMOTHY			Rome	67			
HEBREWS	?						
JUDE	Jude						
1 PETER	Peter				PETER'S LEGACY		
2 PETER				68?			
MARK	Mark						
JOHN			Ephesus?	85	JOHN'S LEGACY	CLOSING	CONTINUING
1 JOHN							
2 JOHN	John						
3 JOHN							
REVELATION			Patmos	96			

There are various opinions as to the order of writing. For example, some place Galatians later and Mark earlier.

content, such as the spoken words of Jesus, was already being shared with the people in oral form, having been memorized precisely.

3. Note the three periods of apostolic literature. Approximately how long was each period? There was a fifteen-year interim of "silent years" between the central and closing periods. The destruction of Jerusalem took place in A.D. 70. Is any connection suggested between that event and the hiatus of writing?

4. The books' ministries to the local churches are identified by what three words (for the three main periods)? What is involved in each of the ministries?

5. Note the three Pauline periods. Scan the lists of books written during those times.

6. The gospel according to Mark is identified as Peter's legacy, because the apostle Peter was a key reporter to Mark of the narrative of Jesus' life.

7. Observe the different kinds of writings authored by John (gospel, epistle, vision).

8. The epistle of James stresses good works in the life of the believer. Why would such a message be the first one to be sent out in written form to the people of God?

9. In what sense was the book of Revelation logically the *last* written communication to the church?

D. TRANSMISSION

Transmission is the process by which the biblical manuscripts have been copied and recopied down through the ages, by hand or machine. God caused or allowed each of the original New Testament autographs to disappear from the scene, but not before copies were already in the hands of His people.[10]

Copies of the New Testament books were handwritten by scribes until the middle of the fifteenth century A.D. when Gutenberg invented movable type for the printing press. Scribal errors have been made in the copies,[11] but God has preserved the text from doctrinal error to this present time. Thousands of Greek and non-Greek manuscripts of all or part of the New Testament text, supportive of the text's purity, exist today. Benjamin B. Warfield says that the purity is unrivalled:

> Such has been the care with which the New Testament has been copied,
> — a care which has doubtless grown out of true reverence for its holy

---

10. One of God's reasons for not preserving the original autographs might have been man's proneness to worship material objects. Also, even if a genuine biblical autograph existed today, how could one *prove* that it was an original autograph?
11. Even Bibles printed in the "modern" twentieth century have printers' errors!

works, — such has been the providence of God in preserving for His Church in each and every age a competently exact text of the Scriptures, that ... the New Testament [is] unrivalled among ancient writings in the purity of its text as actually transmitted and kept in use. . . .[12]

So when you are holding a copy of the New Testament in your hands, you may rest assured that it is a wholly dependable translation, which represents the original, inspired autographs of the first century. As divine author, God wrote an infallible book (inspiration); as divine protector, He has preserved the text from doctrinal error (transmission).

E. CANONIZATION

Canonization is the identification of a writing as being part of the Scripture. It was not enough that God inspired the *writing* of each book of the Bible. He also gave to His people, in a collective sense,[13] the spiritual perception to *recognize* in each of these books genuine marks of divine inspiration and authority.[14] With the Holy Spirit's guidance, they knew what spurious writings to reject, as well as what genuine writings to accept. It was a long human process over a few hundred years, many of the details of which are veiled in obscurity. But it is clear that God's supernatural hand, working through humans, brought His inspired writings into the canon and excluded other writings.

1. *Order of the New Testament books.* The canon of the New Testament is the list of all the New Testament books that God inspired. Although the last New Testament book was written by A.D. 100, for the next couple centuries questions persisted concerning whether some books, such as 3 John, were inspired. By the end of the fourth century A.D. the canon was solidified, being composed of twenty-seven books.

Five of the New Testament books are historical in content; twenty-one are epistles (letters); and one is apocalyptic (revelation of visions). The order in which they appear in our Bible is this:

History: Matthew, Mark, Luke, John, Acts

Epistles: Romans, 1 and 2 Corinthians, Galatians, Ephe-

---

12. Benjamin B. Warfield, *An Introduction to the Textual Criticism of the New Testament*, p. 12.

13. The canon was not determined by any one person or council, or even at any point of time. The canon kept growing over a period of years, with God's people in *that* collective sense recognizing the signs of inspiration in the books that eventually would be grouped as one covenant (testament) of twenty-seven books.

14. Authority is the basis for canonicity. Since God sealed each book with authority, it is He who originally canonized each book.

CHART 2

CANONICAL ORDER
OF N.T. BOOKS

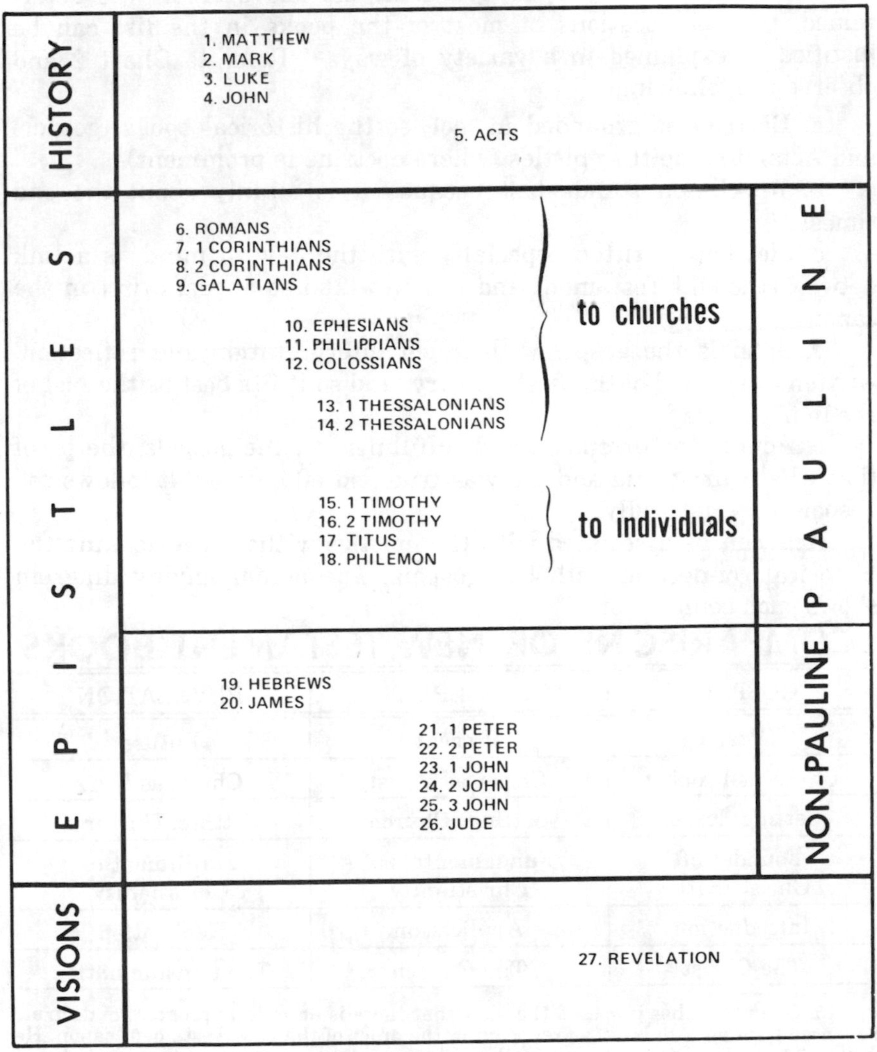

HISTORY	1. MATTHEW 2. MARK 3. LUKE 4. JOHN 5. ACTS	

E P I S T L E S	6. ROMANS
	7. 1 CORINTHIANS
	8. 2 CORINTHIANS
	9. GALATIANS
	
	   10. EPHESIANS
	   11. PHILIPPIANS
	   12. COLOSSIANS
	
	      13. 1 THESSALONIANS
	      14. 2 THESSALONIANS
	
	   15. 1 TIMOTHY
	   16. 2 TIMOTHY
	   17. TITUS
	   18. PHILEMON
	
	to churches
	
	to individuals
		P A U L I N E

	19. HEBREWS
	20. JAMES
	      21. 1 PETER
	      22. 2 PETER
	      23. 1 JOHN
	      24. 2 JOHN
	      25. 3 JOHN
	      26. JUDE
		NON-PAULINE

VISIONS	27. REVELATION	

> sians, Philippians, Colossians, 1 and 2 Thessalo-
> nians, 1 and 2 Timothy, Titus, Philemon, He-
> brews, James, 1 and 2 Peter, 1, 2, and 3 John,
> Jude

Visions: Revelation

We do not know how or by whom the above order was determined, but the locations of most of the books in the list can be
justified or explained in a variety of ways.[15] Refer to Chart 2 and
observe the following:

a. Doctrine is grounded in fact, so the historical books (gospels
and Acts) precede the epistles (where doctrine is prominent).

b. Revelation stands last because it is mainly about the end
times.

c. Matthew, written especially with the Jew in mind, is a link
between the Old Testament and the New and so appears first in the
canon.

d. John is the gospel with much interpretation and reflection,
written at the end of the first century, and so it fits best as the last of
the four gospels.

e. Acts is the extension and fulfillment of the gospels, the proof
that what Christ said and did was true and efficacious. It follows the
gospels very naturally.

Acts can be associated with the epistles without overlooking the
historical connection with the gospels. The accompanying diagram
shows such comparisons.[16]

COMPARISONS OF NEW TESTAMENT BOOKS

GOSPELS	ACTS & EPISTLES	REVELATION
Past	Present	Future
Christ as Prophet	Christ as Priest	Christ as King
Setting: Israel	Setting: Church	Setting: Universe
Founder of Christianity	Fundamentals of Christianity	Fulfillment of Christianity
Introduction	Application	Realization
The Christ	The Church	The Consummation

15. One writer has proposed the view that there is an orderly progress of doctrine
advanced from book to book, as reflected in the order of the New Testament canon. He
writes, "As the several books gradually coalesced into unity it might be expected that
. . . they would on the whole tend to assume their relative places, according to the law
of internal fitness . . . ." (Thomas D. Bernard, *The Progress of Doctrine in The New
Testament*, p. vii).

16. Adapted from W. Graham Scroggie, *Know Your Bible*, 2:16.

f. Paul wrote most of the New Testament books (at least thir-teen[17]), and his books were among the earliest to be written (see Chart 1). So his are the first of the epistles (Romans-Philemon).

g. The order of Paul's letters in the canon has various expla-nations.[18] The first nine (Romans-2 Thessalonians) were written to churches; the last four (1 Timothy-Philemon) were written to indi-viduals. The key opening epistle, Romans, is the classic book on salvation and the Christian walk. The Corinthian letters and Gala-tians, listed together, treat problems of the churches. Ephesians, Philippians, and Colossians are usually kept together because all three were written from prison in Rome, and all three focus on deeper Christian living. The Thessalonian letters are last among the letters to churches; these look into the future, about Christ's second coming.

h. Paul's letters to individuals (1 Timothy-Philemon) appear last. They were among the last letters Paul wrote (see Chart 1). In the canon his letters to Timothy appear first. Timothy was Paul's closest companion and was serving in the key city of Ephesus. Philemon is Paul's shortest letter and contains the least doctrine of all his writ-ings. The message of his letter to Titus is similar to the message of the Timothy letters and follows them accordingly.

i. The last eight letters are non-Pauline. For that reason alone they would be placed *after* Paul's letters, because the apostle was looked up to as the key writer of Scriptures (cf. 2 Pet. 3:15,16). They were the last books of the New Testament to be recognized as inspired writings by the church leaders and councils, and that late recognition also would explain why they were placed at the end of the list of New Testament books.

j. Hebrews and James are placed together because both are addressed to Hebrew Christians. If Paul wrote Hebrews it is interest-ing to observe that it is located next to the other Pauline epistles.

k. The last three epistles (2 John, 3 John, Jude) are short one-chapter books, which is one reason for their little exposure to the early church and hence their being placed near the end of the canon.

2. *Forming of the New Testament canon.* The original writing (composition) of each inspired New Testament book was one thing. The way all twenty-seven were brought together into one volume (canonization) was a different work of God, but no less supernatural. The sovereign hand of God was in the canonization as much as in the

---

17. If Paul wrote Hebrews, then he authored fourteen books.
18. There is a descending length in Paul's epistles, with one exception (Ephesians is longer than Galatians). It is unlikely that the order of so many books would be determined by mere length, however.

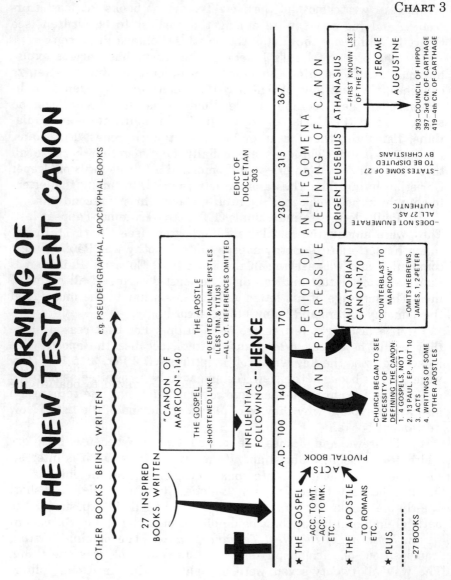

FORMING OF THE NEW TESTAMENT CANON

OTHER BOOKS BEING WRITTEN

e.g. PSEUDEPIGRAPHAL, APOCRYPHAL BOOKS

27 INSPIRED BOOKS WRITTEN

"CANON OF MARCION"-140

THE GOSPEL
—SHORTENED LUKE

THE APOSTLE
—10 EDITED PAULINE EPISTLES
(LESS TIM. & TITUS)
—ALL O.T. REFERENCES OMITTED

INFLUENTIAL FOLLOWING -- HENCE

A.D. 100   140   170   230   315   367

PERIOD OF ANTILEGOMENA AND PROGRESSIVE DEFINING OF CANON

EDICT OF DIOCLETIAN 303

PIVOTAL BOOK

ACTS

★ THE GOSPEL
—ACC. TO MT.
—ACC. TO MK.
ETC.

★ THE APOSTLE
—TO ROMANS
ETC.

★ PLUS
- - - - - - - - - - -
=27 BOOKS

—CHURCH BEGAN TO SEE NECESSITY OF DEFINING THE CANON
1. 4 GOSPELS, NOT 1
2. 13 PAUL. EP., NOT 10
3. ACTS
4. WRITINGS OF SOME OTHER APOSTLES

MURATORIAN CANON-170

"COUNTERBLAST TO MARCION"

—OMITS HEBREWS, JAMES, 1, 2 PETER

ORIGEN

—DOES NOT ENUMERATE ALL 27 AS AUTHENTIC

EUSEBIUS

—STATES SOME OF 27 TO BE DISPUTED BY CHRISTIANS

ATHANASIUS

—FIRST KNOWN LIST OF THE 27

JEROME

AUGUSTINE

393—COUNCIL OF HIPPO
397—3rd CN. OF CARTHAGE
419—4th CN. OF CARTHAGE

composition. If that were not so, an inspired book might have been excluded from the canon, and an uninspired book might have been included in the group. In fact, both of those threats hung over the church for a couple hundred years. For example, there were strong objections by some about accepting the following books (known as antilegomena)[19] as canonical: Hebrews, James, 2 Peter, 2 and 3 John, Jude and Revelation. At the same time, support was given by some church leaders to regard many other writings as Scripture, including books now within the Apocrypha[20] (e.g., 1 and 2 Maccabees, Tobit, Ecclesiasticus) and Pseudepigrapha[21] (e.g., 1 and 2 Enoch, Martyrdom of Isaiah, Testaments of the Twelve Patriarchs).

Study carefully the accompanying Chart 3 to learn the highlights of the gradual forming of the New Testament canon. Relate the following to the chart:

a. The twenty-seven inspired books were written in the period A.D. 45-95. During and after those years noninspired books were also being written.

b. The Gospel. The four gospels were brought together after the last one (John) was written, and they were called *The Gospel*.

c. The Apostle. In the same manner, the inspired writings of Paul "came together" soon after they were written, and they were identified under the one heading *The Apostle*.

d. Acts. Luke's Acts of the Apostles was early regarded by church leaders as a pivotal book, (the one that connected *The Gospel* with *The Apostle*), because it is the sequel to the gospel narrative and gives the historical background to the life and ministry of the apostle Paul.

e. Plus. The letters of other writers (Peter, James, Jude) and the Apocalypse of John (Revelation) were also recognized to bear divine authority.

f. We do not know when all twenty-seven (no more, and no less) books of the New Testament came together *for the first time* and were regarded by leaders of the Christian church as the completed canon of the second volume of Scripture. But whenever it was, the recognition was not once-and-for-all. Questions, objections, and disputes over the canon were to arise from within and from without the Christian communities. So the period A.D. 100-400 was one of *progressive defining* of the canon. Concerning some of the New Testament books, there were few or no questions regarding their divine authority. The antilegomena books were the major cause for the extended delay of consensus by the Christian church (Period of Antilegomena).

g. A few highlights of that period of defining the canon are shown

---

19. The word *antilegomena* means literally, "spoken against."
20. Apocrypha are noninspired writings regarded as canonical by some people.
21. Pseudepigrapha (literally, "false writings") are spurious writings whose authors sought canonical status for them. (This motive explains false authorship of the books.)

on Chart 3.[22] Answer the following questions on the basis of the chart:

(1) The heretic Marcion rejected the Old Testament entirely and accepted what parts of the New Testament as authoritative?

(2) Marcion attracted a large group of followers to his view. His movement was stopped in the next decades in what two ways?[23]

(3) Origen and Eusebius were prominent early church leaders. How did they regard the twenty-seven-book list?

(4) In A.D. 303 Emperor Diocletian issued the decree that all Christian Scriptures be destroyed. By that time there was general agreement on what constituted the New Testament canon. The persecution served to broadcast throughout the Empire just what the Christian Scriptures were.

(5) Whose is the first known list of the twenty-seven-book New Testament? What is its date? What other two theologians and three councils accepted the twenty-seven-book list?

From the middle of the fourth century onward the list of twenty-seven New Testament books was a fixed canon in the eyes of the Christian church. As noted earlier, the canon of twenty-seven books was divinely established from the beginning.

It is fair to ask, From the human standpoint who determined the extent of the New Testament canon? It is important to observe that the list is not the product of any single person or church council. The early church and the New Testament canon grew up together under the ministry of the Holy Spirit. F. F. Bruce writes, "We may well believe that those early Christians acted by a wisdom higher than their own in this matter, not only in what they accepted, but in what they rejected."[24] The Holy Spirit inspired individual writers to compose the original Scriptures, and then He gave discernment and guidelines to the believing community to recognize which books He had inspired.

F. TRANSLATIONS

The original autographs of the New Testament were written in Koine Greek, which was the vernacular of the entire Mediterranean world. If, during the succeeding centuries, translations had not been made into the languages of other nations of the world, converts of the

---

22. See F. F. Bruce, *The Books and the Parchments*, pages 104-13, for a concise description of that period.
23. The Muratorian Canon was so named after L. A. Muratori, who discovered the manuscript of this ancient list.
24. F. F. Bruce, *The Books and the Parchments*, p. 113.

evangelistic crusades would not have had Scriptures to feed upon for their Christian growth, and the prophetic command of Acts 1:8 involving the ends of the earth would have remained an enigma. But, spurred on by the need for new Christians to have the written Word in their mother tongue, many translations were made during the next centuries. It was the natural outcome of Christianity's expansion to foreign lands via the spoken word.

1. *Ancient versions.* One of the key ancient versions was the Syriac Bible, which brought the written Word to lands east of Palestine — eventually to China and India.[25] (See accompanying Map A, Syriac Version.) Translations of the gospels and Acts were made as early as the second century, and by A.D. 425 a standard edition of the Bible (called Peshitta, literally "simple") was being used by the Christians.

MAP A

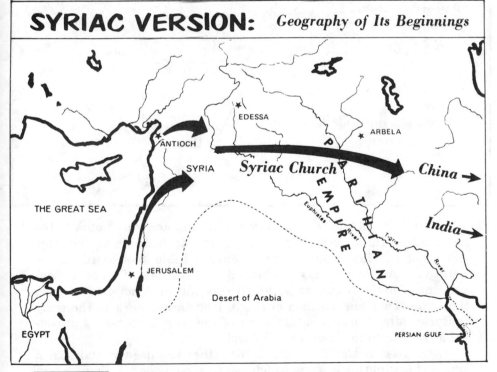

SYRIAC VERSION: *Geography of Its Beginnings*

EDESSA

ARBELA

ANTIOCH

SYRIA *Syriac Church* China →

THE GREAT SEA

Euphrates River

Tigris River

India→

JERUSALEM

Desert of Arabia

EGYPT

PERSIAN GULF →

25. The book of Acts records mainly the missionary labors in the west and northwest. It is interesting to observe that it was a Syrian church (at Antioch) which led that western movement (Acts 13:1 ff.). Yet the Syriac Bible served mainly the people who lived east and north of Palestine.

The Latin Vulgate was the most prominent of the ancient versions. It was the official Bible of Christendom in Europe for a thousand years. The earliest translations appeared in North Africa in the second century (Map B), and Jerome made his standard version during the years A.D. 383-405.[26]

MAP B

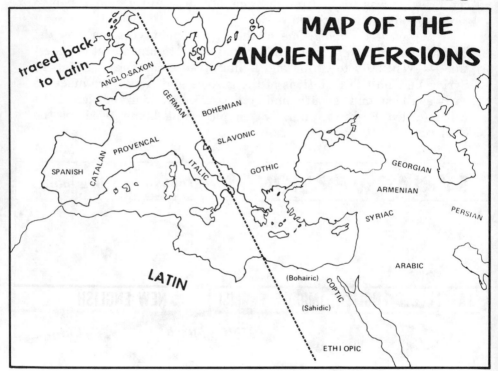

MAP OF THE ANCIENT VERSIONS

traced back to Latin

ANGLO-SAXON

GERMAN

BOHEMIAN

SLAVONIC

PROVENCAL

CATALAN

ITALIC

SPANISH

GOTHIC

GEORGIAN

ARMENIAN

SYRIAC

PERSIAN

ARABIC

LATIN

(Bohairic)

COPTIC

(Sahidic)

ETHIOPIC

Map B shows later European versions that are traced back to the Latin Bible. Those versions are west of the dashed line on the map. Note that the first English (Anglo-Saxon) Bible was based on the Latin version. Observe also on Map B the locations of other ancient versions of neighboring lands, which versions were not derived from the Latin. That phenomenon of active translation work in the early centuries after Christ is a testimony of the New Testament's universal attraction to the hearts of all people.

2. *English Bible*. The English Bible that you use for study has a long and fascinating history, which can be seen when the English text is traced back to its origins. You will appreciate your Bible more

26. Jerome translated the four gospels in A.D. 383, and during the next year he completed the remainder of the New Testament.

when you know the paths over which God has brought it to you. The next few pages are a survey of that history. Study it not just to learn facts of God's program but to enhance your regard for the large variety of English versions, past and present.

a. The earliest versions. The Christian message reached Great Britain by the beginning of the fourth century A.D., when the Latin Bible was the people's Scripture. When English became Britain's new vernacular with the arrival of Germanic-speaking Angles, Saxons, and Jutes in the course of the fifth century, the need for English Scriptures arose. Chart 4 shows some of the main partial or complete English translations of the Bible that were made from about A.D. 700 to 1539. Note the three periods of the English language: *old, middle,* and *new.* The *new English* period extends from the time of the Reformation to the present.

CHART 4

EARLIEST VERSIONS

OF THE ENGLISH BIBLE

400	1100	1520	
LATIN	**OLD ENGLISH**	**MIDDLE ENGLISH**	**NEW ENGLISH**
	BEDE'S	ROLLE'S	TYNDALE'S VERSIONS
	Bible poems c.700	Psalter c.1300	N. T. 1525 - first printed Eng. N. T.
	John's Gospel c.735	Parts of N. T.	Pent. 1530
			Jonah 1531
	Alfred the Great (d.901)	2 WYCLIF	Rev. Pent. and N. T. 1535
	—parts of the Bible	VERSIONS	Rev. N. T. 1535
	Abbot Aelfric (10th cent.)	1380-84 (from Latin)	COVERDALE'S BIBLE
	—parts of O. T.		-1535
		1. Nicholas of Hereford	—first printed Eng. Bible
		—plus another?	
		2. John Purvey	MATTHEW'S BIBLE
		—rev. of Nicholas	1537
			—by John Rogers
			—mixture of Tyn. and Cov.
	Anglo Saxon Paraphrases		TAVERNER'S - 1539
	700-1000		
			GREAT BIBLE
			—by Coverdale 1539
			Henry VIII: "In God's name, let it go abroad among our people."

Note the active program of translation during the first decades of
the *new English* period, including work by William Tyndale and
Miles Coverdale. It was the Reformation that brought a revival of
translation activity, spurred on by renewed interest in Hebrew and

CHART 5

KING JAMES VERSION

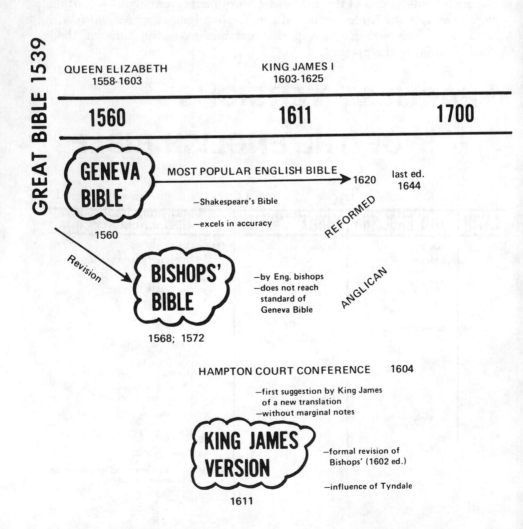

Greek Bible manuscripts, and by Gutenberg's invention of movable type for the printing press.

b. King James Version. The King James Version (KJV), also called the Authorized Version, was the outcome of much translation activity beginning with Tyndale (Chart 4). Scan Chart 5 and observe how it continues the survey of Chart 4. Note on Chart 5 the entry of the four major versions: Great Bible, Geneva Bible, Bishops' Bible, and King James Version.

The Geneva Bible excelled in accuracy and was very popular. It contained marginal notes with an interpretation of Reformed theology. For that reason it was rejected by the Church of England, and a new revision of the Great Bible, containing marginal notes of Anglican theology, was made by English bishops. That Bishops' Bible first appeared in 1568.

The tension and unrest over the two "competing" versions (Geneva and Bishops'), in addition to arguments over other versions, led King James I to call for a new version with no marginal notes of any theological interpretation. The version was made by fifty-four scholars over a period of seven years. It soon became the most popular English Bible, and it is still the most quoted and most memorized text. F. F. Bruce writes of it, "By sheer merit the Authorized Version established itself as The English Bible."[27]

Two important values of the King James Version are its literal rendering and literary style, which strongly support analytical study.

c. English versions after the King James Version. The modern missions era of translation activity began around 1800. It is aptly called "modern" because the era has not yet ended. In fact, one of the brightest aspects of the Christian witness today is the unprecedented production of new Bible translations. Portions of Scripture are reaching people of many languages and cultures in the remotest parts of the world. And in America new English versions and paraphrases, written in contemporary style, are geared to such needy mission fields as homes without a church and campuses with drifting youth. For the serious Bible student who wants to analyze a Bible text that is virtually the same as the original (minus the translation factor), various excellent versions are available, such as the *New American Standard Bible* (NASB) and the *New International Version* (NIV).

Revision of Bible versions is an important activity of this modern era. The first major revision, known as the English Revised Version, appeared in 1881. It was a revision of the King James Version. Chart

---

27. F. F. Bruce, *The Books and the Parchments*, p. 229.

6 shows that and other highlights of the modern era. Use the chart to answer the following questions:

CHART 6

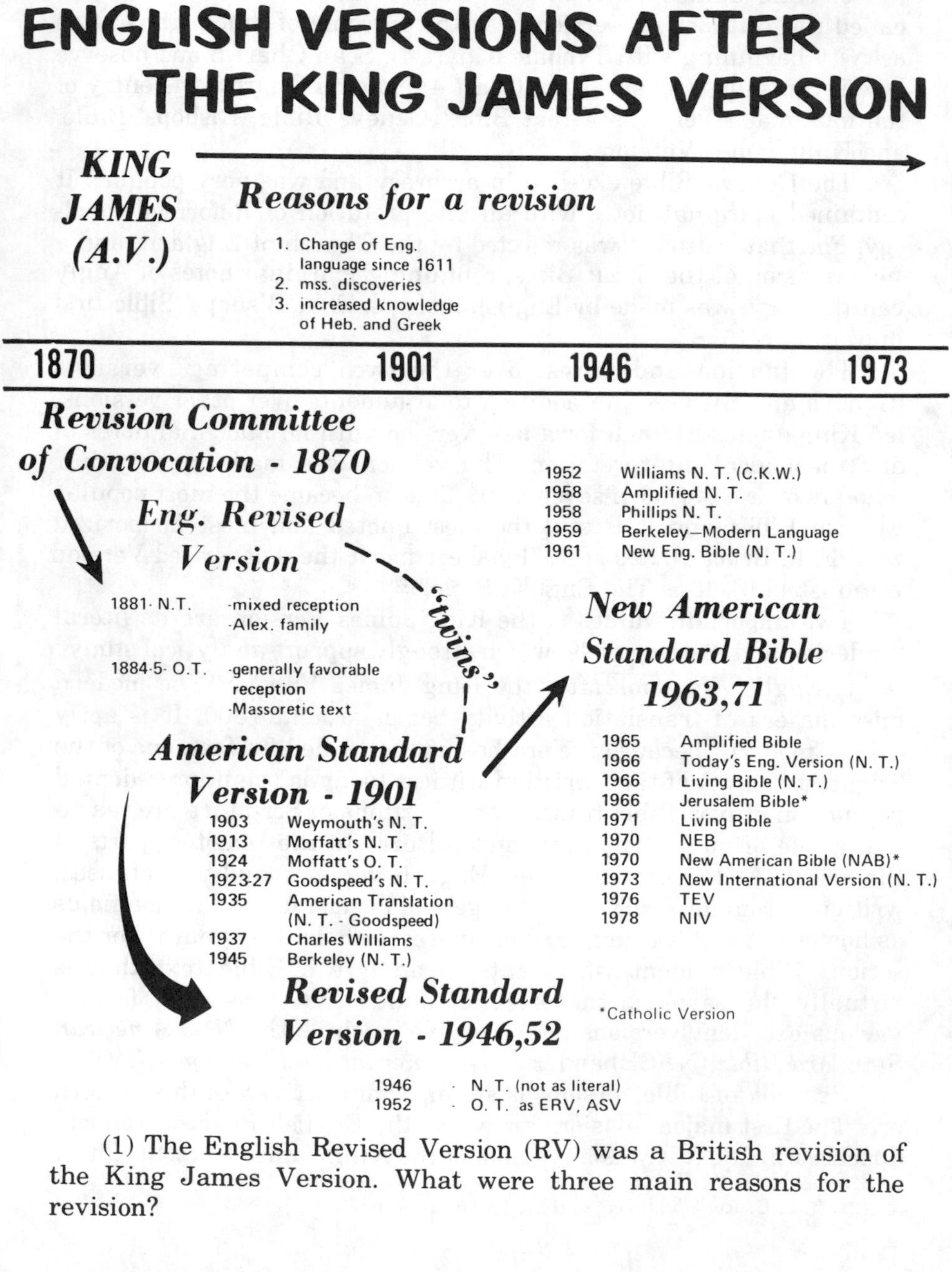

ENGLISH VERSIONS AFTER THE KING JAMES VERSION

KING JAMES (A.V.)

Reasons for a revision

1. Change of Eng. language since 1611
2. mss. discoveries
3. increased knowledge of Heb. and Greek

1870	1901	1946	1973

Revision Committee of Convocation - 1870

Eng. Revised Version

1881- N.T.   -mixed reception
              -Alex. family

1884-5- O.T. -generally favorable reception
              -Massoretic text

"twins"

American Standard Version - 1901

1903	Weymouth's N. T.
1913	Moffatt's N. T.
1924	Moffatt's O. T.
1923-27	Goodspeed's N. T.
1935	American Translation (N. T. - Goodspeed)
1937	Charles Williams
1945	Berkeley (N. T.)

Revised Standard Version - 1946,52

| 1946 | - N. T. (not as literal) |
| 1952 | - O. T. as ERV, ASV |

1952	Williams N. T. (C.K.W.)
1958	Amplified N. T.
1958	Phillips N. T.
1959	Berkeley—Modern Language
1961	New Eng. Bible (N. T.)

New American Standard Bible 1963,71

1965	Amplified Bible
1966	Today's Eng. Version (N. T.)
1966	Living Bible (N. T.)
1966	Jerusalem Bible*
1971	Living Bible
1970	NEB
1970	New American Bible (NAB)*
1973	New International Version (N. T.)
1976	TEV
1978	NIV

*Catholic Version

(1) The English Revised Version (RV) was a British revision of the King James Version. What were three main reasons for the revision?

(2) The American Standard Version (ASV) was a "twin" of the RV, produced for the American reader. The American and British committees collaborated in some of their work. How many years intervened between the KJV and ASV?

(3) The Revised Standard Version (RSV) was a revision of the ASV. What was the span of time between it and the ASV?

(4) The *New American Standard Bible* (NASB) was a revision of the ASV. When was the whole Bible in this revision first published?

(5) The *New International Version* (NIV) was a new translation. When was the whole Bible published?

(6) How many of the other versions on Chart 6 are you familiar with?

Thus, the Bible has come a long way — *from God to us.* And the most thrilling part of it all is that, not counting the necessary translation difference, "we hold in our hands to-day a Bible which differs in no substantial particular from the originals of the various books as they came from the hands of their authors."[28]

III. REVIEW QUESTIONS

1. In what ways is the New Testament related to the Old?

2. What were the main stages of the New Testament's coming *from God to us,* beginning with *revelation?*

3. What is divine revelation? What is the difference between general revelation and special revelation?

4. How were the original Scriptures inspired by God? Were the original autographs inerrant?

5. Do we have any portion of the original autographs? Are the existing ancient copies of the Bible inerrant in every letter and word? If not, how confident can we be that they accurately represent what the authors originally wrote?

6. Were the four gospels the first New Testament books to be written? Which of these books was written after the other two: Ephesians, gospel according to John, Romans?

7. What is meant by canon of the New Testament? How was the extent of the canon determined?

8. Is there an order of progression in the books of the New Testament canon? If so, identify.

9. What is the approximate date of the first known twenty-seven-book canon?

10. What was the most important ancient version of the New Testament?

---

28. G. T. Manley, *The New Bible Handbook*, p. 19.

11. What ecclesiastical difference gave rise to the project of making the King James Version?

12. What is the difference between a free paraphrase and a literal translation?

13. The *New American Standard Bible* (NASB) is a revision of what version? Is the *New International Version* (NIV) a revision of a version?

IV. SELECTED READING

DIVINE REVELATION

Chafer, L. S. *Systematic Theology,* 1:48-60.

Henry, Carl F. H. *Revelation and the Bible.*

Manley, G. T. *The New Bible Handbook,* pp. 6-8.

Packer, J. I. "Revelation and Inspiration." In *The New Bible Commentary,* pp. 24-30.

Warfield, B. B. "Revelation." In *The International Standard Bible Encyclopedia,* 3:2573-82; and *The Inspiration and Authority of the Bible,* pp. 71-102.

INSPIRATION

Clark, Gordon H. "How May I Know the Bible Is Inspired?" In *Can I Trust My Bible?,* edited by Howard F. Vos, pp. 9-34.

Gaussen, L. *Theopneustia: The Plenary Inspiration of the Holy Scriptures.*

Geisler, Norman L., and Nix, William E. *A General Introduction to the Bible,* pp. 26-124.

Hodge, C. *Systematic Theology,* pp. 151-86.

Manley, G. T. *The New Bible Handbook,* pp. 8-18.

Pache, René. *Inspiration and Authority.*

Thiessen, Henry. *Introduction to the New Testament,* pp. 78-97.

Walvoord, John W., ed. *Inspiration and Interpretation.*

TRANSMISSION

Bruce, F. F. *The Books and the Parchments,* pp. 176-90.

Geisler, Norman L., and Nix, William E. *A General Introduction to the Bible,* pp. 211-48; 267-96; 344-93.

Mickelsen, A. Berkeley. "Is the Text of the New Testament Reliable?" In *Can I Trust My Bible?,* edited by Howard F. Vos, pp. 155-69.

Skilton, John H. "The Transmission of the Scriptures." In *The Infallible Word,* edited by N. B. Stonehouse and Paul Woolley.

Thiessen, Henry C. *Introduction to the New Testament,* pp. 31-51.

CANONIZATION

Bruce, F. F. *The Books and the Parchments,* pp. 104-13.

Geisler, Norman L., and Nix, William E. *A General Introduction to the Bible,* pp. 127-47; 179-207.

Harris, R. Laird. "What Books Belong in the Canon of Scripture?" In *Can I Trust My Bible?*, edited by Howard F. Vos, pp. 67-87.

Harrison, Everett F. *Introduction to the New Testament*, pp. 91-128.

Manley, G. T. *The New Bible Handbook*, pp. 32-39.

Riggs, J. S. "Canon of the New Testament." In *The International Standard Bible Encyclopedia*, 1:563-66.

Souter, Alexander. *The Text and Canon of the New Testament*, pp. 146-54.

Stanton, V. H. "New Testament Canon." In Hastings' *Dictionary of the Bible*, 3:529-42.

TRANSLATION: ANCIENT AND MODERN VERSIONS

Bruce, F. F. *The Books and the Parchments*, pp. 194-252.

Geisler, Norman L., and Nix, William E. *A General Introduction to the Bible*, pp. 316-43; 394-446.

Kubo, Sakae, and Specht, Walter. *So Many Versions?*

2

Setting of the New Testament

No Scripture was born in a vacuum. The New Testament books had their antecedents, and they were cradled in a contemporary setting that involved every phase of life. If we are aware of those backgrounds before we begin a study of the New Testament, the biblical message will be clearer and stronger and more real. That is why the study of the New Testament's setting is so important.

I. HISTORICAL AND RELIGIOUS SETTING

The earthbound ingredients of history are people, places, things, actions, and time. God is the Lord of all history, and His blend of the ingredients is sovereignly exercised. That is why there was nothing accidental about the historical and religious setting of the New Testament. We may not always perceive the divine design, but it is important that by faith we recognize its presence.

All the years before Christ, beginning with the time of Adam and Eve, looked forward to His appearance on the earthly scene. That was the pre-Christian era. Study Chart 7 and answer the following questions:

1. The pre-Christian era is of what three parts?
2. About when were the first Scriptures written?
3. Over how many years was the Old Testament written?
4. Over how many years was the New Testament written?
5. Does the chart suggest a meaning of the designation "silent years?" If so, what?
6. Ponder the significance of the eras labelled Pre-Bible and Whole-Bible. What are your reflections concerning spiritual accountability of people living in the two eras?

Let us now focus on the two immediate pre-Christian settings of

CHART 7

HISTORICAL SETTING OF THE NEW TESTAMENT

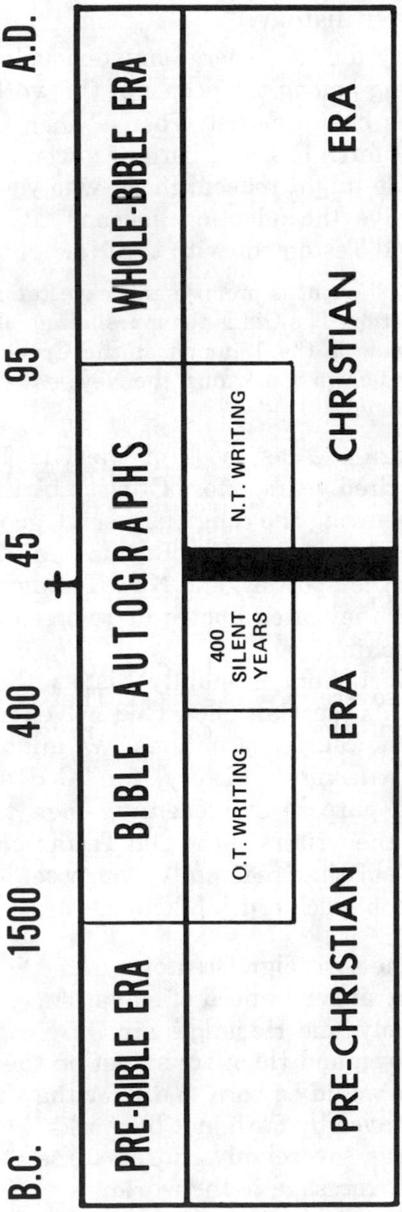

B.C.	1500	400	† 45	95	A.D.
PRE-BIBLE ERA	BIBLE AUTOGRAPHS			WHOLE-BIBLE ERA	
	O.T. WRITING	400 SILENT YEARS	N.T. WRITING		
PRE-CHRISTIAN ERA			CHRISTIAN ERA		

the New Testament, namely the Old Testament and the four hundred silent years.

A. OLD TESTAMENT HISTORY

Christianity did not emerge mysteriously out of a vacuum. God had been moving among the people of the world, especially Israel, for many centuries before Christ. Then, "when the fulness of the time came, God sent forth His Son, born of a woman, born under the Law, in order that He might redeem those who were under the Law, that we might receive the adoption as sons" (Gal. 4:4-5). Erich Sauer connects the Old Testament with the New in these words:

> The Old Testament is promise and expectation, the New is fulfillment and completion. The Old is the marshalling of the hosts to the battle of God, the new is the Triumph of the Crucified One. The Old is the twilight and dawn of morning, the New is the rising sun and the height of eternal day.[1]

Even though the last book of the Old Testament was written about four hundred years before Christ's birth, our knowing the Old Testament is knowing the religious, social, geographical, and, in part, the political setting of the New. Besides, the Old Testament was the Bible of Jesus, the apostles, and New Testament writers. When they spoke or wrote, they often quoted or referred to the Old Testament's history and teaching.

The Old Testament is mainly history, but it is *sacred* history. That is, it reveals especially how God moves in and through the lives of people and the courses of nations. We might also say that the Old Testament is *redemptive* history, for "God actively directs human history for the purpose of redeeming men to Himself."[2] The Holy Spirit inspired the writers of the Old Testament to record what would adequately reveal that redemptive purpose. Thus, the writers have much to say about such crucial facts as these:

1. God is the sovereign Creator.
2. Man is a sinner in need of salvation.
3. God is holy, and He judges sin.
4. God is love, and He offers salvation to sinful man.
5. A savior would be born to die for the sins of man.
6. Man is saved by faith, not by works.
7. Israel was sovereignly chosen to be God's channel of the redemptive message to the world.

---

1. Erich Sauer, *The Dawn of World Redemption*, p. 186.
2. J. Barton Payne, *The Theology of the Older Testament*, p. 3.

8. All history will culminate at the throne of the sovereign God.

Read this list again and observe, from your present acquaintance with the New Testament, how each truth is also a vital doctrine of the New Testament. Also note how the following comparisons[3] are represented in the list:

OLD TESTAMENT HISTORY	NEW TESTAMENT HISTORY
foreshadow	fulfillment
promise	performance
problem	solution
commencement	consummation

B. FOUR HUNDRED SILENT YEARS

Around 400 B.C. God ceased speaking to His people and the world through any new portions of the written Word. For four hundred years the prophets' pens would be dry, hence the designation "four hundred silent years." But prophets would still preach, and God would still speak by His Spirit to a continuing remnant of saints who were studying the Bible that they had (Old Testament) and watching for their Messiah's coming. And God would always remain the sovereign mover of history on the local and world-wide scene. God knew when He would be sending His Son to the world, and He used the four hundred silent years to prepare the world for that coming.

Four hundred years made a vast difference in the setting of Judaism. Compare, for example, the ending of the Old Testament and the opening of the New Testament. The last historical events of the Old Testament are the returns, under Ezra and Nehemiah, of the exiled Jews from Babylon to Jerusalem.[4] The first pages of the New Testament record the birth of Jesus Christ. The accompanying chart lists some other changes in that four hundred-year picture.

Many factors — historical, political, religious, cultural — brought on the changes of those four centuries. In the following pages the highlights of the changes will be surveyed, for the purpose of visualizing and feeling the setting of the New Testament.

Basically, there were three backgrounds in whose shadows Christ moved, the church was born, and the New Testament books were

---

3. Comparisons are from W. Graham Scroggie, *Know Your Bible*, 2:15-16.
4. Ezra and Nehemiah are the last history books of the Old Testament. The book of Malachi, listed last in the canon, is the last prophetic message of the Old Testament.

THE HOLY LAND,

BEFORE AND AFTER THE 400 SILENT YEARS

	400 B.C.		A.D.
LEADERS, PREACHERS	*Ezra Nehemiah Malachi*	**400**	*John the Baptist Jesus*
WORLD RULING POWER	*Persia (east)*		*Rome (west)*
RELIGIOUS GROUPS	*no major groups*	**Silent**	*Scribes, Pharisees Sadducees, Herodians Sanhedrin*
VERNACULAR	*Hebrew*		*Aramaic and Greek*
PLACE OF WORSHIP	*Temple*	**Years**	*Temple and synagogues*

written. Those backgrounds are Hebrew, Greek, and Roman. As you study these, try to relate to them parts of the New Testament with which you are already familiar.

1. *Hebrew background*. The Hebrew background of the New Testament is primarily religious because the Hebrew people, the Jews, are the ones to whom the gospel message was first sent (Rom. 1:16).[5]

a. Three centers of the life of Judaism (Jewish religion). With the Babylonian exile in 586 B.C. the Jews entered a phase of being scattered around the world such that by the time of Christ every large city of the Roman Empire had its large colony of Jews, and towns and villages together contained them by the thousands. When the church's first missionaries (Paul and others) moved out to the "ends of the earth" (Acts 1:8), Jews were among the first contacts made (see Acts 13:5).

During the silent centuries, the greatest impressions made upon Judaism originated in the three great centers of Babylon, Alexandria, and Jerusalem. Observe on Map C the relative location of those cities.

(1) *Babylon*. Changes in Judaism that originated in Babylon were carried over into Jerusalem during the silent years, because there was a continuing program of migration of Jews from Babylon to Jerusalem, which had begun under Ezra and Nehemiah. Some of the major changes, not all good, were:

(a) Theology — The exile had eliminated idolatry and had fostered a pure monotheism ("one God").

(b) Tradition — The Law was amplified to include other writings, mainly Mishnah and Haggada, which were together known as Talmud. Mishnah was a book of man-made rules of living; Haggada was the theology and commentary of the rabbis. Rabbis formulated their own tradition. The Jews became more and more steeped in traditionalism during those years.

(c) Worship — Synagogues were established as the local places of worship. By New Testament times synagogues were located throughout the Mediterranean world. The apostle Paul usually sought out the synagogue when he first arrived in a city on his missionary journeys (see Acts 13:5).

(d) Culture and education — The new professions of teachers and interpreters of the Law, called rabbis and scribes, originated here. Scholarship was advanced, and culture was developed.

---

5. The first book in the New Testament canon is Matthew, a gospel directed to the immediate audience of first-century Jews.

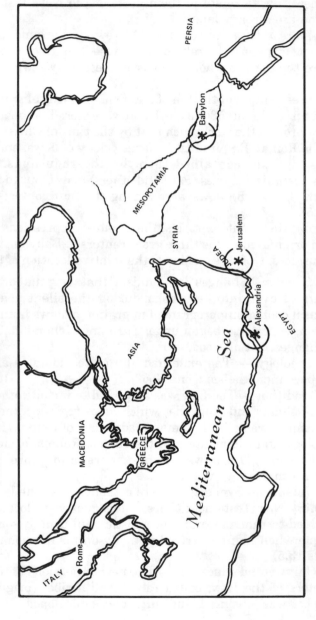

THREE CENTERS OF JUDAISM DURING THE
SILENT CENTURIES

This first centre of Jewish life in Babylon was marked, then, by the creation of the traditional law and theology, and the dominance of a cultured class of scribes and rabbis who, in their zeal to preserve the laws and traditions of Israel, reduced the Jewish religion to a mass of outward ordinances and forms.[6]

Exercise: Refer to an exhaustive concordance[7] and note how often the word *scribe* appears in the New Testament. Do the same for *rabbi*; *tradition*; and *synagogue*. (Include the plural forms in this word study.)

(2) *Alexandria*. A large number of Jews migrated to Egypt a few months after the destruction of Jerusalem in 586 B.C.[8] When Alexander the Great founded Alexandria in 332 B.C., the Jews constituted an eighth of the population of Egypt — in Alexandria, almost a half. He favored them very highly and assigned them a special section of the city. Alexandria became the capital of the Jewish Dispersion (Diaspora), and the events and movements of that city affected the life of Judaism for centuries to come.

Since Alexandria was a Greek-speaking city, the Jewish population gave up its Palestinian Hebrew vernacular as it began learning Greek. Eventually the Jews were without Scripture in their new vernacular, so the need arose for a Greek translation of the Hebrew Old Testament. Such a translation (later called the Septuagint) was soon made — the Pentateuch by 280 B.C., and the whole Old Testament by 180 B.C.

The Jews prospered and multiplied in Egypt during the silent years, such that by New Testament times there were almost one million Jews residing there. Egypt was not far from Judea, and the contacts between Jews of both lands were very close. (Read Matthew 2:13-18, one of the first stories of the New Testament, which is about baby Jesus' parents' escape with Him to Egypt, to flee Herod.) The contributions of the Greek background, including the Septuagint translation, to the New Testament setting will be discussed later.

(3) *Jerusalem*. Approximately 450 B.C. Ezra and Nehemiah had led about 50,000 Jews back to Judea from exile in Babylon. Those remained in the land, rebuilding the walls of Jerusalem and trying in small measure to preserve their religious heritage. But before long the people gave up their allegiance to God and, in their vain pursuit

---

6. Henry Kendall Booth. *The Background of the Bible*, p. 130.
7. The *New American Standard Exhaustive Concordance of the Bible* is recommended for word studies of this book.
8. The story is told in Jeremiah 41-44.

of holiness, surrendered faith for works. The one bright note was that there always remained a faithful remnant in the land who awaited the Messiah.[9]

It was during those silent years that two ruling classes of the Jewish religion appeared: the Sadducees and the Pharisees. As rival religious sects, they became rival political parties by New Testament times.

The Sadducees were the political party of the Jewish aristocratic priesthood. They were not popular with the common people. Among their false doctrines were: (a) denial of the resurrection of the body and future retribution, and (b) denial of the existence of angels and spirits.

The Pharisees were the religious leaders of the Jews, often identified in the New Testament with the scribes. They were the most influential leaders and were very popular with the people. The Pharisees taught such sound doctrines as divine providence, immortality of the soul, and a messianic hope. But they were rigid legalists, and by Jesus' day their sect had degenerated into an empty religion. (Read Luke 11:37-54.)

Below is a comparative summary of the two groups.

PHARISEES AND SADDUCEES

PHARISEES	SADDUCEES
name means "the separated ones"	name may be from a word meaning the "righteous ones"
largest and most influential sect	the aristocratic minority
extreme legalism	external legalism
little interest in politics	a major concern with politics
believed in immortality, resurrection, spirits, and angels	denied these doctrines
regarded rabbinic tradition highly	accepted as authoritative only the written Old Testament

Exercise: Refer to an exhaustive concordance and compare the frequency of the names *Sadducees* and *Pharisees* in the New Testament.

---

9. The book of Malachi, though written around 400 B.C., prophetically describes the evil generations of Jews during the intertestamental period. Read Luke 2:25-38 for two examples of believers of this period.

b. Six periods of Jewish history (international politics). The interval between the Old and the New Testaments is a dark period in the history of Israel. The life and fortunes of the Jews depended on what nation was the world power at the time. That was so because, as Map C shows, the land of Judea was located in the center of the world at that time, and it was all too easily preyed upon by the nation in power.

The interval is divided into six periods, named according to those in power.[10] See Chart 8.

CHART 8

SIX PERIODS OF JEWISH HISTORY BEFORE CHRIST ✝

400 B.C.	334	324	204	165	63	5 B.C.
PERSIAN	ALEXANDRIAN	EGYPTIAN	SYRIAN	MACCABEAN	ROMAN	

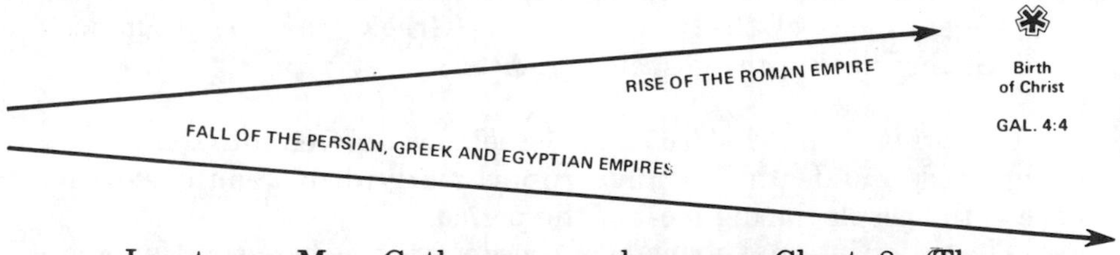

RISE OF THE ROMAN EMPIRE

Birth of Christ

GAL. 4:4

FALL OF THE PERSIAN, GREEK AND EGYPTIAN EMPIRES

Locate on Map C the names shown on Chart 8. (The name Maccabean is not a geographical term.) Highlights of each of the periods, because each of those contributed to the background of the New Testament, will be briefly described below. Overall, the four hundred-year interval is the story of the fall of the Persian, Greek, and Egyptian empires, and the rise of the Roman Empire.[11]

(1) *Persian Period* 400-334 B.C.[12] Palestine was under the rule of the high priests, who were responsible to the governor (satrap) of Syria, a province of Persia. The period was mild and uneventful, for the most part, as far as the Jews were concerned.

---

10. The dates of some periods are not firmly fixed for classification because there are different views concerning precisely when a new period began. The dividing dates as such are not that crucial. The date of 5 B.C. is the date of Jesus' birth. The apparent discrepancy of the number 5 is explained by an error in calculations when the calendar of the Christian era was formed in A.D. 525. (See Robert L. Thomas and Stanley N. Gundry, *A Harmony of the Gospels,* pp. 324-28.)

11. The Syriac nation was not a major power.

12. Transparency charts showing all the details of the intertestamental period are in Moody Press's *New Testament Time Line,* Charts 1-3 (artist Bill Hovey).

(2) *Alexandrian Period* 334-324 B.C. Alexander the Great revolutionized the world, showed much favor to the Jews, and exposed them to the process of Hellenization. The brief period of rule came to an end with Alexander's sudden death. By Jesus' day many Hellenized Jews had adopted the Greek ways, customs, and speech and had been freed from an exclusive spirit of Hebrew tradition and ancestry.

(3) *Egyptian Period* 324-204 B.C. This was the post-Alexandrian reign of the world by four Egyptian generals who were successors to Alexander. For part of the time Judea was allowed self-rule. Often the land was the battleground for wars between Syria and Egypt.

During this period the first copies of the Greek Septuagint were distributed (Pentateuch, 280 B.C.).

Some Bible students hold that the seventy-member Sanhedrin council of New Testament times originated around 250 B.C. That council performed the judicial functions of the Great Synagogue council of Ezra's day (450-400 B.C.).

Exercise: Refer to an exhaustive concordance and note the various appearances of the word *council* (Greek: *sunedrion*, hence "Sanhedrin") in the gospels and Acts.

(4) *Syrian Period* 204-165 B.C. "Israel now entered into the valley of the shadow of death."[13] Uninterrupted martyrdom was the experience of the people during most of the period.

The major internal struggle of these years was between Hellenistic Jews and Hasidim Jews. The latter resisted all forms of diluting their Hebrew heritage. The Pharisees were successors to that group.

Many noncanonical writings were beginning to appear during this period.[14] The two main kinds were: 1. apocryphal (e.g., 1 and 2 Maccabees) — books recognized by the Roman Catholic Church as canonical, but rejected by Protestants; 2. pseudepigraphal (e.g., 1 Enoch) — spurious writings excluded from the canon by all.

It is interesting to observe that during this period, by 180 B.C., all the books of the Old Testament were translated into Greek by the Alexandrian translators.

(5) *Maccabean Period* 165-63 B.C. This has been called the Period of Independence. Politically, it was a time of revolt by Jewish leaders

---

13. Henry E. Dosker, "Between the Testaments," in *The International Standard Bible Encyclopedia*, 1:456.
14. Persecution is often the backdrop of writing activity, especially apocalyptic writing, which concerns judgment for the oppressor and deliverance for the oppressed.

against Syrian forces. Religiously, it was a time of restoring worship of the Lord to the re-dedicated Temple.

During this period Palestine was geographically divided into the three familiar divisions of Judea, Samaria, and Galilee. Also, it was during this time that the rival religious sects (Pharisees and Sadducees) became rival political enemies.

(6) *Roman Period* 63-4 B.C. In 63 B.C. the Roman general Pompey brought Palestine under Roman control. He organized the Decapolis league of ten cities southeast of the Sea of Galilee to balance the power of Judea. Antipater was appointed governor of Judea, and Herod the Great was king of Judea by Roman senatorial grant from 37 to 4 B.C.

For the most part there was little interference by Rome in the religious life of Palestine. The Jews paid taxes to Rome and were subject to the rulers appointed over them by Rome. The conflicts and struggles of the Jews of that day were mainly of the heart, and the darkness and sin were overwhelming. This is James Stalker's description of the Jewish world to which Jesus came:

> A nation enslaved; the upper classes devoting themselves to selfishness, courtiership, and skepticism; the teachers and chief professors of religion lost in mere shows of ceremonialism, and boasting themselves the favorites of God, while their souls were honeycombed with self-deception and vice; the body of the people misled by false ideals; and seething at the bottom of society, a neglected mass of unblushing and unrestrained sin.[15]

When Jesus was born (5 B.C.) the political situation was generally stable, but opposition to the Messiah's coming was quickly demonstrated by King Herod's reactions and decree. (Read Matthew 2:1-18.)

Exercise: 1. Read all of Matthew 2 and make a note of different things that are part of the New Testament setting that you have studied so far. 2. Review all you have learned about the Hebrew Background of the New Testament. In the next pages you will be studying the important Greek Background.

2. *Greek Background*. The Greek background of the New Testament is chiefly cultural, including such things as language and philosophical perspective. Many of the influences of that Hellenistic culture were very important, because they paved the way for the

---

15. James Stalker, *The Life of Jesus Christ,* pp. 35-36.

world-wide proclamation of God's message of salvation in New Testament times.

a. The Greek Bible. As noted earlier, the need for a translation of the Hebrew Old Testament into Greek arose because Greek had become the new vernacular of the Jews in Egypt. In fact Greek was by then the lingua franca of the world, as a result of the world conquests of Alexander the Great.

Alexandrian scholars translated the first five books of the Law (Pentateuch) by 280 B.C., and by 180 B.C. all the books had been translated. Over the next two centuries that "modern version" (later called the Septuagint) of the Old Testament was circulated around the Greek empire, so that by the time of Jesus and the apostles it was widely used.[16] The Hebrew Old Testament was still cherished by Jews as God's Holy Scriptures, and rightly so. Fix these things in your mind as you study the accompanying Chart 9.

CHART 9

THE GREEK SEPTUAGINT

AND THE CHRISTIAN GREEK BIBLE

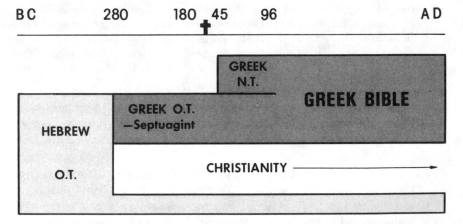

Some of the significant contributions of the Septuagint to the New Testament setting are:

(1) The New Testament writers had a Greek theological vocabulary to work with as they wrote their books in Greek. For example, the Hebrew word *Torah*, which referred only to God's Law, had been translated *nomos* in the Septuagint, even though in those days *nomos*

---

16. Very many of Jesus' quotes of Old Testament passages are from the Septuagint version. This is true also of the New Testament authors.

referred to the whole range of codified custom, not exclusively to God's Law. For almost two hundred years Jews reading *nomos* in the Septuagint gradually began seeing it as meaning only God's Law in those passages where it should be so interpreted. So by the time the New Testament writers did their composing, the word *nomos* very adequately served the theological purpose, and their readers identified the word with God's Law, without having to make a mental adjustment to a secular word. In other words, the Greek *nomos theou* (law of God), as in Romans 7:22, was perceived precisely the same as the Hebrew *torah haElohim* (law of God), as in Nehemiah 8:8.

(2) When the New Testament canon was complete, the Septuagint Old Testament and the Greek New Testament formed a unity, the Greek Bible.

(3) The Greek Bible made God's whole written revelation accessible to the whole world, where Greek was the lingua franca.

(4) This "modern version" of Scripture prepared the way for the Jews' acceptance of God's revelation in a language other than the revered Hebrew language. The barrier of Scripture being rejected in a so-called unholy language was not a problem during the first centuries after Christ.

b. Greek language. By New Testament times Koine Greek was the international language, an ideal channel for communication in the world-wide program of the early church. Christ, the apostles, and early disciples of Palestine spoke Greek (as well as Aramaic); the Scriptures were in Greek; and the audiences of the preached gospel throughout the Roman Empire understood and spoke Greek.

c. Greek philosophy and mystery religion. During the silent years the mind of the Greek thinkers was reaching out to discover the secrets of life and the universe. Because of that, it might be concluded that the Greeks were a ready audience for the message of Christianity. But they were not that prepared, as G. T. Manley writes:

> We must not, of course, exaggerate the preparedness of the Graeco-Roman world for the acceptance of Christianity. It needed three centuries of intensive evangelization and heroic witness-bearing to overcome the pride and self-satisfaction begotten of so mighty and dazzling a civilization. But its external order, its deep spiritual aspirations, and its groping after truth, all assured the presence in it of good soil when the Sower came with His seed which is the word of God.[17]

The answers to the questions of the searching Greeks were in the Hebrew Scriptures, but the philosophers and false religionists re-

---

17. G. T. Manley, ed., *The New Bible Handbook,* p. 293.

jected that revelation and posited their own answers. Some books of
the New Testament, such as Ephesians and Colossians, were written
partly with those philosophers in mind, and the appeal was to accept
God's full revelation by His Son Jesus Christ (see Eph. 3:1-13; Col.
2:2-3,8).

Among the leading philosophers and religionists of the period
were:

(1) *Plato* (427-347 B.C.) — This world is only a shadow of eternal
realities.

(2) *Aristotle* (384-322 B.C.) — Reality resides in individual things
themselves.

(3) *Zeno* (c. 300 B.C.), founder of the Stoics — Live according to
nature.

(4) *Epicurus* (c. 300 B.C.), founder of the Epicureans — Pursue
pleasure.

Exercise: Read Colossians 2:4-23 and observe the different things Paul
        writes about —
        a. false philosophy
        b. false doctrines
        c. Christ, and truth about Him

3. *Roman background.* The Roman background of the New Testament is mainly political and social. The status of the Roman
Empire from its birth (eighth century B.C.) to the time of Christ can
be represented by the two words *expansion* and *peace*:

EXPANSION
- Founding of Rome — eighth century B.C.
- Organization of republican form of government — fifth century B.C.
- Wars — fourth to first century B.C.

PEACE
- Rule of emperors — beginning with Augustus, 27 B.C.
- *Pax Romana* ("Roman peace") — law and order in the empire

Unity and political stability of the Roman Empire at the time of
Christ's birth was one of the bright aspects of the Roman background
of the New Testament. Of this Erich Sauer writes, "Never before or
since in history has there been an empire that has united in itself all
the civilized peoples of its time as did the Roman."[18]

18. Erich Sauer, *The Dawn of World Redemption*, p. 177.

The Greek influence had not died away, however. Sauer writes, "Although the Romans were the military and political masters of the world, *culturally* they were conquered by the Greeks...."[19] The Roman Empire was like a reservoir of the Hellenistic culture, which had spread throughout the Mediterranean world from the time of Alexander the Great.

Some of the characteristics of the Roman background are briefly noted here:

a. World Centralization. The unifier was the emperor, the ruler of the Mediterranean world. Worship of the emperor was inevitable, and so religious clash with Christianity was unavoidable. As an example, Paul was executed by Nero (reign: A.D. 54-68), and John was exiled on the Island of Patmos (Rev. 1:9) during Domitian's reign (A.D. 81-96).[20]

b. World Communication. The highways and sea lanes of the Roman Empire made world traffic possible, and when the time came for the missionary journeys of the early Christians the cities were easily accessible. (See Maps N, O, and P of Paul's missionary journeys, pp. 220, 222, 225.)

The Roman system of roads and bridges also helped expedite mail deliveries between cities.

c. World Peace. Although the reigns of some emperors were marred periodically by times of war (such as Augustus, who ruled from 30 B.C. to A.D. 14), the Roman period was a time of peace. That gave rise to the slogan *Pax Romana*. The benefit of international peace to the church's birth and growth cannot be overstated. When you are studying in the New Testament you will not read about the kinds of wars that were so commonplace in the years of Old Testament history.

d. World Spiritual Disorder. Erich Sauer describes the spiritual disarray: "Rome became a venerator of all deities, often horribly grotesque, senselessly confused, ill-formed sickly phantasies. The entire Mediterranean world resembled a gigantic cauldron of mixture."[21]

Aristocratic society wallowed in moral depravity, idleness of wealth, pursuit of pleasure. The middle class lived on a higher plane morally and had strong religious feelings. Members were searching for the truth but never finding it. Many religions found their way into people's hearts. From Egypt came the worship of Isis and Osiris; from Persia, the cult of Mithras; from Asia Minor, the cult of Cybele. Many

19. *Ibid.*, p. 176.
20. See Chart 12 for a list of the Roman emperors.
21. Erich Sauer, *The Dawn of World Redemption*, p. 181.

gods and idols, representing secret and nature religions, were among those who moved in from the Orient. But none brought redemption of sinners, none brought eternal salvation.

"When the fulness of time came, God sent forth his Son" (Gal. 4:4). Concerning preparation, the time was right, for the law had served its disciplinary and instructive purposes. The time also was right concerning the political, religious, and social climate, because those were conducive to the ministry of the gospel; and it was right regarding need, with a spiritual vacuum waiting to be filled.

The world of Jesus' day was ruled by Gentile Rome. The particular people to whom He primarily ministered were Jews of Palestine

CHART 10

WORLD OF JESUS' DAY

ROMAN EMPIRE	JEWISH PEOPLE
POLITICAL SETTING	
—Unification of the Mediterranean world —Safe and easy communication —Universal language —Universal peace	—Under the yoke of Rome —Expectation of a Deliverer, of their own race —Sanhedrin (the Jewish organ of local government) had only limited power
MORAL SETTING	
—Degradation —"To corrupt and be corrupt is the spirit of the times" (Tacitus)	—Generally strict standards —Sadducees sponsored moral compromise
INTELLECTUAL SETTING	
—Greek and Roman culture highly developed	—Education a prominent part of the Jews' life
RELIGIOUS SETTING	
—Heathen idolatry —Mystic religions —Philosophic religions —Spiritual vacuum	—Generally intensely religious as to externals —Religious life molded by three sects: 1. Pharisees: rigid legalists; self-righteous; middle class 2. Sadducees: free thinkers; worldly; upper class 3. Essenes: mystic pietists; ascetics —Synagogues and rabbis: a thriving institution of worship which arose after the exile —A believing remnant: there were some who looked and prayed for the advent of the Messiah (Read Luke 2:21-39.)

(see Matthew 15:24). Chart 10 is a summary tabulation intended to describe those two worlds of Jesus' day, Gentile and Jewish.

When you read the New Testament, try to visualize the hearts of people — Jew and Gentile — throughout the Roman Empire, hearts that are confused and guilt-ridden. As you do that, you will better understand and appreciate the words and ministry of Jesus, the preaching of the early apostles, and the letters of the New Testament writers.

Review Questions

1. Compare New Testament history with these four descriptions of Old Testament history: foreshadow, promise, problem, commencement.

2. What is meant by "the four hundred silent years"?

3. Compare Judaism of 400 B.C. with Judaism of Jesus' time, concerning vernacular, places of worship, and religious groups.

4. What were the three geographical centers of Judaism during the silent centuries?

5. When did the Sadducees and Pharisees originate?

6. Name the six periods of Jewish history during the silent years. Which was the Period of Independence? What was the political state of Palestine when Jesus was born?

7. What did the Greek Septuagint version contribute to Christianity's first century? To what extent did Jesus and the apostles use that version?

8. What were the contributions of the Roman background to the early Christian church and the New Testament?

II. POLITICAL SETTING

Because the New Testament writings have a historical setting, it is natural that they include references to secular rulers of the Bible lands, rulers who were governing the people at that time. This is the political setting of the New Testament.

The gospels and Acts contain most of the New Testament's references to the secular rulers. The average Bible student has difficulty identifying and associating the references, because of confusion over different *kinds* of rulers. (There were kings, governors, procurators, emperors.) The purpose of this section of study is to distinguish between the different titles of rulers, identify the lands of their rule, and learn the names of the rulers who appear in the Bible account.

A. THE LANDS

All the action of the New Testament takes place in lands of the Roman Empire. That was the "world" of such references as Acts 17:6. The territorial scope of Roman supremacy is shown on Map D, The Roman Empire.[22] Observe the boundaries of the Empire when Jesus was born (5 B.C.). The capitol of the Empire was Rome, Italy. (See Map E, page 64, for its location.) Where on Map D is Palestine located (not identified by name)? Compare its size with other lands, such as Egypt. (See Map L, page 207.)

MAP D

The land of Palestine was a small part of the Roman Empire, but a key part, because of its strategic location. Practically all the gospels and much of Acts have Palestine as their geographical setting. When Jesus was born, Palestine was divided into various provinces and sections, as shown on Map F, Palestine During Jesus' Ministry.[23] Study the map, and observe 1. familiar provinces (e.g., Galilee); 2. less familiar areas (e.g., Trachonitis); 3. familiar cities (e.g., Jerusalem).

22. This map is from *Wycliffe Bible Encyclopedia*, 2:1480.
23. More about the geography of Palestine will be said later in this chapter.

B. THE TASK OF RULE

The ruler of the Roman Empire was the emperor. To rule effectively and peacefully so many distant lands from his throne at Rome was the burden of his government. How this was done in the case of Palestine, the homeland of the Jews, will be shown in the next pages.

C. THE TITLES OF RULERS

The provincial system of government set up by Emperor Augustus involved rulers over countries and over provinces of those countries. The names and brief descriptions of their titles are given below. Before you read the descriptions, study Chart 11, Rulers of the Roman Empire. Observe the three geographical realms of rule and the three associated titles of rulers.

1. *Emperor*. The emperor was the absolute ruler of the Roman Empire. A surname of the early Roman emperors was "Caesar" (e.g., Caesar Augustus, meaning Emperor Augustus). When Paul said, "I appeal to Caesar" (Acts 25:11), he was referring to the emperor, who at that time was Nero.

The names of the emperors during New Testament times are shown on Chart 12, New Testament Time Chart. Who was emperor a. when Jesus was born?; b. when Jesus was crucified?; c. when Paul was first imprisoned in Rome?; d. when the last New Testament book (Revelation) was written?

2. *King*. Kings[24] were the highest local rulers of territories in the Roman Empire, subject to the central authority of the emperor at Rome. The king's office was approved by the Roman senate. During New Testament times Palestine, in whole or in part, was ruled by kings of the Herodian dynasty (succession of rulers from the same family). (See Appendix A, The Herodian Family.) The dynasty began with Herod the Great in 37 B.C. and ended with the death of Herod Agrippa II in A.D. 70.

Study carefully the names of kings of territories in Palestine as shown on Chart 12.[25] Who was king of all Palestine when Jesus was born? What three kings succeeded him? Over what lands did each rule? Locate those lands on Map E. What two kings ruled over all Palestine at any one time, between 37 B.C. and A.D. 70?

Read the following New Testament references to the kings. As you read, associate the geography and time.

a. Herod the Great — Matthew 2:1-19; Luke 1:5

---

24. Some kings are referred to as ethnarchs. A tetrarch (e. g., Herod Antipas) was a ruler of a fourth part of a kingdom or province.
25. The lists of kings and governors on Chart 12 go as far as A.D. 70, which was the critical date of the destruction of Jerusalem.

CHART 11

RULERS OF THE ROMAN EMPIRE

—appearing in the New Testament

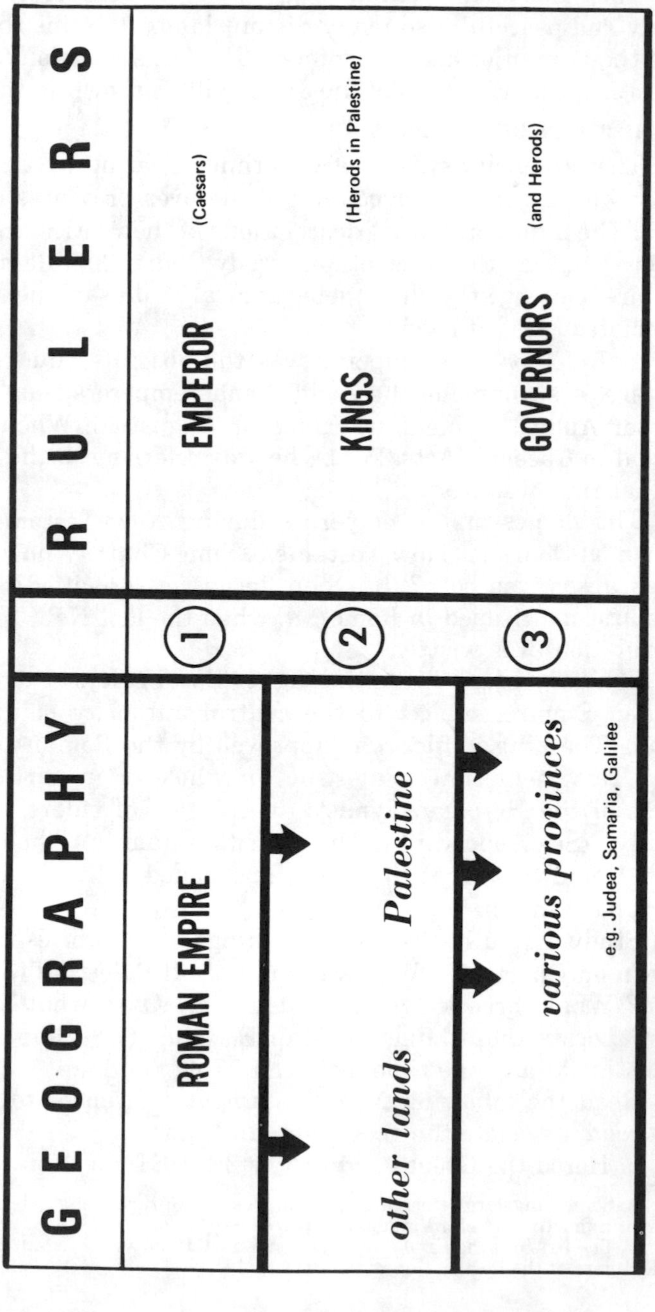

GEOGRAPHY		RULERS	
ROMAN EMPIRE	①	EMPEROR	(Caesars)
other lands → Palestine →	②	KINGS	(Herods in Palestine)
various provinces → e.g. Judea, Samaria, Galilee	③	GOVERNORS	(and Herods)

b. Herod Antipas — Mark 6:14-29; Luke 3:1; 13:31-35; 23:7-12

c. Archelaus — Matthew 2:22

d. Herod Philip — Luke 3:1

e. Herod Agrippa I — Acts 12:1-24

f. Herod Agrippa II — Acts 25:13—26:32

3. *Governor*. Governors (procurators) were rulers of designated territories, appointed by the emperor and directly responsible to him. Much of their work involved finances, such as taxes. They also had supreme judicial authority, such as Pilate used regarding Jesus. Their official residence was in Caesarea (see Map E). The area of their responsibility was usually that area not ruled by a contemporary king. For example, Herod Antipas was a tetrarch of Galilee *while* Pilate was governor of Judea, Samaria, and Old Idumea.[26] (See the locations of those areas on Map E.)

Most of the New Testament references to governors are to Pilate, Felix, and Festus. Observe their names on Chart 12. According to the chart, was there ever any overlapping of governors ruling? When was the first governor of Palestine appointed? Who ruled Palestine alone while there was no governor between A.D. 41-44?

Exercises: a. Note in an exhaustive concordance all the appearances of the word *governor(s)* in the New Testament. Read a few of the verses. b. After Paul's arrest in Jerusalem he had contact with three rulers: King Agrippa, Governor Felix, and Governor Festus. Read Acts 23:1—26:32. Observe all the references to the three rulers (and to the emperor ["Caesar"], 26:32). Refer to Chart 12 to see why all four rulers come into the picture of the account at the same time.

4. *Other titles*. Proconsuls were deputy consuls serving in the Roman provinces for one year, with unlimited power in military and civil situations. Two New Testament references are Sergius Paulus (Acts 13:7) and Gallio (Acts 18:12).

All the preceding discussion has been about secular rulers in Palestine. It should be kept in mind that in each local Jewish community there were also religious leaders, who molded and to a large extent ruled the personal and religious lives of the Jews. Those were the Jewish priests and the Sanhedrin (council), which was like a Jewish Supreme Court. More will be said about these in later studies. For now, study Chart 13, High Priests During New Testament Times.

---

26. The geographical domains of the governors are not shown on Chart 12. Refer to a Bible dictionary for identification of a governor's territory.

NEW TESTAMENT

CHART 12

DATE	EVENTS		EMPERORS (CAESARS)
B.C. 37			
10			
A.D.	BIRTH OF JESUS (5 B.C.)		Augustus (30 B.C.—A.D. 14)
10			
20			
30	Ministry of John the Baptist		Tiberius (14-37)
	Ministry of Jesus; Death and Resurrection		
	Paul's conversion Acts 9:1-19*a*		
40	Famine Acts 11:28		Gaius Caligula (37-41)
	Paul's first journey Acts 13:1—14:28		
	Council of Jerusalem Acts 15:1-15		
50	Paul's second journey Acts 15:36—18:22		Claudius (41-54)
	Paul's third journey Acts 18:23—21:17		
	Paul's first Roman imprisonment		
	Acts 27:1—28:31		Nero (54-68)
60	Paul's second imprisonment		
	Paul's martyrdom		Galba (68-69)
			Otho (69)
			Vitellius (69)
70	Destruction of Jerusalem		Vespasian (69-79)
80			Titus (79-81)
90	LAST NEW TESTAMENT BOOK WRITTEN		Domitian (81-96)
100			Nerva (96-98)
110			Trajan (98-117)
120			

NEW TESTAMENT BOOKS WRITTEN

TIME CHART

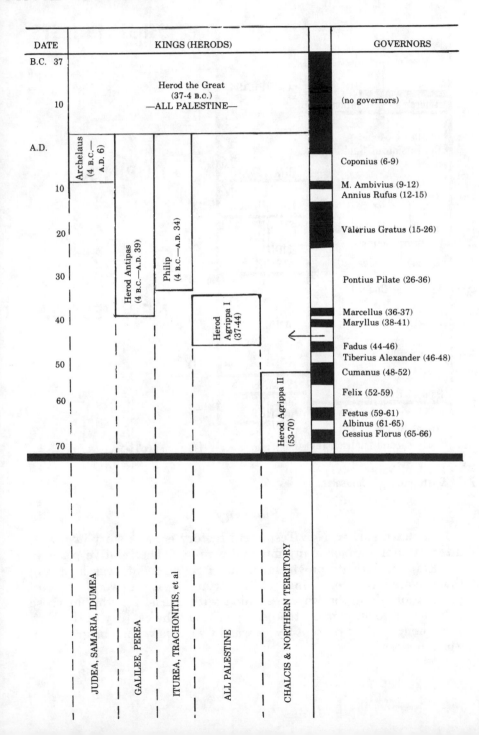

DATE	KINGS (HERODS)		GOVERNORS
B.C. 37			
10	Herod the Great (37-4 B.C.) —ALL PALESTINE—		(no governors)
A.D.	Archelaus (4 B.C.—A.D. 6)		
10			Coponius (6-9)
			M. Ambivius (9-12) Annius Rufus (12-15)
20	Herod Antipas (4 B.C.—A.D. 39)	Philip (4 B.C.—A.D. 34)	Valerius Gratus (15-26)
30			Pontius Pilate (26-36)
40		Herod Agrippa I (37-44)	Marcellus (36-37) Maryllus (38-41)
			Fadus (44-46) Tiberius Alexander (46-48)
50			Cumanus (48-52)
60	Herod Agrippa II (53-70)		Felix (52-59)
			Festus (59-61) Albinus (61-65) Gessius Florus (65-66)
70			

JUDEA, SAMARIA, IDUMEA

GALILEE, PEREA

ITUREA, TRACHONITIS, et al

ALL PALESTINE

CHALCIS & NORTHERN TERRITORY

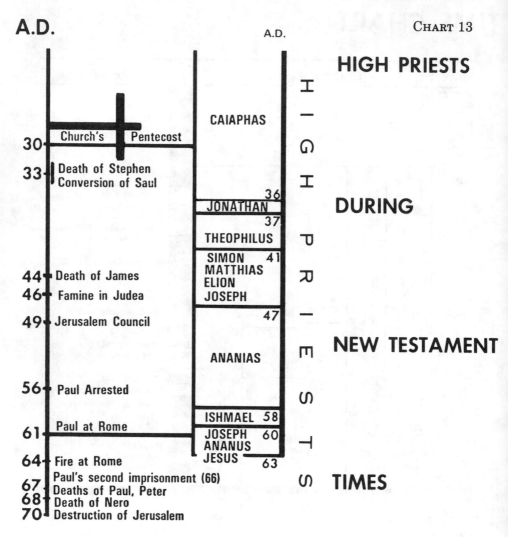

A.D.   A.D.   CHART 13

HIGH PRIESTS

CAIAPHAS

30 – Church's | Pentecost

33 – Death of Stephen
Conversion of Saul

JONATHAN   36
DURING

THEOPHILUS   37

SIMON   41
MATTHIAS
ELION
JOSEPH

44 – Death of James

46 – Famine in Judea

49 – Jerusalem Council   47

ANANIAS

NEW TESTAMENT

56 – Paul Arrested

ISHMAEL   58

61 – Paul at Rome

JOSEPH   60
ANANUS
JESUS   63

64 – Fire at Rome

67 – Paul's second imprisonment (66)
Deaths of Paul, Peter
68 – Death of Nero
70 – Destruction of Jerusalem

HIGH PRIESTS TIMES

Summary

As noted earlier, New Testament history is not a story involving international wars or many internal conflicts. The relative peace of the Empire, with its provincial form of government, was a setting that favored the beginnings of Christianity. There were times of persecution along the way, beginning with Christ's birth, but those only served to strengthen the people of God. The century of the New Testament — the first century — was in various ways a bright era of world history.

Review Questions

1. How extensive geographically was the Roman Empire when Jesus was born?

2. What is the geographical setting of practically all the gospels and much of Acts?

3. Name three provinces of Palestine in Jesus' time.

4. Fill in the correct titles of rulers: The _____ ruled over the Roman Empire; _____ ruled over lands, such as Palestine; and _____ ruled over provinces, such as Galilee.

5. Who was emperor when Jesus was born? Who was king of Palestine at that time?

6. What was the office of Pilate, Felix, and Festus?

7. In what capacity did the high priests rule in New Testament times?

8. What was the Sanhedrin?

III. PHYSICAL SETTING

The physical setting of the Bible is one of the best reminders to us that its message is about real people, just like us, living in real places in actual time. An acquaintance with and appreciation of that physical setting helps make the Bible come alive. In the following pages we will be studying the geography, climate, and everyday living of New Testament times.

A. GEOGRAPHY

Much of the New Testament is action, and action involves places. That is why geography is a key ingredient of the Bible's setting.

Someone has said, "To visualize is to empathize." If you want to help yourself *feel* the action of ancient Bible history, visualize *where* it was taking place as you read the Bible text. This should be one of the strongest motivations for you to learn the geography of the New Testament.

Three basic New Testament maps will be studied in this section. These maps show the large areas of setting. Other related and more detailed maps appear at appropriate places throughout the book. It is important to have a good grasp of the large, overall geographical setting before zeroing in on the details of the smaller areas.

1. *The New Testament world.* Map E, The New Testament World,[27] shows where most of the action of the New Testament took place. Compare the extent of this area with that of the Roman Empire (Map D, page 56).

---

27. This is from *Unger's Bible Handbook,* p. 728.

Answer the following questions or record observations, based on Map E:

a. Is the phrase "from Jerusalem to Rome" an accurate measure of the length of the New Testament world?

b. The name *Palestine* does not appear on the map. It borders the southeastern Mediterranean Sea and extends from below Tyre to the Dead Sea and beyond, south of Jerusalem. (See Map F, p. 65.) What strikes you about Palestine's size, compared to other lands of the Empire?

c. Most of the action of the four gospels is in Palestine. Much of the action of Acts, and the setting of the epistles, is in Asia Minor, Macedonia, and Achaia (Greece). Locate these on the map.

d. Considering Jerusalem as the geographical source of the Christian church, into what direction of the compass does the New Testament report the expansion of Christianity?[28]

MAP E

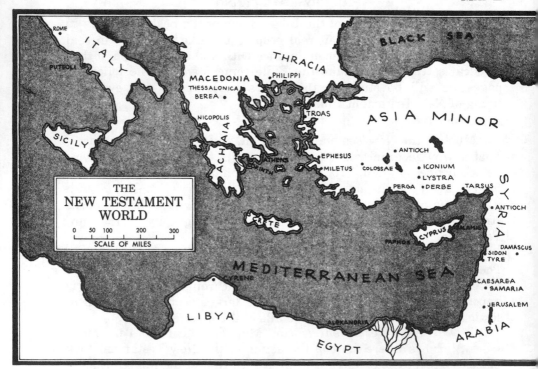

28. Christianity did expand into other directions in the early centuries. That story is described in non-canonical but accurate historical documents.

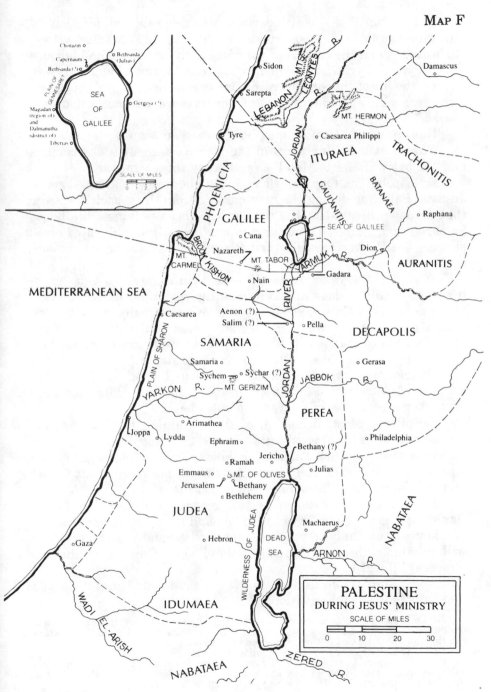

Chorazin
Bethsaida (Julias)
Capernaum
Bethsaida (?)

PLAIN OF GENNESARET

SEA OF GALILEE

Magadan (region of) and Dalmanutha (district of)
Tiberias

Gergesa (?)

SCALE OF MILES
0   1   2

Damascus

Sidon

LEBANON MTS.
LEONTES R.

MT. HERMON

Sarepta

Tyre

JORDAN R.

Caesarea Philippi

ITURAEA

TRACHONITIS

PHOENICIA

BROOK KISHON

GALILEE

Cana

Nazareth

MT. TABOR

MT. CARMEL

GAULANITIS

BATANAEA

Raphana

SEA OF GALILEE

YARMUK R.

Dion

AURANITIS

Gadara

Nain

MEDITERRANEAN SEA

RIVER JORDAN

Caesarea

Aenon (?)
Salim (?)

Pella

DECAPOLIS

PLAIN OF SHARON

SAMARIA

Samaria

Sychem
Sychar (?)
MT. GERIZIM

Gerasa

JABBOK R.

YARKON R.

PEREA

Arimathea

Joppa
Lydda

Ephraim

Ramah

Emmaus

Jerusalem
MT. OF OLIVES
Bethany

Bethlehem

Jericho

Bethany (?)

Julias

Philadelphia

NABATAEA

JUDEA

WILDERNESS OF JUDEA

Gaza

Hebron

DEAD SEA

Machaerus

ARNON R.

IDUMAEA

WADI EL-ARISH

ZERED R.

NABATAEA

PALESTINE
DURING JESUS' MINISTRY

SCALE OF MILES
0   10   20   30

2. *Palestine*.[29] As noted earlier, the geographical location of Palestine in Bible times was strategic. Of that, G. T. Manley writes, "Palestine lay on the cross-roads of ancient civilization. The highway from Egypt to Syria and beyond, which ran through Palestine, was one of the most important roads in the ancient world both for commerce and for strategy, and its importance has not yet disappeared."[30]

This crossroads location may be observed on Map D.

What part Palestine plays in the New Testament books is summarized below. Refer to Map F as you study these summaries.

a. Gospels. The four gospels report the journeys and missions of Jesus in Palestine during His brief career. From the gospels we learn that Jesus spent most of His time in the three provinces of Judea, Samaria, and Galilee. Three surrounding areas that He visited occasionally are Perea, Decapolis, and Phoenicia. Locate the six regions on Map F.

After about a year of limited service in Judea, most of Jesus' itinerant work was done in and around the region of Galilee, though His trips between Galilee and Jerusalem afforded many opportunities of ministry along the way. Of the many cities and villages that He visited on His evangelistic tours, only about twenty are mentioned by name in the gospels. Most of those appear on Map F.

b. Acts. Most of Acts 1-12 takes place in Palestine. Most of the remaining chapters (13-14, 16-28) focus on the missionary journeys and other experiences of Paul in the lands beyond.

c. Epistles. Most, if not all, of the remaining twenty-two New Testament books originated outside Palestine and were written to residents mostly of non-Palestinian lands. But the messages of the epistles focused on the Holy Land, for the simple reason that Christ and the church and Christianity were born there.

3. *Jerusalem*. Jerusalem is the geographical heart of Christianity. It was the Holy City in both Old and New Testament times; it is a key city on the international scene today; and all world history will culminate there at the end of time, when Christ is enthroned forever (Phil. 2:9-11).

Study Map G, Jerusalem In New Testament Times,[31] as you make the following observations:

29. The name *Palestine* is derived from the Hebrew *eres Pelistim*, meaning "land of the Philistines." Philistia was a small region in the southwest, but by the fifth century B.C. the name was applied to the entire land of Canaan.
30. G. T. Manley, *The New Bible Handbook*, p. 425.
31. This map is from Merrill F. Unger, *Unger's Bible Handbook*, p. 488. For a helpful description of the geography of Jerusalem, see the article "Jerusalem" in *The New Bible Dictionary*, J. D. Douglas, ed., pp. 614-20.

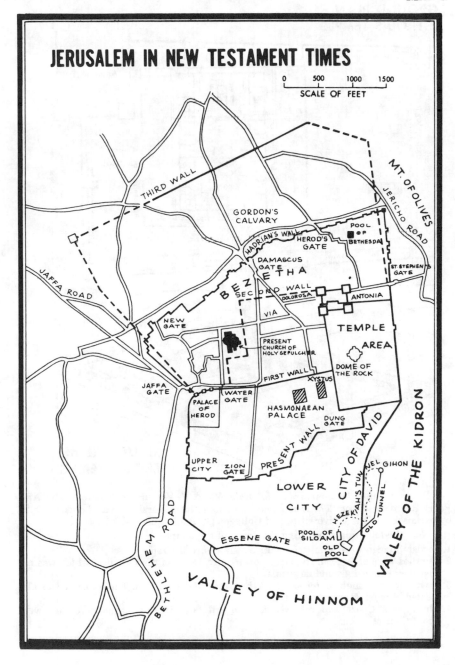

JERUSALEM IN NEW TESTAMENT TIMES

0   500   1000   1500
SCALE OF FEET

THIRD WALL

MT. OF OLIVES

JERICHO ROAD

GORDON'S CALVARY

POOL OF BETHESDA

HEROD'S GATE

JAFFA ROAD

HADRIAN'S WALL

DAMASCUS GATE

ST. STEPHEN'S GATE

BEZETHA

SECOND WALL

VIA DOLOROSA

NEW GATE

ANTONIA

VIA

PRESENT CHURCH OF HOLY SEPULCHER

TEMPLE AREA

DOME OF THE ROCK

FIRST WALL

XYSTUS

JAFFA GATE

WATER GATE

PALACE OF HEROD

HASMONAEAN PALACE

DUNG GATE

CITY OF DAVID

UPPER CITY

ZION GATE

PRESENT WALL

LOWER CITY

HEZEKIAH'S TUNNEL

EL GIHON

OLD TUNNEL

VALLEY OF THE KIDRON

BETHLEHEM ROAD

ESSENE GATE

POOL OF SILOAM

OLD POOL

VALLEY OF HINNOM

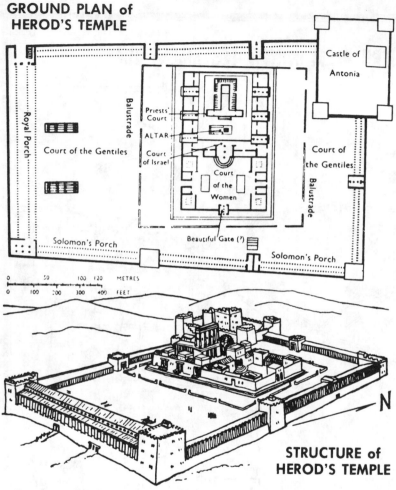

GROUND PLAN of HEROD'S TEMPLE

Castle of Antonia

Royal Porch

Balustrade

Priests' Court

ALTAR

Court of the Gentiles

Court of Israel

Court of the Women

Court of the Gentiles

Balustrade

Solomon's Porch

Beautiful Gate (?)

Solomon's Porch

0   50   100 120   METRES
0   100   200   300   400   FEET

STRUCTURE of HEROD'S TEMPLE

N

Drawings after *Dictionnaire de la Bible, V,* ed. F. Vigouroux, © Letouzey et Ané, Paris. Reproduced from *The New Bible Dictionary* (Inter-Varsity Press, London, 1962), by permission of the Universities and Colleges Christian Fellowship.

Note the following concerning the areas of the temple:

1. Jewish laymen were admitted as far as the Court of Israel.
2. Gentiles were allowed in the large outer court, Court of the Gentiles, which was not considered sacred ground as such.
3. Jewish women might enter as far as the Court of the Women. The treasury was also located here (cf. Mark 12:41—42.
4. The Priests' Court, was reserved for the priests and Levites, and here they went about their services.

a. The original city of Jerusalem in Old Testament times covered only the ridge marked on this map as "City of David."

b. In Jesus' time the north wall of Jerusalem was in the location of Hadrian's wall shown on the map. Soon after the crucifixion, Agrippa I commenced building the third wall in the north, which was never completed before the Roman destruction of Jerusalem in A.D. 70.

c. Note the locations of the Temple area, Herod's palace, Pool of Bethesda, and Gordon's Calvary (traditional site of Jesus' crucifixion). Study the accompanying ground plan and drawing of Herod's Temple.

B. TOPOGRAPHY

One of the best ways to recall the locations of New Testament cities is to picture the physical features of the land where they are located. This also helps you understand why a city originated where it did, and why journeys followed certain routes. Study the general features of Palestine as shown on Map H. The natural contours of the land run north-south. As you move from west to east on the map, you will observe six major kinds of contour.

Observe the following about each of these.

① COASTAL PLAIN This follows the coast up to the promontory of Mount Carmel. Relatively few cities were located here during Bible times, partly because of the absence of navigable harbors.

② SHEFELAH (also called *Lowlands*). Here the terrain begins to ascend from the low coastal plain. Many cities sprang up here, in part because of the semifertile soil.

③ HILL COUNTRY (also called *Judean Hills*, and *Cis-Jordan Hills*). The average elevation of these is two thousand feet. Draw on the map a slightly sweeping curve from Mt. Carmel to Jerusalem. This north-south ridge bisects the lands of Samaria and Judea. The ridge becomes prominent again north of Galilee, after the break at the Plain of Esdraelon, just southwest of the Sea of Galilee. The two major north-south travel routes were along the Cis-Jordan Range and the Jordan Valley. Most of the cities of Christ's ministry lie along the Judean Hills and around the Sea of Galilee. Many cities were built along this ridge, especially because of the natural fortifications that were needed in Old Testament times.

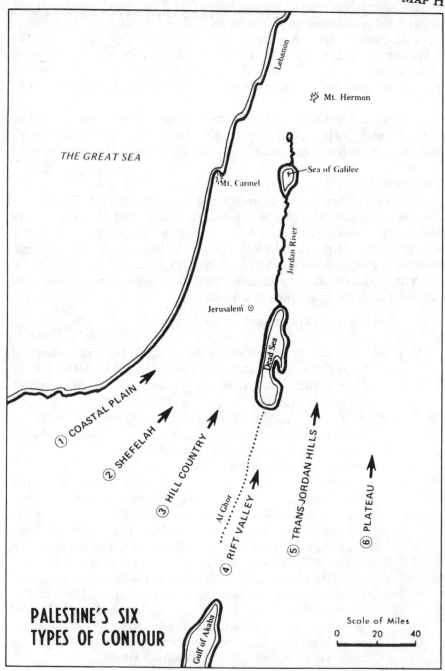

THE GREAT SEA

Lebanon

Mt. Hermon

Sea of Galilee

Mt. Carmel

Jordan River

Jerusalem ⊙

Dead Sea

① COASTAL PLAIN

② SHEFELAH

③ HILL COUNTRY

Al Ghor

④ RIFT VALLEY

⑤ TRANS-JORDAN HILLS

⑥ PLATEAU

PALESTINE'S SIX
TYPES OF CONTOUR

Gulf of Akaba

Scale of Miles

0   20   40

④ RIFT VALLEY This is the most consistent feature of the north-south contour. Its average width is about ten miles. For the entire length of Palestine, the depression is below the level of the Great Sea (Mediterranean). Follow this depression from north to south on Map H as you read the descriptions given below.

Valley west of Mount Hermon. The Jordan River originates here, north of the Sea of Galilee. Between the Lebanon and Hermon ranges, the rift valley is very prominent.

Sea of Galilee. The sea is 685 feet below the level of the Great Sea. This beautiful area was inhabited by many people in New Testament times.

Jordan River. The river is entirely below sea level, from the Sea of Galilee to the Dead Sea. The hot and humid climate of this valley discouraged the building of cities. Jericho was an exception (see Map F).

Salt Sea (Dead Sea). This is 1,286 feet below sea level. What main river flows into it? The sea has no outlet, hence its dense and rich mineral content. A few cities were located on its shores in Old Testament times.

Al Ghor (Araba). A hot, dry valley. No cities were located here.

Gulf of Aqaba. Solomon built a fleet of ships at the north end of this gulf (1 Kings 9:26).

⑤ TRANS-JORDAN HILLS The rugged hills rise sharply from the low rift valley to the high plateau. Few cities were located here.

⑥ PLATEAU From the fertile tableland of the north to the semidesert south, this plateau was the scene of relatively little New Testament history. Its rolling land was used mostly for grazing livestock. Jesus ministered at times in the cities of Decapolis and Perea (see Map F, page 65).

As you proceed with your survey of the New Testament, especially the four gospels and Acts, visualize the topography that you have just studied. For example, when you read that "a certain man was going down from Jerusalem to Jericho" (Luke 10:30), you should be able to visualize a *descending* road, one moving down off the ridge.

C. WEATHER AND CLIMATE

Palestine is in the same latitudes as the southern United States. Its climate is controlled generally by the prevailing westerly winds from the Mediterranean Sea. However, because of the diversity of topography, the climate varies considerably from place to place. Overall, there are two seasons: warm, dry summers, and cool, wet winters. The rainy season lasts from November to March, the rains being unusually heavy at the beginning and end of the season (from which come the terms "early" and "latter" rains).[32] Average temperature ranges for Jerusalem, representing recent records, are forty-one to fifty-four degrees Fahrenheit in January and sixty-five to eighty-five degrees in August. The moderating effect is caused by the more constant temperatures of the Mediterranean Sea.

The climate of Galilee, where Jesus lived most of His life and accomplished most of His public ministry, was more pleasant in the summer months than that of Judea and the south Jordan Valley. Hot desert winds (sirocco) plagued the plateau lands east of the Jordan. This was one of the main reasons for sparse population there in biblical times.[33]

Climate is distinguished from weather in that climate is the prevailing atmospheric condition over a period of time, whereas weather is the condition at a particular time. The accompanying weather map (Map I) of the Bible lands shows the weather pattern that prevailed there on the last of the Passover (Pesah) week, April 22, 1978. The weather on that day in the environs of Jerusalem was typical for the date and place: partly cloudy, mild (around 70° F.), light wind. A high pressure ridge extended from Egypt to Syria and blocked the frontal systems (North Africa to Asia Minor) from moving into Palestine. The Passover week is in the transition between the cool, wet winter and warm, dry summer seasons, and so extreme weather is not the rule during those weeks. The weather was very supportive of the hundreds of thousands of Jews who traveled to Jerusalem to worship on Passover, the most important festival of the year.

D. EVERYDAY LIFE IN PALESTINE

The New Testament was written by Orientals about Orientals. People of Western cultures need to keep that in mind to better appreciate the Bible stories and testimonies coming out of those ancient times. Fortunately, the foundational doctrines, such as man's sinfulness and God's holiness, which are taught in that Oriental setting are timeless and universal. So the Bible is not a closed book to those not acquainted with the everyday life of the inhabitants of

---

32. The early rain softened the ground for ploughing; the latter rain watered the seed.
33. The above observations are based on the reasonable assumption that Palestine's climate has not changed much since New Testament times.

MAP I

WEATHER MAP OF THE BIBLE LANDS April 22, 1978 1200 GMT

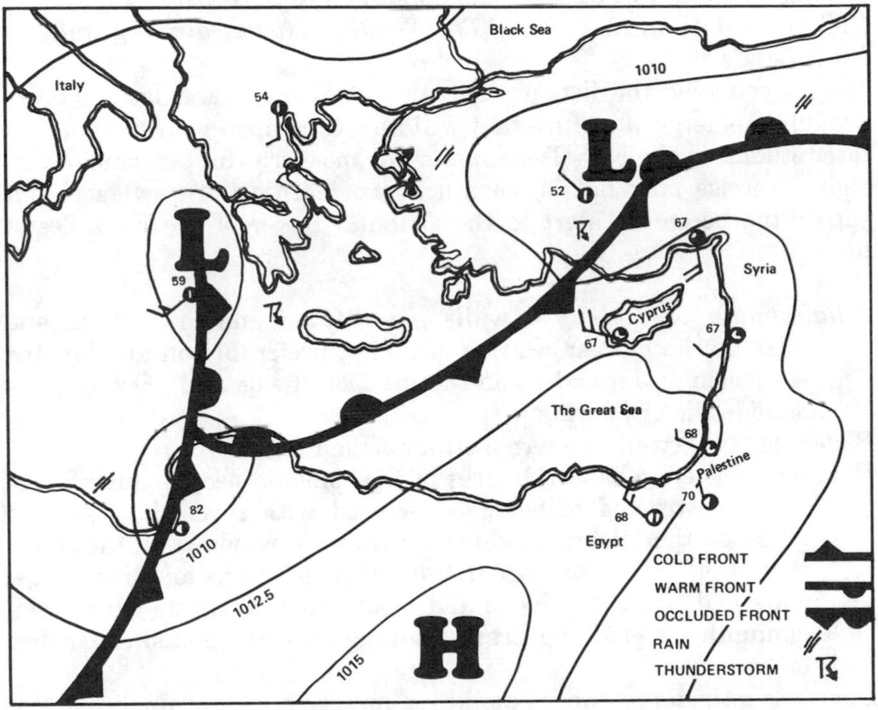

Black Sea

Italy

1010

54

L

52

Cyprus

Syria

59

67

67

67

The Great Sea

68

Palestine

82

68

70

1010

Egypt

1012.5

COLD FRONT

WARM FRONT

OCCLUDED FRONT

RAIN

H

1015

THUNDERSTORM

Palestine. But it can be sharper and clearer if that setting at least is mentally visualized and felt.

Bible dictionaries and commentaries are among the best sources for learning the local settings of the New Testament text. Also, there are books that specifically discuss this subject, such as A. C. Bouquet, *Everyday Life in New Testament Times*; and Fred H. Wight, *Manners and Customs of Bible Lands*.[34] It is beyond the scope of this introductory chapter to describe in detail the typical, everyday life in Palestine during New Testament times. The following list is included, however, to suggest a thumbnail sketch of such a setting.[35] No attempt has been made to show how life in New Testament times had advanced beyond the patterns of the centuries before Christ. By and

34. An interesting chapter on this subject, written in narrative style, is "Israel at Home," by John B. Taylor, in his book *A Christian's Guide to the Old Testament*, pp. 12-20. This is highly recommended reading.

35. All of these items are described, at least briefly, in Fred H. Wight's *Manners and Customs of Bible Lands*, from which this list is constructed. It should be understood that all the items are not necessarily part of every setting.

large, the basic patterns and traditional ways had remained the same. The descriptions are of Jewish life in Palestine. For the Greek setting of cities throughout the Roman Empire, consult Charles F. Pfeiffer and Howard F. Vos, *The Wycliffe Historical Geography of Bible Lands*.

As you read the list, use a little imagination and let a picture gradually emerge, a picture that will be etched upon your memory for later studies in the New Testament. The most fruitful outcome of this short exercise may not be so much the learning of new facts but rather the becoming alert to the Oriental flavor of the New Testament.

A Palestinian town or city — walls, gates, towers, narrow streets, and busy marketplaces; location of a city, preferably on an elevated site, such as Jerusalem on Mount Zion; fields and grazing plots outside the city limits.

Water supply — wells, cisterns, streams, and reservoirs.

Houses[36] — average size of houses of the common people: one room;[37] roofs constructed of beams overlayed with reeds, bushes, and grass; earthen floors; mud-brick walls; few windows on the street side; fireplace on the floor in the middle of the room; furnishings: mats and cushions, chairs and stools, storage chest, lampstand, handmill for grinding grain, cooking utensils, goatskin bottles, broom.

Domestic animals — dogs, donkeys, mules, horses, camels, sheep, goats.

Foods — barley and wheat bread, oil, buttermilk, cheese, fruits (olives, figs, grapes, raisins, pomegranates), vegetables, grain, honey; eggs, meat, and poultry were eaten, but not regularly; fish was a major food in the cities around the Sea of Galilee; generally, the people ate two meals a day: breakfast, and late dinner (about 5 p.m.).

Dress — both men and women: inner garment (tunic); girdle for the tunic; outer garment (mantle) used as shelter from wind, rain, cold, heat, and as a blanket at night; turban (head); sandals; women only: longer tunics and larger mantles, veil (entirely covering the head in public), elaborate ornamentations (earrings, bracelets).

---

36. The average Israelite spent less time in his abode than does the average person of Western culture.

37. Houses with more than one room were built around an open courtyard. For further descriptions of this and other related subjects consult the excellent book by A. C. Bouquet, *Everyday Life in New Testament Times*.

Education — Jewish children educated mainly by their parents: Hebrew religion and Scripture, reading and writing, practical skills; advanced training for leaders: such as in schools of the prophets, and by tutors.

Worship — worship by the Jewish family in each home; called worship meetings in public areas;[38] Temple worship in Jerusalem: regular participation by residents of the vicinity; participation at the annual religious feasts by Israelites from far and near.

Trades and professions — agriculture (grain, grapes, olives, figs), sheep-raising, fishing, hunting, pottery, carpentry, masonry, metal work, tentmaking, merchants, physicians.

Women's tasks — grinding grain; weaving; making clothes; washing; care of flocks; carrying water; cooking; housecleaning; rearing and educating the children; children of the home, especially girls, helped in these daily chores.

Taxes — poll (income tax), tributum (property tax), duties (food, transfer of property, sale of slaves), land tax, customs (on exports), purchase tax.

Travel — usually in groups, for the sake of safety; mode: most often by animals, sometimes by foot; meals: lunch brought along, as the main source; overnight lodging: at homes, sometimes inns.

The following two paragraphs illustrate how one writer has used his imagination, based on known facts, to describe the everyday life of the average Israelite. Do the same in your own thinking as you study the stories of the New Testament.

Tucked away along the winding streets of the town of Ramah, five miles north of Jerusalem, you will find the tiny one-roomed dwelling where Benaiah lives with his family. He lives much the same sort of life as the people around about him, never far from starvation level, cooped up in the city through the cold rainy months of winter and longing for the springtime when he can get out into the fields and work his ground.

. . . .

For beds the family shared two straw mats which were laid on the bare, earthen floor; for blankets they used the cloaks which were their normal outdoor garb. The little oil lamp burned dimly on a ledge in the

---

38. As noted earlier, during the Babylonian Captivity the Jews began worshiping regularly in meeting places, later called synagogues (from the Greek *synagoge*, "place of assembly"). They probably continued that tradition upon returning to their homeland, though there is no specific reference to it in the postexilic books of the Old Testament. By New Testament times the synagogue was a well-established institution.

corner. It was never allowed to go out except when the fire was alight in the daytime. It was the only box of matches they had! However, it gave very little light and so once you had settled down for the night it was impossible to get up without waking the whole household (farmyard and all!) and a caller late at night was never welcome.[39]

E. THE HEAVEN-EARTH SETTING

As much as the Bible concerns people and nations, with all their frailties and sins, it is unique because the dimension of miracle controls its story. In its pages, heaven touches earth, God comes down and works through man. This heaven-earth setting pervades the entire Book. He who wants to know what God is communicating in the temporal, local setting must accept and believe the supernatural dimension, for the message is meaningless without it. More will be said about that below, as we think about how to approach the New Testament and what to look for in our study of its pages.

Review Questions

1. What was strategic about the geographic location of Palestine?

2. In what provinces did Jesus minister mostly?

3. The epistles were written to Christians residing where?

4. In what ways is Jerusalem the geographical heart of Christianity?

5. Moving from west to east, name Palestine's six kinds of contour.

6. What are the two seasons in Palestine?

7. What wind orientation controls Palestine's weather?

8. What is Jerusalem's average weather around the time of Passover (late part of April)?

9. Describe the setting of a typical house and family in a small town of Galilee during the adolescent days of Jesus.

10. What was the average education of Hebrew children?

IV. How to Approach the New Testament

It is very helpful in New Testament studies to be acquainted with the setting, which has been discussed in the preceding pages. It is also helpful and even necessary to have the right approach in studying the New Testament. Without the right approach and clear guideposts, valuable time can be lost when studying the testament's many historical facts, theological doctrines, and end-time prophecies. Also, one

---

39. Taylor, *A Christian's Guide to the Old Testament*, pp. 12,17.

might become discouraged and confused over difficult or obscure portions of the text. But those pitfalls can be avoided in various ways, some of which are discussed below. As guideposts, they help the Bible student keep on track whenever he makes detailed, analytical studies of the Bible text. Those guideposts will reappear in the later survey studies of the individual books of the New Testament.

A. VIEW THE NEW TESTAMENT AS THE FULFILLMENT AND INTERPRETER OF THE OLD TESTAMENT

The Old Testament pointed forward to the New Testament, and so when passages in the latter look "Old" (e.g., lamb sacrifice, Sabbath, Temple), it should not surprise or confuse us. Every New Testament reference to the Old is natural, sound, and necessary. If you are convinced of that, you will feel at home in all passages that refer back to the pre-Christian era. Such passages include (1) prophesied events of Christ's life and His ministries; (2) applications of the Old Testament's doctrines of sin and salvation (e.g., in the book of Hebrews); and (3) prophesied events of end-times (e.g., about Israel).

This approach to the New Testament rests on the foundation that both testaments are the one Book, the Bible. In that Book is the story of God revealing more and more of Himself and His redemptive work to men. Norman Geisler writes of this:

> Christ at once sums up in Himself the perfection of the Old Testament precepts, the substance of Old Testament shadows, and types, and the fulfillment of Old Testament forecasts. Those truths about Him which bud forth in the Old Testament come into full bloom in the New Testament; the flashlight of prophetic truth turns into the floodlight of divine revelation.[40]

Such an approach supports the principle that a knowledge of the Old Testament is one of the best preparations for a study of the New Testament.

How does the accompanying diagram illustrate the relationship of the New Testament to the Old?

B. SURVEY THE NEW TESTAMENT BEFORE ANALYZING IT

It is important to "image the whole, then execute the parts." That is because a general survey study gives perspective and setting for the analysis of the small detailed parts. The main purpose of this book is to lead the student in such a survey of the New Testament. Values and procedures of survey study will be discussed in the next chapter.

---

40. Norman Geisler, *Christ: The Theme of the Bible*, p. 68.

C. RECOGNIZE THE KEY REVEALED TRUTHS OF THE NEW TESTAMENT

Key revealed truths underlie all the details of the whole New Testament text.[41] You are on firm ground when you recognize those truths as you study a Bible passage. Some of the main ones are discussed below.[42]

1. *Redemption is the prominent subject of the New Testament revelation.* From beginning to end the whole Bible is the story of redemption — God's work of bringing sinners back into fellowship with Him, through the death of His Son. Christ is the Redeemer, and because He is the central figure of the New Testament, the prominence of redemption in its pages is natural.

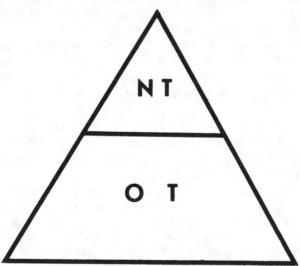

The price of the sinner's redemption was Christ's death on the cross. So the cross is prominent throughout the New Testament. Of that cross Erich Sauer writes,

> The cross is . . . the central event of His work on earth. It is the central act of God in the whole history of the universe. It is the most marvellous revelation of the will of God to save, "so that each that believes in Him should not be lost but have eternal life" (John 3:16).[43]

Because redemption is the prominent subject of the New Testa-

---

41. The Bible itself is the revelatory source of those key truths. That will become more apparent to you as you survey the various books of the New Testament.

42. Actually, the list of key New Testament truths is extensive. After you have studied this selected list, add others that come to your mind. And also keep in mind that *all* Bible truths are important.

43. Erich Sauer, *From Eternity to Eternity,* p.56.

ment, we may expect that each of its twenty-seven books contributes to this theme, in varying degrees, depending on the individual purpose of each book. This also is saying that we are not to read into every passage the doctrine of redemption, when the doctrine is *not* there.

2. *Sin is man's basic, desperate problem.* Redemption is prominent in the New Testament because it is God's merciful response to man's basic problem, sin, whose wages are eternal death (Rom. 6:23). So, just as we may expect to read much in the New Testament about salvation, we may expect to observe equivalent emphasis about sin. For example, Romans 1:18—3:20 is about *sin*; the following section, Romans 3:21—5:21 is about *salvation*.

It is because sin estranges man from God that He judges it as the arch-enemy it really is. And that is why He gave His Son to die on the cross. His death is the exact measure of the sins of mankind: "He died for all" (2 Cor. 5:15).

3. *The human race has no hope outside God's grace.* This truth is taught throughout the New Testament, just as it is prominent in the Old Testament. Paul writes that sinners, because they are separate from Christ, have no hope and are "without God in the world" (Eph. 2:12). But God's grace is the shining ray of hope. In the New Testament the word *grace* appears about one hundred thirty times, thus bathing the passages with the bright hope of salvation through the gift[44] of God's love.

What are your answers to the following: (a) Reconcile how God can forgive a murderer. (b) What makes God so longsuffering in His dealings with sinful man? (c) If a sinner cannot be saved by doing good works, where is there hope? (d) How can God let redeemed sinners into heaven? All these questions are answered by the one word *grace*.

Sinners who refuse the gift of God's grace — being clothed in Christ's righteousness — will spend eternity in the pain and agony of separation from Him. God's grace does not contradict or cancel His holiness. That is why we may expect to read much about judgment in the New Testament (e.g., the book of Revelation, which is mostly judgment). All the divine attributes are absolutely perfect and eternally concurrent. When God sends awful judgment for sin, because He is a holy God, He does not thereby nullify His grace.

4. *The gospel is a universal message.* Jesus and His disciples preached the gospel ("good news") first to the Jews, because they were

---

44. The Greek word (*charis*), which is translated *grace*, is sometimes translated *gift* (e.g., Rom. 6:23).

of the favored nation whose roots were in Abraham, to whom was given the promise of eternal blessing (Gen. 12:1-3; 17:1-8). In this connection it should be observed that the story of the gospels is a transition between the Old Testament law and the post-Pentecost church era. Israel rejected the Messianic message, and with that rejection came the extension of the call to the Gentile world. Of that John F. Walvoord writes,

> The fulfillment of the promise of God to David was postponed, and into the foreground came the undeclared purpose of God to call out from every nation a new company, composed of both Jew and Gentile, independent of all His promises to Israel, having its own calling and destiny.[45]

So Israel was not the exclusive audience of gospel preaching — the priority of the divine program was only with regard to time: "first for the Jew, then for the Gentile" (Rom. 1:16, NIV). Before long in the historical books (gospels-Acts) the gospel is preached to Gentiles as well as to Jews. That universal audience of the gospel is what Jesus had in mind when He gave the commission to His disciples, "You shall be My witnesses both in Jerusalem, and in all Judea and Samaria, and even to the remotest part of the earth" (Acts 1:8). Throughout the New Testament the gospel is seen as the power of God for salvation to *every one* who believes (Rom. 1:16).

5. *The work of Christ is wholly dependent on the person of Christ.* Jesus could do what He did only because of who He was, the true God-man. For example, He could perform miracles because He was God. He was a *genuine* substitute for mankind on the cross because He was genuinely human. And He was an *acceptable* sacrifice because He was sinless and perfect. Because of His humanity, He could identify with those being tempted — He Himself suffered when He was tempted (Heb. 2:18).

The problem with those who reject the works of Jesus (such as His performing of miracles) is that those persons do not believe Him to be who He truly is.[46] Throughout the New Testament the vital relationship of Jesus' person and His works constantly is brought before us. The life and ministry of Christ is an enigma if His divine-human nature is denied.

6. *Miracles are signs of revelation from God.* The New Testament abounds with miracles, most of them performed by Christ. Their basic purpose was to be signs, or revealing truths. For example, John

---

45. John F. Walvoord, *The Holy Spirit*, p. 81.
46. Cf. Mark 8:27-31.

writes that the miracles of Jesus were signs attesting who He was, "the Christ, the Son of God" (John 20:31; cf. Mark 8:27-29). There are secondary purposes in the New Testament miracles, such as alleviation of pain in healing a disease, or infliction of judgment for sin, but the primary purpose is to reveal truth about the miracle worker, Christ.

7. *The Holy Spirit is an active worker in this age.* All Persons of the Trinity are always ministering in behalf of every creature. Their ministries are equally important, though of different character. The Old Testament records many of the Holy Spirit's ministries for the non-elect, and the New Testament teaches His manifold work mainly in the experience of Christians. Walvoord compares the two eras (Old and New Testament) concerning the Holy Spirit's work: ". . . the age of grace shines with all the more brilliant luster, the exceeding abundance of all the ministries of the Spirit to all saints constituting a display of the grace of God such as the world has never seen before."[47]

You will find in your study of the New Testament many extended passages about the person and work of the Holy Spirit (e.g., Romans 8).

8. *All world history moves onward to the last days.* All world history is in God's sovereign control. He directs or permits the course of events in a person's or nation's career according to His sovereign and perfect will. And all will culminate at the climactic event of the enthronement of Jesus Christ. (Read Philippians 2:9-11.)

The historical periods of New Testament history are these:

HISTORY	N. T. COVERAGE
the life of Christ	4 Gospels
the birth and first years of the church	Acts 1-12
the church's early years of expansion	Acts 13-28; Epistles; Revelation 1-3
world history of end times	Revelation 4-21

A quick scanning of the New Testament shows that very few details of world history are prophesied concerning the two millennia before end times. But grand truths, which give deep and wide and far-reaching perspective, appear in the Bible text from time to time. For example, "all things . . . whether thrones or dominions or rulers or authorities . . . have been created through Him and for Him" (Col. 1:16). It is important for the Bible student not to demand (and so

---

47. John F. Walvoord, *The Holy Spirit,* p.77.

invent) detailed descriptions of history, whether predicted or reported. He should embrace the grand truths, and interpret and apply them as they were intended by God. When he does that, the full sufficiency of New Testament history and prophecy will be apparent.

D. ACCEPT THE NEW TESTAMENT AS GOD'S FINAL INSTRUCTIONS FOR LIVING

It is possible for Christians to live lives pleasing to God.[48] If that were not so, all the New Testament's commands, exhortations, promises, and helps would be one vast fraud.

The New Testament contains God's final instructions for living. It was written almost two thousand years ago, when it joined the corpus of Scripture that had been the Bible of Jesus (Old Testament). It remains timeless in its application. That is why the apostle Paul, writing to his friend Timothy about their ancient Bible, asserted dogmatically, "All Scripture is inspired by God and profitable for teaching, for reproof, for correction, for training in righteousness; that the man of God may be adequate, equipped for every good work" (2 Tim. 3:16-17). In the same context, Paul had reminded Timothy that it was the sacred writings that had given Timothy "the wisdom that leads to salvation through faith which is in Christ Jesus" (2 Tim. 3:15). So it is correct to say that all spiritual lessons derived from passages in the New Testament have something to say, directly or indirectly, about these two timeless, vital life truths: *way to* God, or *walk with* God. The Bible is that contemporary. And so we must open our hearts to its message. In the words of Edward J. Young,

> In approaching the Bible ... we need to remember that it is sacred ground. We must approach it with humble hearts, ready to hear what the Lord God says. The kaleidoscopic history of negative criticism is but further evidence that unless we do approach the Bible in a receptive attitude, we shall fail to understand it. Nor need we be ashamed to acknowledge that the words of Scripture are of God. ... The attempt to explain them as anything less than Divine is one of the greatest failures that has ever appeared in the history of human thought.[49]

V. REVIEW QUESTIONS

1. Write a list of four relationships between the New Testament and the Old Testament.

2. Why is it important to survey the New Testament as a whole before analyzing its individual parts (e.g., chapter study)?

48. Cf. Hebrews 11:6.
49. Edward J. Young, *Introduction to the Old Testament,* pp. 10-11.

3. Write out (as many as you can recall) a list of New Testament key truths discussed in the chapter.

4. In your own words, what are the divine practical purposes of the New Testament?

VI. SELECTED READING

HISTORICAL, RELIGIOUS, AND POLITICAL SETTING OF THE NEW TESTAMENT

Bruce, F. F. "Between the Testaments." In *The New Bible Commentary.* Rev. ed. Edited by D. Guthrie and J. A. Motyer, pp. 59-63.

Dosker, Henry E. "Between the Testaments." In *The International Standard Bible Encyclopedia,* 1:455-58.

Gundry, Robert H. *A Survey of the New Testament,* pp. 3-20; 33-55.

Harrison, Everett F. *Introduction to the New Testament,* pp. 3-56; 91-128.

Lace, O. Jessie, ed. *Understanding the New Testament,* pp. 11-63.

Manley, G. T. *The New Bible Handbook,* pp. 276-97.

Metzger, Bruce M. *The New Testament: Its Background, Growth and Content.*

Mounce, Robert H. "Is the New Testament Historically Accurate?" In *Can I Trust My Bible?* Edited by Howard Vos, pp. 173-90.

Pfeiffer, Charles. *Between the Testaments.*

Pfeiffer, R. H. *History of New Testament Times.*

Russell, D. S. *Between the Testaments.*

Snaith, Norman H. *The Jews from Cyrus to Herod.*

Tenney, Merrill C. *New Testament Survey,* pp. 1-58; 65-120.

————. *New Testament Times.*

GEOGRAPHICAL SETTING

Adams, J. McKee. *Biblical Backgrounds,* pp. 52-85; 136-214.

Aharoni, Yohanan. *The Land of the Bible.*

Baly, Dennis, *The Geography of the Bible,* pp. 125-266.

Jeremias, Joachim, *Jerusalem in the Time of Jesus.*

Orni, Efraim, and Efrat, Elisha. *Geography of Israel.* An excellent, large map of Palestine appears in a flap under the back cover.

Pfeiffer, Charles F. *Baker's Bible Atlas.*

Pfeiffer, Charles F., and Vos, Howard F. *The Wycliffe Historical Geography of Bible Lands.*

The Sacred Land. Excellent topographical maps.

Smith, George Adam. *The Historical Geography of the Holy Land.*

EVERYDAY LIFE IN BIBLE TIMES

Bailey, A. E. *Daily Life in Bible Times.*

Bouquet, A. C. *Everyday Life in New Testament Times.*

Corswant, W. A. *A Dictionary of Life in Bible Times.*

Freeman, James M. *Manners and Customs of the Bible.*

Grosvenor, Gilbert, ed. *Everyday Life in Ancient Times.*

Heaton, E. W. *Everyday Life in Old Testament Times.*

La Sor, William Sanford. *Daily Life in Bible Times.*

Manley, G. T. *The New Bible Handbook,* pp. 428-38.
Miller, M. S., and Miller, J. L. *Encyclopedia of Bible Life.*
Moldenke, Harold N., and Moldenke, Alma L. *Plants of the Bible.*
National Geographic Society. *Everyday Life in Bible Times.*
Prichard, James B. *The Ancient Near East in Pictures.*
Wight, Fred H. *Manners and Customs of Bible Lands.*

3

The Survey Method of Study

The fruits of Bible study are largely determined by *how* the Bible is studied, that is, by the method used. Of the various methods of Bible study, survey and analysis are primary. Survey is more than just reading a book. It is important to know what is involved in this method so we can use it to fullest advantage in our study of the New Testament books. The next few pages discuss especially the purposes and procedures of survey study. Further directions and suggestions for survey are given throughout the remainder of this manual in connection with each New Testament book. In the latter half of this chapter we shall see how to use this manual as a guide to our own survey studies.

I. PURPOSES AND PROCEDURES OF SURVEY STUDY

A. THE FULL SCOPE OF BIBLE STUDY

Bible study is of three phases, in the following order:[1]
> *Observation* — seeing what the text says
> *Interpretation* — determining what the text means
> *Application* — applying the text to life

In survey study we are especially engaged in the observation phase, though the other two phases are also involved.

Survey, as applied to the study of a book of the Bible, is an overall view of the book, made from various perspectives. Other names given to this method are synthesis, overview, panoramic study, skyscraper view, bird's eye view.

Picture the whole (survey); then analyze the parts (analysis).

---

1. The order is very important. For example, one is not prepared to interpret a Bible text (*interpretation*) until he has first seen what the text really says (*observation*).

This is the correct procedure for in-depth Bible study. To scrutinize isolated verses without having seen the complete context is to forfeit the richer experiences of Bible study. Survey should always precede analysis, in order to obtain an overall perspective, a general idea of the major emphases of the biblical book, and an orientation to the surrounding texts that subsequently will be analyzed.

This study manual does not involve analysis; hence, we will always be in the survey process for all twenty-seven books of the New Testament. At times we will tarry over details, but only in connection with the survey at hand.

B. PURPOSES AND AIMS OF SURVEY STUDY

Survey should be made before analysis because of two main purposes of survey study.

(1) *To see each part in its intended emphasis.* Making a survey of the highlights of a book before analyzing the details is a guard against the two extremes of overemphasizing *or* minimizing the point of any one part of Scripture.

(2) *To see each part in its relation to the other parts.* Knowing one's bearing in the forest of many facts is a tremendous help in Bible study. An individual verse studied in isolation could be both obscure and difficult. A major rule of interpretation is to interpret a verse in light of its context. This points to a value of survey study — it helps to keep you aware of context, both near and far.

Related to the above purposes are some other important things that survey study aims to accomplish.

1. *Observing the total structure of the book.* A book of the Bible is not just a mass of words. The words are meaningful because their writer, inspired by the Spirit, organized them around themes in such a way as to express the intended truths and impress the inquiring reader. For example, what impresses you about the overall structure of Hebrews, shown in the accompanying diagram?

The apostle Paul was aware of structure in the text of his Scriptures, as evidenced by such comments as Ephesians 6:2. Read this verse. What was Paul observing about the structure of the Ten Commandments (Exod. 20:1-17) when he said, "which is the first commandment with a promise"? Was he suggesting a meaning in the structure? If so, what?

2. *Observing the content of the book.* In survey study we are

interested in *what* the Bible says (content) as well as *how* the Bible says it (structure). Of course, in surveying the content we do not tarry over details, as we would do later in analyzing the text. Here we keep our eyes open to highlights such as key events, prominent persons, emphasized truths. Those are the best clues for us in determining the book's main theme.

THE BOOK OF HEBREWS

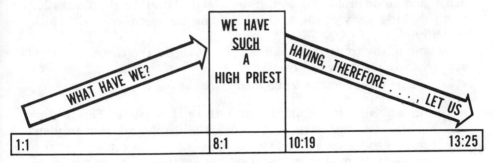

3. *Getting the feel of the book's atmosphere.* Your personal involvement in the Bible text will greatly help to make your study effective. Survey study helps you catch the tone of the book you are studying, as though "you were there."

4. *Relating each book to the others and to the New Testament as a whole.* This is best and most easily done after a survey of the books has been made.

5. *Deriving spiritual lessons from the book's overall thrust.* In survey study we see especially what the important issues of life are, because we constantly are observing *emphasized* truths. We should never lose sight of this practical goal as we proceed with our survey studies.

C. PROCEDURES OF SURVEY STUDY

After you have studied the background of the writing of a particular book of the New Testament (e.g., date and authorship), you are ready to survey the Bible text itself. There are various possible procedures to follow in survey study. Basically, however, three main stages are involved: (1) making the initial acquaintance of the book; (2) working with the individual segments; and (3) seeing how the book holds together. The progression within each stage, and from stage to stage, is *from obscurity to sight.* Stated in other ways, the progression is from first impressions, to repeated impressions, to enduring impressions; or, from the random and indefinite, to the organized and defined.

Your attitude in the initial stages of survey should be one of expectancy and patience. With expectancy, your vision will be keen, and you will discover golden nuggets of truth that otherwise would be hidden. With patience you will not give in to such enemies as discouragement and weariness.

A fresh approach is important in Bible study. In survey, read the book as though you have never read it before, in order to awaken your heart and mind from the dangerous sleep of letting the fantastic, earth-shaking story of the evangel become commonplace, trite, and ordinary.

Some of the things that you will be doing in the three stages of survey study are described below.[2]

1. *Stage One*: *Getting acquainted with the book.*

a. Scanning. Scan the book in one sitting if possible. This is the cursory reading, intended to break the ice, launch you on your project, and give you a taste of good things to come. It is not necessary to read every word or line at this time, especially of long books. If your Bible has paragraph divisions, reading the first sentence of each paragraph will suffice. If your Bible has chapter or paragraph headings, note those as you scan the book.

b. First Impressions. Write down your first impressions of the book. First impressions are not always enduring, nevertheless, they are necessary. You should always seek to be impressed, although you do not need to ask yourself in machine-like regularity, "How does this impress me?" The question is pertinent at the close of your reading; during the course of reading, maintain a spirit of openness and pliability so that you can be impressed.

c. Atmosphere. Try to identify the atmosphere of the book as a whole. This is not always detectable at an early stage. Atmosphere words are tone words, such as *love, conflict.*

d. Keys. List any key words and phrases that stand out as of this first reading. You may not find many of these in this first reading. But you will notice some.

2. *Stage Two*: *Working with the individual segments.*

a. Using the set of segment divisions supplied by this manual,[3] scan

---

2. The stages, as such, will not be identified in the survey studies of the succeeding chapters. Basically, however, the procedures will be followed as described here.
3. Most of the segment divisions appear on the survey charts.

each of the segments and determine the main subject of each. (A segment is a group of paragraphs that represents a unit of thought. A segment may be longer or shorter than a chapter.[4])

NOMENCLATURE OF BOOK UNITS

BOOK OF THE NEW TESTAMENT				
DIVISION			DIVISION	
SECTION		SECTION		
SEGMENT	SEGMENT	SEGMENT		
para-graph				
para-graph				
para-graph				

b. Assign a segment title to each unit and record these on paper. (A segment title is a strong or picturesque word or short phrase, preferably taken from the text, intended to serve as a clue to at least one main part of the segment. For example, a segment title for Hebrews 1:1—2:4 could be *Angels*.) The value of this step of survey is not only in the segment title itself, but also in the mental process of beginning to identify parts and movements of the book.

c. Now that you have begun to look at smaller parts, record any new observations and impressions of the book. Throughout this manual, suggestions of areas of study are given to help you in your survey process. But it is important for you to develop and use your own ingenuity and originality regarding what to look for (observations) in Bible study.

---

4. The terminology used in this book is as follows: a segment is a group of paragraphs; a section is a group of segments; and a division is a group of sections. This breakdown is shown in the accompanying diagram on book units.

3. *Stage Three*: *Seeing how the book holds together.*

Up to this point most of your observations have been about individual items. In this last stage you should be especially interested to observe how those individual items blend together into a pattern. This will help you see the theme more clearly and in more depth in its full scope. Again, remember that it is important to learn not only *what* God said (content) but *how* He said it (structure).

a. Look for groups of material. Such groupings might be about places, people, things, doctrines, speeches, events, and so forth. For example, Matthew 5-7 appears to be a long sermon by Jesus.
b. Compare the beginning and end of the book. This comparison will tell you much about the book, especially if it is narrative.
c. Look for a key turning point in the book. Not every book has such a pivotal point. The example of Hebrews, cited earlier, illustrates the principle of pivot.
d. Look for a climax. If the book has a climax, try to observe a progression leading up to that point.
e. Read your list of segment titles a few times, and see if you can detect any movement in the action, if the book is historical; or in doctrine, if the book is nonhistorical. Read again your listing of the main subject of each segment. Keep working on this until you can formulate a simple outline of the book. Use paper and pencil freely. The observations you made earlier in this stage will be of great help here.
f. Try to state the book's theme in your own words. Assign your own title to the book, a title that will reflect that theme.
g. After you have completed your survey of the Bible text, refer to the survey chart included in the study guide, and compare it with your own studies.

II. Using This Manual as a Guide for Survey Study

The main purpose of this study guide is to help you see for yourself much of what each book of the New Testament says. This independent kind of study is aptly represented by the word *discovery*. When your personal experience is discovery, the New Testament will come alive to you in many ways. Dr. James M. Gray, who excelled in developing and teaching the survey method of study, rightly maintained that one's own original and independent study of the broad pattern of a Bible book, imperfect as the conclusions may be, is of far more value to the student than the most perfect outline obtained from someone else. This is not to minimize the work of others, but to emphasize that recourse to outside aids should be made only *after* the student has taken his own skyscraper view.

In serving as a guide, however, this book also includes instructive material to support and supplement your own independent study. The book is neither a commentary nor a so-called introduction to the New Testament; yet it includes a little of the kind of material found in both of those resources.

The various guides and supporting materials contained in this book are described below.

A. GUIDES

The suggestions for survey study vary throughout the book, depending on which New Testament book is being studied. The kinds of guides remain constant, however, from book to book.

1. *Directions.* Specific directions about such things as what to look for, and where, constitute the major part of your survey. You will constantly be urged to record your observations, of whatever kind they are, on paper. Your faithfulness in doing this may make the difference between mediocre and excellent study. As someone has well said, "The pencil is one of the best eyes."

2. *Questions.* Answering questions is an effective learning experience. Whenever possible, write out your answers. If you faithfully answer the questions and follow all the directions, you will subconsciously be establishing habits and methods of effective Bible study.

3. *Uncompleted charts.* Occasionally you will have the opportunity to record observations on an uncompleted chart that appears in the manual. If you prefer to record these on paper instead, be sure to refer to the chart as you record. Charts as visual aids are effective in representing a panoramic view of Scripture, which is what survey is all about.

4. *Applications.* Ways to apply the messages of the New Testament books are suggested at the end of each survey. For example, biblical commands will be seen as defining God's timeless standards; history as furnishing "example . . . written for our instruction" (1 Cor. 10:11); testimonies and prayers as inspiring and challenging; and prophecy as warning and comforting the reader. Also, it is highly recommended that you spend time meditating over key words and phrases, which you underline in your Bible during the course of your survey. This meditation is one of the best fruits of marking your Bible.

5. *Further study.* Some readers using this study manual will

want to look further into the subjects suggested at the end of each chapter. The continuity of the book will not be jeopardized, however, if these optional studies are passed over.

B. SUPPORTING MATERIALS

Along with suggestions for your own survey of the New Testament books, various kinds of instructive material are given to support your study.

1. *Background.* The background and setting of each New Testament book is given at the beginning of each study unit. Much of this information (e.g., date written, authorship) is not always provided in the Bible text; thus its inclusion here. The treatment can only be brief, because of limitations of space. You might want to refer to supplementary sources for more extensive research.

2. *Comments.* Comments and descriptive notes appear in each study unit to furnish substantive positions from which you may launch your surveys.

3. *Maps.* Much of the New Testament is history, or with historical background, so it is important to visualize the historical setting. Maps will appear from time to time to help you in the mental focusing.

4. *Historical charts.* Historical charts similar to Chart 12 show the settings of Bible passages and books. You will find this visual aid valuable for survey study.

5. *Completed survey charts.* Near the end of the survey of each New Testament book, a completed survey chart appears. Unless you are instructed otherwise, postpone looking at each chart until after you have completed your own survey of the particular book. This will keep the door open for you personally to experience the joys of discovery. Actually, the survey charts that are shown are not exhaustive. You may want to add your own observations and outlines to them.

6. *Outline.* A brief outline of the Bible book is given here for quick reference. Most of the points of the outline will have emerged in the course of your survey studies.

7. *Bibliography.* For each book of the New Testament a few selected works, such as commentaries, are cited as recommended reading, especially for extended studies.

C. TOOLS FOR SURVEY STUDY

Here is a basic list of recommended study tools:

1. *A good study version of the Bible.* This should have easy-to-read print and should include cross-references. An edition without

commentaries and outlines is best for independent study. Having such an edition will encourage you to focus on the Bible text itself. Unless otherwise cited, all Scripture quotations in this book are from the *New American Standard Bible.* The *New International Version* (NIV) is also recommended for survey study.

2. *An exhaustive concordance.*[5] Often you will want to see how many times (and where) a particular word appears in a New Testament book. Such a concordance shows the pattern with one glance.

3. *A one-volume commentary.*[6] You may use this occasionally, mainly in connection with difficult passages or such things as customs, geography, and history. Actually most of your independent study is accomplished without this kind of outside aid.

4. *Pencil and paper.* Always keep a pencil in your hand while studying, either to mark your Bible or to jot down observations on paper. This advice cannot be overemphasized. Some students like to use a notebook in addition to separate sheets of paper. Recording not only provides a permanent record of what has been observed in Bible study, it also initiates other lines of inquiry.

5. *Colored pencils.* Here is an illustration of how valuable a colored pencil can be. As you survey a book, you might underline in blue every reference to the mercy of God. You would do the same for a few other subjects, using other colors.[7] A comparative study of these underlined references can then be very revealing.

III. A CONCLUDING THOUGHT

Solid Bible study, whether survey or analysis, is a thrilling challenge to all believers. If you are in earnest about making your own personal study of the New Testament fruitful, you can identify with the following four words: thirst, toil, time, teachableness. Think about those as you launch on your survey of the New Testament.

IV. REVIEW QUESTIONS

1. What are the three phases of Bible study, in the correct order? Justify the order.

2. What basically is survey study? How does it differ from analysis?

3. Why should survey be made before analysis?

---

5. The *New American Standard Exhaustive Concordance of the Bible* is recommended for survey study using the NASB text, and James Strong's *The Exhaustive Concordance of the Bible* for the KJV text.

6. *The Wycliffe Bible Commentary* and *The New Bible Commentary*, revised edition, are two excellent sources.

7. The use of color loses its effectiveness whenever it is overdone. Hence, the advice here is to use this particular method of underlining for only a *few* major subjects.

4. What are the three general stages of survey study discussed in this chapter? Can you recall some of the things that are done in each stage?

5. What are the values of firsthand, independent Bible study?

6. In what ways does this book serve as a guide to your firsthand study of the Bible? What supporting materials does it furnish to supplement your own personal study?

7. What basic study tools are recommended for your survey studies?

8. Why is the habit of recording observations so important?

V. Selected Reading

Further descriptions of this survey method of study by the author are found in the following:

Jensen, Irving L. *Acts: An Independent Study,* pages 41-54.
———. *Enjoy your Bible,* 44-56.
———. *Independent Bible Study,* pp. 106-13.

Part 1

THE EVENT

The Life of Christ

Christianity is built upon the foundations of divinely controlled historical fact. Christian doctrine, Christian conversion, Christian living, and Christian service would not exist, or at the most would be false, if such great events as Christ's birth, death, and resurrection were not historical facts, sovereignly planned and accomplished by God.

It is not by accident that the first books of the New Testament canon (the four gospels and Acts) are historical narratives. God first establishes the factual evidence of Christ's career and the church's origins, for upon this is built the whole structure of Christian doctrine and life as revealed in Scripture.

The historical books are more than narrative, however. They throb with key doctrines, sure commands, warm exhortations, and promises. They are truly a volume of Scripture by themselves.

The first four historical books, the gospels, focus on one person: Jesus Christ. So the theme of Part 1 is THE EVENT: The Life of Christ.

> Matthew
> Mark
> Luke
> John

4

The Life of Christ

The opening verse of the New Testament introduces the reader to Jesus Christ, whose life is infinite in dimension and one-of-its-kind. So the natural starting point for an overview of the New Testament is to survey the earthly life of Christ, as reported by the four gospels.

Each gospel is selective in what it reports of Jesus' life, and so the fullest biography is in the composite picture given by the *combination* of all four gospels.[1] This chapter surveys the composite picture. Focus on the individual parts of that picture will be made later when each gospel is surveyed separately.

Your study approach in this chapter is mainly deductive, that is, you will confirm the points made, by checking them with the Bible texts furnished. In the following surveys of each gospel (Chapters 5-8), your approach will be mainly inductive, as you engage in more of the independent, discovery kind of study.

I. BEFORE THE EVENT OF BETHLEHEM

The thirty-three-year span of Christ's earthly career is small as compared to His eternal existence. There were antecedents leading up to His birth in Bethlehem; and sequels since His death and resurrection are still shaping world history. Before we survey the periods of Jesus' earthly career, it would be enlightening to consider some subjects that are related to His life in an anticipatory way.

A. THE PREINCARNATE CHRIST

The birth of Jesus in Bethlehem was the first event of His earthly career as the incarnate ("in the flesh") Son of God. He had been

---

1. Even the combination of all four gospels contains only a relatively small portion of Jesus' career (see John 21:25). But all has been recorded that faithfully and fully composes the divinely designed, biblical portrait of Christ.

CHART 14

CHRIST FROM ETERNITY TO ETERNITY

THE PREINCARNATE CHRIST   **THE ASCENDED LORD**

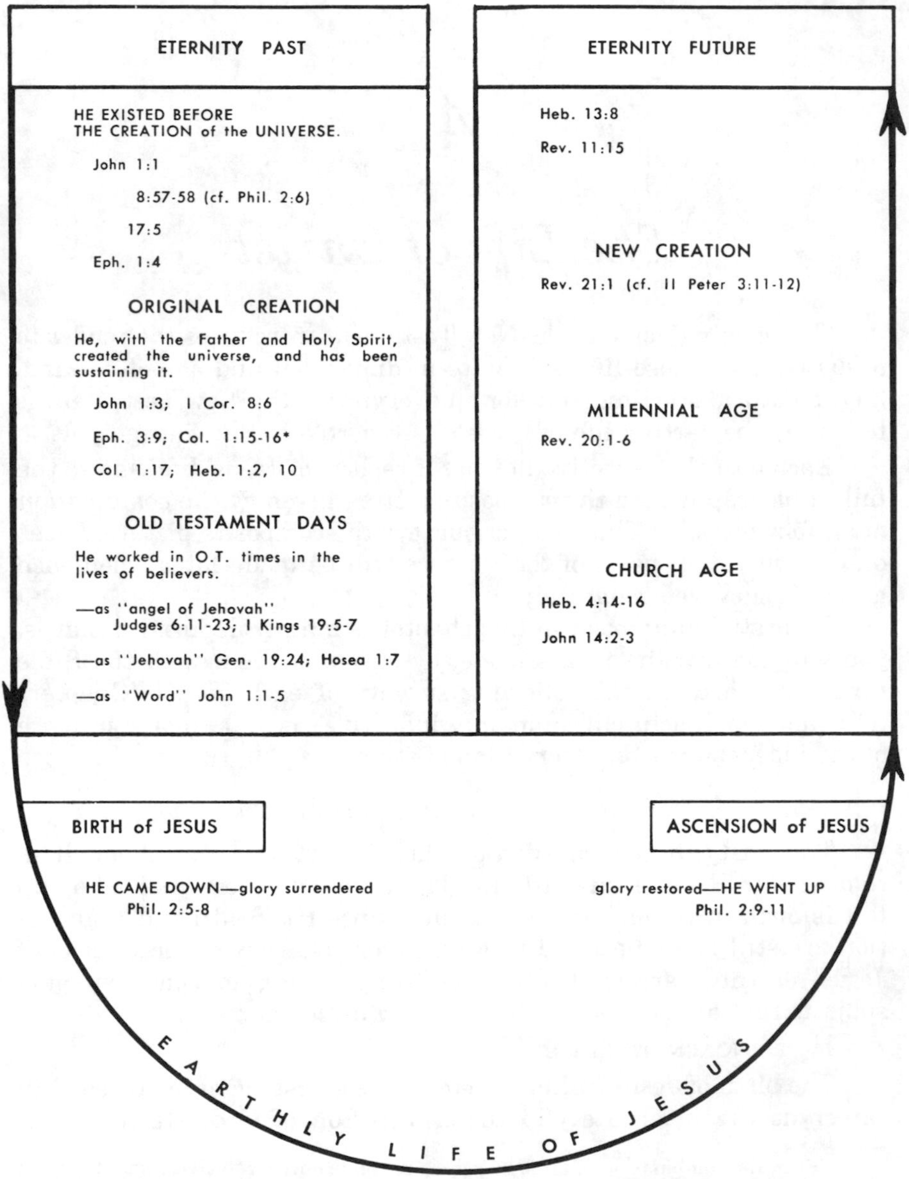

ETERNITY PAST

HE EXISTED BEFORE
THE CREATION of the UNIVERSE.

John 1:1

         8:57-58 (cf. Phil. 2:6)

         17:5

Eph. 1:4

ORIGINAL CREATION

He, with the Father and Holy Spirit, created the universe, and has been sustaining it.

John 1:3; I Cor. 8:6

Eph. 3:9; Col. 1:15-16*

Col. 1:17; Heb. 1:2, 10

OLD TESTAMENT DAYS

He worked in O.T. times in the lives of believers.

—as "angel of Jehovah"
    Judges 6:11-23; I Kings 19:5-7

—as "Jehovah" Gen. 19:24; Hosea 1:7

—as "Word" John 1:1-5

ETERNITY FUTURE

Heb. 13:8

Rev. 11:15

NEW CREATION

Rev. 21:1 (cf. II Peter 3:11-12)

MILLENNIAL AGE

Rev. 20:1-6

CHURCH AGE

Heb. 4:14-16

John 14:2-3

BIRTH of JESUS

HE CAME DOWN—glory surrendered
Phil. 2:5-8

ASCENSION of JESUS

glory restored—HE WENT UP
Phil. 2:9-11

EARTHLY LIFE OF JESUS

* Some translators translate "primeval Creator" instead of "firstborn."

existing before that time, as the preincarnate Christ. Like the Father and the Spirit, He did not have a beginning — He has always existed, from eternity past. When John says (referring to Jesus) that the Word was "in the beginning" (John 1:1), he is simply declaring that when creation's time began its course (Gen. 1:1), the Word, or Jesus, was already existing.

The Bible does not furnish many specific details about the preincarnate Christ or, for that matter, about the ascended Lord. That which it does tell us is vital for us to know. Study Chart 14. Then read each Bible reference shown and record in a few words the essence of each verse.

Note especially Christ's humiliation (from throne to cross) in Philippians 2:5-8 and Christ's exaltation (from cross to throne) in Philippians 2:9-11.

B. THE ANCESTORS OF JESUS

Divine design in the ancestral line of a person is supremely manifested in the ancestry of Jesus. All the prophetic words concerning Him, uttered in the centuries before He was born, were spoken according to a perfect, divine plan and fulfilled with the same accuracy. Of the things prophesied of Him, four were very prominent:

1. He was to be of the human race (Isa. 9:6a).
2. He was to be of the Messianic covenant line (Gen. 22:18; 49:10).
3. He was to be of the royal line of David (2 Sam. 7:14, 16; Isa. 11:1).
4. He was to be "The mighty God" (Isa. 9:6).

The two New Testament genealogies of Jesus (Matt. 1:1-17; Luke 3:23-38) bring out the above four fulfillments. To acquaint yourself with these genealogies, read the two lists and note the likenesses and differences. It might help you compare the two lists if you record them in parallel columns. (Record both in advancing order, like Matthew's.)

Chart 15 shows the prominent features of the two lists. Both genealogies are of Jesus: Luke gives the ancestors of Jesus' mother, Mary; and Matthew gives the ancestors of Jesus' legal father, Joseph.

Notes on Chart 15

1. How far back in the human race does each genealogy go? Account for the difference, keeping in mind that Matthew wrote especially with the Jew in mind.

2. Note that the brothers Nathan and Solomon were the forefathers, respectively, of Heli (father of Mary) and Jacob (father of

Joseph). Which brother succeeded David on the throne? (See 1 Kings 1:13.)

CHART 15

GENEALOGIES OF CHRIST

Luke's list gives the <u>real</u> descent of Jesus,
  which could only be through Mary (Jesus being physically conceived
  of the Holy Ghost, not of Joseph).

This is Mary's genealogy.

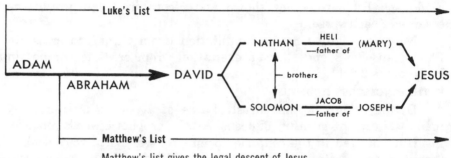

Matthew's list gives the <u>legal</u> descent of Jesus,
  which could only be through the male, Joseph.

This is Joseph's genealogy.

3. Matthew divides his list into three groups (rounded off to fourteen generations each, for convenience): Abraham to David (theocracy); David to Babylon (monarchy); Babylon to Christ (hierarchy). A survey of the Old Testament reveals that Israel's history was generally dark and tragic during those periods.

4. Matthew uses the word *egennesen* ("begat," KJV; "born," NASB; "father," NIV), which in Jewish genealogies usually referred to a son but sometimes referred to even more distant offspring, such as a grandson. For example, Matthew 1:8 says "Joram *egennesen* Osias," but 1 Chronicles 3:11-12 indicates that there were three descendants of Joram before Osias was born. Such genealogical "gaps" are not errors in the Bible, but rather word usage that gives the appearance of error.

Now let us see how the genealogy of Jesus fulfilled the four prophecies listed earlier in this section.

1. *Son of Man*. Jesus was identified literally with the human race, born in real human flesh (cf. Gal. 4:4). Luke emphasizes His identity with the entire human race by going back to the first man, Adam. Matthew brings out the "human" aspect of this race (though

Jesus was not bound by any limitations of humanity) by citing names with moral blots (e.g., Rahab) and by singling out the captivity of Judah in Babylon.

2. *Messiah*. Four times in the first eighteen verses of Matthew Jesus is identified as the Christ (the word is from the Greek *chrio*, "anoint"), a title equivalent to Messiah. Matthew also emphasizes this Messianic aspect in the opening statement, in which he identifies Jesus as the "son of Abraham" (1:1). Also, Matthew's list of names begins with Abraham. It was with Abraham that God first made His covenant with Israel, promising her everlasting blessing (see Gen. 12:2-3; 17:3-8). Jesus came not only to be the hope of the world, but also the Deliverer of Israel.

3. *King*. Matthew calls Jesus "the son of David" (1:1). He repeats the phrase "David the king" twice in 1:6. The royal line of David, continued through Solomon his heir, is recorded by Matthew. It is noteworthy that the bloodline of Jesus (Mary's descent), recorded by Luke, also reaches back to David.

4. *Son of God*. Both genealogies are careful to guard the truth of Jesus' deity, because His birth was of supernatural conception by the Holy Spirit (see Matt. 1:20). Joseph was Jesus' *legal* father only. Matthew says that Joseph was "the husband of Mary, of whom was born Jesus" (1:16). The phrase "of whom" is in the feminine form in Greek and refers *only* to Mary. Note how, a few verses later (v. 23), Matthew explicitly identifies Jesus as God.

The reading of Luke 3:23 also guards the truth that Jesus was conceived of the Holy Spirit, not of Joseph. The verse literally reads "And Jesus . . . being (as was supposed, son of Joseph),[2] of Heli." Heli was Mary's father, and thus Jesus' grandfather. So Luke's list begins with the recognition of a supernatural virgin birth of the Son of God. (Observe that Luke ends the list with a reference to the divine creation of the father of the human race, Adam, "of God" Luke 3:38.)

It is interesting to observe that the other two gospels, Mark and John, identify Jesus as God in the very first verses. Mark 1:1 records the grand genealogical fact: "Jesus Christ, the Son of God." John 1:1 says clearly, "The Word was God."

C. JESUS THE GOD-MAN

When Jesus walked this earth He could not have done what He did unless He was who He was. In fact, He did what He did to show

---

2. The closing parenthesis placed here can be justified by the original Greek, and also makes more sense. See A. T. Robertson, *A Harmony of the Gospels for Students of the Life of Christ*, p. 261. Compare the *Berkeley Version*, and the *New International Version* of this verse.

people who He really was. When Jesus came to the peak and turning point of His preaching and sign-working ministry, the great question He asked was a question of identification: "Who do people say that the Son of Man is?" (Matt. 16:13). The words "Son of Man" refer to His human nature. When Peter told Jesus who *he* believed Jesus to be, he recognized Jesus' deity: "Thou art the Christ, the Son of the living God" (Matt. 16:16).

The gospels do not present Jesus as two persons, that is, God *and* man. He is always one Person, but with two natures. He is of real and true divine nature, and He is of real and true human nature. The two natures are indissolubly united in the one Person. Jesus is no less God because of His humanity, and no less human because of His deity. Each nature resides with the other, and both make up His true personality. Jesus is not God *and* man: Jesus is *God-man*.

II. SETTING OF JESUS' EARTHLY LIFE

The Palestinian setting of New Testament times has been discussed briefly in Chapter 2. A few aspects of the setting as related to Jesus' earthly career are noted below.

A. CITIES AND VILLAGES

The cities and villages named in the gospels were located mainly in the three provinces of Judea, Samaria, and Galilee. Three surrounding areas were Perea, Decapolis, and Phoenicia. Locate these sections on Map F, p. 65.

NEW TESTAMENT CITIES

JUDEA	SAMARIA[3] AND GALILEE	OTHER
1. Jerusalem	7. Sychar	16. Bethsaida (Julias)
2. Bethlehem	8. Samaria	(Luke 9:10)
3. Bethany	9. Nain	17. Gergesa
4. Ephraim	10. Nazareth	18. Caesarea Philippi
5. Jericho	11. Cana	19. Tyre
6. Emmaus	12. Magdala	20. Sidon
	13. Capernaum	21. Bethabara (Bethany
	14. Chorazin	beyond Jordan)
	15. Bethsaida (west side of Sea of Galilee) (Mark 6:45)	

After about a year of limited public ministry in Judea, Jesus carried on most of His itinerant work in and around the region of

3. Travel in Samaria was usually avoided by Jews because of the religious antagonism between the Jews and the Samaritans. Jesus, however, freely moved about and ministered in Samaria (e.g., John 4:4-42.)

Galilee, though His trips from Jersualem to Galilee afforded many opportunities of ministry along the way. Of the many cities and villages that He visited on His evangelistic tours, only about twenty are mentioned by name in the gospels. See the accompanying lists. How many of these places can you visualize on a map of Palestine? Refer to Map F to check your locations.

B. POLITICAL REGIONS

During Jesus' life the governing of Palestine was parcelled among various rulers, all of them directly or indirectly responsible to Rome. Chart 16 lists the rulers, their domain, and dates.

RULERS OF PALESTINE DURING JESUS' LIFE   CHART 16

TERRITORIES	R U L E R S			
			P R O C U R A T O R S	
JUDEA AND SAMARIA	HEROD the GREAT (43-4 B.C.)	ARCHE-LAUS (4 B.C.-A.D. 6)	Coponius Ambibulus Rufus Gratus	PONTIUS PILATE (A.D. 26-36)
GALILEE AND PEREA	HEROD ANTIPAS (4 B.C.-A.D. 39) (Killed John the Baptist)			
ITUREA AND TRACHONITIS (northeast of Sea of Galilee)	PHILIP (4 B.C.-A.D. 34)			

Notes on Chart 16

1. Herod the Great died in 4 B.C., not long after Jesus was born.[4] (See Matt. 2:1, 19.)

2. Archelaus was the ruler whom Joseph avoided on arriving in Palestine from Egypt (Matt. 2:22).

---

4. Jesus was born around 5 or 6 B.C. It is an acknowledged fact that our present calendars are in error by a few years. See A. T. Robertson, *A Harmony of the Gospels for Students of the Life of Christ*, pp. 262-67, for a discussion of this.

CHART 17

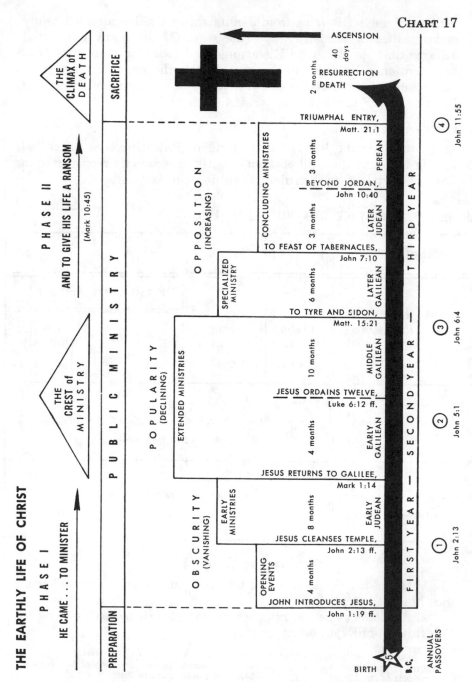

THE EARTHLY LIFE OF CHRIST

PHASE I — HE CAME . . . TO MINISTER

PHASE II — AND TO GIVE HIS LIFE A RANSOM (Mark 10:45)

THE CREST of MINISTRY

THE CLIMAX of DEATH

PREPARATION — PUBLIC MINISTRY — SACRIFICE

OBSCURITY (VANISHING) — POPULARITY (DECLINING) — OPPOSITION (INCREASING)

OPENING EVENTS — EARLY MINISTRIES — EXTENDED MINISTRIES — SPECIALIZED MINISTRY — CONCLUDING MINISTRIES

JOHN INTRODUCES JESUS, John 1:19 ff.
4 months

JESUS CLEANSES TEMPLE, John 2:13 ff.
EARLY JUDEAN
8 months

JESUS RETURNS TO GALILEE, Mark 1:14
EARLY GALILEAN
4 months

JESUS ORDAINS TWELVE, Luke 6:12 ff.
MIDDLE GALILEAN
10 months

TO TYRE AND SIDON, Matt. 15:21
LATER GALILEAN
6 months

TO FEAST OF TABERNACLES, John 7:10
LATER JUDEAN
3 months

BEYOND JORDAN, John 10:40
PEREAN
3 months

TRIUMPHAL ENTRY, Matt. 21:1

DEATH
2 months

RESURRECTION

ASCENSION
40 days

BIRTH — B.C. 5

FIRST YEAR — SECOND YEAR — THIRD YEAR

ANNUAL PASSOVERS
① John 2:13
② John 5:1
③ John 6:4
④ John 11:55

3. Pontius Pilate was the Roman procurator of Judea during Jesus' public ministry (Luke 3:1), who officially condemned Jesus to death.

III. JESUS' PUBLIC MINISTRY

When the stories of the four gospels are brought together into one narrative or harmony, a picture of Christ's life emerges that shows all the important aspects of His redemptive career.

As recorded by the gospels, the life of Jesus was of three different and quantitatively unequal parts:

1. *Preparation years*, relatively obscure, about thirty years in all.
2. *Public ministry,* the highlights recorded in detail, about three and one-half years.
3. *Sacrifice,* the crucial events of Jesus' ministry, transpiring over a period of only a few weeks.

Chart 17 shows the periods and movements of Jesus' career. First study the chart very carefully. Then read the observations to which special attention is called.

Notes on Chart 17

1. Mention was made above of *three* periods of Jesus' life: preparation, public ministry, sacrifice. Notice on Chart 17 the two phases of Jesus' life: to minister (serve), and to die. Observe that the peak of His public ministry (measured by public acclaim) was reached at least a year before His death. His death was *the* crucial event.

2. Jesus' public ministry lasted for about three and one-half years. The annual Passovers mentioned in John[5] are datelines that indicate that duration. Without John's gospel, which alone records Jesus' early Judean ministry, the public ministry of Christ would appear to be much shorter.

3. Each year of Jesus' ministry was of a different sort:

a. First Year: OBSCURITY. No public fanfare attended Jesus' opening ministries, but gradually He moved from the shades of obscurity to the spotlight of public attention.
b. Second Year: POPULARITY. The peak of Jesus' popularity was reached rather quickly, but from then on His acceptance by the multitudes declined just as rapidly.
c. Third Year: OPPOSITION. Open opposition already having been

---

5. This survey manual takes the position that the unnamed feast of John 5:1 was a Passover feast.

manifested, it was only a matter of time and divine schedule before the hour of the cross would arrive.

4. The highest box on the chart represents the main core of Jesus' ministries — His *extended* ministries. Before that, there were the opening events (four months); then the ministries of the early Judean period (eight months). When Jesus had completed His extended ministries, He turned His face and His footsteps toward Jerusalem, engaging in specialized and concluding ministries on His way to the cross.

5. The extended ministries of Jesus were performed in Galilee. Most of His services were rendered in this northern province, the land of His youth and young manhood. Observe the other geographical regions of ministry, including the short one in Perea just before His death.

6. As an exercise, read the references that are cited on Chart 17 at the beginning of each new period of Jesus' ministry. Try to keep those events in your mind as you proceed in your study of Jesus' career, for they are signposts of junctions in that career.

The purpose of the above survey of Jesus' public ministry is to give you a perspective of the *total* earthly career of Jesus before you survey the *partial* coverage of each of the four gospels. For example, when you study Luke's account you should be aware that Luke skips over most of the first year of Jesus' public ministry. See Chart 35, p. 163, which shows the coverage by Luke as compared to Jesus' total career.

The full Bible text of all four gospels is brought together in one chronological sequence, using four parallel columns, in sourcebooks that are commonly referred to as harmonies of the gospels.[6] Whenever you analyze the comparative text of the four gospels in such a sourcebook, use Chart 17 as a reference point to keep the general perspective in mind.

As you survey each of the four gospels in the succeeding chapters, you occasionally will want to refer to the charts of Christ's earthly life (17, 21, 29, 35, or 44), in order to locate the particular passage or section in the sweep of the total public ministry of Christ. The importance of such a chart in a survey of the four gospels cannot be overemphasized.

---

6. A recommended sourcebook that uses the *New American Standard Bible* (NASB) text is Robert L. Thomas and Stanley N. Gundry, *A Harmony of the Gospels.* A harmony using the *American Standard Version* (ASV) is A. T. Robertson, *A Harmony of the Gospels for Students of the Life of Christ.*

IV. WHY FOUR GOSPELS?

The biography of Jesus is written in four separate books in the Bible, composed by four different authors at different times. The natural question is, Why the multiple reporting? — especially since much content is duplicated in the books.[7] It is clear that God had good reasons for His design of four separate gospel records, rather than one, in the Bible's canon.

The Bible does not tell us explicitly what those reasons were, though one suggestion is made by Luke in Luke 1:1-4. But a comparison of the gospels reveals at least five purposes for the multiple format, as noted below.

Note: Chart 18 identifies Matthew, Mark, and Luke as synoptic (literally, "with" + "seeing") gospels. This is because of the many similarities of the three records. John's gospel, written many years later, has fewer parallel passages and includes much doctrinal content, involving more interpretation. So John is set off from the other three as the "Fourth Gospel."

A. CONTENT

A varied view of the content is the prime reason for four gospels. For example, four different portraits of Jesus, taken from different angles, with different background and lighting, are shown. That would not be possible with just one biography. Other subjects concerning the life of Christ, such as the message He preached and the works He performed, can also be treated by the book's author in the same way. "We spend more time, and . . . feel more at home, in the four successive chambers than we should have done in one long gallery."[8]

B. COMMUNICATION

Communication with different audiences is another important reason for four gospels. In the first century the three main cultural groups to be reached were the Jews, Romans, and Greeks. Matthew, Mark and Luke wrote their gospels with those people, respectively, in mind. John's gospel crosses all cultural lines and has the universal church in mind. Even today the communication distinctive holds true, though for other situations.

C. CLARITY

Each gospel is a complement to the other three, so that which

7. See D. Edmond Hiebert, *An Introduction to the New Testament*, 1:160-90, for a discussion of the Synoptic Problem, which is How does one account for the likenesses and differences among the first three gospels?

8. Thomas D. Bernard, *The Progress of Doctrine in the New Testament*, p. 59.

may appear unclear or incomplete in one gospel is clarified and brought into focus by consulting the others.

CHART 18

COMPARISONS OF THE FOUR GOSPELS

	Matthew	Mark	Luke	John
PORTRAITS OF JESUS	The Prophesied King	The Obedient Servant	The Perfect Man	The Divine Son
PROMINENT WORDS	"fulfilled"	"straightway"	"Son of man"	"believe"
CULTURES OF THE ORIGINAL READERS	Jews (Jesus, Son of Abraham)	Romans (Action: no genealogy)	Greeks (Jesus, Son of Adam)	Church (Jesus, Son of God)
OUTLOOK AND STYLE OF THE WRITERS	Teacher	Preacher	Litterateur	Theologian
OUTSTANDING SECTIONS	Sermons	Miracles	Parables	Doctrines
PROMINENT IDEAS	Law	Power	Grace	Glory
BROAD DIVISION	"SYNOPTIC GOSPELS" —stressing the humanity of Christ, from the outward, earthly side			"FOURTH GOSPEL" —stressing the deity of Christ

D. CONFIRMATION

The impact of four independent witnesses to the same facts is impressive, especially in view of the different yet noncontradictory reports that are given of the same events.

E. QUANTITY

If one account had been written to include the material of the four gospels, without duplication, that single gospel would have been considerably shorter than the present four gospels. The gospels make up about half the bulk of the New Testament. The intended emphasis of the gospel story is reiterated by the very space devoted to it.

V. A Concluding Exercise

Here is an interesting comparative study that will give you a first-hand feel of some of the composition differences of the four gospels. Use Chart 19 as your worksheet. Compare the four pictures of Christ as He is portrayed in the concluding words of each gospel. (The passage of John shown on the chart is the last part of the gospel,

CHART 19

FOUR PICTURES OF CHRIST

MATT. 28:18-20
ROYAL LAWGIVER

AUTHORITY	18 Jesus said: ALL AUTHORITY in heaven } to on earth } me	JESUS' ABSOLUTE AUTHORITY
ORDINANCE LAWS	Go therefore MAKE DISCIPLES BAPTIZING in name of { Father Son Holy Spirit TEACHING . . . all that I have COMMANDED YOU	
	I am with you ALWAYS 20	JESUS' CONTINUING PRESENCE

MARK 16:16-20
MIGHTY WORKER

16

20

LUKE 24:50-53
FRIEND OF MAN

50

52

53

JOHN 20:28-31
SON OF GOD

28

31

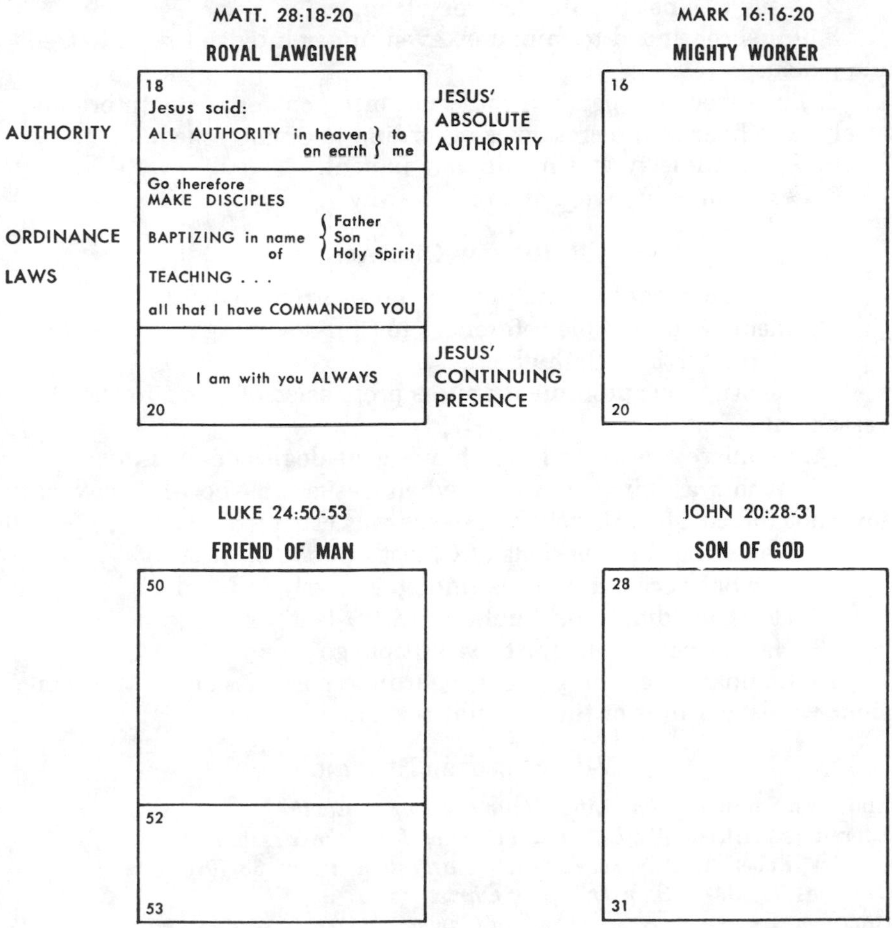

before the epilogue.) Record key words and phrases of the biblical text in the boxes and record your own outlines in the margins. A title for each passage is suggested as a starter. The passage of Matthew is completed as an example.

VI. APPLICATIONS

Important spiritual lessons can be learned from the larger aspects of Jesus' earthly career, which we have just surveyed. Consider the following facts, and see what practical applications you can derive from them:

1. Most of the years of Jesus' life were *preparatory* to His public ministry.

2. Jesus was not popular for very long.

3. Jesus continued to minister, even under intense fire of hatred and jealousy.

4. The severest opposition could not bring on Jesus' death prematurely. The hour of the cross was according to divine schedule.

5. Jesus' ministry was in life *and* in death.

6. Jesus came to give, not to take away.

VII. REVIEW QUESTIONS

1. What is meant by the phrase "preincarnate Christ"?

2. Identify some Bible references to Christ's living and ministering before His birth at Bethlehem.

3. Identify four prominent things prophesied of Jesus in the Old Testament.

4. Compare Luke's and Matthew's genealogies of Jesus.

5. Who was king of Judea when Jesus was born? Who was governor (procurator) there when Jesus was crucified?

6. Name the three periods of Christ's public ministry.

7. In what period did Jesus minister mostly in Galilee?

8. How long did Jesus' public ministry last?

9. Name five reasons for the multiple gospels.

10. Compare the four gospels regarding: portraits of Jesus; prominent words; cultures of the original readers.

VIII. SELECTED READING

Andrews, Samuel J. *The Life of Our Lord upon Earth*.
Edersheim, Alfred. *The Life and Times of Jesus the Messiah*.
Gundry, Robert H. *A Survey of the New Testament*, pp. 63-77.
Guthrie, Donald. *A Shorter Life of Christ*.
Harrison, Everett F. *A Short Life of Christ*.

Hiebert, D. Edmond. *An Introduction to the New Testament,* 1:160-90. The chapter is a survey of the Synoptic Problem.

Jensen, Irving L. *The Life of Christ.*

Morgan, G. Campbell, *The Crises of the Christ.*

Robertson, A. T. *Epochs in the Life of Jesus.*

Stalker, James. *The Life of Jesus Christ.*

Tenney, Merrill C. *New Testament Survey,* pp. 199-225.

Thomas, Robert L. and Gundry, Stanley N. *A Harmony of the Gospels,* pp. 265-68; 302-8; 313-37. Charts appear on pages 347-49.

Vos, Howard F. *The Life of Our Lord.*

5

Matthew: Jesus and His Promised Kingdom

The Person of Jesus Christ is the key to all history, its grand miracle, and humankind's only hope. Who is Jesus, and what did He do while on earth to make all history revolve around Him? Is He the Messiah — the Christ — foretold in the Old Testament? Is He really the King of kings and Lord of lords? Those are some of the questions that Matthew wanted to answer as he wrote his record and reflections of the life of Christ. The opening sentence of the gospel, which in the original Greek text has but eight words, includes four personal names: Jesus, Christ, David, Abraham. This is a strong clue as to what we may expect to find as we survey this first of the four gospels.

I. Preparation for Study

In Bible study it is always helpful to prepare the mind and heart for the task and journey that lie ahead, which in our case will be surveys of each of the New Testament books. The preparation for surveying an individual book may be of various kinds, such as orientation, comparison with other Scripture, reflection on a problem, anticipation of instruction. For each survey of a New Testament book, brief activities of preparation will be suggested by the manual, and your diligence here will greatly enhance the survey study itself.

1. Review your study of the survey method (Chapter 3), especially the purposes and procedures of survey, and how to use the manual in that way.

2. Review your study of the geography of Palestine in New Testament times (Map F, page 65), including the cities and villages that are cited in the four gospels (Chapter 4).

3. Think Matthew. You are about to survey Matthew, and so it is important to concentrate just on that book. If thoughts of passages of other books come to mind as you study, try to set those aside until you have completed your survey at hand. Follow this suggestion for all twenty-seven books of the New Testament. (From time to time there will be occasions when this survey guide will suggest that you *do* refer to other books, for designated reasons.)

4. Think of Matthew's gospel as the historical connecting link between the Old and New Testaments. This is shown on Chart 20. Matthew is preeminently the gospel of fulfillment.

Where on the chart do you place the "four hundred silent years"?

CHART 20

Matthew as a link

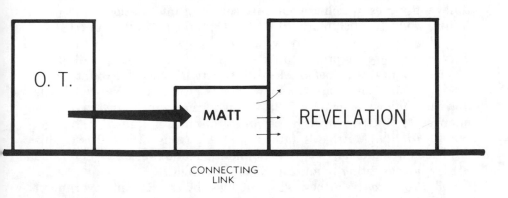

O. T.

MATT → REVELATION

CONNECTING
LINK

PROPHECY   **FULFILLMENT**

5. When Matthew's gospel was written and first distributed in the A.D. 50s, the early church was in its third decade of existence. (See Survey of Acts, Chart 52, p. 214.) Hebrew Christians of the local churches knew from Jesus' preaching and from the church's experiences, such as with the Gentile Cornelius,[1] that Jesus' message of salvation was for Gentiles as well as Jews. Alert students of Scripture also knew such passages as Genesis 12:1-3 taught them that the Lord's covenant with their spiritual father Abraham had included Gentiles in the total scope of His redemptive plan. (Read the passage.) Visualize a meeting of the members of a local church in Antioch of

---

1. This was reported later by Luke in Acts 9-12.

Syria (Map E, p. 64) when a copy of Matthew's gospel is first read in their presence. Most of the members are Hebrew-Christians. Do you suppose that one thing they are attuned to is how Matthew might show that the gospel message is for both Jew and Gentile?

II. BACKGROUND

In the first decades of the early church the book of Matthew was the most highly revered and widely read of the four gospels. Before we survey the text of such a book, let us first become acquainted with its background.

A. THE MAN MATTHEW

As with the other three gospels, authorship of this first gospel account is not identified by name in the text itself. Tradition is unanimous in ascribing the writing to Matthew, son of Alphaeus.

Very little is known of the personal life of Matthew. Read the following verses, which are our only source of information about him: Matthew 9:9-13; 10:3; Mark 2:14-17; 3:18; Luke 5:27-32; Acts 1:13-14.

What was the last activity of the disciple Matthew in the New Testament story, according to Acts 1:13-14? That meeting took place at least twenty years before Matthew wrote his gospel account.

1. *Name.* The name Matthew means "the gift of Yahweh." His Jewish name was Levi (Mark 2:14; Luke 5:27), which may have been changed to Matthew when he became a disciple of Jesus.

2. *Family.* Matthew's father was Alphaeus (Mark 2:14). This Alphaeus was probably not the one mentioned in Mark 3:18 and Luke 6:15, who was father of another disciple, James.

3. *Profession.* Matthew was employed by the Roman government as a tax collector ("publican," Matt. 10:3 [KJV]), a profession bitterly hated by the people because of the personal profit and political corruption involved with the job.

4. *Wealth.* Matthew probably was wealthy (tax collectors usually were), and that is illustrated by the big banquet that he hosted in his house (Luke 5:29).

5. *Call to discipleship.* Matthew's name is not connected with any incident in the New Testament other than his call (Mark 3:13-19; Luke 6:12-16). He no doubt had heard Jesus' preaching on different occasions before the day of the original call. Do you think it is possible that one reason he was chosen was that Jesus saw in him the potential of authoring the important gospel account?

6. *Death.* Matthew probably died a natural death, though some traditional sources say he died as a martyr.

B. TITLE

The title assigned to this gospel by the early church was "The Gospel According to Matthew." The word *gospel* means "good news." Why, then, are the words "according to" more accurate than "of"?

C. ORIGINAL READERS

It is very clear from the content of this Bible book that it was written especially for the immediate audience of Jews.[2] Inasmuch as the first hearers of the *spoken* gospel were mainly Jews,[3] it does not surprise us that one of the four gospels was directed especially to them and answered questions uppermost in their minds about Jesus, such as: Was Jesus truly descended from David? What was Jesus' attitude toward the Old Testament law? Did He come to establish the kingdom promised in the Old Testament? Curiosity about these questions is why Matthew was so widely read in the first decades of the early church.

This gospel is not exclusively Jewish, however. Throughout the account, Jesus' ministry is related to all the people of the world, such as in the Great Commission of 28:19-20, and in Jesus' identification with the human race by calling Himself the Son of man (e. g., 16:13). So Matthew's account was intended also for Gentile readers of the first century, and increasingly so in the centuries that followed.

D. DATE AND PLACE WRITTEN

A possible date for the writing of Matthew is A.D. 58.[4] That was before the destruction of Jerusalem (A.D. 70) and shortly before Luke wrote his gospel account. (See Chart 1, p. 20.) There is strong reason to believe that Matthew was the first of the four gospels to be written.

Matthew might have written this gospel from Jerusalem or Antioch of Syria. The history of the manuscript's circulation from place to place, and of copies made from it, is not known to us today. "Each of the four Gospels, with its distinctive picture of Christ, seems to have circulated at first in the churches of a particular area, but shortly after the appearance of the fourth the four appear to have been bound up together and acknowledged by the churches at large as the authoritative fourfold Gospel of Christ."[5]

E. PURPOSE AND THEME

One of the main reasons for studying each gospel *separately* is

---

2. You will observe this later when you survey the book.
3. Jesus and the disciples were the first to preach and teach the gospel, according to the four gospels and Acts.
4. Bible students differ in assigning a date to Matthew. It could have been written as early as A.D. 44. Most date it in the A.D. 50s. The date depends largely on whether Mark or Matthew was the first gospel written.
5. F. F. Bruce, *The Books and the Parchments*, p. 93.

that each author's purpose can thereby be discovered. The divine purpose of four gospel records was to give four perspectives of the one message of glad tidings. Henry Thiessen writes, "We emphasize, then, that each writer was confronted with a definite need; that he formed a definite purpose for his Gospel; and that he selected his materials, under the guidance of the Holy Spirit, with that object in view."[6]

The main purpose of Matthew in writing this account was to show Jesus as King of the promised kingdom. He sought "to connect the memories of his readers with their hopes; to show that the Lord of the Christian was the Messiah of the Jew," the King of the promised kingdom.[7]

There is much in this gospel about the great Jewish themes of law, prophecy, Messiah, kingdom, Israel. And there are many references to the fulfillment of Old Testament prophecy. All of this points to the grand theme noted above, that Jesus is the King of the promised kingdom.

However, as noted earlier, the gospel of Matthew is not solely Jewish oriented. There are many parts of it, as we shall see in our survey study, that present the gospel as a message to the whole world. That is why from the very beginning it was read by Gentiles as well as by Jews. The large ministry of this gospel in the early decades of the church is described by Tasker:

> It provided the Church with an indispensable tool in its threefold task of defending its beliefs against attacks from Jewish opponents, of instructing converts from paganism in the ethical implications of their newly-accepted religion, and of helping its own members to live a disciplined life of fellowship based on the record of the deeds and words of their Lord and Master, which they heard read week by week in the orderly and systematic form provided by this evangelist.[8]

In order to fulfill his purposes of writing, Matthew, under the Spirit's guidance, selected certain parts of Christ's life and ministry for recording. How much he used of the four-gospel composite picture is shown on Chart 21. Note the Matthew chapter and verse references at the bottom of the chart. Jesus' Sermon on the Mount is recorded in Matthew 5-7. During what period of His ministry was that preached?

---

6. Henry C. Thiessen, *Introduction to the New Testament,* p. 135.
7. See W. Graham Scroggie, *Know Your Bible,* 2:37.
8. R. V. G. Tasker, *The Gospel According to St. Matthew,* in Tyndale New Testament Commentaries, pp. 17-18.

CHART 21

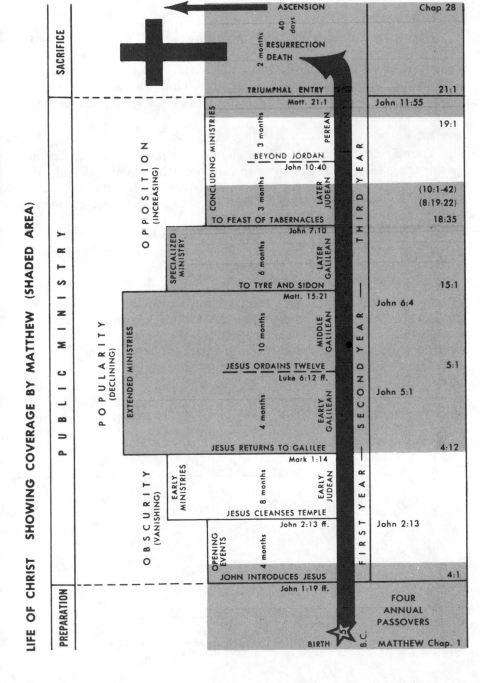

LIFE OF CHRIST SHOWING COVERAGE BY MATTHEW (SHADED AREA)

PREPARATION	PUBLIC MINISTRY			SACRIFICE	

PUBLIC MINISTRY

OBSCURITY (VANISHING)

POPULARITY (DECLINING)

OPPOSITION (INCREASING)

ASCENSION — Chap 28

40 days

RESURRECTION

DEATH

2 months

TRIUMPHAL ENTRY — 21:1

Matt. 21:1 — John 11:55

PEREAN — 19:1

BEYOND JORDAN
John 10:40

CONCLUDING MINISTRIES

3 months

LATER JUDEAN — (10:1-42) (8:19-22)

TO FEAST OF TABERNACLES — 18:35
John 7:10

SPECIALIZED MINISTRY

6 months

LATER GALILEE

TO TYRE AND SIDON — 15:1
Matt. 15:21 — John 6:4

EXTENDED MINISTRIES

10 months

MIDDLE GALILEE

JESUS ORDAINS TWELVE — 5:1
Luke 6:12 ff.

4 months

EARLY GALILEE — John 5:1

JESUS RETURNS TO GALILEE — 4:12
Mark 1:14

EARLY MINISTRIES

8 months

EARLY JUDEAN

JESUS CLEANSES TEMPLE
John 2:13 ff. — John 2:13

OPENING EVENTS

4 months

JOHN INTRODUCES JESUS — 4:1
John 1:19 ff.

BIRTH — B.C. 5

FIRST YEAR — SECOND YEAR — THIRD YEAR

FOUR ANNUAL PASSOVERS

MATTHEW Chap. 1

III. SURVEY

A. PREPARING TO SURVEY

Open your Bible to the gospel according to Matthew and rapidly turn the pages of its twenty-eight chapters. As you do this, get a general overview of the book, just as a tourist would view New York City from the top of its highest skyscraper. This is what survey study is all about — seeing the layout of the book as a whole and getting the feel of its content.

B. FIRST READING

Your first reading of Matthew should be a mere scanning. Spend two or three minutes per chapter to view only the prominent features of each chapter.[9] Do not try to be exhaustive in this stage of your study. The main purpose of this scanning is to make a first acquaintance by identifying things that stand out.

1. What are your first impressions of the book?
2. Did you feel any tone or atmosphere as you scanned the book?
3. Did any key words or phrases stand out?

C. WORKING WITH INDIVIDUAL SEGMENTS

Now you will want to scan the book a little more slowly, segment by segment. Recall from your earlier study of the survey method that a segment is a unit of study, sometimes the length of a chapter, sometimes longer or shorter. Refer to Chart 22 (p. 120) and observe that Matthew is divided here into thirty-three segments. How many begin with verse 1?

Mark the beginning of each segment on the pages of your Bible at this time. Then scan each segment and record on paper a segment

SEGMENT TITLES OF MATTHEW

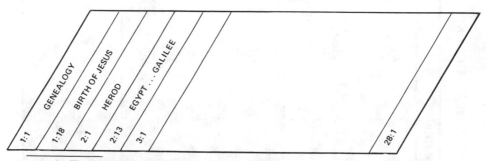

9. The original Bible autographs did not have chapter divisions, or for that matter, paragraph and verse divisions. Such divisions are helps to us today for reference and for identification of small units of thought.

title for each.[10] One suggested way to record these titles is on an oblique chart, as shown here.

What are some of your new impressions of Matthew's gospel after this scanning?

Did you observe any of the following: main characters; main events; discourses of Jesus; opposition to Jesus?

D. SEEING HOW THE BOOK HOLDS TOGETHER

1. Compare the opening verse (1:1) with the concluding verses (28:19-20). For example, compare what is suggested by "son of David" and "all authority." Also, compare the first two chapters with the last two.

2. Read the first two verses of each chapter.[11] Write a list of Matthew's contents, just based on these verses. Do you observe any groups of chapters, for example, *actions, discourses, events,* and so forth? A clue to a group of chapters is when a new chapter shows that it is continuing what went before. For example, the prominent quotation marks in NASB at 6:1 and 7:1 show that these spoken words follow what went before, in the preceding chapters.

3. Compare 4:17 and 16:21. Note the phrase, "from that time." These are key clues to the structure of Matthew's account. What does each verse suggest concerning what follows in the gospel account? Does this support observations you have already made of the content of chapters 4-16 and 16-28? If not, scan these two divisions again until you have seen this. Justify the words *proclamation* and *passion* in this outline of Matthew 4:12—28:20:[12]

4:12—16:20   PROCLAMATION   "began to preach"
16:21—28:20   PASSION   "began to show"

4. Note the discourses or sermons that are recorded in 4:12—16:20. Mark these in your Bible.

5. Scan the *passion* division (16:21—28:20) again. What parts of the account are about, or related to, Jesus' death?

6. Scan 1:1—4:11 again. Review your segment titles for the six segments, and identify the general contents of this division of the account. Relate this division to the two that follow it, namely, *proclamation* and *passion.*

7. Have you observed any more key words in Matthew? Consult

10. A segment title is a strong word or phrase, preferably taken from the text, intended to serve as a clue to at least one main part of the segment. The sum total of segment titles is *not* intended to be a comprehensive outline of contents.
11. For quick scannings like this you need not adhere strictly to the segment divisions, hence the chapter designation.
12. The new division in Matthew begins at 4:12, even though the clue verse, cited earlier, is 4:17. In the context, 4:17 refers back to the starting point, 4:12.

MATTHEW
JESUS AND HIS PROMISED KINGDOM

MATTHEW CONTAINS
15 PARABLES
20 MIRACLES

KEY VERSES: 1:1 "The book of the generation of
Jesus Christ, the son of David, the
son of Abraham."

2:2 "Where is he that is born King of the Jews?
for we have seen his star in the east, and are
come to worship him."

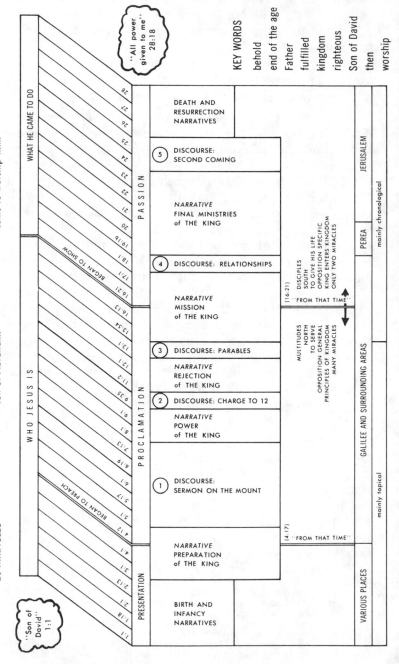

"Son of David" 1:1

"All power given to me" 28:18

PRESENTATION	BIRTH AND INFANCY NARRATIVES
	NARRATIVE PREPARATION of THE KING
PROCLAMATION	① DISCOURSE: SERMON ON THE MOUNT
	NARRATIVE POWER of THE KING
	② DISCOURSE: CHARGE TO 12
	NARRATIVE REJECTION of THE KING
	③ DISCOURSE: PARABLES
	NARRATIVE MISSION of THE KING
	④ DISCOURSE: RELATIONSHIPS
PASSION	NARRATIVE FINAL MINISTRIES of THE KING
	⑤ DISCOURSE: SECOND COMING
	DEATH AND RESURRECTION NARRATIVES

WHO JESUS IS   WHAT HE CAME TO DO

BEGAN TO PREACH   BEGAN TO SHOW

[4:17] "FROM THAT TIME"   [16:21] "FROM THAT TIME"

MULTITUDES
NORTH
TO SERVE
OPPOSITION GENERAL
PRINCIPLES OF KINGDOM
MANY MIRACLES

DISCIPLES
SOUTH
TO GIVE HIS LIFE
OPPOSITION SPECIFIC
KING ENTERS KINGDOM
ONLY TWO MIRACLES

VARIOUS PLACES   GALILEE AND SURROUNDING AREAS   PEREA   JERUSALEM

mainly topical   mainly chronological

KEY WORDS

behold
end of the age
Father
fulfilled
kingdom
righteous
Son of David
then
worship

an exhaustive concordance and note how frequently these words appear in Matthew: king, kingdom, fulfilled. How does this support the earlier discussion of Matthew's theme?

8. Does Matthew's account have a climax? If so, what is it?

E. SURVEY CHART

The organization of Matthew's writing is shown on the survey chart, Chart 22.

Notes on Chart 22

1. Matthew is divided into three major divisions. What are they? Compare the word *presentation* with your observation of the content of 1:1—4:11, which you made earlier.
2. A two-part outline is shown at the top of the chart. Those two phrases of the message about Christ appear in all four gospels, most prominently in Mark. What is significant about the *order* of the two parts?
3. Note the study of contrasts made at the pivotal point of 16:21. For example, before 16:21, Jesus' ministry was mainly to the multitudes; after 16:21, to the disciples; and so forth.
4. Observe at the bottom of the chart what part of Matthew is mainly topical in arrangement, and what part is mainly chronological. Note also the geographical settings.
5. Note how many chapters are devoted to the birth and infancy narratives, and how many to the death and resurrection narratives.
6. In between the two narrative sections noted in point 5. is a series of five discourses, each discourse being introduced by a narrative section. Study this alternating arrangement on the chart very carefully. It represents the core of Matthew's gospel.[13] Note the subjects of the five numbered discourses, and the outline about Jesus as King in the narrative sections.
7. The conclusion of each discourse is identified in the Bible text with words such as these: "when Jesus had finished these words" (7:28). Read in your Bible the five conclusions.
8. Observe that the book opens with a reference to Jesus' kingship ("Son of David," 1:1), and closes on the same note ("all authority has been given to me," 28:18). What comparison had you noted earlier?

---

13. The importance of Jesus' spoken words is seen in the fact that of Matthew's 1,071 verses, 644 contain spoken words of Jesus.

IV. PROMINENT SUBJECTS

The purpose of these studies is to focus on selected, prominent subjects of the New Testament book, without making any detailed analysis. Again, in keeping with the survey method, our interest is mainly in the highlights of the passages involved.

A. OLD TESTAMENT REFERENCES

Listed below are major subjects, appearing throughout this gospel, which would be of special interest to Jews with Old Testament background. Read the verses cited.

• "Holy city"; "holy place" — 4:5; 24:15; 27:53.
• "Son of David" — 1:1, 20; 9:27; 12:23; 15:22; 20:30-31; 21:9, 15; 22:42, 45.
• Fulfillment of Old Testament prophecy — 1:22; 2:5, 15, 17, 23; 4:14; 8:17; 12:17; 13:35; 21:4, 42; 26:31, 54, 56; 27:9-10.
• Jewish customs — 15:1-2; 27:62.
• Law of Moses — 5:17-19, 21, 27, 31, 33, 38, 43; 7:12; 11:13; 12:5; 15:6; 22:36, 40; 23:23.
• "Kingdom of heaven" — (more than thirty references: consult a concordance).
• Old Testament prophets — (thirty-nine references: e. g., 3:3).

The preceding references illustrate the classic couplet:

> The New Testament is in the Old concealed;
> The Old Testament is in the New revealed.

Everything about the Old Testament points to the New, so that when we read the opening chapters of this "link" book, Matthew, it is very clear that "the coming of Jesus was no afterthought, no isolated event, but rather the actual realization in history of the agelong plan and purpose of God."[14]

B. MATTHEW'S GENEALOGY (1:1-17)

There are two New Testament genealogies of Jesus. (They were briefly discussed in Chapter 3.) Matthew organizes his listing into three groups, as he states in 1:17. What are the time periods of those groups? Identify them on Chart 23.

Jewish readers of Matthew's gospel knew Old Testament history, the key events and periods of which are shown on Chart 23. They could very easily visualize those things as they read 1:17. Why do you think Matthew emphasized those three periods of ancestral roots?

Observe in 1:1-2 that Matthew traces Jesus' genealogy only as far

---

14. "Introduction to Matthew," in *The Westminster Study Edition of the Holy Bible*, p. 21.

CHART 23

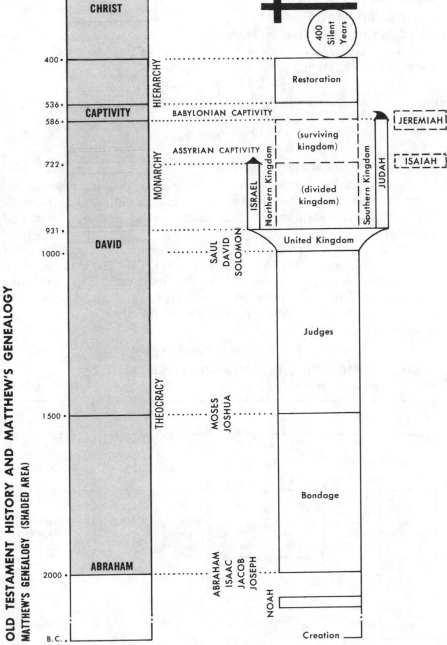

OLD TESTAMENT HISTORY AND MATTHEW'S GENEALOGY
MATTHEW'S GENEALOGY (SHADED AREA)

CHRIST

400

HIERARCHY

Restoration

536

CAPTIVITY

586

BABYLONIAN CAPTIVITY

(surviving kingdom)

JEREMIAH

ASSYRIAN CAPTIVITY

MONARCHY

722

ISRAEL
Northern Kingdom

(divided kingdom)

JUDAH
Southern Kingdom

ISAIAH

931

1000

DAVID

SAUL
DAVID
SOLOMON

United Kingdom

Judges

THEOCRACY

1500

MOSES
JOSHUA

Bondage

2000

ABRAHAM

ABRAHAM
ISAAC
JACOB
JOSEPH

NOAH

B.C.

Creation

400 Silent Years

back as Abraham, whereas Luke goes to Adam (Luke 3:38). What does Matthew have in mind?

C. PRESENTATION (1:1—4:11)

This first short division of the gospel covers the first thirty years of Jesus' earthly life. Only a few experiences are reported. Record them, for the following passages:

> 1:1-17—genealogy
> 1:18—2:23—
> 3:1-12—
> 3:13-17—
> 4:1-11—

D. SERMON ON THE MOUNT (5:3—7:27)

Jesus preached this sermon on a mountain, probably near Capernaum. It was mainly for the benefit of His disciples. Did the multitudes hear the sermon? To answer this, read Matthew 7:28 and Luke 6:17.

Read Jesus' sermon in one sitting, if possible. Try reading it in a modern paraphrase. Picture yourself sitting on the ground with others, and hearing these words for the first time. What are your impressions? Did Jesus preach the sermon to tell how a person can become a Christian, or how a person who is already a believer should live the Christian life?

CHART 24

JESUS' SERMON ON THE MOUNT MATTHEW 5:3-7:27

What the Kingdom Is all About

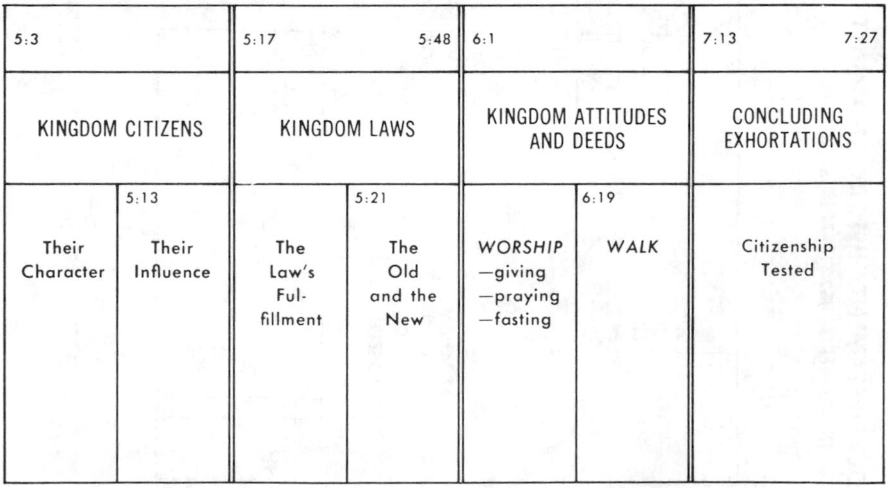

5:3		5:17	5:48	6:1		7:13	7:27
KINGDOM CITIZENS		KINGDOM LAWS		KINGDOM ATTITUDES AND DEEDS		CONCLUDING EXHORTATIONS	
	5:13		5:21		6:19		
Their Character	Their Influence	The Law's Ful- fillment	The Old and the New	WORSHIP —giving —praying —fasting	WALK	Citizenship Tested	

This sermon may be outlined in various ways. Chart 24 suggests an arrangement of thought.

Note the title given to the sermon. Early in His ministry, Jesus wanted to make clear to His disciples and to the multitudes just what kind of a kingdom He had come to establish.

Scan the three chapters of Matthew and observe how the outlines of Chart 24 grow out of the text. This exercise will give you a good general grasp of the passage.

Where is the familiar "Lord's Prayer" quoted in the text?

E. PARABLES OF THE KINGDOM (13:1-53)

This group of parables, spoken on one particular occasion, is the third main discourse of Matthew's account. (What are the first two?)

Jesus' favorite method of teaching was by parables (nearly forty are recorded in the gospels, in addition to many parabolic illustrations).[15] The master teacher well knew that a strong witness of the gospel is the positive proclamation of its truth. While He took time out to defend the gospel from the verbal attacks of His opponents, He spent most of His time teaching the doctrines of the kingdom.

A biblical parable has been described as "an earthly story with a heavenly meaning." It is a comparison of two things to convey a spiritual truth. It is revelation by illustration, given to aid understanding. Jesus did not teach the mysteries of the kingdom to the crowds, because they were not ready for deep truths (13:10-15; cf. Col. 1:26). G. Campbell Morgan illustrates this veiling aspect of parables by the following contemporary parable: "There is a sense in which the sun is hidden by the piece of smoked glass which the boy holds before his eyes, and yet without such an instrument he could not look upon the sun at all. Essential light unveiled, blinds. Its veiling is the opportunity of vision."[16]

Make a list of all the parables of this discourse. Observe that they teach about the kingdom of heaven. Their perspective is not of the ultimate millennial reign of Christ on earth, but of the present formation of His spiritual kingdom, between His first and second advents.[17]

Record a main teaching of each of the parables.

F. SECOND COMING (OLIVET DISCOURSE) (24:1—25:46)

The last discourse of Jesus recorded in Matthew is the Olivet

15. Lists and brief descriptions of all the parables appear in W. Graham Scroggie, *A Guide to the Gospels*, pp. 278-86; 549-51; 663-64.
16. G. Campbell Morgan, *The Gospel According to Matthew*, p. 141.
17. See John F. Walvoord, *Matthew: Thy Kingdom Come*, pp. 95-97.

discourse[18] of chapters 24-25. It is a prophetic message of Jesus' second coming, which He delivered on Tuesday of Passion Week, a few days before His crucifixion. Here are Christ's descriptions of the end of this age, prior to the establishment of His kingdom on earth, *especially as the kingdom relates to Israel and Israel's program.*

Matthew's recording of the Olivet discourse may be divided into six parts, shown on Chart 25.

CHART 25

SIX SECTIONS OF THE OLIVET DISCOURSE MATTHEW 24:4-25:46

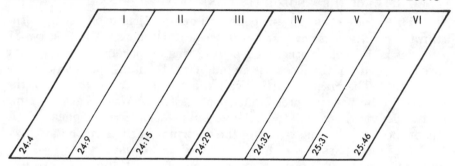

Scan the entire passage and try to account for the dividing points.

The underlying prophecy of this discourse is, *tribulation first, then Christ's return to earth.* In what sections of Chart 25 is this sequence emphasized?

How you interpret this discourse is determined largely by how you view prophecies of the Bible concerning the Millennium. Chart 26 shows the course of Israel's history in the premillennial scheme of world events. Read Acts 1:6-8 and observe that just before Jesus' ascension to heaven, the disciples were still asking when the kingdom would be restored.[19] Jesus' answer did not deny the fact of a restored kingdom. What did He correct, however? It may be observed here that premillennialists view the millennial kingdom on earth as a fulfillment of Old Testament promises, which were preeminently to Israel as a nation. The zenith of Christ's glorious reign will be in heaven for eternity.

The key event on Chart 26 is Christ's second coming to the earth. It is also the key event of the Olivet discourse. Read Matthew 24:3,

---

18. So named because Jesus and His disciples were on the Mount of Olives at this time. The panorama of Jerusalem and its Temple from this spot was beautiful and awe-inspiring (Mark 13:1).

19. The story of Israel's kingdom in Old Testament times was tragedy. The promised messianic kingdom was to be a glorious, miraculous restoration.

CHART 26

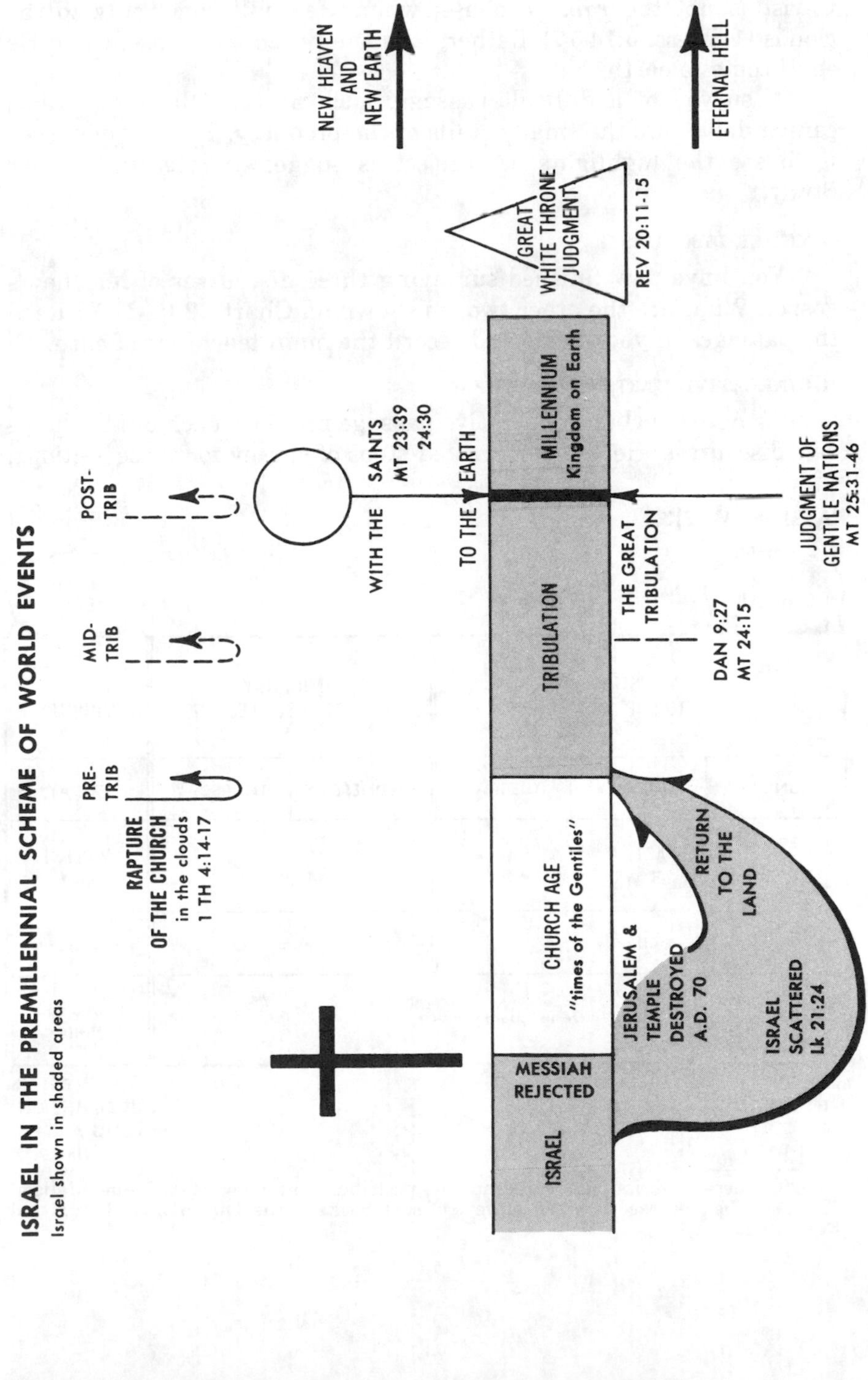

ISRAEL IN THE PREMILLENNIAL SCHEME OF WORLD EVENTS

Israel shown in shaded areas

NEW HEAVEN AND NEW EARTH

ETERNAL HELL

GREAT WHITE THRONE JUDGMENT

REV 20:11-15

MILLENNIUM
Kingdom on Earth

PRE-TRIB

MID-TRIB

POST-TRIB

RAPTURE OF THE CHURCH
in the clouds
1 TH 4:14-17

WITH THE SAINTS
MT 23:39
24:30

TO THE EARTH

TRIBULATION

THE GREAT TRIBULATION

DAN 9:27
MT 24:15

JUDGMENT OF GENTILE NATIONS
MT 25:31-46

CHURCH AGE
"times of the Gentiles"

RETURN TO THE LAND

JERUSALEM & TEMPLE DESTROYED
A.D. 70

ISRAEL SCATTERED
Lk 21:24

MESSIAH REJECTED

ISRAEL

27, 30, 37, 42, 44, 46; 25:13, 31. In the Olivet discourse this coming of Christ is not the *rapture* phase, when He shall come only to the clouds (1 Thess. 4:14-17). Rather, it is the *revelation* phase, when He shall come to earth.[20]

A survey of a difficult passage, such as the Olivet discourse, cannot delve into the small details of the prophecy. The key of survey is to see the highlights. (A project is suggested later in Further Study.)

G. OTHER DISCOURSES

You have now finished surveying three discourses of Matthew's gospel. What are the other two, as shown on Chart 22 (p. 120)? Read the passages in your Bible and record the main teachings of each.

H. NARRATIVE UNITS OF MATTHEW

As noted earlier, a narrative passage precedes each of Matthew's five discourses. Here are suggested steps of survey for these sections:

PASSION WEEK   CHART 27

KING EXTOLLED					KING MOCKED
MINISTRY TO PUBLIC			MINISTRY TO DISCIPLES		SOLITARY MINISTRY
SUNDAY	MONDAY	TUESDAY	WEDNESDAY	THURSDAY	FRIDAY
ACTIVE DAYS			QUIET DAYS		VIOLENT DAY
authority			compassion		submission
Jesus speaks much					Jesus speaks little

RIDING INTO THE CITY ON A COLT (Mt 21:1-11)

DRIVEN OUT OF THE CITY BEARING A CROSS (Jn 19:17)

20. These descriptions represent the pretribulation view of premillennialism. These will be discussed later, in surveys of such books as the Thessalonian letters and Revelation.

1. List the narrative units, including the chapter and verse locations. Secure the information from Chart 22.
2. Read the narratives and record such things as main persons and events of each. Construct an outline of each section.
3. Observe how each narrative leads into each discourse. This will show the togetherness of Matthew's composition and also will explain why Jesus chose the particular subjects of the discourses He gave.

I. DEATH AND BURIAL OF THE KING (26:1—27:66)

Jesus' last week before His death is known as Passion Week. Chart 27 shows Jesus' general involvements during that week. He was crucified on Friday.

Jesus not only prophesied His death and resurrection; He also knew the exact days of their fulfillment. Read Matthew 26:1-2. Then read Exodus 12, which describes the origin of Israel's Passover memorial. What was the Passover a type of, in Old Testament days? How significant was it that Jesus was slain on the very holiday that pointed to Him?

Chart 28 shows how much of Passion Week was reported by Matthew. Compare the outline with that of Chart 27.

CHART 28

EVENTS LEADING TO THE CROSS MATTHEW 26:1-27:66

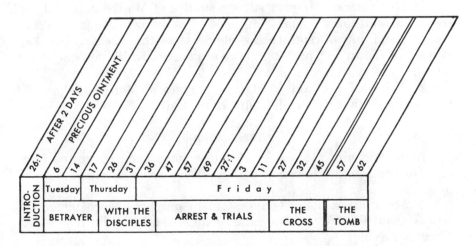

Read the full passage of 26:1—27:66, paragraph by paragraph, for major impressions. Record paragraph titles on the chart. (Examples are shown.) This will help you get an overall view of Jesus' experiences during those days.

Record what this account of Matthew teaches you about: Jesus; the disciples; the rulers; the multitudes.

J. RESURRECTION AND GREAT COMMISSION OF THE KING (28:1-20)

The resurrection was the supreme authentication of the kingship of Jesus. Only the King of kings could say truly, "All authority has been given to Me in heaven and on earth" (Matt. 28:18). Ponder the uniqueness of Christianity among the religions of the world because of its claim of a living Savior who has been resurrected from the grave.

As you read this concluding chapter of Matthew, try to imagine how the events must have impressed all the people, especially the Jews. For example, a distinctive element of Matthew's report, not found in the other gospels, is that of the earthquake. "And, behold, a severe earthquake had occurred" (28:2). Read 1 Corinthians 1:22, and observe that Jews looked to supernatural signs as divine credentials of the true Messiah. Might this have prompted Matthew, writing especially for the Jews, to include this event in his report?

Read the last paragraph of Matthew again (28:16-20). In what ways does it serve as a conclusion to Matthew's account?

V. KEY WORDS AND VERSES

1. Think back over your survey studies of Matthew. Recall the theme of Matthew's account. State it in your own words. Did any verses stand out as representing elements of this theme? Two key verses are shown on Chart 22. There are others, which you may have found.

2. Write a list of key words and phrases of Matthew. Compare your list with that shown on Chart 22 (p. 120).

VI. APPLICATIONS

Applications of the text of Matthew have been suggested from time to time in the previous studies. Here are a few more of the prominent ones:

1. The fulfillments of Old Testament prophecy teach important truths about God. What are some of these, and how do they affect Christian living?

2. God "made" the nation of Israel (Gen. 12:2) and has blessed it even as He promised (Gen. 12:2-3). What spiritual lessons can you, whether Gentile or Jew, apply to your life from this?

3. Write a list of spiritual applications that Christians can make from the truth of the kingship of Jesus Christ.

4. Why is the Lord so concerned how Christians conduct their lives (e.g., Sermon on the Mount)?

5. What important truths and applications does the Olivet discourse teach concerning Christ's second coming?

6. Is Matthew a message for Jew and non-Jew today? Support your answer.

VII. REVIEW QUESTIONS

1. What are the opening verses (1:1-17) of Matthew about?

2. In what sense is Matthew a link in the Bible?

3. What title did the early church assign to this account?

4. Who were the original readers of Matthew?

5. When and where might it have been written?

6. What is the theme of Matthew?

7. Did Matthew report much of the first year of Jesus' public ministry?

8. What are the three main divisions of the account? Identify the chapter and verse locations.

9. How many major discourse sections are there in Matthew? How does each conclude in the Bible text?

10. Identify by subject: chapters 5-7; chapter 13; chapters 24-25.

11. List various items and characteristics of Matthew's account that were of special interest to Jews.

12. Name five key words of Matthew and quote a key verse.

13. How does this gospel conclude?

VIII. FURTHER STUDY

Subjects suggested for extended study, which are beyond the scope of survey, are the following:

1. Of the thirty passages in Matthew that are peculiar to that gospel (that is, not found in Mark, Luke, or John), most have a bearing on the theme of Christ as King. Refer to a harmony of the gospels[21] and observe in general the parts of Jesus' life that are reported only by Matthew. Look for direct or indirect references to kingdom.

2. Make a comparative study of the New Testament phrases "kingdom of heaven" and "kingdom of God."[22]

---

21. For example, Robert L. Thomas and Stanley N. Gundry, *A Harmony of the Gospels*.
22. The former is Matthew's usual designation. The English word *kingdom* is a contraction of the phrase "king's domain." Consult W. E. Vine, *An Expository Dictionary of New Testament Words*, 2:294-96, for a discussion of the two phrases noted above.

3. Make a detailed study of the Olivet discourse. Compare the other two New Testament end times passages: Mark 13 and Luke 21. Refer to commentaries for help.

4. Study the various views held concerning the date of Matthew's writing. Learn the reasons offered for the differing positions (a) that Mark was the first gospel written, and (b) that Matthew was the first gospel.

5. What do you think would be the feelings of the Jewish-Christian members of a local church upon reading Matthew's account for the first time: (a) if *Matthew* was the first gospel written and distributed; (b) if *Mark* already had been written and distributed?

IX. Outline

Here is a brief outline of Matthew, to be used as an additional reference point in your surveys.

MATTHEW: Jesus and His Promised Kingdom

PRESENTATION	1:1—4:11
Birth and Infancy Narratives	1:1—2:23
Preparation of the King	3:1—4:11
PROCLAMATION	4:12—16:20
First Ministries	4:12-25
Discourse: Sermon on the Mount	5:1—7:29
Power of the King	8:1—9:34
Discourse: Charge of the Twelve	9:35—11:1
Rejection of the King	11:2—12:50
Discourse: Parables	13:1-53
Mission of the King	13:54—16:20
PASSION	16:21—28:20
Death Foretold	16:21—17:27
Discourse: Relationships	18:1—19:1*a*
Final Ministries of the King	19:1*b*—23:39
Discourse: Second Coming	24:1—25:46
Death and Resurrection of the King	26:1—28:20

X. Selected Reading

GENERAL INTRODUCTION

Gundry, Robert H. *A Survey of the New Testament,* pp. 83-90.
Tasker, R. V. G. "Gospel of Matthew." In *The New Bible Dictionary,* pp. 794-97.
Tenney, Merrill C. *New Testament Survey,* pp. 141-52.
Wessel, Walter W. "Gospel of Matthew." In *The Zondervan Pictorial Bible Dictionary,* pp. 516-18.

COMMENTARIES

Atkinson, B. F. C. "The Gospel According to Matthew." In *The New Bible Commentary.*

Kent, Homer A. "The Gospel According to Matthew." In *The Wycliffe Bible Commentary.*

Lange, John Peter. *The Gospel According to Matthew.* Rev. ed.

Lenski, R. C. H. *The Interpretation of St. Matthew's Gospel.*

Morgan, G. Campbell. *The Gospel According to Matthew.*

Robertson, A. T. *Commentary on the Gospel According to Matthew.*

Walvoord, John F. *Matthew: Thy Kingdom Come.*

OTHER RELATED SOURCES

Dunnett, Walter M. *An Outline of New Testament Survey.*

Edersheim, Alfred. *The Temple: Its Ministry and Services.*

Jensen, Irving L. *Jensen's Bible Study Charts.*

———. *The Life of Christ.*

McClain, Alva J. *The Greatness of the Kingdom.*

Robertson, A. T. *A Harmony of the Gospels for Students of the Life of Christ.*

Scroggie, W. Graham. *A Guide to the Gospels.*

———. *Know Your Bible,* vol. 2.

Stalker, James. *The Life of Jesus Christ.* Rev. ed.

Strong, James. *The Exhaustive Concordance of the Bible.*

Thomas, Robert L., ed. *New American Standard Exhaustive Concordance of the Bible.*

Vine, W. E. *An Expository Dictionary of New Testament Words.*

6

Mark: The Servant Jesus

For a few decades after Christ's ascension, the world did not have the full written gospel record. During those years the redemptive message of the gospel was being proclaimed mainly by word of mouth (read Acts 15:7), based on trustworthy recollections of eyewitnesses. And at least some of those recollections were being written out on scrolls for a more permanent record. We do not know the exact circumstances of the writing of each of the four gospels, but we are confident that each appeared on schedule according to a divine plan. Mark was one of the four.

I. PREPARATION FOR STUDY

First, recall things you learned about Matthew's gospel, such as: how many chapters; its purpose and emphasis; key words; three-part structural outline; major discourses.

From this point on, *think only Mark*. Occasionally you will make comparisons with Matthew, but your concentration during this survey of Mark should always be on Mark. In order to help you shift gears from Matthew to Mark, the following biographical material on the man Mark is included.

II. BACKGROUND

A. THE MAN MARK

1. *Birth and early life.* Mark was born some ten to fifteen years after Jesus of Nazareth and Saul of Tarsus, so he may have been in his late teens at the time of the crucial events of Jesus' public ministry. His parents gave him the Hebrew name of John (*Johanan*, "Jehovah is gracious"), and his Roman surname of Mark[1] may have

---

1. The Greek *Markos* is from the Latin *markus*, "large hammer."

been adopted at a later time in his life (see Acts 15:37). Concerning his having two names, D. Edmond Hiebert writes: "Either name might be used according to circumstances. In Jewish circles he would appropriately be known as John, but in a Gentile environment he would be called by his Latin name. The fact that his Hebrew name is never used in the epistles shows that the Gentile world was his main sphere of activity."[2]

Colossians 4:10 indicates that Mark was a cousin of Barnabas, a key person in Acts 4-15. Mark's mother Mary was a devout woman of prosperous means. Her home, which may have been located in the Valley of Kidron very near the Garden of Gethsemane, was dedicated to God. Her dedication is confirmed by Luke, who records in Acts 12:12-17 that in the early days of the Christian church, after James the Elder had been slain by Herod Agrippa, and while Peter was in prison for the testimony of the gospel, she was courageous and faithful to the extent of letting her house be the meeting place for the local band of believers. It is possible that Jesus visited that home during His lifetime and even partook of the Last Supper there.

Many feel that the unnamed "young man" of Mark 14:51 was Mark himself. (Read Mark 14:43-52.) E. M. Blaiklock suggests this imagined (though not impossible) story behind the Mark account:

> In the long room on the roof of the house of Mary, the rich widow lady of Jerusalem, the Lord and His band meet for what was to be the Last Supper. In his room below, awake and alert, for he sensed the danger which lurked about the house, lay Mary's son, John Mark. He heard the hurried steps of Judas on the stairway without, and listened with sharper care. And then the noise of feet, and the rest depart.
>
> On a sudden impulse the boy seizes a linen sheet from his bed, wraps it round his body and follows. He watches under the olive trees, sure that some crisis is at hand. A flare of torches, and the betrayer is there. With a boy's reckless loyalty he shouts some protest, and angry hands lay hold of him. Slipping out of his sheet Mark escapes. Perhaps he bore a cruel and mutilating sword-slash across his fingers, for an old tradition says that in the early Church Mark was called "the Stumpfingered."[3]

Indelible were the impressions being made as young John Mark grew up in the environs of a professing holy city and in the shelter of a genuinely devout home. He must have been an eyewitness of some events of Jesus' life. He could not escape crossing the trail of the Son

2. D. Edmond Hiebert, *An Introduction to the New Testament: The Gospels and Acts,* 1:89.
3. E. M. Blaiklock, *Mark: The Man and His Message,* pp. 9-10.

of God. And all the while he was being prepared for a later work in the service of the gospel, studying the Scriptures and learning the current languages of the metropolis — Aramaic, Greek, and Latin.

Mary had a house and a family, and they were given to God. And God had a Son and a gospel, and they were given to the world. Mary's Mark and God's gospel were brought together, and millions of souls since then have cherished the possession of that union, the gospel according to Mark.

2. *Conversion*. Though the devout Judaistic heritage formulated the recollections of Mark's earlier life, there came the day in his life when, like his mother, he was confronted with the claims of the man of Galilee, and was compelled to answer the question, "Who do you say that I am?" (Mark 8:29). Peter may have been the disciple used of God to lead Mark to Christ, and this may be why Peter speaks of Mark as "Mark my son" (1 Pet. 5:13). Details of Mark's conversion experience, however, are not given in the New Testament record.

3. *Christian ministry*. Two gospel writers, Matthew and John, were apostles of Jesus. The other two, Mark and Luke, were not of the chosen twelve. The New Testament verses where Mark's name appears reveal some of the highlights of Mark's experience in Christian service. Read each passage, the context surrounding it, and record biographical notes about Mark in each case.

Passage	Date A.D.	Place[4] and Ministry	Colaborers
Acts 12:12,25	46		
13:5	47		
13:13	47		
15:37-39	49		
Col. 4:10	61		
Philem. 23-24	61		
2 Tim. 4:11	67		
1 Pet. 5:13	68		

Observe among other things the variety of colaborers, and the fact of Paul's and Mark's reconciliation after the separation of Acts 13:13. What do you think helped Mark to mature spiritually between his turning back at Perga (Acts 13:13) and his writing of the gospel at Rome some twenty years later? Blaiklock comments on this, "He was taking up the task he abandoned at Perga. . . . In Mark's Gospel . . .

---

4. For the places involved in some of the passages, follow the views that Paul wrote Colossians from Rome; "Babylon" was a symbolical reference to Rome; and Timothy was living at Ephesus when Paul wrote 2 Timothy.

we meet the man who failed and tried again, the man who, by a friend's help, rebuilt a testimony, and left that testimony in a deathless book."[5]

As noted earlier, the Gentile world was Mark's main sphere of activity, throughout his Christian ministry. One support of this observation is that his Hebrew name John (Johanan) is never used in the epistles, but only his Roman name Mark.

4. *Mark's character.* A character sketch of Mark based on the Bible is at best only partial. But from the verses about him and the gospel written by him, there emerges a portrait of an energetic servant of Christ — a servant who was impulsive, hasty, alert, zealous, friendly, cooperative, humble, and honest. Mark matured over the years, just as his spiritual father Peter did. At the peak of that divine maturing process he had the intense joy of penning the "unadorned and unpretentious, but quite overpowering"[6] gospel according to Mark.

5. *Death.* Mark died not long after Peter's A.D. 67 martyrdom, according to tradition.

B. TITLE

A common title appearing in ancient Greek manuscripts of Mark is *Euaggelion kata Markon* (Gospel according to Mark). The account is the "gospel of[7] Jesus Christ" (1:1), *according to* the divinely inspired writer, Mark.

C. AUTHORSHIP

Although the human author is not identified in the gospel, internal evidence from the text itself agrees with the external witness of the early church Fathers that John Mark was the author.[8]

It is generally held that Peter was Mark's informant of eyewitness stories about Jesus. It is possible that Peter was referring to this forthcoming manuscript by Mark when he wrote 2 Peter 1:15. (Read the verse in the context of its two preceding verses.)

Here is a possible reconstruction of that Mark-Peter relationship: Some time near the close of the earthly lives of Peter and Paul, a gospel record of the ministry of Jesus was taking shape in the mind and heart of Mark, by the moving of the Holy Spirit. At the time, both Mark and Peter were living in Rome. Mark's gospel was to be a brief

---

5. Blaiklock, *Mark*, pp. 14-15.
6. C. F. D. Moule, *The Gospel According to Mark*, p. 4.
7. The *New International Version* reads, "gospel about Jesus Christ."
8. Among these are the Greek fathers Papias (A.D. 70-155), Justin Martyr (A.D. 100-165), Clement of Alexandria (A.D. 150-217), Irenaeus (A.D. 120-192), Origen (A.D. 185-254), Eusebius (A.D. 270-340); and the Latin fathers, Tertullian (A.D. 150-220), and Jerome (A.D. 340-420). (Most dates are approximate.)

eyewitness account of Jesus' life. But Mark, not being one of the twelve apostles of Jesus, obviously did not see or hear firsthand very much of Jesus' ministry. This is where Peter came into the picture. Peter's close relationship with Jesus, as one of His apostles, fitted him superbly for sharing with Mark the eyewitness data for writing. We may wonder why Peter, a gifted writer, was not chosen to write the gospel. We are satisfied that God knew what kind of gospel record He wanted written, and that Mark was the person so fitted for the task. So it was Peter the informant, Mark the writer, and God the inspirer.

D. PLACE AND DATE OF WRITING

Mark wrote his book while living in Rome. There are two main views as to the date of writing: early and late.[9] This survey guide follows the latter view, that the gospel was finished around A.D. 68, soon after Peter's death and before the fall of Jerusalem (A.D. 70).[10] According to this view, Matthew, Luke, and Luke's other book Acts, had already been written. (See Chart 1, p. 20.) Matthew was the account that would have spread the gospel to the Jews scattered around the Mediterranean world. How Mark's gospel met the needs of Romans is described by Henry Thiessen:

> The Book of Acts records the onward march of Christianity through Syria, Asia Minor, Macedonia, Greece, and to Italy. No doubt a good many of the Gentiles who were saved during this time were Romans. Acts shows in various ways how the Roman officials were friendly to Paul. *Finally the time came when a Gospel was needed that was designed especially for the Romans* [italics added].[11]

E. ORIGINAL READERS

Mark's gospel was written especially for Gentile readers in general and Roman laymen in particular.[12] The Roman mind was impressed more by action and power than by discourse and dialogue. (See Chart 18, p. 108.) W. Graham Scroggie writes:

> Reason and philosophy, so convincing to the Greek would mean little to the Roman, who was a man of action rather than contemplation. "The

---

9. Each view has strong arguments in its support. For a defense of an early date of A.D. 50, see W. Graham Scroggie, *A Guide to the Gospels,* pp. 170-71. Henry C. Thiessen defends the late view in *Introduction to the New Testament*, pp. 145-46. Any view on the date of Mark's writing must be tentative, for as Everett Harrison observes, "We do not possess the data for a precise dating of the Gospel" (Everett F. Harrison, *Introduction to the New Testament*, p. 177).

10. Mark had prophesied the city's fall in part of chapter 13 of his gospel.

11. Henry C. Thiessen, *Introduction to the New Testament*, p. 145.

12. Among evidences of a non-Jewish audience is Mark's explanation of Jewish and Aramaic terms and customs not clear to the average Roman (e. g., 5:41; 7:2-4, 11, 34). Other non-Jewish characteristics: a paucity of Old Testament quotations; telling the reader the location of the Mount of Olives (13:3); no mention of the Jewish law.

Gospel for him must present the character and career of Jesus from the Roman ... point of view, as answering to the idea of Divine power, work, law, conquest, and universal sway. To the Roman these are the credentials of Jesus, no less essential than prophecy to the Jew, and philosophy to the Greek."[13]

This accounts for the style and content of the writing, as will be noted below. If Mark wrote the book in Rome, the first readers were no doubt residents of that city. They might even have asked him to compose such a gospel.

F. STYLE

Three characteristics of this gospel identify its style: rapid action, vivid detail, picturesque description. These will be observed in your survey study.

G. PURPOSE AND THEME

With the Roman outlook in mind Mark stressed the *actions*, not so much the words, of Jesus in his reporting the life of Christ and recording the claims of the gospel.

The opening verse (1:1) identifies Mark's evangelistic purpose: to record the historical facts of Christ's earthly life, which were the foundations of the glad tidings of salvation. The apostles and other saints were continuing to proclaim that gospel, which originated in the historical facts. Mark was inspired to show Christ as the ever-active servant, "living and working among men, in the fulness of His energy, the Servant Who stooped to conquer ... "[14]; "for even the Son of Man did not come to be served, but to serve, and to give His life a ransom for many"(10:45). This *servant portrait* of Jesus is drawn naturally by such a man as Mark. Everett Harrison writes of this, "As one who ministered to Barnabas and Paul and also to Peter, Mark was a suitable figure to relate the ministry to Jesus in such a way as to emphasize his mission in terms of humble service."[15]

Just a few years before Mark wrote his gospel, Nero had burned Rome (A.D. 64) and blamed the Christians for it, in order to launch open persecution against them. Mark might have written his account to encourage the persecuted saints. (See 10:30, the only synoptic reference to persecutions.)

Chart 29 shows the coverage that Mark gives to the public ministry of Christ (the shaded areas represent Mark's coverage). Such

---

13. W. Graham Scroggie, *A Guide to the Gospels*, p. 169.
14. W. Graham Scroggie, *Know Your Bible*, 2:27.
15. Everett F. Harrison, *Introduction to the New Testament*, p. 175.

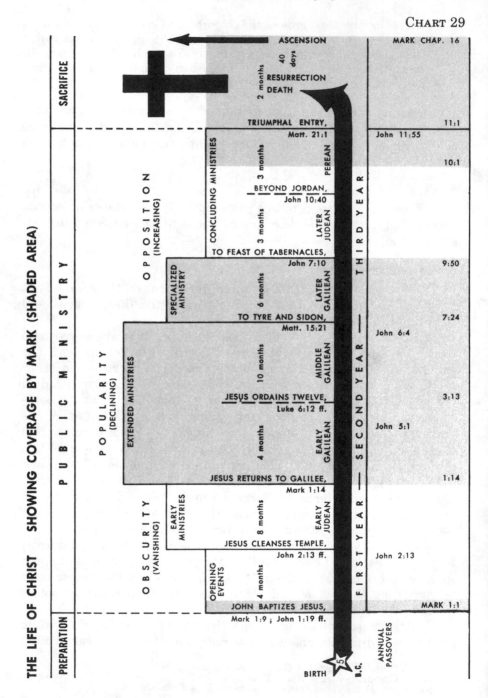

THE LIFE OF CHRIST   SHOWING COVERAGE BY MARK (SHADED AREA)

PREPARATION | PUBLIC MINISTRY | SACRIFICE

OBSCURITY (VANISHING) | POPULARITY (DECLINING) | OPPOSITION (INCREASING)

ASCENSION — MARK CHAP. 16

40 days

2 months — RESURRECTION DEATH

TRIUMPHAL ENTRY, Matt. 21:1 — John 11:55 — 11:1

CONCLUDING MINISTRIES

3 months — PEREAN — 10:1

BEYOND JORDAN, John 10:40

3 months — LATER JUDEAN

TO FEAST OF TABERNACLES, John 7:10 — 9:50

SPECIALIZED MINISTRY

6 months — LATER GALILEAN

TO TYRE AND SIDON, Matt. 15:21 — 7:24

John 6:4

EXTENDED MINISTRIES

10 months — MIDDLE GALILEAN

JESUS ORDAINS TWELVE, Luke 6:12 ff. — 3:13

John 5:1

4 months — EARLY GALILEAN

JESUS RETURNS TO GALILEE, Mark 1:14 — 1:14

EARLY MINISTRIES

8 months — EARLY JUDEAN

JESUS CLEANSES TEMPLE, John 2:13 ff. — John 2:13

OPENING EVENTS

4 months

JOHN BAPTIZES JESUS, Mark 1:9 ; John 1:19 ff. — MARK 1:1

BIRTH   5 B.C.

FIRST YEAR — SECOND YEAR — THIRD YEAR

ANNUAL PASSOVERS

selectivity is always divinely inspired. What are your observations of Mark's coverage, from this chart? How far into Christ's public ministry do chapters 1-9 go? What is the reporting of chapters 10-16? How much of Jesus' first year does Mark report?

III. SURVEY

A. PREPARING TO SURVEY

It is important in survey study to know *what* you are looking for. Recall from your earlier studies that among the main activities that constitute the *what* of survey study are (not necessarily in this order):

1. Discovering the book's overall *theme*
2. Observing *patterns* and *movements* in the literary structure, or organization, of the book
3. Noting *highlights* of the book, and finding *clues* for the study of its various parts
4. Getting a *feel* of the book's atmosphere and approach.

Keep these goals always before you as you make your survey study of Mark.

As a starter, to get a little feel of the book, do these three things: (a) turn the pages of the book, noting the number of chapters and their length; (b) observe the length of each verse of chapter 1, and note the first word of each verse; (c) read aloud 1:1-13.

B. FIRST READING

1. Scan the book of Mark in one sitting if possible. It is not necessary to read every word or line at this time. If your Bible has paragraph divisions, reading the first sentence of each paragraph will suffice for now. If your Bible has chapter or paragraph headings, note them as you scan the book.
2. Write down your first impressions of the book.
3. What is the atmosphere of the book as a whole?
4. List any key words and phrases that stand out after the first reading.
5. Compare the opening verse (1:1) with the concluding verses (16:19-20) of the gospel.

C. SURVEYING INDIVIDUAL SEGMENTS

1. First identify the sequence of twenty segments in Mark, as these are laid out on Chart 30. As an aid for the studies that follow, mark in your Bible the beginning of each segment. (Reasons for the segment dimensions will be seen later.)

CHART 30

SEGMENT TITLES OF MARK

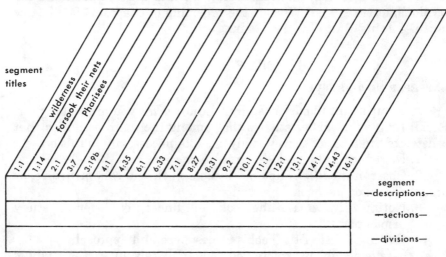

segment titles

wilderness
forsook their nets
Pharisees

1:1 1:14 2:1 3:7 3:19b 4:1 4:35 6:1 6:33 7:1 8:27 8:31 9:2 10:1 11:1 12:1 13:1 14:1 14:43 16:1

segment —descriptions—

—sections—

—divisions—

2. Now scan the book of Mark again, segment by segment. Assign a segment title to each unit. Record these on Chart 30 (examples are given).

3. Go through the segments again and record the main subject of each segment, in as few words as possible. (A main subject may not be similar to a segment title, because segment titles are not intended necessarily to represent main subjects.)

4. What other things have you observed about the book of Mark, in addition to your first impressions? Make a list of those. Compare your observations with the following partial list:

a. Most of the different actions in Mark are very short, like candid snapshots. Recall your earlier observations of the length of verses in chapter 1 and of the repeated first word of each verse.

b. Most of the text reports events, with little comment. Mark is a book of continuous action. "It moves at a breathless pace, portraying Jesus as incessantly active."[16] One writer says that "Mark's words are little pictures."

c. Some of the most awesome and soul-shaking events are recorded in what appears to be calm, matter-of-fact fashion. Look for some of those in chapter 1.

d. The word *immediately* appears often.

16. D. Edmond Hiebert, *An Introduction to the New Testament: The Gospels and Acts*, 1:97.

e. The narrative does not report the birth and infancy of Jesus.

f. Although most of the gospel is narrative, two long teaching sections appear in 4:1-34 (parables) and chapter 13 (prophecy).[17]

g. Mark frequently reports personal gestures of Jesus (3:5; 5:41; 7:33; 8:23; 9:27; 10:16); emotions of Jesus (3:5; 6:6, 34; 8:12; 10:14, 21); and people's reactions to Jesus' ministries (1:27; 2:7; 4:41; 6:14; 7:37; 14:1). Read the verses cited, and add others to the list from your own observations.

5. The writing style of Mark can be described as graphic, vigorous, concise, clear, orderly, and dynamic. Can you think of different examples from the text that illustrate those descriptions?

D. SEEING HOW THE BOOK HOLDS TOGETHER

Mark, like the other three gospels, is a unified story of selected parts of Jesus' life. Let us see how the author organized his material.

1. *Looking for a key turning point in the narrative.* It is clear from all four gospels that Jesus came to earth to minister by *life* and by *death*. Mark 10:45, which may be used as a key verse for Mark, states that very clearly. (Read the verse.) Where in Mark's gospel does Jesus move from the *ministration* phase to the *sacrifice* phase by explicitly telling of His coming death? The answer is: at 8:27. (Read that verse and the following verses.) This is the pivotal or turning point in the action of Mark's gospel.

Observe Jesus' key question and Peter's answer in 8:27-30. Then study the following diagram, which is a key outline for Mark's gospel.

KEY OUTLINE OF MARK

JESUS REVEALS HIS IDENTITY MAINLY BY WHAT HE DOES	WHO DO MEN SAY I AM?	JESUS PRESSES THE CLAIM THAT HE IS THE CHRIST
8:1-26	8:27-30	8:31—16:20

Up to 8:27 Mark shows how Jesus revealed His true identity mainly by His deeds.[18] Then (8:27-30) Jesus inquires about His reputation. He learns that people have not seen Him as the Son of God, but only as an emissary sent from God (such as John the Baptist

---

17. A comparison of the four gospels shows these percentages reporting Christ's words: Mark, forty-three percent; Luke and John, each nearly fifty percent; and Matthew, sixty percent.

18. In His contacts with the multitudes, Jesus also revealed His true identity by *word*, but Mark stresses the *works* ministry.

CHART 31

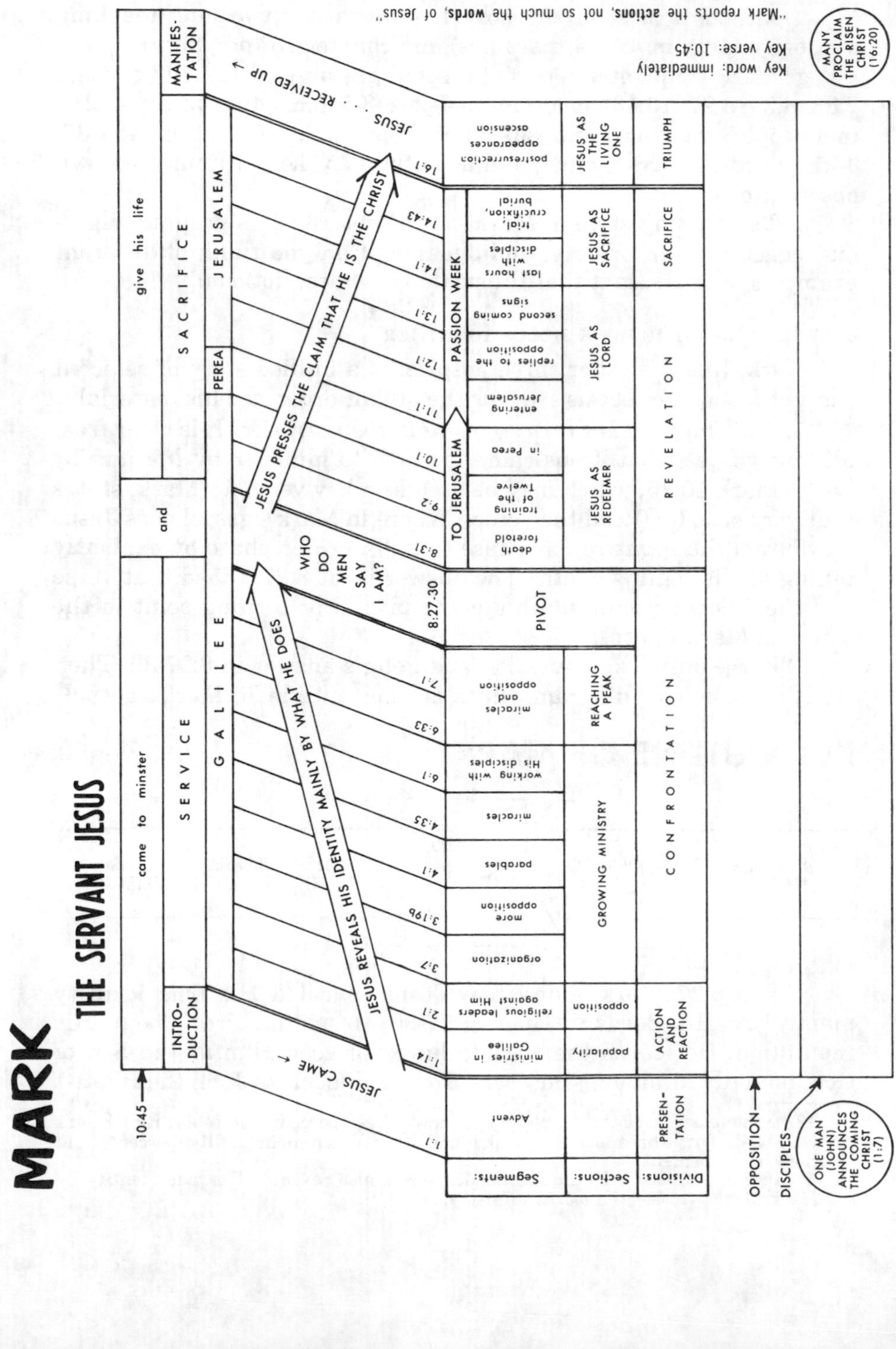

MARK

THE SERVANT JESUS

10:45 — came to minster and give his life

"Mark reports the actions, not so much the words, of Jesus"

Key word: immediately
Key verse: 10:45

MANY PROCLAIM THE RISEN CHRIST (16:20)

ONE MAN (JOHN) ANNOUNCES THE COMING CHRIST (1:7)

JESUS CAME →
JESUS REVEALS HIS IDENTITY MAINLY BY WHAT HE DOES
JESUS PRESSES THE CLAIM THAT HE IS THE CHRIST
JESUS ... RECEIVED UP →

WHO DO MEN SAY I AM?

	INTRO-DUCTION	SERVICE							PIVOT	SACRIFICE							MANIFES-TATION
		GALILEE								PEREA	JERUSALEM						
										TO JERUSALEM	PASSION WEEK						

Segments:	Advent	ministries in Galilee	religious leaders against Him	organization	more opposition	parables	miracles	working with His disciples	miracles and opposition		death foretold	training of the Twelve	in Perea	entering Jerusalem	replies to the opposition	second coming signs	last hours with disciples	trial, crucifixion, burial	postresurrection appearances ascension
	1:1	1:14	2:1	3:7	3:19b	4:1	4:35	6:1	6:33	7:1	8:31	9:2	10:1	11:1	12:1	13:1	14:1	14:43	16:1
Sections:		popularity	opposition								JESUS AS REDEEMER		JESUS AS LORD			JESUS AS SACRIFICE		JESUS AS THE LIVING ONE	
Divisions:	PRESEN-TATION	ACTION AND REACTION			GROWING MINISTRY				REACHING A PEAK		REVELATION				SACRIFICE			TRIUMPH	
			CONFRONTATION																

OPPOSITION →
DISCIPLES →

or Elijah). Jesus knew that to extend His public ministry by giving more of the same kind of revelation would not change the people's reactions. Basically, he had fulfilled the *deeds* phase of His ministering ("For even the Son of Man came . . . to serve," 10:45a). Now He must proceed to the second task, that of giving His life ("and to give His life a ransom for many," 10:45b). This was not the life of a mere man, but of Messiah, the Christ — the anointed one (*krino*) — who Peter, by revelation, confessed Him to be (8:29). And so, Jesus began to teach His disciples very explicitly that He (the Christ) must suffer, be rejected, be killed, and after three days rise again. The story of Mark from this point on, then, is the story of *sacrifice*.

Observe how the strategic center of Mark, which was just described, is shown on the survey of the whole book, Chart 31.

2. *Looking for groups of material*. Refer back to Chart 30, page 142, where you recorded segment titles and segment main subjects. Study your series, and look for groups of segments according to similar subjects. Record those as sections.

Note on Chart 31 that the segment divisions are the same as on Chart 30. Some segments do not begin at the first verse of the chapter (e. g., 1:14; 3:7). Refer to your Bible text and justify why the divisions are made where they are. The segment subjects shown on Chart 31 will help you here.

The bulk of a survey chart shows how the small individual segments combine to make groups of material with a common subject. For example, the two segments beginning at 14:1 and 14:43 are identified on the chart as the section *Jesus as sacrifice*.

As noted in Chapter 3, one of the advantages of a survey chart over the standard outline is that various topical outlines can be viewed simultaneously. Also, a survey chart is a vivid visual reference for context as one analyzes an individual segment.

A division, which is a group of sections, is determined in the same manner as a section. Study the divisions shown on Chart 31. Observe the following on this survey chart:

a. Compare the opening segment (1:1-13) and the concluding segment (16:1-20).

b. What outlines show two main divisions in the book?

c. Study the various sectional and divisional outlines.

d. Note the geographical pattern of Mark's account. Relate this geographical pattern (Galilee, then Jerusalem) to the three-part outline around the pivotal 8:27-30, studied earlier.

e. At some time in your study, record at the bottom of the chart the various oppositions to Jesus and the part the disciples play in the gospel record. (You may want to do this exercise later on.)

f. What is the climactic part of Mark's account? In what ways is it a climax?

3. *Identifying a Main Theme.* In your own words, what is the main theme of Mark? Your survey study should supply the answer. Also try assigning a title to Mark, one that would coincide with the theme. Observe the title shown on Chart 31 — *The Servant Jesus.*

4. *Your Own Summary of Mark's Gospel.* Try writing out your own summary of Mark's gospel. To do this, use all the survey studies you have made of the gospel account, together with everything supplied by this study guide. A sure way of staying on track as you move through the account is to follow the progression of the survey on Chart 31, segment by segment and section by section. As an example of what such a summary is, the following is supplied. Casually view its format; then write out your own summary.

> *Announced and anointed for a redemptive ministry (Presentation, 1:1-13), Jesus preached and worked in the company of the multitudes, attracting many (Popularity, 1:14-45) and angering not a few (Opposition, 2:1—3:6). Jesus anticipated the day when He would no longer minister on this earth, and so He began to organize a band of close disciples (Organization, 3:7-35) while He continued to teach (Parables, 4:1-34) and perform miracles (Miracles, 4:35—5:43). Although He delegated more and more responsibility to the disciples (6:1-32), He nevertheless remained the tireless servant of the multitudes, constantly revealing His true identity by eventually coming to the moment when this phase of His ministry concluded (Peak of Advance, 6:33—8:30). From this point on, as He set His face toward Jerusalem for the last time, He pressed the claim of His being the Christ. He explicitly told of His coming death and resurrection (Jesus as Redeemer, 8:31—10:52); claimed divine authority and prophesied of the future (Jesus as Lord, 11:1—13:37). Then the death plot was drawn up (Plot, 14:1-11); Jesus spent His last hours of fellowship with His disciples (With Disciples, 14:12-42); and He was tried, crucified, and buried (14:43—15:47). Raised from the dead by God, He appeared to His disciples and gave them the mandate of world-wide evangelization, as He was received up into heaven (Triumph, chap. 16).*

IV. PROMINENT SUBJECTS

A. PRESENTATION (1:1-13)

Mark quickly gets to the main theme of his account, which is the *service* and *sacrifice* of Jesus the servant, by using just thirteen verses to introduce Jesus and His main ministry. Mark does this in the organization of his writing by omission (e. g., the nativity of Jesus is not included) and condensation (note how this is done for the wilderness temptations, 1:12-13).

Read the *presentation* passage. How does a condensed, brief opening passage like this call attention to itself? Does this illustrate the principle that emphasis can be made by brief content as well as by long content? Record how each paragraph points forward to the upcoming public ministry.

1:1 _____ .
1:2-8_____ .
1:9-11 _____ .
1:12-13 _____ .

Who are the main characters of this opening passage of Mark?

Refer to Chart 29, page 140. How much of Jesus' three-year public ministry is spanned by Mark 1:1-13?

B. ACTION AND REACTION (1:14—3:6)

This part of Mark covers much of the four-month period of Jesus' second year, after He returned to Galilee for His extended ministries (Chart 29). It includes a short time of popularity (*action*), followed quickly by opposition (*reaction*). (See Chart 31, p. 144.)

Read each part of this ministry, and record your identifications of the main parts:
1. Popularity 1:14-45
2. Opposition 2:1—3:6

C. CONFRONTATION (3:7—8:30)

Mark shows incessant confrontation of Jesus with the religious leaders and the multitudes. The leaders always opposed Jesus; the multitudes usually followed the leaders, but at times they showed interest in this man of Galilee (either out of curiosity or because they were impressed by His miracles). Refer again to Chart 31. What three sections make up the division called *confrontation*?

Read the gospel account and record things that support the following outline:
1. Growing Ministry (3:7—6:32)
   a. Scope of the Ministry (3:7-12)
   b. Helpers in the Ministry (3:13-19)
   c. Opposition to the Ministry (3:20-35)
   d. Ministry in Word (Parables, 4:1-34)
   e. Ministry in Works (Miracles, 4:35—6:32)
2. Reaching a Peak (6:33—8:26)
3. Pivot (8:27-30)

D. MIRACLES (4:35—6:32)

Because he emphasizes the *works* of Jesus,[19] miracles occupy a prominent place in Mark's gospel. Jesus' miracles were performed to show His power and authority and to attest that He was sent from God. Read this passage on miracles, and record observations on *power* according to the outline shown:

power over nature	(4:35-41)
power over demons	(5:1-20)
power over death	(5:21-24, 35-43)
power over disease	(5:25-34)
power restricted	(6:1-6*a*)
power delegated	(6:6*b*-13)
power recognized	(6:14-29)
power at rest	(6:30-32)

E. TURNING POINT OF JESUS' PUBLIC MINISTRY (8:27—9:1)

This is the pivotal point of Jesus' public ministry, the time at which He turned His eyes toward His death and resurrection. As Jesus reminisced with His disciples about the two and one-half years He had just completed of ministering to the multitudes, His one great concern was, "Who do people say I am?" According to the disciples' answer (8:28), He had failed to get across to the people who He really was. It must have been gratifying to hear Peter's reply, "Thou art the Christ" when Jesus directed the question to Peter personally.[20]

We know that this conversation between Jesus and the twelve marked a turning point in Jesus' ministry, because then for the first time He began to tell His disciples *explicitly* that He must die and be raised again the third day (8:31). He had hinted at it before and had foretold the events in parables and figures (e. g., John 2:19; 3:14), but He had not spelled it all out openly in clear words, (cf. 8:32*a*).

Jesus was miles away from Jerusalem at the time of the pivotal point of 8:27-30. (See accompanying Map J.) On His way to the holy city His main attention would be focused on His disciples, to prepare them for the months and years ahead. He would also have limited contacts with the multitudes, and intense discussions with His opponents. In all of this He would, by showing Himself as Redeemer, Lord, Sacrifice, and the ever-living One, be pressing the claim that He was

---

19. Mark rightly reports the parables of Jesus, as well (4:1-34), because the *words* and *works* of Jesus cannot be divorced. There are eighteen miracles in Mark. Proportionately more space is given to miracles in Mark than in the other gospels.

20. As reported by Matthew (Matt. 16:17), Jesus told Peter that His Father had revealed the truth of Jesus' messiahship and deity to Peter.

the Christ, the anointed Messiah. How do those four identifications appear on the survey, Chart 31 (p. 144)?

LAST MINISTRIES OF JESUS

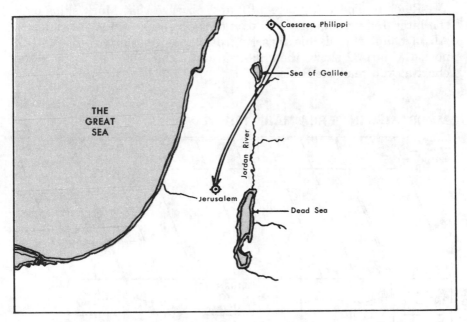

Record what the three paragraphs of 8:27—9:1 teach about the following:

Person of Christ	8:27-30
work of Christ	8:31-33
followers of Christ	8:34—9:1

F. JESUS' TRANSFIGURATION (9:2-13)

The "high mountain" where the transfiguration took place was probably Mount Hermon (9,200 feet), about twelve miles northeast of Caesarea Philippi. (See Map F, p. 65.)

One factor that made Jesus' transfiguration especially impressive upon the hearts and minds of Peter, James, and John was *when* it took place — just about a week after the pivotal session around the questions "Who do people say that I am?" (8:27). For in the transfiguration experience, the prominent spoken words are those of Jesus' Father, and they also are about Jesus' identity: "This is My beloved Son, listen to Him!" (9:7). After you have read the entire passage, relate it to 8:27-30. Then reflect on how an experience like the transfiguration, at the time it occurred, would prepare the way for all that was to follow — in Jesus' life and also in the disciples' experiences.

G. MINISTRIES IN PEREA[21] (10:1-52)

Refer to Chart 29, page 140, and observe that Mark skips over the later Judean ministry and part of the Perean ministries of Jesus. All of chapter 10 is his reporting of the latter part of the Perean period. Chart 32 shows the organization of that chapter. Refer to the chart as you read the Bible text.

CHART 32

MINISTRIES IN PEREA MARK 10:1-52

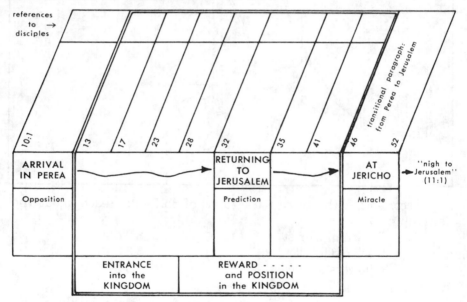

When we keep in mind that Jesus left Caesarea Philippi to go to Jerusalem to be crucified, and that He never sought to postpone His death, then we will see that His ministries for the next six months in Judea and Perea (Chart 32) were not delaying tactics but rather foreordained appointments of a divine calendar. In short, Jesus went to Perea because it was not yet His time to die, and because He had a work to do in those regions in the meantime.

What is chapter 10 mostly about: words or works?

21. The name Perea does not appear in the Bible, but it is the region referred to as "beyond the Jordan" (10:2). (See Map F, p. 65.) The Greek of that phrase, *peran tou Iordanou*, indicates how the word Perea was derived.

Relate the teachings of Jesus to His impending death, resurrection, and glorification.

What is the context of 10:45, which is the verse chosen as a key verse of Mark?

H. DEATH, BURIAL, AND RESURRECTION OF JESUS (15:22—16:8)

Read the three parts of this account, in one sitting. Note all the short verses. What are your overall impressions of Mark's record? Compare this passage with all that goes before it.

Some hold that the original writing of Mark concluded at 16:8. If that were so, what are your impressions of such a conclusion?

I. THE LAST TWELVE VERSES OF MARK (16:9-20)

There are major differences of opinion among textual critics[22] as to whether the original autograph of Mark ended with verse 8, verse 20, or some other ending. Read the marginal notes at 16:8, 16:9, and 16:20 in the NASB.[23] One project for Further Study is based on this.

For this survey study, set aside all considerations of a short or long ending of Mark. Approach the passage as the authentic conclusion to Mark's gospel, and answer the following:

1. What are the various contents?
2. Who are the characters?
3. What do the last two verses report?
4. What earmarks of *conclusion* do you observe in the last two verses?

V. KEY WORDS AND VERSES OF MARK

You have already observed the word *immediately* as a key word of Mark.[24] Usually the word *and* is not designated as a key word, but for Mark, the book of *continuous action*, it is a prominent word, appearing very often. Did you observe any other words, which may be called key words, as you surveyed Mark?

We have already suggested 10:45 as a key verse of Mark, one representing Jesus' redemptive ministry in the role of Servant. In your survey did you see other verses that may be called key verses of Mark?

---

22. Textual criticism (also called "lower criticism") is the discipline of reconstructing the Bible text as it probably appeared in the original manuscripts. The whole discipline is based on thousands of manuscripts, no one of which is part of *the* original writing. See Norman L. Geisler and William E. Nix, *A General Introduction to the Bible*, pp. 358-93.

23. Most Bibles with marginal notes refer to this disputed question.

24. The Greek word *utheos* appears about forty times in Mark, translated in different versions as "immediately," "straightway," "forthwith," "anon," and so forth. It appears more often in Mark's account than in the other three gospels combined.

VI. APPLICATIONS

1. Mark was raised in a devout, God-fearing home. What are your reflections about God's often calling servants from such homes, to carry on His work?

2. Mark matured spiritually during the years after Christ's ascension. What do you learn from Mark's experiences, regarding what contributed to his maturity?

3. Mark's account stresses the fact of *real events* — one after the other — in Jesus' life. How does that strengthen one's Christian faith?

4. What would you answer someone who asked you, on the spot, "Who do you say Jesus is?"

5. Jesus was the Christ — the Anointed One. What does this teach about His Father and about Himself? How are you brought into the picture?

6. List some major spiritual truths that you have learned in your survey of Mark.

VII. REVIEW QUESTIONS

1. When was Mark born, and how old was he when he died?

2. What were the highlights of Mark's Christian service?

3. How did each of the following men influence Mark's life: Barnabas, Paul, Peter?

4. What kind of person was Mark?

5. For whom was this account originally written? What are some evidences of this?

6. Name some characteristics of Mark's writing, such as style.

7. What is the purpose and theme of Mark's account?

8. What is the pivotal point of the book? What three-point outline can be built around this?

9. What outline of Mark is suggested by the key verse 10:45?

10. Name some prominent passages of Mark.

11. What is one key word of Mark?

VIII. FURTHER STUDY

1. Study various sources on the unsettled question of the date of Mark's writing. Correct interpretation of the Bible text, of course, does not depend on the date, otherwise, God would have included the date in the text. But observations concerning such things as background (e. g., how much of the recorded gospel the readers were

already exposed to) are made from the conclusions of date. Think of other things that do depend on date.

2. Study the question about the "long" or "short" ending of Mark. Among other things, compare Bible versions to see how the translators and publishers have represented their conclusions regarding the question. Also, arrive at your own answer to this question, "If verses 9-20 are not genuine, why did God in His providence allow them to pass for genuine, in most Bibles, for so long?"

IX. OUTLINE

MARK: The Servant Jesus
    SERVICE OF JESUS   1:1—9:1
        Presentation   1:1-13
        Popularity and Opposition   1:14—3:6
        Growing Ministry   3:7—6:32
        Reaching a Peak   6:33—8:26
        Turning Point   8:27—9:1
    SACRIFICE OF JESUS   9:2—15:47
        Jesus as Redeemer   9:2—10:52
        Jesus as Lord   11:1—13:37
        Jesus as Sacrifice   14:1—15:47
    TRIUMPH OF JESUS   16:1-20

X. SELECTED READING

GENERAL INTRODUCTION

Harrison, Everett F. *Introduction to the New Testament,* pp. 171-83.
Hiebert, D. Edmond. *An Introduction to the New Testament,* 1:81-113.
Scroggie, W. Graham. *A Guide to the Gospels*, pp. 161-238.
Tenney, Merrill C. *New Testament Survey*, pp. 153-65.
Thiessen, Henry Clarence. *Introduction to the New Testament*, pp. 139-49.

COMMENTARIES

Cole, R. A. *The Gospel According to St. Mark*. Tyndale New Testament Commentaries.
Earle, Ralph. *Mark: The Gospel of Action*. Everyman's Bible Commentary.
Hendriksen, William. *Exposition of the Gospel According to Mark*. In his New Testament Commentary Series.
Hiebert, D. Edmond. *Mark: A Portrait of the Servant*.
Lenski, R. C. H. *The Interpretation of Mark*.
Morgan, G. Campbell. *The Gospel According to Mark*. Unexcelled for its thematic studies in the gospel.

OTHER RELATED SOURCES

Blaiklock, E. M. *Mark: The Man and His Message*.

Burgon, John W. *The Last Twelve Verses of the Gospel According to St. Mark*.
Geisler, Norman L., and Nix, William E. *A General Introduction to the Bible*.
Jensen, Irving L. *Life of Christ*.
Morgan, G. Campbell. *The Parables and Metaphors of Our Lord*.
Robertson, A. T. *Word Pictures in the New Testament*. Vol. 1.
———. *Making Good in the Ministry*. pp. 1-174. A description of Mark's
    biography.
Vine, W. E. *An Expository Dictionary of New Testament Words*.

7

Luke: The Son of Man Among Men

The gospel of Luke is the longest book of the New Testament, and of the four gospels it gives the most comprehensive picture of the life and ministry of Christ. After one has completed a study of Matthew and Mark, the pages of Luke's gospel are a warm and vibrant invitation to walk over new paths.

Luke and John are the two gospel writers who state in the biblical text something of their purpose in writing.[1] Luke, writing to his friend Theophilus, puts it this way: "It seemed fitting for me as well ... to write it out for you in consecutive order ... so that you might know the exact truth about the things you have been taught."[2] So as Luke was inspired to write his account, the *content* he had in mind was the "exact truth," and the *form* he had in mind was "consecutive order." He was not implying that the accounts of the gospel story written by other authors were inadequate or deficient, but rather that *he also was led* to write an account, of the kind identified by his words of purpose. And his reporting, inspired by the Holy Spirit, became part of the twenty-seven-book New Testament canon.

All survey and analytical study of the Bible text involves (1) what the Bible says (*content*) and (2) how it says it (*form*). Our survey of this third gospel will focus therefore on both of the following, which Luke had in mind as he wrote: (1) the content of exact truth and (2) the form of consecutive orderliness. Before doing that, however, we will study the background and setting of this inspired work, to better appreciate and understand its message.

---

1. Luke 1:1-4; John 20:30-31; 21:24-25.
2. Luke 1:3-4.

155

I. Preparation for Study

Review Chart 18, page 108, which shows comparisons of the four gospels. Luke is one of the three synoptic gospels. Note especially how it is compared with Matthew and Mark, which you have just surveyed in the preceding chapters. Among other things, the writer Luke is identified as a litterateur, a man of letters, for he was gifted and probably trained in the art of composition. We may expect to observe evidences of this training as we survey his book.

Think more about content (*what* the Bible says) and form (*how* it says it). The Holy Spirit moved in the heart and mind of each author of Scripture as he wrote, without dictating what the author should write.[3] We do not know the exact process used by the Holy Spirit to guide each writer, but we know that the end product — the Scripture itself — is the authoritative Word of God. The human author's choice of words, style, and plan of composing reflects his own personality, training, and background. Does this process of inspiration account for differences in the four gospels? If so, what kind of differences?

To what extent do you think Jews, living at the time of Jesus' birth, knew of and looked for the promised coming of Jesus as their Messiah? After you have thought about that, read Luke 2:22-38 and observe the expectations of two saints, Simeon and Anna.

To know the writer of this gospel is to appreciate more fully the book he has written. From the sparse biographical data about Luke contained in the gospels and Acts, an unusually full portrait of the man can be composed. The following pages are about the man Luke. Careful study of the descriptions is good preparation for your survey studies.

II. Background

This gospel was inspired and written according to divine design and schedule, eventually to be listed as the forty-second book of the sixty-six-book library in the Bible. Let us see how it came to be.

A. THE MAN LUKE

1. *Birth and early life.* Luke was born of Greek parents, a heritage that made him probably the only Gentile writer of the New Testament. He was born at about the same time as Jesus and Paul. Two possible birthplaces are Antioch of Syria and Philippi of Macedonia. His parents gave him the name of Lucas, a shortened

---

3. In a few places of Scripture the method of inspiration did involve word-for-word dictation (e.g., the Ten Commandments). See Norman L. Geisler and William E. Nix, *A General Introduction to the Bible*, pp. 34-36; 43-47.

form of the Roman name Lucanus. He studied for the medical profession, and this advanced education might have been received at either Athens or Tarsus. From the content and style of his books, we may speculate that history and literature were two of his favorite subjects.

2. *Conversion.* Luke was not a disciple of Jesus during Jesus' earthly ministry. While living in Antioch he may have been converted under the ministry of Paul, such as is referred to in Acts 11:25-26.[4]

3. *Profession and ministry.* Luke was a man of various talents and callings:

a. Physician. "Luke, the beloved physician" (Col. 4:14).[5] If he studied medicine at the university in Tarsus, then he and Paul may have first met at the university, because it is very possible that Paul studied there, his hometown school.

b. Historian. His interest in history is shown by the many historical datelines cited in the gospel (e. g., 1:5, 26, 56; 2:1-2, 21-22, 36-37, 42; 3:1-2).

c. Writer. Luke's gospel is considered by many to be a literary masterpiece. It reveals a highly trained composer, who had a very large vocabulary, vivid style, historical outlook, and gift of communication. The combination of Luke's gospel and Acts makes Luke the writer of more content of the New Testament than any other author.

d. Evangelist and pastor. He was Paul's colaborer on the apostle's missionary journeys, remaining with him until Paul's death (read Col. 4:14; 2 Tim. 4:11; Philem. 24). Apparently Luke never married.

4. *Luke's character.* Luke's writings serve as character prints. What he included and emphasized in his gospel and Acts reveals much about what kind of man he was. We see him as kind, humble, joyful, bright, pious, and gentle. He had a keen sense of the might, justice, and holiness of God. He was surely a man of prayer, because he reported praise and intercession often in his writings. For example, read the songs recorded at 1:46-55 (Mary); 1:67-79 (Zacharias); 2:13-14 (angels); 2:25, 29-32 (Simeon). Also, Luke's gospel refers to the prayers of Jesus more than do Matthew and Mark, and it contains three parables on prayer not found in the other gospels. Luke was also a man of love and sympathy for the underprivileged and those of

---

4. More is known of Luke from his Acts book than from the gospel. In the former he is one of Paul's companions in the "we" sections (to be studied later).

5. Note the medical terms and descriptions in these passages: Luke 4:38-39; 8:43-44; 13:11; 16:20-21. Also it is significant that of the six miracles recorded by Luke and not found in the other gospels, five are miracles of healing: 7:11-18 (widow's son); 13:11-17 (eighteen-year infirmity); 14:1-6 (man with dropsy); 17:11-19 (ten lepers); 22:50-51 (ear healed).

humble estate; for women, children, and the poor; and for the out-casts, such as the Samaritans. He was truly a saint who identified himself with needy humankind, and thus was the very appropriate divine choice as the writer of the gospel of "The Son of Man Among Men."

5. *Death*. One tradition says Luke died as a martyr in Greece. According to the anti-Marcionite "Prologue to Luke," written around A.D. 170, "at the age of eighty-four he fell asleep in Boeotia, full of the Holy Spirit."

B. AUTHORSHIP

The author of this third gospel is nowhere named in the book,[6] but tradition and internal evidence strongly support Lucan author-ship. Concerning tradition, Guthrie observes, "At no time were any doubts raised regarding this attribution to Luke, and certainly no alternatives were mooted. The tradition could hardly be stronger."[7]

The same author wrote both Luke and Acts. (Compare Luke 1:1-4 and Acts 1:1.) The internal evidence of Acts points to Luke as its author, and this evidence in turn supports the accepted Lucan au-thorship of the third gospel.[8]

C. PLACE AND DATE OF WRITING

The place of writing is unknown; it could have been Caesarea or Rome. Luke wrote his gospel around A.D. 60, not much earlier than writing Acts (c. A.D. 61). Read Acts 1:1 for Dr. Luke's reference to his gospel as "the first account."

D. SOURCES OF INFORMATION

Luke had access to other early written records of the life and ministry of Jesus (cf. Luke 1:1-2), and he also interviewed many people who had been eyewitnesses of the events of Jesus' life (Luke 1:2). While Paul was imprisoned at Caesarea before his voyage to Rome, Luke had ample opportunity for such interviewing in the cities of Palestine. Paul himself, though not an eyewitness, must have had some influence on Luke's production of this gospel, even as Peter influenced Mark. Direct disclosure of some parts of the gospel came by the Holy Spirit; *all* the gospel was divinely inspired, or God-breathed.

---

6. Luke is mentioned by name only three times in the New Testament. These occurrences are in prison epistles of Paul: Colossians 4:14; 2 Timothy 4:11; Philemon 24.

7. Donald Guthrie, *New Testament Introduction*, p. 99.

8. See Hiebert, *An Introduction to the New Testament*, pp. 114-24; and Thiessen, *Introduction to the New Testament*, pp. 150-54.

E. ORIGINAL READERS

Luke wrote this gospel especially for his friend Theophilus ("lover, or loved, of God"; see Acts 1:1; Luke 1:3). Theophilus may have been an influential Christian layman of Greece, possibly even a convert of Luke. When Luke's gospel began to circulate throughout the Roman Empire in the first century, the readers particularly attracted to it were people of Greek culture, the culture that glorified wisdom, beauty, and the ideal man. The excellent literary style of this third gospel must have afforded a special attraction to such readers.

Luke had all mankind in mind when he wrote this gospel, which is one reason the title of Jesus, "Son of Man," appears throughout the book. Also, he traces Jesus' genealogy back to Adam, not just to Abraham (see Chart 15, p. 100).

F. PURPOSE AND THEME

As noted earlier, Luke states his purpose in 1:1-4 — to write a consecutive, chronological account of the full and exact truth of Jesus' ministry. Also, because there are *four* gospels instead of *one*, we may conclude that the gospel of Luke is intended to complement the other three gospels by telling the story of Jesus from a different angle and for a different viewer. When the four gospels are compared, differences of the following kind are seen, as shown in the accompanying chart.

COMPARISON OF FOUR GOSPELS

	MATTHEW	MARK	LUKE	JOHN
Jesus as:	King of Israel	Servant of the Lord	Son of Man	Son of God
Reader:	Jew	Roman	Greek	World
Prominent ideas:	Law	Power	Grace	Glory

The theme of Luke concerns "Jesus the Nazarene, who was a prophet mighty in deed and word in the sight of God and all the people" (Luke 24:19). Luke presents Jesus as the Son of Man among men (19:10), the perfect God-man (cf. 1:35) who alone offers to all nations (24:47) the salvation of God (3:6). He emphasizes the universality of salvation, and the word faith appears often in his gospel.[9]

9. Faith is also a key truth in Paul's writings, and the close relationship of Paul and Luke might partly account for Luke's emphasis of this foundational doctrine. In the New Testament, the word *faith* appears more than 240 times, and only 53 times outside of Paul's and Luke's writings.

IV. SURVEY

A. PREPARING TO SURVEY

As a starting acquaintance with Luke's gospel, observe how many chapters there are in the book. Then turn the pages of your Bible and note the average length of Luke's chapters. After that, compare the opening historical paragraph (1:5-7) and the concluding one (24:50-53). What are your observations?

B. FIRST READING

Now scan the book of Luke in one sitting if possible. It is not necessary to read every word or line at this time. If your Bible has paragraph divisions, reading the first sentence of each paragraph will suffice. If your Bible has chapter or paragraph headings, note those as you scan the book.

The purpose of this initial scanning is to get the feel and atmosphere of the book and to catch its major purposes. Write down your first impressions of the book and any key words and phrases that stand out as of this reading.

C. WORKING WITH INDIVIDUAL SEGMENTS

Refer to Chart 34, page 162, and note that Luke is divided into twenty-four segments. All the segments begin at verse 1, with what exceptions?

CHART 33

SEGMENT TITLES OF LUKE

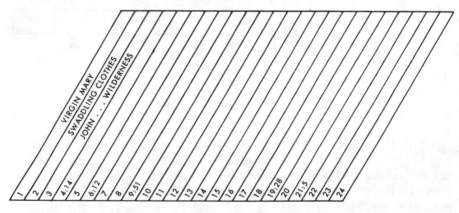

Now go through the book of Luke once again (still in cursory fashion), and assign a segment title to each segment. Recall that a segment title is a strong word or short phrase, preferably taken from the text, intended to serve as a clue to at least one main part of the segment. Some Bible students like to memorize these titles as an aid in recalling the movement of the entire book. Record your titles on a worksheet similar to Chart 33.

What are some of your impressions of this gospel so far?

What have you noticed so far about these subjects:

1. the various groups Jesus spoke to and worked with
2. the constant action in the book — Jesus moving from place to place
3. how much speaking, compared to working, that Jesus did
4. where miracles mainly appear
5. where parables mainly appear?

D. SEEKING INTEGRATING RELATIONSHIPS

The gospels are not unorganized collections of the recorded words and deeds of Jesus. Each gospel is a unified story of selected parts of Jesus' life. The Holy Spirit's inspiration determined the selectivity in each case. A general chronology is followed, with some parts written mainly with a topical organization in mind.

Let us now look at the organization of Luke.

1. Observe from Chart 34 that main divisions are made at 4:14; 9:51; and 19:28. In order to understand the reasons for these divisions, we need to know the overall plan of Jesus' life. Chart 35 shows this plan. The shaded area indicates how much of Jesus' life is reported by Luke.[10] Observe the locations of Luke 4:14; 9:51; 19:28.

Read 4:14-15. Is Jesus engaged in public ministry here? Scan all that happens before 4:14, and the reason for a main division at 4:14 will become evident. Make a brief outline for these sections: 1:1—2:20; 2:21-52; 3:1-20; 3:21-38; 4:1-13.

Now read 9:51. Note the geographical reference. It is at this point in Luke that Jesus enters the later Judean and Perean ministries (see Chart 34) on His way to Jerusalem.

Read 19:28, and justify a main division at this point in the gospel.

2. It is interesting to observe where in Luke most of the miracles occur, and where the parables abound. Below is a list of each group. Record in the segment spaces of Chart 34 a check mark (✔) for each miracle, an (X) for each parable, and you will observe the respective concentrations.

Miracles: chap. 4: unclean demon, Simon's mother-in-law; chap. 5: fishes, leper, palsy; chap. 6: withered hand; chap. 7: centurion's

10. The full biographical content of the chart is arrived at by comparing all four gospels. No one gospel includes all the events, but Luke's gospel is regarded as the most generally representative biography. About half its material is not found in the other gospels.

CHART 34

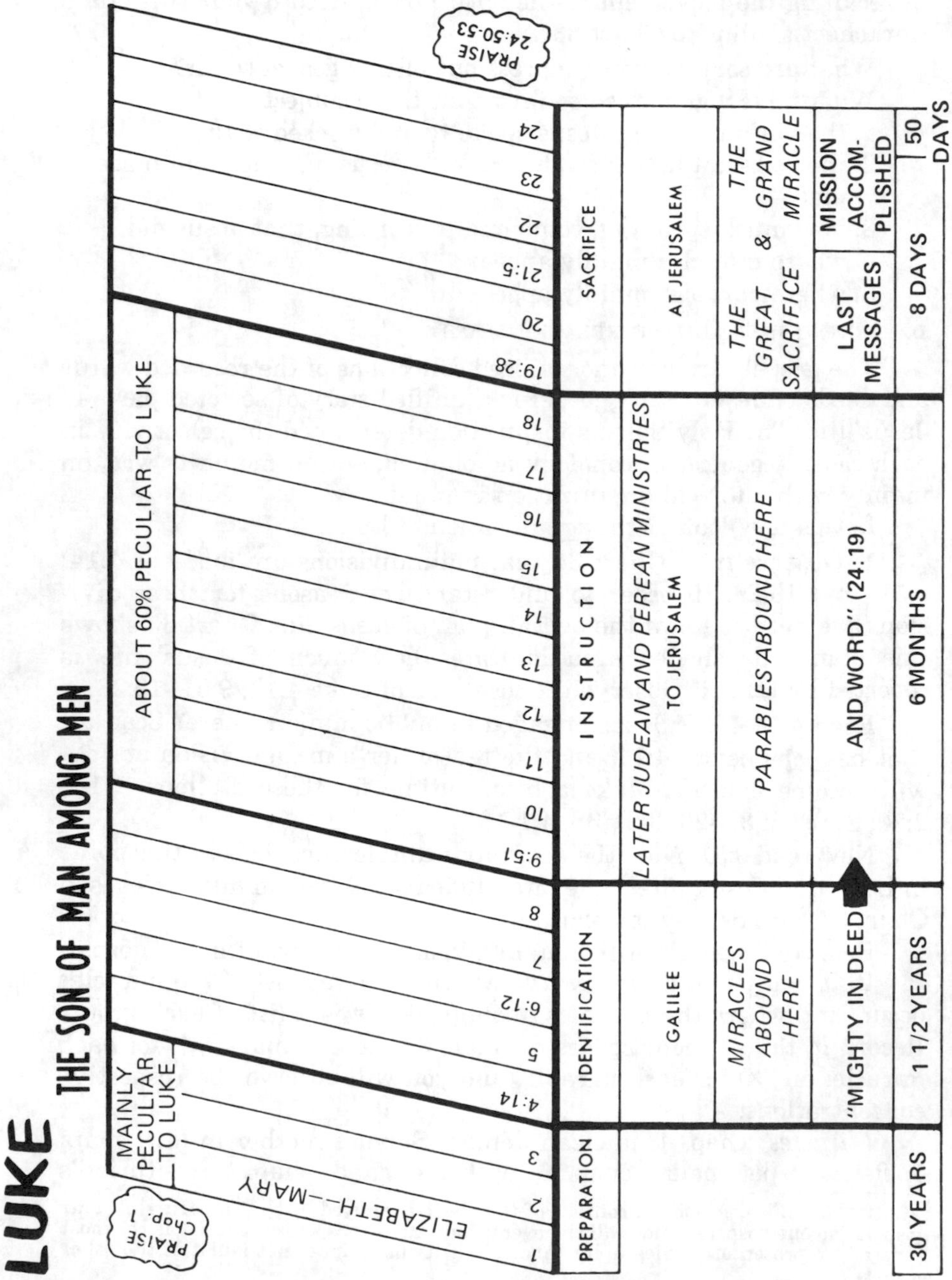

LUKE
THE SON OF MAN AMONG MEN

PRAISE Chap. 1

PRAISE 24:50-53

ELIZABETH—MARY

MAINLY PECULIAR TO LUKE

ABOUT 60% PECULIAR TO LUKE

PREPARATION	IDENTIFICATION	INSTRUCTION	SACRIFICE
	GALILEE	LATER JUDEAN AND PEREAN MINISTRIES TO JERUSALEM	AT JERUSALEM
	MIRACLES ABOUND HERE	PARABLES ABOUND HERE	THE GREAT & GRAND SACRIFICE / THE GREAT & GRAND MIRACLE
	"MIGHTY IN DEED	AND WORD" (24:19)	LAST MESSAGES / MISSION ACCOMPLISHED
30 YEARS	1 1/2 YEARS	6 MONTHS	8 DAYS / 50 DAYS

1 2 3 4:14 5 6:12 7 8 9:51 10 11 12 13 14 15 16 17 18 19:28 20 21:5 22 23 24

KEY VERSES: 19:10; 24:19

KEY PHRASE: "SON OF MAN"

CHART 35

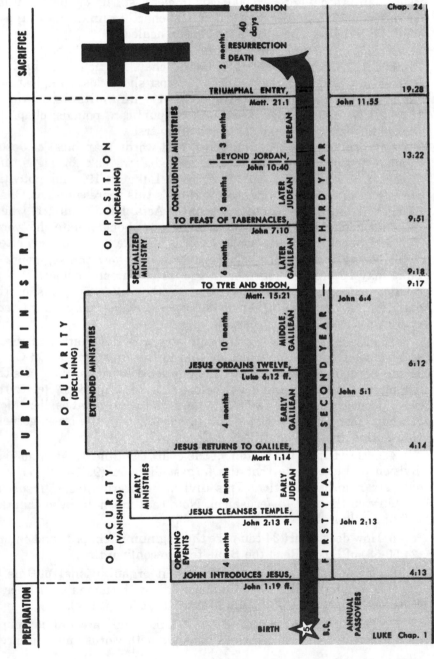

LIFE OF CHRIST SHOWING COVERAGE BY LUKE (SHADED AREA)

PREPARATION

PUBLIC MINISTRY

SACRIFICE

OBSCURITY (VANISHING)

POPULARITY (DECLINING)

OPPOSITION (INCREASING)

OPENING EVENTS

EARLY MINISTRIES

EXTENDED MINISTRIES

SPECIALIZED MINISTRY

CONCLUDING MINISTRIES

ASCENSION

40 days

2 months RESURRECTION

2 months DEATH

TRIUMPHAL ENTRY,
Matt. 21:1

3 months PEREAN

BEYOND JORDAN,
John 10:40

3 months LATER JUDEAN

TO FEAST OF TABERNACLES,
John 7:10

6 months LATER GALILEAN

TO TYRE AND SIDON,
Matt. 15:21

10 months MIDDLE GALILEAN

JESUS ORDAINS TWELVE,
Luke 6:12 ff.

4 months EARLY GALILEAN

JESUS RETURNS TO GALILEE,
Mark 1:14

8 months EARLY JUDEAN

JESUS CLEANSES TEMPLE,
John 2:13 ff.

4 months

JOHN INTRODUCES JESUS,
John 1:19 ff.

BIRTH

B.C.

FIRST YEAR — SECOND YEAR — THIRD YEAR

Chap. 24

19:28

John 11:55

13:22

9:51

9:18

9:17

John 6:4

6:12

John 5:1

4:14

John 2:13

4:13

ANNUAL PASSOVERS

LUKE Chap. 1

servant, widow's son; 8:1—9:50: sea calm, man in tombs, twelve-year issue, Jairus's daughter, 5,000 fed, unclean spirit; chap. 11: dumb devil; chap. 13: eighteen-year infirmity; chap. 14: man with dropsy; chap. 17: ten lepers healed; chap. 21: ear healed.

Parables: chap. 7: two debtors; chap. 8: sower; chap. 10: Good Samaritan; chap. 11: friend at midnight; chap. 12: rich fool; chap. 13: fig tree, mustard seed, leaven; chap. 15: lost sheep, lost coin, lost son; chap. 16: unrighteous steward; chap. 17: unprofitable servants; 18:1—19:27: unjust judge, Pharisee and publican, pounds; chap. 20: wicked husbandman; chap. 21: signs of fig tree.

Concerning the deeds (miracles) and words (parables) of Jesus, compare 1 Corinthians 1:22: "For indeed Jews ask for signs, and Greeks search for wisdom." Also, read Luke 24:19, and note the phrase "mighty in deed and word." How is this represented on Chart 34? Recall that Luke wrote the book of Acts. Read Acts 1:1, where Luke identifies what his gospel account was about. Relate the words "do" and "teach" with the two key words of Luke 24:19 already cited.

3. Study the outlines on Chart 34 to see how the segments of Luke may be brought together in groups of common subject. Try to relate each of your segment titles to the different parts of the outlines. If you choose to do more survey study, you may want to add your own outlines to this chart.

The climax of Jesus' earthly ministry was His death and resurrection, so all four gospels include this in their last pages. On Chart 34 this reporting is identified by the one word *sacrifice*. What are the two main divisions of Luke just before this, leading to it? Relate the two outline words to the two words *deed* and *word* cited earlier. Most of what Luke reports in 1:1—4:13 is not found in the other gospels. How is this division identified on Chart 34?

4. Observe from the bottom of the chart the time duration of each division of Luke. Note that the largest division (9:51—19:27) is of only six months' duration. This division concerns Jesus' *transient* ministry on the way to Jerusalem. Note that much of these chapters is found only in Luke.

5. How does Chart 34 compare the beginning (chap. 1) and ending (24:50-53) of Luke? Read the Bible text to confirm this.

6. What would you say is the main organizational outline of Luke, according to Chart 34? Compare this with the main outlines of Matthew (Chart 22, p. 120) and Mark (Chart 31, p. 144).

7. The structural organization of Luke's full account is simple and precise, which also describes his style with words and sentences.

V. PROMINENT SUBJECTS

The subjects that are identified below, because of their prominence in Luke, reveal something of that gospel's theme.

A. THE PERFECT HUMANITY OF CHRIST

Luke presents Jesus as Son of God (e.g., 1:35), but he shows Him especially as Son of man. This gospel is the fullest account of the birth, childhood, domestic and social life of Jesus. It underscores His human feelings (e.g., 10:21; 19:41; 22:44). And many of His social contacts are reported, for example with Simon (7:36-50); with Martha and Mary (10:38-42); with Pharisees (11:37-52; 14:1-24); with Zaccheus (19:1-10).

Prayers of Jesus are prominent throughout the book, which fact again emphasizes His humanity. In the four gospels fifteen occasions of Christ praying are reported, eleven of which are found in Luke. Much teaching about prayer also is given in this third gospel (e.g., 11:5-13; 18:1-8; 21:36).

The genealogy of Jesus as recorded by Luke (3:23-38) also identifies Jesus intimately with the human race, by tracing the descendants back to Adam (3:38). Recall your earlier study of this in Chapter 4 (Chart 15, p. 100).

B. PRAISE AND THANKSGIVING

Recall your earlier observation of praise at the beginning and end of this gospel (1:9; 24:52). Read the following passages, found only in Luke, which are the source of great hymns of the church:[11]

Ave Maria	1:28-31
Magnificat	1:46-56
Benedictus	1:68-79
Gloria in Excelsis	2:14
Nunc Dimittis[12]	2:29-32

Note the reference to men glorifying God in these passages: 2:20; 5:25, 26; 7:16; 13:13; 17:15; 18:43. Refer also to an exhaustive concordance, and observe how often the word *blessed* appears throughout this gospel.

C. HISTORICAL PERSPECTIVE

The *factual* basis of the gospel is underscored by the inclusion of many references to dates and secular rulers. Also, the organization of the book has a historical perspective. For example, Luke begins his gospel as one might expect a historian to do — by describing

---

11. Scroggie has called these "the last of the Hebrew Psalms, and the first of the Christian hymns" (*A Guide to the Gospels*, p. 371).
12. The Latin title refers to the Bible text, "now ... let ... depart."

background and preliminary events first. He leads up to *the great event*, the coming of Jesus. In this connection it is interesting to observe that the first direct reference to Jesus is not made until verse 31 of chapter 1. For the first thirty verses Luke is setting the stage; and then, bursting forth in all their glory, appear the beautiful words "You will . . . bear a son, and you shall name Him Jesus."

D. THE RELATED MINISTRIES OF JOHN THE BAPTIST AND JESUS (1:1—4:13)

On Chart 34, page 162, the section 1:1—4:13 is called *preparation.*[13] Two preparations are meant by this: the preparation of the people through the ministry of John the Baptist, and the preparation of Jesus for His public ministry. Study Chart 36 to see how Luke interweaves the two preparations into his account. Follow the numbers for Luke's order.

CHART 36

PREPARATION LUKE 1:5-4:13

Preparation of the People		Preparation of Jesus	
6 B.C.			
1 Announcement of John's Coming	1:5-25	2 Announcement of Jesus' Coming	1:26-56
3 Birth of John (5 B.C.)	1:57-58	4 Birth of Jesus (5 B.C.)	2:1-20
Infant John Presented in Temple	1:59-79	Infant Jesus Presented in Temple	2:21-39
Maturing Years of John	1:80	Maturing Years of Jesus	2:40-52
A.D. 26			
5 John Preaching in Wilderness	3:1-20	6 Baptism of Jesus	3:21-38
		7 Temptations of Jesus	4:1-13

Observe from Chart 36 the following arrangement of interchange:

Announcement of John's coming   1:5-25
     — announcement of Jesus' coming   1:26-56
Birth of John   1:57ff.
     — birth of Jesus   2:1ff.

Keep in mind as you study 1:5—2:52 how such an arrangement emphasizes the likenesses of John and Jesus, and the differences. Which of the two birth accounts is longer?

One of Luke's reasons for interweaving the stories of John and Jesus is to magnify Jesus. For example, in the first two chapters of Luke, we read how John came on the scene first, followed by Jesus. People rejoiced when John was born, as well as when Jesus was born.

---

13. Actually, 1:1-4, an introduction to the epistle, stands by itself.

But there was everything about the narrative that spotlighted *Jesus* as the main person, the source of all blessing. Further, in their public ministries, John comes on the scene first, followed by Jesus. Here John can speak for himself, and what he has to say focuses all attention on the One whom he precedes, because he speaks this way of Christ: "He who is mightier than I is coming, and I am not fit to untie the thong of His sandals" (3:16).

Jesus' baptism (3:21-22) and temptations (4:1-13) are reported by Matthew, Mark, and Luke. Read the Luke passages, and observe how the experiences prepare Jesus for His public ministry.

What truths revealed by Luke 1:5—4:13 stand out prominently in your mind?

E. THE CHRISTMAS STORY (2:1-20)

This particular reporting of Jesus' birth appears only in Luke's gospel. The beauty of the narrative is unsurpassed in all of literature. Do not let the familiarity of the story keep you from seeing its significant and wonderful truths. Survey the passage and record your major impressions.

F. IDENTIFICATION BY MIRACLES (4:14—9:50)

One way Jesus identified Himself was by miracles.[14] The miracles demonstrated His power and, in particular, His deity. Twenty miracles are reported in this gospel, six of which are not in the other gospels.

CHART 37

THE FOUR MIRACLES OF LUKE 8:22-56

Subject	Storm vv. 22-25	Demoniac vv. 26-39	Issue of Blood vv. 43-48	Jairus' Daughter vv. 40-42; 49-56
Realm of miracle	nature			
Occasion				
Persons involved				
Appeal made				
Faith demonstrated				
Manner and extent of miracle				
Effect				
Main instruction of the miracle				

14. This revelation of His nature is prominent in John's gospel, to be studied later.

As examples of miracles in Luke, read the four that are recorded in 8:22-56. Over what did Jesus exercise His power in each instance? Record this and other items listed on Chart 37.

G. INSTRUCTION BY PARABLES (9:51—19:27)

We have already seen that parables abound in the third main division of Luke (9:51—19:27). In the entire gospel thirty-five parables are recorded, nineteen of which are unique to Luke's account.[15] Jesus' favorite method of teaching was by parables. Luke records a group of six parables in 15:1—17:10. Read the passage, and record some of your observations on Chart 38.

CHART 38

GOD'S GRACE AND MAN'S RESPONSIBILITIES LUKE 15:1-17:10

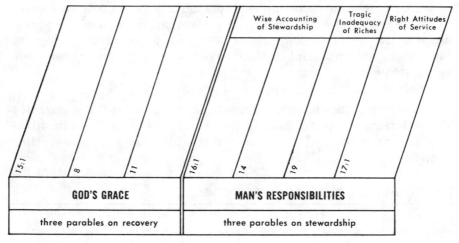

				Wise Accounting of Stewardship	Tragic Inadequacy of Riches	Right Attitudes of Service
15:1	8	11	16:1	14	19	17:1
GOD'S GRACE			MAN'S RESPONSIBILITIES			
three parables on recovery			three parables on stewardship			

H. KINGDOM TEACHING (17:11—19:27)

One of the important subjects of Jesus' teaching was that of the kingdom. Jesus knew, as the prophets had taught, that in the end times He would be sitting on the Davidic throne. That was the kingdom especially oriented to Israel, according to covenant promises. But Jesus had in mind now a *larger* kingdom, as large and universal as the gospel itself, existing right now ("the kingdom of God is within you," 17:21, KJV).

Multitudes of Jesus' contemporaries had false views about the kingdom, hence His instruction concerning it. Read 19:28, noting the phrase "after He had said these things." Then read 17:11—19:27,

15. For a list of parables and miracles found only in Luke *and* of those found in all the synoptic gospels, see W. Graham Scroggie, *A Guide to the Gospels*, pp. 351-52.

where "these things" are recorded. Study the passage to learn what Jesus was teaching (whether by word or works) about the present kingdom.

I. THE GREAT SACRIFICE (22:1—23:56)

At 22:1 Luke begins his account of the darkest episode of Jesus' life. He tells of the satanic plot to betray Jesus (22:1-6); the sad last hours of Jesus with His disciples (22:7-46); the cruel scorn hurled against Him by the religious rulers and the mobs that they incited (22:47—23:25); the agony of scourging and crucifixion (23:26-56).

Read the entire passage, and record observations and impressions on the accompanying Chart 39.

CHART 39

EVENTS OF THURSDAY AND FRIDAY (PASSION WEEK) LUKE 22:1-23:56

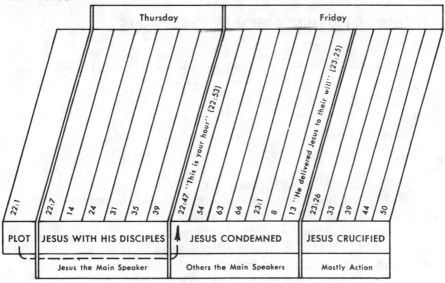

J. THE GRAND MIRACLE (24:1-53)

The tone of praise and blessing that pervades the first chapter of Luke reappears now at the last chapter. From the chamber of the empty tomb the triumphant message echoes forth in matchless glory, "He is not here, but He has risen" (24:6). When Luke wrote his narrative about thirty years had transpired since Jesus' resurrection; but the glory of the event had not subsided. Read the last four verses of Luke's gospel and you will be convinced that intense joy must have filled his heart as he laid down his pen on completion of his writing task. Could any book close on a more triumphant note?

K. OTHER PROMINENT SUBJECTS OF LUKE

1. The work of Christ in redemption. References to grace and the glad tidings occur throughout the book. Christ is the gracious Savior of mankind (19:10).

2. The work of the Holy Spirit. The Holy Spirit is referred to more in Luke than in Matthew and Mark combined. Read 1:15, 35, 41, 67; 2:25-26; 3:22; 4:1, 14, 18; 10:21; 24:49.

3. Christ's ministry to Gentiles. For example, read 2:32.

4. The needs of the humble estate. Women, children, and outcasts appear often in Luke's story. For example, women are mentioned in all but five of the chapters.

5. Various identifications of Jesus. Near each main junction of Luke's gospel, shown below, there is recorded an identification of Jesus.

LUKE'S IDENTIFICATIONS OF JESUS

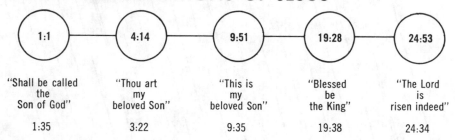

1:1	4:14	9:51	19:28	24:53
"Shall be called the Son of God"	"Thou art my beloved Son"	"This is my beloved Son"	"Blessed be the King"	"The Lord is risen indeed"
1:35	3:22	9:35	19:38	24:34

6. The Emmaus story (chap. 24).

7. The medical terms, and descriptions with medical interest, which support authorship by a physician.

8. Angels. Scroggie writes, "There are more glimpses of the unseen world in this than in any other Gospel. It resounds with angel songs, and with the music of their wings."[16]

9. Short passages found only in Luke include:
   a. Christ weeping over Jerusalem (19:41-44; cf. 13:34-35)
   b. The sweat at Gethsemane (22:44)
   c. Mercy to the thief on the cross (23:40-43).

10. The words of Christ are prominent in Luke's gospel. About half of the account's verses are Christ's words (586 of 1,151 verses).

VI. KEY WORDS AND VERSES

A key verse for Luke is 19:10: "For the Son of Man has come to seek and to save that which was lost." Other suggested key verses are

---

16. W. Graham Scroggie, *A Guide to the Gospels*, p. 380.

24:19 and 4:18-19. A key phrase is "Son of Man," found twenty-five times in this gospel. It was Jesus' favorite title for Himself, used only by Him, with one exception in the New Testament.[17] What key words did you observe in your survey study?

VII. APPLICATIONS

1. How deep is your gratitude and joy over Christ, if He is your Savior?

2. Why is it so important to magnify Christ in all your ways? What do you learn about that from John the Baptist?

3. What lessons about humility do you learn from Jesus, as that quality is made prominent in Luke?

4. What are your relationships with people of low estate?

5. Are you introducing the Son of Man to the people around you?

VIII. REVIEW QUESTIONS

1. In your own words, describe the man Luke.

2. Who were the original readers of this gospel?

3. What is the theme of Luke? Compare Luke's purposes in writing with those of Matthew and Mark.

4. Of what part of Jesus' three-year public ministry does Luke report very little?

5. What are the four main divisions of this gospel account?

6. Where in the account do miracles and parables, respectively, abound?

7. How does 1:1—4:13 fit into the organization of Luke's account?

8. What is a key phrase of Luke? Quote a key verse.

9. Name five prominent subjects of Luke.

IX. FURTHER STUDY

1. John the Baptist served in the transitional period between the Old and New testaments. Study this subject further with the help of a Bible encyclopedia and Bible dictionary.

2. Study Jesus' use of parables in His teaching ministry.[18]

3. Worship of God is a prominent subject of the first two chapters of Luke. Using such helps as a concordance, commentary, and Bible encyclopedia, extend your study of this subject to other passages in the Bible. Consider such areas as the object of worship; way of access to God; heart attitudes; forms of public worship; fruits of worship;

---

17. Stephen referred to Jesus this way (Acts 7:56).
18. Two recommended outside sources on this subject are G. Campbell Morgan, *The Parables and Metaphors of Our Lord*; and Herbert Lockyer, *All the Parables of the Bible*.

idolatry. Some Bible passages to be read are: Exodus 20:5; 1 Kings 11:33; 1 Chronicles 29:20; Psalm 27:4; 95:6; 96:9; 100:4-5; Isaiah 2:8; 44:17; Matthew 4:8-10; John 4:20-26; Philippians 2:9-11; 1 Timothy 2:5; Hebrews 8:5; 10:20, 24-25; 1 Peter 2:9; Revelation 4; 5:5-14; 7:9-12.

4. Study the basic conflict between the *religion* of Pharisaism and the *life* of Christianity.

5. Study the important subject of prayer in Luke.

X. Outline

LUKE: The Son of Man Among Men

PREPARATION	1:1—4:13
Births of John and Jesus	1:1—2:52
Preaching of John, and Baptism and	
Temptations of Jesus	3:1—4:13
IDENTIFICATION	4:14—9:50
Jesus' Message Identified, Demonstrated,	
and Opposed	4:14—6:11
Middle Galilean Ministry Begins	6:12—7:50
Last Months of Jesus' Galilean Ministry	8:1—9:50
INSTRUCTION	9:51—19:27
Ministries Around Jerusalem	9:51—11:54
Teaching in Cities and Villages	12:1—14:35
Six Parables	15:1—17:10
Kingdom Teaching	17:11—19:27
SACRIFICE	19:28—24:53
Last Messages	19:28—21:38
The Great Sacrifice	22:1—23:56
The Grand Miracle	24:1-53

XI. Selected Reading

GENERAL INTRODUCTION

Gundry, Robert H. *A Survey of the New Testament*, pp. 93-101.
Hiebert, D. Edmond. *An Introduction to the New Testament*. 1:114-59.
Scroggie, W. Graham. *A Guide to the Gospels*, pp. 329-92.
Tenney, Merrill C. *New Testament Survey*, pp. 169-83.
Thiessen, Henry C. *Introduction to the New Testament*, pp. 150-61.

COMMENTARIES

Geldenhuys, Norval. *Commentary on the Gospel of Luke*. The New International Commentary on the New Testament.
Godet, F. *A Commentary on the Gospel of Luke*. Reprint. 2 vols.
McNicol, J. "The Gospel According to Luke." In *The New Bible Commentary*.

Morgan, G. Campbell. *The Gospel According to St. Luke*.

Morris, Leon. *The Gospel According to St. Luke*. The Tyndale New Testament Commentaries.

OTHER RELATED SOURCES

Hobart, W. K. *The Medical Language of St. Luke*.

Morgan, G. Campbell. *Parables and Metaphors of Our Lord*.

Ramsey, William. *The Bearing of Recent Discoveries on the Trustworthiness of the New Testament*, pp. 222-300.

Robertson, A. T. *Luke the Historian in the Light of Research*.

Strong, James. *The Exhaustive Concordance of the Bible*.

Tenney, Merrill C., ed. *The Zondervan Pictorial Bible Dictionary*.

Thomas, Robert L., ed. *New American Standard Exhaustive Concordance of the Bible*.

Vine, W. E. *An Expository Dictionary of New Testament Words*.

8

John: Life in Jesus, the Son of God

About forty years after the first New Testament book was written, God inspired the aged apostle John to compose the last of the gospel accounts, known today as the fourth gospel. In many ways it is distinct from the other three gospels and serves as a capstone revelation of the life and ministry of Christ. Today it is often the first New Testament book recommended to new Christians for study. That is because it has a combination of many desirable features that make it a primer for reading and study: it clearly presents foundational truths; it combines fact and interpretation; it presents the way of salvation succinctly and persuasively (e.g., 3:16); its very setting and atmosphere are universal; and it is picturesque and attractive in varied forms. Some of those qualities will become evident as you survey this fascinating portion of Scripture.

I. PREPARATION FOR STUDY

1. First, think about why God would want a fourth gospel written, since the combination of the three that had been written — Matthew, Mark, and Luke — was so comprehensive and instructional. A sweeping general view of the first century, involving the facts of the gospel, will suggest some answers to the question. Study Chart 40, observing the following:

a. The three words *originate, recorded,* and *interpreted* identify each of the century's three periods.

b. The *first period* (up to A.D. 33) is that of the historical origins. For example: Jesus was born; Jesus was crucified; Jesus was resurrected.

c. The *second period* (from Jesus' ascension to the destruction of Jerusalem, in A.D. 70) is when the three synoptic gospels were written. They mainly report the facts of Christ's life. They also include Jesus' teaching and as much of the writer's interpretation as God deemed necessary for that time.

CHART 40

PLACE OF JOHN'S GOSPEL IN FIRST-CENTURY HISTORY

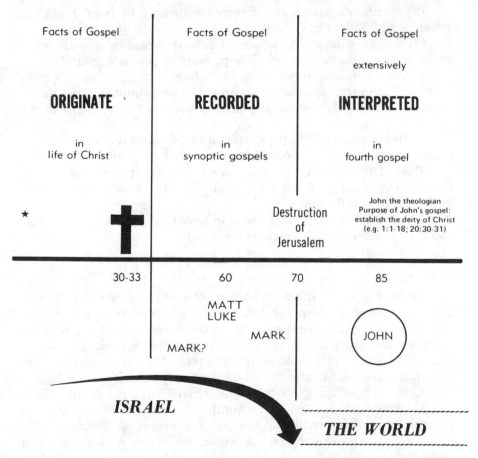

d. The *third period* begins after the fall of Jerusalem and reaches to the end of the century. It was a time of consolidation, organization, and reflection in the Christian communities of the Mediterranean world. In A.D. 85 God inspired John to write the fourth gospel, to include key facts of the gospel but extensively to interpret those facts for the reader. John writes as the reflective theologian, with a main purpose of establishing the foundational truth of the deity of Christ.

Do you see the logical order of:

HISTORICAL FACTS → REPORTED FACTS → INTERPRETATIONS

e. John's gospel also fits into the transitional scheme of God's revelatory program:

(1) The Old Testament prophets, Jesus, and the early disciples preached first to Israel.

(2) Matthew's gospel was directed primarily to Jews; Mark's to Romans; and Luke's to Gentiles.

(3) John's perspective was particularly worldwide, with references to Jew, Roman, and Greek kept more in the background.

2. Now consider other aspects before beginning your survey studies. For example, what is perhaps the most-quoted verse in the New Testament? Do you see any significance that it is in this fourth gospel by John?

3. Review Chart 18, page 108, and think especially of John's gospel as you observe the comparisons of the four gospels.

4. Read the opening verse of each of the synoptic gospels. (Read Luke 1:5 in place of Luke 1:1.) Then read the first verse of John. What are your reflections?

5. Prepare your heart and mind to have open eyes and a receptive spirit as you survey this precious book of God.

II. BACKGROUND

A. AUTHOR

Authors of many Bible books are not identified by name. This is so in the case of the gospel of John. The traditional view is that John the apostle, sometimes referred to as John the evangelist, was the author; hence the title, gospel of John, or gospel according to John.[1] (The titles of our Bible books were not a part of the originally inspired text, but were added later for identification purposes.) According to 21:20, 23-24, the "disciple whom Jesus loved" was the author. Read 13:23; 19:26; 20:2; 21:7 for other similar descriptions of this disciple. In each case, John could be the disciple meant. If John was the author, why do you suppose he would not name himself in those passages?

---

1. Another view is that a close disciple of the apostle, referred to as John the elder, was the book's author. See A. M. Hunter, *The Gospel According to John*, pp. 12-14.

Listed below are some descriptions and other facts concerning the apostle John. Study these carefully to become acquainted with the author. Be sure to read all verses cited.

1. *Family*

a. John was a son of Zebedee (21:2) and Salome (cf. Matt. 27:56; Mark 15:40; John 19:25). Since Salome was a sister of Jesus' mother Mary, Jesus and John were cousins. That would partly explain the close association between the two.

b. John was a brother of the apostle James. Jesus surnamed both men Boanerges, or "sons of thunder," a name indicating perhaps a fiery personality (cf. Luke 9:52-56).

c. Zebedee, James, and John were fishermen at the Sea of Galilee. Zebedee was probably well-to-do (Mark 1:19-20).

2. *Christian ministry*

a. John may have been a disciple of John the Baptist when Jesus called him to His service (Mark 1:20). His age at that time may have been around twenty-five, and he lived to be about one hundred.

b. John was a Palestinian Jew, a close companion of Peter, a contemporary of the events of his gospel.

c. John became a leader of the Jerusalem church (Gal. 2:9).

3. *Writings*

John wrote three epistles and Revelation in addition to his gospel. Because Revelation refers mainly to the last days, the statement may be made that, as John the Baptist prepared the way for the first coming of Jesus, the apostle John has prepared the way for Christ's second coming.

4. *Later life*

There are only a few historical references to John after the events of the gospels. Read these:

Acts 4:1-22; 8:14-15 — John with Peter
Galatians 2:9 — One of John's contacts with Paul
Revelation 1:1, 4, 9 — John's exile experience, around
A.D. 95

5. *Character*

From New Testament biography and epistles, a composite personality image of John is seen, though the image is incomplete in some respects. John was a man of courage, fervor, loyalty, spiritual perception, love, and humility. The subject of love is a keynote of his epistles. Of this Merrill Tenney writes, "As Christ tamed his ardor and purified it of unrestrained violence, John became the apostle of love whose devotion was not excelled by that of any other writer of the New Testament."[2] (See 1 John 4:7.)

A little may be learned about the man John from the book he wrote, although one is not usually aware of the author, as John's gospel is being studied. From that standpoint, the authorship may rest in anonymity, as suggested symbolically by someone's remark that "this gospel was written by the hand of an angel."

B. PLACE AND DATE OF WRITING

The latter years of John's life were spent around Ephesus, hub city of Asia Minor, where the apostle was teaching, preaching, and writing. The advanced nature of John's gospel points to the fact that the other three gospels had already been written, and that a period of time had elapsed since their writing. Now the church's need was for a restatement of the same story of Christ, but with more reflection and interpretation combined with the narrative. On the basis of all this it may be concluded that John wrote his gospel toward the end of the century, or around A.D. 85, while he was ministering at Ephesus.[3]

Ten years later, around A.D. 95, John was exiled by Emperor Domitian to the Island of Patmos, where he wrote the book of Revelation (cf. Rev. 1:9).

C. ORIGINAL READERS

By the time John wrote his gospel the church had matured in its transition from a Jewish exclusivism (cf. Acts 10) to a universal outreach. Recall from your study of Luke, written about twenty-five years earlier, that the third gospel had helped men understand the broader scope of Christ's message by showing the gospel's universal application. By the time of the appearance of John's gospel it was very natural for the message of this fourth gospel to be directed to the world at large. There are many internal evidences of this universal outreach. For example, John knew as he wrote that not many of his readers would be Jews. So he translated Hebrew and Aramaic words (e.g., Siloam, 9:7; Gabbatha, 19:13; and Golgotha, 19:17), and he explained Jewish religious practices (e.g., the burial custom of 19:40). There are many other characteristics of his writing that reveal its universal application.

Despite this universal flavor of the fourth gospel, it has been observed that the account "is saturated with the thoughts, imagery, and language of the Old Testament."[4] This confirms the unity of both testaments of the Bible.

---

2. Merrill C. Tenney, *New Testament Survey*, p. 189.
3. John's gospel is sometimes called "The Ephesian Gospel."
4. A. Plummer, quoted by W. Graham Scroggie, *A Guide to the Gospels*, p. 426.

D. STYLE OF WRITING

There is a basic simplicity about the language and structure of the fourth gospel, whereas the meaning of its message ranges from the perspicuous (e.g., 3:16) to the mystical (e.g., 1:1). Luther wrote, "Never in my life have I read a book written in simpler words than this, and yet the words are inexpressible." Another theologian has expressed it this way: "The noble simplicity and the dim mystery of the narration, the tone of grief and longing, with the light of love shedding its tremulous beam on the whole — these impart to the Gospel of John a peculiar originality and charm, to which no parallel can be found."[5]

John is a book of contrasts, moving quickly from grief and sadness to joy and gladness, from the storms of opposition to the peace of fellowship, from condescension earthward to ascension heavenward, from doubt to faith, from life to death. Any attentive reader of this gospel must be stirred within as he ponders what its narrative has to do with him.

E. PURPOSES AND THEME

The three different writings of John (gospel, epistles, Apocalypse [Revelation]) reveal three different basic purposes of the author.

1. *The gospel*: the evangelic founding and nurturing of the church.

2. *The epistles*: the organic shaping of the church.

3. *The Apocalypse*: the eternal future of the church.[6]

It is interesting to observe that one author should be divinely assigned such a wide range of content for writing.

Chart 41 shows how Christ's ministry is written about in each of the three groups of the New Testament, as well as in the Old Testament.

John explains specifically in 20:30-31 why his gospel was written. It was primarily to win *unbelievers* (Jew and Gentile) to a saving faith. John also must have had in mind the confirming of *believers* in their faith,[7] so that the church would have a stronger witness.

Read 20:30-31 for John's purpose in reporting the "signs" of Jesus in his gospel. The miracles were called "signs" by John because they *signified* vital spiritual truths. John wanted his readers not only to learn those spiritual truths, but to come to a personal relationship

---

5. August Tholuck, quoted in John Peter Lange, *Lange's Commentary on the Holy Scriptures*, 17:vii.

6. Ibid., 17:15.

7. *The New English Bible* translates 20:31 as "recorded in order that you may hold the faith that Jesus is the Christ, the Son of God."

with Jesus through faith in Him as the Christ, the Son of God. The theme of his account may be stated as "Life in Jesus, the Son of God." Keep in mind the words *believe* and *life* as key words of John's gospel. What is the connection between signs, belief, and life?

CHART 41

CHRIST IN THE BIBLE

OLD TESTAMENT	GOSPELS AND ACTS	EPISTLES	REVELATION
HIS MINISTRY	HIS MINISTRY	HIS MINISTRY	HIS MINISTRY
PROPHESIED	INITIATED	INTERPRETED	CONSUMMATED
		AND APPLIED	AND HIS CLAIMS
			VINDICATED
(MESSIAH)	DEATH AND RESURRECTION ——————————————————→		GLORY (KING)

John also had other purposes in mind, subordinate but related to those mentioned above. One was to refute the heresy of Docetism, which denied the true humanity of Jesus (observe John's "answer" in 1:14). Another was to expose the unbelief of Judaism[8] (e.g., "He came to his own country, but his own people did not receive him," 1:11, TEV).

F. RELATION TO THE SYNOPTIC[9] GOSPELS

The four canonical gospels record an identical "good news" about the same God-man, Jesus. Yet each gospel has its own unique function. The one gospel markedly different from the other three is John's. Some of these differences are shown on Chart 42.

Most of the comparisons shown on Chart 42 refer to the gospels' contents *as a whole*. For instance, Jesus is no less Son of God in the synoptics than He is in John. Study the chart.

G. RELATION TO THE NEW TESTAMENT CANON

We have already seen that John is the author of a gospel, three epistles, and the Apocalypse. Chart 43 shows his gospel as a link in the chain binding together the three groups of New Testament books

---

8. The word *Jew* appears about seventy times in the gospel.
9. The word *synoptic* is used to identify the similarity of Matthew, Mark, and Luke. The word itself is from the Greek *synoptikos*, which means "seeing the whole together."

(history, epistles, visions). Observe on the chart these other interlocking connections in the whole New Testament canon:

CHART 42

THE SYNOPTICS AND JOHN

The Synoptics	John
chiefly concerned with Jesus' ministry in the north, around Galilee	gives more coverage to Jesus' ministry in the south, around Judea
much emphasis on "kingdom" inheritance	more emphasis on the person of Jesus ("I am's") and eternal-life inheritance
Jesus as Son of David, Son of man	Jesus especially as Son of God
the gospel of the infant church	the gospel of the maturing church
the earthly story	the heavenly meaning
Jesus' sayings generally short (e.g., parables)	more of the long discourses of Jesus
comparatively little commentary by the gospel writer	much commentary by John
only one mention of a Passover	three, possibly four, Passovers cited (on this basis it is concluded that Jesus' public ministry lasted 3½ years)

1. Luke wrote a gospel, supportive of the other three; and Luke wrote Acts.
2. Paul's credentials are established in Acts.
3. Paul wrote the Pauline epistles, supportive of the general epistles.
4. John wrote three epistles, supportive of the other general epistles.
5. John wrote Revelation.

H. COVERAGE OF JESUS' LIFE

The four gospels differ from each other on how much they report of Jesus' life. Whatever each author included or excluded was determined by a divinely inspired selectivity with a view to the particular gospel's purposes.[10] We have already seen what proportion of Christ's life recorded is covered by each of the synoptic gospels. Chart 44 shows the coverage of John's gospel, as indicated by the shaded areas.

CHART 43

INTERLOCKING ATTESTATION
OF N.T. BOOKS

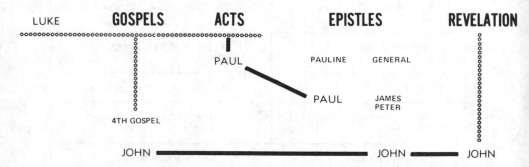

1. Observe that John gives a full coverage of the first year of Jesus' ministry. What region of Palestine was primarily involved?

2. John also gives extensive coverage of the last months of Jesus' ministry. Like the other three gospels, he gives special attention to Jesus' death and resurrection.

3. Read in your Bible the four references to Passovers cited on the chart. (Some hold that the "feast" of 5:1 was not of Passover time.)[11]

4. Observe that one verse, 7:1, covers the entire six-month period of Jesus' specialized ministry. (The synoptic gospels give an extensive coverage of that period.) Why would an author, such as John, include in his gospel narrative only certain events of Jesus' life?

---

10. For example, Matthew omits Jesus' first miracle in Cana; Mark omits the nativity story; Luke omits Jesus' meeting with the Samaritan woman; John does not record Jesus' ascension to heaven. (Neither does John report Jesus' nativity and genealogy, youth, wilderness temptations, or transfiguration.)

11. The text of 5:1 reads "a feast of the Jews." Some ancient manuscripts read "the feast . . . ," suggesting that *the* main Jewish feast of the Passover was meant. Bible students have interpreted this unnamed feast in various ways: Passover, Pentecost, Tabernacles, Purim, Dedication.

THE LIFE OF JESUS   SHOWING COVERAGE BY JOHN (SHADED AREA)

SACRIFICE & VICTORY			

ASCENSION — 21:25

40 days

2 months — RESURRECTION

2 months — DEATH

TRIUMPHAL ENTRY, — 12:12
Matt. 21:1 — John 11:55

CONCLUDING MINISTRIES

3 months — PEREAN

BEYOND JORDAN, — 10:40
John 10:40 — 10:22-39

3 months — LATER JUDEAN

TO FEAST OF TABERNACLES, — 7:2—10:21
John 7:10

SPECIALIZED MINISTRY

6 months — LATER GALILEAN — 7:1

TO TYRE AND SIDON, — John 6:4 — Chap. 6
Matt. 15:21

OPPOSITION (INCREASING)

EXTENDED MINISTRIES

10 months — MIDDLE GALILEE

JESUS ORDAINS TWELVE, — Chap. 5
Luke 6:12 ff. — John 5:1

POPULARITY (DECLINING)

4 months — EARLY GALILEAN

JESUS RETURNS TO GALILEE, — 4:43-54
Mark 1:14 — 4:42

EARLY MINISTRIES

8 months — EARLY JUDEAN

JESUS CLEANSES TEMPLE, — John 2:13
John 2:13 ff.

OBSCURITY (VANISHING)

OPENING EVENTS

4 months — JOHN INTRODUCES JESUS, — 1:19
John 1:19 ff.

BIRTH ⭐ 5 B.C. — ANNUAL PASSOVERS — John 1:1-18

PREPARATION | PUBLIC MINISTRY

FIRST YEAR — SECOND YEAR — THIRD YEAR

THE GEOGRAPHY OF JOHN'S GOSPEL

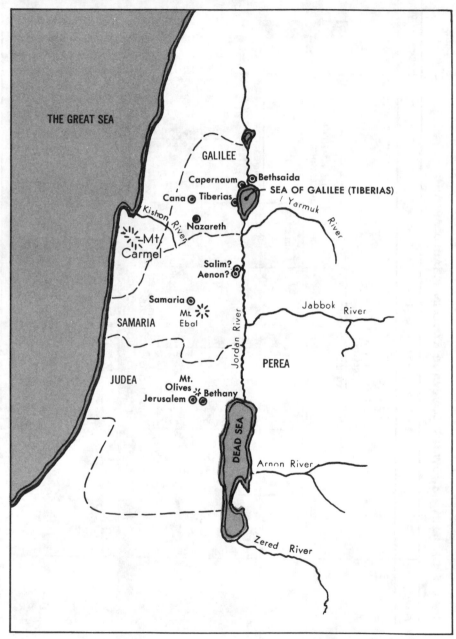

I. GEOGRAPHY

Map K shows the geographical places mentioned in John's gospel. Refer to this as you survey the book.

III. SURVEY

A. PREPARING TO SURVEY

We have studied the background of the fourth gospel in order to have a greater appreciation for how it came into being. Now as we enter the stage of survey study, our goal is to learn what this gospel emphasizes regarding Jesus' life and ministry.

Open your Bible to the gospel of John and rapidly turn the pages of its twenty-one chapters. As you do this prepare your mind to get a general overview of this book. Have you ever tried thumbing through a magazine first for a casual acquaintance and then returning to read the individual articles and features?

Two things that you should observe in this preliminary glance are the lengths of the chapters and the topical headings at the top of the pages of your Bible.[12]

For your survey studies you should be using a Bible edition in which you will not hesitate to make pencil notations. Always keep a pencil in your hand as you read the Bible text, and use it to record your observations.

B. FIRST READING

Your first reading of the text of John should be a scanning. Spend about an hour (averaging three minutes per chapter) viewing only some of the prominent features of each chapter.[13] Do not try to be exhaustive in this stage of your study. The main purpose of scanning is to make a first acquaintance by identifying the book's major contents.

Things to look for in scanning are main characters (e.g., Lazarus, chap. 11), main events, and key words and phrases. You may choose to read only the first verse or two of each paragraph in a chapter, rather than all the verses of the chapter. (For survey study, keep training your eyes to see things without tarrying over the details.)

What are some of your first impressions of John's gospel after your first reading?

---

12. NASB uses a helpful set of topical headings.

13. Of course, the original autographs did not have chapter divisions, or, for that matter, verse divisions. Such divisions are helps to us today for reference and for identification of small units of thought.

C. WORKING WITH INDIVIDUAL SEGMENTS

Note on Chart 45 that the first verse of each chapter of John begins a new segment, and three additional segments are made: at 1:19; 10:40; and 12:36*b*. Mark those additional segment indicators in your Bible.

Read John's gospel segment by segment, recording segment titles on Chart 45 as you read.

What are your further impressions of this gospel? Have key words and phrases begun to stand out?

CHART 45

SEGMENT TITLES OF JOHN

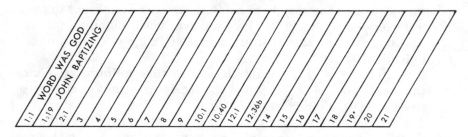

D. SURVEYING THE STRUCTURE OF THE BOOK[14]

Keep in mind your set of segment titles as you move about in this stage of survey. Do you see any grouping of material in John's gospel, such as groups of miracles?

Try to identify any turning points, such as when Jesus becomes a prisoner. Read the Bible text and justify why new segment divisions are made at 1:19; 10:40; and 12:36*b*.[15]

Compare the first and last segments of John. Also, compare the first verse of John and the last verse.

Do you sense a forward movement in the account?

Is there a climax? If so, where?

How does John identify the purpose of his account, in 20:30-31? What title would you give to the gospel, based on this purpose?

Chart 46 is a completed survey chart showing various outlines that you will be referring to as you now use the following study suggestions. The answers are not always found on the chart itself. Refer to the Bible text as much as possible.

---

14. For a discussion of various structures of John's gospel, read Merrill C. Tenney, *John: The Gospel of Belief*, pp. 25-53; and William Hendriksen, *Exposition of the Gospel According to John*, pp. 64-66.

15. The reasons for beginning divisions at these points will be seen later.

JOHN
LIFE IN JESUS, THE SON OF GOD

KEY VERSES:
20:30-31

OBJECT of BELIEF:

"Behold the Lamb of God"

DISCIPLES' BELIEF GROWING

GATHERING OF HIS OWN (6:35-51)

CONFLICT WITH JEWS

PEOPLE'S UNBELIEF INTENSIFYING

MINISTERING TO HIS CLOSE DISCIPLES

CRUCIFIED BY HIS ENEMIES

RESURRECTION AND APPEARANCES TO HIS DISCIPLES

PRO-LOGUE

ERA OF INCARNATION BEGINS

YEARS OF CONFLICT

THE GREAT PAUSE

DAY OF PREPARATION
discourse and prayer

HOUR OF SACRIFICE
-cross-

DAWN OF VICTORY
-resurrection-

EPILOGUE

PUBLIC MINISTRY

PRIVATE MINISTRY

THREE YEARS

FEW DAYS

SIGNS WROUGHT
(MIRACLES)

SELF REVEALED
(DISCOURSES)

Chapter
2—Water to Wine
4—Nobleman's Son Cured
5—Sick Man Healed

Chapter
6—5,000 Fed
6—Walking on Sea
9—Blind Man Healed
11—Lazarus Raised

Chapter
14—The Father's House
15—Vine and the Branches
16—Promises of Jesus
17—High-priestly Prayer

Chapter
20—Resurrection
21—Postresurrection Appearances
21—Draught of Fishes

KEY WORDS

believe (98)
world (78)
Jew (71)
Know (55)
glorify (42)
My Father (35)
verily, verily (25)
light, darkness
love
truth
abide, life
witness, testify
Word
judgment
name

Chapter references: 1:1 1:19 2:1 3 4 5 6 7 8 9 10:1 10:40 12:1 12:36b 14 15 16 17 18 19 20 21

*—Four Passovers of John: 2:13; 5:1; 6:4; 11:55
•—Peculiar to John

Notes on Chart 46

1. Most of the chart divides the gospel of John into how many main divisions?

2. How does 1:19 begin a new section? That is, how is 1:1-18 different from 1:19ff.? What is 1:1-18 called, on the chart?

3. Generally speaking, to whom is Jesus extending His ministry in 1:19—12:36*a*? Who are the special objects of His ministry in 12:36*b*—17:26?

4. What verses of chapter 5 show beginnings of opposition to Jesus?

5. Study the outline of Chart 46 concerning the people's unbelief, and compare this outline with the one shown of the disciples' belief. As you study John, keep in mind both of these developments. Are there progressions? climaxes?

6. The hour of 12:36*b* has been called "The Great Pause." How is this a turning point in the gospel? For help in answering this, identify the "they" of 12:37 and "his own" of 13:1. Then refer to Chart 46, and note the various outlines that have a turning point at 12:36*b*.

7. In what chapter does Jesus' arrest take place? Where is the resurrection recorded? How are chapters 20-21 related to this resurrection?

8. Do the verses 20:30-31 appear to conclude the main story of the gospel? If so, how do you account for the inclusion of chapter 21? Observe that 21:24-25 has a reference to the *writing* of the fourth gospel, as does 20:30-31. Could you say that John has two endings? What might be an author's purpose in doing this? Chart 46 shows chapter 21 as an epilogue. Compare this with the prologue of 1:1-18.

9. From Chart 46, how long is the time period of 1:19—12:36*a*? Compare this with the time period of the last half of the gospel. As was noted earlier, of the gospel writers, only John reports Jesus' early Judean ministry, without which record the duration of Christ's ministry would seem to be only two and one-third years. To show how selective the gospel writers were, it may be noted that John reports events of only about twenty individual days of Jesus' public ministry. Read 21:25 for an explanation of the necessity of such selectivity. Did the Bible authors depend on the guidance of the Holy Spirit in selecting what should be included in their writings?

10. What is the content of the last half of John mainly about, miracles or discourses?

11. Study the key outline shown just below the main horizontal line (*Era of incarnation begins*, etc.). What are the *time* words of this

outline? How does the outline represent the survey of the book that has been made up to this point?

Compare this outline with the ones shown on Chart 47.

CHART 47

FOUR MAIN SECTIONS

OF JOHN'S GOSPEL

1:1	5:1	12:36b	18:1 21:25
IDENTIFICATIONS	CONFLICTS	PREPARATIONS	CRISES
TRUE CLAIMS	*FALSE CHARGES*	*INTIMATE FELLOWSHIP*	*REDEMPTIVE WORK*
INTRODUCTIONS TO THE PEOPLE	OPPOSITION BY THE JEWISH RULERS	INSTRUCTIONS FOR THE DISCIPLES	EXPERIENCES IN TRIUMPH

12. Note the key words and phrases shown on the chart. (The numbers after some words indicate how often the word appears in the text.) Each key word (e.g., "believe") suggests an important subject developed in John's gospel.

13. Note also by Chart 46 that 20:30-31 are given as key verses for this gospel. What are the key words of those verses? Observe on Chart 46 what chapters record the signs. In performing the signs, was Jesus' main purpose one of alleviating distress? How does 20:31 furnish an answer to this question?

14. Observe on the chart the outline *Signs wrought; Self revealed*. Actually, in both main sections of John's gospel Christ was revealing who He was. In the last section, however, He pressed His claim more explicitly and revealed it fully in His death and resurrection.

15. What title is assigned to this gospel? How does it relate to the suggested key verses? Suggest a title of your own.

IV. Prominent Subjects

A. THE PROLOGUE (1:1-18)

This passage is unexcelled in the Bible for its compactness of the gospel message. The first three words repeat the first three words of Genesis, and two verses later John makes the summary statement that all things were made by the "Word" (v. 3). From that point on, however, John's object in the prologue is not to expand on the matchless cosmogeny of Genesis, but to show how this Creator Jesus was involved in His Father's plan of redemption for the fallen human race.

COMPARISONS OF JOHN 1:1 AND 1:14

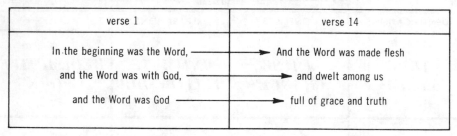

verse 1	verse 14
In the beginning was the Word, ⟶	And the Word was made flesh
and the Word was with God, ⟶	and dwelt among us
and the Word was God ⟶	full of grace and truth

In 1:1—4:54 John shows Jesus as the object of belief (see Chart 46). Read the prologue and observe how Jesus is identified as the One to believe. The accompanying diagram of comparisons further illustrates such unique revelations. How do these verses make it clear that the "Word" must be Jesus Christ? Where in the prologue is Jesus Christ first identified by name? How does the title "Word" identify a main ministry of Jesus to this world? In answering this, consider the meaning of the phrase "he has explained Him" (1:18).

B. JESUS' MEETING WITH NICODEMUS (3:1-21)

Before this point in the gospel John has not recorded many actual spoken words of Jesus. A few of Jesus' commands (e.g., "Come, and you will see," 1:39; "Follow me," 1:43) and a few prophecies (e.g., "You shall see greater things than these," 1:50; "In three days I will raise it up," 2:19) appear. But any extensive treatment on the subject of salvation is limited to the words of the gospel writer (1:1-18) and of John the Baptist (1:29-34).

Now in the design of his gospel, John breaks forth with the story of one of the greatest confrontations of Jesus with an unsaved man. The man was Nicodemus, an influential leader of the Jews. The subject of the conversation was the urgency and way of salvation.

Nicodemus's informant was none other than the "teacher come from God."

Little did John know that one of the verses (3:16) of this passage would become a universal "golden text" of Christians in the centuries to follow.

Read the passage and observe how Jesus reveals Himself to be both divine Teacher and Life Giver.

C. YEARS OF CONFLICT (5:1—12:36*a*)

At chapter 5 the author begins to record instances of open opposition to Jesus by the Jewish rulers.[16] A key sentence of chapter 5 is, "For this reason the Jews began to persecute Jesus" (v. 16, TEV). Refer to the survey chart of John (Chart 46, p. 187), and observe that the section 5:1—12:36*a* is called *Years of conflict*. The chapters of this conflict section cover about two years of Jesus' public ministry, which were marked by a growing hate of the Jewish rulers against Jesus because of His claims to Messiahship and divine sonship. Those religionists had one goal: kill Jesus.

Many of the multitudes gave a sympathetic ear to Jesus' claims, and demonstrated their support by giving Him a royal reception as He rode into Jerusalem on a donkey (12:14). There were many persons from the multitude who believed on Him.

And then there were Jesus' close friends and disciples. For the most part they are in the background in John's gospel during these chapters, but all references to them reveal a loyal group of followers. (Judas was the exception.)

Throughout this period of conflict with His enemies, Jesus faithfully performed His mission. He told who He was, He demonstrated who He was, and He invited all people to believe on Him to be saved. When that mission was over, He "no longer continued to walk publicly among the Jews" (11:54), for He was ready now to accomplish a more private ministry to the twelve disciples.

The climax of opposition came in the hour of crucifixion, recorded by John in chapter 19. The antagonism of the rulers and people against Jesus during these last two years of His public ministry was incessant. Even some of Jesus' disciples opposed Him on occasion.

After writing the *Conflicts* section John chose to include a long *Day of preparation* section (12:36*b*—17:26) dealing with Jesus' intimate fellowship with His disciples just preceding His arrest and trial. The interrelationships of these four parts of John's gospel are shown in the accompanying diagram.

16. In most instances in the gospels, the word *Jews*, in context of opposition to Jesus, refers to the Jewish rulers.

INTERRELATED PARTS OF JOHN'S GOSPEL

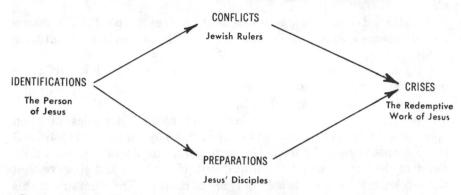

Compare this diagram with Chart 47, page 189.

D. FAREWELL DISCOURSES (14:1—16:33)

Anyone who asks the question, "What kind of person was Jesus?" will find innumerable answers in John's gospel. This is particularly true in the section 12:36b—17:26. Chapters 14-16 contain three farewell discourses of Jesus, which were delivered to His disciples on the evening before His crucifixion. The first discourse, chapter 14, was probably spoken in the upper room where the Last Supper (chap. 13) was held.[17] The last phrase of 14:31 suggests that Jesus and His disciples left the house and started walking east toward the Garden of Gethsemane. The second discourse (15:1—16:4a) and the third (16:4b-33) may then have been spoken as the group moved quietly through the city.[18] The high-priestly prayer of chapter 17 was prayed before Jesus and His disciples crossed the Kidron Valley on their way to Gethsemane.

The accompanying diagram breaks down passage 14:1—16:33 into the three discourses and suggests a title for each discourse. Use these suggestions as starters for further study. Among other things, study what the passages teach about the *Person* of Jesus.

E. HIGH-PRIESTLY PRAYER (17:1-26)

Jesus' high-priestly prayer in chapter 17 has been called the New Testament's noblest and purest pearl of devotion. A Christian cannot read this chapter without being warmed in heart over the tremendous

---

17. Some Bible students prefer to regard 13:31-38 as part of this first discourse. The content is not affected either way.

18. It is difficult to say where the second discourse ends and the third begins because of the constantly recurring subjects that Jesus spoke about in this informal conversation with His disciples. Actually all three farewell discourses could be called one discourse, because they are so intimately related.

fact that his Lord prays to the Father on *his* behalf.

We would like to be able to reconstruct the setting of this five-minute prayer of Jesus but no details are given in the account, other than that Jesus lifted up His eyes to heaven (17:1), and spoke the words in the presence of the eleven disciples (cf. 18:1). Few details, but an awesome truth: the Son of God speaking to His Father in heaven about His disciples.

THREE DISCOURSES OF JOHN 14:1—16:33

FIRST DISCOURSE		SECOND DISCOURSE		THIRD DISCOURSE	
14:1	14:31	15:1	16:4a	16:4b	16:33
The Father's House		Vine and the Branches		Promises of Jesus	

The prayer is clearly of three main parts:

1. Jesus prays for Himself (17:1-5)
2. Jesus prays for His disciples (17:6-19)
3. Jesus prays for the church (17:20-26)

When you study the chapter, think of the heart needs of the disciples at that time. Also, think how Jesus was feeling at that time, knowing what trying experiences were awaiting Him in the next hours. Let these studies be the background of applying the prayer to your own life.

F. HOUR OF SACRIFICE (18:1—19:42)

After the high-priestly prayer of chapter 17 the succession of events was this:

> Soul agony of Gethsemane[19]
> Arrest
> Trials
> Scourging
> Crucifixion
> Death

Jesus did not try to delay or avoid any of these experiences. To the very end, His attitude was one of obedience to His Father's will: "The

---

19. John makes only the brief mention of Jesus' entering the Garden of Gethsemane with His disciples (18:1).

cup which the Father has given Me, shall I not drink it?" (18:11; cf. Matt. 26:1-2). That Jesus was not a fatalist concerning such a sovereignly fixed program is shown throughout the gospels by the intensity of His human emotions in the midst of each trying experience. This man of sorrows, acquainted with grief, was "obedient to the point of death, even death on a cross" (Phil. 2:8).

1. *Trial* (18:12—19:16). Jesus was confronted by two different realms of authority in His trial. The political rulers were Roman, and the religious rulers were Jewish. Shown below are the two confrontations, with three stages in each. Note how much is reported by John.

    a. Jewish Trial.
        (1) Before Annas (18:12-14, 19-23).
        (2) Informal trial by Sanhedrin before dawn (18:24; Matt. 26:57, 59-68; Mark 14:53, 55-65; Luke 22:54, 63-65).
        (3) Formal trial after dawn (Matt. 27:1; Mark 15:1; Luke 22:66-71).
    b. Roman Trial.
        (1) First appearance before Pilate (18:28-38; cf. Matt. 27:2, 11-14; Mark 15:1-5; Luke 23:1-5).
        (2) Before Herod Antipas (Luke 23:6-12).
        (3) Final appearance before Pilate (18:39—19:16; cf. Matt. 27:15-26; Mark 15:6-15; Luke 23:13-25).

2. *Death* (19:17-42). The redemptive fruits of Christ's death are glorious, but the hour of His death was mankind's darkest hour. Even nature itself echoed this, with the darkening of the sun and the violent earthquake (Matt. 27:51; Luke 23:45).

John's account of Jesus' death is brief but weighty. He paints six portraits, identified below:

Identity recognized	19:17-22
Goods confiscated	19:23-24
Mother cared for	19:25-27
Life given	19:28-30
Death verified	19:31-37
Body buried	19:38-42

G. RESURRECTION CHAPTER (20:1-31)

The resurrection of Jesus was both prescheduled of His Father and unanticipated by the disciples. Jesus had clearly instructed His disciples earlier about His forthcoming death and resurrection (Matt. 16:21; Mark 8:31; Luke 9:22), but they did not understand the meaning then, nor did they even remember the words later. Understanding would come through believing, and believing would come through signs. John 20 records some of the signs that restored the disciples to Jesus in a personal and new relationship to Him as the risen Lord. How utter defeat can suddenly and miraculously turn to victory is one of the glowing truths of this chapter.

Recall 20:30-31. The word *signs* is a key word of the verses. What signs are recorded in John 20? Observe in the chapter how often the word *see* (and related words) appears in the chapter.

V. KEY WORDS AND VERSES

Read again the list of key words shown on Chart 46, page 187. Add to the list the other key words that you have observed. Note also the key verses indicated on the chart: 20:30-31. There are other key verses in John. Did you observe any in the course of your survey?

VI. APPLICATIONS

1. Why is belief in the deity of Christ a key ingredient of saving faith?
2. When is your faith in Christ as miracle worker the strongest? How would you describe the *healthy* faith-life?
3. Christ is the believer's interceding High Priest. How does this truth affect your daily life as a Christian?
4. What does Christ's interest in individual persons teach you?

VII. REVIEW QUESTIONS

1. Describe John's home background and his character. What was his approximate age at death?
2. What New Testament books did John write?
3. When and where was the fourth gospel written?
4. Who were the original readers?
5. What is the purpose of this gospel?
6. Compare this gospel account with the synoptic gospels.
7. Did John report more of Jesus' first or second year of public ministry?
8. What is the prologue (1:1-18) about?
9. What is "The Great Pause" of John?
10. Complete the five-point outline of John beginning with *Era of incarnation begins*.
11. Name three key words.
12. What is the main point of 20:30-31?
13. What is the epilogue (chap. 21) about?

VIII. Further Study

1. Study the references in John to Jesus' deity. There is at least one reference in each chapter, which references are the following: 1:49; 2:11; 3:16; 4:26; 5:25; 6:33; 7:29; 8:58; 9:37; 10:30; 11:27; 12:32; 13:13; 14:11; 15:1; 16:28; 17:1; 18:11; 19:7; 20:28; 21:14.

Include in your study personal recognitions of Jesus' deity by these persons: John the Baptist (1:34); Nathaniel (1:49); Peter (6:69); Christ[20] (10:36); Martha (11:27); Thomas (20:28); John (20:31).

2. Christ appears under many titles in this gospel, such as "the Word," "Creator," "Only Begotten of the Father," "Lamb of God." John also records several "I am" testimonies of Jesus, including those appearing in these verses: 6:35; 8:12; 8:58 (cf. Exod. 3:14); 10:11; 11:25; 14:6; 15:1. Make a study of these identifications.

3. The gospels give no detailed description of the process of Roman crucifixion. The text usually reads only briefly, as in John 19:18, "They crucified him." Can you suggest a reason for that relative silence? Consult a Bible dictionary for a full description of crucifixion as a Roman form of execution. Also, read Psalm 22:1-21 for a description of some of the physical, mental, and spiritual agonies of Jesus on the cross. Consult the dictionary also about the burial customs of Jesus' day.

4. Study the subject of miracles in the gospel of John. For an outside source on the general subject of miracles, consult C. S. Lewis, *Miracles*.

IX. Outline

JOHN: Life in Jesus, the Son of God

ERA OF INCARNATION BEGINS	1:1—4:54
Prologue	1:1-18
Witnesses and Discoveries of Jesus	1:19-51
Miracle Worker and Voice of Authority	2:1-25
Teacher Come from God	3:1-36
"This Is Indeed the Christ"	4:1-54
YEARS OF CONFLICT	5:1—12:36a
Persecution Against Jesus Begins	5:1-47
Bread of Life Refused	6:1-71
Attempts to Arrest Jesus	7:1-53
Light of the World Rejected	8:1—9:41
The Good Shepherd Spurned	10:1-39
The King of Israel Enters Jerusalem	10:40—12:36a

---

20. This is one of Jesus' own claims to deity. Only God Himself can rightfully claim deity. Since Jesus is God, He could make such a claim.

X. Selected Reading

GENERAL INTRODUCTION

Edersheim, Alfred. *The Life and Times of Jesus the Messiah.*
Gundry, Robert H. *A Survey of the New Testament*, pp. 101-11.
Guthrie, Donald. *New Testament Introduction*, pp. 237-335.
Hiebert, D. Edmond. *An Introduction to the New Testament*, 1:191-242.
Iverach, James. "John, Gospel of" in *International Standard Bible Encyclopedia*, 3:1720-27.
Scroggie, W. Graham. *A Guide to the Gospels*, pp. 393-470.
Tenney, Merrill C. *New Testament Survey*, pp. 185-97.

COMMENTARIES

Godet, F. L. *Commentary on the Gospel of John.* 2 vols.
Hendriksen, W. *Exposition of the Gospel According to John.* 2 vols. In his New Testament Commentary Series.
Hunter, A. M. *The Gospel According to John.*
Lange, John Peter. *The Gospel According to John.*
Morgan, G. Campbell. *The Gospel According to John.*
Tasker, R.V.G. *The Gospel According to St. John.* The Tyndale New Testament Commentaries.
Westcott, B. F. *Commentary on John.*

OTHER RELATED SOURCES

Griffith-Thomas, W. H. *The Apostle John: His Life and Writing.*
Orr, James. *The Resurrection of Jesus.*
Robertson, A. T. *Epochs in the Life of Jesus.*
———. *A Harmony of the Gospels.*
Scroggie, W. Graham. *St. John: Introduction and Notes.*
Strong, James. *The Exhaustive Concordance of the Bible.*
Tenney, Merrill C. *John: The Gospel of Belief.*
Thomas, Robert L., ed. *New American Standard Exhaustive Concordance of the Bible.*

Part 2

THE SEQUEL

The Church, Christ's Body

Broadly speaking, the group of people that is the main object of attention in the New Testament is the church. The gospels present Christ as the Foundation and Head of the church. The book of Acts records the beginning and early history of the church. The epistles offer instructions for the church, and the book of Revelation prophesies end times and describes the eternal reign of the church with Christ.

The above capsule sketch shows how important Acts is in the full canon of the New Testament.

Acts

9

Acts: The Beginnings of the Christian Church

Acts is the church's standard textbook on the first three decades of its history and its ageless global task of evangelization. The book is clearly the sequel to the gospels; its story of the church is the wonderful continuation of the unique and fantastic story of Christ's earthly life. Beyond this, Acts provides the key for the fuller understanding of the epistles, which follow Acts in the New Testament canon and interpret the gospel that Christ lived and preached.

I. PREPARATION FOR STUDY

Reflect on the core of the gospels' history: Jesus came from heaven and then returned to heaven, accomplishing His Father's will while He was here on earth. That was His time-bound, eternity-affecting life. The gospels tell the story of that wonderful life, but only a few pages relate the events of the few weeks of his postresurrection ministry. The Bible's history would conclude with an abrupt void if the account of what the resurrected Christ did to men's hearts was limited to only a few instances, such as the two men's reaction, "Were not our hearts burning within us while He was speaking to us?" (Luke 24:32) and Thomas's, "My Lord and my God!" (John 20:28). Acts was designed by God to complete the story of the gospels, by showing the gospel of the resurrected Christ at work. That work was the transforming of men's hearts to make them witnesses of the Way, through the ministry of the Holy Spirit sent to earth for that purpose. This is all illustrated by Chart 48.

Acts was not written to furnish a system of doctrine for the church, or even to do much interpreting of the tremendous truths of

201

the gospel. That task was assigned by the Spirit of God to those who were later inspired to write the epistles. Acts reports the gospel in action, and it is the Christian student's opportunity to seek out the universal, timeless, historically-backed principles, by which he and the church may live and serve God.

CHART 48

RELATION OF ACTS TO THE GOSPELS

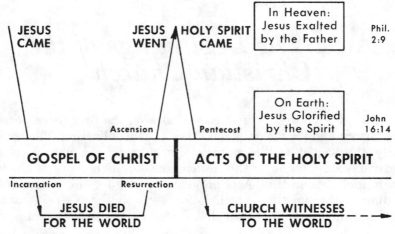

As you survey the story of Acts, think of it as a historical link book and a doctrinal demonstration book. Concerning doctrine, what does it demonstrate?

II. BACKGROUND

A. TITLE

The short name usually assigned the book is Acts.[1] The full name Acts of the Apostles is traceable back to the second century. When the book was originally written, its author Luke probably combined it with his earlier writing, the gospel of Luke. Then when his gospel was joined to the other three gospels, Acts stood alone. Here are some observations:

1. The key word in the longer title is Acts. These are not the dreams, theories, or speculations of the apostles, but their acts, their deeds, things they actually accomplished.

---

1. Various titles were ascribed to this book in the early days of its circulation. The three most common ones were "Acts of the Apostles" (found in the *Muratorian Fragment* on the Canon, of the late second century); "Acts of Apostles" (fourth-century *Vaticanus* and *Beza* manuscripts); and "Acts" (fourth-century *Sinaiticus* manuscript).

2. The phrase *of the apostles* probably refers to the main apostles during the years of the book's record. Of those apostles, Peter and Paul were the key leaders.

3. It is recognized that the book records the acts of the Holy Spirit as He worked through the apostles. In that sense the book could be called The Acts of the Holy Spirit. The Holy Spirit's name appears about seventy times in the book.

B. AUTHOR

Most authorities agree that Luke was the writer of Acts. Extant ancient witnesses, dating as early as A.D. 170, are practically unanimous about that. The strongest internal evidence for Lucan authorship is the fact that Acts and the third gospel are both addressed to Theophilus, and Acts refers to a "first account," which obviously was the gospel. (Compare Luke 1:1-4 and Acts 1:1-5.)

Other internal evidences for Lucan authorship of Acts, based on a comparison with the gospel, include (1) the similar style and language of the two writings; (2) the natural connection between the ending of the gospel and the beginning of Acts; (3) similarities such as the prominent place of women in both narratives. Further, the writer of Acts accompanied Paul on many of his travels (as the "we" sections of Acts reveal: 16:10-17; 20:5—21:18; 27:1—28:16),[2] and of the number of close associates of Paul, Luke is most clearly identified as that fellow-traveler.[3]

The writing style of Acts is as clear and organized as that of Luke's gospel. Blaiklock describes it further: "Vivid, rapid in its movement, sure and purposeful in brief summary or leisurely report, amazingly evocative of atmosphere, economical of words, but never drab in colour, the book holds the reader from its dedication to the end."[4]

For biographical information on Luke, refer back to those descriptions given in Chapter 6.

C. DATE AND PLACE OF WRITING

Luke probably wrote Acts while in Rome, toward the end of Paul's two-year imprisonment there, or about A.D. 61. He could not have completed his writing earlier than that, since Acts records that imprisonment (Acts 28:30), which is dated around A.D. 59-61. The Holy Spirit's design was not to include any more of Paul's life or of

---

2. Luke no doubt was also with Paul at other times in the book of Acts, even when Luke uses the third person in the narrative. (Richard B. Rackham, *The Acts of the Apostles*, p. xxvii.)

3. See Rackham, p. xvi, for evidences of this identification.

4. E. M. Blaiklock, *Acts of the Apostles*, pp. 12-13.

the church's experience in this book, and so He inspired Luke to write at that time.

That Luke did not write Acts at a later date is obvious from the following:

1. The Jewish war of A.D. 66-70, climaxing in the holocaust of the destruction of Jerusalem (A.D. 70), is not even alluded to.

2. Nero's anti-Christian policy, following the great fire of Rome (A.D. 64), finds no place in the account.

3. Though Paul was in prison at the close of Acts, there is no suggestion in the narrative that his death was imminent. Very likely he was soon released. After traveling for a few years in evangelistic work, even as far as Spain, Paul probably was arrested again and placed in the execution cell at Rome, where he wrote 2 Timothy, his "dying letter," and then finally was executed shortly before Nero's suicide. (Date of the latter was June 8, A.D. 68.)

D. SOURCES OF INFORMATION

Luke the master writer was also the master researcher. For his gospel he needed to interview many witnesses for their firsthand accounts of the life of Jesus. Research of oral and written sources also was required for Acts, but he had personally seen and heard much of its history or had learned about it from his intimate companion Paul. Chart 49 shows the most probable sources of information for Luke's Acts.

CHART 49

LUKE'S SOURCES FOR WRITING ACTS

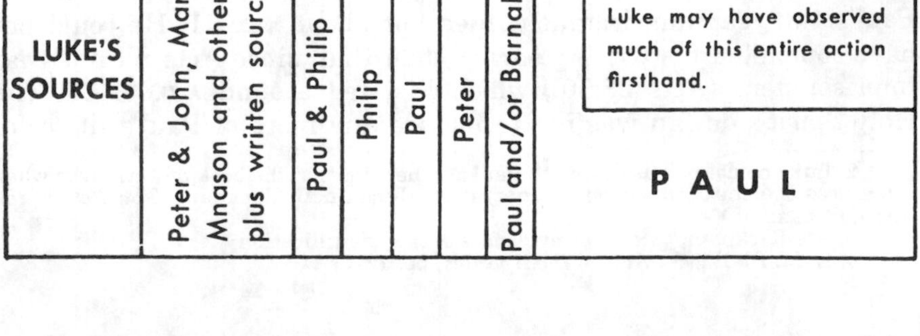

OUTLINE OF ACTS	EARLY DAYS		TRANSITION			MISSIONARY EXPANSION			
		6:1 8:1	9:1	9:32	11:24	12:25	16:10-17	20:5—21:18	27:1 28:16
LUKE'S SOURCES	Peter & John, Mark, Mnason and others, plus written sources		Paul & Philip	Philip	Paul	Peter	Paul and/or Barnabas	"WE" "WE" "WE" Luke may have observed much of this entire action firsthand. P A U L		

Notes on Chart 49

1. Luke personally observed much, as is indicated by the three "we" sections.[5] Also it should be noted that Luke may have witnessed the action of portions of Acts where he does *not* use "we" in his narrative. This may have been true regarding the large section of Acts 20:5 to 28:31.

2. Luke's main informant was Paul, who was able to supply not only the events of his conversion and missionary ministry but also other facts of the early church's history, such as Stephen's message and martyrdom (chapters 6-7).

3. The remainder of the source material for Acts concerned the early days of the church. Most of it probably was secured orally from other sources, such as Barnabas, Philip, Peter, James, John, Mark, and Mnason (e.g., Acts 21:16). Luke probably consulted with them at such cities as Jerusalem, Antioch of Syria, and Caesarea.

E. RELATION TO THE OTHER NEW TESTAMENT BOOKS

Originally, Luke's two writings — his gospel and Acts — probably were circulated as one work, because the narrative of his Acts was the natural sequel to the story of his gospel. But when John's record was published as the final gospel at the end of the first century, Luke's gospel was weaned from Acts and linked with the other three gospels to become known corporately as "The Gospel."[6] At about the same time, Paul's writings were being collected and identified under the one title, "The Apostle." Thus seventeen New Testament books were brought together and reduced to two units. Moreover, these two units found their common link in Acts, as shown on Chart 50.

---

5. A "we" reference is one where the writer (in this case Luke) is a participant in the action (e.g., Acts 16:10).

6. This was a natural fusion, since all four books recorded the same message, though from four different vantage points. W. Graham Scroggie compares the gospels with the other twenty-three books of the New Testament as follows:

Gospels	*Acts-Revelation*
The Christ	The Church
Introduction of the Gospel	Progress of the Gospel
Into the World	In the World
Christ for Us	Christ in Us
Christ Revealed Historically	Christ Revealed Mystically

Chart adapted from *Know Your Bible*, 2:59.

CHART 50

RELATION OF ACTS TO THE NEW TESTAMENT

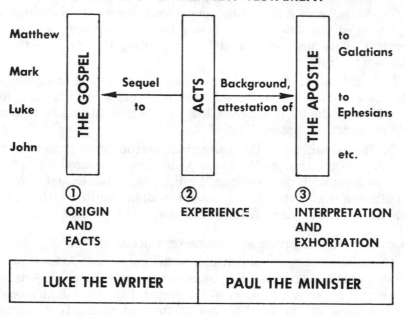

F. GEOGRAPHY

The mission assigned to the early church, spelled out in Acts 1:8, was universal. The performance of that mission in the years of Acts retained the universal quality, because the home base of the missionaries kept moving. The advance reported by Luke in Acts was generally from east to west: Jerusalem to Antioch (Syria) to Ephesus to Rome. (See Map L, and visualize the Palestinian Christians' view into the west.) Actually, Christianity spread in all directions from Jerusalem after Christ's ascension. Why do you think Acts records only the westward advance?[7]

---

7. For a history of the expansion of Christianity in the other directions, see church history volumes such as Kenneth Scott Latourette, *A History of the Expansion of Christianity*, 1:86-113. Latourette cites one tradition that arose in the early centuries of the church concerning missionary work beyond Roman frontiers: "Sometimes in the early centuries of Christianity the tradition arose that the Twelve Apostles had parcelled among themselves the known world. One form of this tradition declared that Thomas received the Parthians as his assignment; Matthew, Ethiopia; and Bartholomew, part of India" (p. 101).

MAP L

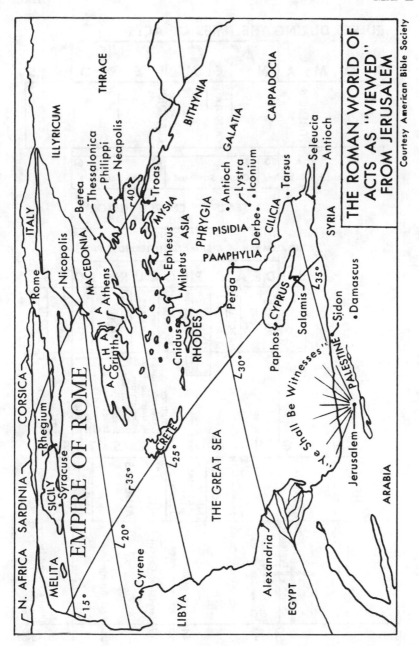

THE ROMAN WORLD OF ACTS AS "VIEWED" FROM JERUSALEM

Courtesy American Bible Society

RULERS DURING THE TIMES OF ACTS

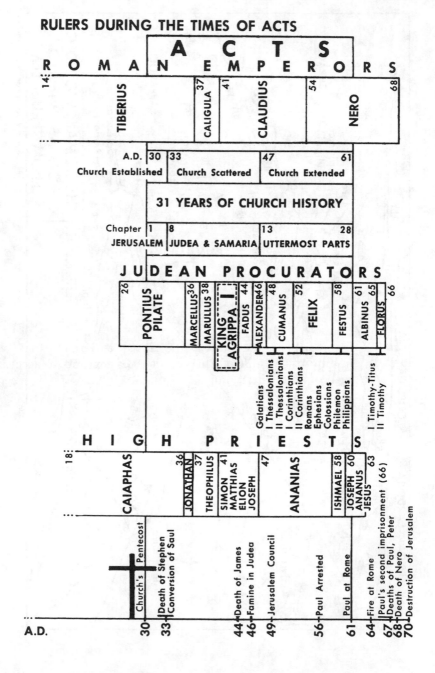

G. RULERS DURING THE TIMES OF ACTS

Chart 51 shows the times of reign of the Roman emperors, Judean procurators, and high priests during the three decades of the Acts history. Among other things, the chart helps you see what emperor, procurator, and high priest were ruling contemporaneously, at any one time of Acts. For example, identify the emperor, procurator, and high priest ruling at the time of Acts 8, when the church was scattered.

H. PURPOSES

Three words may be used to suggest the overall *grand* purposes of Acts: registration, vindication, edification.

1. *Registration.* The written record of the history of redemption makes up a substantial part of both the Old and New Testaments. The experiences of individual believers, as well as those of the corporate people of God, are registered in the Bible, thereby demonstrating before the audience of the ages that redemption is real, dynamic, and worthy to be sought. God moved Luke to record the narrative of the early church in the Holy Scriptures in order to show the church's relation (a) to the past (continuation) and (b) to the future (propagation).

a. Continuation. Luke's own words reveal this aspect of the narrative. His purpose in the third gospel was to record, like the writers before him, the origins of Christianity "To compile an account of the things accomplished among us" (Luke 1:1). The first verse of Acts, by citing "all that Jesus began . . . to do and teach" implies that Luke intends to show how Acts *continues* the story of Jesus as the ascended, exalted One (Acts 1:2, 9).

b. Propagation. Throughout Acts the thrust is one of extension, propagation, multiplication, and advance. Externally, the advance is from Jerusalem to Rome; internally, it moves from a Jewish hearing to a universal audience. All in all, the church makes fantastic progress in its first three decades of life, and Luke accurately registers this phase of its history.

2. *Vindication.* Acts was written soon after the last event of its narrative. Why was there no delay or waiting period, as with the gospels? As we approach the question we must recognize that although each book of the Bible was written primarily for the ages, its publication date was ordained by God so that its message could fill a contemporary need as well. A study of the times in which Luke wrote reveals that Acts apparently was given to the Roman world to let the

history and message of the church *vindicate its claim to divine origin*. The church needed to make clear to the Roman government that Christianity was not to be associated with Judaism, though both claimed the same God and same Old Testament Scriptures. In fact, Luke emphasized in Acts that the leaders of Judaism considered Christians as heretical and blasphemous, and that this formed the basis for most of the persecutions of the disciples of that day. There was a divine purpose in such a clarification of the church's identity at this time, for in just a few more years rebellion of Jewish authorities against the Roman Empire would lead to war. That war would eventually culminate in the destruction of Jerusalem (A.D. 70) by the Romans. Thus Rome would know that the Christians were not part of any rebellion brewing against the Empire.[8]

The authenticity of Luke's gospel is shared by Acts because of the one author. And, since Paul's conversion and divine call were reported by Luke in Acts, the message of Paul's letters ("The Apostle") was thus given a strong acceptance. Furthermore, Acts provided evidence of the apostleship of other New Testament writers, such as Peter and James. So in a real sense Acts served as the pivotal book of the New Testament. At the same time it must be recognized that this vindicative purpose of Acts was not one of the main reasons it was written.

3. *Edification*. The primary purpose of Acts must have been edification, for it was inspired and written to profit for teaching, reproof, correction, and instruction in righteousness — a ministry of edifying of the church of God. A soul may learn how to be saved from Acts, but the book was written primarily for the believer's instruction in how to live and serve God. Your study of Acts should be geared to learning what the book teaches about Christian living and the mission of the church of which you are a part. And the fruits of studying Acts are multiplied when it is studied in connection with the epistles of the New Testament, for which it provides the setting and background.

III. SURVEY

A. PREPARING TO SURVEY

Recall your study in Chapter 1 of the complex environment of Christianity in the first century. Three major forces (combinations of such things as culture, religion, knowledge, and tradition) controlled the environment that formed the life and makeup of the peoples

---

8. See F. F. Bruce, *Commentary on the Book of the Acts*, pp. 17-24, for a discussion of this apologetic purpose of Luke.

described in Acts. Those three forces were the Jewish, Greek, and Roman elements.[9] The following summary will help you visualize that setting of the three decades covered by Acts. (Recall Chapter 3.)

Judaism was one important element of the culture. Negatively, it was known for its false sects, its hard and impenetrable traditions, its rejection of Jesus as the Messiah, and its zealous patriotism. Positively, it stood for a belief in one God, the Old Testament Scriptures as the revelation of God, a search for salvation, the salting influence of a believing remnant, a sense of destiny, and a faithful attendance at the worship services of the Temple in Jerusalem and the synagogues scattered throughout the Empire.

Hellenism was another ingredient that vitally affected the environment. Among its major contributions were a philosophical spirit of inquiry that invaded its many religions, an attractive culture that sought the good and the beautiful, and, above all, its vernacular (Koine) Greek language, the universal communication medium of the Roman world by which the gospel was spread quickly and efficiently.

The *Roman Empire* gave the church political and governmental advantages. It guaranteed law and justice in hostile situations; it provided roads, bridges, and seaways for travel; and it promoted an underlying religious tolerance of the new religion of Christianity.

Before beginning your survey study, think of answers to this question, "Why might God have wanted a book like Acts to be a part of the canon of Scripture?"

B. FIRST READING

Scan the book of Acts in one sitting. You may choose to read only the first verse of each paragraph. Read enough to get the feel of the book. If possible, read aloud. What are your impressions? Is there much action in Acts? Are there many sermons? many characters? Have any words or verses stood out as being prominent, from this scanning?

C. SURVEYING THE INDIVIDUAL SEGMENTS

First note on Chart 52, page 214, how the text of Acts is divided into segments. Each segment begins at verse 1 with the exceptions shown below. Read the Bible text to justify these beginnings:

1. 8:1*b* — The phrase of 8:1*a*, "And Saul was in hearty agreement with putting him to death" is appropriately associated with the end of the Stephen story.

2. 9:32 — Chapter 9 gives the story of Paul's conversion. Verse 31 is a fitting conclusion to that story; verse 32 picks up the Peter

9. For further study see E. M. Blaiklock, *Acts of the Apostles*, pp. 20-44.

account again, therefore it seems logical to begin a new segment here.

3. 15:36 — Paul's second missionary journey begins at this point, therefore it is well to make a division here.

4. 18:23 — The start of the third missionary journey is almost obscured in the narrative. A new division (and therefore new segment) is necessary here.

5. 21:18 — The point that one chooses to distinguish between the end of the third journey and the subsequent events at Jerusalem is rather arbitrary. We shall use 21:18 as the beginning of the new section.

Mark the above-mentioned dividing points in your Bible, to help your survey study.

Now quickly read each segment of Acts. Record segment titles on a worksheet similar to those used in your earlier studies (e.g., Chart 45, Segment Titles of John). When you have chosen titles for all the segments of Acts, scan the list and try to visualize the progression of the narrative from beginning to end. You now will begin to sense a movement or flow in the narrative of Acts. Record any new observations and impressions of the book.

Your survey so far has been groundwork. From this point on, the structure of Acts is what you will examine.

D. SEEING HOW THE BOOK HOLDS TOGETHER

Having seen the content of individual chapters (or more accurately, segments), your task now is to determine Luke's narrative organization. It would be an oversimplification to say that because Acts is history Luke simply followed the chronology of events and recorded them in diary fashion. Remember that Acts does not exhaustively record everything that transpired in the first decades of the early church. Luke, inspired of the Holy Spirit, selected the events and items that he would include to best serve the book's purposes. Selectivity and nondiarylike composition, plus the inclusion of many sermons and addresses, happily afford the potential of all the beauty, interest, and appeal that can be found in a true literary work.

This part of your study does not involve another reading of the entire book of Acts as such. Instead, you will find that you must continually page through the book or certain sections of it as you proceed from subject to subject. As you discover different parts of the structure of Acts, record those on the worksheet chart where you have recorded segment titles.

1. *Groupings of segments.* The easiest way to begin the search for Acts' organization is to identify groupings of chapters as determined

by similarity of subject. In history, the three items of persons, events, and places usually steer the narrative. Consider each of those separately, using the following questions as directive helps in locating groupings.

a. Who is the main character of the first few chapters of Acts? What was his title or work? How long does he stay in the narrative of Acts? (Refer to an exhaustive concordance for a quick answer to this question.)

b. Who is the main character of the last chapters? Where is he first introduced? At what chapter does he reappear to remain the key person?

c. From your study so far, is any part of Acts not represented by one main character?

d. Now try events. We have already spoken of Paul's missionary journeys. How many were there? Where did each begin and end? If Paul was not always on missionary journeys in Acts, account for the remainder of his Acts years. Repeat this study for Peter's life, earlier in Acts.

e. Consider the events of the church. Does Acts record its beginning? Where? Then what were its periods of experience? (Note: This stage of survey is looking for *groupings*. Hence, the question just given does not ask for experiences, but periods of experience.)

f. Evangelism is a prominent theme in Acts. In the early chapters of Acts the gospel was generally preached where and to whom? Was there a change in audience, generally speaking, on Paul's missionary journeys? What do chapters 10 and 11 contribute to your answers to this question?

g. You have already observed that geography plays a vital part in Acts, especially in terms of the expansion of the gospel. Consider where Acts begins and where it ends. Relate that to 1:8. Using the geography of this verse as an outline for the whole book of Acts, identify the three geographical sections on your worksheet chart.

h. Other survey studies either may be made now or reserved to a later time in your project. Two suggested subjects are: "Persecution," and "Progress of the Gospel."

2. *Major movements in Acts.* Progress in some direction is the normal pattern of composition. The book of Acts is no exception. From what you have already read and studied of Acts, try to identify its major movements. You have already noted the geographical expansion of the gospel witness. In the account does persecution increase, wane, or remain constant? Is there a climax of any sort in the book?

ACTS

THE EARLY CHURCH'S WITNESS OF THE GOSPEL

Author: Luke
Date Written: A.D. 61
Key Word: Witness
Key Verse: 1:8

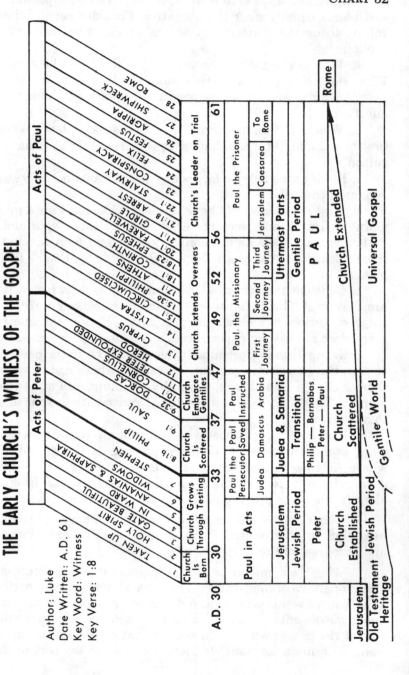

Look also for turning points or strategic centers about which the narrative pivots. Are there any transition sections or any notable contrasting sections?

Compare the beginning (e.g., chap. 1) and end (e.g., chap. 28) of Acts. What are your observations? What is the last word of Acts? What does that suggest?

On the basis of your survey studies so far, how would you identify the theme of Acts? From that theme, what title would you suggest for the book?

E. SURVEY CHART OF ACTS

Chart 52 shows ways of identifying the structure of the text of Acts. You have already observed many of those things in your survey study. Refer to this chart as you read the brief discussion below.

1. The twenty-eight chapters of Acts fall into three main divisions, with dividing points at 8:1*b* and 13:1. What outlines show this threefold organization? The geographical outline is a natural unfolding of 1:8. The outline on the church shows a progression of the church in the Acts narrative.

2. Acts can also be divided into two main parts, according to main characters. In chapters 1-12, Peter plays the leading role, whereas in chapters 13-28 everything centers on Paul's activities.

3. Note the divisions related to Jew and Gentile. In the early chapters of Acts, the Jews make up most of the audience of the gospel. In chapters 10-12 the church sees its responsibility to extend the invitation of the gospel to Gentiles as well. This was a transitional period for the church. From chapter 13 on, the field is the world.

4. Paul as a missionary served well when at liberty (13:1—21:17) and remained loyal when in bonds (21:18—28:31).

5. A main outline of Acts is on the church and appears under the main horizontal line of the chart.

6. Note the outlines about Paul in Acts.

7. Geographically, where does Acts begin? Where does it end?

8. The dates shown on the chart are not obtained from the text of Acts, but are shown here to give chronological perspective.[10] What is the time span of Acts? How long was each missionary journey?

IV. PROMINENT SUBJECTS

The number of prominent subjects in Acts is unusually large. Only a few of those can be identified here.

---

10. For a good system of New Testament chronology, see the study graph chart *New Testament Chronological Chart*, revised edition (1968), by James L. Boyer, Moody Press, Chicago. Professor Boyer also gives a clear presentation of the factors that determine the assigning of dates to New Testament events.

A. THE CHURCH IS BORN (2:1-47)

Acts 2 records a new experience in the history of God's people, involving the Holy Spirit. The time was the Feast of Pentecost,[11] one of the three great festivals of Jerusalem attended by Jews from all parts of the world. In the design of God the day had arrived for the beginning of an extended ministry of the Spirit in the lives of believers.

Pentecost day was the time when the church was born. There had been an invisible organism of believers in Old Testament days and during Jesus' earthly ministry, but now the people of God — known as the church[12] — would be experiencing and serving in a new relationship to a more fully revealed God. That extended revelation was by the incarnate Christ ("God . . . has . . . spoken . . . in His Son," Heb. 1:1-2) and the indwelling Spirit (John 16:13-15). In light of that, it is accurate to say that the Pentecost day of Acts 2 was the birthday of the church.

The following outline of chapter 2 shows the highlights of Luke's recording:

Event	2:1-4
Reaction	2:5-13
Explanation	2:14-36
Response and Sequel	2:37-47

From chapter 2 to the end of the book, Luke shows the active role of all three persons of the Trinity during the first three decades of the Christian church.[13] See Chart 53.

B. STEPHEN'S LIFE AND DEATH (6:1—8:1*a*)

Stephen is usually remembered for his martyrdom. That was his ministry "by death" (cf. Phil. 1:20). (In Acts 22:20 "witness" means *martyr*.) We should also remember him, however, for his brief but faithful ministry "by life" as one of the seven deacons serving in the "business" phase of the Jerusalem church (see 6:2-3). The twofold story of Stephen is organized in Acts as illustrated in Chart 54.

---

11. Read Exodus 23:16; 34:22; Leviticus 23:15-21; Numbers 28:26; Deuteronomy 16:10, 16, 17.

12. The first appearance of the word *church* (assembly) in Acts is at 2:47. Before this it appears only three times in the New Testament: Matthew 16:18; 18:17 (twice).

13. When a generalization is made concerning the *prominent* functions of the three Persons of the Godhead during the years of Bible history, it may be said that the Father is most prominent in the Old Testament, the Son in the Gospels, and the Holy Spirit in Acts.

CHART 53

THE ROLE OF THE THREE PERSONS OF THE GODHEAD

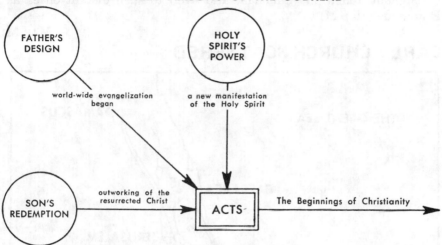

When Stephen was falsely accused by religious opponents, the high priest invited him to defend himself. The essence of his speech (7:2-53) was that the religionists of his day were the guilty ones, even as their forefathers had been: "You people of this day are just like your ancestors, you always resist the Holy Spirit. Only you are worse than your fathers; they killed God's messengers who prophesied of the Messiah, but you have killed the Messiah Himself!" (Acts 7:51-53, author's paraphrase).

The rulers and people became more incensed, and they stoned Stephen to death. His dying words were, "Lord, do not hold this sin against them!" (7:60).

CHART 54

STEPHEN'S LIFE AND DEATH

PART I	By Life	Ministry of Serving Tables	6:1-6
		Fruit of the Ministry	6:7
PART II	By Death	Ministry of Words and Miracles	6:8—8:1a
		Fruit of the Ministry	8:1b ff.

C. SAUL SAVED (9:1-19*a*)

Persecution against the believers in Jerusalem scattered them throughout Judea and Samaria, and even to such distant cities as Damascus (Map M).

MAP M

EARLY CHURCH SCATTERED

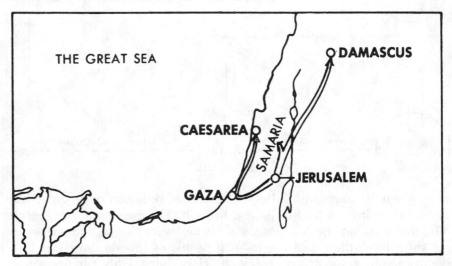

It was when the persecution had reached a peak through the fanatic labors of the arch-persecutor Saul[14] (8:1-3), that God came down and struck him to the ground. In Blaiklock's words, "The rabid persecutor was a tormented man, soon to be brought to surrender, and destined to be the greatest name in the history of the Church."[15] The wonderful, miraculous conversion of a man who called himself the chief of sinners is the subject of Luke's reporting in 9:1-19*a*.

D. THE CHURCH EMBRACES GENTILES (9:32—12:25)

In the early chapters of Acts most of those who believed in Christ were Jews. That is understandable, since the gospel was the fulfillment of the Jews' Scriptures; Jesus and His disciples were Jews; and His mission was primarily to the house of Israel. The disciples were thus now taking it for granted that the gospel was mainly for Jews, with Gentiles brought into the fellowship of the church *only* via the

14. Saul is called Paul (a Roman name) for the first time in Acts 13:9. After that, Luke always refers to him as Paul. (Paul uses "Saul" in describing his conversion experience in 22:7, 13; 26:14.) The significance of the two names will be discussed later.
15. E. M. Blaiklock, *The Acts of the Apostles*, The Tyndale New Testament Commentaries, p. 79.

Jewish institutions. The time had come for God to emphasize more than ever before that the gospel was for Gentile as well as Jew. Peter, leader of the church at that time, was the logical one to whom God would give such instruction. How God did that is the story of most of 9:32—12:25.

The scattering of the Jewish believers, which began on the day of Stephen's death, was the first break in the solidarity of Jewish exclusivism that God would eventually liquidate. It was inevitable that Spirit-filled disciples should touch human hearts with whom they came in contact, regardless of race or religion. That is illustrated in the unrestricted expansion of the church as recorded by Luke in 8:1*b*—9:31 and summarized so triumphantly in 9:31.

But God wanted the Jews to hear clearly and in unambiguous words that the gospel was universal. So He led His disciples into the experiences recorded in 9:32—12:25. The entire section might be called "The Church Embraces Gentiles."

Read 11:18 as a key verse of this section. What other similar verses do you observe?

Note: The problem of Gentile salvation was to reappear at a later time. It was part of Paul's reason for writing Galatians, and it was the subject of discussion at what is now called the Jerusalem Council (Acts 15).

E. PAUL THE MISSIONARY (13:1—21:17)

For about ten years (A.D. 47-56) Paul had the privilege and responsibility of leading the evangelization crusade of the early church in three missionary journeys (see Chart 52, p. 214). There was one major interruption — the Jerusalem Council — between the first and second journeys (15:1-35).

SUMMARY OF PAUL'S MISSIONARY JOURNEYS

JOURNEY	DATE	REGION	MILEAGE	ACTS
1	47-48	S.E. Asia Minor	1,500 mi.	13:1—14:28
2	49-52	Macedonia, Achaia	3,000-4,000 mi.	15:36—18:22
3	52-56	W. Asia Minor	4,000 mi.	18:23—21:17

Chapter 13 begins an entirely new section in Acts.[16] Antioch replaces Jerusalem as the base of operations or the mother city of the church. Saul (soon to be Paul) replaces Peter as the central figure of the evangelistic program. A mission field of all races and religions

---

16. The last verse of chapter 12 might be considered as part of chapter 13.

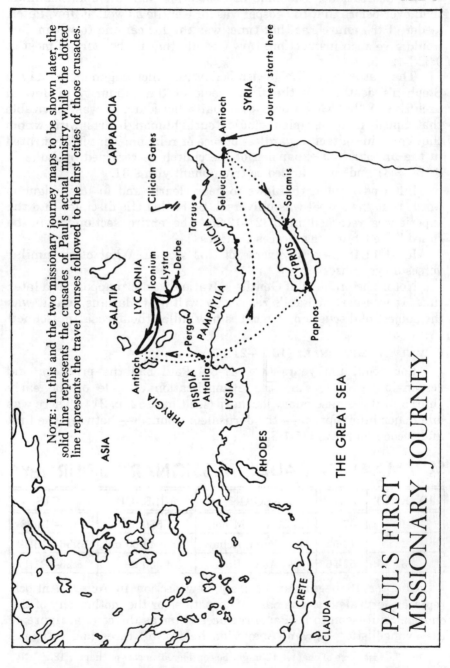

NOTE: In this and the two missionary journey maps to be shown later, the solid line represents the crusades of Paul's actual ministry while the dotted line represents the travel courses followed to the first cities of those crusades.

PAUL'S FIRST
MISSIONARY JOURNEY

SUMMARY OF PAUL'S FIRST MISSIONARY JOURNEY

A.D. 47-48 (12 to 18 months)

13:1	13:4	13:13				14:21	14:26 14:28
COMMISSION	MISSION (A) Island	MISSION (B) Inland				MISSION (C) Return	HOMECOMING
	CYPRUS: 1 SALAMIS 2 PAPHOS	14:1 1 ANTIOCH OF PISIDIA	2 ICONIUM	14:7 3 LYSTRA	14:20 4 DERBE	LYSTRA ICONIUM ANTIOCH PERGA ATTALIA	ANTIOCH OF SYRIA
	1 Salamis Ministry: 2 Paphos Ministry: Opposition: Miracle: Spiritual Fruit:	1 Antioch Ministry: Opposition: Altered strategy: Spiritual Fruit: 2 Iconium Ministry: Opposition: Spiritual Fruit: 3 Lystra Ministry: Miracle: Problem: Opposition: 4 Derbe Ministry: Spiritual Fruit:				RETURN VISITS Ministry: Spiritual Fruit:	MISSIONARY REPORT

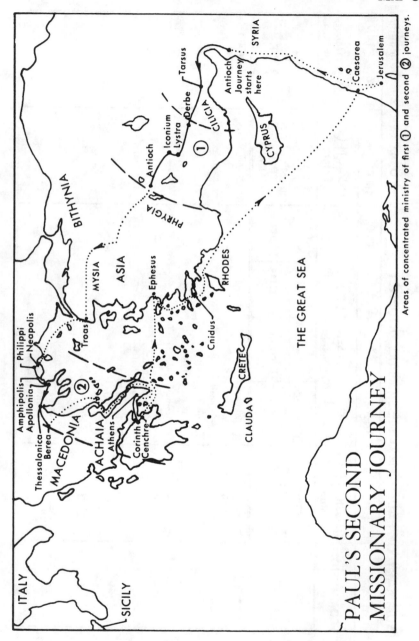

Areas of concentrated ministry of first ① and second ② journeys.

PAUL'S SECOND
MISSIONARY JOURNEY

CHART 56

SECOND MISSIONARY JOURNEY   A.D. 49-52
Acts 15:36—18:22

	Antioch (15:36)	Syria Cilicia (15:41)	Mysia Troas (16:6)	Philippi (16:11)	Thessalonica (17:1)	Berea (17:10)	Athens (17:15)	Corinth (18:1)	Ephesus Caesarea Antioch (18:18 / 18:22)
		ASIA MINOR		MACEDONIA			ACHAIA		
PREPARATION & COMMISSION		MISSION (A)		MISSION (B)			MISSION (C)		RETURN
PERSONNEL									
DURATION									
ITINERARY DETERMINANTS									
MINISTRIES								I and II Thess. written from Corinth[17]	
KEY MESSAGES									
OPPOSITION & DELIVERANCE									
SIGNS & MIRACLES									
SPIRITUAL FRUIT									
KEY VERSES									

17. It was in response to the report from Timothy concerning the Thessalonians (cf. Acts 18:5 and 1 Thess. 3:6) that Paul wrote the letters.

becomes the church's obligation, while the Jerusalem church continues to minister primarily to Jews. Home missions work in the homeland of Jerusalem, Judea, and Samaria continues, but foreign missions work to Asia and Europe is added to the responsibility of the apostles.

Maps and charted summary-worksheets of Paul's three missionary journeys are included in the accompanying pages to help your survey of these important chapters of Acts.

Notes on the missionary journeys

1. World evangelization was the plan that Jesus shared with His apostles (1:8). At 13:1 it was the time to execute such a plan. We observe from the text that it was not Saul or the church, but the Holy Spirit who took the initiative of this new venture (13:2). It was God's plan, and it was God's work. The missionaries were to be His instruments in the work (cf. 14:26-27).

2. It was during Paul's missionary journeys that the apostle was inspired to write some of the New Testament epistles, and it is obvious from them that the interpretations and implications of the ABC's of the gospel message were becoming deeper and more advanced by revelation from God.

3. The end of Paul's second journey and the beginning of his third are so briefly and casually recorded by Luke that the reader of Acts is hardly aware that a new missionary crusade has begun. The second journey closes at 18:22, and in the very next verse,[18] although a period of time is spent at Antioch, Paul is off to the work again, moving about Galatia and Phrygia.

GEOGRAPHICAL COVERAGE ON MISSIONARY JOURNEYS

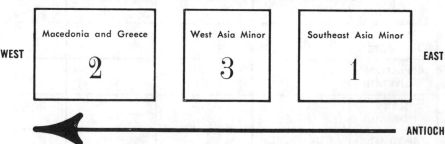

4. Observe that Paul bypassed western Asia Minor on his second journey and did most of his work in Macedonia and Greece. So it was

---

18. The *Berkeley Version* and the *New International Version* accurately make a new paragraph at 18:23, indicating the third journey's commencement here.

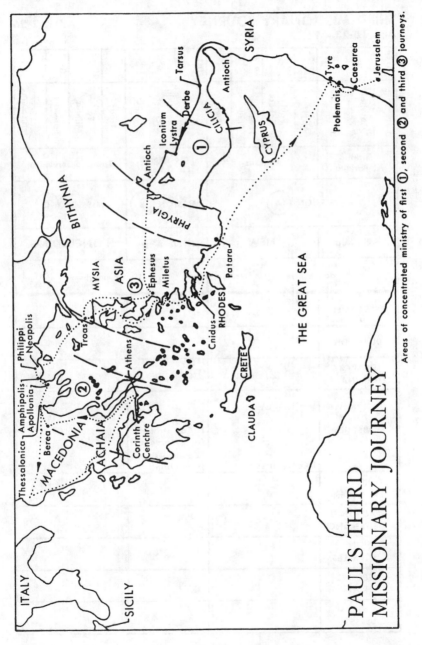

PAUL'S THIRD
MISSIONARY JOURNEY

Areas of concentrated ministry of first ①, second ② and third ③ journeys.

THE GREAT SEA

ITALY

SICILY

CLAUDA

CRETE

RHODES

CYPRUS

SYRIA

BITHYNIA

PHRYGIA

ASIA

MYSIA

MACEDONIA

ACHAIA

Thessalonica
Amphipolis
Apollonia
Philippi
Neapolis
Berea
Athens
Corinth
Cenchre
Troas
Ephesus
Miletus
Cnidus
Patara
Antioch
Iconium
Lystra
Derbe
Tarsus
Antioch
CILICIA
Tyre
Ptolemais
Caesarea
Jerusalem

CHART 57

THIRD MISSIONARY JOURNEY
Acts 18:23—21:17

A.D. 52-56

18:23	18:24	19:1	19:8	19:21	20:1		20:7	20:13	20:17	21:1	21:17
Galatia & Phrygia	Apollos	Paul to Ephesus	Teaching & Preaching	Riot	Macedonia & Greece		Troas	To Miletus	Farewell	To Jerusalem	
Galatia & Phrygia	Ephesus				Macedonia & Greece		Troas to Jerusalem				
MISSION (A)					MISSION (B)		MISSION (C)				
Follow-up	NEW				Follow-up		CONCLUDING				
about 3 years					10-14 months						
PERSONNEL											
DURATION											
ITINERARY DETERMINANTS											
MINISTRIES	I Cor. written				II Cor. written from Macedonia Romans written from Corinth						
KEY MESSAGES											
OPPOSITION & DELIVERANCE											
SIGNS & MIRACLES											
SPIRITUAL FRUIT											
KEY VERSES											

very natural for his third tour that he should be led to spend most of his time (three years) in western Asia Minor (with Ephesus at the hub).

F. PAUL THE PRISONER (21:18—28:31)

Paul the missionary became Paul the prisoner, and he remained in bonds for the remainder of the story of Acts. Luke knew he was not writing a complete biography of Paul, so any awareness that Paul might be given later opportunity to serve God in even greater ministries did not deter Luke from closing his account where he did. Borne of the Holy Spirit, the physician-author designed Acts to close with an action-packed account of the appearances of Paul the prisoner in defense of his Christian testimony. These were appearances before an angry mob, a disorganized council, and confused rulers — all of that leading to his finally reaching Rome (28:14), the goal of his heart (Rom. 1:10-11; 15:22-24). Blaiklock writes, "Paul's was the most significant life ever lived, and when he came to Rome, the purpose for which he had toiled and striven was virtually achieved."[19]

Map Q shows the route over which Paul was taken to Rome (27:1—28:14), and Chart 58 is a survey of these last chapters of Acts.

V. KEY WORDS AND VERSES

A key word of Acts is *witness*, which appears in its various forms about twenty times. Some other key words and phrases are "and it came about," "but when," "preached," "boldly," "Jews," "Greeks." What other words did you especially observe in your survey?

Acts 1:8 is often identified as a key verse of Acts, especially since an outline of Acts (geography) is in the verse. What other key verses did you observe?

VI. APPLICATIONS

Various applications of Acts have already been made in the course of this chapter, so additional ones will not be cited. As you think back over your survey, what spiritual applications remain with you indelibly?

VII. REVIEW QUESTIONS

1. When and where did Luke write Acts?
2. What were his purposes in writing?
3. What were Luke's sources of information?

---

19. E. M. Blaiklock, *Acts of the Apostles*, p. 12.

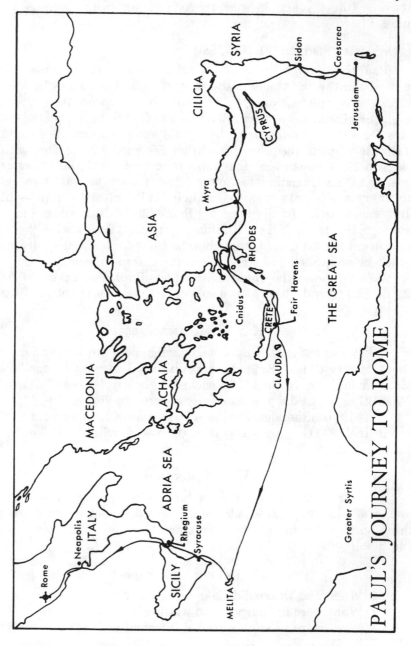

PAUL'S JOURNEY TO ROME

CHART 58

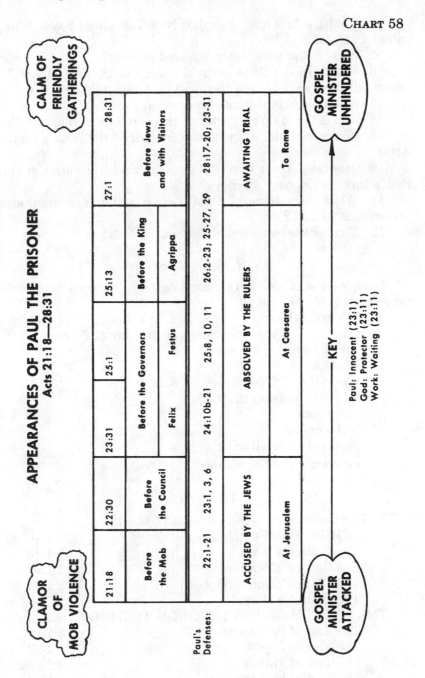

APPEARANCES OF PAUL THE PRISONER
Acts 21:18—28:31

CALM OF FRIENDLY GATHERINGS

CLAMOR OF MOB VIOLENCE

GOSPEL MINISTER UNHINDERED

GOSPEL MINISTER ATTACKED

21:18	22:30	23:31	25:1	25:13	27:1	28:31
Before the Mob	Before the Council	Before the Governors		Before the King		Before Jews and with Visitors
		Felix	Festus	Agrippa		

Paul's Defenses: 22:1-21   23:1, 3, 6   24:10b-21   25:8, 10, 11   26:2-23; 25-27, 29   28:17-20; 23-31

ACCUSED BY THE JEWS   ABSOLVED BY THE RULERS   AWAITING TRIAL

At Jerusalem   At Caesarea   To Rome

KEY

Paul: Innocent (23:1)
God: Protector (23:11)
Work: Waiting (23:11)

4. Compare Acts with the other New Testament books. Why is it called a pivotal book?

5. What is the time period covered by Acts?

6. What are the three main divisions of the text of Acts? Can you recall three outlines built around that threefold structure?

7. Where in Acts is Paul's conversion recorded?

8. Who is the main character of chapters 1-7? of chapters 13-28?

9. How would you describe the content of the middle section of Acts?

10. Generally, what were the geographical itineraries of each of Paul's three missionary journeys?

11. What were some of Paul's examination appearances as a prisoner, in 21:18ff.?

12. What is the last word of the text of Acts?

VIII. Further Study

Here is a list of subjects for further study, selected from the wide range of subjects in Acts:

> the early church
> ministries of the Holy Spirit on the day of Pentecost
> life of Peter
> life of Paul
> use of the Old Testament in Acts
> miracles, prayers in Acts
> demonism
> idol worship
> personal evangelism
> persecution of Christians.

IX. Outline

ACTS: The Beginnings of the Christian Church

THE CHURCH IS BORN	1:1—2:47
The Church's Work	1:1-14
The Church's Workers	1:15-26
The Church's Spirit Baptism	2:1-21
The Church's Gospel	2:22-47
THE CHURCH GROWS THROUGH TESTING	3:1—8:1a
The Test of Popularity	3:1-26
The Test of Loyalty	4:1-22
The Test of Things	4:23—5:11
The Test of Fortitude	5:12-42

X. Selected Reading

GENERAL INTRODUCTION

Bruce, F. F. *The Acts of the Apostles*, pp. 1-64.
Hiebert, D. Edmond. *An Introduction to the New Testament*, pp. 243-81.
Manley, O. T., ed. *The New Bible Handbook*, pp. 344-50.
Robertson, A. T. "Acts of the Apostles." In *The International Standard Bible Encyclopedia*, 1:39-48.
Thiessen, Henry C. *Introduction to the New Testament*, pp. 177-88.

COMMENTARIES

Blaiklock, E. M. *The Acts of the Apostles*. The Tyndale New Testament Commentaries. Political and cultural background is given on pages 20-44.
Bruce, F. F. *Commentary on the Book of Acts*. The New International Commentary on the New Testament. This is one of the best commentaries on Acts available today.
Lange, John Peter. *Commentary on the Holy Scriptures: Acts*.
Morgan, G. Campbell. *The Acts of the Apostles*.
Rackham, Richard B. *The Acts of the Apostles*.
Scroggie, W. Graham. *The Acts of the Apostles*.

OTHER RELATED SOURCES

Foakes-Jackson, F. J., and Lake, Kirsopp, eds. *The Beginnings of Christianity*.

Goodwin, Frank J. *A Harmony of the Life of St. Paul*.

Jensen, Irving L. *Acts: An Independent Study*.

Kent, Homer A., Jr. *Jerusalem to Rome: Studies in the Book of Acts*.

Purves, George T. *The Apostolic Age*.

Robertson, A. T. *Epochs in the Life of Paul*.

Sauer, Erich. *The Dawn of World Redemption*.

Stalker, James. *The Life of St. Paul*.

Walvoord, John F. *The Holy Spirit*.

Part 3

THE MESSAGE

Christ the Savior,
Sanctifier, and
Coming King

Twenty-one of the twenty-seven New Testament books are epistles. This kind of writing, with its personal characteristics, is a very natural follow-up of the historical kind represented by the four gospels and Acts. As the Christian church was expanding geographically in the first decades after the day of Pentecost (Acts 2), communication from individual to individual, from group to group, and from individual to group was usually by letter. The characteristic common to all the New Testament epistles was the spiritual bond in Christ, between the writer and the reader(s). It was a personal, intimate relationship, and so the epistle was an appropriate channel for sharing personal testimony and delivering exhortations and commands, in addition to interpreting the grand truths of the gospel.

Of the twenty-one epistles, thirteen bear the name of the apostle Paul, and are referred to now as the Pauline epistles. The remaining letters are non-Pauline epistles, and were written by Peter, James, John, Jude, and an anonymous author (Hebrews).

Philip Schaff says the New Testament epistles "compress more ideas in fewer words than any other writings, human or divine, excepting the Gospels." The subject of the epistles is Jesus Christ. Their message is that He is the sinner's Savior, the Christian's sanctifier, and the King who one day will return to rule over His kingdom forevermore. The world desperately needs to hear that message.

Pauline epistles		*Non-Pauline epistles*
Romans	Colossians	Hebrews
1, 2 Corinthians	1, 2 Thessalonians	James
Galatians	1, 2 Timothy	1, 2 Peter
Ephesians	Titus	1, 2, 3 John
Philippians	Philemon	Jude

10

Paul and His Letters

In so many different ways the apostle Paul must be regarded as a key servant of God in the New Testament's story of the church, "given to Christianity when it was in its most rudimentary beginnings."[1] James Stalker writes that the early Christian community "was in the utmost need of a man of extraordinary endowments, who, becoming possessed with its genius, should incorporate it with the general history of the world; and in Paul it found the man it needed."[2] It was God, in His sovereign ways of foreknowledge, who brought the two together at the right time.

The purpose of this chapter is to furnish background for the surveys of each of Paul's letters, by looking briefly at the man, his life, and his ministry, including the letters he wrote.

I. THE MAN PAUL

A brief description of the man Paul is given below. We will see more of the apostle and his ministry as we survey each of his epistles in the chapters that follow. Refer to outside sources for extended treatment of Paul's life and ministry.[3]

A. NAME

Paul's Hebrew name was *Saul* ("asked of God"); his Roman name was *Paul* ("little").[4] Very possibly he had both names from childhood. In his epistles the apostle always refers to himself as Paul. Consult an exhaustive concordance for all the references to the two names in the

---

1. James Stalker, *The Life of St. Paul*, pp. 7-8.
2. Ibid., p. 8.
3. James Stalker's book, *The Life of St. Paul*, is an excellent condensed biography.
4. Bruce writes, "The apostle, as a Roman citizen, must have had three names — *praenomen, nomen gentile* and *cognomen* — of which Paullus was his *cognomen*. . . . The apostle's *praenomen* and *nomen gentile*, unfortunately, have not been preserved." F. F. Bruce, *Commentary on the Book of Acts*, pp. 264-65.

New Testament. Read Acts 13:9, which is the turning point in Acts for the changeover of designation from Saul to Paul. After 13:9, the author of Acts always refers to him as Paul. But Paul uses the name Saul in describing his conversion experience in Acts 22:7, 13; 26:14.

B. DATE AND PLACE OF BIRTH

Paul was born about the time of Jesus' birth,[5] in the city of Tarsus, of the province of Cilicia. (See Map E, p. 64.)

C. FAMILY

Paul's father was a native of Palestine, a Roman citizen, merchant by trade, and a strict Pharisee. His mother was probably a devout woman. Paul had at least one sister and one nephew (Acts 23:16).

THREE PHASES OF PAUL'S LIFE

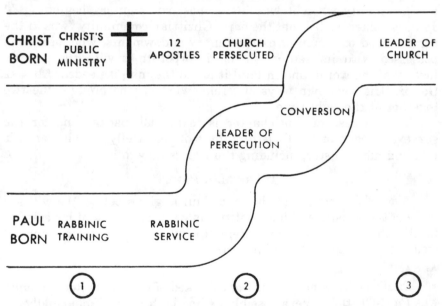

D. EDUCATION

In his youth Paul learned the trade of tent-making. He may have matriculated at the famous university in Tarsus, one of the three major universities of the Roman Empire. His rabbinical training was under Gamaliel at Jerusalem.

5. This is a strong likelihood when one considers that in A.D. 33 (Stephen's death) Paul was a "young man" (Acts 7:58), and in A.D. 61 he calls himself an aged man (Philem. 9).

E. POSTSCHOOL YEARS

Paul probably served in synagogues outside of Palestine after his rabbinical training, and he returned to Jerusalem some time after Christ's ascension. He soon became the leader of the persecution of the Christian church.

F. CONVERSION

Paul's conversion to Christ came at the height of his opposition to the church, on the road to Damascus. Acts 9:1-19a reports the experience. (Recall your survey of Acts.) The sovereign ways of God are remarkably demonstrated in Paul's three-phased life (early training; church persecutor; church leader) in relation to Christ and the early church. This is shown on the accompanying diagram. What are your impressions?

G. MISSIONARY-AUTHOR

Many of Paul's New Testament letters were written during the years of his missionary labors. Chart 59 shows how these two ministries overlapped each other.[6] (For Scripture references to each item, see Appendix B, p. 518.)

CHART 59

OUTLINE OF HIGHLIGHTS OF PAUL'S LIFE

Birth of Paul	around the time of Christ's birth
Conversion of Paul	A.D. 33
First missionary journey	47-48
GALATIANS written after first journey[7]	48
Apostolic council at Jerusalem	49
Second missionary journey	49-52
I and II THESSALONIANS written during second journey	52
Third missionary journey	52-56
I and II CORINTHIANS written during third journey	55
ROMANS written during third journey	56
Arrest in Jerusalem	56
Journey to Rome	60-61
In Rome awaiting trial, under guard	61
PHILEMON, COLOSSIANS, EPHESIANS, PHILIPPIANS written from prison	61
Paul released, revisits churches, resumes evangelistic ministry	62-66
I TIMOTHY, TITUS written	62-65
Paul arrested, imprisoned at Rome	66-67
II TIMOTHY written from prison	67
Paul executed	67

---

6. Some of the dates on the chart can only be approximated.
7. Some hold that Galatians was not written until a later date, for example after the third missionary journey, around A.D. 56.

H. CHARACTER

A study of Paul's character as revealed by Acts and his writings shows him to be one of the most unique Christians of the New Testament. A. T. Robertson's interpretation of that character revelation is given here:

> Passing by Jesus himself, Paul stands forever the foremost representative of Christ, the ablest exponent of Christianity, its most constructive genius, its dominant spirit from the merely human side, its most fearless champion, its most illustrious and influential missionary, preacher, teacher, and its most distinguished martyr. He heard things in the third heaven not lawful to utter (II Cor. 12:4), but he felt himself a poor earthen vessel after all (II Cor. 4:7). He sought to commend himself in the sight of God to every man's conscience, for he had seen the light of the gospel of the glory of Christ and was the servant of all for Jesus' sake (II Cor. 4:3 ff.).[8]

I. TRIALS AND DEATH

Paul was released from his first Roman imprisonment (Acts 28:16-31), but he was incarcerated again after about four years of freedom. His second letter to Timothy was written from prison, and the letter reveals that he did not expect to be released (2 Tim. 4:6). His trial was probably very brief, and according to tradition he was beheaded. Stalker describes the scene, as he imagines it:

> The trial ended, Paul was condemned and delivered over to the executioner. He was led out of the city with a crowd of the lowest rabble at his heels. The fatal spot was reached; he knelt beside the block; the headsman's axe gleamed in the sun and fell; and the head of the apostle of the world rolled down in the dust. So sin did its uttermost and its worst. Yet how poor and empty was its triumph! . . . ten thousand times ten thousand welcomed him in the same hour at the gates of the city which is really eternal. Even on earth Paul could not die . . . in ten thousand churches every Sabbath and on a thousand thousand hearths every day his eloquent lips still teach that gospel of which he was never ashamed.[9]

II. PAUL'S LETTERS

The epistolary form of most of the New Testament (21 of 27 books) is one of its unique characteristics, distinct from all other sacred writings of the world. Hiebert compares that form with the Old Testament legal document form:

---

8. A. T. Robertson, *Epochs in the Life of Paul*, p. 4.
9. James Stalker, *The Life of St. Paul*, p. 143.

CHART 60

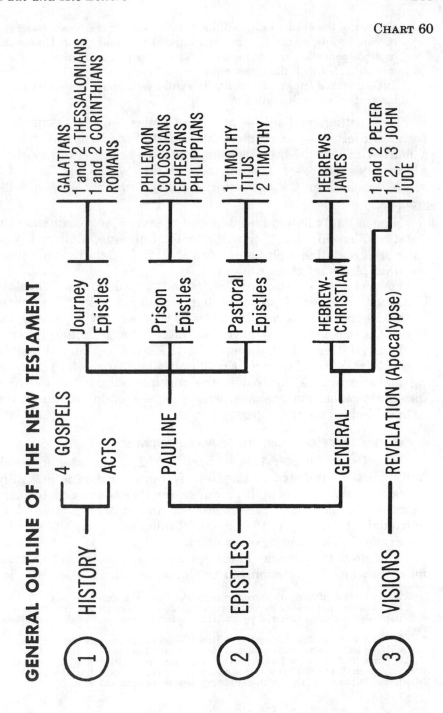

GENERAL OUTLINE OF THE NEW TESTAMENT

1 HISTORY

4 GOSPELS
ACTS

2 EPISTLES

PAULINE

Journey Epistles

GALATIANS
1 and 2 THESSALONIANS
1 and 2 CORINTHIANS
ROMANS

Prison Epistles

PHILEMON
COLOSSIANS
EPHESIANS
PHILIPPIANS

Pastoral Epistles

1 TIMOTHY
TITUS
2 TIMOTHY

GENERAL

HEBREW-CHRISTIAN

HEBREWS
JAMES

1 and 2 PETER
1, 2, 3 JOHN
JUDE

3 VISIONS

REVELATION (Apocalypse)

The use of the epistle as a medium of revelation in the New Testament reveals the difference between the ages of law and grace. Under the legal dispensation the demands of God were set forth in legal documents, sealed with the direct authority of God; in the age of grace God further makes known His will to His children through loving letters of instruction and exhortation.[10]

The writings of Paul — at least thirteen of twenty-one New Testament letters — constitute a major part of the New Testament.[11] A fourteenth book, Hebrews, also might have been written by Paul. All twenty-seven New Testament books are shown on Chart 60, which breaks down the list into three major groups. What are the groups?

Nine of Paul's letters are addressed to seven Gentile churches (in Galatia, Thessalonica, Corinth, Rome, Colossae, Ephesus, and Philippi). Locate these places on Map L, p. 207. (Galatia is a region; the other places are cities.)

Four of Paul's letters are addressed to individuals (Timothy, Titus, and Philemon). Paul wrote four "prison epistles."[12] The epistle to the Hebrews, whoever the author, was written especially for Jewish Christians and may have been intended as a circular letter.

Paul's letters are not listed in the New Testament in the chronological order of their writing. Study Chart 61 carefully, observing the progressions involved in the ongoing additions to the New Testament canon. For example, what progression do you see in the main subjects of the three groups?

A. THE NEW TESTAMENT LISTING OF PAUL'S LETTERS

As noted in Chapter 1 (see Chart 2, p. 23), the order in which Paul's epistles are listed in the New Testament canon is generally topical, involving two main groups: epistles addressed to local churches (Romans to 2 Thessalonians); and epistles addressed to individuals (1 Timothy to Philemon). Within each group the epistles are arranged in descending order of length.[13]

1. *Letters to churches.* These epistles teach the proper order of the church and her relationship to Christ the Head. They also in-

---

10. D. Edmond Hiebert, *An Introduction to the Pauline Epistles*, p. 14.
11. Of course Paul wrote other letters during the course of his life. But these were noncanonical. Only those inspired by the Holy Spirit became part of the New Testament.
12. Those were written during Paul's first Roman imprisonment. Second Timothy, Paul's "dying letter," was written during his second imprisonment.
13. There is one minor exception to this order, because Galatians is slightly shorter than Ephesians. We do not know if this descending order of length had any bearing on the original formation of the canonical listing, whenever that took place.

PROGRESSIVE ADDITIONS OF PAUL'S EPISTLES TO THE CANON OF THE NEW TESTAMENT

CHART 61

GROUP	SETTING	EPISTLE	DATE A.D.	MAIN SUBJECTS	GENERAL PURPOSES	
I TRAVEL EPISTLES	between first and second journeys	GALATIANS	48	SALVATION at Present and in the Future	EVANGELIZING	TO CHURCHES
	second journey	1 and 2 THESSALONIANS	52			
	third journey	1 and 2 CORINTHIANS	55			
		ROMANS	56			
II PRISON EPISTLES	first Roman imprisonment	COLOSSIANS	61	CHRIST and the Christian Life	EDIFYING	
		EPHESIANS				
		PHILEMON				
		PHILIPPIANS				
III PASTORAL EPISTLES	release	1 TIMOTHY	62	CHURCH and its Workers	ESTABLISHING	TO INDIVIDUALS
		TITUS	62			
	second Roman imprisonment	2 TIMOTHY	67		personal farewell	

struct the church regarding her position, possessions, privileges, and duties.

Romans has naturally the first place in order, since it is the foundational epistle of the doctrines of salvation. Romans shows the material out of which God forms the church: man lost in sin, hopeless, helpless. It also shows how God by His mighty power transforms this unpromising material into living stones of which the church is built, Christ Himself being the chief cornerstone. Here is the canonical order:

> Romans
> 1 and 2 Corinthians
> Galatians
> Ephesians
> Philippians
> Colossians
> 1 and 2 Thessalonians

2. *Letters to individuals.* The message of these epistles applies especially to individual Christians, concerning Christian living and service. This is the order:

> 1 and 2 Timothy
> Titus
> Philemon

B. DIFFERENT ORDERS OF STUDYING THE NEW TESTAMENT BOOKS

There are various orders that may be followed in studying the books of the New Testament. A few of these have already been identified. The different orders are these:

1. *Canonical order.* This follows the list of books as it appears in our New Testament. It is the order of our surveys in this study volume.

2. *Chronological order.* See Chart 1, p. 20, (entire New Testament) and Chart 61 (Paul's letters). Here one studies the books in the order of their first public appearances in the first century.

3. *General groups.* This order is shown on Chart 60, page 239.

4. *Doctrinal content.* There are various possible orders using this approach. Below is one suggestion, which is charted on Chart 62. This chart shows a logical order (Matthew to Revelation, with the epistles built around Acts) combined with a doctrinal progression (*salvation; Christ; church; consummation*).

a. basic facts of the gospel — Matthew, Mark, Luke
b. further reflections of the gospel — John
c. sequel to the gospel — Acts

d. salvation (soteriology) —
  (1*a*) Romans: The way of salvation
  (1*b*) Hebrews: The person of salvation
  (2*a*) Galatians: Liberation by the gospel
  (2*b*) James: Compulsion of the gospel
e. Person and work of Christ (christology) —
  (1*a*) Ephesians: Christ and the church
  (1*b*) Colossians: Christ and the cosmos
  (2*a*) Philippians: Joy in Christ
  (2*b*) Philemon: Forgiveness in Christ
f. church (ecclesiology) —
  (1*a*) 1 Corinthians: Problems of a church
  (1*b*) 1 Timothy: Pastoral care of a church
  (1*c*) Titus: Traits of a good church
  (2*a*) 2 Corinthians: Ministry vindicated
  (2*b*) 2 Timothy: Ministry accomplished
g. last things (eschatology) —
  (1*a*) 1 Thessalonians ⎫
  (1*b*) 2 Thessalonians ⎭ Lord's (second) coming
  (2*a*) 1 Peter ⎞
  (2*b*) 2 Peter ⎬ Christian's living
  (2*c*) Jude ⎠
  (3) Revelation: God and Christ on the throne

C. THE MAIN PURPOSES OF PAUL'S LETTERS

The main purposes of Paul's letters are seen when they are compared with the gospels and Acts. The gospels emphasize especially the facts of Christ's redemptive ministry; the epistles interpret those facts and tell the redeemed ones how to live the Christian life. In the gospels Christ announces His purpose to build the church (Matt. 16:16-18). Acts shows the church in the first stages of construction. The epistles show how the church is built, what materials are used, and what are the positions, relationships, privileges, and duties of the members of its glorious and mysterious fellowship.

Prominent in all Paul's epistles are the exhortations and commands based on the doctrines. Seemingly simple duties are based on sublime truths that originate with the Person and work of Christ. Difficult commands (e.g., "present your bodies a living and holy sacrifice," Rom. 12:1) are justified as being reasonable and consistent. Paul's epistles make it very clear that God offers all the help needed to fulfill His commands.

Little did Paul and the other writers of the New Testament

CHART 62

MAIN SUBJECTS OF THE NEW TESTAMENT BOOKS

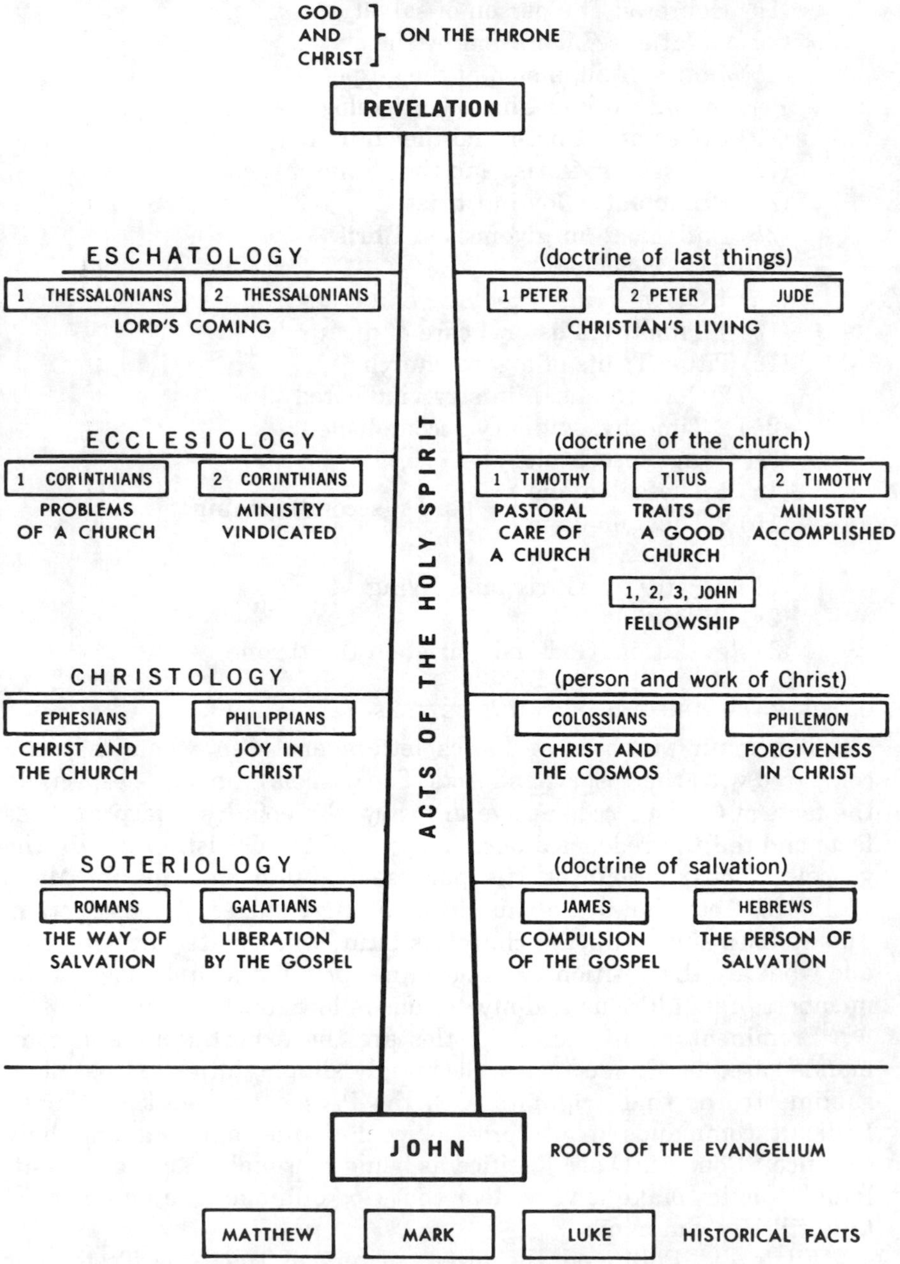

GOD
AND   — ON THE THRONE
CHRIST

REVELATION

ESCHATOLOGY   (doctrine of last things)

| 1 THESSALONIANS | 2 THESSALONIANS | | 1 PETER | 2 PETER | JUDE |

LORD'S COMING   CHRISTIAN'S LIVING

ECCLESIOLOGY   (doctrine of the church)

| 1 CORINTHIANS | 2 CORINTHIANS | | 1 TIMOTHY | TITUS | 2 TIMOTHY |

PROBLEMS   MINISTRY   PASTORAL   TRAITS OF   MINISTRY
OF A CHURCH   VINDICATED   CARE OF   A GOOD   ACCOMPLISHED
                          A CHURCH   CHURCH

| 1, 2, 3, JOHN |

FELLOWSHIP

CHRISTOLOGY   (person and work of Christ)

| EPHESIANS | PHILIPPIANS | | COLOSSIANS | PHILEMON |

CHRIST AND   JOY IN   CHRIST AND   FORGIVENESS
THE CHURCH   CHRIST   THE COSMOS   IN CHRIST

SOTERIOLOGY   (doctrine of salvation)

| ROMANS | GALATIANS | | JAMES | HEBREWS |

THE WAY OF   LIBERATION   COMPULSION   THE PERSON OF
SALVATION   BY THE GOSPEL   OF THE GOSPEL   SALVATION

ACTS OF THE HOLY SPIRIT

JOHN   ROOTS OF THE EVANGELIUM

| MATTHEW | MARK | LUKE | HISTORICAL FACTS |

epistles realize the impact their letters would make on the lives of people for two thousand years. One church historian has evaluated the epistles thus:

> The Epistles of the New Testament are without a parallel in ancient literature. . . . Tracts for the times, they are tracts for all times. Children of the fleeting moment, they contain truths of infinite moment. They compress more ideas in fewer words than any other writings, human or divine, excepting the Gospels. They discuss the highest themes which can challenge an immortal mind — God, Christ, and the Spirit, sin and redemption, incarnation, atonement, regeneration, repentance, faith and good works, holy living and dying. . . . And all this before humble little societies of poor, uncultured artisans, freedmen and slaves.[14]

III. REVIEW QUESTIONS

1. What do Paul's two names mean, literally? Which name appears first in the New Testament text?
2. Where and when was Paul born?
3. Describe Paul's education.
4. What may have been Paul's activities during Jesus' public ministry?
5. What letters of Paul were written in connection with his missionary journeys?
6. Describe Paul's character.
7. When did Paul die?
8. List the books of the New Testament under each of these groups: History, Epistles, Visions.
9. How many epistles did Paul write? In what chronological order did he write them?
10. What are the two groups of New Testament listings of Paul's letters?
11. Describe various orders in which one may study the New Testament books.
12. What are the main purposes of Paul's letters?

IV. SELECTED READING

Ball, Charles Ferguson. *The Life and Journeys of Paul.*
Bruce, F. F. *The Letters of Paul: An Expanded Paraphrase.*
———. *Paul: Apostle of the Heart Set Free.*
Conybeare, W. J., and Howson, J. S. *The Life and Epistles of St. Paul.*

---

14. Philip Schaff, *History of the Christian Church*, 1:740-41.

Farrar, F. W. *The Life and Work of St. Paul.*
Goodwin, Frank J. *A Harmony of the Life of St. Paul.*
Hiebert, D. Edmond. *An Introduction to the Pauline Epistles.*
———. *Personalities Around Paul.*
Kelso, James L. *An Archaeologist Follows the Apostle Paul.*
Longenecker, Richard. *The Ministry and Message of Paul.*
Moe, Olaf. *The Apostle Paul.*
Ramsay, W. H. *The Cities of St. Paul.*
Robertson, A. T. *Epochs in the Life of Paul.*
Stalker, James. *The Life of St. Paul.*

11

Romans: God's Salvation for Sinners

Romans is Paul's masterpiece, a key that unlocks the door to vast treasures of Scripture. People who have read and studied this epistle cannot find words sufficient to describe its worth. "The most profound book in existence" (Coleridge). "Cathedral of the Christian faith" (Godet). "The chief part of the New Testament and the very purest Gospel" (Luther). "A thorough study of this epistle is really a theological education in itself" (Griffith Thomas).

The uniqueness of Romans is not for its telling a different gospel or new teaching, but for its spelling out the ABC's of the gospel of salvation in Christ, in clear, full scope, so that there can be no question concerning any important aspect of that gospel. Romans tells, for example, how sinful man can be restored to fellowship with his Creator, the holy God. It was of divine design that, by interpreting the truths already spoken by Jesus, one epistle should be written especially to explain such truths to people. Paul was the man chosen to be the writer, and Romans was the epistle. Under the guidance of the Holy Spirit this longest of the epistles has been placed by the people of God first in the order of New Testament epistles.

I. Preparation for Study

In order to appreciate the important place that Romans occupies in Scripture, it is necessary to understand something of fallen man's utter lack of righteousness as revealed throughout human history.

A review of the moral history of the race as set forth in the books of the Bible up to the book of Romans shows that man is, and always has been, an utter failure as regards righteousness. When Adam was tempted in the Garden of Eden he proved himself a failure, and all of Adam's descendants have done the same. "All have sinned" (Rom. 3:23). "There is none righteous, not even one" (3:10).

From Adam to Abraham God patiently dealt with the sons of man, wooing them to His compassionate heart, giving them opportunity after opportunity to choose Him and His way, and so to find His favor. But the human race as a whole rejected Him, and the result was utter failure — failure so great that God "gave them over" and allowed them to go their own wicked ways (Rom. 1:24, 26, 28).

Then God tested the nation of Israel, the Jews. This is the story of Genesis 12 to the end of Malachi. Everything was given Israel to afford a perfect opportunity to choose the righteous ways of God: special privileges, perfect instruction, marvelous revelations, miraculous protection, and matchless covenants and promises. But again there was utter and complete failure — failure so great that when Israel chose, with others, to crucify the Lord Jesus and refused to listen to the voice of the Holy Spirit through the apostles, God rejected her and scattered the people throughout the earth, allowing them to go on in their own blindness and darkness.

In the book of Romans God is saying to the readers of the whole world — Jew and Gentile — that though they have failed to attain a righteousness acceptable to a holy God, this righteousness may be received as a gift from Him, through faith, in the person of His righteous Son. It is their only hope for now and eternity.

II. Background

A. AUTHOR

According to the text of 1:1, Paul was the author. Note the three ways Paul identifies himself in the verse. In your own words write down what is involved in each identification. Most of what is known about Paul's life is given to us in the book of Acts.

B. DATE WRITTEN

Paul wrote Romans from Corinth toward the end of his third missionary journey, around A.D. 56.

C. THE CITY OF ROME IN A.D. 56

When Paul wrote this letter Rome was the largest and most important city of the world (estimated population: one to four million). Emperor Nero had just begun to rule (A.D. 54-68), and anti-Christian persecutions had not yet begun. The city's population was made up of the usual mixture of a large city: wealth, poverty, capitalism, slavery, citizens, aliens, religion, worldliness. There was a large number of Jews living in Rome at the time, for about a dozen synagogues were located throughout the city. Hiebert writes, "Around the various synagogues of the Jews there gradually grew up a considerable following of Gentiles more or less in active sympathy with their religion. Here, as elsewhere in the Empire, these 'God-fearers' furnished fertile ground for the spread of Christianity."[1]

D. ORIGINAL READERS

The letter was addressed to the saints in Rome (1:7), a mixed group of Jews and Gentiles, the latter group probably constituting the majority (cf. 1:13; 2:17). These Christians had migrated to Rome from various parts of the Mediterranean world. Some no doubt were converts of Paul's and Peter's itinerant ministries. It is possible also that included in the number were "visitors from Rome" (Acts 2:10) who had been present at Jerusalem on the day of Pentecost and had returned to Rome with the message of Christ. Paul had not as yet visited the church at Rome when he wrote the epistle.

E. OCCASION AND PURPOSE OF WRITING

Paul had various things in mind in writing this letter. Among them was his desire to tell the Roman Christians of his plan to visit them and enlist their support for his proposed tour to Spain (15:23-25). The letter also would pave the way for Paul's personal visit by giving instruction to the Christians regarding the basic truths of salvation and Christian living. This intent of setting forth a solid interpretation of the gospel must be the underlying purpose of the epistle, and almost two thousand years of church history have demonstrated successful fulfillment of such a divine purpose.[2]

III. SURVEY

A. PREPARING TO SURVEY

1. Keep in mind that a single Bible book is a structure composed of various parts. Recall from an earlier study that we are using the following terms to represent individual units of that total structure:

a. Paragraph: A paragraph is a group of sentences (usually verses) making up one thought unit (e.g., Rom. 9:1-5).

b. Segment: A segment is a group of paragraphs, often the length of one chapter, sometimes shorter or longer (e.g., Rom. 2:17—3:8).

c. Section: A section is a group of segments, such as Romans 1:18—3:20.

---

1. D. Edmond Hiebert, *An Introduction to the Pauline Epistles*, pp. 166-67.
2. Paul did not include the whole range of doctrines in his letter, evidenced by the little he wrote about the church and eschatology.

d. Division: These are the largest units of a book. For Romans, there are four divisions: prologue; doctrine; practice; epilogue. These will be located later.

2. Turn the pages of Romans in your Bible, for quick, first impressions. How many chapters in this letter? Are any exceptionally long? What is the first and last word of the letter? Does Paul quote the Old Testament often? (NASB clearly shows Old Testament quotes by using all capitalized letters.)

B. FIRST READING

Scan the book of Romans, chapter by chapter, in one sitting. It is not necessary to read every word at this time, but it is important to read the first and last verses of each chapter. For this first reading do not tarry over the text as though you were analyzing it. Otherwise, the weight of sixteen chapters will suddenly bear down heavily upon you, and you will be discouraged from pursuing your survey.

Did you observe any repeated words, especially in the first verse of each chapter? Is there a prevailing atmosphere throughout, or does the atmosphere change along the way? Regarding the kind of content, how does chapter 16 compare with all the other chapters?

C. SURVEYING THE INDIVIDUAL SEGMENTS

Now refer to Chart 63 (survey of Romans) and note that the epistle is divided into twenty segments. Note that all the segments begin with the first verse of each chapter, with these exceptions: 1:18; 2:17; 3:9; 3:21; 9:30; 12:9; 15:14. Mark these segment divisions in the Bible version that you are using as the basic text of your survey. Then scan through Romans segment by segment and assign a segment title to each. Record the titles by whatever method you are using for this.

What new impressions do you have of Romans? Have key words begun to appear?

D. STRUCTURE OF ROMANS

The next step in survey study is to look for groups of segments according to content or any turning point in the book. Do not refer to the outlines on Chart 63 until you have first tried to arrive at your own outlines. Even if you do not arrive at a complete outline for the book, the time spent here in independent study is well spent, for you will begin to get acquainted more intimately with *what* Paul was writing as you try to discover *how* he wrote those truths. This is the search for *structure*, or organization, of the book.

Try answering these questions on the basis of your survey of the twenty segments of Romans:

1. What is the first segment about? In what ways does it serve as a prologue (introduction) to the book?

2. Paul's letters are composed mainly of doctrinal and practical passages. Which comes first in Romans? Where does the concentration of the second kind of passage begin? How is the opening sentence of this second kind a clue to what follows in the division?

3. The last two segments (15:14-33 and 16:1-27) make up the epilogue. How do they conclude the letter? What are the last three verses of the letter?

4. Now you have viewed the four main divisions of Romans: *prologue; doctrinal; practical; epilogue.* Where are they identified on Chart 63?

5. Where in the epistle does Paul write much about sin and judgment? about justification? about Israel?

6. Try to group the segments between 1:18 and 11:36 according to similar content. These groups are called sections. Is there a logical progression of general doctrinal content in the sequence of the sections? If so, what is it?

7. Before referring to the outlines on Chart 63, survey the segments and sections of Romans some more.

E. SURVEY CHART OF ROMANS

Observe on Chart 63 that the prologue is made up of three parts: salutation; personal testimony; and introduction of the theme. Locate these in the Bible text.

The first eleven chapters are mainly *doctrinal.* In those chapters Paul presents the great truths of the gospel. What are the main doctrines involved? How does the doctrinal division (1:18—11:36) end? Is that a clue that a change of subject follows?

The remaining chapters, 12-16, are mainly *practical.* In those chapters Paul shows the practical working out of the doctrines taught in chapters 1-11. Read Philippians 2:12-13 for what Paul writes about working out one's salvation.

There is an ascending progression of subject in the sections of 1:18—11:36, shown by the arrow. The progression moves from the wrath of God *(God's holiness in condemning sin)* to the glory of God *(God's glory the object of service).* Study the other parts of the outline as they fit into this progression. From the outline of 12:1—15:13 note also what should be the ultimate object of all Christian service.

Though the practice of Christianity may involve the most menial of tasks, all such practice is placed by the Bible on a very high plane. Observe how the practical section of Christian service begins at the peak of the Christian's consecration (12:1-2) and ends at the peak of God's glory (15:8-13). All the commands and exhortations are recorded in between. Read those two passages at this time.

Study the threefold outline at the very bottom of the chart, beginning with *Deadliness of sin.* Another way to word this outline is: Need of salvation; Way of salvation; Results of salvation.

Some look on chapters 9-11 as parenthetical, because in those chapters Paul's subject is a special people, Israel, whereas in the sections preceding and following those chapters he speaks about *all* people and *all* Christians. But the Jews are brought into the discussion of the epistle in other parts of Romans, such as the first chapters, and Gentiles are very prominent in chapters 9-11. Therefore the outlines of Chart 63 consider those chapters to be an integral part of Paul's theme, not parenthetical. That will be discussed later as a prominent subject of Romans.

To help get a mental image of the full scope of Paul's epistle, study the other outlines shown on Chart 63. The easiest outline to remember for Romans is the one that begins *sin; salvation*; and so forth. In your own words, what is each of the sections about? Compare your segment titles with these subjects.

IV. PROMINENT SUBJECTS

A. WHOLE WORLD CONDEMNED (1:18—3:20)

The theme of Romans is salvation by faith in Christ (1:16-17), but Paul's starting point is showing why that salvation is needed: because the whole world is guilty of sin and condemned to eternal death. The first section of Romans is divided into these four parts:

> The pagan world condemned (1:18-32)
> The self-righteous condemned (2:1-16)
> The Jew condemned (2:17—3:8)
> The whole world condemned (3:9-20)

1. *The pagan world condemned* (1:18-32). These verses represent the classic Bible passage referred to for answers to such questions as, Are the heathen lost? and, Is it fair that those who never in their lifetime hear or read a gospel message should be eternally condemned? Paul firmly declares that God's wrath is justly revealed against unevangelized sinners because God gives them sufficient knowledge of Himself to induce reverent worship and obedience, making this revelation of Himself both in their conscience (1:19) and through nature (1:20). But when men thus introduced to God refuse to worship and serve Him (1:21-23), God gives them up to their own

CHART 63

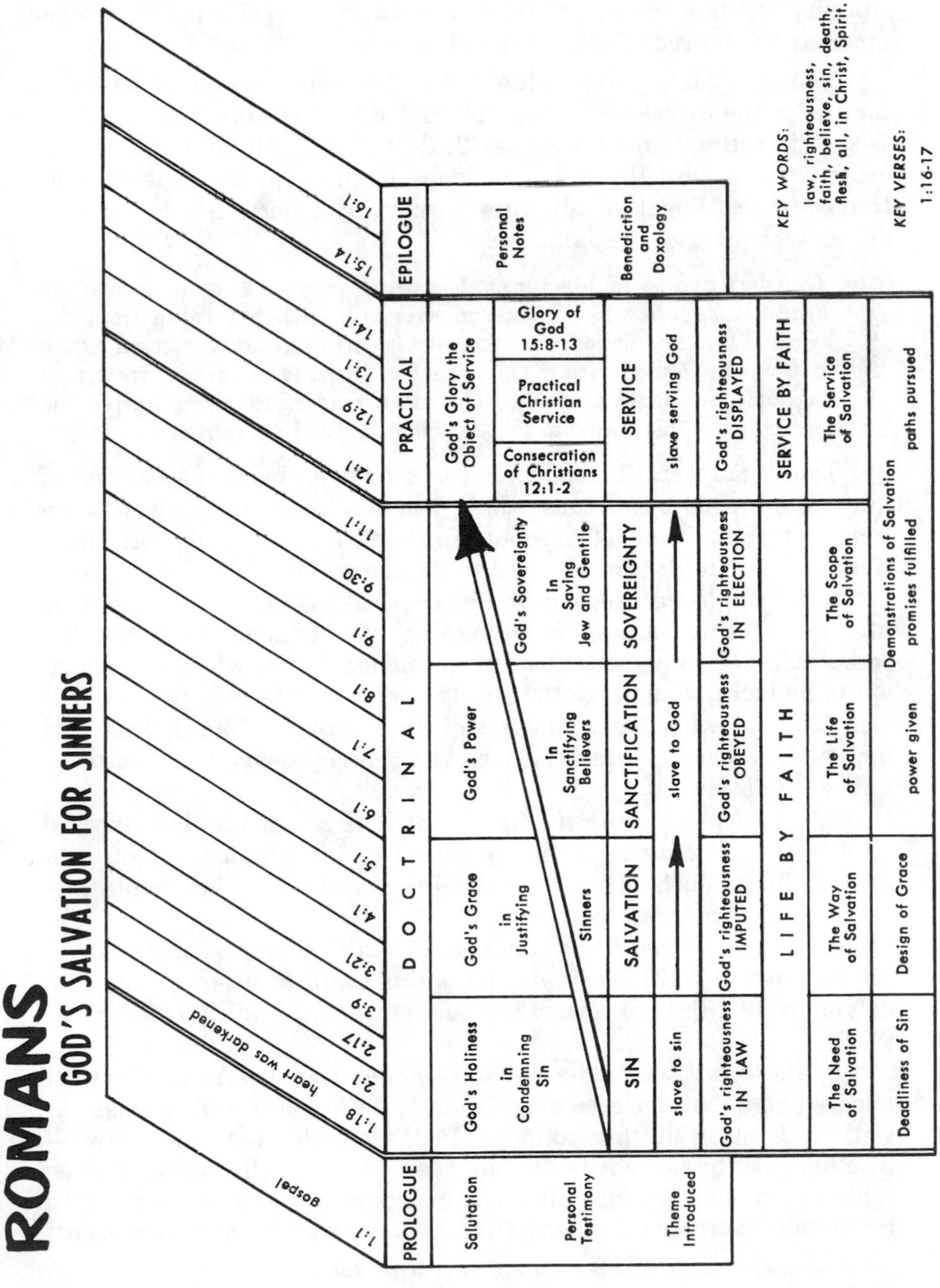

ROMANS
GOD'S SALVATION FOR SINNERS

KEY WORDS:
law, righteousness, death, faith, believe, sin, death, flesh, all, in Christ, Spirit.

KEY VERSES:
1:16-17

	PROLOGUE	DOCTRINAL			PRACTICAL	EPILOGUE
		SIN	SALVATION	SANCTIFICATION	SOVEREIGNTY	SERVICE	
Salutation		God's Holiness in Condemning Sin	God's Grace in Justifying Sinners	God's Power in Sanctifying Believers	God's Sovereignty in Saving Jew and Gentile	God's Glory the Object of Service
Personal Testimony						Glory of God 15:8-13 / Practical Christian Service / Consecration of Christians 12:1-2	Personal Notes
Theme Introduced		slave to sin		slave to God		slave serving God	Benediction and Doxology
		God's righteousness IN LAW	God's righteousness IMPUTED	God's righteousness OBEYED	God's righteousness IN ELECTION	God's righteousness DISPLAYED
		SIN	LIFE BY FAITH			SERVICE BY FAITH
		The Need of Salvation	The Way of Salvation	The Life of Salvation	The Scope of Salvation	The Service of Salvation
		Deadliness of Sin	Design of Grace	power given	Demonstrations of Salvation promises fulfilled	paths pursued

Chapter references: 1:1 gospel, 1:18, 2:1 heart was darkened, 2:17, 3:9, 3:21, 4:1, 5:1, 6:1, 7:1, 8:1, 9:1, 9:30, 11:1, 12:1, 12:9, 13:1, 14:1, 15:14, 16:1

ways (vv. 24-26), and those ways lead them into the fearful depths of iniquity pictured in verses 26-32. The wrath of God must be understood as His hatred of sin, not of the sinner.

The concluding paragraph of 1:28-32 presents the dark picture of man after the threefold "giving up" of God. The climax of this picture is seen in the statement of verse 32, that those guilty of these crimes commit them with the full knowledge of the penalty of death that they deserve. Worst of all, they rejoice in others, and encourage others who practice the same sins.

> This dark and painful picture of the pagan world . . . is a picture of the degradation into which mankind ever sinks when turning from the truth of God and no longer restrained by his grace. It was given as the reason why Paul gloried in the gospel and desired to have it proclaimed in Rome. It should arouse all Christian readers to-day to hasten the preaching of this gospel as the only hope of the human race.[3]

The pagan world is condemned in the sight of God not because of ignorance of God but because their reaction to the light given them concerning God is one of rejection, unthankfulness, vanity, presumption, and evil deeds. They are all without excuse.

2. *The self-righteous condemned* (2:1-16). The self-righteous moralist of this passage is a legalist who believes that the life acceptable to God is the zealous performance of that which *he* considers to be morally right. But the only source of infallible judgment is God Himself, who is absolutely righteous, fair, and good. And God applies His standard and declares the self-righteous moralist to be guilty for his sin.

3. *The Jew condemned* (2:17—3:8). The sin of the Jew exposed here is that of outward religion devoid of inner spirit. These religionists find their haven in formal religion and are willing to pay any price of outward worship.

4. *The whole world condemned* (3:9-20). After writing that all have sinned (3:9-12) and that such sin is totally cancerous and God defying (3:13-18), Paul clearly records the verdict "Guilty before God" (3:19).

In these last verses he not only pronounces God's final verdict upon sinners, but declares every man to be helpless and hopeless as well. It is clear at this point in Paul's epistle that God's law — whether it is the law written in the heart (2:15), or the law written on tablets of stone — cannot save a man. If such a one is to be justified there must be some other way than through such law. Paul presents

3. Charles R. Erdman, *The Epistle of Paul to the Romans*, p. 31.

that other way in the next two and a half chapters (3:21—5:21). The diagnosis of man's fatal disease has been ascribed: *the heart cannot do good* (3:12). It is not righteous, nor does it have the power to attain righteousness. In the next chapters the prescription of cure is written, telling how sinful man can be given a heart of righteousness. No diagnosis without an offer of cure — such is the method of the holy and gracious God.

B. JUSTIFICATION (3:21—5:21)

All the world is guilty before God, because all have sinned and have fallen short of God's glory. "But now," writes Paul, "a way to get right with God has been revealed . . . provided by God, through faith in Jesus Christ, for all who believe in Him" (3:21-22).[4] This is the bright message of this second main section of Romans.

Paul writes here about God's grace in justifying sinners, as he follows this train of thought:

Justification defined (3:21-31)
Justification illustrated (4:1-25)
Justification's fruits (5:1-21)

Paul writes also about three other doctrines in connection with justification. Definitions of the four divine works are given here. (Read the verses where they appear in the text of Romans.)

1. *Justification* (3:24, 26, 28). In justification God *declares* a sinner righteous on the basis of his faith in Jesus Christ. Such a believer is legally declared to be in good standing with God.

2. *Redemption* (3:24). Christ's work of redemption for a soul is the offering of His life as a ransom, to give (1) deliverance from the penalty of the law, sin as a power, and the bondage of Satan; and (2) release to a new relationship to God and a new life in Christ.

3. *Propitiation* (3:25). Propitiation is not man's appeasement of God's wrath for sin, but God's merciful provision of forgiveness for that sin (cf. Heb. 2:17). The shedding of Christ's blood effected this propitiation. Read Hebrews 9:5 and note the reference to the mercy seat, which in the Old Testament was the place where the high priest sprinkled blood to provide a sacrifice for the people's sins. The Greek word translated "mercy seat" is the same word translated "propitiation" in Romans 3:25.

4. *Remission* (3:25). In the ten appearances of this word in the New Testament (KJV), the word *sins* is always included (e.g., "remission of sins"). Remission of sins is the canceling, pardoning, passing over of sins against the soul, made possible by the shedding of blood

---

4. F. F. Bruce, *The Letters of Paul*, p. 191.

(cf. Heb. 9:22). Christ appeared "to put away sin by the sacrifice of Himself" (Heb. 9:26*b*).

Now read 3:24-25 in the light of the above definitions, and observe the interrelations of those four works of Christ on behalf of the sinner.[5] The good news for the people of the world, all of whom are guilty before God because of their sin, is that God in His grace offered His Son as a sacrifice to pay the penalty of sin. He who places his faith in Jesus Christ is counted as righteous, and therefore receives the gift of eternal life. Abraham believed God, and his faith (not works, nor religion, nor law) was counted unto him for righteousness. God accepts the sinner in the same way He accepted Abraham (4:24), and showers him with all the cherished fruits of justification, including eternal life, joy, and love (5:1-21).

C. SANCTIFICATION (6:1—8:39)

The doctrine of sanctification is one of the most practical and vital doctrines involving *every* believer. Sanctification is a work of God in three phases of the believer's experience: past, present, future. It began in his life the moment he was saved (past), when he was positionally made holy, in Christ (cf. 1 Cor. 1:2, 30). As a progressive experience it continues throughout his earthly life (present), God working in his heart, conforming him more and more to the image of Christ. The believer's sanctification is completed (future) when he is raptured and sees his Lord face to face and is made like Him (1 John 3:2).

Sanctification in the believer's present life involves the negative *separation* from evil, and the positive *setting apart* for God's worship and service. In these three chapters Paul writes mostly about this present phase of sanctification — victorious Christian living. For study, the section may be divided into three parts, as shown on Chart 64.

CHART 64

VICTORIOUS CHRISTIAN LIVING   (ROMANS 6-8)

	6:1 PRINCIPLES	7:7 PRACTICE	8:1 POWER 8:39
a key subject	surrender	self	Spirit

1. *Principles of Christian living* (6:1—7:6). The basic problem in Christian living is *sins* (the problem of *sin* having been settled once

5. The Greek translated "remission" in the KJV is translated "passed over" in the NASB.

and for all for the Christian when he was saved). In Romans 6-8 Paul is writing about sins, and the temptations that come to Christians daily to commit sins. In 6:1—7:6 he lays down the principles that should govern Christians in their everyday walk. Three such principles are:

a. Double identification (6:1-11). The Christian is identified with Christ in death *unto sin* and resurrection *unto God.* Key thoughts: dead and alive.
b. New servitude. (6:12-23). The Christian is now a bondslave of righteousness. Key thoughts: before and after.
c. Total liberation. (7:1-6). The Christian has been liberated from the old life (indictment of the law) to the new life (compulsion of the Spirit). Key thoughts: old and new.

2. *Practice of Christian living* (7:7-25). Before the new birth the Christian had only the old, corrupt nature inherited from Adam; after the new birth he has also the new, divine, spiritual nature imparted by God. The co-existence of the two natures accounts for the conflict that goes on within him when temptation comes. How is this conflict depicted in 7:14-25? What is the key to victory (7:25)?

3. *Power of Christian living* (8:1-39). Victory in the daily spiritual conflicts is possible through Christ by the power of the Holy Spirit. Observe the many truths taught about the Spirit in this chapter.

Victory today (8:1-17), glory to come (8:18-30), and fellowship with God forever (8:31-39) are the happy fruits of God's work of sanctification in the heart of the believer.

D. ISRAEL (9:1—11:36)

Paul writes about Israel in Romans to make his treatise on salvation complete. This is necessary because Israel is the special object of divine attention for practically all of Old Testament history (beginning at Genesis 12), and for much of the New Testament. Coupled with this is the fact of an indissoluble covenant extending to the end of time, which God made with Israel.

In chapters 9-11 of Romans Paul is writing especially about Israel and Gentiles as entities, not individuals. In chapters 1-8 he has discussed the salvation of individuals — Jew or Gentile. Now he can focus his attention on the salvation of the nation of true Israel by comparing it with the salvation of Gentiles.

Chart 65 shows a brief outline of this section of Romans. Follow this outline as you read the Bible text.

CHART 65

GOD'S SOVEREIGNTY IN SAVING JEW AND GENTILE

9:1	9:6	9:30 10:21	11:1	11:30 11:36
INTRODUCTION	GOD'S SOVEREIGNTY	MAN'S RESPONSIBILITY	GOD'S PURPOSE	CONCLUSION
Paul's Concern for Israel	(over Jew and Gentile)	(Jew and Gentile)	for ISRAEL (related to Gentile)	God's Purpose for Mankind

In chapters 9-11, when writing about the Jews, Paul moves chronologically in the direction shown on Chart 66.

CHART 66

PAUL WRITES ABOUT THE JEWS

PAST ⟶	PRESENT ⟶	FUTURE
(Israel Selected) (9:6-29)	(Israel Rejected) (9:30—10:21)	(Israel Accepted) (11:1-29)

Paul shows in each successive chapter that "the key to all of God's *past* dealings with Israel is the *sovereignty* of God; that the key to all God's *present* dealings with Israel is the *salvation* of God; and that the key to all God's *promised* dealings with Israel is the *sincerity* of God."[6]

There is also a progression in the expression of Paul's feelings for Israel at these three junctions in this section:

1. Heaviness — "great sorrow and unceasing grief" (9:2).
2. Desire — "My heart's desire and prayer to God for Israel is, that they might be saved" (10:1, KJV).
3. Hope — "God has not rejected His people" (11:2).

God has not finished His dealings with Israel. Their present rejection by God is neither total (11:1-10) nor final (11:11-32). Partial blindness of Israel will persist "until the full number of the Gentiles has come in" (11:25, NIV; cf. Acts 15:14-18). Christ will return to earth at that time, to deliver Israel (11:26-27).

Chart 67 shows Israel in relation to the present church age.

---

6. John Phillips, *Exploring Romans*, p. 143.

CHART 67

ISRAEL IN RELATION TO THE CHURCH AGE

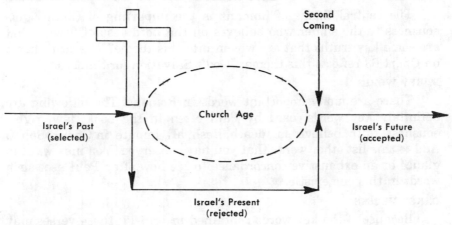

E. CHRISTIAN CONDUCT (12:1—15:13)

This division of Romans, entitled *practical* on Chart 63 (p. 253), contains a host of valuable exhortations and commands for everyday Christian conduct. Use Chart 68 as a guide in your study of the segments.

CHART 68

PRACTICAL CHRISTIAN SERVICE ROMANS 12:1-15:13

12:1	12:3	12:9 12:21	13:1	13:8	13:11 13:14	14:1			15:8 15:13
	Christian Servant		Christian Citizen			Christian Brother			
						Christian's Position on Questioned Practices			
							14:13	15:1	
Introduction	Gifts for Service	Obligations to Others	Subjection to Authorities	Attitude of Love	Armor of Light	Principle of Liberty (tolerance)	Principle of Love (care)	Example of Christ (obedience)	Conclusion
Consecration of Christian									Glory of God

V. Theme, Key Words and Verses

A. THEME

The central theme of Romans is the imparting of God's righteousness to the sinner who believes on the Lord Jesus Christ. What are some key truths that are woven into this theme? The title shown on Chart 63 reflects this theme: "God's Salvation for Sinners."

B. KEY WORDS

There are many important words in Romans. The following are definitely key words, used by Paul often in the book: law, righteousness, faith, believe, sin, death, flesh, all, impute, in Christ, Spirit. Add to this list other words that you have observed. You may want to glance at an exhaustive concordance to see how often Paul uses such words in this one epistle.

C. KEY VERSES

Because of the key words contained in 1:16-17, these verses may be considered key verses for Romans. What other key verses did you observe in your survey?

VI. Applications

Record a list of applications to daily living that you have observed in Romans. Include what the letter assures the believer regarding the *power* to live pleasing to God.

VII. Review Questions

1. In what three ways does Paul identify himself in 1:1?
2. When and where was Romans written? To whom?
3. Why did Paul write this letter?
4. How many chapters are there in Romans? Name the four main divisions.
5. Where (chapter, verse) does the practical division begin?
6. Complete the outline of the epistle:
   SIN; _____ ; _____ ; _____ : _____ .
7. What key verses represent the theme of Romans? State the theme, in your own words.
8. Name five key words of Romans.
9. Where is the Israel section in Romans? Why is this subject included in the letter?
10. Define justification, redemption, propitiation, remission, sanctification.

VIII. Further Study

1. Go through the entire letter to the Romans and make a list of the various doctrines that are taught (e.g., justification).

2. With the help of outside sources study the subject of Israel in Bible prophecy, especially concerning the end times.

IX. Outline

ROMANS: God's Salvation for Sinners

PROLOGUE	1:1-17
DOCTRINE	1:18—11:36
God's Holiness in Condemning Sin	1:18—3:20
God's Grace in Justifying Sinners	3:21—5:21
God's Power in Sanctifying Believers	6:1—8:39
God's Sovereignty in Saving Jew and Gentile	9:1—11:36
PRACTICE	12:1—15:13
The Christian Servant	12:1-21
The Christian Citizen	13:1-14
The Christian Brother	14:1—15:13
EPILOGUE	15:14—16:27

X. Selected Reading

GENERAL INTRODUCTION

Harrison, Everett F. *Introduction to the New Testament*, pp. 280-92.

Hiebert, D. Edmond. *An Introduction to the Pauline Epistles*, pp. 164-205.

Mickelsen, A. Berkeley. "The Epistle to the Romans." In *The Wycliffe Bible Commentary*, pp. 1179-83. A comprehensive outline of the epistle is included.

Scroggie, W. Graham, *Know Your Bible*, 2:162-75.

COMMENTARIES

Bruce, F. F. *The Epistle of Paul to the Romans.*

Erdman, Charles R. *The Epistle of Paul to the Romans.*

Hodge, Charles. *Commentary on the Epistle to the Romans.*

Newell, William R. *Romans Verse by Verse.*

OTHER RELATED SOURCES

Bruce, F. F. *The Letters of Paul.*

Chafer, L. S. *He That Is Spiritual.* Discussion of sanctification.

Walvoord, J. F. *Israel in Prophecy.*

Wuest, Kenneth S. *Romans in the Greek New Testament.*

12

The Corinthian Letters

1 Corinthians: Problems of a Local Church
2 Corinthians: Paul's Apostolic Ministry

The Corinthian letters immediately follow Romans in the New Testament canon, though in point of time they were written just before Romans (see Chart 1, p. 20). Their location in the canon shows a topical progression when one considers *general emphases*.[1] Observe how this is shown in the accompanying diagram.

THE GOSPEL OF JESUS CHRIST

NEW TESTAMENT ORDER	EMPHASES
GOSPELS ACTS	HISTORICAL FACTS
ROMANS	INTERPRETATIONS
1 and 2 CORINTHIANS	APPLICATIONS

The Corinthian letters *apply* the Roman letter's *interpretations* of the historical books' *facts*. Seen from another view, the church, which is the subject of the Corinthian letters, is the outcome of salvation, which is the subject of Romans.

I. PREPARATION FOR STUDY

A. PAUL'S JOURNEYS

Review Paul's missionary journeys and his ministry of writing New Testament letters (Chapter 7). This will help you see clearly just

---

1. This observation holds only in the large, overall sense. For example, there is much interpretation in the gospels and Acts, just as there is much application in Romans and much interpretation in the Corinthian letters.

where the Corinthian letters fit in the chronological sequence of his writings. It will help to adjust your perspective, having just studied Romans.

B. THE LOCAL CHURCH

The Corinthian letters, especially 1 Corinthians, focus on the operations of the local church. Observe in an exhaustive concordance how often the word *church(es)* appears in the letters. Reflect on the importance of this vital organism of God's working. New Testament references to *church* are of three different kinds:

1. *Invisible church* — all believers, whether alive or dead, who are members of Christ's Body. (Read Ephesians 1:22-23; 5:23, 25-27.)
2. *Visible church at large* — a constituency of all believers living at any one time (Acts 8:3; cf. "churches" in Acts 9:31).
3. *Visible local church* — a fellowship of believers who worship in a given locality (e.g., Corinth, 1 Cor. 1:2). It is possible for persons to have their names on the membership roll of a church, and not be believers (cf. Rev. 2-3).

A local church, such as the church of Corinth, is a geographically confined fellowship of believers, a visible outworking of the invisible church. It is important to have clearly in mind just what the invisible church is and whom it comprises. Read 1 Corinthians 10:32, and note the reference to three groups: Jews, Gentiles, and the church of God.[2] Chart 69 identifies these in the stream of the human race.[3] Refer to this chart in the discussion that follows.

In the early generations of the human race there were no group distinctions, such as Jew and Gentile. All the descendants of Adam were as one family, "children of men," and God spoke to the whole race, seeking to get all people to obey Him and fellowship with Him. The race as a whole refused to do this, although there were some individuals who responded acceptably. Men persisted in doing their own will rather than God's will, and they became utterly rebellious and disobedient. God allowed men to go on in their self-chosen ways.

But from the multitudes of the world living around 2000 B.C. God selected one man, Abraham. From him He made a nation that was to be His chosen people, special representatives to whom and through

---

2. Most Bible versions, including NASB, do not distinguish between the visible church and invisible church by the printing of the word *church*. (This is true also of the original Greek autographs.) In all of those versions the translator used the small letter *c*. The student must determine from the context what church is meant.

3. If Chart 69 included events of the last days, it would recognize Paul's prophecy of the rebirth of Israel (cf. Rom. 11:26).

whom He could speak and act. The top line of Chart 69 represents the descendants of Abraham, known as Jews or Israelites. The name Gentiles shown on the bottom line represents all other people.

CHART 69

THE STREAM OF THE HUMAN RACE

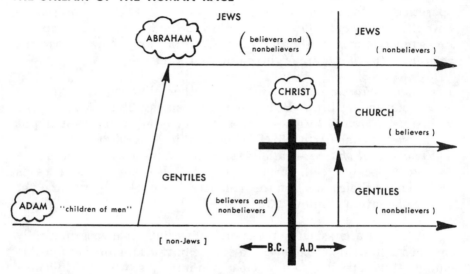

Not all Jews were believers, just as not all Gentiles were unbelievers. For nearly two thousand years God patiently dealt with that chosen nation of Israel and sought to get more than just a remnant to obey and represent Him. But the nation as a whole repeatedly refused to do that, although there were individual Israelites who obeyed. The nation became so corrupt and rebellious that God allowed them to go on in their self-chosen ways. The pattern was the same as for the human race before the time of Abraham.

Finally the day came when God sent His only begotten Son into the world, to redeem lost sinners (whether Jew or Gentile) and form a new, unique people, the church, Christ's Body (1 Cor. 12:27). That invisible church is composed of all twice-born men, women, and children, who have received a divine nature from God upon believing on Jesus Christ as their Savior.

Not long after Christ's death, resurrection, and ascension, the Holy Spirit came down from heaven to indwell and empower the first members of that church. From the very beginning the believers at Jerusalem worshiped together as a local church, and when some moved to other cities, they started local churches there. And all the local churches together made up the visible church at large. The visible church at large is God's representative body of Christians on earth today, through whom He speaks to nonbelieving Jews and nonbelieving Gentiles.

II. BACKGROUND OF THE CORINTHIAN LETTERS

Ancient Corinth was very similar to today's large cities of the world. It was a busy, cosmopolitan, commercial center known by all. The first Christian church of Corinth had an equally strong likeness to many urban churches of today. As you anticipate surveying the Corinthian letters try to *visualize* the setting of those letters. In doing so you will find it very easy and natural to apply their teachings to the twentieth century. Assuredly the letters were written not only for a local congregation of one generation, but for Christians everywhere, throughout the entire Christian age.

A. CORINTH: THE CITY AND ITS PEOPLE

When Paul visited Corinth for the first time in A.D. 50 on his second missionary journey, he must have been impressed by its stately buildings and bustling commerce. This Greek city was widely acclaimed as the hub of the Roman Empire's commerce, a strategic position that Paul no doubt coveted for the advantage of propagating the gospel of Jesus Christ.

The following descriptions will help you appreciate what Paul saw, learned, and experienced concerning the city and its people.

1. *Name.* The Greek name *Korinthos* means "ornament."

2. *Geography.* Observe on Map R the strategic location of Corinth on the four-mile-wide isthmus between the Ionian and Aegean seas.[4] Shippers moving cargo between Italy and Asia Minor via Corinth avoided the dangerous voyage around the southern tip of Greece. Small ships were moved across the isthmus by tramway, or cargo of the larger ships was transferred to transports waiting at the eastern port.[5]

3. *History.* Corinth's ancient history revolves around two events: (1) the destruction of the old city by the Roman general Mummius, 146 B.C.; and (2) the rebuilding of the city by Julius Caesar, with its gaining of status as a Roman colony, 46 B.C. How old, then, was the new city when Paul first visited it?

---

4. For the geographical setting of Corinth on Paul's three missionary journeys, see Map L, p. 207.

5. For an excellent description of the sights that Paul saw on his first visit to Corinth, consult Charles F. Pfeiffer and Howard F. Vos, *The Wycliffe Historical Geography of Bible Lands*, pp. 477-87.

4. *Population*. Estimates of size in Paul's day vary from 100,000 to 700,000. There was a mixture of races (Roman, Greek, Oriental) and a large distribution of mobile occupations (e.g., sailors and businessmen). A very large proportion of its population was composed of slaves.

GEOGRAPHY OF CORINTH,   Map R
SHOWING CORINTHIAN GULF AND CANAL

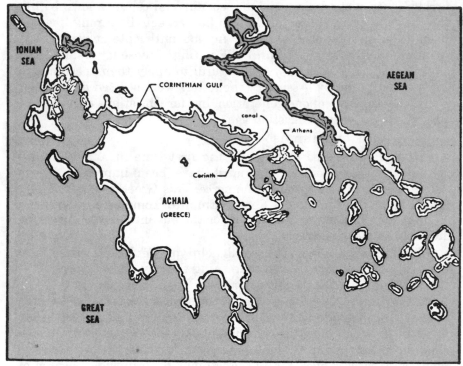

5. *Political status*. Corinth was a Roman colony, the capital of the province of Achaia. Gallio was proconsul of the province during Paul's visit (Acts 18:12).

6. *Moral condition*. The depraved character of the old city of Corinth, exemplified by prostitute priestesses serving in the temple of Aphrodite,[6] goddess of beauty and love, was carried over into the new city of New Testament times. The very Greek word *korinthiazomai* ("to act the Corinthian") came to mean "to commit fornication." One writer has described Corinth as "a seaman's paradise, a drunkard's heaven, and a virtuous woman's hell."[7]

---

6. This Greek goddess was identified with the Roman goddess Venus.
7. Joseph M. Gettys, *How to Study 1 Corinthians*, p. 10.

7. *Activities.*

a. Commerce. Movement of shipping across the isthmus was Corinth's number one business. Some of its own manufactured products included items of pottery and brass.

b. Education. Study of the arts and sciences flourished. There were studios of language and schools of philosophy. Yet Paul, raised in the environment of the university at Tarsus, and trained under the great teacher Gamaliel, was keen to detect an intellectualism that was both smug and superficial. (Read some of Paul's references to knowledge and wisdom in such passages as 1 Corinthians 1:20-21, 27; 2:1-8).

c. Sports. Corinth was a famous sports center, with its Isthmian Games (similar in some ways to the Olympics) held every two years. It is interesting to observe that corruption in sports events was widespread at that time.[8] (Read Paul's references to sports in 1 Corinthians 9:24-27).

d. Religion. Corinth was a city of many gods and various cults. Judaism was one of its Oriental religions. The Jews' synagogue was Paul's favorite place of contact for reaching people with the gospel message when he first arrived in Corinth (see Acts 18:1-4).

B. THE FIRST CONTACT OF PAUL WITH THE CORINTHIANS

Read Acts 18:1-18a for the historical record of Paul's first evangelistic ministry in Corinth. This visit took place on the apostle's second missionary journey, A.D. 50. Answer the following questions on the basis of the Bible text.

1. Does the text indicate when Aquila and Priscilla were converted to Christ? Read these other New Testament references to this couple, and try to decide when they might have become believers (if they were not already believers when Paul first met them, Acts 18:2): Acts 18:18b, 26; Romans 16:3; 1 Corinthians 16:19; 2 Timothy 4:19.

2. What different verbs of the Acts passage are used to describe Paul's *word* ministry (e.g., "reasoned," v. 4)?

3. To what different groups did Paul minister?

4. What were the different reactions to Paul's message? How many conversions were there?

5. Account for Paul's action of verse 6.

6. What do you think constituted Paul's "teaching the word of God" (18:11)?

7. One of the important things Paul did while in Corinth was to

---

8. Pfeiffer and Vos, *Wycliffe Historical Geography*, p. 485.

write the two epistles to the Thessalonians.[9] Read 2 Thessalonians
3:1-2 for references to Paul's ministry at Corinth at this time. (Cf. 1
Thess. 2:15.)

C. THE FIRST CHURCH OF CORINTH

The organized church at Corinth began around A.D. 50 as a small
nucleus of believers, most of whom were Gentiles (e.g., Justus, Acts
18:7); and some of whom were Jews (e.g., Crispus, Acts 18:8). Their
meeting place from the start might have been an upper chamber of
the house of one of the group, such as Crispus.

Most of the members were probably of the poorer or middle-class
strata (cf. 1 Cor. 1:26 ff., which only suggests this observation).

The church members were slow to mature in their Christian faith
and conduct (cf. 1 Cor. 3:1 ff.). That was part of the heavy burden
borne by Paul, which he referred to as "the care of all the churches" (2
Cor. 11:28). Apollos was the church's pastor-teacher for part of the
time between Paul's second and third missionary journeys. (Read Acts
18:24—19:1. Also read the seven references to Apollos in 1 Corinthians 1:12; 3:4-6, 22; 4:6; 16:12. The last reference concerns a
proposed second tour of duty by Apollos in Corinth.)

First Corinthians 1:12 and 9:5 suggest only the *possibility* that
Peter may have ministered to the church at Corinth.

D. CONTACTS AFTER THE FIRST VISIT AND BEFORE THE FIRST EPISTLE

Two possible contacts that Paul had with the Corinthian converts
after his first visit and before writing 1 Corinthians were these:[10]

1. A short visit to Corinth to combat an incipient opposition to
the apostle's ministry and to correct other evils. Apparently his
mission was not effective.[11] (Read 2 Corinthians 2:1; 12:14; 13:1-2.
Note the reference to a forthcoming "third time" visit.)

2. A letter referred to in 1 Corinthians 5:9. At least part of the
letter was written to correct existing evils in the church. The letter is
not part of the New Testament canon and was therefore not divinely
inspired Scripture.[12]

---

9. There was probably an interim of a few months between the writings of the two
epistles.

10. Different views are held on this obscure subject, because of the relative silence
of the New Testament. You might want to consult various authors for a full discussion.

11. This unrecorded visit is placed before 1 Corinthians by A. T. Robertson and A.
Plummer, *First Epistle of St. Paul to the Corinthians*, pp. xxi-xxv; and by Henry Alford,
The Greek Testament, 2:52-54. The visit is placed after 1 Corinthians by Merrill
Tenney, *New Testament Survey*, p. 298; and by S. Lewis Johnson, "First Corinthians"
in *The Wycliffe Bible Commentary*, p. 1228.

12. Paul obviously wrote many letters in his lifetime besides those that were
inspired.

III. BACKGROUND OF 1 CORINTHIANS

A. TIME AND PLACE WRITTEN

Paul wrote this letter on his third missionary journey, toward the end of his three-year ministry in the city of Ephesus (1 Cor. 16:8).[13] The year of writing was A.D. 55. Read Acts 19:1-20 for a description of the very fruitful work he was doing at Ephesus, in the power of God, while in absentia he was trying to help the Corinthian church with its problems.

B. OCCASION

Paul was a traveling evangelist who took to heart the follow-up work of nurturing the young converts whom he had led to Christ. He learned of the Corinthians' problems through reports (see 1:11 and 5:1) and inquiries (7:1, 25; 8:1; 11:2; 12:1; 15:1; 16:1) originating with members and leaders of the church (cf. 1 Cor. 16:17.) If he had already made a short visit since founding the church, he also knew of some of the problems firsthand.

C. PURPOSES

Among Paul's purposes in writing one of his longest letters were these: (1) to identify the basic problems underlying the reports and inquiries; (2) to offer solutions by way of doctrine and example; (3) to give extended teaching on related doctrines; (4) to give at least a short defense of his apostleship; (5) to exhort the believers in the ways of a full, mature Christian life. One writer has called the book, "The Epistle of Sanctification."

D. STYLE

Alford describes Paul's style with these words:

> The depths of the spiritual, the moral, the intellectual, the physical world are open to him. He summons to his aid the analogies of nature. He enters minutely into the varieties of human infirmity and prejudice. . . . He praises, reproves, exhorts, and teaches. Where he strikes, he heals. His large heart holding all, where he has grieved any, he grieves likewise; where it is in his power to give joy, he first overflows with joy himself.[14]

E. AUTHENTICITY

First Corinthians is one of the best-attested epistles as to authorship and unity of content.

---

13. See Acts 20:31; see Acts 19:8, 10 for the time element.
14. Henry Alford, *The Greek Testament*, 2:57.

IV. SURVEY OF 1 CORINTHIANS

A. FIRST READINGS

By now you have established some patterns for surveying a Bible book, so all the various steps will not be repeated here nor in the chapters that follow. Be sure to include:

1. first quick scanning, followed by a slower scanning
2. observing of key words, phrases, atmosphere
3. assigning segment titles (For 1 Corinthians each chapter is a new segment, with these two changes: 11:2 replaces 11:1 as a beginning, and chapter 1 may be divided into two segments: 1:1-9 and 1:10-31.)
4. comparing the beginning and end of the book
5. looking for turning points, progressions, and climax, if any.

B. CORRELATIONS

You can move out in various directions in your study from this point on. Some "search missions" are suggested below. Your ultimate aim, of course, should be to correlate all your observations into one overall picture of 1 Corinthians. (Note: Be sure to read every Bible reference cited below.)

1. Look for groupings of chapters according to a common subject. A clue to this is Paul's use of phrases such as, "I have been informed" (1:11; 5:1) and "Now concerning" (7:1, 25; 8:1; 12:1; 16:1 [cf. 11:2]). Actually, as to general structure, 1 Corinthians is one of the simplest of Paul's epistles. Justify the twofold outline shown on Chart 70: *acknowledging reports; answering inquiries.* What kinds of problems are discussed in chapters 1-6? What kinds of questions are discussed in chapters 7-15?

2. How do 1:1-9 and 16:1-24 serve as introduction and conclusion, respectively?

3. First Corinthians is one of the most practical of all Paul's epistles. Make a note of all the problems explicitly mentioned by Paul in the epistle. Group those according to common subject, and compare your conclusions with the outlines of Chart 70.

4. After recognizing a problem in the Corinthian church, Paul offers solutions, including examples of his own personal experiences. As you survey the chapters of this letter, keep aware of these three subjects: problems, solutions, examples.

5. Go through the epistle and mark in your Bible every block of positive doctrine, contrasted with the discussions of the various evils

of the Corinthian church. (The length of each block will vary from a paragraph to more than a chapter.) Note also where Paul gives personal testimony.

6. What chapters would you consider key chapters for the particular subjects they present?

7. What primary doctrines of the gospel appear from time to time throughout the epistle? Did you notice, for example, references to the death of Christ? (Check a concordance for the twelve direct references to this subject under these words: blood, cross, crucified, died, sacrificed.)

8. How would you describe the style of this epistle? Writers have observed that it is the most varied of all Paul's epistles. It ranges from the informal, conversational style, to a "lofty and sustained solemnity."[15] Did you observe in your reading such literary devices as logic, poetry, narration, exposition, and the frequent use of questions?

C. SURVEY CHART

Study the survey chart, Chart 70. Observe the following:

1. There are three groups of problems. How do they differ from each other?

2. The three cited guides in the solution of problems are verses of chapter 15. How does each verse help in solving spiritual problems of Christians?

3. Why do you think Paul discussed questions about the resurrection body last in the letter?

4. Note the title on the chart. Someone has said that "no epistle tells us so much about the life of a primitive local church." If a title was made to include the solutions to the church's problems, a key phrase might be "Victory through Christ" (15:57).

V. PROMINENT SUBJECTS OF 1 CORINTHIANS

A. PROBLEMS OF A CONGREGATION (1:10—6:20)

Paul deals with four main problems, identified by the following five passages, in these chapters:

1. Divisions within the membership (1:10—4:21). How does 1:12 identify one quarrel?
2. Church's neglect of the problem of fornication (5:1-8).
3. Evil fellowship (5:9-13).
4. Lawsuits in the public courts (6:1-11).
5. Libertine attitude concerning fornication (6:12-20).

---

15. Ibid.

CHART 70

1 CORINTHIANS

PROBLEMS OF A LOCAL CHURCH

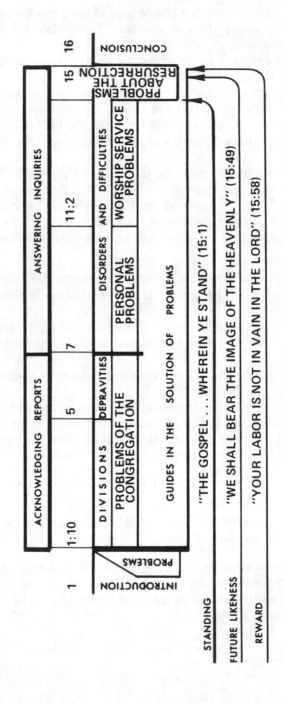

INTRODUCTION

PROBLEMS

ACKNOWLEDGING REPORTS

ANSWERING INQUIRIES

CONCLUSION

1   1:10   5   7   11:2   15   16

DIVISIONS   DEPRAVITIES   DISORDERS AND DIFFICULTIES

PROBLEMS OF THE CONGREGATION

PERSONAL PROBLEMS

WORSHIP SERVICE PROBLEMS

PROBLEMS ABOUT THE RESURRECTION

GUIDES IN THE SOLUTION OF PROBLEMS

STANDING   "THE GOSPEL . . . WHEREIN YE STAND" (15:1)

FUTURE LIKENESS   "WE SHALL BEAR THE IMAGE OF THE HEAVENLY" (15:49)

REWARD   "YOUR LABOR IS NOT IN VAIN IN THE LORD" (15:58)

KEY WORDS: LOVE, RESURRECTION, CROSS, SPIRIT, BODY, GIFTS, CORRUPTION, WISDOM

KEY VERSE: 15:57

The severity of Paul's reproof (e.g., "I say this to your shame," 6:5) is an indication of the awfulness of the spiritual cancers that plagued the church he founded.

B. MARRIAGE (7:1-40)

G. Campbell Morgan correctly observes that no attempt is made in 1 Corinthians to state the Christian doctrine of marriage in its fullness and completeness.[16] Besides, false conclusions are easily made from chapter 7 if the local Corinthian situation and the larger context of Paul's epistles are not recognized. Let us look at these briefly.

1. *Local Corinthian situation.* We do not know exactly how the Corinthians' questions were worded. If we did, some of the difficult aspects of chapter 7 might disappear. For example, the Corinthians' former heathen exaltation of celibacy could have prompted them to ask Paul if celibacy for Christians was not the state that all Christians should cherish. To which Paul's reply was, "[True,] . . . it is good for a man not to touch a woman, [*nevertheless,*] . . . let each man have his own wife, and let each woman have her own husband. [Because if this normal pattern for the human race is broken, fornication is inevitable]" (7:1).

Another local situation about which we can only speculate is the kind and extent of "distress" (7:26) that was threatening the Corinthian Christians at that time. It could very well have been severe persecution, in which case Paul's counsel to the Corinthians was to postpone marriage for the time being (e.g., 7:26-27).

In studying chapter 7 it must also be remembered that sexual immorality ("fornication") was an evil threatening the very survival of the Corinthian church. That problem must have had much to do with how Paul answered the questions about marriage.

2. *Paul's full teaching on marriage.* A reading of all Paul's letters reveals that the apostle commended marriage as a high and holy estate. Read, for example, Ephesians 5:22-23. In 1 Timothy 4:3 Paul speaks of "forbidding to marry" as a doctrine of demons (4:1). In 1 Corinthians 7:12-16 Paul discusses the problems of mixed marriages with unbelievers. In 2 Corinthians 6:14 his advice is that the unmarried Christian can avoid such problems by not marrying an unbeliever. Many other references outside 1 Corinthians could be cited here.

C. CHRISTIAN LIBERTY (8:1—11:1)

This long section of the letter concerns a delicate situation the

16. G. Campbell Morgan, *The Corinthian Letters of Paul*, p. 65.

material object of which is neutral or non-moral. The Corinthians' question was, May we as believers eat meat that has been offered in sacrifice unto idols (see 8:4)? Meat of itself is amoral, that is, neither right nor wrong. But could a Corinthian Christian go to a meat market sponsored by a heathen temple and buy meat that had been left over from a heathen sacrifice? Was this associating himself anew with the former life of heathenism? Did the Corinthian believer have to consider what *other people* (especially immature believers) would think if he did that, even though both he and God knew that he had no intention of fellowship in the heathen circle? Those were some of the things that were on Paul's mind as he formulated this lengthy discourse on what must have been a stormy issue in the Corinthian congregation. Its application to similar problems of Christian living today is both clear and vital.

The outline of Chart 71 shows how Paul teaches and exhorts concerning the problem. Read the chapters and observe the *specific* things Paul wrote, within each group of *principles*.

D. SPIRITUAL GIFTS (11:2—14:40)

After dealing with problems of worship and service concerning veiled women (11:2-16) and abused communion service (11:17-34), Paul writes three chapters about operations of the church in its gospel ministry.

- Chapter 12 is about spiritual gifts, or divinely endowed capacities for service.
- Chapter 14 compares two of these gifts (prophecy and tongues).
- Chapter 13 is the classic treatise on love, the grace that makes gifts fruitful.

Read 14:1 and observe how the subjects of each of the three chapters are represented by the verse. (Note: The order of chapters given above is a logical order. Scan the three chapters and determine why Paul inserted chapter 13 in the middle.)

The lists of gifts found in chapter 12 are not exhaustive. Read Romans 12:6-8 and Ephesians 4:11, and keep those lists in mind as you study 1 Corinthians 12. Also read these related passages: Romans 1:11; 12:6; 1 Corinthians 4:7; 2 Timothy 1:6; Hebrews 2:4; 1 Peter 4:10.

In chapter 14 Paul compares two spiritual gifts that were being exercised in the church at Corinth: (1) prophecy — the divine gift of revealing the will of God, meeting the need that later was to be filled by the written New Testament; (2) tongues — the divine gift of expressing praises to God in words unintelligible to the hearers. The words are intelligible to those who have been given the gift of interpretation (12:10).

CHART 71

1 CORINTHIANS 8:1-11:1

HOW TO KEEP YOUR CHRISTIAN LIBERTY FROM BECOMING A STUMBLING BLOCK TO OTHERS (8:9)

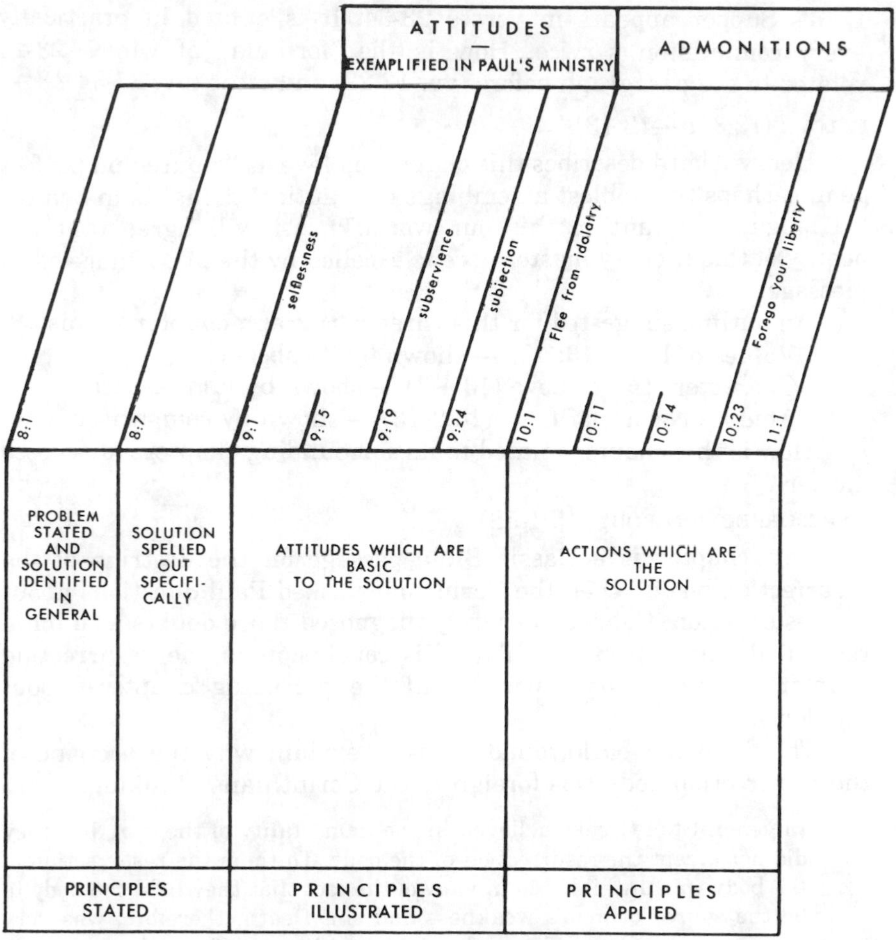

ATTITUDES — EXEMPLIFIED IN PAUL'S MINISTRY			ADMONITIONS	

Labels: selflessness, subservience, subjection, Flee from idolatry, Forego your liberty

References: 8:1, 8:7, 9:1, 9:15, 9:19, 9:24, 10:1, 10:11, 10:14, 10:23, 11:1

PROBLEM STATED AND SOLUTION IDENTIFIED IN GENERAL	SOLUTION SPELLED OUT SPECIFICALLY	ATTITUDES WHICH ARE BASIC TO THE SOLUTION	ACTIONS WHICH ARE THE SOLUTION
PRINCIPLES STATED		PRINCIPLES ILLUSTRATED	PRINCIPLES APPLIED

The structure of chapter 14 is shown by Chart 72. Read the chapter through once, underlining strong words and repeated words. Note, for example, every reference to edification. What is the main point of each paragraph? Compare your observations on this with the keynotes shown on Chart 72.

The first four paragraphs (14:1-25) compare the gifts of speaking in tongues and prophesying and show how the latter gift excels.[17]

The two paragraphs of 14:26-36 give instructions regarding the order of the worship service, especially with reference to the two spiritual gifts.

E. LORD'S SUPPER (11:17-34)

The fullest statement of the New Testament ordinance of the Lord's Supper appears in verses 23-34. It is quoted in practically every communion service. How is the "formula" of verses 23-26 related to the paragraph before (vv. 17-22) and after (vv. 27-34)?

F. LOVE (12:31*b*—13:13)

Henry Alford describes this chapter on love as "a pure and perfect gem, perhaps the noblest assemblage of beautiful thoughts in beautiful language extant in this our world."[18] All will agree that the beauty of this literary masterpiece is excelled by the importance of its message.

An outline suggested for this three-paragraph chapter is this:

　　Values of Love (13:1-3) — shown by its absence
　　Characteristics of Love (13:4-7) — shown by its presence
　　Abiding Nature of Love (13:8-13) — shown by comparison

How is this chapter related to its surrounding chapters (discussed earlier)?

G. RESURRECTION BODY (15:1-58)

This chapter is a classic Bible passage on the doctrine of the resurrection body. When the Corinthians asked Paul questions about the resurrection, the apostle surely diagnosed those doubts as a main root of all their problems. Thus his conclusion to the resurrection chapter is also a conclusion to all the preceding chapters about problems.

The following background helps to explain why the doctrine of the resurrection body was foreign to the Corinthians' thinking:

> In general the Greeks believed in the immortality of the soul, but they did not accept the resurrection of the body. To them the resurrection of the body was unthinkable in view of the fact that they held the body to be the source of man's weakness and sin. Death, therefore, was very welcome, since by it the soul would be liberated from the body; but

---

17. Observe in the lists of chapter 12 how the gift of tongues is always cited last: 12:10, 28, 30.
18. Henry Alford, *The Greek Testament*, 2:57.

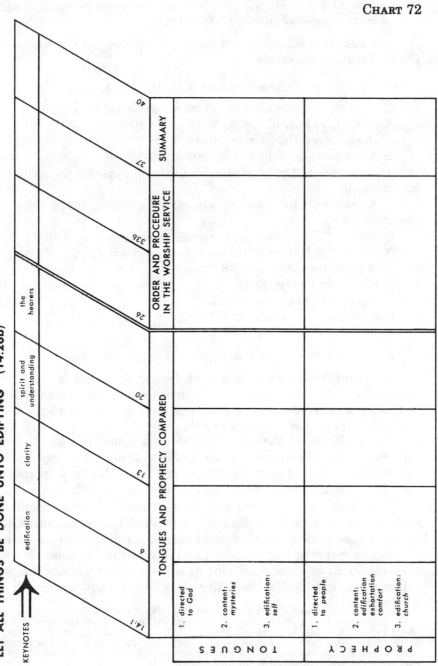

1 CORINTHIANS 14:1-40
"LET ALL THINGS BE DONE UNTO EDIFYING" (14:26b)

KEYNOTES

edification | clarity | spirit and understanding | the hearers

TONGUES AND PROPHECY COMPARED | ORDER AND PROCEDURE IN THE WORSHIP SERVICE | SUMMARY

TONGUES
1. directed to God
2. content: mysteries
3. edification: self

PROPHECY
1. directed to people
2. content: edification exhortation comfort
3. edification: church

resurrection was not welcome, because this would constitute another descent of the soul into the grave of the body.[19]

The following outline shows the approach Paul took in answering the Corinthians' questions.

The resurrection body (15:1-58)

Question: "Is there a resurrection of the dead?" (15:12)
Answer: The Fact of the Bodily Resurrection (15:1-34)
1. Declaration: Christ was raised, 1-11
2. Argument: Saints shall be raised, 12-19
3. Declaration: Christ was raised, giving hope for the believer's future, 20-28
4. Argument: Christ was raised, giving meaning to the believer's present, 29-34
Question: "With what body are the dead raised?" (15:35)
Answer: The Nature of the Resurrection Body (15:35-57)
1. Supernatural body, 35-38
2. Heavenly image, 39-49
3. Incorruptible character, 50-57
Conclusion: "Be steadfast" (15:58)

VI. SUMMARY AND THEME OF 1 CORINTHIANS

In 1 Corinthians Paul makes an honest diagnosis of the young church of Corinth, and he shows solutions for its problems and shares testimony so that the young congregation that he founded can be restored to its former spiritual health.

The problems of the congregation as a group include disunity, sophisticated intellectualism, neglect of discipline of its members, evil fellowships, and civil lawsuits. Those are the problems "reported" to Paul by concerned believers in the church (1:10—6:20).

Then there are personal problems of the individual members, problems about which the church wrote Paul for his counsel (7:1—15:58). Those involve the responsibilities of marriage, the question of whether to marry or not to marry, and whether to eat meat that had been sacrificed to idols. Paul also answers questions about the worship service, specifically about the place of man and woman in the

---

19. S. Lewis Johnson, "First Corinthians" in *The Wycliffe Bible Commentary*, p. 1255. Among the Greek philosophers, Epicureans denied any existence beyond death; Stoics held that death brought a merging of the soul in deity, and so a loss of personality; Platonists absolutely denied bodily resurrection. It is possible also that some of the Jewish converts of the Corinthian church had been influenced by the Sadducees' denial of resurrection (cf. Acts 23:8).

service, abuses of the Lord's table, and an evaluation of spiritual gifts in the ministry of the gospel.

Paul devotes the last chapter of the main body of the epistle to the cardinal doctrine of the Christian faith: the resurrection. Every church has its problems, but what about man's most desperate plight — the appointment with death? Resurrection "in Christ" (15:22) is Paul's answer, and it is that truth that brings the apostle to the peak of the epistle, in the praise, "thanks be to God, who gives us the victory through our Lord Jesus Christ" (15:57), coupled with the appeal to be "steadfast, immovable, always abounding in the work of the Lord" (15:58).

How would you identify the theme of 1 Corinthians, in one sentence? From that theme derive a title.

VII. Key Words and Verses of 1 Corinthians

What key words and verses did you observe in the course of your survey? Compare those with the ones listed on Chart 70. Related to the key word *cross*, there are fourteen direct references to Calvary in the letter, in words such as "crucified," "died." Hence the book has been called "the epistle of the doctrine of the Cross in application."

VIII. Applications from 1 Corinthians

1. Two main values of studying 1 Corinthians are: seeing God's diagnosis of our own spiritual maladies; and learning His prescriptions for cure. Write a list of some of the maladies and prescriptions that you consider to be crucial in the life of a local church today.

2. Try writing out your own reflections on the superlative quality of love, as measured by 1 Corinthians 13. Include the excelling and distinctive characteristic of love that relates the Christian to other persons.

3. What do you think contributes to spiritual problems in the early months and years of a born-again believer's spiritual life? Why do spiritual problems often arise very early in the life of a newly organized local church?

IX. Review Questions on 1 Corinthians

1. Were the Corinthian letters written before or after Romans?
2. Distinguish between: local church, visible church at large, invisible church.
3. Describe the city of Corinth when Paul first visited it.

4. What does the word *korinthiazomai* mean literally, and how was it used?

5. Describe Paul's first activities in founding the local church at Corinth.

6. Describe the first church at Corinth.

7. What two contacts did Paul have with the Corinthians after his first visit and before he wrote the first letter?

8. When and where was 1 Corinthians written?

9. Why did Paul write this letter?

10. Identify the main divisions of the structure of 1 Corinthians.

11. What are the three groups of problems discussed?

12. List key words, and identify a key verse of the letter.

13. Identify these by chapter number: marriage, spiritual gifts, love, resurrection body.

X. FURTHER STUDY OF 1 CORINTHIANS

With the help of outside sources study further the phenomenon of speaking in tongues *(glossolalia)*.[20] Concerning the situation at Corinth, there are two different views as to the exact nature of the tongues: (1) they were the same kind of utterances such as were spoken on the day of Pentecost (Acts 2:1-13) — languages foreign and unintelligible to the speakers, but native and intelligible to different groups of hearers; or (2) they were ecstatic utterances of a nonexistent language, understood by the listeners only through an interpreter.

Include in your studies these areas:

a. the false and the true

b. temporary gift or permanent gift

c. recent spread of the "tongues movement" in the Christian world.

XI. OUTLINE

1 CORINTHIANS: Problems of a Local Church

INTRODUCTION	1:1-9
DIVISIONS	1:10—4:21
Party Strife	1:10-31
The Mysteries of God Revealed	2:1-16
The Unity of God's Servants	3:1-23
Paul's Defense of His Ministry	4:1-21

20. Condensed descriptions are given in Merrill C. Tenney, ed., *The Zondervan Pictorial Bible Dictionary*, pp. 859-60; Merrill F. Unger, *Unger's Bible Dictionary*, pp. 1107-8; John F. Walvoord, *The Holy Spirit*. Various books and articles are available on this subject.

XII. BACKGROUND OF 2 CORINTHIANS

Paul's second letter to the Corinthians is the most personal of his writings. It is filled with personal testimonies and has been called his *Apologia Pro Vita Sua* ("defense of his life").

A. BIOGRAPHICAL SETTING

The background of the second Corinthian letter is closely involved with that of the first. For this reason the complete sequence is summarized below, some of which is review. Observe how each letter fits into the chronology.

1. Founding of the Corinthian church, on Paul's second missionary journey, A.D. 50 (Acts 18:1-18a). Paul was about fifty years old. He remained at Corinth for about eighteen months, living with Aquila and Priscilla, and working part time in the tent-making business to support his evangelistic ministry.

2. Arrival at Ephesus on the third missionary journey, A.D. 52. Paul had these two contacts with the Corinthian church before writing 1 Corinthians from Ephesus:

a. A short visit to combat an incipient opposition to the apostle's ministry, and to correct other evils. His mission was apparently not effective. (Read 2 Corinthians 2:1; 12:14; 13:1-2. Note the reference to a forthcoming "third time" visit.)

b. A letter referred to in 1 Corinthians 5:9. At least part of this so-called previous letter was written to correct existing evils in the church. The letter was noncanonical.

3. A three-year teaching and evangelistic ministry in Ephesus, on his third missionary journey (Acts 19:8, 10; 20:31; 1 Cor. 16:8), including a fruitful ministry (Acts 19:10-12, 17-20) and severe trials

(Acts 19:9; 19:21—20:1; 20:31; 2 Cor. 1:8). *Paul writes 1 Corinthians* toward the end of this mission, around A.D. 55. Titus may have been the one to deliver the letter to Corinth. (If the short visit mentioned above was not *before* writing 1 Corinthians, it would be placed here.)

4. A "painful" letter to the church (2 Cor. 2:3-4; 7:8).[21] This may have concerned an offense given to Paul in person during the short visit cited above. (See 2 Cor. 2:5-11.) Titus may have been the bearer of this letter to Corinth.[22]

5. Departure from Ephesus, and a ministry at Troas, discontinued when Paul could not find Titus (2 Cor. 2:12-13). See ② on Map S. Was Paul ill at Troas? (See 2 Cor. 4:17 ff.)

6. To Macedonia, for a ministry there (③ on Map S; Acts 20:1-2; 2 Cor. 2:13).[23] Troubles multiply (2 Cor. 7:5). Titus arrives from Corinth; he shares mixed news:

a. of a spiritual awakening in the Corinthian church (2 Cor. 7:6 ff.)

b. of problems still existing in the church (e.g., 2 Cor. 10:2, 10, 12; 11:4; 12:16, 20-21).

Paul writes 2 Corinthians from Macedonia to prepare the way for his third visit. Titus (with two companions) delivers the epistle to the church (2 Cor. 8:6, 16-24).

7. Paul's final visit to Corinth — three months of ministering (Acts 20:2-3). (See Romans 16:21-23 for names of Paul's associates at this time.) *Paul writes Romans.* He escapes a plot against his life (Acts 20:3) and continues on to Jerusalem (Acts 20:3—21:17).

B. THE WRITING OF 2 CORINTHIANS

1. *Date.* A.D. 56 and 57, depending on how soon after 1 Corinthians (A.D. 55) the letter was written.

2. *Place written.* Macedonia (7:5). One tradition assigns Philippi as the city of origin.

3. *Original readers.* All the saints of Achaia (Greece) are included with those of Corinth in the salutation of 1:1. This may be explained

---

21. Some view the letter referred to by "I wrote" (2 Cor. 2:4) as being 1 Corinthians, and the sinning brother as the one of 1 Corinthians 5:1-5.
22. S. Lewis Johnson, "The First Epistle to the Corinthians" in *The Wycliffe Bible Commentary*, p. 1228.
23. Paul's *original* plan (cf. 2 Cor. 1:15-16) was to go from Ephesus to Corinth directly by sea, then to Macedonia, then back to Corinth (thus a "second benefit" for the Corinthians, 2 Cor. 1:15), finally on to Jerusalem. His changed plan (Acts 20:3; 1 Cor. 16:5-8) was to go first to Macedonia, then to Corinth, then to Jerusalem via Macedonia. The reason for delaying his visit to Corinth was to "allow the Corinthians by God's help to remedy the evils, and then to arrive in their midst." (R. C. H. Lenski, *The Interpretation of St. Paul's First and Second Epistles to the Corinthians*, p. 858). One consequence of this change was that the Corinthians charged Paul with not being a man of his word (2 Cor. 1:17).

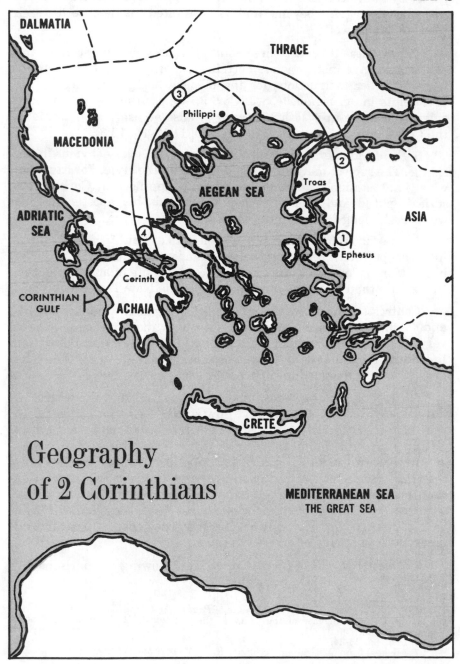

DALMATIA

THRACE

MACEDONIA

Philippi

AEGEAN SEA

Troas

ADRIATIC
SEA

ASIA

Ephesus

Corinth

CORINTHIAN
GULF

ACHAIA

CRETE

Geography
of 2 Corinthians

MEDITERRANEAN SEA
THE GREAT SEA

partly by Paul's concern that news of the opposition against him was spreading to regions beyond, and so he wanted his defense to reach those people as well.

4. *Purposes.* At least three main purposes can be seen in the epistle: a. to give instruction in doctrine and practical exhortations; b. to give further instructions for the offering being gathered for the poor saints in Jerusalem (e.g., 2 Cor. 9:1-5); c. to make an extended defense of Paul's apostleship in view of false accusations by some in the Corinthian church (e.g., 2 Cor. 10:10; 11:13-15; 13:3).

5. *Style and characteristics.* Variety of style is very obvious in the epistle. The subject matter usually determines the style. For example, when Paul assumes the role of shepherd of the flock at Corinth, his style is placid and relaxed. When he defends his apostleship, his words rush along like a mighty torrent.

In this "most letter-like of all the letters of Paul,"[24] the apostle is intensely personal, revealing the intimate joys and fears of his tender heart. More is learned about the character and life of an apostle from this epistle than from any other portion of the New Testament.

Contrasts abound in the epistle: glorying and humiliation, life and death, sorrow and consolation, sternness and tenderness. One is very much aware in reading 2 Corinthians that for Paul the Christian life means going all out for Christ, or it is not real life at all. The color gray cannot be detected in this book.

6. *Unity of the book.* Some modern critics hold that the original 2 Corinthians was not as long as it now stands (i.e., that chaps. 10-13 were not part of the letter).[25] It should be recognized, however, that in no ancient manuscript of this epistle is there "any trace of a division at any point in the letter, or any variation in the arrangement of the material; and in no early Christian writer is there any suggestion that the document is composed of parts of different letters, or that it was not all written at one time to meet one particular situation."[26] In your survey studies you will be observing evidence of a structural unity in the company of diversity of parts.

7. *Compared with 1 Corinthians.* The following comparisons are suggested by W. Graham Scroggie:[27]

----

24. R. V. G. Tasker, *The Second Epistle of Paul to the Corinthians*, p. 10.
25. For an able defense of the unity of the full text of 2 Corinthians, consult Tasker, pp. 23-35.
26. Ibid., pp. 23-24.
27. Adapted from W. Graham Scroggie, *Know Your Bible*, 2:142-43.

FIRST AND SECOND CORINTHIANS COMPARED

1 Corinthians	2 Corinthians
objective and practical	subjective and personal
insight into the character of an early church	insight into the character and ministry of Paul
deliberate instruction	impassioned testimony
warns against pagan influences	warns against Judaistic influences

XIII. SURVEY OF 2 CORINTHIANS

A. FIRST SCANNING

Spend five to ten minutes scanning the entire letter, reading only the first two verses of each paragraph. What does this reveal about the *general* contents of the letter? Most of the New Testament epistles have the customary opening and closing salutations. Observe the length of these in chapters 1 and 13.

B. A FIRST READING

This is the one-sitting reading that can be completed easily in fifty minutes. Try reading aloud. Do not tarry over any of the details. Read to be impressed. Make mental notes, and record some of your impressions.

C. SEGMENT TITLES

Observe on Chart 73 that 2 Corinthians is divided here into twelve segments (not including the introduction and conclusion). Mark the segment divisions in your Bible. Then read each segment, and assign a segment title to each.

The locations of segment dividing points not beginning with the first verse of a chapter are based on the following considerations:

1:3-11. This is an opening testimony of Paul. Actually, his testimony carries over into the next verses and paragraphs (in fact throughout the epistle), but there appears to be a new beginning at 1:12.

1:12—2:13. Observe the many references to Paul's *coming* to Corinth. This is the main reason for not making a new division at 2:1, but carrying the segment through 2:13.

2:14—4:6. This segment is about Paul's ministry *specifically*, such as preaching (4:5).

4:7—5:10. At 4:7 Paul begins to talk about the "outward man," "earthen vessels," the "body." The subject continues throughout the segment.

5:11—7:3. At 5:11 Paul returns to the subject of ministry, especially the *message* of that ministry ("ministry of reconciliation," 5:18).

7:4-16. Some Bibles make a new paragraph at 7:5 instead of at 7:4.[28] However, in view of the subjects *comfort* and *tribulation* in 7:4, and of the connective "for" in 7:5, it seems better to include 7:4 with the new division.

12:14—13:10. The common connecting phrase is "the third time" (12:14 and 13:1). This is the basis for including 12:14-21 with 13:1-10.

D. CORRELATION: SEEING HOW THE BOOK HOLDS TOGETHER

Use the survey Chart 73 as the point of reference for the remaining studies.

1. *Main divisions.* Read chapters 8 and 9 and observe the common subject here. Refer to the survey, Chart 73, and note that this passage is the second of three main divisions in the epistle. Scan chapters 1-7 again, and look for testimonial and doctrinal passages. Then scan chapters 10-13 and observe how frequently Paul defends his apostleship. Read 13:3 for Paul's reasons for devoting four chapters to the subject of defending his ministry.

How are the three main divisions identified in various ways on Chart 73? It is difficult to find a logical development of the theme of each division that could be represented by any detailed outline.[29] The explanation of this absence of strict logical structure is to be found in the intimate, personal quality of the letter, one that pulsates with emotion. As someone has observed, "Feeling cannot be reduced to system; it vanishes under the dissecting knife."

2. *Paul's ministry.* What are the two main parts of the epistle on this subject? Read the segments of the division, "Vindication of Paul's Ministry." Try to arrive at an outline of this division. Start by observing the main point of each segment.

3. *Tone.* Be alert to change of tone as you move through the epistle. What does the chart show?

4. *Biographical setting.* The three main divisions are related to the historical setting. Study the two outlines by T. Zahn that appear at the top of the chart, keeping in mind the setting discussed earlier. As we have seen, Paul sent this letter to prepare the way for his visit to Corinth, which he wanted to be a success.

5. *Testimony.* Much of 2 Corinthians is Paul's testimony. This is

28. Observe, for example, how 7:5 picks up the narrative that had been temporarily suspended at 2:13. It is for this reason that the section 2:14—7:4 is often viewed as a parenthesis in the epistle.

29. A simple outline is given in Alfred Plummer, *Second Epistle of St. Paul to the Corinthians*, pp. xx-xxi.

CHART 73

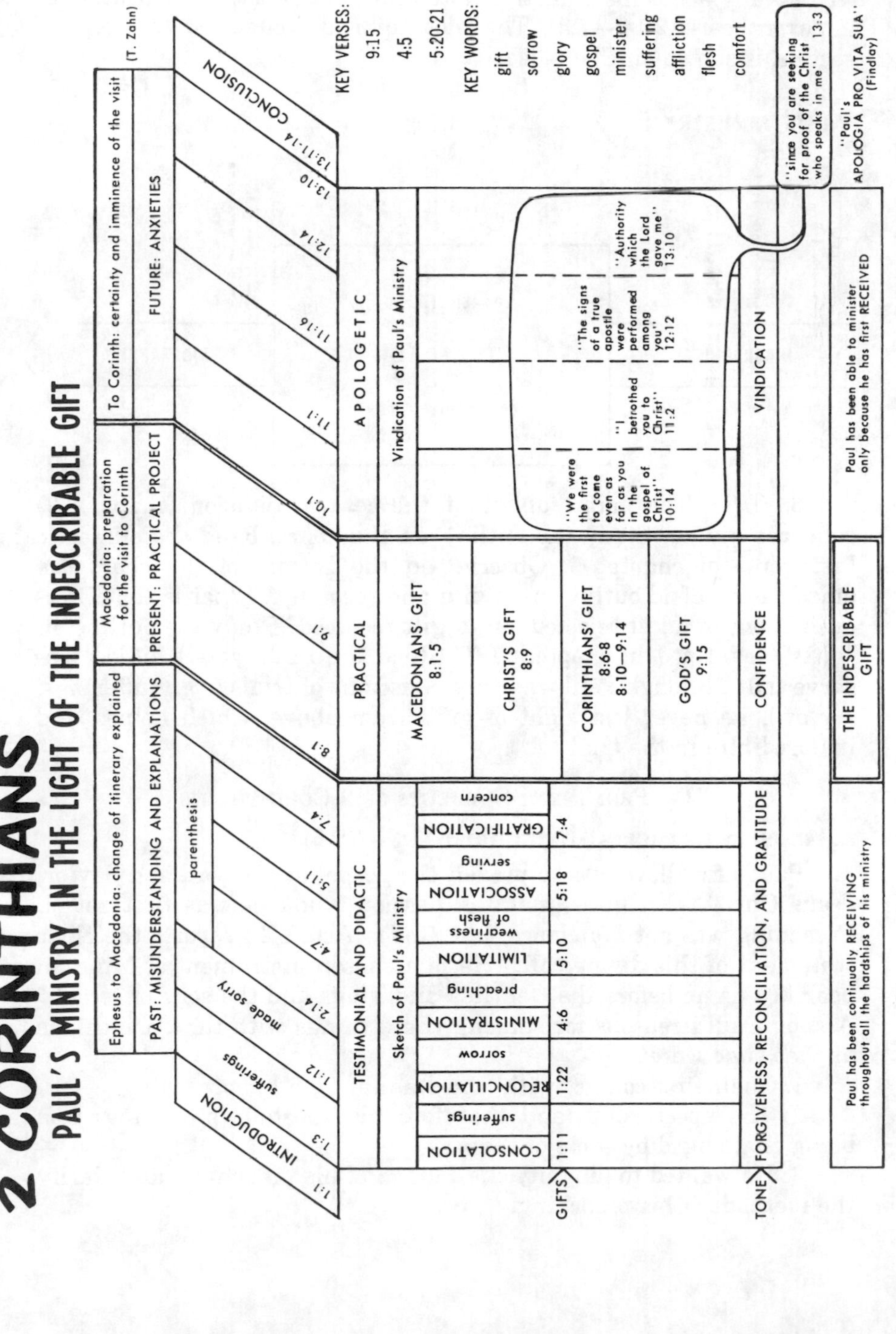

2 CORINTHIANS
PAUL'S MINISTRY IN THE LIGHT OF THE INDESCRIBABLE GIFT

	Ephesus to Macedonia: change of itinerary explained	Macedonia: preparation for the visit to Corinth	To Corinth: certainty and imminence of the visit (T. Zahn)
	PAST: MISUNDERSTANDING AND EXPLANATIONS	PRESENT: PRACTICAL PROJECT	FUTURE: ANXIETIES

INTRODUCTION 1:1	TESTIMONIAL AND DIDACTIC	PRACTICAL	APOLOGETIC	CONCLUSION 13:11-14

Sketch of Paul's Ministry

Vindication of Paul's Ministry

1:3 suffering	1:12 suffering	2:14 made sorry	4:7 parenthesis	5:11	7:4	8:1	9:1	10:1	11:1	11:16	12:14	13:10

CONSOLATION 1:11	RECONCILIATION 1:22	MINISTRATION 4:6	LIMITATION 5:10	ASSOCIATION 5:18	GRATIFICATION 7:4
sufferings	sorrow	preaching	weariness of flesh	serving	concern

GIFTS

MACEDONIANS' GIFT 8:1-5

CHRIST'S GIFT 8:9

CORINTHIANS' GIFT 8:6-8 8:10—9:14

GOD'S GIFT 9:15

"We were the first to come even as far as you in the gospel of Christ" 10:14

"I betrothed you to Christ" 11:2

"The signs of a true apostle were performed among you" 12:12

"Authority which the Lord gave me" 13:10

TONE: FORGIVENESS, RECONCILIATION, AND GRATITUDE | CONFIDENCE | VINDICATION

THE INDESCRIBABLE GIFT

Paul has been continually RECEIVING throughout all the hardships of his ministry

Paul has been able to minister only because he has first RECEIVED

KEY VERSES:
9:15
4:5
5:20-21

KEY WORDS:
gift
sorrow
glory
gospel
minister
suffering
affliction
flesh
comfort

"since you are seeking for proof of the Christ who speaks in me" 13:3

"Paul's APOLOGIA PRO VITA SUA" (Findlay)

especially true of the first division (1:3—7:16), where the apostle writes fully about his ministry. Note on Chart 73 the identification of a parenthesis (2:14—7:3). The biographical context of this topical section is shown on Chart 74.

CHART 74

PAUL'S MINISTRY

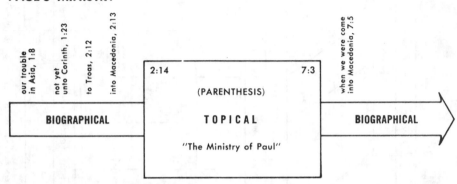

6. *Gifts*. The main subject of the central division (chaps. 8-9) concerns giving. Study the outline on the chart. Read the climactic last verse of chapter 9. Observe on the bottom of the chart the epistle's threefold outline on giving and receiving. What is the difference between a gift rejected and a gift received? Study the outline on "gifts" developed in chapters 1-7. (Read the Bible verses cited.) Observe that although Paul was very conscious of trials (e.g., sufferings, sorrow), he never lost sight of gifts from above, which helped and inspired him in the trial.

XIV. PROMINENT SUBJECTS OF 2 CORINTHIANS

A. MINISTRY OF PROCLAIMING CHRIST (1:3—7:16)

Paul's first love was to preach the gospel of his Lord and Savior, Jesus Christ. God gave him this passion when he was first saved. Preaching was not *his* choice, but *God's*. Acts 9:15 reports the clear statement of this divine call: "He is a chosen instrument of Mine, to bear My name before the Gentiles and kings and the sons of Israel." Among Paul's reasons for sharing these things with the Corinthians at that time were:

1. Their first contact with him was through his preaching.

2. His apostleship (and therefore his apostolic preaching) was being challenged by some of them.

3. He wanted to magnify the Person of his preaching, and clarify the methods of his preaching.

4. He wanted the Corinthians to learn important spiritual lessons applicable to laymen as well as to preachers, since both are witnesses of the gospel.

It is in the parenthesis of 2:14—7:3, noted earlier, that Paul teaches much about the Christian ministry. Chart 75 shows the subjects of the three segments.

CHART 75

2 CORINTHIANS 2:14-7:3

THE PARENTHESIS

THE MINISTRY OF THE GOSPEL		
2:14	4:7	5:11 7:3
GLORIOUS NATURE of the Gospel	FRAIL BEARERS of the Gospel	BELOVED HEARERS of the Gospel

Tenney breaks down this section into the following outline:[30]

The Nature of the Ministry	2:14—3:18
The Sincerity of the Ministry	4:1-6
The Perseverance of the Ministry	4:7-15
The Prospect of the Ministry	4:16—5:10
The Sanctions of the Ministry	5:11-19
The Example of the Ministry	5:20—6:10
The Appeal of the Ministry	6:11—7:3

In the same section a study of ambassadorship (5:20) may be made:

An ambassador for Christ	(5:11—7:3)
1. his motivations	5:11-15
2. his message	5:16-21
3. his marks	6:1-10
4. his fellowship	6:11—7:3

Every Christian is to minister in some way in God's vineyard, as a witness of the gospel. Paul was a preacher-teacher-missionary, but his testimony about his experiences can be applied to any kind of

30. Merrill C. Tenney, *New Testament Survey*, p. 300.

Christian service, when the universal, timeless principles are identified.

B. CHRISTIAN GIVING (8:1—9:15)

This passage is the New Testament's classic treatise on Christian giving. The setting is that of a fund-raising project that the Corinthians had begun a year earlier.[31] In his first letter Paul called this a "collection for the saints" (1 Cor. 16:1). Some of the Jewish Christians living in Jerusalem were poverty-striken, and it was the apostle's conviction that financial help at that time would carry them through the critical experience. Paul was also wise enough to know that the spiritual benefits derived from the project by the donors would far outweigh the monetary worth of the gift itself. He saw here the implications of a *communion* of saints, and a reminder of the greatness of divine grace. It is no wonder then that he devoted such a large amount of the epistle to the mundane subject of fund-raising.

Various explanations have been offered as to what brought on this poverty situation at Jerusalem. Some of these are mentioned below:

> Augustine suggests that the poverty at Jerusalem was the result of the community of goods (Acts iv. 32) . . . without careful organization of labour. . . . But there were other causes. Jerusalem had a pauperized population, dependent on the periodical influx of visitors. The Jewish world, from Cicero's time at least, supported the poor of Jerusalem by occasional subventions. As the Christian Jews came to be regarded as a distinct body, they would lose their share in these doles; and the "communism" of Acts iv. 32 was but a temporary remedy. Most of the converts were, therefore, poor at the outset. They were probably "boycotted" and otherwise persecuted by the unconverted Jews (1 Thess. ii. 14; Jas. ii. 6; v. 1-6), and their position would be similar to that of Hindoo Christians excluded from their caste, or Protestants in the West of Ireland.[32]

The setting is far removed from all of us, but the timeless principles that are involved bridge all the gaps. Observe in the passage the two supreme examples: Christ's gift (8:9) and God's gift (9:15).

---

31. The interval of one year is cited in 8:10 and 9:2. It has been pointed out by some, however, that the Greek text translated "a year ago" should read "last year" (NIV), which would make the interval something less than a year. (See R. V. G. Tasker, *The Second Epistle of Paul to the Corinthians*, p. 123.)

32. A. T. Robertson and A. Plummer, *First Epistle of St. Paul to the Corinthians*, p. 382.

C. CREDENTIALS OF PAUL'S MINISTRY (10:1—13:10)

Paul devotes four chapters (or thirty percent) of the entire letter to vindicating his apostolic ministry. At one point in this section he states bluntly why such a vindication is necessary: "since you are seeking for proof of the Christ who speaks in me" (13:3). Not all the Corinthians were guilty of such suspicion or antagonism. In fact, most of them were *with* Paul, and were anxious to support his ministry in every way (read 7:16). The instigators of opposition to Paul were men from outside the Corinthian fellowship (cf. 11:4) who were trying to lure some of those Christians away from their loyalties. "These were of the Judaistic agitators who dogged the footsteps of Paul across Asia Minor and into Europe, impugning his message and attacking his person."[33] As long as there was this thorn in the group, Paul would do everything he could to remove it and the festering that it threatened.[34]

We can understand the urgency of such an apologetic stand before the entire Christian world of the first century. A false gospel (11:4) and the true were being broadcast simultaneously around the world, and people were asking, Who are the gospel's true ministers, and who are the false? Paul's second letter to the Corinthians gave the answer, not only to the church at Corinth, but to people everywhere, of all time. As you survey these four chapters, look especially for the credentials of a true witness for Christ in the great work of the gospel.

D. BIOGRAPHICAL NOTES

This letter is the only source of the following unique experiences of Paul:

1. escape from Damascus, 11:32-33
2. his revelations and visions, 12:1-6[35]
3. his thorn in the flesh, 12:7
4. five Jewish scourgings; two Roman scourgings; three shipwrecks; many perils, 11:23-27.

E. OTHER IMPORTANT SUBJECTS

Other important subjects discussed by Paul in 2 Corinthians include:

1. the Old and New covenants contrasted (chap. 3)
2. Christ's substitutionary atonement (5:21)
3. the gospel of reconciliation (5:18-20)

---

33. W. Graham Scroggie, *Know Your Bible*, 2:139.
34. Read the following passages, which reveal something of the dark side of the Corinthian scene at this time: 11:3-4; 12:20-21; 13:5-7, 11.
35. Consult commentaries for identification of "a man" in 12:2.

4. separation from worldliness (6:14—7:1).

What key truths are taught in these passages: 4:7-12; 4:16-18; 5:1-10; 5:17-21; 6:4-10; 8:9; 9:8; 11:23-33; 12:1-10; 13:14?

XV. Key Words, Verses and Theme for 2 Corinthians

Note the key words listed on Chart 73, p. 287. Each of the words *glory* and *minister* (and their cognates and synonyms) appear about twenty times in the letter.

Read in your Bible the key verses cited on the chart. Did you observe other key verses in the epistle?

Note that the title on the chart reflects the two main subjects of the epistle: *ministry* and *gift*. In your own words, state the theme of 2 Corinthians.

XVI. Applications from 2 Corinthians

A large variety of spiritual applications may be made of this letter because it is so personal. What practical truths are taught about these:

1. suffering and trial of Christians
2. death
3. ambassadors for Christ
4. Christian giving
5. how to deal with false accusation and false teaching?

XVII. Review Questions on 2 Corinthians

1. Where was Paul when he wrote 2 Corinthians?
2. Why did Paul write this letter?
3. Describe the letter, in regard to general contents and style.
4. Compare 1 and 2 Corinthians.
5. The structure of 2 Corinthians is of how many main divisions? Identify the contents of each.
6. Why did Paul write so much to vindicate his ministry?
7. What were some of the credentials which he submitted for himself?
8. What is meant by "apologia pro vita sua"?
9. Name key words of the letter.
10. Quote a key verse.

XVIII. Further Study of 2 Corinthians

Using outside sources, study the interesting experiences of Paul as recorded in 12:1-6 (visions and revelations) and 12:7 (thorn in the flesh).

XIX. OUTLINE

XX. SELECTED READING FOR CORINTHIAN LETTERS

GENERAL INTRODUCTION

Hodge, Charles. *An Exposition of the First Epistle to the Corinthians*, pp. iii-xxi.

Hughes, Philip Edgcumbe. *Paul's Second Epistle to the Corinthians*. The New International Commentary on the New Testament, pp. xv-xxxvi.

Morris, Leon. *The First Epistle of Paul to the Corinthians*. The Tyndale New Testament Commentaries, pp. 15-23.

Tasker, R. V. G. *The Second Epistle of Paul to the Corinthians*. The Tyndale New Testament Commentaries, pp. 15-38.

COMMENTARIES

Broomall, Wick. "The Second Epistle to the Corinthians." In *The Wycliffe Bible Commentary*.

Johnson, S. Lewis. "First Corinthians." In *The Wycliffe Bible Commentary*.

Lenski, R. C. H. *The Interpretation of St. Paul's First and Second Epistle to the Corinthians*.

Morris, Leon. *The First Epistle of Paul to the Corinthians*.

Plummer, Alfred. *Second Epistle of St. Paul to the Corinthians*. The International Critical Commentary.

Robertson, A., and Plummer, A. *First Epistle of Paul to the Corinthians*.

OTHER RELATED SOURCES

Vincent, Marvin R. *Word Studies in the New Testament*.

Vine, W. C. *Expository Dictionary of New Testament Words*.

13

Galatians: Set Free from Bondage

The epistle to the Galatians was Paul's first God-breathed *(theopneustia)* writing, delivered to the churches of Galatia during the decade of his missionary labors.[1] (See Chart 1, p. 20.) We have already surveyed Romans and the Corinthian letters of this period. Recall from your study of Chapter 1 that James and Galatians were probably the first New Testament books to be written (James A.D. 45; Galatians, A.D. 48). In our surveys of these letters we shall observe that both concerned themselves with the subject of *works*. But each book stressed a different, though not contradictory, aspect of that common subject. James was addressed to the error of loose antinomianism (from *anti*, "against" and *nomos*, "law"), which said that because a person is saved by grace through faith, works thereafter are not important. (Read James 2:14-26.) Galatians was addressed to the error of what might be called *Galatianism*, which said that one is *saved* through faith and *perfected* by the keeping of the law, thus salvation is by faith *plus* works. Stated positively, Galatians teaches *liberation by the gospel*; James teaches *compulsion of the gospel*. This is the comparison shown on Chart 62, p. 244. It is easy to see from this why a study of Galatians made in conjunction with a study of James brings out the stable, balanced New Testament teaching on the place of *works* in the doctrine of salvation.[2]

From the above description of the emphasis of Galatians it is understandable why Martin Luther, released from the legalistic shackles of the Roman church, embraced this letter as his favorite Bible book. This attraction has been shared by multitudes before and

---

1. The date of writing Galatians is an unsettled question, as is noted later in the chapter. This book follows the position of the early writing.
2. If these two letters were the first two books to be written, it is interesting to observe that this balance was the first message to the early church.

after Luther. One writer has called the epistle "The Magna Charta of Spiritual Emancipation."

I. Preparation for Study

Review Paul's three missionary journeys (Chapter 10, especially Chart 59, p. 237), and note especially the cities of Galatia that he visited on the first journey (Map N, p. 220). Locate the cities on Map T. Did Paul visit these cities again on his later journeys? Did he ever visit cities in north Galatia for an evangelistic ministry, as far as the Bible record is concerned?

Read Acts 13:1—14:28, which is Luke's reporting of Paul's first missionary journey. Study especially the ministries and events at the four Galatian cities shown on Map T. These are the cities where Paul won converts and founded the churches to which he wrote Galatians. Note: Paul's return trip on the first missionary journey (Acts 14:21-27) might be called a second visit to the people. Observe that as of Acts 14:23, churches in the area were already being established.

II. Background

A. AUTHOR

The writer is identified in the text as "Paul, an apostle" (1:1; cf. 6:11). Read Galatians 1:2 and observe that other Christians joined Paul in greeting the Galatian churches: "all the brethren who are with me."

B. ORIGINAL READERS

The text identifies the original readers as "the churches of Galatia" (1:2; cf. 3:1), hence the title, "Galatians." The other places in the New Testament where the reference to "Galatia" appears are these: Acts 16:6; 18:23; 1 Corinthians 16:1; 2 Timothy 4:10; 1 Peter 1:1.

It is interesting to observe that this is the only Pauline epistle addressed as such to a *group* of churches. Some of Paul's epistles (e.g., Ephesians) were intended to be circulated among churches, even though one church was designated as the original recipient.[3]

Where were the "churches of Galatia" located? Two different views are held on this: (1) the North Galatian view — churches of northern cities, supposedly founded on Paul's second missionary journey when he passed through the northern districts of Asia Minor; (2) the South Galatian view — churches founded on Paul's first mission-

---

3. In 2 Corinthians 1:1 Paul addresses the church at Corinth *and* "all the saints who are throughout Achaia."

The Geography of Galatians

ary journey to such southern cities as Lystra and Derbe. (See Further Study for brief descriptions and defenses of each of these views.)

The position taken by this book is that the "churches of Galatia" were located in the southern cities evangelized by Paul on his first missionary journey. The following suggestions for orientation are geared to this position.

Study Map T, which shows the geography of Galatians. Note again the locations of these cities: Antioch, Iconium, Lystra, and Derbe. Try to fix their locations in your mind in order to help you *visualize* the setting of the Bible text that you will be surveying.

It is generally believed that most of the Galatian believers were of Gentile background. How is that supported by the following verses in Galatians: 4:8; 5:2; 6:12?

What do the following verses tell you about the Galatian churches and about Paul's relationship to them: 1:6-7; 1:8-11; 3:1-5; 4:12-15; 4:19-20; 5:7-9?

C. DATE AND PLACE WRITTEN

The date of Galatians depends on which view of its recipients — North Galatian or South Galatian — is correct. In accord with the latter view, Paul wrote Galatians after his first missionary journey (Acts 13-14) and before the Jerusalem Council (Acts 15). If the Jerusalem Council had already convened, Paul would no doubt have referred to its decisions in his letter, since both the Council and the letter addressed the same problem. The Jerusalem Council was held in A.D. 49, so A.D. 48 may be assigned to the epistle. The epistle of James (A.D. 45) was probably the only other New Testament book predating Galatians.

Paul may have written the letter at Antioch of Syria, Jerusalem, or between the two cities.

D. SETTING

The first opposition that the Gentile Christians of Galatia encountered after their conversion was persecution from Jewish unbelievers of their own hometowns (cf. Acts 13:45-50; 14:21-23). Apparently the Christians withstood those attacks, for Paul does not refer to such a problem in his epistle. Satan changed his tactics against the Galatians and used Jewish Christians from without (probably from Jerusalem) to cast a pall of doubt over Paul's evangelistic ministry among the Gentile Galatians. "Where the blustering storm of opposition failed the subtle influences of persuasion had met with more success."[4]

---

4. C. F. Hogg and W. E. Vine, *The Epistle to the Galatians*, p. 7.

It all happened very fast. Soon after Paul left the cities of Galatia on his first missionary journey, Judaizers arrived and told the new converts that they had not heard the *whole* gospel (1:6-7). Those troublemakers taught that salvation was by (1) faith in Christ, *plus* (2) participation in Jewish ceremonies (e.g., circumcision). In other words, the Gentile converts of Galatia were not saved if they had not also become Jews. Read the following verses of Galatians, and note the various false doctrines taught by the opponents of Paul: 1:6-9; 2:16; 3:2-3; 4:10, 21; 5:2-4; 6:12. Also record how each of the following verses identify those false teachers: 1:7; 3:1; 4:17; 5:10, 12.

Why do you think it was difficult for many Jews in Paul's day to accept the doctrine of *salvation through faith alone*? One writer answers with these words, "Two thousand years of Jewish tradition were in their bones."[5] What were some of the ingredients of that tradition (e.g., forefathers, the Temple)? Read Acts 6-7 to see how one Jew, Stephen, saw the deeper significance of the sacred Jewish institutions, as they pointed to a Messiah not only on the throne of David but also on the throne of the universe.[6]

E. PURPOSES

Some of Paul's main purposes in writing this epistle were:

1. to expose the false teachings of the Judaizers who were undermining the faith of the new converts

2. to defend Paul's apostleship, which was being challenged by the Judaizers

3. to emphasize that salvation is through faith alone, not faith plus law

4. to exhort the Galatian Christians to live in the liberty brought by Christ (5:1) and bring forth the fruit of the Spirit (5:22-23).

F. CHARACTERISTICS OF THE EPISTLE

Distinguishing marks of the epistle include the following items.

1. *Many contrasts*. These will be seen in your survey study.

2. *Strong statements*. Paul was justifiably incensed over the destructive work of the troublemakers. Twice in the opening chapter he writes, "Let him be accursed." "Every sentence is a thunderbolt" is one writer's view of the epistle. William Neil describes Paul here as "a man with a brilliant mind, a trenchant controversialist, a fearless fighter . . . a man whose life was 'hidden with Christ in God.'"[7]

---

5. William Neil, *The Letter of Paul to the Galatians*, p. 4.
6. Stephen was probably a Hellenistic Jew speaking the Greek language and adopting Greek customs. The speech of Acts 7 was delivered to an audience in Jerusalem about 15 years before Galatians was written.
7. Neil, *Paul to the Galatians*, p. 89.

3. *Clear distinction between faith and works as the condition for salvation*. The book has been used of God to bring spiritual awakening to such men as Martin Luther and John Wesley. Luther said this of Galatians: "It is my epistle; I have betrothed myself to it: it is my wife."

4. *Classic treatment of Christian liberty*. This is why, as cited earlier, the epistle has been called "The Magna Charta of Spiritual Emancipation."

5. *No congratulations or words of praise*. It was not that there was nothing commendable about the Galatians' spiritual lives. The epistle was written under strain of urgency, over a situation of emergency. Paul would be having personal interaction with the churches later, when he could inspire them through commendation.

G. GALATIANS IN RELATION TO OTHER NEW TESTAMENT BOOKS

We have already compared Galatians and James. Two other interesting comparisons are made below.

1. *Galatians and Romans*. The subject of works is prominent in Romans as well as in Galatians. Romans exposes the error of legalism, which says that a person is saved by works. The subject of justification by faith appears often in both epistles. (Read Galatians 2:16-17; 3:11, 24; 5:4; Romans 3:20, 24, 28; 5:1, 9.) The large subject of salvation is treated more fully in Romans. It has been said that Galatians is the "rough block" of what appears in more finished form in Romans, written eight years later.

2. *Galatians and 2 Corinthians*. Much of 2 Corinthians is devoted to a defense of Paul's apostleship (e.g., 2 Cor. 10-13), because Paul's opponents were stirring up the Corinthian believers by challenging his credentials as an apostle. In the first two chapters of Galatians Paul defends his apostleship, which was challenged by the same kind of troublemakers. When you are surveying Galatians 1-2, recall the *apologia* chapters of 2 Corinthians 10-13.

III. SURVEY

A. PREPARING TO SURVEY

1. Visualize the young Christians of a church of Galatia about to read Paul's letter for the first time. Keep in mind the antecedents of the epistle:

    a. Paul's first missionary journey

    b. conversion of residents of Galatia

    c. Paul returns to home base, Antioch

d. troublemakers and false teachers harass the Galatian Christians.

2. Take a casual look at Galatians in your Bible, observing such things as number and length of chapters.

B. FIRST READING

Read the entire book in one sitting. Aim here to get the feel of the book. Approach the text, as much as possible, with "an innocence of the eye," that is, as though you had never seen it before. What are your impressions?

Scan the book for the general content of its chapters. Is there an opening salutation in the first chapter? What would you consider to be the concluding section of the letter?

How do the first two chapters differ from the others as to content? Which group has more commands: chapters 3-4, or 5-6?

What key words, phrases, and subjects of the epistle have stood out as prominent so far in your survey? How would you describe the atmosphere of the book?

C. INDIVIDUAL SEGMENTS AND PARAGRAPHS

Refer to Chart 77, page 302, and note that Galatians is here divided into eight segments, including the introduction and conclusion. Each segment is a group of paragraphs. Because Galatians has only six chapters, we will begin this phase of survey with the paragraph units. The aim here is to identify the main subject of each paragraph without tarrying over any details.

Refer to Chart 76 and note the set of paragraph divisions (i.e., chapter-verse reference). Mark those divisions in your Bible. Then read each paragraph, and assign a paragraph title.[8]

D. IDENTIFYING GROUPS OF SEGMENTS AND PARAGRAPHS

Now read your entire group of paragraph titles. Could any of those be grouped together under a common subject? You may or may not see any groupings from your paragraph titles. Do not hesitate to glance back at the Bible text for clues to groups.

Think next in terms of segments. Do you see any ways to group segments according to common subject?

What part of the epistle is mostly practical?

What part is mostly doctrinal?

What part is mostly autobiographical?

---

8. A paragraph title has the same kind of function as a segment title. It is a word or short phrase, taken directly from the Bible text, which represents a main subject of the paragraph.

E. SURVEY CHART

Study Chart 77, which shows the structure of Galatians. Note the following:

1. The epistle is clearly divided into three parts of two chapters each. Observe that the practical section follows the doctrinal. Paul always bases his applications on firmly established doctrinal truths.

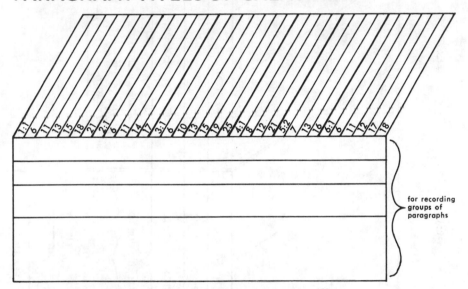

CHART 76

PARAGRAPH TITLES OF GALATIANS

for recording groups of paragraphs

2. A new division is made at 5:2 in order to show 5:1, with its theme of liberty, as a concluding verse to the previous section about liberty (e.g., note the word *free* in 4:26, 30-31).

3. The first ten verses of the letter are seen here as the introduction. Some versions and commentaries consider only 1:1-5 or 1:1-9 as the introduction. What are the functions of the paragraph 1:6-10?

4. The conclusion of the epistle is identified as 6:11-18. If it were not for verse 11, can you see why only 6:17-18 might be considered as the conclusion?

5. Observe how each of the three divisions of the letter is identified, in the different outlines. Compare the outlines with your own observations of groups of paragraphs.

6. The title "Set Free from Bondage" reflects the key verse 5:1, with its reference to a "yoke of slavery." What is the practical command of 5:1?

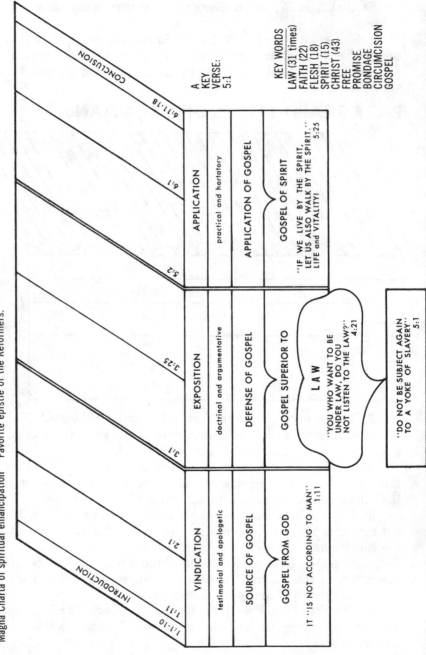

GALATIANS
SET FREE FROM BONDAGE

"Magna Charta of spiritual emancipation" Favorite epistle of the Reformers.

	INTRODUCTION	VINDICATION	EXPOSITION	APPLICATION	CONCLUSION
	1:1-10	testimonial and apologetic	doctrinal and argumentative	practical and hortatory	6:11-18
		SOURCE OF GOSPEL	DEFENSE OF GOSPEL	APPLICATION OF GOSPEL	
		GOSPEL FROM GOD	GOSPEL SUPERIOR TO LAW	GOSPEL OF SPIRIT	

IT "IS NOT ACCORDING TO MAN" 1:11

"YOU WHO WANT TO BE UNDER LAW, DO YOU NOT LISTEN TO THE LAW?" 4:21

"IF WE LIVE BY THE SPIRIT, LET US ALSO WALK BY THE SPIRIT." 5:25 LIFE and VITALITY!

"DO NOT BE SUBJECT AGAIN TO A YOKE OF SLAVERY" 5:1

A KEY VERSE: 5:1

KEY WORDS
LAW (31 times)
FAITH (22)
FLESH (18)
SPIRIT (15)
CHRIST (43)
FREE
PROMISE
BONDAGE
CIRCUMCISION
GOSPEL

IV. PROMINENT SUBJECTS

A. PAUL'S TESTIMONIES (1:1—2:21)

The first two chapters of Galatians record various testimonies of Paul, as summarized below. Paul's main purpose in sharing those testimonies was to show that God, not man, was the source of his calling to the ministry.

1. *Divine source of Paul's message* (1:1-24). Read the chapter and note the various ways Paul emphasizes that his message was by revelation from God, and not by instruction from man. Refer to Chart 78 for help in the biographical notes of the passage.

CHART 78

THE CHRONOLOGY OF GALATIANS 1:11-2:10

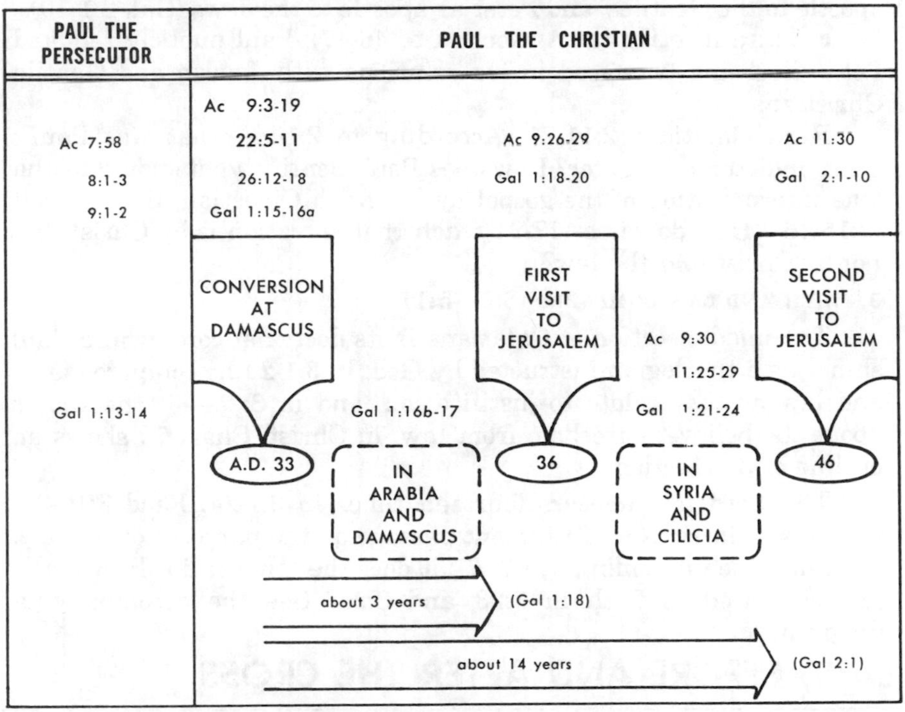

2. *Human endorsement of Paul's mission* (2:1-10). In this passage Paul shows that his mission to the Gentiles (of which the Galatian churches were a part) was wholeheartedly endorsed by the Jewish leaders of the Jerusalem church. As you read the text, observe how Paul did that.

3. *Confrontation with Peter* (2:11-21). This is the concluding

passage in the two-chapter testimonial section of the epistle. The fact of Paul's encounter with Peter served to support his proof that he was not preaching the gospel under the rule of anyone, including the apostles from Jerusalem. One can appreciate why Paul was so deeply disturbed over the problem about Jewish laws for Christians, when even a pillar of the church, like Peter, would compromise on the issue.

Paul's confrontation with Peter probably took place soon after Paul had returned to Antioch from Jerusalem. It was the third meeting of Paul and Peter, and not a pleasant one.

a. First meeting (at Jerusalem, A.D. 36). Paul became acquainted with Peter, and visited with him for fifteen days (Gal. 1:18).

b. Second meeting (at Jerusalem, A.D. 46). Paul and Peter joined "right hands of fellowship" in the ministry of the gospel, Paul as apostle to the Gentiles, and Peter as apostle to the Jews (Gal. 2:1-10).

c. Third meeting (at Antioch, A.D. 46-47). Paul publicly rebuked Peter for being two-faced in his relations with Jewish and Gentile Christians.

Read Galatians 2:11-21. According to 2:14a, what was Paul's sharp indictment of Peter? How does Paul identify what should be the true interpretation of the gospel by a Jewish Christian, like himself (2:15-16)? How do verses 17-21 teach that salvation is by Christ, but not by Christ *and* the law?

B. FAITH AND LAW COMPARED (3:1—5:1)

The middle section of Galatians is its doctrinal core, where Paul shines as a theologian instructed by God. In 3:1-24 he compares faith and law as they relate to justification, and in 3:25—5:1 he writes about the believer's freedom from law, in Christ. Chart 79 shows an outline of this section.

The word *law* appears fourteen times in 3:1-24. Read 3:10-24, which is a classic New Testament passage on the purposes of the law. What are the law's ministries? What does the law *not* do? How is the law compared to faith in 3:23 and 3:25? See the accompanying diagram.

LAW, BEFORE AND AFTER THE CROSS

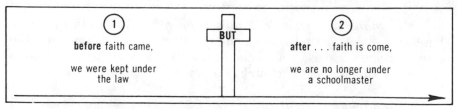

CHART 79

GALATIANS 3:1—5:1

Justification is by faith in Christ alone, as shown by:					
①	②	③	④		⑤
THE CHRISTIAN'S NEW EXPERIENCE	GOD'S COVENANT WITH ABRAHAM	THE LIMITED MINISTRY OF THE LAW	THE CHRISTIAN'S NEW STANDING	PARENTHESIS (4:12-20)	ILLUSTRATIONS FROM OLD TESTAMENT HISTORY
3:1	3:6	3:19	3:25	4:12	4:21 5:1
FAITH AND LAW COMPARED			FREEDOM IN CHRIST		

The apostle never suggests in any of his writings that God's law and Christian freedom are contradictory or unmixable. In 3:24 and 5:1 he shows that they are intimately related. The accompanying diagram illustrates this.

LAW AND LIBERTY

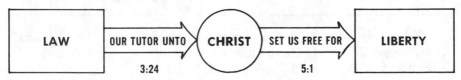

The Jewish agitators in the Galatian churches were luring the new Gentile converts back to the yoke of legalistic bondage. Paul wanted to show the Galatians that their newfound emancipation from the law brought them into a new and intimate relationship to God, through His dear Son.

C. WALKING BY THE SPIRIT (5:2-26)

The key repeated word of this segment is *Spirit*. Paul's appeal for walking by the Spirit is based on the truth of the believer's standing: "If we live by the Spirit" (5:25). It is in the context of this passage that the familiar verses are found listing the "fruit of the Spirit" (5:22-23).

V. Key Words, Verses and Theme

Observe the list of key words shown on Chart 77, page 302. Does the frequent repetition of some words indicate something of Paul's method of writing this letter?

Galatians is clearly a book of contrasts. Note how many of the key words appear in the contrasts of Chart 80.[9]

Chart 80

CONTRASTS IN GALATIANS.

CHAPTER	The Lower	The Higher
1—2	lost in Adam all die physically in Adam another gospel (false) man's reasoning	saved in Christ all live spiritually in Christ the genuine gospel God's revelation
3—4	law works curse of death condemnation by works servants in bondage (defeat) old covenant (symbolized by Hagar)	grace faith blessing of life justification by faith sons in freedom (victory) new covenant (symbolized by Sarah)
5—6	living in the flesh works of the flesh falling from grace world or self the object of glorying	walking in the Spirit fruit of the Spirit standing firm in grace the cross the sole object of glorying

What key verses did you observe in your survey of Galatians? Compare your choices with the following list: 1:15-16; 2:16*a*; 2:20; 3:3; 3:13; 3:24; 4:4-6; 5:1; 5:22-23; 5:25; 6:2, 5; 6:15.

In your own words, state a theme for Galatians.

VI. Applications

Some of the areas of application to be derived from Galatians are shown here:

1. One's salvation. What really are the conditions for salvation that a person must fulfill?

2. One's Christian growth (sanctification). Does this come by self-effort? What is the source of strength?

3. One's liberty. What are the believer's privileges of freedom in Christ? Is the church of Christ supposed to be uniform in custom and

---

9. List is adapted from Merrill F. Unger, *Unger's Bible Handbook*, p. 659.

habit in all respects? Did Paul urge Gentile Christians to act like Jewish Christians, or Jewish Christians to act like Gentile Christians?

4. Are there boundaries and limitations in this Christian freedom? If so, what are they?

5. Is the phrase "keep standing firm" of 5:1 a suggestion of boundary in Christian living? What about the common New Testament phrase "in Christ"?

VII. REVIEW QUESTIONS

1. Recall some of the high points of Paul's life. Where does the writing of Galatians fit in?

2. Where were the churches of Galatia located?

3. When did Paul first meet the Galatians? Did he have any part in the founding of the local churches in the different cities?

4. Why is it held that Paul wrote Galatians *before* the Jerusalem Council of Acts 15?

5. Why did Paul write to the churches of Galatia so soon after completing his evangelistic mission to them?

6. What was the local setting that brought on this letter?

7. Name four main purposes of the epistle.

8. What are some of the distinguishing marks of the epistle?

9. Compare Galatians with James, Romans, and 2 Corinthians.

10. Identify by outlines the three divisions of this epistle.

11. Quote a key verse.

12. Name five key words of Galatians.

VIII. FURTHER STUDY

1. Study further the comparisons of law and Spirit in Scripture. Use outside sources, including an exhaustive concordance and *Nave's Topical Bible*. The accompanying Chart 81 suggests some areas of study.

2. Refer to outside sources for arguments used to support the North Galatian and South Galatian views.[10] Background and summary are given below.

The North Galatian and South Galatian Views

In Paul's day the term *Galatia* had two connotations. One was

---

10. For support of the South Galatian view, see Robert Gundry, *A Survey of the New Testament*, pp. 260-62; Merrill C. Tenney, *New Testament Survey*, pp. 265-67; and D. Edmond Hiebert, *An Introduction to the Pauline Epistles*, pp. 79-83. For support of the North Galatian view, see Everett F. Harrison, *Introduction to the New Testament*, pp. 259-64; and W. Graham Scroggie, *Know Your Bible*, 2:148-50.

ethnic, and the other was provincial. A summary of the historical
background will explain the reason for the differences:

250 B.C.   Migratory Celtic tribes (Gauls) moved in from the west
           and north and settled down in Asia Minor, mostly in the
           northern half.

189 B.C.   The people were conquered by the Romans.

 25 B.C.   Augustus made the region a Roman province, calling it
           Galatia (after "Gaul").

A.D. 41   The original boundaries were extended southward to
           include such cities as Derbe and surrounding areas.

CHART 81

LAW AND SPIRIT IN GOD'S TIMETABLE

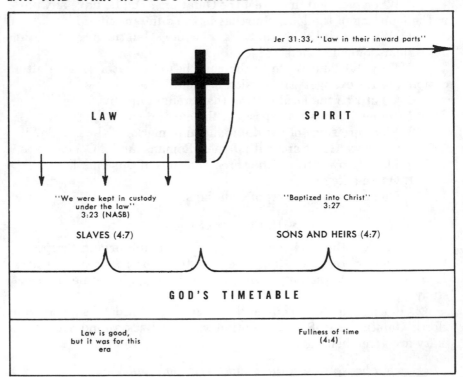

Here are the two views and some arguments that are advanced to
defend each:

1. "Churches of Galatia" were churches in the northern regions.

a. This is "ethnic" Galatia, using the term in a *popular* sense.

b. The churches were founded on Paul's second or third missionary journey (see Acts 16:6; 18:23).

c. This area was the true Galatia, in race and language.

d. There were more Gentiles in the northern cities, hence the problem referred to in Galatians would more likely exist there.

e. The early church Fathers understood the term "Galatia" to mean the northern region.

2. "Churches of Galatia" were churches in the southern regions.

a. This is "provincial" Galatia, with the term used in an *official* sense.

b. The churches were founded on Paul's first missionary journey (Acts 13-14).

c. We know of no churches existing at this early date in the northern parts of Galatia.

d. Barnabas, who accompanied Paul on the first journey but not on the second, is mentioned more than once in Galatians 2, as if he were well known to the readers (2:1, 9, 13).

e. The letter was written *before* the Jerusalem Council (Acts 15), and therefore before the second missionary journey; otherwise Paul would surely have referred to the Council's decree favoring Gentile Christian freedom from the Mosaic law, which is the main problem being addressed in Galatians.

f. This is the view generally held today.

IX. OUTLINE

X. SELECTED READING

GENERAL INTRODUCTION

Harrison, Everett F. "The Epistle to the Galatians." In *The Wycliffe Bible Commentary*, pp. 1283-85.

Hendriksen, William, *Exposition of Galatians*. In his New Testament Commentary series, pp. 3-25.

Ross, Alexander. "The Epistle to the Galatians." In *The New Bible Commentary*, pp. 1089-92.

COMMENTARIES

Cole, R. A. *The Epistle of Paul to the Galatians.*

Lightfoot, J. B. *The Epistle of Paul to the Galatians.*

Luther, Martin. *A Commentary on St. Paul's Epistle to the Galatians.*

OTHER RELATED SOURCES

Goodwin, Frank J. *A Harmony of the Life of St. Paul.*

Stalker, James. *The Life of St. Paul.*

Tenney, Merrill C. *Galatians: The Charter of Christian Liberty.*

14

Ephesians: Christ and the Church

Each of Paul's letters is classified in one of two groups: (1) *early*, written during the years of the missionary journeys; and (2) *later*, written after Paul's arrest at Jerusalem (Acts 21). Ephesians is one of the later letters, of a smaller group known as the "prison epistles." All of the epistles we have studied so far are of the early group.

I. PREPARATION FOR STUDY

It will help you prepare to study Ephesians if you first become acquainted with the prison epistles as a group and think about what it meant for Paul to experience imprisonment while writing.

A. THE GROUP OF PRISON EPISTLES

The prison epistles were among Paul's later letters written during the apostle's first imprisonment in Rome. Study Chart 82 and observe the following:

1. There are two groups of New Testament epistles: Pauline and general. How many general epistles?

2. What early Pauline letters have we not studied yet?

3. How many groups of later epistles are there?

4. Name the prison epistles. The order shown on the chart is the probable order of writing.[1] The identification Christological indicates the general theological content of the letters, namely the Person and work of Christ.[2]

5. 2 Timothy was also written from prison, but it is not of the group *prison epistles*.

---

1. The order that we are following in the surveys of this study guide is the canonical order, which is also the order of appearance in our Bible.
2. Philemon is a very personal note, with no direct, formal theological teaching.

THE PLACE OF THE CHRISTOLOGICAL EPISTLES IN THE NEW TESTAMENT

NEW TESTAMENT

HISTORY	EPISTLES		APOCALYPSE
	Pauline	General	

HISTORY
- MATTHEW
- MARK
- LUKE
- JOHN
- ACTS

EPISTLES — Pauline

EARLY (during missionary journeys)
- GALATIANS
- 1 THESSALONIANS
- 2 THESSALONIANS
- 1 CORINTHIANS
- 2 CORINTHIANS
- ROMANS

LATER (after arrest at Jerusalem)

FIRST IMPRISONMENT ("prison epistles") — CHRISTOLOGICAL
- COLOSSIANS
- EPHESIANS
- PHILEMON
- PHILIPPIANS

RELEASE — PASTORAL
- 1 TIMOTHY
- TITUS

SECOND IMPRISONMENT
- 2 TIMOTHY

EPISTLES — General
- JAMES
- HEBREWS
- JUDE
- 1 PETER
- 2 PETER
- 1 JOHN
- 2 JOHN
- 3 JOHN

APOCALYPSE
- REVELATION

B. PAUL THE PRISONER

All four of the prison epistles contain direct references to Paul's imprisonment. Read Ephesians 3:1; 4:1; 6:20; Philippians 1:7, 13; Colossians 4:3, 18; Philemon 10, 13, 22, 23. Paul had previously experienced being jailed (2 Cor. 11:23), but the first Roman imprisonment was of long duration and involved extensive ministry outreach. Read Acts 28:16-31 for Luke's reporting of some activities from part of that period.

C. PLACE OF WRITING

It is generally held that the prison epistles were written at Rome, during the imprisonment of Acts 28. Some advocate either Caesarea or Ephesus as the place of writing.[3]

D. ORDER OF WRITING

Colossians, Ephesians, and Philemon were written first, dispatched at the same time by the same messengers. (Read Ephesians 6:21-22; Colossians 4:7-9; Philemon 12.) Philippians was written at a later time. (The date will be discussed when that epistle is studied later.)

II. BACKGROUND

A. AUTHOR

Twice in the text of Ephesians, Paul is identified as the author. Read 1:1 and 3:1. Internal evidences of style and content, as well as the external witness of tradition, support this observation.

Paul was about sixty-five years of age when he wrote the letter. He referred to himself as "the aged" when he wrote to Philemon at this same time.

B. DATE AND PLACE OF WRITING

A date assigned to the writing of Ephesians is A.D. 61. This is based on Paul's writing the epistle during his first imprisonment in Rome, which lasted at least two years (A.D. 61-62). At that time he also wrote Colossians, Philemon, and Philippians, as noted above. Read Acts 28:30-31. Were circumstances favorable to Paul to meditate, study, and write during this imprisonment? John Bunyan wrote the classic *The Pilgrim's Progress* while in prison. Have you read of other "prison masterpieces"? How do you account for such a phenomenon, from the human standpoint? Of course, in the case of a canonical book like Ephesians, God was the originator and user of the writing's setting.

---

3. See D. Edmond Hiebert, *An Introduction to the Pauline Epistles*, pp. 205-11, for a discussion of this.

C. DESTINATION

1. *Main views*. There are two main views regarding the original destination of Ephesians.

a. The church of Ephesus. This view is supported by the reading of 1:1, and by the traditional title assigned the epistle by the early church Fathers: "To Ephesians" (Greek, *Pros Ephesious*). Also, such verses as 4:17 and 6:21-22 point to a *specific* church as being addressed, whatever that church was.

b. A circuit of various unspecified churches. This view is based mainly on the fact that some important ancient manuscripts omit the phrase "at Ephesus" (Greek, *en Epheso*) in 1:1.[4] Also, the epistle as a whole lacks the usual Pauline personal greetings, and so appears to be a circular letter.[5]

Each of the above views has its strengths and weaknesses. Perhaps the answer is found in combining the two views. In the words of one writer, "The epistle was written to the Ephesians and addressed to them, but ... the Apostle intentionally cast it into a form which would make it suitable to the Christians in the neighboring churches and intended that it should be communicated to them."[6]

Refer to a detailed map of Asia Minor (Map V, p. 337) for the location of the churches of some cities near Ephesus that would have read Paul's letter sooner or later. Read Acts 19:8-10; 20:31 for references to Paul's three-year ministry to people living in Ephesus and the regions round about.

2. *The city of Ephesus*. The Christians living in and around Ephesus to whom Paul wrote this sublime epistle were cosmopolitan and well informed about world affairs. This is because of the city's strategic location. Ephesus was recognized as the "first" city of the province of Asia, even though Pergamum, ninety miles to the north, was its capital. Try to imagine some of the native characteristics of the congregation at Ephesus from the following brief notes about the city.

a. Commerce. Ephesus was one of the three leaders of international trade, the other two being Alexandria of Egypt and Antioch of Syria. Note on Map E, p. 64, the city's trade-oriented location.

b. Arts and sciences. The city was a haven for philosophers, poets, artists, and orators. Corinth, across the Aegean Sea, was one of its rivals in those disciplines.

---

4. Main examples are the two primary uncials, Sinaiticus and Vaticanus (fourth century), and the Chester Beatty papyri (third century).
5. An exception is 6:21.
6. D. Edmond Hiebert, *An Introduction to the Pauline Epistles*, p. 266.

c. Religion. The worship of Diana (Greek, *Artemis*) was the dominant religion of this area. The temple of Diana was world famous. Read Acts 19:23-27, noting among other things from the passage that Demetrius boasted that "all of Asia and the world" worshipped Diana (19:27). Many of the Ephesians also identified with the imperial cult of Augustus and with various forms of magic (cf. Acts 19:13-19; Eph. 6:12). When you study Ephesians try to recall from time to time that its original readers were converts from the darkness of those idolatries.

3. *The church at Ephesus.* Read the following passages for what they reveal concerning the Ephesian church. Look for such things as first converts, leaders, and organizational growth.

a. Pentecost converts from Asia. A.D. 30 — Acts 2:9

b. Before Paul's extended campaign at Ephesus. A.D. 52 — Acts 18:18-21; 18:24-26

c. During the extended campaign. A.D. 52-56 — Acts 19

d. Paul recalling the past. Acts 20:17-27

e. Charge to the Ephesian elders. A.D. 55-56 — Acts 20:28-38

f. Charge to Timothy. A.D. 64 — 1 Timothy 1:3

Also read Acts 19:17-20 for one glimpse of this group before and after their conversion (A.D. 55). Little did the Christians know then that the bonfire of their heathen books would bring forth out of its ashes an object of spiritual gold — one short book of Ephesians — just six years later.

Most of the Ephesian congregation were Gentile converts, though the number of Jewish Christians was not small. Note the two references to "Jews and Greeks" in Acts 19:10, 17. Because their conversion took place in A.D. 55 and Ephesians was written in A.D. 61, the people of the congregation were relatively young in the Lord when they read Paul's letter for the first time. The church itself served as a "mother church" to the others of the province. By the time the apostle John became a spiritual shepherd of the Asian Christians toward the end of the first century, the Ephesian church was regarded as the headquarters of Christian missions, having succeeded Antioch of Syria (which had succeeded Jerusalem). Observe in Revelation 1:11 the location of the name Ephesus in the list of the seven churches. Does the location suggest something to you?

D. OCCASION AND PURPOSE OF EPHESIANS

Ephesians does not give a clue concerning any specific problem in the Ephesian church to which the epistle might have been directed. By "specific problem" is meant such things as heresy (e.g., Colossians); internal strife (1 Corinthians); false accusations (2 Corinthians); false doctrine (Galatians). But when Paul wrote Ephesians he still must have been thinking of such evils as doctrinal heresy threatening the neighboring church at Colossae, which he specifically refers to in his letter to the Colossians. (Observe on Maps E and V, pp. 64 and 337, how close Colossae was to Ephesus.) No church is ever immune to doctrinal defilement, so it could be that the apostle's positive teachings in Ephesus on the pure knowledge of Christ were directed at the same kinds of problems that were vexing the Colossian church. Also, the Christians at Colossae would eventually be reading Ephesians, as it made the rounds of the churches of Asia. Hiebert writes on this: "Judging from its close relation to Colossians, it appears that the conflict which caused the writing of Colossians likewise called forth this epistle. The Colossian conflict revealed to Paul the need for a fuller statement of God's program for the universe as it centers in Christ in His relationship to the Church."[7]

No doubt there were individual problems in the Ephesian church. But the basic need for the young Christians there was to grow spiritually in the Lord, by (1) an increasing awareness of their relationship to Him and His ministry to them through the Spirit, and (2) the day-to-day experience of walking in that light. Paul was inspired to address this epistle to that basic need for spiritual growth. The letter still serves the same function today for the children of God.

E. GENERAL CHARACTERISTICS

Ephesians is a book of grand superlatives. It is the sublimest of all Paul's epistles and has been called "The Grand Canyon of Scripture." There are very few personal notes and biographical references and, as noted earlier, controversies and problems are not discussed here. Paul is not thereby ignoring the practical mundane issues, as though they were unimportant. (At least half the epistle is practical in purpose.) Rather, the apostle has a vision of the heavenly realm, and in the quiet and calm of his imprisonment he is inspired by the Spirit to share that with his readers.[8] Philip Schaff describes this aspect of the epistle:

> It certainly is the most spiritual and devout, composed in an exalted and transcendent state of mind, where theology rises into worship, and meditation into oration. It is the Epistle of the Heavenlies. . . . The aged apostle soared high above all earthly things to the invisible and eternal realities in heaven. From his gloomy confinement he ascended for a

7. Ibid.
8. The word *heaven(s)* appears four times, and *heavenly places* (or *heavenlies*) four times, in Ephesians.

season to the mount of transfiguration. The prisoner of Christ, chained to a heathen soldier, was transformed into a conqueror, clad in the panoply of God, and singing a paean of victory.[9]

The distinctive language and style of Ephesians reflects the richness and depth of its message. Someone has observed that the letter contains forty-two words (e.g., "obtained an inheritance," 1:11) not found in any other New Testament book, and forty-three not used by Paul in his other writings. One of the prominent features of Paul's style in Ephesians is its long sentences, described as follows by one writer: "The sentences flow on as it were in the full strong tide, wave after wave, of an immense and impetuous sea, swayed by a powerful wind, and brightened and sparkling with the golden rays of a rising sun." This suggests something of the excitement and inspiration in store for all who study the Bible text.

CHART 83

COLOSSIANS AND EPHESIANS COMPARED

COLOSSIANS	EPHESIANS
CHRIST AND THE COSMOS	CHRIST AND THE CHURCH
Emphasis on Christ Head of the Church	Emphasis on the Church Body of Christ
MORE PERSONAL; LOCAL	LESS PERSONAL; LOFTY
COMBATS ERROR DIRECTLY	COMBATS ERROR INDIRECTLY
TONE: intensity and tumult of a battlefield	TONE: calmness of surveying the field after victory

F. RELATION TO OTHER NEW TESTAMENT BOOKS

1. *Prison epistles.* We have already seen that the four epistles — Ephesians, Philippians, Colossians, and Philemon — were written about the same time. This would account for at least some of the similarities of these books. Ephesians, Philippians, and Colossians were written to local churches of those cities; Philemon, although

---

9. Philip Schaff, *History of the Christian Church*, 1:780.

written particularly to a personal friend of Paul, was also addressed to the church that met in Philemon's house (Philem. 2; cf. Col. 4:15), which was in or near Colossae.

2. *Ephesians and Colossians*. Ephesians and Colossians have been called twin epistles because of their many likenesses. Phrases of 78 of Ephesians' 155 verses are very similar to phrases in Colossians. This is explained by the same general purpose for which both epistles were written: to show the relationship between Christ and His church as assurance and correction to young Christians growing and maturing in the Lord.

But the two epistles are far from being *identical* twins. Some differences are shown on Chart 83.

3. *Galatians, Ephesians, and Philippians*. You have just finished surveying Galatians, which Paul wrote about thirteen years before he wrote the prison epistles. In your first reading of Ephesians you will quickly detect many differences between the letters, including one of tone. Chart 84 compares Galatians, Ephesians, and Philippians.

CHART 84

GALATIANS, EPHESIANS AND PHILIPPIANS COMPARED

	GALATIANS	EPHESIANS	PHILIPPIANS
STYLE	mainly logical and argumentative	doctrinal and hortatory	informative and consoling
A MAIN SUBJECT	SALVATION	CHRIST	LIFE OF JOY
PURPOSE	CORRECTIVE	INSTRUCTIVE	INSPIRATIONAL
TONE	sharp, rebuking	calm, victorious	tender, joyful

III. SURVEY

A. FIRST READING

1. Scan the letter of Ephesians in one sitting.

2. Write down your first impressions of the book.

3. What is the atmosphere of the book as a whole?

4. List a few key words and phrases that stand out as of this reading.

B. PARAGRAPHS AND SEGMENTS

1. Before reading the letter again, mark paragraph divisions in your Bible at the following verses: 1:1, 3, 15; 2:1, 11, 19; 3:1, 14, 20; 4:1, 7, 14, 17, 25; 5:3, 6, 15, 21, 25; 6:1, 5, 9, 10, 14, 18, 21, 23.

2. Now read the letter paragraph by paragraph. Assign a title for each paragraph. Doing this exercise helps you get an initial momentum in survey study.

3. Is there an introduction and conclusion to the letter? What are the verses?

4. Did you notice any major turning point in the book? If so, where?

5. Add to the list of key words and phrases, which you began earlier in this study.

6. Did you observe any personal references, such as names of people?

7. Where in Ephesians do prayers of Paul appear?

C. OBSERVING THE STRUCTURE OF THE LETTER

Now you will want to see how the various parts of Ephesians are related to each other. Two key things to look for in this structure study are (1) main turning point and (2) groupings of paragraphs.

1. *Main turning point.* You probably have already observed that there is a change in the epistle at the end of Chapter 3. How is this supported by the following:

a. the content of 3:20-21

b. the last word of 3:21

c. the first two words of 4:1

d. the general content of chapters 4-6 as compared with 1-3? (For example, which chapters are predominantly practical?)

2. *Groupings of paragraphs.* Some groups of paragraphs are not always easy to detect in the early stages of study. What subject appears in the paragraph 5:21-24, and continues into the next paragraphs? Where then does a new general subject begin? Identify the group beginning at 5:21 with a title. Try to identify other groups in the epistle.

How does the paragraph 6:10-20 serve as a concluding paragraph to the epistle (not counting the paragraph 6:21-24)?

D. SURVEY CHART

Chart 85 is a survey chart of Ephesians. Refer to it after you have completed most of your overview of the contents and structure of the letter. Observe the following on the chart:

1. Ephesians is divided into two main parts. Which is mainly doctrinal, and which is mainly practical?

2. "Our Heritage in Christ" is related to "Our Life in Christ" by the word *therefore* (see 4:1). What is the practical lesson suggested by this?

3. Note the two sections *we in Christ* and *Christ in us*. Scan chapter 1 for the many appearances of the phrase "in him" (and similar phrases). Then read 3:20 (cf. 3:17) for the phrase "works within us," which anticipates the development of the theme *Christ in us* in the chapters to come.

4. The passage 3:2-13 is shown as a parenthesis in chapter 3. Read the chapter and observe why 3:2-13 is parenthetical.

5. Observe the commands shown at the top of the chart (e.g., *know*). Read each verse in the Bible text. Relate the command words to the outlines shown below them on the chart. Compare these outlines with your own studies made so far.

IV. PROMINENT SUBJECTS

A. PRAYER AND PRAISE

The opening passage 1:3-14 has been called a "hymn of grace." How does the following outline represent the doctrines of the hymn?

Salvation: The Father planned it (1:4-6)
Salvation: The Son paid for it (1:7-12)
Salvation: The Spirit applied it (1:13-14)

Two notable prayers appear at 1:15-23 and 3:14-21.

1. *Prayer of 1:15-23.* This prayer is closely related to the hymn of 1:3-14. That hymn was Paul's testimony of praise to God for the boundless spiritual blessings in Christ. The prayer of 1:15-23 is the apostle's intercession for saints, that they may know the extent of their blessings in Christ. So in 1:3-14 the appeal to the reader is for a heart of praise; in 1:15-23 the appeal is for a spirit of wisdom. The Christian who earnestly covets and cultivates both of these is the maturing Christian, growing daily in the grace and knowledge of Jesus Christ.

Prayer of 3:14-21. Read the prayer. Compare it with 1:15-23.

B. DOCTRINE

Ephesians is a storehouse full of many doctrines of the Christian

EPHESIANS
CHRIST AND THE CHURCH

INTRODUCTION						CONCLUSION
1:3	1:15	2:1	3:2	3:14	4:1	5:21	6:10	6:21

1:1	KNOW 1:18	REMEMBER 2:11	FAINT NOT 3:13	WALK WORTHILY 4:1		PUT ON 6:11
	BLESSINGS IN CHRIST	EXPERIENCE OF SALVATION	GROWING KNOWLEDGE AND STRENGTH	CHRISTIAN CONDUCT		CHRISTIAN ARMOR
	position and possessions	PAST: without Christ PRESENT: with Christ	present and future	church unity	daily walk	domestic duty	THE CONFLICT

PARENTHESIS —PAUL'S TESTIMONY

PRAISE	PRAYER	EXHORTATION	TESTIMONY AND PRAYER	COMMANDS AND EXHORTATIONS

OUR HERITAGE IN CHRIST			OUR LIFE IN CHRIST

Therefore

"I pray that you may know your resources in Christ"

"I pray that you may live consistent with your faith in Christ"

WE IN CHRIST	CHRIST IN US

IN HIM 1:4

IN US (cf. 3:20)

WORK OF GOD	WALK OF THE CHRISTIAN
heavenly standing	earthly walk

| —every blessing | —access | —power | —unity | —joy | —prayer |
| —sealing | —growth | —revelation | —holiness | —thanksgiving | —word |

HOLY SPIRIT

Key Verses
2:19-20
1:22-23

Key Words
church
in Christ
in Him
heavenly places
according to
power
riches
glory
one
love
walk
even as
grace
spiritual
Spirit
mystery

faith, as already noted. Observe where the following appear in the letter:

1. Salvation: as a deliverance *from*, and deliverance *unto*.

2. Union with Christ: an inscrutable yet real relationship.

3. The church universal: as the Body of Christ, who is its Head.

4. Holy Spirit: the source of every blessing and power in the Christian life.

5. Will and work of God: for man's benefit and God's glory.

6. What doctrines are taught by these oft-quoted passages: 2:4-10; 2:19-22?

C. PRACTICE

At least half the epistle is devoted to the practical walk of the believer in Christ. The Christian's *walking* (4:1) and *standing* (6:11) are based on his *sitting* (2:6). His life in Christ (chaps. 4-6) is drawn from his heritage in Christ (chaps. 1-3).

Chapters 4-6 are the chapters of the plains and the cities where Christians reveal by their deeds who they really are. In 1:1—3:21 the apostle has written much about the Christian's heavenly standing; now he says some things about the believer's earthly walk. In the first half of Ephesians the emphasis is on the Christian's position *in Christ*. Now the spotlight turns on Christ's living *in the Christian*.

The armor passage of 6:10-17 is a classic Scripture portion describing the weaponry of the Christian's spiritual warfare. Paul has just finished telling Christians how they ought to conduct their lives, giving them command upon command that must be obeyed if God is to be glorified. Now he speaks as a general to his army troops and, pointing to the arsenal of the superhuman armor, he assures them of victory if they will but use the divine resources.

V. KEY WORDS AND VERSES

1. *Key words*. There are many key words in Ephesians (Chart 85). If you had to limit the list to ten, which ones would you choose?

2. *A key verse*. Look for a verse that represents the theme of the letter. You may find more than one.

3. *Main theme*. In your own words, what is the main theme of Ephesians?

4. *Title*. Assign a title to Ephesians to coincide with the main theme you have determined. Note the one given on Chart 85.

VI. APPLICATIONS

What three different areas of a Christian's life are suggested by the outline: church unity, 4:1-16; daily walk, 4:17—5:20; domestic duty, 5:21—6:9? Write a list of applications derived from these parts of the epistle.

Add other important applications to the list.

Read Revelation 2:1-7 for a brief description of the Ephesian church's spiritual state thirty-five years after Paul wrote Ephesians. What are your reflections?

VII. REVIEW QUESTIONS

1. How old was Paul when he wrote Ephesians? Where was he when he composed the letter?

2. Regarding to whom Ephesians was originally sent, what are the two main views? What are your conclusions?

3. How would you describe the average member of the church at Ephesus in the year A.D. 61?

4. Reconstruct the story of how the Ephesians were first saved, and how the local church came to be organized.

5. Do you think the message of Ephesians was too deep for the young converts at Ephesus? Who should be reading and studying Ephesians today?

6. What relationship was there between the church at Ephesus and churches in surrounding cities (e.g., Colossae)?

7. What were some of Paul's reasons for writing this letter to the churches of Asia?

8. What are some of the main doctrines taught in Ephesians?

9. Identify some of the letter's characteristics, such as style and tone.

10. Compare Ephesians and Colossians. How do you account for the many likenesses?

11. From what you have learned in your survey of Ephesians, how can this epistle realistically help Christians today?

VIII. FURTHER STUDY

You may want to make an extended study of different subjects that appear throughout the epistle. Topics suggested for such study are listed below:

1. Paul as seen in the epistle. For example, see 3:1, 8, 13; 6:19-20.

2. The Ephesian Christians as seen in the epistle. See 1:15; 2:11; 3:13; 4:1 ff.; 6:10 ff.

3. God the Father.

4. God the Son.

5. God the Holy Spirit (see the outline on Chart 85).
6. The "heavenlies."
7. The subjects of faith, hope, love, prayer, power.
8. Eternity.

IX. Outline

EPHESIANS: Christ and the Church

OUR HERITAGE IN CHRIST	1:1—3:21
Spiritual Blessings in Christ	1:1-14
Prayer for Spiritual Wisdom	1:15-23
Once Dead, Now Alive	2:1-22
Paul's Testimony and Prayer	3:1-21
OUR LIFE IN CHRIST	4:1—6:24
Preserving Church Unity	4:1-16
Daily Walk of Christians	4:17—5:20
Conduct in the Christian Home	5:21—6:9
The Christian's Armor	6:10-24

X. Selected Reading

GENERAL INTRODUCTION

Hiebert, D. Edmond. *An Introduction to the Pauline Epistles*, pp. 254-82.
Westcott, B. F. *Saint Paul's Epistle to the Ephesians*, pp. xix-lxviii.

COMMENTARIES

Bruce, F. F. *The Epistle to the Ephesians*.
Hodge, Charles. *A Commentary on the Epistle to the Ephesians*.
Martin, Alfred. "The Epistle to the Ephesians." In *Wycliffe Bible Commentary*.

OTHER RELATED SOURCES

Baxter, J. Sidlow. *Explore the Book*, Vol. 4.
Miller, H. S. *The Book of Ephesians*.
Moule, H.C.G. *Ephesian Studies*.

15

Philippians: Life in Christ

Philippians was probably the last of the four prison epistles to be written, but in the New Testament canon it is placed second, following Ephesians. It is the brightest and most joyful of all Paul's writings, and one of its ministries has been to rejuvenate the spiritual life of multitudes of Christians.

I. Preparation for Study

Review the things learned in Chapter 14 about the prison epistles. Recall that Paul wrote Ephesians, Colossians, and Philemon at the same time, and shortly thereafter he wrote to the church at Philippi.

II. Background

A. AUTHOR

Paul was the author of this epistle. He names his colaborer Timothy (Timotheus) in the salutation of 1:1 because Timothy was with him when he wrote the letter. (Cf. Col. 1:1; Philem. 1.)

B. DESTINATION

1. *The city of Philippi.* The opening verse of Philippians identifies its destination as a congregation of the city of Philippi. Let us first consider the city itself.

a. Geography. Refer to Map V, page 337, which shows the geographical setting of the prison epistles. Observe the following:

(1) Philippi was a city of the province of Macedonia.

(2) The city is just inland (about ten miles) from the coastal town of Neapolis. (Read Acts 16:11-12, which records Paul's stopover at Neapolis on his first visit to Philippi.)

(3) Observe that Philippi is located on the Egnatian Way, a major overland route of Macedonia. When Paul sent Epaphroditus back to Philippi from Rome (2:25), the trip no doubt was via the Appian Way through Italy (see map), followed by an eighty-mile boat trip across the Sea of Adria, then the land journey on the Egnatian Way.

(4) Observe other coastal cities that Paul visited after leaving Philippi on his second missionary journey: Amphipolis, Apollonia, Thessalonica, Berea, Athens, Corinth.

b. Name. In 350 B.C. the city was named Philippi, after Philip of Macedon, father of Alexander the Great. Its former name was *Krenides* (Little Fountains).

c. Political status. The city became a Roman colony in 42 B.C. "It was a miniature Rome ... exempt from taxation and modeled after the capital of the world."[1] Luke recognized its popular acclaim by calling Philippi "the chief city of that part of Macedonia" (Acts 16:12).[2]

d. Population. Estimates range from 200,000 to 500,000 residents, as of Paul's time. Most of those were Greeks, with a smaller contingent of Jews and Romans. Read Acts 16:13 and observe where Paul held his first evangelistic meeting in the city. Might this suggest that there was no synagogue (Jewish place to worship) in the city, since Paul usually had his first public contacts with the people in the synagogue?

One writer has described the typical citizen of Philippi thus: "The Macedonians, like the old Romans, were manly, straightforward and affectionate. They were not skeptical like the philosophers of Athens, nor voluptuous like the Greeks of Corinth."[3]

e. Economics. Philippi was a relatively wealthy city, known for its gold mines and exceptionally fertile soil. A reputable school of medicine was located there. It is interesting to associate this latter fact with the view held by many that Philippi was Dr. Luke's hometown.

2. *The church at Philippi.* When Paul wrote Philippians, the congregation at Philippi was about ten years old. Here is a thumbnail sketch of the congregation:

a. Origins. Among the first converts were Lydia and the town's jailer. Read Acts 16:13-15 and 16:23-34, respectively, for the account of those conversions. Observe among other things that the other

---

1. Robert H. Mounce, "The Epistle to the Philippians," in *The Wycliffe Bible Commentary*, p. 1319.
2. Actually, Amphipolis was the capital of the district that included Philippi.
3. Quoted in J. Sidlow Baxter, *Explore the Book*, 6:181.

members of the two families were also saved at that time. Luke identifies Lydia as "a worshiper of God" (Acts 16:14), which indicates that she was a proselyte to the Jewish religion when Paul first met her. The first meeting place of the new Christians at Philippi was probably the home of Lydia (Acts 16:15, 40).

b. First church of Europe. Philippi is commonly referred to as the birthplace of European Christianity, since the first converts of any known organized missionary work in Europe were gained here. The occasion was Paul's second missionary journey of A.D. 49-52, as recorded in Acts 15:36—18:22. The year of Paul's first contact at Philippi was around A.D. 50.

c. Membership and organization. Most of the congregation were Greeks, though the fellowship included some converted Jews. The average family was of the middle class, of moderate financial means. By the time Paul wrote the epistle, the church had an organizational structure that included the church offices of bishops (overseers) and deacons. (Read Philippians 1:1.)

d. Early days. When Paul left the new Philippian converts after his first ministry in Philippi, his companion Luke remained behind, and no doubt helped in a follow-up ministry of encouraging and instructing the new Christians. Read the following passages which support this observation:

Acts 16:10-13: Luke joins Paul's missionary party at Troas to go to Macedonia, as indicated by the repeated pronoun "we." (Luke was the author of Acts.)

Acts 16:40; 17:1-4: Luke is not part of Paul's party that left Philippi. Conclusion: Luke must have remained behind.

Acts 20:5-6: Luke rejoins the group when Paul passes through Philippi on the last part of his third missionary journey, about six years later (A.D. 56).

C. PLACE AND DATE OF WRITING

Paul wrote Philippians from his prison quarters at Rome, around A.D. 61-62.[4] Read Acts 28:16-31 for Luke's report of those two years of imprisonment.

D. PURPOSES

Paul had two main reasons for writing to the church at Philippi at this time. One was circumstantial; the other was instructional.

1. *Circumstantial.* Read the following passages and observe what message Paul wanted to relay to the Philippians: 2:19-24; 2:25-30; 4:2-3; 4:10-19.

---

4. References to the "palace" (1:13) and "Caesar's household" (4:22) are evidence that the letter came from Rome.

2. *Instructional*. All of Paul's epistles fulfill the purposes as described in 2 Timothy 3:16-17. Some of the things the apostle wanted to share with the saints at Philippi were:

a. encouragement to put Christ first in everyday living. Possibly nowhere else in the New Testament is the Christ-centered life more vividly portrayed than in this letter. Read 1:20-21 and 3:7-14.

b. appeal to beware and to correct spiritual problems (e.g., 4:2-3).

c. instruction in Christian doctrines (e.g., 2:6-11).

E. CHARACTERISTICS

Philippians has been called Paul's love letter to the saints at Philippi because its informal, personal style reveals so much of the apostle's affectionate character. The epistle contains less censure and more praise than does any other epistle.

Because Paul's purpose in writing was more practical than doctrinal, no detailed outline is apparent in the structure of this personal letter. However, Paul does teach about the doctrines of the Person and work of Christ in the epistle.

Paul does not quote the Old Testament in the letter, and the vocabulary includes sixty-five words that are not found in any of Paul's other epistles.

F. PLACE IN THE NEW TESTAMENT

Each of the twenty-seven New Testament books has particular functions in the volume of Scripture. Refer to Chart 62, page 244, and note that Philippians is identified as a Christological letter. How is it compared with Philemon? (Compare it also with Ephesians and Colossians on the chart.)

H. C. G. Moule has compared Philippians with other Pauline writings in this way:

> Looking at the other epistles, each with its own divine and also deeply human characteristics, we find Philippians more peaceful than Galatians, more personal and affectionate than Ephesians, less anxiously controversial than Colossians, more deliberate and symmetrical than Thessalonians, and of course larger in its applications than the personal messages to Timothy, Titus, and Philemon.[5]

III. SURVEY

A. FIRST READING

Read Philippians in one sitting, without lingering over any details. After this scanning, answer the following:

---

5. H.C.G. Moule, *Philippian Studies*, p. 5.

What are your main impressions?

What is the general atmosphere of the letter?

Were you conscious of any organized outline as you read?

Did you observe any turning points in the epistle? If so, where?

What strong words or phrases stand out in your mind as of this reading?

B. SUBSEQUENT READINGS

Mark paragraph divisions in your Bible at these locations: 1:1, 3, 12, 27; 2:1, 5, 12, 19, 25; 3:1, 15; 4:1, 4, 8, 10, 21. Then read the letter again, more slowly than the first time. Assign paragraph titles.

Scan the epistle again, looking for *groups* of paragraphs with similar content. For example:

1. Which paragraphs contain mainly Paul's testimonies regarding his experiences?

2. Which paragraphs record the ministries of colaborers of Paul?

3. Which paragraphs contain warnings?

4. Which paragraphs are mainly hortatory (containing exhortations and commands)?

5. Which paragraphs are mainly about personal relationships between Paul and the Philippians?

6. Look for other groupings.

7. Compare the opening and closing salutations of the letter.

On the basis of these groups, and other individual clues, have you been able to detect any general outline of content in the epistle? (Some Bible students feel there is no organized structure as such in Philippians, partly because of the letter's very personal nature. The survey, Chart 86, will suggest some general patterns, which may be seen in the epistle without forcing an outline on it.)

C. SURVEY CHART

The survey shows something of the structure and highlights of Philippians. Observe the following:

1. A main division is made at 1:27, instead of at 2:1. Read the Bible text and note that paragraph 1:27-30 is more similar in content to 2:1-4 than it is to 1:12-26.

2. A main division is made at 4:2 instead of at 4:1. Read 4:1 and observe that it serves better as a conclusion to what goes before than as an introduction to what follows.

3. The content of the epistle can be categorized under the headings of three key ideas: testimony, examples, and exhortations. Compare this with your earlier study of groups of paragraphs.

4. The four-part outlines are of a topical nature (i.e., life in

Christ, motives in life, Spirit, joy). Each outline shows how the particular topic appears in at least one verse of each of the four segments. The subheadings that represent the title "Life in Christ" are: *Christ our LIFE, Christ our PATTERN, Christ our GOAL*, and *Christ our SUFFICIENCY*.

5. Note the title assigned to Philippians, "Life in Christ." How do the outlines on the chart support that title?

IV. PROMINENT SUBJECTS

Some of the main subjects that appear in Philippians are: (1) joy in Christ — the words *rejoice* and *joy* appear seventeen times in the epistle; (2) unity of believers in Christ — key passages are 1:27—2:18 and 4:1-9; (3) keeping *above* hard circumstances of every day life; (4) growing in the Lord; (5) the gospel — the word appears nine times in the letter.

Favorite passages memorized by many Christians include 1:21-26; 3:7-11; 3:12-16; 4:4-7; 4:8; 4:11-13; 4:19.

Two important passages of Philippians are briefly discussed below.

A. CHRIST'S EMPTYING (2:5-11)

This paragraph is one of the most glorious passages in the entire Bible. It is a doctrinal book in miniature, teaching truths about the Person and work of Christ. It is a handbook of Christian living, summing up Christian behavior in one sublime, opening appeal.

The passage is usually referred to as the kenosis passage, named after the key Greek word *ekenosen* ("emptied," v. 7). The unstated question of the text is, Of what did Jesus empty Himself when He came to earth? Those who hold that Jesus of Galilee was only human answer that Jesus emptied Himself of deity. The marginal note of the *New American Standard Bible* gives the interpretation that Jesus "laid aside His privileges." Compare this with the interpretation that Jesus surrendered the *independent* exercise of some of His relative attributes (e.g., "not my will, but thine, be done").[6]

Read the passage. What is its main subject? What is the opening, practical exhortation? How do the words *humiliation* and *exaltation* represent the two parts of the paragraph?

B. CHRIST OUR GOAL (3:1—4:1)

Chapter 3 is the mountain peak of Philippians, challenging and inspiring its Christian readers with the highest of goals (e.g., 3:14).

---

6. Cf. Henry C. Thiessen, *Introductory Lectures in Systematic Theology*, p. 296.

PHILIPPIANS
LIFE IN CHRIST

A KEY VERSE 1:21

KEY WORDS:
Day of Christ
In Christ
Rejoice
Gospel
Spirit
Mind
Love
Joy
All

	TESTIMONY	EXAMPLES	EXHORTATIONS	KEY VERSES
	1:1	1:27	3:1	4:2	4:23	

[despite imprisonment]
"For to me to live is Christ and to die is gain (1:21)."

"Conduct yourselves in a manner worthy of the gospel of Christ (1:27). Have this attitude in yourselves which was also in Christ Jesus (2:5-11)."

"More than that I count all things to be loss (3:8). That I may know Him, and the power of His resurrection (3:10). Forgetting what lies behind, I press toward the goal (3:13, 14). Citizenship in heaven (3:20)."

"Have no anxiety about anything (4:6-7). I have learned to be content in whatever circumstances I am (4:11). I can do all things (4:13). My God shall supply all your needs (4:19)."

KEY VERSES:
Life in Christ
Motives
Spirit
J O Y

Christ our LIFE	Christ our PATTERN	Christ our GOAL	Christ our SUFFICIENCY
GLORIFY CHRIST (1:20)	BE LIKE CHRIST (1:27)	GAIN CHRIST (3:8)	BE CONTENT IN CHRIST (4:11)
SUPPLY of the SPIRIT 1:19	FELLOWSHIP in the SPIRIT 2:1	WORSHIP by the SPIRIT 3:3	GRACE through the SPIRIT 4:23

THE CHRISTIAN LIFE — AN ABIDING JOY (2:17-18)

REJOICE:	REJOICE:	REJOICE:	REJOICE:
in fellowship of saints (1:3-11).	in the ministry for the saints (2:1-18).	that your hopes are in Jesus (3:2-16).	always over all things (4:4-9).
over afflictions (1:12-30).	in fellowship of Timothy and Epaphroditus (2:19-30).	that your citizenship is in heaven (3:20).	in bounties of God's people (4:10-19).

J O Y

Read the segment with these three different parts in mind:

Commands — 3:1-3
Testimonies — 3:4-14
Appeals — 3:15—4:1

Observe the goals Paul writes about. How is Christ related to each?

Throughout Philippians the Person of Jesus Christ is central. There can be no rejoicing outside of Him. He is the Christian's life (1:21), his supreme example (2:5-11), his great goal (3:10), and his gracious provider (4:13). No wonder Paul's passion and goal was "That I may know Him, and the power of His resurrection and the fellowship of His sufferings" (3:10).

C. CHRIST OUR SUFFICIENCY (4:2-23)

The structure of Philippians may be seen as a threefold unit:

PRESENT 1:1 ATTITUDES	1:27 AIMS AND ASPIRATIONS	PRESENT 4:2 SUFFICIENCY 4:23

How is each subject related to each other, and to the general scope of the Christian life?

Read 4:2-23 and observe different references to the Christian's sufficiency in Christ. How do these assurances affect the believer's aims and aspirations?

V. THEME, KEY WORDS AND VERSES

Write a list of key words and phrases that best represent Paul's emphases in this letter. Then identify a theme, and choose a key verse that reflects that theme.

Chart 86 shows 1:21 as a key verse. One writer has commented on this verse: "This outlook on life transformed misery into melody, prisons into palaces, and Roman soldiers into souls to be won for Christ."[7]

VI. APPLICATIONS

Have you ever wondered what the author of a New Testament book was thinking about during the minutes after he finished writing? Here is how one writer has reconstructed the scene in Paul's prison quarters after the apostle had finished dictating his Philippian letter:

The voice is silent; the pen is laid aside. In due time the papyrus roll, inestimable manuscript, is made ready for its journey. And perhaps as

_____
7. John Phillips, *Exploring the Scriptures*, p. 239.

it now lies drying, the Missionary and his brethren turn to further conversation on the beloved Philippian Church, and recall many a scene in the days that are over ... and they speak again of the brightness of the Philippian Christian life, and the shadows that lie on it here and there; and then, while the Praetorian sentinel looks on in wonder, or perhaps joins in as a believer, they pray together for Philippi, and pour out their praises to the Father and the Son, and anticipate the day of glory.[8]

That was almost two thousand years ago. Only God knows how many lives the letter has touched since. Like all Scripture, it is always new, always contemporary. Has it spoken to your heart? Write a list of applications that you have derived from the letter in the course of your survey.

What does Philippians teach about these experiences and areas of Christian living:
• joy in Christ
• sufficiency in Christ
• industry and rewards
• justifiable motives?

VII. REVIEW QUESTIONS

1. What made the geographical location of Philippi a strategic one?

2. How would you describe a typical citizen of this Macedonian city?

3. What was Paul's first contact in Philippi?

4. What picture do you have of the Philippian congregation when Paul wrote the epistle?

5. How many years had intervened between the first conversions at Philippi and the writing of the letter?

6. What was Luke's interest and ministry in Philippi?

7. Where was Paul when he wrote Philippians? What persecution had he experienced in Philippi on his first visit to the city? Relate these two observations to the keynote of *joy* in the epistle.

8. What were Paul's purposes in writing Philippians?

9. List some of the main subjects discussed in the letter.

10. What is the prevailing tone of Philippians?

11. Is much censure or rebuke found here?

12. What chapters of the epistle are identified by each of the following different kinds of content: testimony, examples, exhortations?

---

8. H.C.G. Moule, *Philippian Studies*, pp. 253-54.

VIII. FURTHER STUDY

1. The doctrine of the Person of Christ is a major doctrine of the New Testament. With the help of outside sources, such as a book on doctrine, study the following:

a. the humanity of Christ: Was it real and perfect? Did Jesus have to be *human* in order to make man's salvation possible? If so, why?

b. the deity of Christ: Was Jesus truly God? Did Jesus have to be *God* to make salvation possible? If so, why?

c. Jesus as God-man: How could Jesus be truly God and truly man at the *same time*?

2. Make an extended study of *joy* as that experience is written about in other parts of Scripture. Among other things, aim at a biblical definition of genuine joy.

3. Spend further time studying what Philippians reveals about Paul and about the Christians at Philippi. For the latter, refer to such verses as 1:5, 27, 29-30; 3:2; 4:2, 10, 14-18.

IX. OUTLINE

PHILIPPIANS: Life in Christ

Salutation	1:1-2
CHRIST OUR LIFE	1:3-26
CHRIST OUR PATTERN	1:27—2:30
CHRIST OUR GOAL	3:1—4:1
CHRIST OUR SUFFICIENCY	4:2-20
Greetings and Benediction	4:21-23

X. SELECTED READING

GENERAL INTRODUCTION

Hiebert, D. Edmond. *An Introduction to the Pauline Epistles*, pp. 283-304.
Martin, Ralph P. *The Epistle of Paul to the Philippians*, pp. 15-54.
Scroggie, W. Graham. *Know Your Bible*, 2:220-28.

COMMENTARIES

Davidson, F. "The Epistle to the Philippians." In *The New Bible Commentary*.
Moule, H.C.G. *Philippian Studies*.
Mounce, Robert H. "The Epistle to the Philippians." In *The Wycliffe Bible Commentary*.

OTHER RELATED SOURCES

Bruce, F. F. *The Letters of Paul: Expanded Paraphrase*.
Robertson, A. T. *Paul's Joy in Christ*.
Tenney, Merrill C. *Philippians: The Gospel at Work*.

16

Colossians: Christ Is All and in All

Colossians is another of Paul's four prison epistles, similar in many ways to his letter to Ephesus. The church addressed was very small and inconspicuous, but the letter itself had all the credentials of a message from God. Its readers could not help but notice that it magnifies the Person and work of Jesus Christ. Those who study the book today discover new insights into the depths and riches of intimate fellowship with Christ, who "is all, and in all" (3:11).

I. PREPARATION FOR STUDY

You have just completed your survey of Philippians, whose setting and tone are very different from those of Colossians. Prepare yourself mentally to expect differences, keeping in mind that diversity of peoples, church situations, and experiences brings on such differences.

Refer to Chart 1, page 20, again and note when Colossians was written — almost midway in the writing series of the twenty-seven books.

II. BACKGROUND

A. AUTHOR AND DESTINATION

Colossians 1:1 identifies the author as Paul, and recognizes Paul's co-worker Timothy in its greeting. Verse 2 identifies the readers as "the saints and faithful brethren in Christ who are at Colossae." Paul also directed the Colossian church to share the letter with the church at Laodicea (4:16; cf. 2:1). The title of the book, "Colossians," is derived from the destination.

B. THE CITY OF COLOSSAE

See Map U (Environs of Colossae) and note that Colossae was one of the "tri-cities" of the Lycus Valley. This area was about one hundred miles inland from Ephesus. (See also Map V for the larger setting.) Five centuries before Christ, Colossae was hailed as "the great city of Phrygia." By Paul's time, it was just a small town. A main reason for the change was the rise of the neighboring cities of Laodicea and Hierapolis, when the trade route between Ephesus and the Euphrates Valley was diverted away from Colossae.[1]

MAP U

ENVIRONS OF COLOSSE

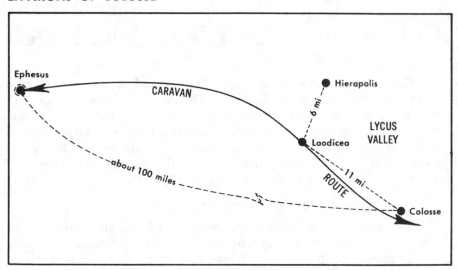

When Paul wrote Colossians, there was a Christian congregation meeting in each of these three cities (4:13).

The inhabitants of Colossae were mainly Greeks and Phrygians, with an unusually large Jewish population. The area was famous for its soft wool.

C. THE CHURCH AT COLOSSAE

An exact and full picture of the Colossian church cannot be determined from Scripture, but the following description shows a pattern. Paul's evangelistic and teaching ministry at Ephesus, on his third missionary journey, may have had much to do with the founding of the church at Colossae.[2] From Colossians 1:3-4 (cf. 2:1) some conclude that the people of the congregation for the most part were

---

1. Laodicea was known as "the metropolis of the valley," and Hierapolis, "the sacred city."
2. The journey (A.D. 52-55) is recorded in Acts 18:23—21:17. Read especially 19:10, 26.

MAP V

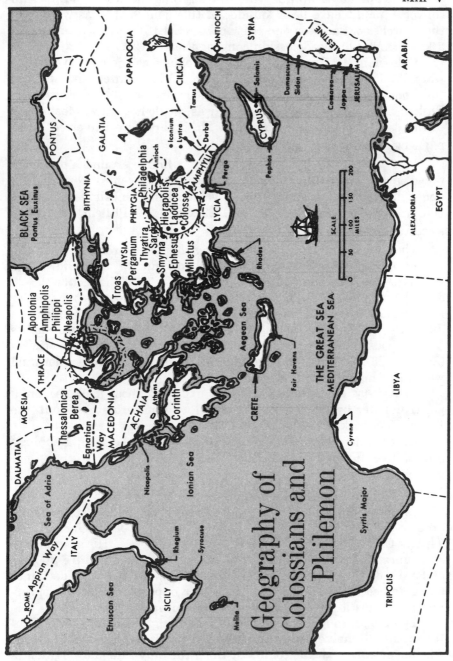

Geography of Colossians and Philemon

strangers to Paul. Epaphras, who possibly was one of Paul's Ephesian converts, might have been founder of this church (1:7) as well as of the churches of Laodicea and Hierapolis (cf. 4:13). At any rate, he was a key member of the Colossian congregation (4:12).

Colossians 4:17 suggests that Archippus was the church's pastor when Paul wrote the epistle. (Cf. Philem. 2.) The church assembled in the home of Philemon, who was one of its active members (4:9; Philem. 1, 5-7). How large the group was, we do not know. Most of the members were of Greek background. The others were converted Jews.

D. PLACE AND DATE OF WRITING

Paul wrote this epistle from prison at Rome, around A.D. 61. As noted earlier, his letters to Philemon and the Ephesians were written and delivered at the same time. Tychicus and Onesimus were the bearers of the letters. (See Eph. 6:21-22; Col. 4:7-9; Philem. 12, 23-24.)

E. OCCASION FOR WRITING

The immediate occasion for writing this letter was heresy in the church at Colossae. Epaphras reported to Paul the false views and evil practices in the church at that time. (Cf. 1:7-8). The section 2:8-23 describes those rather explicitly, though Paul does not name or identify any heresy itself. Among the heresies involved were: (1) a Judaistic legalism, involving circumcision (2:11; 3:11), ordinances (2:14), foods, holidays, and so forth (2:16); (2) a severe asceticism (2:16, 20-23); (3) worship of angels (2:18); and (4) glorification and worship of human knowledge (2:8).

Paul very ably challenged and exploded those heresies on a positive note, by a pure presentation of countertruths about the Person and work of Jesus Christ.

Read Philemon 23 to learn what may have befallen Epaphras after delivering his report to Paul.

F. THEME AND TONE

The main theme of Colossians is well represented by the text, "Christ is all, and in all" (3:11). As someone has said, "Paul does not preach a system nor a philosophy, but a person — Jesus Christ." The deity of Christ, the efficacy of His death on the cross, His sovereignty and supreme lordship, and His continuing mediatorship, are all part of Paul's doctrinal message, because these were the very doctrines being denied by the false teachers. Other important subjects appearing in the epistle will be observed in our survey study.

The tone throughout the epistle is forthright, positive, bold. Paul takes the offensive, not the defensive position. He would agree wholeheartedly with the comment that "the only safeguard against a false intellectual system is a strong and positive Christian theology." But there is a tone of compassion in the epistle as well, as Paul breathes the spirit of tender love and joy in the midst of sorrow and affliction.

G. RELATION TO OTHER NEW TESTAMENT BOOKS

Review the comparisons of Ephesians and Colossians made earlier (Chart 83, p. 317). The place of Colossians in the foursome of Romans, Galatians, Ephesians, and Colossians may also be noted. What comparisons does Chart 87 make?

CHART 87

DOCTRINAL AND CORRECTIVE EPISTLES

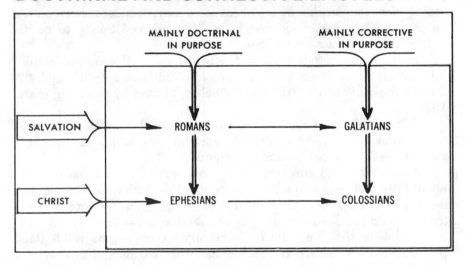

III. SURVEY

A. FIRST SCANNING

Scan the entire epistle in one sitting. List your general impressions.

Do you feel any atmosphere in the letter? Do any words or phrases stand out?

B. PARAGRAPH TITLES

Mark the following paragraph divisions in your Bible, and then on paper record a title for each paragraph: 1:1, 3, 9, 13, 21, 24; 2:1, 4, 8, 16, 20; 3:1, 5, 12, 18; 4:2, 7, 10, 15, 18.

Record any new impressions and observations of the letter.

C. STRUCTURE OF THE BOOK

Read through the epistle a few more times, looking for:

1. organization of content (e.g., introduction, main body, conclusion)

2. kinds of content (e.g., doctrine, practice)

3. any pivot, or climax

4. a prominent theme.

D. SURVEY CHART

Chart 88 is a survey chart of Colossians. After you have looked it over at least in a general way, follow the study suggestions given.

1. Note on the chart the opening and closing benedictions. Also note the two sections identified as *mainly personal*. Read the Bible passages involved, to justify these descriptions. The section called *mainly doctrinal* begins at 1:13 because a major concentration on the subject of Christ is introduced here ("His beloved Son"), to be developed in the verses that follow.

In the survey studies suggested below you will want to find out why major divisions on Chart 88 are also made at 2:4; 3:5; and 4:7. Justify the other observations made below, always by referring to the Bible text.

2. Note the three parts of the main body of the epistle. *Polemical* means that which refutes errors of doctrine. *Hortatory* as used here includes both exhortation and command.

3. Read 2:4 and observe how in this verse Paul begins to write about false teachers who were threatening the Christians at Colossae. Read also the opening phrases of 2:8, 16, 18. What errors or false teachings do you see referred to in the section 2:4—3:4?

4. Note on the chart that the hortatory section begins at 3:5. Read paragraph 3:1-4. You will observe that this paragraph is also of a hortatory nature. But it is included in the previous section (*polemical*, 2:4—3:4) because it is closely related to paragraph 2:20-23. (For example, compare the first phrases of 2:20 and 3:1.)

5. The concluding personal section begins at 4:7, because here Paul begins to bring in personal notes and salutations.

6. Colossians is basically of three kinds of writings: doctrinal, practical, and personal. Note the outline at the top of the chart showing this.

7. Study the other outlines that represent the content of the major divisions of Colossians.

IV. Prominent Subjects

A. THANKSGIVING AND INTERCESSION (1:3-12)

The letter begins on a bright, cheerful note, typical of Paul's

CHART 88

Key Verse: 3:11b

Key Words: mystery, knowledge, wisdom, fulness, perfect, all (16 times in chap. 1), faith, body, love, prayer

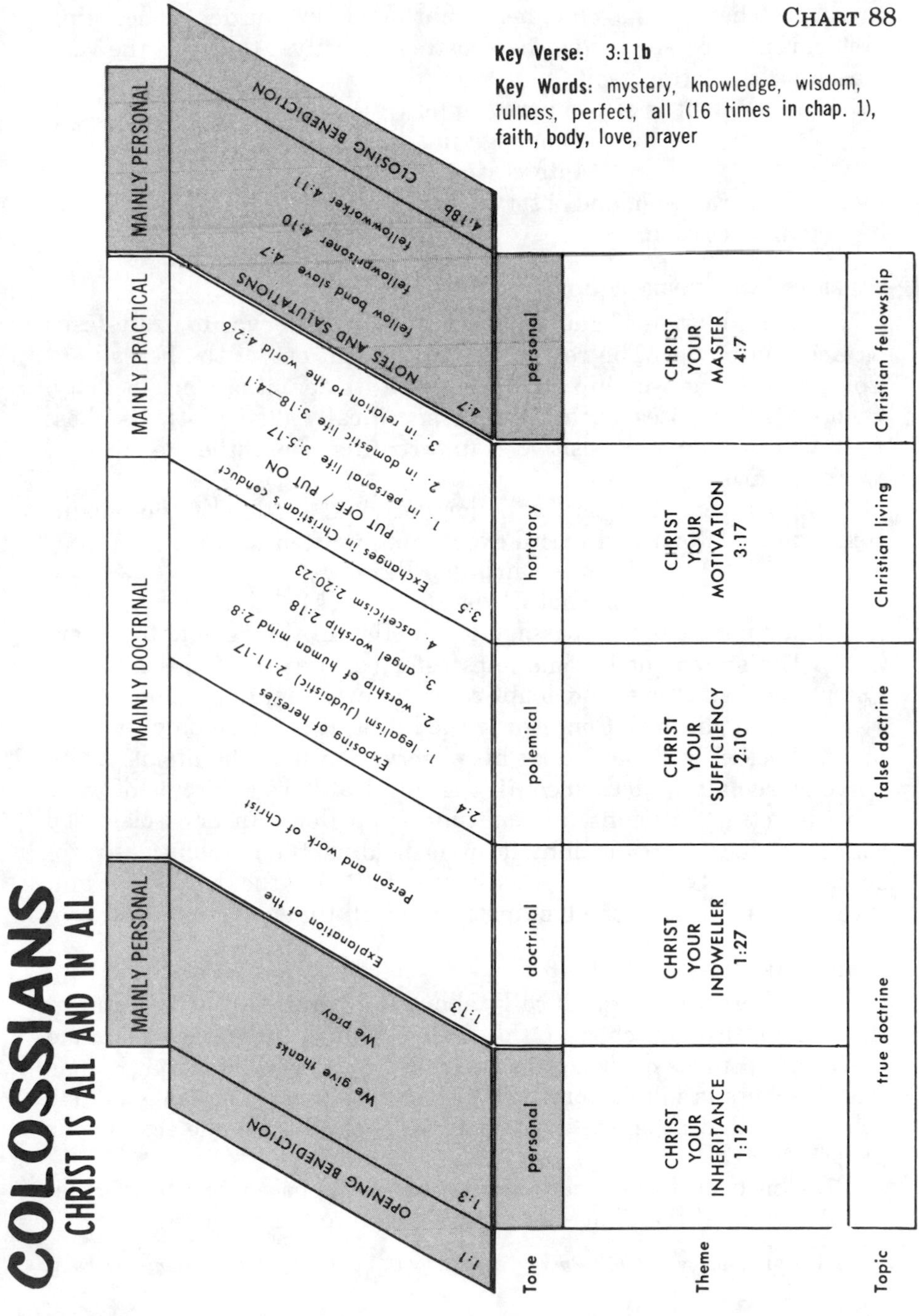

COLOSSIANS
CHRIST IS ALL AND IN ALL

Tone	personal	doctrinal	polemical	hortatory	personal
Theme	CHRIST YOUR INHERITANCE 1:12	CHRIST YOUR INDWELLER 1:27	CHRIST YOUR SUFFICIENCY 2:10	CHRIST YOUR MOTIVATION 3:17	CHRIST YOUR MASTER 4:7
Topic	true doctrine		false doctrine	Christian living	Christian fellowship

MAINLY PERSONAL | MAINLY DOCTRINAL | MAINLY PRACTICAL | MAINLY PERSONAL

OPENING BENEDICTION 1:1

We give thanks
We pray 1:3

Explanation of the person and work of Christ 1:13

Exposing of heresies 2:4
1. legalism (Judaistic) 2:11-17
2. worship of human mind 2:8
3. angel worship 2:18
4. asceticism 2:20-23

Exchanges in Christian's conduct 3:5
PUT OFF / PUT ON
1. in personal life 3:5-17
2. in domestic life 3:18—4:1
3. in relation to the world 4:2-6

NOTES AND SALUTATIONS 4:7
fellow bond slave 4:7
fellowprisoner 4:10
fellowworker 4:11

CLOSING BENEDICTION 4:18b

writings. There is no clue here that a heavy burden concerning problems at Colossae lay on the apostle's heart, yet that was the very reason for the letter itself.

This segment is of two paragraphs:

Thanksgiving 1:3-8

Intercession 1:9-12

Read each paragraph, and observe what constituted Paul's thanksgiving and intercession.

B. PERSON AND WORK OF CHRIST (1:13—2:3)

A major burden of Paul in writing this epistle was to exalt Jesus as God and Savior. The reason for this is that one of the heresies at Colossae was the worship of angels, with its denial of Christ's deity. Before Paul exposed such heresies specifically (2:4—3:4), he chose first to proclaim the positive countertruths about the Person and work of Christ.

The passage itself is the major doctrinal section of the epistle. Read the Bible text and record everything written about:

1. who Christ is (Person)
2. what Christ does (work)

A key phrase of this passage is "in Him all things hold together" (1:17). The statement is sometimes referred to as the Colossian law. The phrase "all things" no doubt refers to every realm, including the spiritual and physical. Concerning the latter, it is interesting that the physical scientist is baffled by his observation that the atoms of the universe remain intact, when all the physical laws say some of their parts (electrons, protons) are mutually repellant. In one scientist's words, "Some inflexible inhibition is holding them relentlessly together."[3] The Scripture of Colossians 1:17, by the hand of Paul, reveals that Christ is the binding force of all things.

C. HERESIES EXPOSED (2:4—3:4)

Paul here writes specifically about the heresies that threatened the life of the churches of the Lycus Valley. He does not name individual persons or groups as such. But it is very clear that he has false teachers in mind, from such phrases as "that no one may delude you" (2:4); "that no one take you captive" (2:8); "let no one act as your judge" (2:16).

1. Chart 89 shows what were probably the bases for the speculative doctrines of the Colossian heresy. Observe the following:

---

3. Karl K. Darrow, *Atomic Energy*, quoted by D. Lee Chesnut, *The Atom Speaks*, p. 67.

a. The false religionists attempted to solve the problem of the great gulf. What was that problem?

b. Two solutions were suggested:

(1) God reaching man by way of emanations from Himself, each successive emanation being of less holiness. How was Jesus regarded, as compared with angels?

(2) Man reaching God in the realm of mental activity.[4] Why was mind and spirit worshiped?

c. Since flesh was regarded as essentially evil, asceticism and legalism were the consequences. What is asceticism? Does the Bible teach that flesh *itself* is evil?

CHART 89

TEACHINGS OF THE COLOSSIAN HERESY

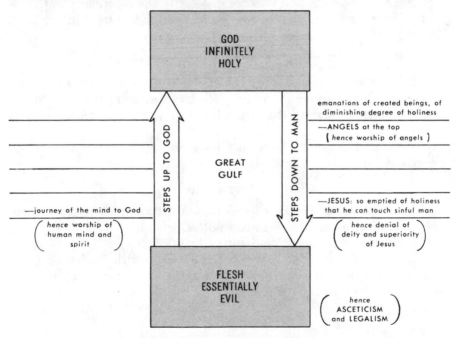

Read 2:4—3:4. What verses refer directly or indirectly to each of the following heresies shown on Chart 89: worship of angels; denial of deity of Christ; speculation; deification of human knowledge; asceticism; Judaistic legalism?

As correctives for the heresies, what different truths about Christ does Paul teach in the passage?

---

4. This was one form of the heresy now referred to as Gnosticism.

D. CHRISTIANITY IN ACTION (3:5—4:6)

Up to this point in the letter, Paul has written about doctrine: first, true doctrine (1:1—2:3); then, false doctrine (2:4—3:4). Now in the typical Pauline pattern, he directs attention to practical Christian living.

Observe references in the passage to specific conduct and specific groups. Follow this outline as you read:

Christian living
1. in personal life 3:5-17
2. in domestic life 3:18—4:1
3. in relation to the world 4:2-6

E. THE FELLOWSHIP OF CHRISTIANS (4:7-18)

Read the passage and observe especially the references to Christian fellowship. For example, how is the word *fellow* used in verses 7, 10, and 11?

V. THEME, KEY WORDS AND VERSES

In your own words identify the theme of Colossians. Note the list of key words shown on Chart 88. How does each word relate to the epistle's theme? Add to the list other key words you noted as you surveyed the letter.

What key verse is cited on Chart 88? What other key verses represent the theme of Colossians?

VI. APPLICATIONS

Many practical truths of Colossians derive from two intimate relationships that the believer has with Christ:
1. *death* — "you have died with Christ" (2:20)
2. *resurrection* — "you have been raised up with Christ" (3:1).

Read the entire epistle again, observing the various applications that derive from the above truths.

VII. REVIEW QUESTIONS

1. How large a city was Colossae in the days of Paul? How far was it from Ephesus?

2. Did Paul have anything to do with the founding of the church at Colossae? If so, what?

3. Name some active members of the congregation. Who may have been the pastor when Paul wrote Colossians?

4. Was Paul acquainted with most of the congregation by sight?

5. Where were the two nearest churches located?

6. Where was Paul when he wrote Colossians, and when did he write?

7. What was the immediate occasion for writing this letter?

8. What serious problems threatened the Colossian church?

9. What approach did Paul use in writing to the church?

10. Whom else besides the Colossians did Paul want to read the letter?

11. What is the main theme of Colossians?

12. Compare the theme and purpose of Colossians with each of the following: Ephesians, Galatians, Romans.

13. What are the different kinds of content in the epistle? Can you recall the outline and show where each new section begins?

14. Does Paul here follow his usual pattern of writing about doctrine, as a foundation, *before* giving appeals for Christian living?

15. What title is assigned to Colossians on the chart?

16. Try to complete this outline:

Christ Your Inheritance; _____ ; _____ ; _____ ; _____ .

17. What are some key words and key verses of Colossians?

VIII. FURTHER STUDY

1. Read through the entire epistle and note the times Christ is mentioned (either as Christ, or by other names and titles). Make a list showing what Paul writes about Him in each instance. This study will support the conclusion that the fundamental thought of Colossians is Christ, the Head of all things.

2. Note all the names of people referred to in the epistle and what Paul writes about each.

3. With the help of outside sources study the false gnostic philosophy of the first centuries, as it appeared in various forms.

IX. OUTLINE

COLOSSIANS: Christ Is All and in All

OPENING BENEDICTION	1:1-2
TRUE DOCTRINE	1:3—2:3
Thanksgiving and Intercession	1:3-12
Person and Work of Christ	1:13—2:3
FALSE DOCTRINE	2:4—3:4
Heresies Exposed	2:4—3:4
CHRISTIAN LIVING	3:5—4:18
Christianity in Action	3:5—4:6
Personal Greetings	4:7-18*a*
CLOSING BENEDICTION	4:18*b*

X. Selected Reading

GENERAL INTRODUCTION

Guthrie, Donald. "Colossians." In *The New Bible Commentary*, pp. 1139-41.

Hiebert, D. Edmond. *An Introduction to the Pauline Epistles*, pp. 215-40.

COMMENTARIES

Ellis, E. Earle, "The Epistle to the Colossians." In *The Wycliffe Bible Commentary*.

Maclaren, Alexander, "The Epistles of St. Paul to the Colossians and to Philemon." In *The Expositor's Bible*.

OTHER RELATED SOURCES

Robertson, A. T. *Paul and the Intellectuals*.

Vincent, Marvin R. *Word Studies in the New Testament*.

17

The Thessalonian Epistles

1 Thessalonians: The Lord Jesus Is Coming Again
2 Thessalonians: He Has Not Come Yet

Christ's first coming to earth was a crucial event in world history; His second coming will be the climactic event. He came the first time to die and be raised to life. When He comes again, it will be to gather to Himself those saved by His death. Paul sums up all the joys and glories of this ingathering by saying simply, "And thus we shall always be with the Lord" (1 Thess. 4:17). It had to be a thrilling experience for the apostle to write the Thessalonian letters[1] and share such a message.

Of Paul's letters, 1 and 2 Thessalonians focus especially on the theme of Christ's return. Here, the apostle not only gives the details of prophecy but he also shows how Christians should be living day by day in light of the Lord's return. That practical emphasis will be evident as you study the epistles.

I. PREPARATION FOR STUDY

Before you begin to read the Thessalonian letters, answer the following questions on the basis of your present knowledge and interpretation of eschatology (doctrine of last things):

1. Will Jesus return to this earth? If so, what signs or events will precede His coming?

2. Will the saints be raptured (caught up) to heaven before Christ returns to the earth? If so, will there be a period between such a rapture and His coming to earth?

3. What will Christ do when He returns?

---

1. The terms *letter* and *epistle* are used interchangeably in this volume, even though a distinction may be made regarding content and style. (E.g., see Dwight M. Pratt, "Epistle," in *The International Standard Bible Encyclopedia*, 2:967.)

4. For how long will Christ remain on earth? Then what?

II. BACKGROUND OF THE THESSALONIAN LETTERS

A. THE CITY OF THESSALONICA

1. *Name*. The city was originally named Therme. When it was refounded by Cassander, around 315 B.C., he named it Thessalonica, after his wife.

2. *Location*. Study carefully the location of Thessalonica, as shown on Map V, page 337. Note the city's strategic position as a seaport and on the Egnatian Way, which was the principal east-west trade and military route between Rome and Asia Minor.[2] How does this strategic location shed light on 1 Thessalonians 1:8?

Observe the other two important cities of this part of Macedonia, Philippi, and Berea, which Paul visited on his second missionary journey. Why did Paul concentrate much of his missionary tours in key cities of the Empire?

Note the location of Corinth on the map. It was from here that Paul wrote both of the Thessalonian letters.

3. *Population*. The population of Thessalonica in Paul's day has been estimated as around 200,000 (about half its present population). Of this number most were Greeks, but there was also a fairly large Jewish segment in the city. From the following description, try to visualize Paul's impressions of the bustling city as he first entered it on his second missionary journey (Acts 17:1):

> With overland caravans thronging its hostelries, with its harbor filled with ship's bottoms from overseas, with old salts, Roman officials, and thousands of Jewish merchants rubbing shoulders in its streets, Thessalonica presented a cosmopolitan picture. It is very suggestive that the Jewish opponents of Paul should have called Paul and his co-workers "world-topplers" (Acts 17:6).[3]

4. *Government*. Thessalonica was made the capital of the province of Macedonia in 148 B.C. It gained the status of a free city in 42 B.C. and elected its own government officials. (Note the reference to city rulers in Acts 17:6.)

5. *Commerce*. As noted earlier, the city was a strategic trade center, with connections by land and sea. This determined its commercial "personality." It was a very prosperous city.

6. *Religion*. Idolatry was the common religion of most of the

---

2. Sections of this fifteen-foot-wide paved highway remain to this day.
3. Charles F. Pfeiffer and Howard F. Vos, *The Wycliffe Historical Geography of Bible Lands*, p. 457.

Greeks. Nearby Mount Olympus, viewed daily by the people, stood as a symbol of the gods. In ancient times, it was at the summit of Mount Olympus that Zeus was believed to gather together all the gods of Greece for a council.

The Jewish community of Thessalonica was either large or influential, or both, as seen from the action of Acts 17:5. The Acts account records that Paul's first evangelistic preaching was done in the city's synagogue (Acts 17:1-4).

There was also a large Roman segment of the populace, with a strong nationalistic devotion to the emperor Caesar (cf. Acts 17:7).

B. THE FIRST CHRISTIAN CHURCH OF THESSALONICA

1. *Paul's evangelistic campaign.* Thessalonica was the second major city visited by Paul for an evangelistic ministry on his second missionary journey (Philippi was the first). Read Acts 17:1-10 for Luke's brief account of this ministry. Observe the following:

a. Upon arriving at the city, Paul first shared the gospel with the Jews in the synagogue. That was his customary procedure. How long did that mission continue?

b. Paul based his ministry on the Scriptures. What does the phrase "reasoned with them" (Acts 17:2) reveal about Paul's method of communicating the gospel to the Thessalonians?

c. Paul tried to establish three basic truths, in this order:

(1) Christ (the promised Messiah, Redeemer) had to suffer and die.
(2) Christ had to rise from the dead.
(3) The Jesus whom he preached was this Christ.
    If you had only the Old Testament today, as Paul had then, how
        would you support each of the above three truths, from those
        Scriptures? For a starting point, see Isaiah 53.

d. Immediate results of Paul's ministry (Acts 17:4-5):

(1) Some Jews were converted.
(2) A great multitude of devout Greeks believed.
(3) A substantial number of leading women believed.
(4) The Jews who rejected Paul's message stirred up a riot.
(5) Paul was forced to leave the city.

e. Paul's later contacts with the Thessalonian Christians:

(1) Twice Paul was hindered from returning to Thessalonica soon after his first visit (1 Thess. 2:17-18).
(2) He sent Timothy to minister in his place (1 Thess. 3:1-2).
(3) He wrote the two epistles.
(4) The apostle made at least two other visits to the area on his third missionary journey (Acts 20:1-4; 2 Cor. 2:12-13). Also, he may have visited the Thessalonian church after his first Roman imprisonment.

2. *Founding and constituency of the church.* The church at Thessalonica was only an infant when Paul wrote the letters, but its fame was widespread because of the miraculous transformation of lives from idolatry to Christianity. From the very beginning, the newborn believers banded together in a Christian fellowship. What evidences of such a fellowship do you see implied in Acts 17:4, 6, 10? When Paul wrote to the group only a few months later, he addressed them as "the church of the Thessalonians" (1 Thess. 1:1). No doubt, the organization of the local church was simple at first. We do know the church had leaders, however, as shown by 1 Thessalonians 5:12.

Most of the church's members were Gentiles, converted from idolatry (cf. Acts 17:4; 1 Thess. 1:9). Some were Jews (Acts 17:4). From 1 Thessalonians 4:11, it has been concluded that for the most part, the people were of the common working class. (See Acts 17:4*b* for a notable exception.) As young converts, the Christians at Thessalonica were a real joy and inspiration to Paul, and were reliable and devoted followers of Christ. The bright tone of the two epistles confirms this.

III. BACKGROUND OF 1 THESSALONIANS

A. AUTHOR

Twice, Paul identifies himself by name in the epistle: at 1:1 and 2:18. The title *apostle* does not appear in this letter or in 2 Thessalonians, Philippians, or Philemon. Some have suggested the reason for this is that any question of Paul's authority does not enter into the discussions of these epistles.

Silvanus (Silas) and Timothy are included in the opening salutation (1:1). Both were intimate co-workers with Paul. Read the following verses concerning each man:

1. Silas: Acts 15:22, 27, 32, 40; 16:19-20; 1 Peter 5:12
2. Timothy: Acts 16:1-3; Philippians 2:19-22; 1 Timothy 1:2; 2 Timothy 4:9, 21.

B. PLACE AND DATE WRITTEN

Paul wrote 1 Thessalonians from Corinth, where the apostle spent eighteen months on the second missionary journey, soon after leaving Thessalonica (Acts 18:1, 11). (Refer to Appendix B, pages 518-19, and fix in your mind the chronology of Paul's life and ministry. Note, among other things, when and where the apostle wrote each of his epistles.)

The date of writing 1 Thessalonians was around A.D. 52.[4] The epistle was among the earliest of Paul's inspired writings.[5] About how old was Paul when he wrote this letter? How old was he when he was saved? (See Appendix B.)

C. OCCASION AND PURPOSES

We have already observed that when Paul was hindered from visiting the Thessalonians (2:17-18), he partly made up for this by doing two things: sending Timothy to minister to them in his place (3:1-5); and writing this epistle after receiving Timothy's report about the church (3:6-13). (Read 3:10 for another thing that Paul, being absent from the Thessalonians, did on their behalf.) This then was the occasion for writing 1 Thessalonians.

Paul had various purposes in mind in writing the letter. Some of the more important ones were:

1. to commend the Christians for their faith (3:6)

2. to expose sins (e.g., fornication, 4:3; and idleness, 4:11) and correct misapprehensions (e.g., about the second coming of Christ, 4:13-17)

3. to exhort the young converts in their new spiritual experience (e.g., 4:1-12)

4. to answer false charges against Paul. Such charges may have sounded like these:

a. Paul was a money-making teacher, attracted by the rich ladies who attended his meetings. For Paul's replies, read such verses as 2:3, 9-10.

b. Paul was a flatterer, with selfish goals in mind. Read 2:4-6.

c. Paul was afraid to appear in person in Thessalonica again. Read 2:17-20.

D. CHARACTERISTICS

Paul's letters to the Thessalonians have the marks of typical New Testament epistles. They are like a doctor's diagnosis and prescrip-

---

4. Some have placed the date as early as A.D. 50.
5. If Galatians was not the first to be written, as many hold, then the Thessalonian letters were Paul's first inspired writings.

tion, blended together in one package. Some of the characteristics of 1 Thessalonians that stand out are:

1. It is intimate, heart-to-heart.

2. Its tone is gentle, affectionate, "a classic of Christian friendship."

3. The epistle is simple, basic.

4. There is an air of expectancy, especially concerning Christ's return.

5. The epistle gives one of the earliest pictures of the primitive New Testament church.

6. There are no quotations from the Old Testament. (We may recall here that most of the Thessalonian Christians were Gentiles, not Jews.)

7. There is not the usual abundance of doctrine in this epistle (4:13-18 being a notable exception).

8. Paul's style of writing in this epistle is very informal, personal, and direct.

9. Much may be learned about Paul in 1 Thessalonians from the way he wrote and what he emphasized. Tact, love, and humility are three qualities that appear often in the epistle.

E. PLACE IN THE NEW TESTAMENT

As noted earlier, the Thessalonian letters were among the earliest of Paul's New Testament writings. Refer to Chart 1, page 20, and note what books were written just before and after those letters.

IV. SURVEY OF 1 THESSALONIANS

A. FIRST READING

Scan the epistle once for first impressions. Then answer the following questions:

1. Is this a long epistle?

2. Is it more practical than doctrinal?

3. Are there many personal references?

4. Did you sense any particular tone or atmosphere in the letter?

5. Does Paul seem to have one specific purpose in writing?

6. What are your personal impressions of the book?

B. PARAGRAPH SURVEY

1. Read the letter again, a little more slowly. Begin to underline words and phrases that strike you as you read.

2. Make a list of the key words and phrases, and add to the list while you continue your studies.

3. Mark paragraph divisions in your Bible, with each paragraph

beginning at these verses: 1:1, 2, 6; 2:1, 7, 13, 17; 3:1, 6, 11; 4:1, 9, 13; 5:1, 6, 12, 23, 25, 28.

4. Read the paragraphs, and assign a paragraph title to each.

5. What are your new impressions of the epistle? What parts stand out prominently?

C. OBSERVING THE STRUCTURE

Now begin to see how the nineteen paragraphs (thought units) of 1 Thessalonians merge together to communicate Paul's message. Things to look for are suggested below.

1. *Introduction and conclusion.* Read the first and last paragraphs of the epistle. What verses would you identify as the introduction and the conclusion?

2. *Blocks of similar content.* Go through the epistle again, and see if you can find any groups of paragraphs that are of similar content, of such kinds as doctrine, exhortation, personal reflections, and biography. Make a note of those.

3. *Turning point.* Sometimes a book has a turning point, such as a change from doctrine to practice. Do you detect any such change in 1 Thessalonians?

4. *High points and climax.* Occasionally, an epistle will reach a high point, or high points, in the course of the writing. A doxology at such a place is often a clue to this. Do you observe any peaks in 1 Thessalonians? Would you say that there is a definite climax toward the end of the epistle? If so, where specifically?

5. *A prominent doctrine.* Observe the references to Christ's return at the end of each chapter. What paragraphs in the epistle deal especially with this event of end times?

D. SURVEY CHART

Chart 90 is a survey chart of 1 Thessalonians, showing the basic structure of the epistle and outlines of various topics. Study this chart very carefully.

Observe the following on the chart:

1. The salutation of 1:1 and the assorted verses of 5:23-28 are viewed here as the introduction and conclusion, respectively.

2. A major division appears at 4:1, dividing the epistle into two main parts. What two outlines show this twofold division? (Note: the first word of 4:1 is "finally," which suggests a change in Paul's train of thought at this point.) Review the survey study made thus far to check whether these twofold outlines represent the epistle's general content.

3. You have already observed that Paul devotes much space to

descriptions of his ministry to the Thessalonians. Note the outline that shows three aspects of that ministry. The segment division shown at 2:17 is based on this observation. Read the paragraphs before and after 2:17 to justify a main division at this point.

Study also the two related outlines that appear just below the *ministry* outline.

4. One of the prominent subjects of the letter is the Lord's return. It was noted earlier that each chapter ends with a clear reference to this future event. The fivefold topical outlines shown on the survey chart are organized around this observation of the five chapter endings. These outlines also reflect the general content of each of the chapters. For example, the word *salvation* for chapter 1 refers to the Thessalonians' conversion, the experience that accounted for their hope of Christ's return (waiting "for His Son from heaven," 1:10). Study the topical outlines on this theme.

5. Observe on the chart that the title given to the epistle is about the Lord's return. The title is worded this way to anticipate the title that will be assigned later to 2 Thessalonians, which is, "He Has Not Come Yet." Note also the key verse.

V. Prominent Subjects of 1 Thessalonians

The prominent subjects of 1 Thessalonians reflect Paul's purposes in writing. Some of the major subjects are in the following list.

1. The second coming of Christ. The key doctrinal passage of the epistle is 4:13-18, on the rapture of the church.

2. Thanksgiving for the Thessalonians' faith and endurance.

3. Encouragement to the church members in their afflictions.

4. Doctrines of various subjects, such as the following:

God the Father	Pastoral responsibility
The Lord Jesus	Gospel
(Note the full title "our	Way of salvation
Lord Jesus Christ" at 1:3;	Believers
5:9, 23, 28.)	The world
The Holy Spirit	Satan

5. Exhortations to holy living.

Some of the prominent subjects cited above are described more fully in the pages that follow.

A. LORD'S RETURN

In our survey study, we observed various references in 1 Thessalonians to Christ's second coming. The first of these appears at 1:10.

CHART 90

1 THESSALONIANS
JESUS IS COMING AGAIN

KEY VERSE: "I pray God your whole spirit and soul and body be preserved blameless unto the coming of our Lord Jesus Christ" (5:23b).

KEY WORDS:
Lord
brethren (17 times)
sanctification
affliction
coming
gospel
word
day

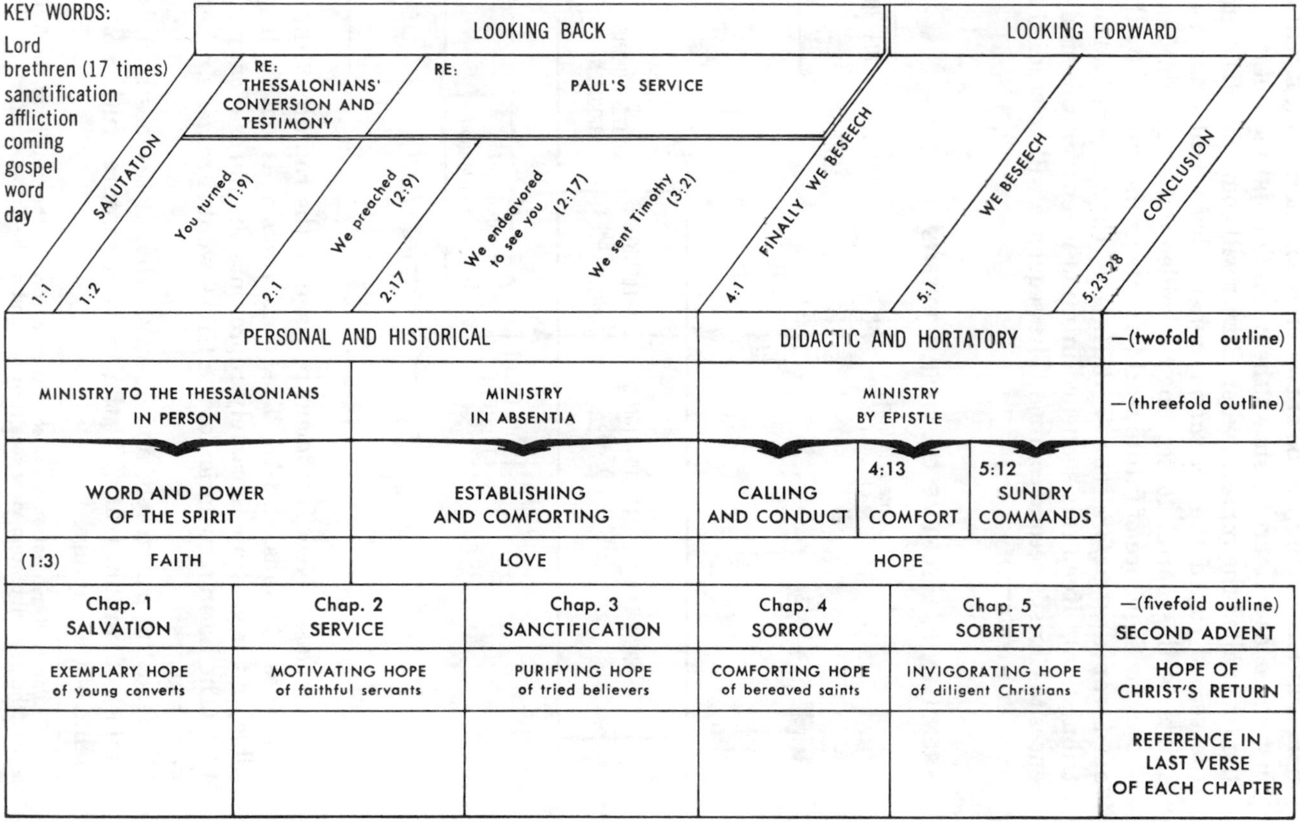

	LOOKING BACK			LOOKING FORWARD
	RE: THESSALONIANS' CONVERSION AND TESTIMONY	RE: PAUL'S SERVICE		CONCLUSION
SALUTATION	You turned (1:9)	We preached (2:9)	We endeavored to see you (2:17)	We sent Timothy (3:2)
1:1	1:2	2:1	2:17	4:1 FINALLY WE BESEECH	5:1 WE BESEECH	5:23-28

PERSONAL AND HISTORICAL		DIDACTIC AND HORTATORY	
MINISTRY TO THE THESSALONIANS IN PERSON	MINISTRY IN ABSENTIA	MINISTRY BY EPISTLE	
WORD AND POWER OF THE SPIRIT	ESTABLISHING AND COMFORTING	CALLING AND CONDUCT	4:13 COMFORT	5:12 SUNDRY COMMANDS
(1:3) FAITH	LOVE	HOPE		

Chap. 1 SALVATION	Chap. 2 SERVICE	Chap. 3 SANCTIFICATION	Chap. 4 SORROW	Chap. 5 SOBRIETY
EXEMPLARY HOPE of young converts	MOTIVATING HOPE of faithful servants	PURIFYING HOPE of tried believers	COMFORTING HOPE of bereaved saints	INVIGORATING HOPE of diligent Christians

—(twofold outline)
—(threefold outline)
—(fivefold outline) SECOND ADVENT
HOPE OF CHRIST'S RETURN
REFERENCE IN LAST VERSE OF EACH CHAPTER

There are different views concerning Christ's second coming. Some hold that His coming will be of two phases; others, that it will involve just one phase. Chart 91 shows the premillennial view of two phases, the first called the *rapture*, when Christ will come *for* His saints; and the second called the *revelation*, when Christ will come *with* His saints to this earth, to set up the millennial kingdom. The chart shows the sequence of future world events as interpreted by the view of a rapture *before* the Tribulation (hence the name, pre-tribulation).[6] Keep this sequence in mind whenever you study references to Christ's second coming. (The sequence will be studied further in later chapters.)

CHART 91

PREMILLENNIAL SCHEME OF WORLD EVENTS

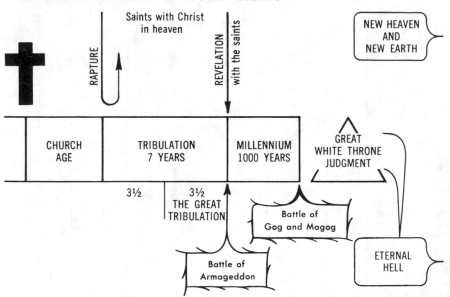

The classic New Testament passage on the rapture of the church is 1 Thessalonians 4:13-18. The word *rapture* is not found in the Bible, but it very appropriately represents the phrase "caught up" of 4:17. (The Latin translation of the Greek word is *rapiemur*, hence our word *rapture*.)

Read the paragraph, and observe what it teaches about (1) the comfort of rapture truth, (2) the basis of rapture truth, and (3) the events of the rapture.

---

6. The mid-tribulation view sees the rapture in the middle of the Tribulation period; the posttribulation view sees it at the end of the Tribulation.

CHART 92

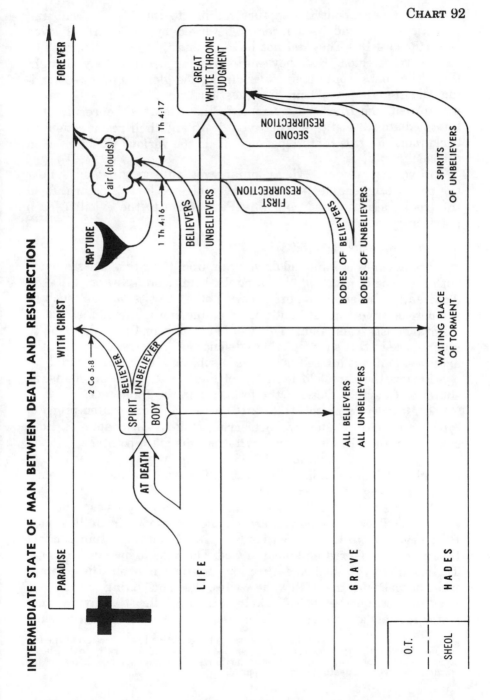

INTERMEDIATE STATE OF MAN BETWEEN DEATH AND RESURRECTION

Paul wrote about the rapture mainly to comfort Thessalonian Christians who had been recently bereaved by the death of loved ones. (Read 4:13.) They did not have doubts that those would some day be resurrected. But they were grieving because they thought their loved ones would miss experiencing the glorious events attending Christ's return. Their big questions were, *When* will we be resurrected, and *How* will it happen? Study Chart 92 concerning the intermediate state of people between death and their resurrection, as background for this rapture passage. Read the various verses cited on the chart.[7]

In your survey of 1 Thessalonians you observed that at or near the end of each chapter there is a reference to Christ's return. Read the passages again, and note why Paul refers to the event in each passage.

B. PAUL'S MINISTRY (1:1—5:28)

The enemies of Paul had driven him from the city of Thessalonica with the hope of aborting his evangelistic mission (see Acts 17:5-15). Apparently, the enemies pursued with other tactics as well, such as slanderous rumors about Paul's personal life, motives, and methods in his evangelistic campaigns. This would account for Paul's devoting so much space in this short epistle to defend his ministry. Just what the apostle said about himself is the main subject of chapters 1 and 2.

Review the threefold ministry of Paul to the Thessalonians, as shown on Chart 90. Observe the following in the Bible text:

1. *Ministry in person* (1:2—2:16). Observe the repeated pronoun "you" in chapter 1, and "we" (referring to Paul) in chapter 2. Both chapters are Paul's testimonies. What are his main points?

2. *Ministry in absentia* (2:17—3:13). Paul regrets that he cannot be with the Thessalonian Christians in person for the time being. What two things does he do for them?

3. *Ministry by epistle* (4:1—5:28). At 4:1 Paul begins especially to exhort the Thessalonians concerning their behavior in daily living. Paul never wrote a letter without appealing for Christian conduct that magnified Christ and pleased God. The apostle here reminds the Thessalonians that he had earlier instructed them about these things when he was with them. Now, he writes, "keep on" living in that way, but "doing still better" (4:1, Berkeley). Healthy Christian living is not static; it is always dynamic. Christians are to keep growing, moving,

---

7. Before Calvary, the spirits of deceased believers went to the blessed of the two regions of Sheol, that part reserved only for God's people. After Calvary, only Sheol's other region, the place of torment (new name "Hades"), remained, since thereafter the spirits of believers at death would go to paradise. (Cf. Luke 23:43.)

abounding. As someone has said, "There is no finality in practical holiness while the Christian remains on the earth."

VI. THEME, KEY WORDS AND VERSES FOR 1 THESSALONIANS

How would you identify the theme of 1 Thessalonians? Observe the theme identified on Chart 90 as a title. Note the key words and verse shown also on the chart. Compare these with your own choices made on the basis of your survey.

VII. APPLICATIONS FROM 1 THESSALONIANS

Paul's first letter to the Thessalonians abounds in practical applications. Reflect on the things you have learned here about the following:
1. the comfort and hope of Christ's return
2. endurance in affliction
3. faithful Christian service
4. maturing as a Christian.

VIII. REVIEW QUESTIONS ON 1 THESSALONIANS

1. On what missionary journey did Paul first visit Thessalonica? Name two nearby cities evangelized about the same time.
2. What was the strategic location of Thessalonica?
3. Describe the average Thessalonian in Paul's day.
4. What was the religious situation in Thessalonica when Paul arrived at the city?
5. What were the main points of Paul's first sermons in the synagogue? What were the results of this ministry?
6. Where was Paul when he wrote 1 Thessalonians? Why did he write the letter?
7. Name some prominent subjects in this epistle.
8. What are some of the letter's characteristics?
9. When did Paul write 1 Thessalonians, as compared with his other epistles?
10. What key doctrinal passage appears in this letter?
11. Where does the second division of a twofold outline of the letter begin? What is the opening word of this division?
12. What subject is common to the end of each chapter?
13. In what chapters does Paul write much personal testimony about his ministry?
14. Where is the classic rapture passage?

IX. FURTHER STUDY OF 1 THESSALONIANS

1. Using outside sources as guides,[8] study what the Bible teaches about the following:

    a. the rapture of the church

    b. the Millennium

    c. the Great Tribulation

    d. Christ's return to earth (epiphany, revelation).

2. Study the different views regarding the time of the rapture (i.e., before, during, or after the Great Tribulation on earth). One of the main differences between premillennialists who believe in a rapture before (pre) the Tribulation period and premillennialists who hold to a rapture after (post) that Tribulation period arises out of the interpretation of the *action* aspect of the rapture (4:17). Pretribulationists believe that at the rapture, the Lord does not come to the earth, but only to the air and clouds above the earth, and that He returns to heaven immediately with the raptured saints. This view sees in the sharp phrase "caught up" the meaning of being transported from one place to another, which in this case is from earth to heaven. (Cf. Acts 8:39; 2 Cor. 12:2, 4; Rev. 12:5.) Posttribulationists, on the other hand, believe that the saints will be caught up to meet the Lord in the air, but that they will immediately escort Him to earth. F. F. Bruce gives the background of such a view:

> When a dignitary paid an official visit or *parousia* to a city in Hellenistic times, the action of the leading citizens in going out to meet him and escorting him on the final stage of his journey was called the *apantesis*; it is similarly used in Mt. xxv. 6; Acts xxviii. 15. So the Lord is pictured as escorted to the earth by His people — those newly raised from death and those who have remained alive.[9]

X. OUTLINE

---

8. Outside sources include Bible dictionaries, encyclopedias, handbooks, and books with the subject titles.

9. F. F. Bruce, "1 Thessalonians," in *The New Bible Commentary*, p. 1159.

XI. BACKGROUND OF 2 THESSALONIANS

A couple of months after Paul had written his first letter to the Thessalonian church, various circumstances led him to write again. This later epistle has been described as "a second prescription for the same case, made after discovering that some certain stubborn symptoms had not yielded to the first treatment."[10] But the epistle is more than that. It answers new questions that have been raised, and it extends Paul's earlier instruction and exhortation to deeper and higher levels. The keynote of the Lord's second coming, as taught in 1 Thessalonians, is also the keynote here. The importance of such a doctrine in the lives of the Thessalonian believers is emphasized.

Much of the background of this epistle is common to that of the first letter. Review the earlier section before studying the new descriptions given below.

A. AUTHOR

Paul identified himself by name in 1:1 and 3:17. The vocabulary, style, doctrine, and atmosphere all indicate that this epistle is as Pauline as the first letter.

B. ORIGINATION AND DATE

Both of the Thessalonian epistles were written from Corinth, during Paul's eighteen-month stay there, on his second missionary journey. The second letter followed the first by no more than a few months, or around A.D. 52. This was before the flare-up at Corinth, recorded in Acts 18:5-17.

C. IMMEDIATE OCCASION AND PURPOSES

Whoever delivered Paul's first letter probably remained at Thessalonica long enough to view the conditions at the church and to bring back a report to Paul. The good parts of the report are the subjects of Paul's commendations in 2 Thessalonians. A negative report was that the Christians were believing the false word that the "day of the Lord" had already come, and therefore the end of all things was upon them. This even caused some of the believers to give up their daily occupations and professions, in anticipation of the shout and trump of heaven heralding the Lord's return. Those were some of the things that Paul wanted to write about in a second, brief letter. So the purposes of the letter were (1) commendation and (2) doctrinal and practical correction.

10. R. H. Walker, "The Second Epistle of Paul to the Thessalonians," in *The International Standard Bible Encyclopedia*, 5:2968.

D. THE TWO EPISTLES COMPARED

Some of the main differences of the two epistles are shown on Chart 93. These will become apparent as you survey 2 Thessalonians.

CHART 93

FIRST AND SECOND THESSALONIANS COMPARED

1 THESSALONIANS	2 THESSALONIANS
describes how the Thessalonians received the Word of God	mentions their progress in faith, love, and patience
teaches the imminency of the Lord's return	corrects misapprehensions about that event
comforts and encourages the saints	assures coming judgment on Christ's foes
concerns the church	concerns Satan, Antichrist, and the world
presents outstanding eschatological passage in 4:13-18	presents outstanding eschatological passage in 2:1-2
tells about the **parousia** (coming, presence)—4:15	tells about the **apocalupsis** (revelation)—1:7
presents the Day of Christ (cf. Phil 1:10)	presents the Day of the Lord (2 Th 2:2)

It will be seen from these comparisons that the two epistles differ mainly over which phase of the Lord's return is in view. In 1 Thessalonians, the first phase (rapture) is the main subject. In 2 Thessalonians, attention is focused on the second phase (revelation). In order to see if the above distinctions are justified it would be necessary for you to analyze carefully the text of the Thessalonian letters. Such analysis is beyond the scope of these survey studies. As a background for examining whether the two epistles are emphasizing two different phases of the Lord's coming, differences between those two phases are shown on Chart 94.[11]

XII. SURVEY OF 2 THESSALONIANS

A. FIRST READINGS

1. Before you read the letter, observe its length. Compare it with that of the first epistle. Also compare the opening and closing verses of both epistles.

2. What are your first impressions after reading the whole epistle in one sitting?

---

11. Adapted from J. Dwight Pentecost, *Things to Come*, pp. 206-7.

3. Does this letter appear to be intimately related to the first one? If so, in what ways?

4. Do you sense a prevailing tone or atmosphere?

5. What key words and phrases stand out?

CHART 94

RAPTURE AND REVELATION COMPARED

FIRST PHASE (RAPTURE)	SECOND PHASE (REVELATION)
Christ comes to claim His bride, the church	Christ returns with the bride
Christ comes to the air	Christ returns to the earth
the tribulation begins	the millennial kingdom is established
translation is imminent	a multitude of signs precede
a message of comfort is given	a message of judgment is given
the program for the church is emphasized	the program for Israel and the world is emphasized
translation is a mystery	revelation is predicted in both Testaments
believers are judged	Gentiles and Israel are judged
Israel's covenants are not yet fulfilled	all of Israel's covenants are fulfilled
believers only are affected	all people are affected
the church is taken into the Lord's presence	Israel is brought into the kingdom

B. PARAGRAPH UNITS

1. Read the epistle paragraph by paragraph, using the following divisions (each reference is the beginning verse of the paragraph): 1:1, 3, 5, 11; 2:1, 5, 13, 16; 3:1, 6, 16. Mark the divisions in your Bible.

2. Assign a title to each paragraph.

3. Make a list of some of the main subjects of the letter.

4. Note every reference in the text to the second coming of Christ. Mark those in your Bible.

5. Where is the most concentration of practical exhortation?

6. Scan through the epistle and note the places of Paul's prayers of benedictions in behalf of the Thessalonians.

C. STRUCTURE OF THE LETTER

1. What verses serve as the introduction? the conclusion?

2. What is the first word of chapter 3? What does this suggest concerning the structure of the epistle? Relate to this what you observe about the last two verses of chapter 2.

3. How does 2:1 introduce what follows?

4. What is the main general content of each of the three chapters? Use this observation to formulate, in your own words, what Paul is communicating in the letter.

D. SURVEY CHART

Chart 95 is a survey chart of this epistle, showing the broad structure of the three chapters as they make up the whole unit. Study this chart carefully, comparing its outlines and observations with your own. Observe the following on the chart:

1. The epistle is basically of three parts, one chapter per part. Study the various outlines of content and purpose. Where is the *exhortation* section?

Here is another comparison of the three chapters (note the different time element in each):

Chap. 1 — before the rapture: persecution (tribulation)

Chap. 2 — before the revelation: Antichrist (man of sin)

Chap. 3 — how Christians should live now

2. Note the focal point: "The day of the Lord has not come yet!" Observe how it relates to what goes before and to what follows. Refer to the Bible text to confirm this.

3. Where does Paul write specifically about persecutions and afflictions? Relate this to the chart's phrase "Don't be disturbed."

4. Where does Paul write much about the man of sin? Relate this to the manifestation of the Lord of glory (chap. 1).

5. Note the outline at the bottom of the chart that relates to the subject *Lord's return*. How are the points developed in the sections of the epistle?

6. Note the different exhortations and commands shown on the chart. What others did you observe in your survey?

7. Compare the title given to this epistle with that of 1 Thessalonians. How do the two titles reveal two different instructional purposes of the epistles?

XIII. PROMINENT SUBJECTS OF 2 THESSALONIANS

A. BEFORE THE RAPTURE: PERSECUTION (1:3-12)

Paul's second Thessalonian letter begins on a bright note, commending the saints for their perseverance and faith in severe trials (1:4). Chapter 1 is background to the problem specifically mentioned

2 THESSALONIANS
HE HAS NOT COME YET

KEY VERSE: "Stand fast, and hold the traditions which ye have been taught, whether by word, or our epistle" (2:15).

KEY WORDS:
Lord
lawlessness
revelation
thanks
sin

PERSECUTION	PROPHECY	PRACTICE

We give thanks—3

We beseech—1

We give thanks—13

We command—6

MAN OF SIN

THE DAY OF THE LORD HAS NOT COME YET! 1, 2

DON'T BE DISTURBED

PERSECUTIONS

STAND FIRM 2:15 . . .

THE LORD WILL STRENGTHEN AND PROTECT YOU—3

WORK 3:12 . . .

PRAY—1
KEEP ALOOF—6
WORK—12

"DO NOT GROW WEARY OF DOING GOOD" (13)

	1	2	3
	COMMENDATION	CORRECTION	EXHORTATION
	MANIFESTATION OF THE LORD IN GLORY	REVELATION OF THE MAN OF SIN	ACTION OF THE WORD OF THE LORD
	— a comfort to the persecuted — a terror to the unconverted (8-9)	— a revelation and consummation of the lawless one	— demands a severance of fellowship with evil and idle men
LORD'S RETURN	Record references to the Lord's return		

in 2:2: *persecution* before the *rapture*. Just how the two are related is discussed below.

Recall the key prophetic passage of Paul's first letter (4:13-18). Paul very clearly foretold the sudden (though not necessarily immediate) event of the rapture of the saints. Then he wrote about the coming, unannounced "day of the Lord," which shall bring destruction and travail (5:1-5). Whether the Thessalonians interpreted these two "comings" as happening at different times, they did associate tribulation with the day of the Lord. When a letter forged with Paul's signature reached them with the message that the day of the Lord had arrived,[12] they were prone to believe it, because of the severe persecution they were going through. But that raised a real problem: If the day of the Lord had already arrived, what about the rapture that Paul had foretold in his letter? Had it taken place, and were they left behind? So in chapter 1 Paul interprets the meaning and purpose of persecution and affliction for saints before the rapture (cf. Heb. 10:32-39).

The word *tribulation(s)* appears twice in this passage. It should not be confused with *the* Tribulation period (or the Great Tribulation period), which shall transpire between the rapture and the revelation (Matt. 24:21) (cf. Chart 91, p. 356). Read the following verses where the word has reference to various kinds of trials that Christians are called upon to endure in their daily walk: John 16:33; Romans 5:3; 12:12; 2 Corinthians 1:4; 7:4; Ephesians 3:13; 1 Thessalonians 3:4.

Ultimate judgment of all unbelievers will fall at the great white throne judgment (Chart 91). Read Revelation 20:11-15 for the description of that most awesome and tragic event. That is the background to verses 8-10 of this Thessalonian passage.

B. BEFORE THE REVELATION: ANTICHRIST (2:1-17)

Chapter 2 is the crux of the second letter. Here Paul treats the problem vexing the Thessalonian Christians. The passage contains one of the New Testament's fullest descriptions of the activity and defeat of Antichrist, called the "man of lawlessness [sin]" in 2:3. (See Chart 96.) The chapter's main point is that the day of the Lord will not come until the Antichrist has first been revealed and worshiped as God by the world.

This is the background of Paul's instructions in chapter 2:

1. In the first letter, Paul instructed the Thessalonians to expect a sudden rapture, when deceased and surviving believers would be

---

12. "by . . . report or letter supposed to have come from us, saying that the day of the Lord has already come" (2:2, NIV).

caught up to be with Christ forever (1 Thess. 4:13-18).

2. In the same letter, Paul wrote that the day of the Lord — a time of judgment for unbelievers — would come upon the unbelieving world unannounced, "just like a thief in the night" (1 Thess. 5:1-3).

3. After receiving that letter, the Thessalonians had continued to be sorely persecuted for their faith. False teaching was circulating that the day of the Lord had already come and brought the Thessalonians' tribulations. The church's natural questions were, Did not Paul write and say that we would be raptured? How, then, could the day of the Lord be upon us?

4. So Paul wrote the second letter, instructing the church that the persecutions they were experiencing were not to be confused with the judgments of the day of the Lord against unbelievers. That was yet to be (2 Thess. 1:7-9). "Now, concerning your confusion about how the rapture relates to all of this: don't be misled or disturbed by any kind of false teaching. The day of the Lord has *not* come yet. That day will not come until after two things have happened: first, the rise of the great rebellion against God, and then the appearance of the man of sin, the instigator of the rebellion."[13]

5. The aim of the apostle in this chapter, therefore, was "to clear away the confusion existing in the minds of the converts by further defining the circumstances attending the Day of the Lord; these are different from the circumstances of the Parousia."[14]

6. Read 2:1-12 again and record all that is written about the man of sin (Antichrist). Then refer to the section Further Study for more descriptions of this archenemy of Christ.

XIV. THEME, KEY WORDS AND VERSES FOR 2 THESSALONIANS

Compose a theme for 2 Thessalonians. This should center on the main subject of the epistle.

Make a list of key words and verses of the letter, as you observed these in your survey studies. Compare your list with what is recorded on Chart 95.

XV. APPLICATIONS FROM 2 THESSALONIANS

This second letter is filled with truths applicable to the Christian life. For example, what is taught about victorious Christian living in 3:1-5, and about the disciplined life in 3:6-15? Go through the three chapters and list the applications you see.

---

13. Summary paraphrase of 2:1-12.
14. C. F. Hogg and W. E. Vine, *The Epistles to the Thessalonians*, p. 245.

XVI. REVIEW QUESTIONS ON 2 THESSALONIANS

1. Does Paul identify himself by name in 2 Thessalonians?
2. When did he write the second letter?
3. What were Paul's reasons for writing?
4. Compare the two letters in five ways.
5. Compare the rapture and the revelation.
    Complete the two phrases:
        BEFORE THE RAPTURE: _____.
        BEFORE THE REVELATION: _____.
6. Compare the lengths of the two letters.
7. Identify a title for each.
8. What is the key point of 2 Thessalonians, regarding Christ's second coming?
9. Identify the contents of each chapter.
10. Where does Paul write most about the Antichrist (man of sin)?

XVII. FURTHER STUDY OF 2 THESSALONIANS

Because the Antichrist is a main character of 2 Thessalonians 2, it will be very helpful for you to read other passages of Scripture about him. (The Thessalonians knew about him from the Old Testament and from Paul's earlier instruction [2:5-6].) Read the following: Ezekiel 38-39; Daniel 7:8, 20; 8:24; 11:28—12:3; Zechariah 12-14; Matthew 24:15; 1 John 2:18, 22; 4:3; 2 John 7; Revelation 13:1-10; 17:8.

Various names by which this Antichrist is identified in Scripture are the little horn (Dan. 7:8; 8:9), the prince that shall come (Dan. 9:26), the willful king (Dan. 11:36), the man of lawlessness (sin) (2 Thess. 2:3), the son of destruction (perdition) (2 Thess. 2:3), that lawless (wicked) one (2 Thess. 2:8), antichrist (1 John 2:18), the beast out of the sea (Rev. 13:1-10).

John wrote about many antichrists in the world, but singled out the Antichrist (1 John 2:18). This Antichrist is a real person, an emissary of Satan, the personification of evil, and the culmination of all that is opposed to God.

Chart 96 shows the temporary reign of Antichrist during the Tribulation period, as it is related to the two phases of Christ's coming — the rapture and revelation. You will want to keep this chronology in mind when you study chapter 2.

CHART 96

THE TEMPORARY REIGN OF ANTICHRIST

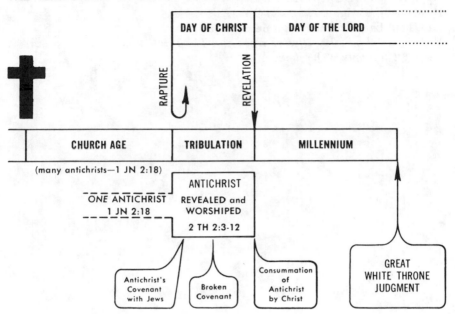

XVIII. OUTLINE

2 THESSALONIANS: Waiting For the Lord's Return

XIX. SELECTED READING FOR THE THESSALONIAN LETTERS

GENERAL INTRODUCTION

Bruce, F. F. "1 and 2 Thessalonians." In *The New Bible Commentary*, pp. 61-62; 1154-55.

Hiebert, D. Edmond. *An Introduction to the Pauline Epistles*, pp. 31-68.

COMMENTARIES

Hiebert, D. Edmond. *The Thessalonian Epistles*.

Hogg, C. F., and Vine, W. E. *The Epistles to the Thessalonians*.

Morris, Leon. *The Epistles of Paul to the Thessalonians*.

Ryrie, Charles C. *First and Second Thessalonians*.

OTHER RELATED SOURCES

Hoyt, Herman A. *The End Times*.
Pentecost, J. Dwight. *Things to Come*.
Tan, Paul Lee. *The Interpretation of Prophecy*.
Walvoord, John F. *The Blessed Hope and The Tribulation*.
————. *The Rapture Question*.

18

The Pastoral Epistles and Philemon

1 Timothy: Godliness and Pastoral Care
Titus: Adorning the Doctrine of God
2 Timothy: Endurance and Separation in the Ministry
Philemon: Appeal for Forgiveness

Paul wrote about half the New Testament's twenty-seven books. The last three that he wrote were 1 Timothy, Titus, and 2 Timothy, in that order. The letters have since been called pastorals, for reasons to be given below. The very fact that these letters were written toward the end of such an outstanding career is a promise of much spiritual insight and inspiration to all who would study the letters.

About a year before writing 1 Timothy, Paul wrote a short letter to Philemon. This letter appears last in the canonical list of Paul's writings, hence it is the last to be studied in this survey series.

The pastoral epistles and Philemon are messages from one heart to another. Here we can learn much about *individual* Christians: Paul and Timothy and Titus; Philemon and Onesimus; and the members of churches in Ephesus and Crete and Colossae. And because human nature does not change from generation to generation, we can easily see why these letters are so contemporary in their message to us.

I. PREPARATION FOR STUDY

It will help you to prepare for your study of each of the pastoral epistles by first viewing them as a group.

Paul's three letters to Timothy and Titus are called pastorals, because for the most part they are Paul's counsel to his assistants who served in the pastoral (shepherd-like) functions of the churches

371

in the regions of Ephesus and Crete.[1] (The word *pastor* appears only once in the New Testament, Ephesians 4:11, and literally means "shepherd." Read Acts 20:28-29 and 1 Peter 5:2-3, where the word *flock* is used, and note the various functions of a spiritual shepherd, such as feeding, guiding, and superintending. Also read Jeremiah 23:1-4.)

The Pauline authorship of these epistles has been challenged by liberal critics, but external and internal evidence strongly supports it.

The place and function of the pastoral letters in the New Testament are seen when they are compared with the other writings of Paul. Study Chart 61, page 241, carefully, and note the following:

1. The epistles are listed in the chronological order of writing. (Some would place Galatians at a later date.)

2. There are three groups of epistles:

travel epistles: written during the years of the missionary journeys
prison epistles: written during Paul's first Roman imprisonment
pastoral epistles: 1 Timothy and Titus written after Paul's release
      from prison; 2 Timothy written during his second Roman imprisonment.

3. The main subjects and general purposes of these three groups were different, broadly speaking. Do you see a progression in each list?

4. The first two groups were addressed to churches;[2] the pastoral epistles were addressed to individuals.

5. The pastoral epistles, especially 1 Timothy and Titus, are about the church and its workers. Sometimes the epistles are referred to as Paul's ecclesiastical letters.

6. Second Timothy has a place all its own, since it is Paul's personal farewell to his most intimate friend and colaborer.

Note: We will study the pastoral epistles in the order of their writing — 1 Timothy, Titus, 2 Timothy. This will be followed by a survey of Paul's letter to Philemon.

---

1. Technically, it might be said that Timothy and Titus were not *pastors*, as we use the term today, since in those early years a church's pastor was chosen from its elders (cf. Acts 20:17, 28-29). Timothy and Titus were not elders of churches at Ephesus and Crete. Timothy's task was "to direct, organize, and supervise the work of the churches and to help repel and reject certain errorists whose efforts were threatening to corrupt that work. He had been temporarily left behind to carry on the work which Paul would do if he were there himself" (D. Edmond Hiebert, *First Timothy*, p. 10). Fortunately, the doctrines and applications of the epistles are unaffected by questions about the men's official title.
2. Philemon was addressed to others besides the man Philemon (see Philem. 1).

II. Background of 1 Timothy

A. THE MAN TIMOTHY

Timothy is one of the most likable and devoted Christians of the entire New Testament. From a human standpoint, his greatest honor was to be chosen as an assistant to the church's foremost missionary leader Paul. He was Paul's closest friend to the very end, but the apostle recognized his higher worth and relationship when he called him a "man of God" (1 Tim. 6:11).

The name Timothy appears twenty-four times in the New Testament. You may want to read these verses to learn more about the man: Acts 16:1; 17:14-15; 18:5; 19:22; 20:4; Romans 16:21; 1 Corinthians 4:17; 16:10; 2 Corinthians 1:1, 19; Philippians 1:1; 2:19; Colossians 1:1; 1 Thessalonians 1:1; 3:2, 6; 2 Thessalonians 1:1; 1 Timothy 1:2, 18; 6:20; 2 Timothy 1:2; Philemon 1; Hebrews 13:23.

1. *Home*. Timothy was a native of Derbe (cf. Acts 16:1 and 20:4), son of a Gentile father and Jewish mother (Acts 16:1, 3). His mother and grandmother are mentioned by name in 2 Timothy: Eunice and Lois (2 Tim. 1:5). Paul was thirty to thirty-five years old when Timothy was born, which means that the apostle was twice Timothy's age when 1 and 2 Timothy were written (cf. 1 Tim. 4:12).

From the time Timothy was a child, he was instructed by his mother in the Old Testament Scriptures (2 Tim. 1:5; 3:14-15). His mother had been taught by her mother Lois. Timothy's Gentile father apparently did not hinder this Jewish religious training.

2. *Name*. The name Timothy (Greek, *Timotheus*) means "honoring God" or "honored by God." Timothy's mother very likely chose the name because of her faith in God.

3. *Conversion*. Timothy and his mother were probably converted when Paul visited Derbe on his first missionary journey (Acts 14:6-7, 20-21). From 1 Corinthians 4:14-17 and 1 Timothy 1:2, we may conclude that it was Paul who led Timothy to the Lord. Timothy was a young man, probably in his late teens, when he was saved.

4. *Ministry*. When Paul and Silas revisited Derbe on the second missionary journey, Christians from that area highly recommended Timothy to Paul as an assistant (Acts 16:1-2). Paul responded, and Timothy was circumcised and ordained to the ministry of the Word (Acts 16:3-5; 1 Tim. 4:14).[3] From that time onward, Timothy was Paul's closest co-worker, serving in these various capacities:

a. Paul's aide on the journeys, doing many of the necessary

---

3. The rite of circumcision in this case was to keep open the door of witness to unbelieving Jews who would learn that Timothy was half Gentile (Acts 16:3).

menial tasks as well as helping in the ministry of the Word

b. Paul's representative to young groups of Christians, in follow-up work, while Paul was ministering in new areas (for examples, read Acts 19:22 and 1 Thessalonians 3:1-2)

c. Paul's companion in prison (cf. Phil. 1:1; Col. 1:1; Philem. 1; Heb. 13:23).

The relationship of the apostle Paul to the younger Timothy has been described by one writer thus:

> That an older man should selflessly love, instruct and repose confidence in a youth and then continue to exhibit such close companionship for approximately twenty years is surely admirable. For a young man to respond with similar respect, confidence, and heartfelt admiration, without jealousy, impatience, or resentment is equally commendable. The relationship of these two men is a remarkable display of Christian virtues at their best.[4]

Paul spent about three years of his third missionary journey in Ephesus (cf. Acts 19:8, 10; 20:31). Timothy was with Paul at this time (cf. Acts 19:1 and 19:22), so that he became well acquainted with the Christians there. This was the area where Timothy was ministering when Paul wrote 1 Timothy approximately seven years later.

5. *Character.* Someone has written, "Timothy was one of the magnificent compensations Paul enjoyed for the cruel treatment he received at Lystra." Various things written in Acts and the epistles furnish the background for a personality profile of this man of God. Try to visualize the man Timothy from these descriptions:[5]

tender, affectionate (1 Cor. 4:17; Phil. 2:20-21)

timid, tactful (1 Cor. 16:10-11: 1 Tim. 4:12; 2 Tim. 1:6-7)

faithful, loyal (1 Cor. 4:17)

conscientious (Phil. 2:19-23)

devoted to God (1 Tim. 6:11)

with a physical infirmity (1 Tim. 5:23).

You will become more acquainted with Timothy the man as you survey the two letters bearing his name.

6. *Death.* The Bible does not reveal any details of the deaths of Paul or Timothy. According to tradition, Paul was executed by Nero, and Timothy suffered martyrdom later under Emperor Domitian or Nerva.

B. THE AUTHOR PAUL

Many things related to the apostle's ministry (e.g., message,

---

4. Homer A. Kent, *The Pastoral Epistles*, p. 19.
5. Sometimes a trait can only be implied from a Scripture passage.

methods, people, places), up to the time of his writing 1 Timothy, form part of the background of the pastorals. So it will be very helpful at this time to view Paul's career in sketch form, observing how 1 Timothy fits into the pattern. For this, study Appendix B, pages 518-19, entitled, "An Approximate Chronology of the Life of Paul." Note especially all references to the man Timothy.

C. THE CHURCHES OF EPHESUS

Timothy's ministry extended to all the local congregations in and around Ephesus, so any reference in this book to the "mother" church at Ephesus includes the satellite churches as well. See Map W, which shows the geographical setting of 1 Timothy. There were, of course, other towns and villages in the vicinity of Ephesus.

Read Acts 20:17-21 for Paul's resumé of his ministry at Ephesus when he brought the gospel to that city for the first time (third missionary journey).

When Paul visited Ephesus after his release at Rome, he discovered that during his absence the church was being plagued with all kinds of spiritual problems. The city itself, with all its corruption and idolatry, was proving to be a spiritual battleground for the congregation of believers. One can well appreciate why this was a problem in many of the first-century churches.

"If it be remembered how vast was the change which most of the members had made in passing from the worship of the heathen temples to the pure and simple worship of Christianity, it will not excite surprise that their old life still clung to them or that they did not clearly distinguish which things needed to be changed and which might continue as they had been."[6]

Paul stayed a while and tried to help the people as much as he could. When he had to leave for Macedonia, he left Timothy at Ephesus to continue what he had started (1 Tim. 1:3).

The congregations of Ephesus were five to eight years old when Paul wrote 1 Timothy. Growing pains were still there, issuing from such important tasks as organizing, teaching, correcting, and unifying. Timothy had a full-time job, helping the leaders of the various congregations fulfill their ministry.

D. DATE AND PLACE WRITTEN

Paul probably wrote this letter from Macedonia, around A.D. 62[7] (1 Tim. 1:3). He expected to return to Ephesus shortly, but he knew of the possibility of a long delay (3:14-15).

---

6. James Stalker sees in this description of the church at Corinth a picture of the average church of Paul's missionary journeys. *The Life of St. Paul*, p. 108.
7. Some hold that Paul wrote from Corinth in Greece.

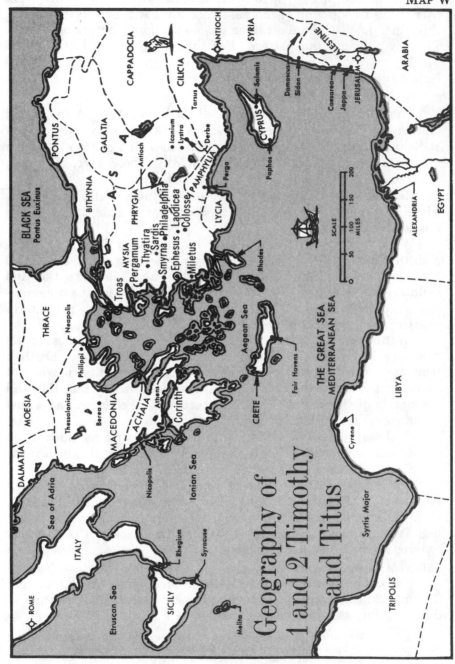

Geography of
1 and 2 Timothy
and Titus

E. OCCASION

It is not difficult to learn from the epistle itself what situation at Ephesus constrained Paul to write at this time. Read the letter through, not tarrying over details, and observe direct or indirect references to the following problems or needs: spread of false doctrine,[8] spiritual coldness, personnel problems, problems of the worship services, problems related to the offices of the church and the care of widows.

F. PURPOSES

Paul's immediate purpose in writing was to urge Timothy to stay on at Ephesus (1:3-4). Timothy must have yearned to be ministering at the side of Paul again. In general, Paul wrote this letter with two purposes in mind, to meet the needs caused by the occasion discussed above: (1) personal — to help Timothy; (2) ecclesiastical — to help the churches of Ephesus.

Underlying both of those aims was Paul's ever-present burden of propagating and preserving the truth of the gospel. The apostle clearly shared this burden with his colaborer when he spoke of the gospel as "the glorious gospel of the blessed God, with which I have been entrusted" (1:11).

III. SURVEY OF 1 TIMOTHY

A. FIRST SCANNING

Read 1 Timothy in one sitting. The purpose of this initial scanning is to get the atmosphere of the book and catch its major purposes. Write down your first impressions of the epistle and any key words and phrases that stand out as of this reading.

B. SEGMENTS AND PARAGRAPHS

Refer to Chart 97 and observe that new segments of this letter begin at the opening verse of each chapter, with these exceptions: at 6:2b in place of 6:1; and an additional unit beginning at 3:14. Mark these segments in your Bible.

Next, mark new paragraph divisions in your Bible, at the following opening verses: 1:1, 3, 12, 18; 2:1, 9; 3:1, 8, 14; 4:1, 6, 11; 5:1, 3, 9, 11, 17; 6:1, 2b, 6, 11, 17, 20. Read the paragraphs and assign a title for each.

Do you observe any groups of paragraphs with similar general content?

What have you noticed so far about these subjects in the epistle:

8. Read Paul's earlier prediction of this in Acts 20:28-30.

Timothy's life and ministry, the church, notes of praise, various kinds of sin?

C. STRUCTURE

Paul's letter is a unit from beginning to end. It is not an unorganized list of miscellaneous thoughts. Let us look at it more closely to see its structural relationships.

1. What is the opening salutation?

2. What would you consider to be the concluding note?

3. Does the word *Amen* appear at any place other than at the end of the letter? What is the function of such a word?[9]

4. Does there seem to be a turning point in the epistle? For example, how does chapter 3 end?

5. How do the opening words of chapter 2 indicate a beginning of something new here? Compare what goes before (chap. 1) with what follows (chaps. 2-3).

6. What reference to the local church is made in 3:15? Are chapters 2 and 3 about the subject of the church? Support your answer.

7. What seems to be the general subject of chapters 4-6?

D. SURVEY CHART

Survey Chart 97 shows some of the structure of this letter. Study it carefully, in the light of your own observations made so far. Among other things, note the following:

1. A major division is made at 2:1. What is the two-part outline?

2. The key of the epistle is shown as 3:14-16. Read the passage. How is it related to what goes before and to what follows? How is this shown on the chart?

3. Study the contents of each chapter as shown on the chart. What is the difference between *church regulations* and *pastoral directions*?

4. Note the outline indicators at the right of the chart, *the man* and *the ministry*. These are two subjects that Paul writes much about in the letter. For example, how is chapter 1, *charge to Timothy*, an appropriate introduction to all that follows?

5. Note the three indicators of hymns on the charts. Read the passages. What is the context of each?

---

9. One writer has pointed out this symmetrical structure of 1 Timothy, centered on the three hymns of the epistle:
   Charge (1:3-16); Hymn (1:17); Charge (1:18-20)
   Charge (2:1—3:15); Hymn (3:16); Charge (4:1—6:2c)
   Charge (6:2d-15a); Hymn (6:15b-16); Charge (6:17-21).
(See Wilbur B. Wallis, "I Timothy," in *The Wycliffe Bible Commentary*, pp. 1368-70.)

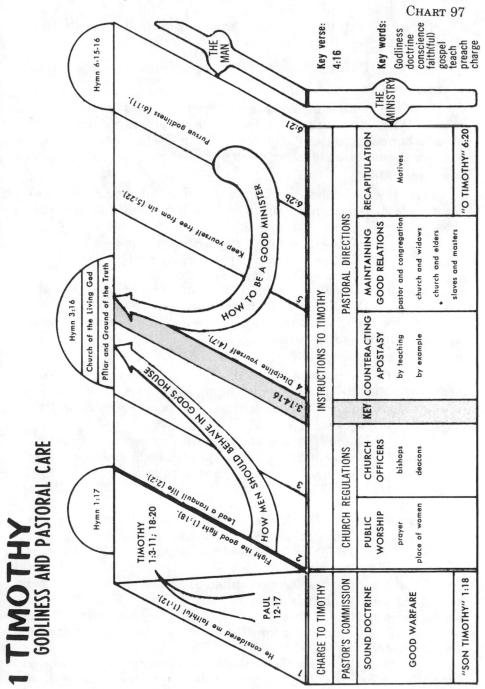

1 TIMOTHY
GODLINESS AND PASTORAL CARE

Key verse: 4:16

Key words:
Godliness
doctrine
conscience
faith(ful)
gospel
teach
preach
charge

THE MAN

THE MINISTRY

Hymn 6:15-16

Pursue godliness (6:11).

6:21

Keep yourself free from sin (5:22).

HOW TO BE A GOOD MINISTER

6:2b

5

Hymn 3:16

Church of the Living God
Pillar and Ground of the Truth

Discipline yourself (4:7).

3:14-16

HOW MEN SHOULD BEHAVE IN GOD'S HOUSE

Hymn 1:17

TIMOTHY 1:3-11; 18-20

Lead a tranquil life (2:2).

Fight the good fight (1:18).

3

2

He considered me faithful (1:12).

PAUL 12-17

1

CHARGE TO TIMOTHY	INSTRUCTIONS TO TIMOTHY			
PASTOR'S COMMISSION	CHURCH REGULATIONS		PASTORAL DIRECTIONS	
SOUND DOCTRINE	PUBLIC WORSHIP	CHURCH OFFICERS	COUNTERACTING APOSTASY	MAINTAINING GOOD RELATIONS	RECAPITULATION
GOOD WARFARE	prayer	bishops	by teaching	pastor and congregation	Motives
	place of women	deacons	by example	church and widows	
				church and elders	
				slaves and masters	
"SON TIMOTHY" 1:18	KEY				"O TIMOTHY" 6:20

6. Note the title for 1 Timothy, shown at the top of the chart. How do the two subjects of the title appear in the letter?

IV. PROMINENT SUBJECTS OF 1 TIMOTHY

A. INTERCESSORY PRAYER (2:1-7)

Read the passage and observe who are the objects of intercessory prayer. What other things are taught about prayer in verses 1-4? What other subjects does Paul write about in the full paragraph, and how are these related to intercessory prayer?

B. WOMEN (2:9-15)

Read the paragraph, noting the different subjects Paul writes about regarding women. Compare your observations with this outline:

> 2:9-10 — A woman's appearance in public
> 2:11-12 — A woman's place in the church
> 2:13-15 — The first woman, Eve

What is the timeless, universal principle taught in each of the first two parts (2:9-10; 2:11-12)? In the paragraph Paul writes about the noble state of Christian womanhood. Where do these descriptions appear: godly life, diligent learning, salvation?

C. CHURCH OFFICERS (3:1-13)

Paul writes here about two kinds of church officers: overseer and deacon (NASB). Before examining the passage closely, read the following descriptions of the two offices, as taught by various New Testament passages.

The organization of local churches in the first century was simple and basic. There were only two offices: *episkopos* and *diakonos*, Greek titles translated by the King James Version as *bishops* and *deacons*, respectively (Phil. 1:1).

1. *Titles*.

a. *Episkopos*. The Greek word means literally "overseer," as it is consistently translated in the *New American Standard Bible*. The word appears in these New Testament verses: Acts 20:28; Philippians 1:1; 1 Timothy 3:1-2; Titus 1:7.

The titles *elder* and *overseer* referred to the same person and were used interchangeably (Acts 20:17, 28; Titus 1:5, 7). The title *overseer* denoted the *function* of the office. The title *elder* (Greek, *presbyteros*) was a carry-over from the Jewish synagogue organization and denoted the *dignity* and *authority* of the office.

b. *Diakonos*. The Greek word translated "deacon" means literally "servant" or "minister." It is distinguished from the common New

Testament word for servant (*doulos*) thus: *diakonos* views a servant in relationship to his work, and *doulos* views a servant in relationship to his master. Consult a concordance for the appearances of these three words: *deacon, minister, servant*.

2. *Functions*.

a. *Overseers* were superintendents of a local church. They were also the teachers and preachers of the congregation, having the responsibility of feeding the flock (Acts 20:28; cf. 1 Pet. 5:2). Other duties included guarding the congregation from spiritual harm (Acts 20:29-31); being examples to the members (1 Pet. 5:3); and visiting those in need (James 1:27). In other words, the title *overseer* of the first centuries was equivalent to the present-day title of *pastor*.[10]

b. *Deacons* were the assistants of the overseers, serving in spiritual matters but especially in the physical, mundane areas of the church's life. Read Acts 6:1-6, which is the description of what may be the first deacon appointments in the New Testament church (even though the word *deacon* does not appear in the Bible text).

On the basis of the previous discussion, would you say that the two offices of the early New Testament church called for very strict qualifications of those who would serve in them? In the light of this, study the qualifications given by Paul in 1 Timothy 3:1-13: qualifications of the overseer (3:1-7); qualifications of the deacon (3:8-13).

D. HYMN OF DOCTRINE (3:16)

Paul may be quoting here from an early creedal hymn used by the Christians. What prime doctrines appear in the stanza? What do you think Paul has in mind by introducing the lines by the phrase, "great is the mystery of godliness"?

E. ANTIDOTE FOR FALSE TEACHING (4:1-16)

False teaching was one threat to the churches that Paul vigorously forewarned against. The apostle's consistent formula was, in effect, destroy false doctrine by sound doctrine. This is the subject of 4:1-16, as Paul turns his attention particularly to Timothy's missions, showing him how he can minister to the needs and problems of the Ephesian churches.

---

10. The two-office organization of the New Testament church gradually merged into this three-office arrangement in the centuries that followed: (1) pastor (as preacher-teacher-shepherd); (2) elders (assisting the pastor especially in spiritual matters); (3) deacons (assisting the pastor especially in physical matters, such as the finances of the church). The thing to note here is that the tasks that needed to be done were always present; the titles given to those who performed the tasks varied from church to church and from century to century.

What false doctrines and teachers does Paul expose in 4:1-5? What sound doctrines does he teach throughout the chapter?

F. WIDOWS, ELDERS, AND SLAVES (5:3—6:2*a*)

Questions and problems that had arisen in the churches about widows, elders, and slaves are now discussed by Paul.

1. *Widows.* Four groups of widows are cited.[11] Only the first group is eligible for church support. Observe in the text the description and disposition given for each group.
- real widows (5:3, 5, 9-10)
- widows with relatives able to support (5:4, 8, 16)
- widows living in wanton pleasure (5:6-7)
- young widows (5:11-15)

2. *Elders* (5:17-25). The word *elder* does not appear after verse 19, but it seems that Paul is still thinking about this group of church leaders until he moves to the next group at 6:1. Following this pattern, observe in the text what these verses teach about elders: 5:17-18, 19, 20, 21, 22, 24-25.

3. *Slaves* (6:1-2*a*). Christian employees have obligations to Christian employers, even as employers have obligations to their employees. Paul here applies the gospel to the slave-master situation that existed in the households of many new converts to Christ in the first century. Are these verses Paul's counsel to servants or to masters? Might there have been a problem in the Christian households about this when he wrote? If so, what was it?

G. WEALTH (6:6-10, 17-19)

Paul gives sound advice to those who are blessed with wealth. How does he relate the following subjects to wealth: godliness, contentment, evil, good works, eternal wealth?[12]

V. THEME, KEY WORDS AND VERSES FOR 1 TIMOTHY

What key words and verses did you observe in your survey of 1 Timothy? Note the ones cited on Chart 97. Observe that *godliness* appears eight times in the letter. This is one of the reasons for including it in the two-part title, "Godliness and Pastoral Care."

VI. APPLICATIONS FROM 1 TIMOTHY

1. Go back over the epistle and read the various things Paul wrote about the Christian pastor. Use the following outline in or-

---

11. Some classify the widows of 5:9-10 as a distinct group, in which case the number of groups is five.
12. The last phrase of 6:5 introduces the paragraphs 6:6-10: "who think that godliness is a means to financial gain" (NIV).

ganizing your reading.[13] What is the value of this instruction to laymen of a local church?

a. His office: 1:1, 11, 12, 18; 2:7; 3:1; 4:11; 6:12.

b. His qualifications: 1:16, 18; 3:2, 4-6; 4:6, 12, 15, 16; 5:21-22; 6:13-14.

c. His duties as preacher: 1:4; 2:7, 8; 3:8-15; 4:6, 7, 11; 5:14-16, 20, 21; 6:1, 2, 4, 17-19, 20-21.

d. His duties as pastor: 1:3, 4, 18-19; 2:1, 2; 3:2, 3, 4-7, 8-13, 15; 5:1-2, 4-16, 20, 21; 6:10, 11, 12, 20.

e. His personal life: 1:5, 16, 18; 3:2, 4, 7, 8, 10, 15; 5:22, 23; 6:6-8, 9, 20.

2. What does this letter teach about the following:

a. the church's obligation to any physical needs of members of the congregation

b. procedures, policies, and principles to be followed when calling a man to serve as pastor

c. the kind of Christian employee that all of us should strive to be

d. the daily conduct of women — whether they are widows, single, or married — which is pleasing to the Lord

e. why church organization and administration need not suppress spiritual vitality.

3. What does 1 Timothy teach about prayer?

VII. REVIEW QUESTIONS ON 1 TIMOTHY

1. In what order were the pastoral epistles written?

2. When did Paul first bring the gospel to Ephesus? How long did he minister there at that time?

3. What does the name Timothy mean? When was Timothy converted? When did he join Paul's missionary party?

4. In what three ways did Timothy serve with Paul?

5. What kind of a man was Timothy?

6. Did Timothy minister to only the "mother" church at Ephesus? What was Timothy's main responsibility?

7. What were some of the problems in the Ephesian congregation when Paul wrote his first letter to Timothy?

8. What were Paul's two main purposes in writing the epistle?

9. What practical lessons can be learned for today from this New Testament book?

10. What are the two main structural divisions of 1 Timothy?

11. In what chapter does Paul give his personal testimony in connection with the charge to Timothy?

---

13. Outline from W. Graham Scroggie, *Know Your Bible*, 1:245.

12. What subjects does Paul write about in the section called *church regulations* (p. 379)?

13. In what chapter does Paul write about widows?

14. Name five key words of this letter.

VIII. FURTHER STUDY OF 1 TIMOTHY

1. With the help of an exhaustive concordance, study the usage of the key word *godliness* in the New Testament. The Greek word is a compound of two roots: *eu* (good), and *sebomai* (revere, adore).[14]

2. The phrase "this is a faithful saying" appears five times in the pastoral epistles. Use the following comparative outline to suggest other studies of the phrase.[15]

Christ's coming — the way of sins' forgiveness (1 Tim. 1:15)
Christ's ministry — the way of noble service (1 Tim. 3:1)
Christ's life — the way of spiritual progress (1 Tim. 4:10)
Christ's world — the way of honorable work (Titus 3:8)
Christ's strength — the way of successful suffering (2 Tim. 2:11)

IX. OUTLINE

1 TIMOTHY: Godliness and Pastoral Care	
CHARGE TO TIMOTHY	1:1-20
Sound Doctrine	1:1-11
Grace and Warfare	1:12-20
INSTRUCTIONS TO TIMOTHY	2:1—6:21
Public Worship in the Church	2:1-15
Church Officers	3:1-16
Antidote for False Teaching	4:1-16
Widows, Elders, and Slaves	5:1—6:2a
Final Instructions and Exhortations	6:2b-21

X. BACKGROUND OF TITUS

Soon after Paul wrote 1 Timothy to his closest friend, he wrote a letter to another co-worker and fellow-servant, Titus. This letter has been called "a priceless and unrivalled manual of pastoral advice." Though written to a church leader, its message is intended for all Christians, just as the other pastoral epistles are. Luther wrote of it: "This is a short Epistle, but yet such a quintessence of Christian

---

14. In one verse (1 Tim. 2:10) another Greek word translated "godliness" appears: *theo* (God) *sebeia* (reverence).

15. W. Graham Scroggie, *Know Your Bible*, 2:243. Scroggie suggests that these sayings may point to "certain Logia current in the early Churches, or the use of liturgical forms."

doctrine, and composed in such a masterly manner, that it contains all that is needful for Christian knowledge and life."[16]

Review what you learned about Titus earlier in this chapter.

A. THE MAN TITUS

1. *Name and family.* The name Titus was a common Latin name in Paul's day. Both of Titus's parents were Greek. Their residence may have been in a city such as Antioch of Syria (cf. Gal. 1:21; 2:1).

2. *Conversion.* Titus may have been converted through the ministry of Paul, as suggested by Titus 1:4. (Cf. 1 Cor. 4:15.)

CHART 98

THE MEN TIMOTHY AND TITUS COMPARED

LIKENESSES	
Both were young and gifted.	
Both were co-workers of Paul.	
Both served in difficult church situations.	
DIFFERENCES	
TIMOTHY	TITUS
half-Jew	wholly Gentile
circumcised by Paul	uncircumcised
served at Corinth and Ephesus	served at Corinth and Crete
nervous and retiring personality	strong and stern personality
prominent in Acts	not mentioned in Acts

3. *Ministry as Paul's assistant.* Titus does not appear by name in the book of Acts, but his first contacts with Paul were during those years. The following is a summary of his ministries with the apostle.

a. He accompanied Paul and Barnabas to the Jerusalem Council of Acts 15. (Read Galatians 2:1-4.)

---

16. Quoted by W. Graham Scroggie, *Know Your Bible*, 2:251.

b. He was Paul's representative at the Corinthian church during Paul's third missionary journey (1) to alleviate tension there (2 Cor. 7:6, 13-14); and (2) to collect money for the poor (2 Cor. 8:6, 16, 23).

c. He was Paul's representative at the Cretan churches after Paul's release from the first Roman imprisonment (Titus 1:4-5).

d. He had a ministry at Dalmatia (2 Tim. 4:10).

4. *Timothy and Titus compared*. Likenesses and differences of the two men are summarized in Chart 98.

5. *Character*. Titus was a consecrated Christian of strong affection, courage, and zeal. He was wise and practical in his dealings with others, commanding their respect. "He knew how to handle the quarrelsome Corinthians, the mendacious Cretans, and the pugnacious Dalmatians."[17]

B. THE EPISTLE TO TITUS

1. *Date and place written*. Paul wrote to Titus soon after writing 1 Timothy, probably while the apostle was in Macedonia, enroute to Nicopolis (3:12), in A.D. 62.

2. *Island of Crete*. Paul had left Titus in the Roman province of Crete, just as he had left Timothy at Ephesus (1:5). This mountainous island is located southeast of Greece (see Map W, p. 376); its dimensions are 160 miles by 35 miles. The accompanying Map X shows where its numerous coastal towns were located in Titus's day.

MAP X

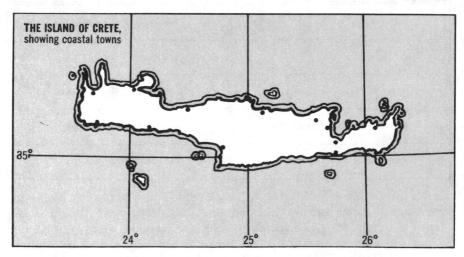

THE ISLAND OF CRETE, showing coastal towns

---

17. Merrill C. Tenney, ed., *The Zondervan Pictorial Bible Dictionary*, p. 857.

These towns were heavily populated, described by one writer as "neither peaceable among themselves, nor very patient of foreign dominion." Morally and socially the Cretans had a bad reputation in the Mediterranean world, illustrated by these two sayings from classical writing: "Cretans are always liars, evil beasts, lazy gluttons" (Epimenides, quoted by Paul in 1:12). "The Cretans are always brigands and piratical, and unjust" (Leonides).

3. *Churches of Crete.* It is not known when or by whom the Cretans were first evangelized. The original nucleus of Christians may have begun on the day of Pentecost, at Jerusalem (Acts 2:11). Paul did not visit the island on any of his missionary journeys. He may have preached in the cities of the island on his brief visit after the Roman imprisonment. (Read Titus 1:5.) By the time he wrote to Titus, however, he had many Christian friends living there (Titus 3:15). The very fact that God included in the canon of the New Testament a letter written indirectly to the Cretan churches that were not widely known to the first-century Christian world tells us that no local church, however small or insignificant in man's eyes, is overlooked by God.

4. *Occasion of writing.* Paul wrote the book of Titus for many of the same reasons he wrote the book of 1 Timothy. These include:

a. disorder and false teaching threatening the local churches (1:10-11)

b. inconsistent living by church members

c. need for instruction concerning church organization.

5. *Purposes of the epistle.* The main purposes of the epistle, in the immediate setting, include (a) to advise Titus in his task of superintending the circuit of Cretan churches as Paul's representative (1:5); (b) to instruct and exhort both Titus and the churches regarding Christian behavior consistent with Christian doctrine (chaps. 1-3); (c) to instruct Titus concerning personal matters (3:12-13).

6. *Main contents.* Your survey of Titus will show the main subjects discussed by Paul in the epistle. The predominant theme is that of maintaining good works as a demonstration of a saving faith. Read the passages 2:11-14 and 3:4-7, which have been called two of the most comprehensive statements of Christian truth to be found in the New Testament.

7. *Place among the pastoral epistles.* Of the pastoral epistles, 1 Timothy and Titus are most alike regarding background and content, and in one sense could be called twin epistles. The three pastoral epistles are compared in the accompanying diagram.

PASTORAL EPISTLES COMPARED

1 TIMOTHY	TITUS	2 TIMOTHY
predominantly pastoral	less pastoral	mainly personal
Guard the gospel (6:20)	Practice the gospel (3:8)	Preach the gospel (4:2)

XI. SURVEY OF TITUS

A. READINGS

Follow the stages and exercises of survey that you have established in your own personal study. Use the suggestions given below to send you on various paths of inquiry.

1. Identify the introduction and conclusion of the letter. What does Paul write about in each part, in addition to the customary greetings?

2. Regard each chapter (not including the introduction and conclusion) as a unit of study. Read the chapters a few times and observe the things Paul writes about and *how* he writes them.

3. Note the two comprehensive doctrinal passages cited earlier (2:11-14 and 3:4-7). What is the *context* of each? What is the *content* of each?

4. You will observe the word *doctrine* as one of the key words of Titus. Note the phrase of 2:10, "that they may adorn the doctrine of God our Savior in every respect." The meaning of "adorn" is "to make attractive" (cf. NIV translation). As you read the text of Titus, observe the many ways Paul exhorts to good deeds, which are the adornment of the gospel. Note the repetition of the phrase "good deeds."

5. What groups of people does Paul write about in each chapter?

B. SURVEY CHART

Study carefully the different structural outlines shown on the survey, Chart 99, and note the following:

1. In this letter Paul writes mainly about three groups: leaders, opponents, and followers. Survey the Bible text to identify who they are.

TITUS
ADORNING THE DOCTRINE OF GOD

	LEADERS	LAITY	GENERAL
MAINTAINING GOOD WORKS	GOD MANIFESTED HIS WORD (1:3)	GRACE OF GOD HAS APPEARED (2:11)	KINDNESS AND LOVE OF GOD APPEARED (3:4)

SALUTATION AND INTRODUCTION — 1:1 — 1:5

CONCLUSION — 3:12 — 3:15

	elders	false teachers		Christian conduct: GROUPS	Christian conduct: GENERAL
	LEADERS	OPPONENTS		FOLLOWERS	
	TEACHERS OF SOUND DOCTRINE	SOWERS OF FALSE DOCTRINE		LIVING TESTIMONY OF SOUND DOCTRINE	
	ORDERLY CHURCH—1:5		SOUND CHURCH—2:1		PRACTICING CHURCH—3:1

KEY VERSES:
2:10b and 3:14

KEY WORDS:
DOCTRINE
GOOD WORKS
TEACH
LOVE
GOD OUR SAVIOUR
FAITH
ADORN

2. Note the outline centered on *doctrine*. How is this outline derived from the Bible text?

3. Note the other outlines appearing on the chart. Relate these to your own observations in the survey process.

4. What title is assigned to the letter? What verse is it derived from?

XII. Prominent Subjects of Titus

A. FALSE TEACHING IN A CHURCH (1:1-16)

After an inspiring greeting (1:1-4), Paul launches into the main subject of his letter without delay. The churches of Crete had some glaring defects, and the apostle wanted Titus to "set things in order" there (1:5).

This first chapter illustrates a consistent principle of the Bible: no diagnosis without prescription for cure. As far as Paul was concerned, the problems of the churches on the island of Crete could be solved, hence the letter to his friend and co-worker.

Read the chapter again and observe these three parts:

1. *Doctrine* (1:1-4). False teaching is best dealt with by true doctrine. What different doctrines does Paul refer to here?
2. *Leaders* (1:5-9). Spiritual, experienced leaders of the church have the responsibility to deal with the problem of false teaching. What qualifications of the leaders are cited here?
3. *False teachers* (1:10-16). Observe the different false teachers and teachings plaguing the Cretan churches.

B. ADORNING THE GOSPEL (2:1-15)

In this chapter Paul turns his attention to the churches' lay members, exhorting them, through Titus, to genuine Christian conduct. Already in the letter he has written much about creedal truth, using such terms as *the faith, the truth, word, preaching, commandment, sound doctrine.* Now he appeals for the kind of Christian conduct that will make that doctrine attractive to people: "Adorn the doctrine of God our Savior in every respect" (2:10*b*; cf. Matt. 5:16). Recall that this verse represents the key thought of the entire epistle.

What exhortations does Paul give to each group cited in chapter 2?

C. THE GOOD WORKS OF A BELIEVER (3:1-15)

In this last chapter of his letter to Titus, Paul masterfully blends the two truths of faith and works, leaving no question unanswered concerning the place of good works in the life of a believer.

Read each of the three paragraphs and observe (1) the reference to "good deeds" in each paragraph; (2) what Paul writes about each subject listed below:

Preparation for good works	3:1-7
Carefulness in good works	3:8-11
Regularity of good works	3:12-15

D. THE GRACE OF GOD (2:11-14; 3:4-7)

As noted earlier, these are two of the most comprehensive statements of the Christian gospel to be found in the New Testament. Compare the two lists of doctrines in the two passages.

XIII. THEME, KEY WORDS AND VERSES FOR TITUS

What key words and verses did you observe in your survey? Compare these with what is shown on Chart 99. Refer to an exhaustive concordance and note how often some of the words are repeated in the letter.

In your own words, how would you identify the theme of Titus?

XIV. APPLICATIONS FROM TITUS

You have seen in your survey of Titus that the main emphasis of the epistle is the adorning of the gospel by good deeds. Think through the epistle once again and see how many practical applications you can recall.

XV. REVIEW QUESTIONS ON TITUS

1. In what different ways did Titus assist Paul in the gospel ministry?

2. Compare Titus and Timothy.

3. Describe the local congregations of Christians on the island of Crete.

4. What were some of Paul's main purposes in writing Titus?

5. What are some prominent emphases of the epistle?

6. Compare this epistle with 1 Timothy.

7. List some key words of Titus, and quote one key verse.

8. Complete the outline: ORDERLY CHURCH; SOUND CHURCH; _____.

9. In what part of the letter does Paul write about false teachers and false teachings?

10. What is the meaning of the phrase, "adorning the doctrine of God"?

XVI. FURTHER STUDY OF TITUS

1. *Word study.* Make a comparative study of all the verses of Titus where the word *work(s)* appears.

2. *Doctrine study.* Atonement, redemption, and sanctification are three doctrines referred to in Titus 2:14. How are the three doctrines related to each other? (Use outside sources, such as a book of doctrine.)

3. After you have studied the book of James, compare James and Titus regarding their emphasis of good works in the life of the believer.

XVII. OUTLINE

TITUS: Adorning the Doctrine of God

Salutation and Introduction	1:1-4
CHURCH LEADERS DEALING WITH FALSE TEACHERS	1:5-16
MAKING CHRISTIAN DOCTRINE ATTRACTIVE BY EXAMPLE	2:1-15
THE GOOD WORKS OF A BELIEVER	3:1-11
Conclusion and Benediction	3:12-15

XVIII. BACKGROUND OF 2 TIMOTHY

The tenderest and most moving of Paul's letters was his last one, known by title as 2 Timothy. Paul was an aged man when he wrote this epistle from a cold, dark dungeon of a Roman prison. He knew he had but a short time left to live, and so the letter is his spiritual last will and testament — his "dying wish" — to friend and co-worker Timothy.

A. BACKGROUND

Some of the background of 1 Timothy already studied is common to that of 2 Timothy and hence need not be repeated. It will help you to review that background now. Below is a look at the particular setting of 2 Timothy.

1. *Date and place written.* Paul wrote this letter from prison at Rome around A.D. 67, about five years after his first letter to Timothy. Refer to the chronology of Paul's life (Appendix B, p. 518-19), and note the setting of the two Roman imprisonments. Part of the sequence is this:

A.D. 58-62 First imprisonment — "prison epistles" written
A.D. 62-66 Release and travels — 1 Timothy written
A.D. 67 Second imprisonment — 2 Timothy written

There was one event in Rome that happened during Paul's time of release and led indirectly to his second imprisonment. That was the burning of Rome, which occurred on July 19, A.D. 64. When Emperor Nero failed to squelch the well-founded suspicion that he had ordered the fires, he blamed the Christians and ordered them to be arrested and punished. For the remainder of his reign Christianity was a *religio illicita* (illegal religion) and waves of anti-Christian persecution rolled across the lands of the Empire. When Paul returned east in the spring of A.D. 66, his enemies had no problem arresting him and transporting him to a prison in Rome.

Read the following verses of 2 Timothy, which point to the fact of this last imprisonment: 1:16-17; 2:3, 9-13; 4:6-8, 16. Study the comparisons of the two imprisonments, as shown on Chart 100.

CHART 100

PAUL'S TWO IMPRISONMENTS COMPARED

FIRST IMPRISONMENT	SECOND IMPRISONMENT
accused by Jews of heresy and sedition	persecuted by Rome and arrested as a malefactor
good living conditions in a rented house (Ac 28:30-31)	poor conditions, in a cold, dark dungeon
many friends visited him	virtually alone
had many opportunities for Christian witness	opportunities restricted
expected freedom (Phil 1:24-26)	anticipated execution (2 Ti 4:6)

2. *Occasion and purpose.* The immediate occasion of the letter was Paul's desire to see Timothy and Mark again (4:9, 11, 21) and to have Timothy bring Paul's cloak, books, and parchments, which the apostle had left at Troas (4:13).[18] The cloak was for the damp of the cell and the cold of the winter. Of the two kinds of writing (books and parchments) that Paul requested, the latter no doubt included the Scriptures (Old Testament), hence the accent, "*especially* the parchments" (italics added).

---

18. Troas may have been the place of Paul's arrest.

Paul's main purpose in writing was to inspire and challenge Timothy to take up the torch of the gospel ministry left by the apostle. It is possible that Timothy had left Ephesus by this time, suggested by 4:12. If so, he probably was engaged in evangelistic work in Macedonia or Asia. If Paul was executed before Timothy could visit him, the letter was that much more significant for Timothy.[19]

Try to imagine how Timothy felt when he received this letter from his friend who just recently had been torn from him by Nero's soldiers. As far as Timothy knew, Paul already might have been executed by the tyrant Nero. Here is how one writer has described the soul of Timothy at that time:

> Timothy stood awfully lonely, yet awfully exposed, in face of a world of thronging sorrows. Well might he have been shaken to the root of his faith. He might almost have tasted a drop of that last despair which gives up to God and wishes that being could cease to be. To such a heart, when some sad weeks had passed away, came this Letter . . . to pour its mighty sympathies into his sorrow and to bid him be strong again in the living Lord Jesus Christ.[20]

3. *Tone.* Paul's last inspired writing has been called "an epistle of mingled gloom and glory." True, there is a pathos about such lines as "I am already being poured out" (4:6) and "Demas has deserted me" (4:10). Paul was ever truthful, and exposing his wounded heart like this could only have spurred Timothy on to the fellowship of suffering. But the prominent tone of the letter, even in references to trials as mentioned above, is triumph, and glory, and deep gratitude. Paul is not despondent; he does not despair. Only a sure hope could give birth to such an exclamation as, "In the future there is laid up for me the crown of righteousness" (4:8).

XIX. SURVEY OF 2 TIMOTHY

A. FIRST READING

1. First mark your Bible to show segment divisions beginning at the following verses: 1:1, 3; 2:1; 3:1; 4:1, 6, 9, 22. Then read the letter through, aloud if possible, in one sitting for first impressions. Be aware of the segment units as you read.

2. What atmosphere do you sense in the letter?

3. What key words and phrases stand out prominently?

---

19. On the view that Timothy may have got to visit Paul, see Frank J. Goodwin, *A Harmony of the Life of St. Paul*, p. 191.
20. H.C.G. Moule, *The Second Epistle to Timothy*, p. 14.

B. SEGMENTS

1. Read the letter again, segment by segment. Assign segment titles. Try to identify a main subject of each segment. Are you beginning to see differences of content of the segments?

2. Do the same for the paragraphs of the epistle, using this set of paragraph divisions: 1:1, 3, 6, 11, 15; 2:1, 8, 14, 20; 3:1, 10, 13, 14; 4:1, 6, 9, 19, 22.

3. Record on paper any new observations and impressions.

C. STRUCTURE

Because this letter is very personal, we are not surprised that it does not have an elaborate organization such as does a doctrinal book like Romans. At the same time, we observe that the master author Paul did not put together the letter in a haphazard way. You probably sensed a togetherness of the composition in the readings you have already made.

1. What would you identify to be the introduction and conclusion of the letter?

2. Review the main subjects that you assigned to the segments. Do any combinations of segments cover any general area of subject? For example, is there a concentrated section of exhortations and warnings?

3. Look more at the paragraphs, and note the flow of Paul's thinking as he writes to Timothy.

4. Identify each segment for its emphasis of any one of the three time elements of past, present, future.

5. Try to arrive at a basic outline for this epistle.

D. SURVEY CHART

Study carefully Chart 101. Note the following:

1. The parting words of 4:6-8 are the climax of the epistle.

2. Study the outline beginning with *thanksgiving for Timothy*. Scan the chapters and account for each part of this outline.

3. Note the three-part major outline, *past — present — future*. Check this out by scanning the epistle again. Do these three time references represent the *general* emphasis of each particular section?

4. The topical outline on the bottom of the chart lists the references to God's Word as these appear throughout the epistle. Observe the variety of references. Do you sense a climax in the brief phrase, "Preach the word"?

5. The three-part outline of *challenge* reveals the major flow of Paul's writing. Read the section 1:3—2:13 and observe the different

ways Paul urges Timothy to suffer hardship *with* him. Then note in 2:14—4:5 the repeated theme of warning to *avoid* evil men. Observe the two subjects of endurance and separation in the title assigned to the epistle.

6. Compare the outlines shown on the chart with your own observations of the epistle's organization.

XX. PROMINENT SUBJECTS OF 2 TIMOTHY

A. FOUNDATIONS OF CHRISTIAN SERVICE (1:3-18)

The burden of Paul's heart was to inspire and challenge his young successor Timothy to keep witnessing for Christ. It was no easy task to tell Timothy that afflictions were part of the price to pay for being faithful to his calling in Christ, especially since the young evangelist was already experiencing deep trials and shedding tears in travail (1:4). But Paul had the answers, learned by experience at the feet of his Master, whom he first had met thirty-four years earlier. The apostle knew that the foundations of the gospel were impregnable, and that if Timothy could be reassured about this, he would not falter.

Read the passage. How does Paul show the following to be foundations for Christian service: home training, 1:3-5; God's work, 1:6-10; divine call to serve, 1:11-14; bond of fellowship, 1:15-18?

B. CHAPTER OF METAPHORS (2:1-26)

After reassuring Timothy about foundations of Christian service, Paul writes about the ministry itself. He is a master in using metaphors to describe persons, things, and actions.[21] In this chapter he uses a number of them, such as *athlete* and *farmer*, to describe the Christian servant and to challenge Timothy to be a good one. Because Paul writes from prison and sees soldiers every day, it should not surprise us that one of the first metaphors he uses is that of *soldier*: "Timothy, be a good soldier of Christ Jesus" (see 2:3).

Read the chapter, observing each metaphor and what Paul teaches in each instance.

C. THE LAST DAYS (3:1-9, 13)

Paul the realist forewarns Timothy about the difficult times — times of stress — which were yet to come upon the world. The apostle identifies the times as "the last days" (3:1). Sometimes the New Testament phrase *last days* refers to the entire Messianic age, including the first century (cf. Acts 2:16-17; 1 John 2:18). Homer Kent

---

21. A metaphor is an implied comparison between two different things.

CHART 101

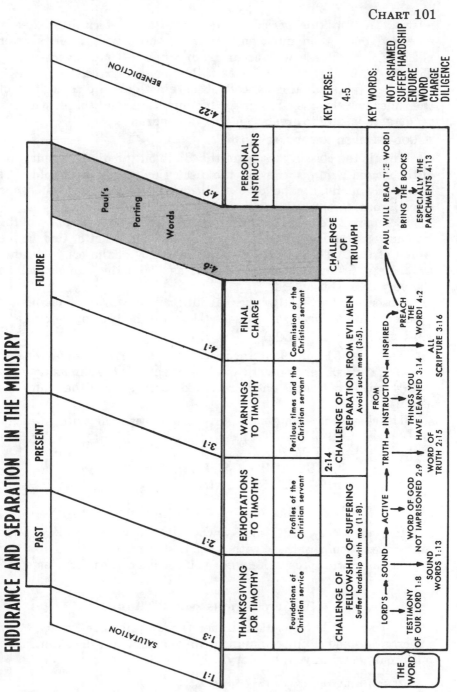

2 TIMOTHY
ENDURANCE AND SEPARATION IN THE MINISTRY

SALUTATION 1:1

PAST   PRESENT   FUTURE

THANKSGIVING FOR TIMOTHY 1:3

EXHORTATIONS TO TIMOTHY 2:1

WARNINGS TO TIMOTHY 3:1

FINAL CHARGE 4:1

Paul's Parting Words 4:6

PERSONAL INSTRUCTIONS 4:9

BENEDICTION 4:22

Foundations of Christian service

Profiles of the Christian servant

Perilous times and the Christian servant

Commission of the Christian servant

CHALLENGE OF FELLOWSHIP OF SUFFERING
Suffer hardship with me (1:8).

2:14 CHALLENGE OF SEPARATION FROM EVIL MEN
Avoid such men (3:5).

CHALLENGE OF TRIUMPH

LORD'S → SOUND ← ACTIVE → TRUTH → INSTRUCTION → INSPIRED

TESTIMONY OF OUR LORD 1:8

WORD OF GOD NOT IMPRISONED 2:9

FROM THINGS YOU HAVE LEARNED 3:14

PREACH THE WORD! 4:2

PAUL WILL READ THE WORD!

SOUND WORDS 1:13

WORD OF TRUTH 2:15

ALL SCRIPTURE 3:16

BRING THE BOOKS ESPECIALLY THE PARCHMENTS 4:13

THE WORD

KEY VERSE: 4:5

KEY WORDS:
NOT ASHAMED
SUFFER HARDSHIP
ENDURE
WORD
CHARGE
DILIGENCE

writes, "Within this period of the last days, which has already extended more than nineteen centuries, there will set in shorter seasons. . . . These will occur from time to time (even during Timothy's lifetime), but conditions will become progressively worse."[22]

When you study this passage observe not only the description of the times but also the strategy for triumph that Paul shares with his readers, to inspire to greater heights of endurance.

D. GOD-INSPIRED SCRIPTURES (3:16-17)

This is the classic passage of the Bible on the divine inspiration of the sacred *writings*. (Review the discussion of this in Chapter 1 of this study manual.) The phrase "inspired by God" translates one Greek word, *theopneustia*, meaning literally "God-breathed."

Compare 2 Peter 1:21, which teaches the divine inspiration of the human *writers*. The Bible has been called "the heart of God in the words of God." The infallibility and inerrancy of the original autographs rest firmly on such testimonies as 2 Timothy 3:16, as well as the very character of God.

Observe what Paul writes about in the verses of chapter 3 preceding the *theopneustia* passage. How are the two related?

E. PAUL'S FAREWELL (4:1-22)

These are Paul's last recorded words, written in a tone of urgency, triumph, and tender care. The chapter is the climax not only of this epistle but of the entire recorded earthly life of the man from Tarsus.

The chapter is of four main parts. What does Paul write, in each?

        4:1-5 TIMOTHY
        4:6-8 PAUL
        4:9-18 MAINLY PAUL
        4:19-22 MAINLY PAUL

XXI. THEME, KEY WORDS AND VERSES FOR 2 TIMOTHY

In your survey of 2 Timothy what did you choose as key words and verses? Compare these with what is shown on Chart 101.

In your own words write what you consider to be the theme of 2 Timothy.

XXII. APPLICATIONS FROM 2 TIMOTHY

1. This last letter of Paul understandably includes many warm exhortations and strong commands. Make a list of the ones that stand out prominently in your memory.

---

22. Homer A. Kent, *The Pastoral Epistles*, p. 281.

2. Write a list of the practical truths taught by 1:7. Do the same for the passages listed below.

2:1-7	Rewards for Christians
2:8-20	Discipline in the Christian life
2:21-25	What to flee and what to follow (cf. chapter 3)
4:1-5	Ministry of the Word
4:6-8	Crown of righteousness

XXIII. REVIEW QUESTIONS ON 2 TIMOTHY

1. Trace briefly the careers of Paul and Timothy between the years of the writing of the two epistles.

2. Compare the two imprisonments of Paul.

3. What were Paul's purposes in writing 2 Timothy?

4. Name a few outstanding passages for which 2 Timothy is remembered.

5. How much of the structure of this epistle can you remember? Where is a climax?

6. Where in the letter does Paul make the challenge of *fellowship of suffering*? Where does he write much about avoiding the fellowship of evil men?

7. Name five different things that Paul writes about the Word, in this epistle.

8. How would you compare 2 Timothy with 1 Timothy and Titus? Reflect on the observation that 2 Timothy is mainly personal, only incidentally pastoral, and less doctrinal than the other two pastoral epistles.

9. Name some key words of 2 Timothy.

10. What are the key teachings of 3:16-17?

XXIV. FURTHER STUDY OF 2 TIMOTHY

Here are four vital subjects suggested for further study:
1. description of the world in last times
2. inerrancy of the original Scriptures
3. crowns as rewards for Christians
4. the ministry of preaching the Word.

XXV. OUTLINE

2 TIMOTHY: Endurance and Separation in the Ministry

Salutation	1:1-2
FOUNDATIONS OF CHRISTIAN SERVICE	1:3-18
A GOOD SOLDIER OF JESUS CHRIST	2:1-26

PERILOUS TIMES AND THE	
CHRISTIAN SERVANT	3:1-17
PAUL'S FAREWELL	4:1-18
Greetings and Benediction	4:19-22

XXVI. BACKGROUND OF PHILEMON

Philemon is the shortest of Paul's writings, written about six years earlier than his last epistle, 2 Timothy. Recall that Paul wrote to Philemon from his first imprisonment, when the apostle also wrote Ephesians, Philippians, and Colossians. One of the reasons Philemon is placed last in the canonical list of Paul's writings is its brevity.

The letter is a masterpiece of graceful, tactful, and delicate pleading for a forgiving spirit. This very personal correspondence of Paul has been described as "a model letter written by a master of letter writing."

A. NAMES IN THE LETTER

1. Philemon was a well-to-do Christian friend of Paul, living in or near Colossae. He was probably the husband of Apphia and father of Archippus, two persons named in Philemon 2. The name Philemon means "loving."

2. Onesimus was a household servant of Philemon, who, after his conversion at Rome, probably came to know Paul intimately. His name means "useful," or "profitable," a common nickname for slaves.

3. The names cited in Philemon 23-24 were studied in connection with the Colossian epistle.

B. OCCASION AND PURPOSE OF THE LETTER

Onesimus had apparently stolen money or goods from his master Philemon (Philem. 18) and fled to Rome like so many other runaway slaves. Through circumstances unknown to us, he became acquainted with Paul, who led him to the Lord (Philem. 10). Paul's immediate concern was for Onesimus's restoration and reconciliation with Philemon. Hence the apostle's tender and moving intercessory letter to his close friend Philemon on behalf of Onesimus.

The bearers of the letter were Onesimus and Tychicus, who also delivered Paul's letters to the Ephesian and Colossian churches. (Cf. Col. 4:7-9.)

C. PLACE AND DATE OF WRITING

Paul wrote to Philemon from prison in Rome, around A.D. 61. That was about the same time he wrote the other three prison epistles, namely Colossians, Ephesians, and Philippians. (See Chart 1, p. 20.)

XXVII. Survey of Philemon

A. READINGS

1. First mark paragraph divisions in your Bible, beginning at the following verses: 1, 4, 8, 12, 17, 22.

2. Read the letter a few times, paragraph by paragraph. Identify the introduction and conclusion.

3. Where in the letter does Paul first make his request? What does he write about in verses 4-7?

4. Identify the main point of each paragraph, and construct an outline of the letter from this.

B. SURVEY CHART

1. Study the survey, Chart 102. Note among other things the orderly progression of thought, as shown by the two outlines: *object of the appeal — the appeal — source of the appeal*; *praise of Philemon — plea for Onesimus — promise of Paul*.

2. Study the entries made in the bottom areas of the chart. Locate the phrases in the Bible text that are the bases for the entries.

3. What title is assigned to the letter?

XXVIII. Prominent Subjects of Philemon

A. PLEA FOR FORGIVENESS

The whole epistle is one Christian's plea to another to forgive and restore a third person. In what different ways does Paul make His appeal to Philemon?

B. SUBSTITUTIONARY ATONEMENT (ILLUSTRATION)

Read verses 17-21 and apply the following phrases, by way of illustration, to the substitutionary work of Christ for the sinner:

"accept him as you would me"   verse 17
"charge that to my account"   verse 18
"I will repay it"   verse 19
"you owe to me"   verse 19

Read the entire epistle and look for other words and phrases similar to those cited above.

XXIX. Theme, Key Words and Verses for Philemon

What key words and verses did you observe in your survey study? Compare those with the ones shown on Chart 102.

What is the theme of Philemon, in your own words?

CHART 102

KEY VERSES—10, 18
KEY WORDS—love, beseech, profitable, servant

PHILEMON
APPEAL FOR FORGIVENESS

"That your goodness should not be . . . by compulsion, but of your own free will" (v. 14, NASB)

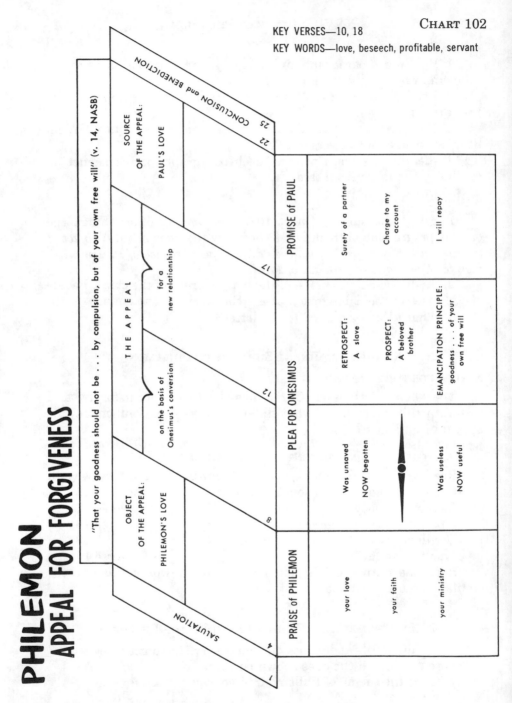

SALUTATION

OBJECT OF THE APPEAL: PHILEMON'S LOVE

THE APPEAL
on the basis of Onesimus's conversion
for a new relationship

SOURCE OF THE APPEAL: PAUL'S LOVE

CONCLUSION and BENEDICTION

1   4   8   12   17   22   25

PRAISE of PHILEMON
- your love
- your faith
- your ministry

PLEA FOR ONESIMUS
- Was unsaved / NOW begotten
- Was useless / NOW useful

RETROSPECT: A slave
PROSPECT: A beloved brother
EMANCIPATION PRINCIPLE: goodness . . . of your own free will

PROMISE of PAUL
- Surety of a partner
- Charge to my account
- I will repay

XXX. Applications from Philemon

1. What examples of tact and wisdom do you see in the letter? For example, observe that Paul does not use such words as *stole* or *fled* when referring to Onesimus.

2. What does this epistle teach about the master-servant relationship, when both are Christians? Compare Colossians 3:22—4:1. Extend this application to related situations today, such as that of employer-employee.

3. "For love's sake I ... appeal to you" for Onesimus (Philem. 9-10). What do you learn about Christian love from this letter?

XXXI. Review Questions on Philemon

1. What brought about the writing of Philemon?
2. When and where was the letter written?
3. How did Paul make his appeal?
4. Outline the epistle.
5. Name some key words and phrases.

XXXII. Further Study of Philemon

Much has been written about the subject of slavery, including what the New Testament says about it. It has been observed, for example, that in his letter to Philemon Paul does not make a frontal attack upon the institution of slavery, which was very widespread throughout the Roman Empire. Rather, he sets forth principles and patterns of Christian conduct and relationships that inevitably must bring about the destruction of the institution, when consistently applied. Study this subject further, using the New Testament and outside helps for your sources.

XXXIII. Outline

PHILEMON: Appeal for Forgiveness

Salutation and Benediction	1-3
PRAISE OF PHILEMON	4-7
PLEA FOR ONESIMUS	8-16
PROMISE OF PAUL	17-21
Conclusion and Benediction	22-25

XXXIV. Death of Paul

Soon after writing his last letter, 2 Timothy, Paul no doubt stood before Nero to hear the sentence of death. The Scriptures are silent concerning the end of the apostle's life. Here is a penetrating reconstruction of what might have transpired, as imagined by one author:

> In all history there is not a more startling illustration of the irony of
> human life than this scene of Paul at the bar of Nero. ON THE
> JUDGMENT-SEAT, clad in the imperial purple, sat a man who in a bad
> world had attained the eminence of being the very worst and meanest
> being in it — a man stained with every crime, the murderer of his own
> mother, of his wives and of his best benefactors; a man whose whole
> being was so steeped in every namable and unnamable vice that body
> and soul of him were, as some one said at the time, nothing but a
> compound of mud and blood; and IN THE PRISONER'S DOCK stood
> the best man the world contained, his hair whitened with labors for the
> good of men and the glory of God.
>
> The trial ended, Paul was condemned and delivered over to the
> executioner. He was led out of the city with a crowd of the lowest rabble
> at his heels. The fatal spot was reached; he knelt beside the block; the
> headsman's axe gleamed in the sun and fell; and the head of the apostle
> of the world rolled down in the dust. . . . The city falsely called eternal
> dismissed him with execration from her gates; but ten thousand times
> ten thousand welcomed him in the same hour at the gates of the city
> which is really eternal.[23]

XXXV. Selected Reading for the Pastoral Letters and Philemon

GENERAL INTRODUCTION

Hiebert, D. Edmond. *An Introduction to the Pauline Epistles*, pp. 305-65.
Tenney, Merrill C. *New Testament Survey*, pp. 331-42.

COMMENTARIES

Erdman, Charles R. *The Pastoral Epistles of Paul*.
Gaebelein, Frank. *Philemon: The Gospel of Emancipation*.
Hiebert, D. Edmond. *First Timothy*. Everyman's Bible Commentary.
Kent, Homer A. *The Pastoral Epistles*.
Stibbs, A. M. "Titus". *The New Bible Commentary*.
Wallis, Wilbur B. "I Timothy," "II Timothy," and "Titus." *The Wycliffe Bible
    Commentary*.

OTHER RELATED SOURCES

Bruce, F. F. *The Letters of Paul: Expanded Paraphrase*.
Ernst, Karl J. *The Art of Pastoral Counselling. A Study of the Epistle to
    Philemon*.
Strong, James. *The Exhaustive Concordance of the Bible*.
Thomas, Robert L., ed. *New American Standard Exhaustive Concordance of
    the Bible*.
Vincent, Marvin R. *Word Studies in the New Testament*.

---

23. James Stalker, *The Life of St. Paul*, pp. 142-43.

The Non-Pauline Epistles

The New Testament may be divided into four main groups: historical accounts, Pauline epistles, non-Pauline epistles, and apocalypse. The five historical books (gospels and Acts) make up almost sixty percent of the Bible text; the Pauline epistles, about twenty-four percent; the non-Pauline epistles, about ten percent; and the apocalypse (Revelation), six percent.[1] So far we have surveyed the books of the first two groups; the remaining two groups follow.

Listed below are the eight non-Pauline epistles. These books are classified as non-Pauline because none bears the name of Paul as author. The anonymous epistle to the Hebrews may have originated with Paul. All the books except Hebrews are sometimes referred to as general epistles. This vague designation was attached to the seven books during the centuries of the early church for a combination of reasons: general or joint apostolic authorship of the group; general scope of the recipients (no local churches addressed); general in content.[2] Actually there is no group title that clearly and fully identifies all the books from Hebrews to Jude in the New Testament canon. We will use the designation "non-Pauline," keeping in mind the unsettled question of authorship of Hebrews.

Hebrews	1 John
James	2 John
1 Peter	3 John
2 Peter	Jude

---

1. The size of each proportion is, of course, no measure of the relative importance of the books involved.
2. D. Edmond Hiebert, *An Introduction to the New Testament*, 3:16. Read this work, pages 15-25, for a discussion of the non-Pauline epistles.

19

Hebrews: Consider Jesus, Our Great High Priest

Hebrews is a unique commentary on the Old Testament. It interprets its history, explaining the fulfillment of its prophecy and revealing the ultimate purpose of all its institutions of worship. The epistle is the Holy Spirit's grand portrait of Christ with the Old Testament as a background. "Consider Jesus" is its urgent appeal to believers who were turning their backs to Jesus. Christians today who are in danger of backsliding and apostasy, who are leaning toward the things of the world from which they have been delivered, have God's clear warning and exhortation in Hebrews. No Christian is immune to the threat of lukewarmness and apathy, and Hebrews speaks about those. The book is that contemporary.

I. PREPARATION FOR STUDY

Before you begin your study of Hebrews, think of various things that cause Christians today to drift away from their close relationship to Jesus. Among other things, this will help you appreciate more the exaltation of Jesus in the epistle.

II. BACKGROUND

A. TITLE

The earliest manuscripts have the simple title *pros Hebraious* ("to Hebrews"). The title was probably not a part of the original epistle, but no doubt was added later by the church.

B. DATE WRITTEN

The interval between A.D. 65 and A.D. 70 may be accepted as the time when Hebrews was written. A date before A.D. 70 is based on the fact that in A.D. 70 Jerusalem, with its Temple, was destroyed by the Roman general Titus. Hebrews gives the clear impression that the Temple was still standing when the epistle was written (see 8:4-5; 10:11), and there is the hint that the removal of the Temple services was not too far distant (12:27). If the Temple had already been destroyed, some mention of it surely would have been made by the writer, because one of his main points was that the Jewish institutions were intended to be superseded by a more perfect system.

That the epistle was written as late as A.D. 65 is supported by the observation that the readers were a second generation of Christians (2:1-4; cf. 5:12), whose leaders probably had passed away (13:7, ASV).

C. AUTHOR

The conclusion of Origen on this subject is the classic statement, "Who wrote the epistle in truth God alone knows."

Various authors have been suggested. The following list shows some of the possibilities:

1. *Paul.* This view is based on (1) affinities in language and concepts between Hebrews and other Pauline epistles; (2) centrality of the Person and work of Christ in Hebrews, as in other Pauline epistles; (3) Paul's association with Timothy (cf. 13:23); (4) the "Pauline" salutation: "Grace be with you all" (13:25).

2. *A co-worker of Paul.* This view accounts for both Pauline and non-Pauline traits of the epistle. Apollos, Luke, and Barnabas are names suggested, most of the evidence pointing to Apollos. Apollos was an Alexandrian Jew (Acts 18:24), worked closely with Paul toward the end of Paul's ministry (Titus 3:13), was well grounded in the Old Testament Scriptures, and was an enthusiastic teacher-preacher. (Read Acts 18:24-26.)

3. *Others.* Least likely authors, but suggested for various reasons, include Aquila, Silas, Philip the Deacon, and Clement of Rome.

D. GROUP ADDRESSED

Whatever is known today of the original readers is derived from the epistle itself. They were from a single congregation of Hebrew Christians, living somewhere in the Roman world (e.g., 2:3; 5:11-12; 6:9-10; cf. 13:23-24). Some think Jerusalem was where the church was located because of the emphasis on the Temple and its institutions. This view is not without problems, however. Alexandria, Caesarea, Antioch in Syria, and Ephesus are also suggested as the home of those Hebrew Christians. There is strong support for the view that Rome was the location. That there was an influential group of Jewish Christians in Rome is confirmed by the Roman epistle (e.g., Rom.

9-11), and by Acts' record of Paul's contacts when in prison at Rome (see Acts 28:17-31). The salutation of Hebrews 13:24 could have been made by Christians who were originally from Italy and were sending back greetings to their friends.

More important than knowing where the readers lived *geographically* is knowing how they fared *spiritually*. The many strong warnings of the epistle indicate that those Hebrew Christians were in a backslidden condition, in danger of apostatizing from Christ and returning to Judaism. Faith, conviction, and enthusiasm were waning (3:6, 9, 12, 14); and prayer, public worship, and the Scriptures were being neglected (2:1; 10:25; 12:12-13). The Christians by now should have been teachers of others, but were still in need of being taught the ABC's of the gospel (5:12).

One circumstance had much to do with the Hebrew Christians' turning back in their Christian walk. That was the threat of persecution from without, with its intimidation to surrender. Earlier those Christians had withstood persecution (10:32-34). But now they were beginning to weaken. Of this, R. C. H. Lenski writes:

> The Jewish Christians stood unshaken during the terror of 64 (year of Nero's burning of Rome). . . . But now, since Peter was dead, since even Paul, their spiritual father, had been removed, since Christianity was permanently branded as criminal, since there was no other apostle to stiffen their courage, some of these Jewish Christians began to weaken. Voices were raised which advocated a return to Jewry. If their synagogues became Jewish as they had been a few years ago they would be safe like the other Jewish synagogues, for Judaism continued to remain a religion that was legally approved in Rome and in the empire.[3]

E. PURPOSES

Someone has said that Hebrews was written to "rekindle a dampened fire." A fainting spirit, dying enthusiasm, and dullness of hearing were the emergency of the hour. The letter of Hebrews was the response, sounding forth in this double chord: (1) teaching and (2) warning and exhortation.

1. *Teaching.* The best antidote for the poison of falsehood and unbelief is the positive declaration of revealed truth. The opening verses of Hebrews disclose that the epistle's main teaching is about three vital subjects:

a. Revelation ("God . . . has . . . spoken" 1:1-4). The written

---

3. R.C.H. Lenski, *The Interpretation of the Epistle to the Hebrews and of the Epistle of James*, p. 21.

revelation of God over the centuries has come in two groups: Old Testament and New Testament. Hebrews shows the relationships between those two Testaments or covenants. And beyond the written Word is the living Word.

b. A person ("by his Son"). Hebrews is the most comprehensive New Testament book portraying Christ as Son of God and Son of Man. "Consider ... Jesus" (3:1) is a key phrase in the epistle. How would a better knowledge of who Jesus was help the Hebrew Christians in their spiritual plight? Andrew Murray answers: "He (the author) unceasingly places their weakness and Christ's person side by side: he is sure that, if they but know Christ, all will be well."[4]

c. A work ("He sat down"). The subjects of Christ's once-for-all sacrifice and His continuing ministries as Priest and King pervade the book. Concerning sacrifice, one has written of Hebrews, "Tear a page and it will bleed."

2. *Warning and exhortation.* Warning and exhortation appear throughout the epistle, aimed at the spiritual condition of the readers. The warnings concern just recompense for sinning against God; the exhortations are positive appeals and encouragements to appropriate the power and privileges of God's children, and incentives to press on to fuller stature as Christians.

There are five main warning sections in Hebrews:

a. Take heed (2:1-4).

b. Do not miss the rest (3:7—4:13).

c. Beware sloth and apostasy (5:11—6:20).

d. Beware willful sinning (10:26-31).

e. Beware disobeying Christ (12:25-29).

Exhortations appear throughout the epistle (e.g., 4:1, 11, 14, 16), but the main hortatory section begins at 10:19.

F. PLACE IN THE BIBLE

The book of Hebrews occupies a very important place in the Scriptures. It is the Spirit's commentary on the Pentateuch, especially the book of Leviticus. The writer uses the Old Testament Scriptures throughout, making at least eighty-six direct references, traceable to at least one hundred Old Testament passages. Hebrews explains the meaning and significance of the whole Jewish ritual. It makes clear that all the ceremonial laws given in the Old Testament, such as the offerings of sacrifices and the ministrations of the priests, were but types pointing forward to Christ, the *great* sacrifice for sin, the *true* Priest, the *one* Mediator between God and man. In Hebrews the

---

4. Andrew Murray, *The Holiest of All*, p. 23.

Christian is taught that he has passed from the realm of shadows into that of reality, that in Christ he has the fulfillment of all the earlier types.

Hebrews has been referred to as the fifth gospel because it tells of Jesus' finished work on earth and His continuing work in heaven. There is no other book in the New Testament that helps us to understand the *present* ministry of Christ as does the book of Hebrews. Many Christians know little about Christ's present work for His people. Hebrews shows us that just as God led the Israelites from Egypt through the barren wilderness, protecting them from danger, supplying all their needs, teaching them, training them, and eventually bringing them into the rich land of Canaan, so Christ is at this present time helping His children, by intercession, inspiration, instruction, and indwelling, to enter into the spiritual rest land of abundant living, a taste of the heavenly glories to come.

G. HEBREWS AND ROMANS COMPARED

Hebrews is often compared with Romans. Hebrews presents the Person of salvation; Romans presents the way of salvation. Hebrews focuses on the ceremonial law of the Old Testament; Romans, on the moral law of all time. "Romans moves from law to grace, and Hebrews, from shadow to substance."[5]

III. SURVEY

A. FIRST READING

1. First note how many chapters there are in Hebrews.

2. Make a cursory reading of Hebrews, in one sitting if possible, to get main impressions and the "feel" of the book. Record your impressions.

3. What words and phrases stand out after this reading?

4. What appears to be the main theme of the book? What are some of the subjects discussed to support the theme?

5. Compare the beginning and end of the book.

6. Where in the book does doctrine give place to the practical? (Practical sections are recognized by the prominence of commands and exhortations.)

B. WORKING WITH THE INDIVIDUAL SEGMENTS

Keep reading the epistle as you work with the individual segments.

1. Refer to the survey Chart 103 and note the breakdown of the

5. John Phillips, *Exploring the Scriptures*, p. 262.

epistle into segments. Mark your Bible to show the beginning of each segment, at these verses: 1:1, 4; 2:5; 3:1; 4:14; 5:11; 7:1; 8:1; 9:1; 9:13; 10:19; 11:1; 12:3; 13:1, 22.

2. Assign a segment title from the Bible text for each segment.

3. Who is the main person of the epistle? What different things are written about Him?

4. Make a list of different subjects of the epistle. After you have done this, compare your list with the following one.

Person of Christ — His humanity and deity

Work of Christ — for example, atonement and intercession

Old and New Covenants — the relation between the two

Sin — especially the sins of unbelief and disobedience

Word of God — written (Bible) and living (Christ)

Faith — for salvation, and for Christian living

Testing and discipline — their purposes and rewards

Christian growth — the marks of spiritual maturity

Old Testament institutions and New Testament counterparts

Purposes of the Levitical ritual law

5. What new key words and phrases are you observing?

6. Look for groupings of segments according to similar subject, and try making a simple, general outline of the epistle.

7. What is the main theme of Hebrews?

C. STRUCTURE OF THE EPISTLE

When various topical studies are outlined on a survey chart, the structure of a book's composition becomes evident. The survey of Hebrews, Chart 103, shows something of the organization of the epistle. Study the chart carefully, then note how the following are shown on the chart.

1. There are thirteen chapters in Hebrews. The chart shows thirteen segments (not all beginning at the first verse of a chapter) plus an introduction (theme, 1:1-3) and epilogue (13:22-25). Five warning sections are parts of those segments. Which warning section is a full segment? Which warning sections conclude a segment? Which is in the middle of a segment?

2. Basically, the epistle has two main divisions: Instruction (1:1—10:18) and Exhortation (10:19—13:25).

3. Study the key outline.

KEY OUTLINE OF HEBREWS

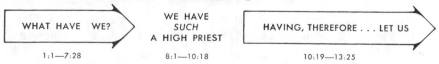

WHAT HAVE WE?	WE HAVE SUCH A HIGH PRIEST	HAVING, THEREFORE . . . LET US
1:1—7:28	8:1—10:18	10:19—13:25

a. What Have We? (1:1—7:28). The suggestion for this question really comes from 8:1*a*, "Now the main point in what has been said is this: We have...." In other words, in chapters 1-7 the author is adding up that which the believer has, in answer to a question "What have we?" One can visualize the Hebrew Christians saying, "Why shouldn't we go back to Judaism — what do we have for being Christians?" The author of Hebrews responds, "You ask, 'What have we?' Let me show you what we have!"

b. We Have Such a High Priest (8:1—10:18). The phrase "We have such a high priest" comes from 8:1. Read the verse again. The author is saying that we have in Jesus a *High Priest*. But the emphasis is on the word *such*. (In the original Greek the word appears first, for emphasis.) The author has shown this superiority in the previous section, chapters 1-7. Observe the outline on Chart 103 that shows Jesus as divine Priest, redeemer Priest, apostle Priest, perfect Priest, eternal Priest. All this adds up to the sum "We have *such* a high priest."

Although 8:1 refers back to the cumulative inventories of chapters 1-7, it also introduces this middle section, 8:1—10:18. In this section the author continues to show the superior priestly ministry of Jesus (e.g., 8:6; 9:11), and he also shows in detail the workings of that ministry.

c. Having, Therefore . . . Let Us (10:19—13:25). Read 10:19-21 for the source of this phrase. Observe the phrase "let us" in 10:22-24. The practical, hortatory division of Hebrews thus begins at 10:19. The exhortations to Christians are all based on the blessed truth that "we have *such* a high priest."

4. Observe on the chart another outline that divides Hebrews into three main parts. Also keep this in mind as you proceed with analysis later on.

5. Note where the five warning sections appear on Chart 103.

6. The outline shown at the bottom of the chart could be worded as follows:

> Christ, the Son of God — His deity (1:1—2:4)
> Christ, the Son of Man — His humanity (2:5—4:13)
> Christ, the Priest — His work (4:14—10:18)
> Christ, the Way — His leadership (10:19—13:25).

7. Observe on Chart 103 the title "Consider Jesus, Our Great High Priest." In the course of your study in Hebrews, try to arrive at a title of your own.

CHART 103

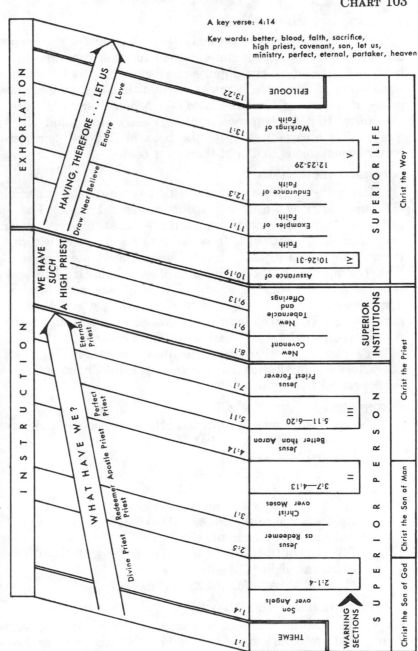

A key verse: 4:14

Key words: better, blood, faith, sacrifice, high priest, covenant, son, let us, ministry, perfect, eternal, partaker, heaven

HEBREWS
CONSIDER JESUS, OUR GREAT HIGH PRIEST

EXHORTATION

HAVING, THEREFORE . . . LET US

Love — Endure — Believe — Draw Near

WE HAVE SUCH A HIGH PRIEST

INSTRUCTION

WHAT HAVE WE?

Eternal Priest — Perfect Priest — Apostle Priest — Redeemer Priest — Divine Priest

Ref	Section		
13:22	EPILOGUE		
13:1	Workings of Faith		
12:25-29	V		SUPERIOR LIFE
12:3	Endurance of Faith		
11:1	Examples of Faith		
10:26-31	IV	Faith	
10:19	Assurance of		
9:13	Tabernacle and Offerings	SUPERIOR INSTITUTIONS	
9:1	New		
8:1	New Covenant		
7:1	Jesus Priest Forever		
5:11—6:20	III		SUPERIOR PERSON
4:14	Jesus Better than Aaron		
3:7—4:13	II		
3:1	Christ over Moses		
2:5	Jesus as Redeemer		
2:1-4	I		
1:4	Son over Angels	WARNING SECTIONS	
1:1	THEME		

Christ the Way — Christ the Priest — Christ the Son of Man — Christ the Son of God

IV. Prominent Subjects

A. PERSON AND WORK OF CHRIST

The main person of Hebrews is Jesus. The author of the epistle is convinced that all that is necessary to restrain from apostasy is to hold up Christ in all the dignity and beauty of His Person and the importance of His work. It might be said that Hebrews consists of a series of pictures of Jesus the Lord. We behold Him in His deity, His humanity, His sacrificial work, His priestly office, and His kingly glory. After a careful study of the book of Hebrews one must feel better acquainted with Christ than ever before.

B. SUPERIORITY OF JESUS

The writer of Hebrews repeats the key word *better* to emphasize the superiority of Jesus regarding man's salvation. The epistle presents a series of contrasts between the *good* things of Judaism and the *better* things of Christ. In seeking to restrain the Jewish Christians from apostasy, the author demonstrates, step by step, that Christ is superior to the prophets through whom God had spoken in times past (1:1-3); superior to angels, through whom the law had been administered (1:4—2:4); superior to Moses, their great leader, (3:1-6); superior to Joshua, who led them into Canaan (4:8); and superior to Aaron, their high priest, (4:14—5:10). Throughout the book the writer's plan is to introduce, one after the other, Old Testament characters and institutions, and then to present Christ and show how far superior He is to any of those.

C. CONTRASTS

The epistle abounds in contrasts. Here are some of them:
Son and angels (1:4—2:4)
Son and Moses (3:1-6)
Canaan rest and God's rest (3:12—4:13)
Christ and Aaron (4:14—5:10)
Spiritual infancy and maturity (5:11-14)
Apostasy and faithfulness (5:11—6:20)
Old and New Covenants (8:1-13)
Offerings of the law and offering of Christ (9:1—10:18)
Faith and sight (11:1-40)
Mount Sinai and Mount Zion (12:18-29)

D. CHRIST THE SON OF GOD (1:1—2:4)

In the opening segment of the epistle the author reveals the dignity and exalted nature of the author of Christianity as the Son of God. Note some of the different ways he points to the deity of Christ in this first segment (locate the Bible texts that support the points).

1. *Divine names*. (e.g., God, 1:8; Lord, 1:10)

2. *Divine works*. (e.g., creation, 1:2; upholding all things, 1:3; purging sins, 1:3)

3. *Divine character*. (1:3)

4. *Divine position and honor*. (e.g., heir, 1:2; seated on the right hand of the Majesty on high, 1:3; rank higher than angels, 1:4-14).

5. *Eternal existence*. (e.g., 1:8)

E. CHRIST THE SON OF MAN (2:5—4:13)

Christ is shown as Son of Man to be man's Redeemer, tasting "death for every one" (2:9). He became the Son of Man that we might become the sons of God. He came to earth that we might go to heaven. He bore our sins that we might partake of His righteousness. He took our nature in order that we might have His nature. Christ became a man in order to restore to man all that he lost through Adam's fall.

As a man Christ lived before men; as a man He died; and as the Son of Man He appears now in the presence of God for the believer. Not only was it necessary for Christ to become a man that He might die, but it was necessary for Him to become a man in order that He might be a merciful and faithful high priest; One who was tempted as we are; One who knows all about us; One who is able to succor them that are tempted (2:17-18). Those are some of the truths of Christ's humanity that the author writes about in this section of the epistle.

F. CHRIST THE HIGH PRIEST (4:14—10:18)

An extensive development of the central subject of Christ as the great High Priest begins at 4:14 and continues until 10:18. Christ's priesthood had already been mentioned at 2:17 and 3:1, but this was with an introductory purpose.

In Judaism the office of high priest was the highest religious office. The writer of Hebrews seeks to show that Christianity also has a High Priest, but One who is superior in every way to the high priests of Judaism. He makes clear that the high priest of Judaism was just a *type* of the great High Priest of Christianity.

In this long section of the epistle the author shows the superiority of the Person and ministry of Christ the High Priest. The range of his discussions is shown on Chart 104.

Recall from your survey the summary statement of 8:1, "We have *such* a high priest." Locate on Chart 103 the five descriptions of Christ as priest, noted earlier. Locate in the Bible text of 1:4—7:28 where each of the five identifications appears.

In 8:1—10:18 Christ is shown as:
        mediator of a better covenant (8:6-13)
        priest of a better tabernacle (9:1-12)
        offerer of a better sacrifice (9:13—10:18)

CHART 104

HEBREWS 4:14-10:18
SUPERIORITY OF CHRIST'S PERSON AND MINISTRY

4:14 SUPERIORITY OF THE PERSON (HIGH PRIEST) 7:28	8:1 SUPERIORITY OF THE MINISTRY (HIGH PRIESTHOOD) 10:18	
"We have a great high priest" (4:14)	"We have such an high priest" (8:1)	"A more excellent ministry" (8:6)
qualifications, order	covenant, tabernacle, sacrifice	

G. REST FOR THE BELIEVER (3:7—4:13)

The keynote of 3:7—4:13 is *rest*. Life's incomparable blessings come only from Christ. The first of blessings in Christ is salvation itself, or *redemption*. Only the redeemed one can enjoy life in its fullness, which is abundant life, or *rest*. The logical order is: *redemption*, then *rest*. The author of Hebrews follows this order in his epistle, as seen in the following outline:

Comparison:	Christ better than angels	(1:4—2:4)
Blessing:	REDEMPTION	(2:5-18)
Comparison:	Christ better than Moses	(3:1-6)
Blessing:	REST	(3:7—4:7)
Comparison:	Christ better than Joshua	(4:8-13)

The above outline shows how the *Comparison* sections are woven around the *Blessing* sections, to support the theme "We have *such* a high priest." The accompanying diagram illustrates that.

SURROUNDING CONTEXT OF ONE "REST" PASSAGE

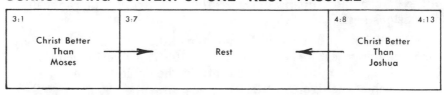

3:1	3:7	4:8 4:13
Christ Better Than Moses →	Rest	← Christ Better Than Joshua

Refer to the Bible text and observe these things taught about *rest*:

1. It is called "His rest" — God's rest (3:18; 4:1, 3, 5, 10). It is called His rest because it is that which He Himself enjoys and which He alone can confer.

2. It is the kind of rest or satisfaction that God enjoyed in His finished work of creation (see Gen. 2:2; Heb. 4:4). And it is the rest He now has in His Son's finished work of redemption.

3. This rest of God is intended for the people of God (4:9). He wants His people to enjoy the same rest and satisfaction in the finished work of Christ that He Himself enjoys.

4. He who has entered into God's rest is the one who has ceased from his own works and is satisfied with the work that God did for him in the Person of Jesus Christ (4:10).

5. Faith enables the believer to enter into this rest of God; unbelief and disobedience prevent him from entering into it (4:2, 11).

6. The rest that God is speaking of in this chapter is a rest far beyond Israel's Canaan rest, although the Canaan rest was a type of the reality. This is evident from 4:8-9. Such rest is the heart rest that comes only by genuine confidence in God and entire satisfaction in all that He does. This rest is for now, although the believer shall not come into the full enjoyment of it until a future time when his body is redeemed and he is forever with the Lord.

H. WARNING SECTIONS

There are five major warning sections in the book of Hebrews. Locate them on Chart 103, page 413. (The list was also cited earlier in this chapter, page 409.) For many Bible students they are the most difficult passages to understand, especially because the warnings of judgment are so severe. Some important things for the student to remember when he analyzes the passages are these:

1. Recognize the context. What leads into the warning section? What does the author write about *after* the section?

2. Observe all parts of the passage very carefully.

3. Do not force your personal explanation upon any difficult passage. The Scriptures themselves — both near and far context — are the most reliable interpreters of the text.

4. Accept by faith even truths you cannot understand.

5. After your own independent study, seek help on difficult portions from outside reliable sources.

I. EXAMPLES OF FAITH (11:1—12:2)

Recall from your survey of the epistle that at 10:19 the author blends instruction into exhortation, and doctrine becomes practice. Observe on Chart 103 that Christ is identified as the way to the superior life. Christ is not only the way to eternal life (John 14:6); He is also the way for Christian living, which 10:19—13:25 describes. The superior Person, Christ, makes possible the superior life in Christ. Christ is both our Priest and our pattern. In this last division of Hebrews, we who know Him as the way *to* God are exhorted regarding the way He would have us live *for* God. We are exhorted to avail ourselves of all the advantages and privileges that are now ours as Christians, and we are exhorted to perform all the duties that belong to us as saved sinners.

The key to successful Christian *living* is faith. Observe on Chart 103 the four sections of 10:19—13:25 on *faith*. The second chapter is the familiar chapter 11 (11:1—12:2), called "The Westminister Abbey of Faith."[6] It is a condensed register of some of the Old Testament's heroes of faith. Here is a brief suggested outline to follow when you study the chapter:

> Faith described (11:1-3)
> Faith as the way to please God (11:4-16)
> Faith and the race of life (11:17—12:2).

The conclusion of 12:1-2 is powerful. A greater example of faith is to be found in Jesus. Noble and great as are the cloud of witnesses of chapter 11, it is Jesus, originator and perfecter of our faith, upon whom we must fix our eyes.

V. THEME, KEY WORDS AND VERSES

The main theme of Hebrews may be stated thus: The knowledge and assurance of how great this High Priest Jesus is should lift the drifting believer from spiritual lethargy to vital Christian maturity. Stated another way: The antidote for backsliding is a growing personal knowledge of Jesus.

Various verses in Hebrews could be cited as key verses representing the epistle's main theme. One such verse is 4:14, "Since then we have a great high priest who has passed through the heavens, Jesus the Son of God, let us hold fast our profession."

What key words did you observe in your readings of Hebrews? Compare your list with the following: better, perfect, eternal, partaker, heaven(ly), blood, faith, sacrifice, covenant, Son, high priest, let us, ministry, love. Refer to an exhaustive concordance to see the appearances of these words in the epistle.

---

6. The abbey in London displays the tombs of Christian statesmen of past centuries, as Hebrews 11 eulogizes the faith lives of Old Testament saints.

VI. Applications

There is a wide range of applications that may be made of Hebrews. Below are listed various suggestions.

1. Warnings about backsliding
2. Exhortations
3. Encouragement
4. Appeal for spiritual inventory
5. Intercessory ministry of Christ
6. Exalting Christ
7. The faith life

The most important teachings of the epistle are referred to in the benediction of 13:20-21: the power of God; the death of Christ; His resurrection life; His present work; the everlasting covenant; the object of Christ's work, namely, to restore again in man the image of God, which has been marred through sin. What different applications are suggested by these truths?

VII. Review Questions

1. What Old Testament book is Hebrews especially related to, concerning Jewish ritual?

2. When was Hebrews written?

3. What names have been suggested as author of Hebrews?

4. What is the source of the title "Hebrews"?

5. Identify the original readers geographically, socially, and spiritually.

6. What are the purposes of this epistle?

7. What is the main theme of Hebrews?

8. How many main sections are there in Hebrews? Identify them by outline.

9. What is 8:1—10:18 about? Relate it to what goes before and what follows.

10. Where in the epistle is the deity of Christ especially discussed?

11. Where is the high priesthood of Christ especially discussed?

12. Identify by content the five warning sections of Hebrews.

13. Name key words of the epistle. What key verse represents the theme?

VIII. Further Study

1. The high priesthood of Jesus is related to the person and office of Melchizedek in 4:14—5:10. Study this Old Testament character,

and arrive at your conclusions why he is a type of Jesus the High Priest.

2. Chapter 1 deals at length with angels. Study further why angels are the first objects of comparison with Jesus in the sequence of 1:1—7:28.

IX. OUTLINE

X. SELECTED READING

GENERAL INTRODUCTION

Ross, Robert W. "Hebrews." In *The Wycliffe Bible Commentary*, pp. 1401-8.
Scroggie, W. Graham, *Know Your Bible*, 2:265-82.

COMMENTARIES

Bruce, F. F. *The Epistle to the Hebrews.*
Lenski, R.C.H. *The Interpretation of the Epistle to the Hebrews and of the Epistle of James.*
Newell, William R. *Hebrews Verse by Verse.*
Westcott, B. F. *The Epistle to the Hebrews.*

OTHER RELATED SOURCES

Murray, Andrew. *The Holiest of All.*
Strong, James. *The Exhaustive Concordance of the Bible.*
Thomas, Robert L., ed. *New American Standard Exhaustive Concordance of the Bible.*

20

James: Faith for Living

One of the earliest, perhaps the first, New Testament book to be written was the epistle of James. Its practical, nondoctrinal emphasis reveals the kind of message that God wanted to share with the Christian community in published form very soon after Jesus ascended to heaven.

I. PREPARATION FOR STUDY

Think about the primary message of Scripture. It is accurate to say that the Bible dwells mainly on two themes: "The Way to God," and "A Walk with God." No one can walk *with* God who has not first been restored *to* God. Much of the New Testament tells us the way a sinner can come to God and be eternally saved. That way is by God's grace, through one's faith in Jesus Christ (Eph. 2:8). The epistle of James, on the other hand, was written to instruct Christians — those who have been reconciled to God through Christ — how to walk with God in this life.

Thoughts, words, and deeds are the ingredients of a person's daily living. The important question here is, What *kind* of thoughts, words, and deeds should be part of the life of a Christian who walks with God? James was written to give us God's answers to that question. Those are some of the things you will be observing as you survey this important book.

II. BACKGROUND

A. THE AUTHOR

To know the author of a book is to understand and appreciate better his writing. We do not have an abundance of information concerning the man James, but what we do know makes us feel that

421

James is no stranger to us after all.[1] And what is more, we as Christians know the divine Author of this epistle in an experiential relationship, which is the master key to our understanding of its message.

So before we survey his epistle, let us think about the man James.

1. *Personal name.* The English name "James" in the New Testament translates the Greek *Iakobos*. This is from the Hebrew *Iakob*, translated "Jacob" in the Old Testament.

2. *Family background.* To learn something of the author's family background, we first need to identify which James this is. Actually, there are four different New Testament persons with the name James:

James the son of Zebedee (Matt. 4:21; Mark 1:19; Luke 5:10)

James the son of Alphaeus (Matt. 10:3; Mark 3:18; 15:40; Luke 6:15; Acts 1:13)

James the father of Judas the apostle (Luke 6:16, Berkeley)

James "the Lord's brother" (Matt. 13:55; Mark 6:3; Gal. 1:19).

There is strong support that the epistle's author was the last-named James. This is the view followed by this study guide. James really was a half brother of Jesus, both having the same mother, Mary, but not the same father. (Joseph was only the *legal* father of Jesus; Jesus was conceived of the Holy Spirit, Matt. 1:20.)

James had sisters and at least three brothers besides Jesus: Joses (Joseph), Simon, and Jude (Matt. 13:55). The home environment in which James was reared must have been an exceptional one, with such devout parents as Mary and Joseph. Yet, the parents could not make their children's decisions concerning belief in Jesus as Savior and Lord (Messiah). When it was that James made his decision is the subject of the next section.

Whether James ever married and raised his own family is an open question. The only passage in Scripture that may suggest his marriage is 1 Corinthians 9:5.

3. *Conversion.* James and the other brothers of Jesus did not believe in Him as Savior and Lord during the years of Jesus' public ministry. Read John 7:2-8. Does this passage suggest what hindered the brothers from believing? How do you account for this unbelief in light of such devout upbringing by Mary and Joseph? What light does Proverbs 22:6 shed on this question?

From Acts 1:14 we learn that James had become a believer

---

1. Practically all our knowledge of James comes from New Testament history. Tradition supplies a few items of interest concerning his life.

sometime before Pentecost day. His conversion may be dated at the time when Jesus appeared to him after His resurrection (1 Cor. 15:7). Or James may have believed just after Jesus' crucifixion. Whenever the experience, it was genuine, for James's entire life was transformed into one of service for Christ, as the book of Acts so clearly reveals.

4. *Christian service.* A biography of James's life shows four main periods, as indicated by Chart 105. For help in background orientation, fix this chart clearly in your mind.

CHART 105

PERIODS OF JAMES' LIFE

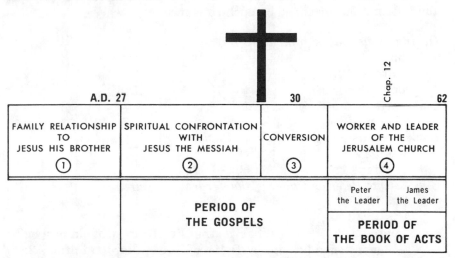

The third period (conversion) is the shortest and most crucial of the four, representing about fifty days between Jesus' death and Pentecost day (Acts 2).[2] James' ministry as a "servant of God and of the Lord Jesus Christ" (James 1:1) could not begin earlier than his conversion. From his earliest days as a believer, James identified himself with the local Christian group at Jerusalem, praying, working, and serving in various capacities (cf. Acts 1:14). Gradually he was recognized as a leader, so that at least by the time Peter, the church's key leader during Acts 1-7, left Jerusalem (Acts 12:17), James was the natural successor. Of this D. A. Hayes writes,

> When he was exalted to this leadership we do not know, but all indications seem to point to the fact that at a very early period James

2. The word *pentecost* means "fiftieth." Pentecost was the Old Testament Festival of Weeks (cf. Lev. 23:15; Deut. 16:9). The day of Pentecost (Acts 2:1) fell on the fiftieth day after the passion Passover.

was the recognized executive authority in the church at Jerus, which was the church of Pentecost and the church of the apostles. ... All Christian Jews would look to Jerus as the primitive source of their organization and faith, and the head of the church at Jerus would be recognized by them as their chief authority.[3]

It was just about this time also that James wrote his epistle, whose content reveals that he was an active Christian worker and leader at the time of writing.

The Bible references shown below reconstruct for us something of the biography of James up to the time of his death. Read all the passages (plus the contexts surrounding them) and record on paper the information furnished by each reference.

During Jesus' public ministry
    John 2:12
    Matthew 12:46-50
    John 7:1-9
Early days as a believer
    1 Corinthians 15:7
Early years as a servant of Jesus Christ
    Acts 1:14
    Galatians 1:18-19 (cf. Acts 9:26)
Successor to Peter as leader of the Jerusalem church
    Acts 12:17
    Acts 15:13
    Galatians 2:1, 9-10 (What is the significance of James being
        mentioned first in Paul's list of three pillars, Galatians 2:9?)
    Acts 21:18-26 (Last appearance of James in the New Testament)

5. *Character*. The biography of a man is incomplete without a description of his character. Review the verses you have just studied in connection with James's life. Recall, for example, that James was a praying man (Acts 1:14). One church historian, Hegesippus (c. A.D. 175), commended James's prayer life especially, noting how he spent long hours interceding for the people, so that his knees became calloused.

The best insight into James's character is gained by reading his own writing. Take a few minutes at this point in your study to read the epistle with one object in mind: learning what kind of man James was. Record your impressions and compare those with the following

3. D. A. Hayes, "Epistle of James," in *The International Standard Bible Encyclopedia*, 3:1563. It should be observed here that the book of Acts does not give much information concerning James's leadership during those decades.

list: a praying man, pure, powerful, practical, plain, persistent, humble, honest, single-minded, upright, and just.

Concerning the last-named trait, James came to be known by the early church as "James the Just," (meaning James the Righteous). It is interesting to note that James's father, Joseph, was "a righteous man" (Matt. 1:19); and that James refers to Jesus as "the righteous" man (James 5:6). *The International Standard Bible Encyclopedia* pursues this thought at length, showing how the younger brother James and his elder brother Jesus were so much alike in personality.[4] The content and style of their messages were very similar.

6. *Death.* A strong tradition is that James was martyred at Jerusalem in A.D. 62. This date is about one year after the closing of the book of Acts and about five years before Paul and Peter were martyred. The manner of death, if Josephus (A.D. 37-95) and others are correct, was by stoning at the order of Ananias the high priest.

B. THE PEOPLE ADDRESSED

The salutation identifies the original readers of this letter as "the twelve tribes who are dispersed abroad." Like many passages in the Bible, this phrase could be interpreted literally or symbolically.

1. *Literal interpretation.* The question is, Were the readers (1) *Jews in general*, representing the twelve families of Israel, living in different parts of the New Testament world, of what is usually called the Dispersion (*Diaspora*); or (2) *Jewish Christians* scattered abroad for various reasons?[5] Read at least part of chapter 1 and see why the first view (Jews in general) is unacceptable.

2. *Symbolic interpretation.* These scattered "twelve tribes" represent the Christian church, God's elect (cf. Gal. 3:7-9; 6:16; Phil. 3:3), living in strange country (this world), far from their land of citizenship (heaven). (Cf. Gal. 4:26; Phil. 3:20; Heb. 12:22; 13:14; 1 Pet. 1:1, 17; 2:11.)

The contents of the epistle itself strongly support the view that James's readers were *Jewish Christians*, wherever they were located. This would be expected, if the epistle was written at a very early date (see Date below), for most Christians in the earliest days were Jews (cf. Acts 1-7).

Indications in the epistle itself that James's readers were Jews include these (read the verses):

---

4. Ibid., 3:1567.
5. *Diaspora* is the Greek word translated "scattered abroad" in 1:1. Persecutions, dating back as far as the Assyrian captivity (721 B.C.), and pursuit of commerce accounted for most of this "dispersion."

1. the reference to "synagogue" ("assembly," KJV), not "church" (2:2)[6]

2. illustrations from the Old Testament (e.g., 2:25; 5:11, 17)

3. the reference to Abraham as "our father" (2:21)

4. the Old Testament name "Lord of Sabaoth" (5:4)

5. no mention of what might be called "pagan" vices, such as idolatry and drunkenness.

C. DATE AND PLACE WRITTEN

The position of this survey guide is that James was the earliest (or one of the earliest) New Testament book to be written. (See Chart 1, p. 20). The date of writing was around A.D. 45-50.

Associate the writing of James with the times of the book of Acts, with the help of Chart 106.

CHART 106

THE WRITING OF JAMES IN RELATION TO ACTS

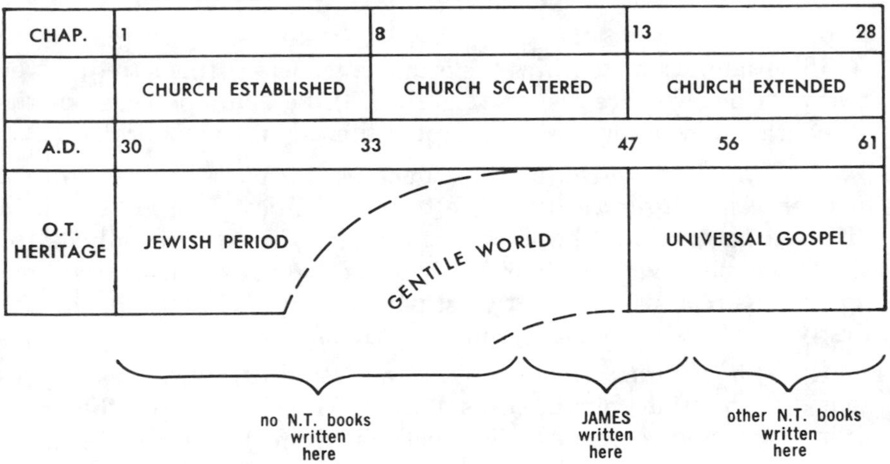

CHAP.	1	8	13	28
	CHURCH ESTABLISHED	CHURCH SCATTERED	CHURCH EXTENDED	
A.D.	30	33	47 56	61
O.T. HERITAGE	JEWISH PERIOD	GENTILE WORLD	UNIVERSAL GOSPEL	

no N.T. books written here   JAMES written here   other N.T. books written here

The view of a later date places the writing of James around A.D. 60, a year or so before James's death.[7] Reasons for the early date include:

1. Church order and discipline in the epistle are very simple.

2. The Jerusalem Council of Acts 15 (A.D. 48 or 49) was still future: "The question of the admission of the Gentiles (into the church which in the earliest years was Jewish) seems not yet to have come to the fore."[8]

---

6. The word *church* does appear, however, in 5:14.

7. Some hold to a late date on such grounds as: James 2:14-26 was written to correct a misinterpretation of Paul's doctrine of justification by faith, contained in such writings as Romans (c. A.D. 56); and references to persecutions fit a late date better than an early date.

8. Henry C. Thiessen, *Introduction to the New Testament*, p. 277.

3. The Judaic emphases on law, moral principles, and works were the immediate concerns of the first decades of the church.

As to the question of the place of writing James, it is very probable that James was living in Palestine when he wrote the epistle.

D. OCCASION AND PURPOSES

Persecution of the Christians, unchristian conduct (e.g., in speech) by many believers, and erroneous views on such doctrines as faith and sin were some of the circumstances that called for this epistle.

Most of the epistle was written to correct evils and to teach right Christian behavior. There is also encouragement and exhortation in things such as the coming of the Lord (e.g., 5:7). The epistle has been called "A Practical Guide to Christian Life and Conduct." More of James's purposes will be observed as you survey the epistle.

E. CONTENT

James emphasizes *conduct* more than *creed*. For this reason James has been called the apostle of good works, an identification linking him with the trio of John, apostle of love; Paul, apostle of faith; and Peter, apostle of hope. There is very little of systematically-presented theology in the book. Specific references to Jesus and the gospel are few, though this does not take away from the Christian spirit that pervades the book.[9] Of this, D. A. Hayes writes, "James says less about the Master than any other writer in the New Testament, but his speech is more like that of the Master than the speech of any of them."[10]

F. COMPARISON WITH OTHER BOOKS

Some interesting comparisons between James and other parts of Scripture are suggested below. You may want to inquire more into this subject a later time.

1. *Proverbs of the Old Testament.* James and Proverbs are both concerned primarily with *conduct*.

2. *Jesus' Sermon on the Mount.* There are many extraordinary likenesses between the book of James and Jesus' Sermon on the Mount.

3. *Paul's writings* (especially Galatians and Romans). The most obvious observation to be made here is a difference of emphasis: Paul

---

9. The two verses containing the name "Jesus" are 1:1 and 2:1. The name "Lord" occurs fifteen times in the epistle.

10. D. A. Hayes, "Epistle of James," in *The International Standard Bible Encyclopedia*, 3:1564.

emphasizes the place of faith, and James, the place of works. There is no contradiction here, however, though some theologians have concluded so.[11] The difference between the two books is accounted for by the two different vantage points. Paul deals with "Justification Before God"; James, "Demonstration Before Men." "Paul saw Christ in the heavens, establishing our righteousness. James saw Him on the earth, telling us to be perfect. . . ."[12]

Refer to Chart 62, page 244, for comparisons of the various New Testament books. Note especially how James and Galatians are compared:

GALATIANS: Liberation by the gospel

JAMES: Compulsion of the gospel

A study of this chart is one good way to survey the main content of the New Testament.

    4. *Other general Epistles.*

        James and 1 Peter — predominantly ethical (Christian behavior)

        Jude and 2 Peter — eschatological (doctrine of last events)

        Epistles of John — Christological and ethical

It is interesting to observe that James, the first author of the New Testament, and John, the last author, both write with a note of authority, emphasizing conduct acceptable to God.

G. STYLE

The book of James is a letter, as its salutation indicates, but its style is more like that of a preacher's sermon, or an Old Testament prophet's appeal. James writes in simple, straightforward sentences. Like Old Testament writings and Jesus' discourses, there are no abstractions, and picture language abounds. Most of the sixty-three Greek words unique to James's letter are picture words, such as *poison, fade.* The epistle bristles with strong, pointed truths, from the first word to the last. Hayes says of James, "He has the dramatic instinct. He has the secret of sustained interest. . . . He is an artist."[13]

H. TONE

A tone of authority pervades the epistle. (There are fifty-four imperatives in the one hundred eight verses.) For this, James has been called "The Amos of the New Testament." But James's forthrightness and severity are blended with warmth and love, evidenced

---

11. The notable example of refuting James is that of Martin Luther, who wrote that James "contradicts Paul and all Scriptures, seeking to accomplish by enforcing the law what the apostles successfully effect by love." (Quoted by Hayes, 3:1566.)

12. Henrietta C. Mears, *What the Bible Is All About*, p. 595.

13. Hayes, 3:1564.

by the repeated words "brethren" and "beloved brethren." Read 1:5, 17; 2:5; 4:6 and 5:11, 19, 20 for some of the more tender sentences of the epistle.

I. PLACE IN THE CANON

Questions over authorship and doctrine delayed general recognition of this book's divine inspiration, but by the end of the fourth century the epistle of James was firmly fixed in the canon of Holy Scripture.

III. SURVEY

As you make your own survey of James, keep from getting involved in details, which is the task of analysis. Look especially for *main emphases* and *broad movements*.

A. FIRST READING

Scan the book in one sitting, reading aloud if possible. You may choose to do this first in a modern paraphrase and then in the version of your study. What are your first impressions of the book? What things stand out? Do you sense a tone or atmosphere in the writing? Do any key words and phrases draw attention to themselves?

B. SUBSEQUENT READINGS

1. Scan the book again, underlining every appearance of the address "my brethren" (or related phrases). How often is this repeated? Is there any pattern concerning where the phrase appears? What does this brief study tell you about the epistle?

2. Compare the opening verses (e.g., 1:1-4) with the closing verses (e.g., 5:19-20).

3. With a pencil, mark paragraph divisions in your Bible at these places: 1:1, 2, 5, 9, 13, 16, 19, 22, 26; 2:1, 5, 8, 14, 18, 19, 21, 25; 3:1, 3, 5*b*, 7, 9, 13; 4:1, 4, 11, 13; 5:1, 7, 13, 19.

4. Now read each paragraph and derive a paragraph title from each.

5. Observe in the epistle every reference to each of the subjects listed below.

    a. references to God, Jesus, Lord
    b. use of questions
    c. specific references to the Old Testament
    d. figurative language (e.g., "vapor," 4:14)

6. What are your new observations and impressions?

C. OBSERVING THE STRUCTURE OF THE EPISTLE

Review the paragraph titles you made earlier. Read the epistle again and identify *groups* of paragraphs according to *common* subject. (These groups are called *segments*.) For example, what paragraphs speak about the common subject of the tongue (speech)? This might be the most difficult part of your study in James because this epistle is not a formal treatise as such, but a series of exhortations written in a pattern whose order is not apparent, for the most part. Take on the challenge of finding an outline, as obscure as one may appear. That is how discoveries are often born. An example of this is the testimony of J. Albrecht Bengel concerning his study of the maxims of Proverbs: "I have often been in such an attitude of soul, that those chapters in the Book of Proverbs in which I had before looked for no connection whatever, presented themselves to me as if the proverbs belonged in the most beautiful order one with another."[14] It may be added here that any time spent in search of structure of a book of the Bible is not lost time, for its fruits keep reappearing in the later stages of analytical study.

The next logical step in determining the structure of a book is to identify sections, which are groups of segments, followed by the identification of divisions, which are groups of sections.

CHART 107

VARIOUS OUTLINES OF JAMES

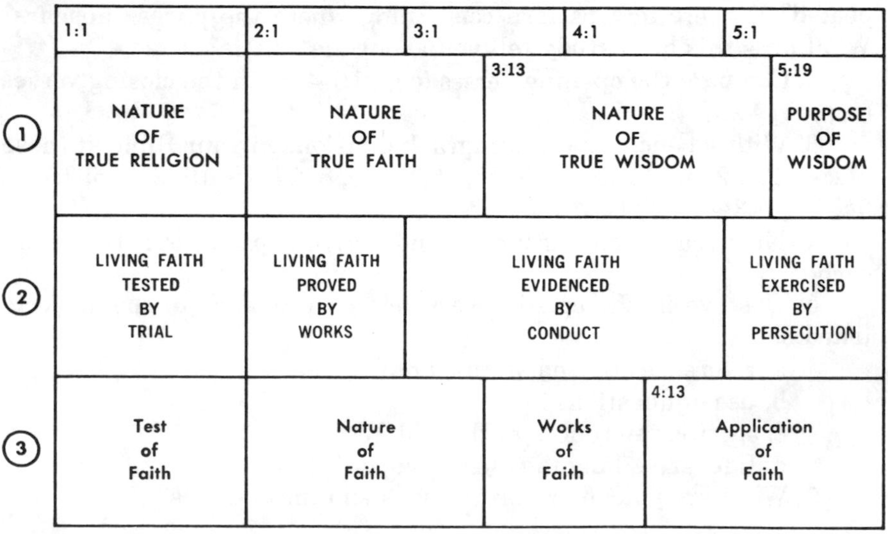

	1:1	2:1	3:1	4:1	5:1
(1)	NATURE OF TRUE RELIGION	NATURE OF TRUE FAITH	**3:13** NATURE OF TRUE WISDOM		**5:19** PURPOSE OF WISDOM
(2)	LIVING FAITH TESTED BY TRIAL	LIVING FAITH PROVED BY WORKS	LIVING FAITH EVIDENCED BY CONDUCT		LIVING FAITH EXERCISED BY PERSECUTION
(3)	Test of Faith	Nature of Faith	Works of Faith	**4:13** Application of Faith	

14. Quoted in John Peter Lange, *Commentary on the Holy Scriptures: Proverbs*, p. 33.

Three outlines by different authors are shown on Chart 107 as examples of various ways in which the structure of James has been outlined.[15] Compare these also with the outlines of Chart 108.

What would you identify as the introduction and conclusion of James, if they are present? Do you observe any turning point or climax in the epistle?

D. SURVEY CHART

Study carefully the survey, Chart 108, and observe the following:

1. There is a formal salutation in James, but no formal closing.

2. The bottom of the chart shows four main divisions in the epistle. There is an ascending progression in the first three: *principles involved; practices for the present; prizes in the future*. The fourth section is like an epilogue, where the writer returns to the subject of *practices for the present* by giving two final exhortations of a very practical nature to his Christian readers.

3. Observe how the epistle is first divided into small sections (first outline under the main horizontal line). Then study the outline of large divisions, on the subject of *faith*. Check out the outlines with your own observations, which you have made of the epistle.

4. What outline of *works* appears on the chart?

5. The division of 1:19—4:12 (*faith at work*) is difficult to break down into an outline. James appears to be writing about various aspects of the outer and inner life of faith. Note the listing of subjects on the chart (*fulfillment, favoritism,* and so forth). Compare this outline with your own work.

6. The title for James given on the chart is "Faith for Living." The intention of this title is to show the necessary ingredient of *faith* in *action*.[16] This very clearly is James's main theme. The key verse chosen for the epistle (2:26) reflects that theme.

IV. PROMINENT SUBJECTS

A. FAITH AND TRIALS (1:1-18)

Recall that the hardships of persecution were part of the setting bringing forth this epistle. The fact that the first subject that James writes about is the hardship of trials tells us that this was a most pressing problem.

---

15. These are outlines, respectively, of (1) Merrill C. Tenney, *New Testament Survey*, pp. 263-64; (2) Merrill F. Unger, *Unger's Bible Handbook*, p. 784; (3) Walter M. Dunnett, *An Outline of New Testament Survey*, pp. 143-44. The three outlines show mainly the compositional unit of *section*.

16. Compare the title of G. Coleman Luck's commentary in the Everyman's Bible Commentary series, *James, Faith in Action*.

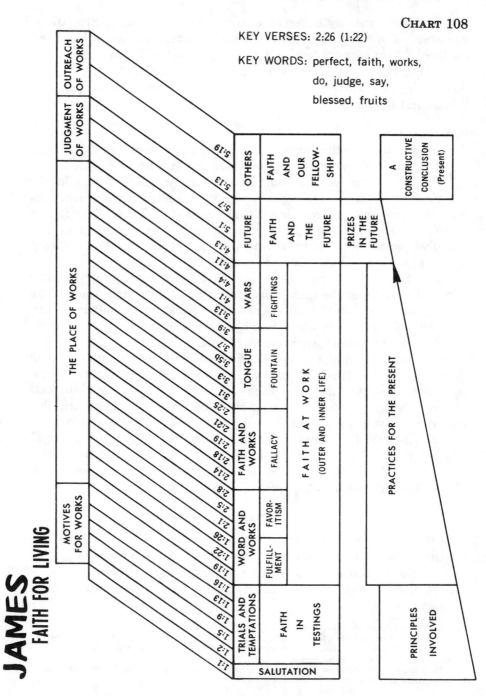

CHART 108

KEY VERSES: 2:26 (1:22)

KEY WORDS: perfect, faith, works,
do, judge, say,
blessed, fruits

JAMES
FAITH FOR LIVING

MOTIVES FOR WORKS	THE PLACE OF WORKS	JUDGMENT OF WORKS	OUTREACH OF WORKS

TRIALS AND TEMPTATIONS — FAITH IN TESTINGS

WORD AND WORKS — FULFILLMENT / FAVORITISM

FAITH AND WORKS — FALLACY

TONGUE — FOUNTAIN

WARS — FIGHTINGS

FUTURE — FAITH AND THE FUTURE

OTHERS — FAITH AND OUR FELLOWSHIP

FAITH AT WORK (OUTER AND INNER LIFE)

PRIZES IN THE FUTURE

A CONSTRUCTIVE CONCLUSION (Present)

PRACTICES FOR THE PRESENT

PRINCIPLES INVOLVED

SALUTATION

1:1 1:2 1:5 1:9 1:13 1:16 1:19 1:22 1:26 2:1 2:5 2:8 2:14 2:18 2:19 2:21 2:25 3:1 3:3 3:5b 3:7 3:9 3:13 4:1 4:4 4:11 4:13 5:1 5:7 5:13 5:19

Observe how much instruction James compresses into three verses, in 1:2-4.

        trials v. 2 — The Situation
        testing v. 3*a* — The Test
        endurance vv. 3*b*, 4*a* — The Immediate Fruit
        maturity v. 4*b* — The Ultimate Fruit

Read the entire segment and observe other truths and applications concerning perseverance under trial.

B. THE FAITH THAT SAVES (2:14-26)

James describes saving faith in different ways. The following outline shows some of those.

The Faith that Saves

A Faith That Produces Works (2:14-18)
    Works are faith's partner (2:14-17)
    Works are faith's demonstrators (2:18)
A Faith That Comes from the Heart (2:19-26)
    It is not mere intellectual assent (2:19-20)
    It is heart obedience (2:21-26)

Read Romans 3:21—5:2 for Paul's teaching about justification by faith. Paul says a person is not justified by works (e.g., Rom. 4:2, 6); whereas in the present passage of James we read that Abraham was justified by works (2:21). Contradictory as the two passages may appear, there is no problem when one considers the context and the perspective of each writer. Paul only denies works as the root of salvation.[17] He is not writing about Christian conduct as such, but about the way to becoming a Christian. James is not denying faith as the way of salvation, but he is maintaining that works will issue from a faith that is genuine. D. A. Hayes writes: "Paul is looking at the root; James is looking at the fruit. Paul is talking about the beginning of the Christian life; James is talking about its continuance and consummation. With Paul, the works he renounces precede faith and are dead works. With James, the faith he denounces is apart from works and is a dead faith."[18]

C. THE TONGUE (3:1-12)

James 3:1-12 is a classic Scripture passage on the tongue. Use the following outline as you study the various truths taught.

    3:1-2 The subject of the tongue introduced
    3-5*a* The influential tongue

---

17. Read such passages as 1 Timothy 6:18; Titus 1:16; 3:8, which show the important place Paul assigns to works as the outcome of salvation.
18. D. A. Hayes, "The Epistle of James," in *The International Standard Bible Encyclopedia*, 3:1566.

     5*b*-6   The destructive tongue
     7-8   The untameable tongue
     9-12   The inconsistent tongue

As you study this passage, reflect on what is involved in these three activities: Thought; Word; Action. Think about motives; ones affected; possibility of misunderstanding; repentance and recovery. If deeds (be "doers of the word," 1:22) are crucial in effective Christian living, are spoken words any less crucial?

D. FACTION AMONG CHRISTIANS (3:13—4:12)

The subject of the previous segment was the Christian and his speech; now it is the Christian and strife. When James wrote about the tongue, there was nothing mediocre in his tone. For he well knew the awesome power of the tongue. When he writes in this passage about strife among believers, his pen is at its sharpest and boldest: "You lust . . . you commit murder . . . you fight and quarrel" (4:2). What a tragic state of affairs, James must have thought, when joint heirs of the Prince of Peace are mauling each other to grab a selfish prize.

James writes much about this problem that defiles a Christian community. As you read the passage, refer to Chart 109[19], observing the different approaches James takes to the problem. What four arguments against selfish faction does he raise?

V. THEME, KEY WORDS AND VERSES

State the theme of James in your own words, based on your survey study.

Compare the key words and verses, which you observed in James, with those shown on Chart 108.

VI. APPLICATIONS

From beginning to end the thrust of James's epistle is application. Write a list of the various areas of application in the book. Compare your list with the following: prayer, trials, lust, service to God, values, good works, faith, love, judging others, the tongue, brotherly love, impartiality, wealth, the Lord's second coming. Derive applications for each area.

VII. REVIEW QUESTIONS

1. Who are the four different New Testament persons with the name James? Which one is most likely the author of the epistle?

2. Recall what is known about James's family background.

---

19. Chart 109 is an abridged analytical chart. The method of constructing analytical charts is taught in my book, *Independent Bible Study*.

CHART 109

FOUR ARGUMENTS AGAINST SELFISH FACTION
JAMES 3:13—4:12

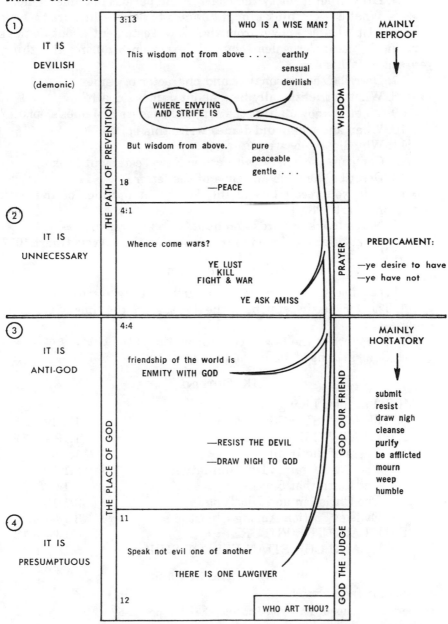

① IT IS DEVILISH (demonic)

THE PATH OF PREVENTION

3:13   WHO IS A WISE MAN?

This wisdom not from above . . .   earthly   sensual   devilish

WHERE ENVYING AND STRIFE IS

But wisdom from above.   pure   peaceable   gentle . . .

18   —PEACE

WISDOM

MAINLY REPROOF

② IT IS UNNECESSARY

4:1

Whence come wars?

YE LUST
KILL
FIGHT & WAR

YE ASK AMISS

PRAYER

PREDICAMENT:
—ye desire to have
—ye have not

③ IT IS ANTI-GOD

THE PLACE OF GOD

4:4

friendship of the world is
ENMITY WITH GOD

—RESIST THE DEVIL

—DRAW NIGH TO GOD

GOD OUR FRIEND

MAINLY HORTATORY

submit
resist
draw nigh
cleanse
purify
be afflicted
mourn
weep
humble

④ IT IS PRESUMPTUOUS

11

Speak not evil one of another

THERE IS ONE LAWGIVER

12   WHO ART THOU?

GOD THE JUDGE

3. What did James not believe about Jesus during His public ministry? What may have been the main hindrance?

4. Draw from memory the chart of the periods of James's life.

5. What do you think brought James to believe in Christ?

6. List what is known from the New Testament about James's part in the local Jerusalem church's experience during the thirty years of Acts' history.

7. Describe the personality and character of James.

8. What is traditionally held about James's death?

9. What is known about the original readers of James's epistle?

10. When and where did James write this epistle?

11. Why did James write?

12. Compare the epistle with other New Testament books.

13. Describe the style and tone of the letter.

14. Can you recall two of the four-point outlines of the book shown on Chart 108?

15. Name five key words and quote one key verse.

16. What title is assigned to the epistle on the survey, Chart 108?

VIII. FURTHER STUDY

Three subjects recommended for further study are:

1. The various dispersions of the Jews, since the time of Christ to the present

2. The place of the law of God in the life of the Christian

3. Comparisons of James and Galatians.

IX. OUTLINE

JAMES: Faith for Living

FAITH IN TESTINGS	1:1-18
FAITH AT WORK	1:19—4:12
Doers of the Word	1:19-27
The Case Against Discrimination	2:1-13
The Faith that Saves	2:14-26
The Christian and His Tongue	3:1-12
Evils of Faction Among Christians	3:13—4:12
FAITH AND THE FUTURE	4:13—5:12
FAITH AND CHRISTIAN FELLOWSHIP	5:13-20

X. SELECTED READING

GENERAL INTRODUCTION

Hiebert, D. Edmond. *The Non-Pauline Epistles*, pp. 32-67.

Knowling, R. J. *The Epistle of St. James*.

McNab, Andrew. "The General Epistle of James." In *The New Bible Commentary*.

COMMENTARIES

Luck, G. Coleman. *James: Faith in Action*. Everyman's Bible Commentary.
Mayor, Joseph B. *The Epistle of James*.
Plumptre, E. H. *The General Epistle of St. James*.

OTHER RELATED SOURCES

Robertson, A. T. *Studies in the Epistle of James*.
Vine, W. E. *An Expository Dictionary of New Testament Words*.

21

1 Peter: Trials, Holy Living, and the Lord's Coming

Shortly before Peter denied his Master, Christ told him, "Simon, Simon, behold, Satan has demanded permission to sift you like wheat; but I have prayed for you, that your faith may not fail; and you, when once you have turned again, *strengthen your brothers*" (Luke 22:31-32, italics added). Little did Peter know at that time how he would eventually be used of God to strengthen not only believers of his own generation, but believers of all generations to come, through the two inspired epistles that he was to write.

I. PREPARATION FOR STUDY

One of the best preparations for studying Peter's letters is to study his biography. That is the reason for the extended treatment of biography in the pages that follow.

II. THE MAN PETER

Peter wrote only two New Testament books. It is interesting to observe that of the notable "triumvirate" of New Testament writers mentioned earlier — Paul, apostle of faith; John, apostle of love; and Peter, apostle of hope — the man who does not appear in the gospels (Paul) authored most of the New Testament books, and the man who is most prominent in the gospels (Peter) wrote the least number of New Testament books.[1]

For some Bible books, we cannot be sure of the identity of authorship (e.g., Hebrews). For some books whose authorship is

---

1. Paul wrote thirteen epistles (fourteen, if he wrote Hebrews); Peter, two; John, five books (gospel, three epistles, Revelation).

438

known, we have sparse biographical information concerning the author (e.g., Jude). However, in the case of 1 and 2 Peter, the gospels and Acts furnish much information concerning the life and character of those epistles' author.

Peter is one of the most interesting characters of the New Testament. The New Testament gives more personal information of Peter than it does of any other apostle of Christ.

A. NAME

Originally, Peter's name was Simon (a common Greek name), the Hebrew equivalent of which is Symeon (Acts 15:14). Jesus gave Simon a new name, prophetically pointing to his future status and position among the Christian circle. That new name was Cephas (Aramaic), or Peter (Greek) (John 1:42). Consult an exhaustive concordance to observe how frequently the name Peter appears in the New Testament, as opposed to only six references to the Aramaic name Cephas. It may be noted here that there is no other Peter in the New Testament.

B. BIRTH

We do not know the date of Peter's birth. His father was a Jew named John or Jonas (also Jona). (Read Matthew 16:17; John 1:42; 21:15-17.) Peter had at least one brother, whose name was Andrew. The family's hometown was Bethsaida of Galilee (John 1:44), located near the north shore of the Sea of Tiberias (Galilee). (See Map F, p. 65.)

C. FOUR PERIODS OF LIFE

The biography of Peter can be divided into four parts: (1) pregospel period, (2) gospel period, (3) early church period, (4) later life period. The highlights of each of those are shown below.

1. *Pregospel period.*

a. Education. Peter probably had the normal elementary education of a Jewish boy in a small town. The description "unlearned and ignorant" of Acts 4:13 (KJV) is better translated "unschooled, ordinary" (NIV) and has reference to Peter's not having had rabbinical training. What amazed the rulers and people was that such unschooled laymen as Peter and John preached and performed with such mighty power.

b. Occupation. Many boys raised in the environs of the Sea of Galilee eventually entered the fishing trade. Peter and his brother Andrew were among those. When Jesus first met them, they were busy about their trade (Matt. 4:18). James and John, sons of Zebedee, were partners with Peter and Andrew (Luke 5:10), who were living at that time in the coastal town of Capernaum (cf. Mark 1:29).

c. Marital status. From Mark 1:30 and 1 Corinthians 9:5 we learn that Peter was a married man during the period of the gospels. We do not know if he had children. (The gospels and Acts provide comparatively little information concerning the families of the disciples and apostles.)

2. *Gospel period*.

The highlights of Peter's life during Jesus' public ministry are listed below. Be sure to read all the Bible passages cited.

a. Connection with John the Baptist. Peter very likely attended the preaching services of John the Baptist, as did his brother Andrew (cf. John 1:35-37, 41-42).

b. There were three calls by Jesus to Peter:

    (1) the new name call: "You shall be called" (John 1:42)

    (2) the new vocation call: "You will be catching men" (Luke 5:1-11)

    (3) the new association call: "He appointed twelve" (Mark 3:13-19).

What three aspects of this ordination are mentioned in Mark 3:14-15? It is interesting to observe that in the four passages where the names of the twelve apostles are listed, Peter's name heads each list (Matt. 10:2-4; Mark 3:16-19; Luke 6:14-16; Acts 1:13-14). At least two reasons may be given for this priority: (a) Peter was among the first disciples called by Jesus for the evangelistic ministry, and (b) Peter's natural aggressiveness made him the spokesman and leader of the group, at least in an unofficial way. Two examples of Peter acting as spokesman are given in John 6:66-69 and Matthew 16:16-20.

c. Peter was one of Jesus' "inner circle." It was natural for Jesus to have in His company from time to time only a small segment of the twelve disciples. Peter, James, and John made up this "inner circle." The gospels record three occasions when the three men were the only apostles accompanying Him. Read the passages and determine the reasons for the limited company.

    (1) At the house of Jairus — Mark 5:37 (also Luke 8:51)

    (2) Mount of Transfiguration — Matthew 17:1 (also Mark 9:2; Luke 9:28)

    (3) Garden of Gethsemane — Matthew 26:37 (also Mark 14:33)

d. Peter was a prominent character during Jesus' passion week. Read carefully each of the following passages, and observe (1) the occasion involved, and (2) what is revealed about Peter's character.

Matthew 26:33-46, 58, 69-75
Mark 11:21; 13:3
Luke 22:8, 61-62
John 13:1-11; 18:10-11

e. Key role among apostles. Peter also played a key role among the apostles during the forty days between Jesus' resurrection and ascension. Before Peter could begin to minister as a "rock" in the gospel's witness, he needed to be restored to fellowship with Christ, which had been broken during the week of Jesus' trial. Read the following passages and note what is said about Peter in each case:

John 20:1-10 (Mark 16:7; Luke 24:12)
1 Corinthians 15:5
John 21:1-23.

In your own words describe the "new" Peter as of the end of the gospel account.

3. *Early church period.*

The most active and eventful period of Peter's life was during the years of the first twelve chapters of Acts, or A.D. 30 to A.D. 47. Chart 110 shows the major events and movements of those chapters, and it also indicates that Peter was *the* main character in chapters 1-7, and that in chapters 8-12 he shared the spotlight with such men as Philip, Barnabas, and Paul.[2]

CHART 110

ACTIVE PERIOD OF PETER'S LIFE
ACTS 1—12

1	3		8:1b	9:32	12
Church Is Born	Church Grows Through Testing		Church Is Scattered	Church Embraces Gentiles	
Jerusalem			Judea and Samaria		
Peter			Philip—Barnabas—Peter—Paul		

The following passages of Acts reveal the place of leadership and responsibility that Peter filled in the small group of twelve chosen

2. See Chart 51, page 208, for the reigns of emperors, procurators, and high priests during those years.

apostles and in the larger group of the local congregation of believers in Jerusalem.[3]

 a. Leader of the twelve apostles (1:15-26).

 b. Powerful preacher (2:14-40; 5:42; 8:25; 10:34-43).

 c. Miracle-worker (3:1—4:22; 5:12-16; 9:32-43).

 d. Other experiences (identify them): 5:1-11; 5:17-41; 8:14-24; 12:1-19 (Except for the reappearance of Peter in chapter 15 in connection with the Jerusalem Council, we might say that Peter fades out of the picture of Acts at 12:17: "And he [Peter] departed and went to another place.") It is not known where that place was.

 e. Apostle to the Gentiles (10:1—11:18).

 f. Speaker at the Jerusalem Council (15:6-11; cf. vv. 12-29). This is the last reference to Peter in Acts. What he was doing while Paul was engaged in missionary journeys and other experiences of Acts 13-28 is the subject of the next era of his life, which we shall call the later-life period.

 4. *Later-life period*.

From a few New Testament references to Peter after the Jerusalem Council, the following reconstruction of his later life may be made:

 a. Evangelistic ministry to Jews (Gal. 2:7-9).

 b. A visit to the church at Antioch (in Syria). Here Paul rebuked Peter for his inconsistency in the manner of having fellowship with Gentiles and with Jews.[4] Read Galatians 2:11-21. What harm was Peter doing?

 c. Evangelistic tour of northern Asia Minor. There is a strong possibility that the northern provinces of Asia Minor not evangelized by Paul were the areas where Peter ministered the gospel as an itinerant evangelist after the Jerusalem Council. This would partly explain Peter's references to believers living in Pontus, Galatia, Cappadocia, Asia, and Bithynia, in the salutation of 1 Peter (1 Pet. 1:1).[5] Peter probably ministered to both Jews and Gentiles at this time.

---

3. The original group of twelve was reduced to eleven with the alienation and death of Judas (Acts 1:16-20), but it was restored to the number of twelve when Matthias was selected to replace Judas (Acts 1:23-26).

4. Peter's behavior on this occasion has been identified in various versions as "insincerity" (RSV), "deception" (Phillips), "playing false" (NEB), and "hypocrisy" (NASB and NIV).

5. Of Peter's relationship to the churches in these areas, Tenney writes, "While there is no statement on record that Peter founded or even visited these churches, there is nothing to preclude his doing so." Merrill C. Tenney, *New Testament Survey*, rev. ed., p. 345.

d. Arrival at Rome. It is generally believed that Peter came to Rome shortly after Paul's release from his first imprisonment.

e. Writing of the epistles. With perhaps a short interval between them, the two epistles of Peter were written during the period A.D. 64-67. At the time of his second letter, Peter knew his death was imminent (2 Pet. 1:14).

D. DEATH

According to tradition, Peter was martyred by Nero in A.D. 67, about the same time his "beloved brother Paul" (2 Pet. 3:15) also was martyred. Origen says that Peter's death was by crucifixion and that the apostle requested he be crucified head downward, because he felt unworthy to die as Christ died.

E. THE CHARACTER AND PERSONALITY OF PETER

The character of Peter has been scrutinized perhaps more than that of any other man or woman of the Bible. It is a happy circumstance that the New Testament reveals much about this interesting man.

A man's character may change radically in his lifetime, such as happens in the conversion of his soul. His basic temperament, however, is part of his permanent image.[6] For example, Peter was always an aggressive man, full of energy. In his early days as a disciple of Jesus, this brought on unfortunate consequences, such as Peter's rash act of cutting off the ear of the high priest's servant, Malchus (John 18:10-11). After Pentecost, Peter was still the man of action, but that basic temperament had undergone some radical experiences, including the Holy Spirit's baptism (Acts 2). This gave birth to a new passion and a mature vision, so that now the yet-aggressive man named Peter was the powerful preacher and courageous leader of the earliest New Testament church community. Peter in Acts is a different *character* from the Peter found in the gospels, but his basic temperament is essentially the same.

Various character traits have been attributed to Peter at some time in his life. Among the descriptions are: unstable, daring, weak, humble, energetic, courageous, devoted as a servant, hasty, strong in faith, impulsive, strong in leadership, self-confident. As to what kind of man he was in the last decade or so of his life, our only source is his inspired writing during those years — the two epistles that bear his name. After you have surveyed the epistles, try arriving at a character identification of the apostle at that time.

---

6. For an interesting and practical discussion of varieties of temperament, see O. Hallesby, *Temperament and the Christian Faith*.

III. BACKGROUND

A. AUTHORSHIP

First Peter is one of those Bible books whose authorship is identified by name. "Peter, an apostle of Jesus Christ, to . . ." (1:1). As to genuineness of this authorship, the epistle is one of the best attested books of the New Testament. When Peter wrote this letter he was an elderly man, as seen from 5:1: "I . . . your fellow-elder" (cf. 5:5, "younger"). How else did Peter identify himself in 5:1?

B. DESTINATION

The natural, literal meaning of 1:1 is that this epistle was sent to people who were living in various Roman provinces of northern Asia Minor, namely, Pontus, Galatia, Cappadocia, Asia, and Bithynia (see Map T, p. 296). They were believers (5:2), and apparently had moved to those regions because of persecution ("aliens, scattered," 1:1). Peter's interest in these areas may have originated in evangelistic work to which he had devoted himself some time between the Jerusalem Council (Acts 15, A.D. 49) and the Neronian persecutions at Rome (A.D. 64). From the Acts account we learn that Paul did not evangelize northern Asia Minor on his missionary tours — in fact, on the one occasion when he began to move northward into this vicinity, he was forbidden by the Holy Spirit, who directed him to Troas, from there to Macedonia (Acts 16:6-12).

It is difficult to determine the exact background of the exiles to whom Peter wrote his epistles. There were probably Gentiles represented in the group as well, suggested by such verses as 2:10 and 4:3-4 (read these).

C. DATE AND PLACE WRITTEN

First Peter was written probably around the time of the outbreak of the Neronian persecution, or A.D. 64.

From 5:13 we may conclude that Peter wrote this epistle from Babylon. If the reference is a literal one,[7] there are two possible places of writing: (1) Babylon on the Euphrates (Mesopotamia), where a colony of Jewish Christians lived as early as A.D. 36; or (2) Babylon on the Nile (a city of Egypt now known as Old Cairo).[8]

Many Bible scholars favor a symbolic interpretation of the name Babylon, seeing it as a reference to Rome. Merrill Tenney sees Babylon here as "a mystic name for Rome, by which Christians applied to it all the evil connotations that had been historically

7. The main argument for a literal interpretation is that the whole verse (5:13) is a simple, matter-of-fact salutation.
8. See G. T. Manley, ed., *The New Bible Handbook*, p. 399.

associated with the Babylon on the Euphrates, and by which they could vent their feelings without being detected."[9] If the purpose of using "Babylon" was to disguise the actual origin, we can understand why the name as Peter used it does not have the *appearance* of mysterious symbolism in the context of the verse.

D. IMMEDIATE SETTING

The Christians addressed by Peter in this epistle were experiencing fiery trials of their faith (1:6-7). Slander by fellow citizens was one of those trials (2:12). Darker still were the shadows of state persecution, which Christians throughout the Roman Empire feared. Everyone knew about those martyred by Nero in Rome. Would the fires spread to the Christians in northern Asia Minor? Peter wrote this letter not to assure the Christians that persecution would not come, but to encourage them to stand true and endure suffering for Christ's sake and with His strength, even when the persecution grew more intense.[10]

E. PLACE IN THE NEW TESTAMENT

Refer to Chart 62, page 244, and note that the Petrine epistles are classified under the subject of eschatology. The emphasis of the two books is how to live the Christian life *in view of* the second coming of Christ. After you have surveyed the letters think of how they are related to other New Testament books.

IV. SURVEY

A. FIRST READING

Scan 1 Peter in one sitting. The purpose of this initial quick reading is to get the feel and atmosphere of the book and to catch its major purposes. Write down your first impressions of 1 Peter and any key words and phrases that stand out as of this reading.

B. PARAGRAPHS

1. First, mark in your Bible paragraph divisions at these verses: 1:1, 3, 10, 13, 22; 2:1, 4, 9, 11, 13, 18; 3:1, 7, 8, 13, 18; 4:1, 7, 12; 5:1, 5, 10, 12.

2. Read the epistle paragraph by paragraph, assigning a title to each paragraph as you read.

---

9. Merrill C. Tenney, *New Testament Survey*, rev. ed., p. 348.

10. To what extent the persecutions at Rome extended to other lands at this time is not exactly known, but "Roman provincial governors tended to reflect the Emperor's will, and especially in any place where powerful elements were ill-disposed to Christianity there might well be a severe outbreak" (Alan M. Stibbs, *The First Epistle General of Peter*, p. 54). At least by the end of the century, in the time when John wrote Revelation, the churches of Asia Minor were undergoing severe persecution.

3. Scan the paragraphs again and note the opening word or phrase of each. Does this suggest anything about Peter's writing?

4. Compare the paragraphs in regard to general kind of content: for example, the amount of doctrine (teaching, such as 1:18-19), as compared with the amount of practical injunctions (such as the command of 2:2).

5. Compare the opening paragraph (1:1-2) and closing paragraph (5:12-14).

6. What new key words and phrases do you observe?

C. STRUCTURE OF THE WHOLE

The organization of a book of the Bible is not always clearly discerned. This is so for 1 Peter. Whatever outline is arrived at for a Bible book, the student should not force any artificial structure onto any part of the book, just for the sake of a homogeneous or symmetrical outline. The suggestions for survey study given below have this counsel in mind.

1. Read your paragraph titles and try to recall the general movement of 1 Peter.

2. The opening and closing paragraphs are typical salutations found in epistles.

3. In constructing an outline, we should always look for *groups* of paragraphs of similar content. One group shows up very clearly in 1 Peter — paragraphs involving servants, wives, husbands, and so forth. Locate these paragraphs in the epistle. Chart 111 shows this group beginning at 2:11 and ending at 3:12. Observe that the opening and closing paragraphs are directed to believers in general. The other paragraphs are addressed to more specific groups. List these in the following outline:

2:11-12 _____.
2:13-17 _____.
2:18-25 _____.
3:1-6 _____.
3:7 _____.
3:8-12 _____.

In this connection also note the appeal of subjection, or submission, directed to each group (e.g., 2:13, 18; 3:1, 7).

4. You no doubt have already observed that the subject of trial and suffering appears often in 1 Peter. Read each verse listed below, and record what is said about suffering in each case. (The first group gives the appearances of the word *suffering* in its various forms as

related to Christ; the second group, as related to believers. The last group shows references to the *subject* of suffering.)

> *Group 1: Christ's suffering*
> 1:11; 2:21, 23; 3:18; 4:1, 13; 5:1
> *Group 2: Believer's suffering*
> 2:19, 20; 3:14, 17; 4:1, 13, 15, 16, 19; 5:9, 10
> *Group 3: Other references*
> 1:6, 7; 2:12; 3:13, 16; 4:4, 12, 14

What combination of two chapters has the most references to suffering?

How is trial related to salvation in 1:5-9?

5. There are important references to Christ's second coming in this epistle. What is taught in 1:8, 13; 2:12; 4:7, 13; 5:4? (There are other references that *imply* this second coming. Look for these.)

D. SURVEY CHART

When the total structural organization of a Bible book is not too clear, it is sometimes helpful to choose a prominent section of the book and, using it as the base or starting point, relate the other sections of the book to this base. The result will be *an* outline of a prominent theme of the book, which will not necessarily represent a standard outline of content.[11] Let us apply this approach to 1 Peter. Keep referring to Chart 111 as you read the following.

1. *A base section.*

Let us choose 2:1-10 as our base section. In these three paragraphs are some wonderful truths basic to Christian living, namely, truths about who Christ is and about what the believer's position is in Christ. (Read the passage.) Let us identify the section by the phrase *unique position*. Note where this appears on Chart 111. Try to think of other representative phrases.

2. *Related sections.*

2:11—3:12. We have already scanned this section, observing that it is about specific Christian groups, appealing especially to a life of submission. Let us call this section *life of submission*.

1:13-25. A strong key command here is "be holy yourselves" (1:15). While other attributes appear in this section as well (e.g., "fear," v. 17; "love," v. 22), we will choose to call this section *life of holiness*.

3:13—5:11. Earlier in our study we observed the concentration of

---

11. I consulted seven authors to compare their outlines of 1 Peter, and I found no two outlines alike, even concerning chapter-verse dividing points. Of the seven outlines, three centered on the subject of suffering, one on salvation, two on Christian living, and one on varieties of questions.

A KEY VERSE: 1:7
SOME KEY WORDS: suffering, trial, hope, revelation, glory, joy, grace, subjection, well-doing, holy, precious.

1 PETER
TRIALS, HOLY LIVING, AND THE LORD'S COMING

GRACE UNTO YOU 1:3	
TRIED WITH FIRE 1:10	
PROPHETS 1:13	
HOLY 1:22	
WORD OF GOD 2:1	
MILK 2:4	
LIVING STONE 2:9	
CHOSEN GENERATION 2:11	
PILGRIMS 2:13	
KING 2:18	
SERVANTS 3:1	
WIVES 3:7	
HUSBANDS 3:8	
ALL 3:13	
SUFFER FOR WELL-DOING 3:18	
BAPTISM 4:1	
WILL OF GOD 4:7	
END OF ALL THINGS 4:12	
FIERY TRIAL 5:1	AMEN
ELDERS 5:5	
YOUNGER 5:10	
GOD OF ALL GRACE 5:12	
GREET ONE ANOTHER	AMEN

INTRODUCTION 1:1

	LIFE OF HOLINESS	UNIQUE POSITION	LIFE OF SUBMISSION	SUFFERING AND GLORY	CONCLUSION
	HOW THEY SHOULD LIVE	GOD'S CHOSEN PEOPLE	HOW THEY SHOULD LIVE	THEIR OUTLOOK ON TRIALS	

SUFFERING AND SALVATION

THEIR OUTLOOK ON TRIALS

1:8 revelation appearing 1:13

2:12 visitation

4:7 4:13 5:4 end revelation

SECOND COMING

references to suffering in this section. Read the passage again to discover what truths are associated with that of suffering. One such truth is *glory*. Underline in your Bible each reference to glory. We will call this section *suffering and glory*.

Observe the word "Amen" at the end of 4:11. Some see here a climactic point in the passage 3:13—4:11. Compare 3:13—4:11 and 4:12—5:11, observing differences and likenesses.

1:3-12. Two subjects seem to be prominent in this section: suffering and salvation. Read the section and observe how Peter relates the two subjects. We will call this section *suffering and salvation*.

3. *Main outlines.*

Note on Chart 111 the wording of the outline that is centered on "God's Chosen People," which is another way of wording the outline arrived at above. Compare the different points of each outline.

References to Christ's second coming are also shown on the chart. What title is assigned to 1 Peter?

V. PROMINENT SUBJECTS

A. THE CHRISTIAN PILGRIMAGE (1:13-25)

One of the key verses of 1 Peter is 1:17, which concludes with the command "conduct yourselves in fear during the time of your stay upon earth." The Christian's pilgrimage on earth should be marked by various life-styles and attitudes. Three of these that Peter emphasizes in this passage are:

> Be Holy (1:15-16)
> Fear God (1:17)
> Love One Another (1:22).

These are basic commands for active consecrated Christian living. Later in the epistle (2:11—3:12) Peter treats specific rules of behavior (e.g., of servants, husbands, wives).

B. REDEMPTION BY CHRIST'S BLOOD (1:18-19)

The lamb as a type and picture of Christ appears from time to time throughout the Bible. Make a list of the various truths taught about the blood of Christ in this passage. Chart 112 shows key references to Christ as a lamb, as these references appear throughout the Bible. Read the context of each passage cited.

C. LIFE OF SUBJECTION (2:11—3:12)

The key word of this passage is *submit*. Read the segment and note how many paragraphs open with that thought. What does the passage teach about submission in the everyday living of citizens, employees, wives, husbands, and members of a local church?

D. SUFFERING AND TRIAL (3:13—5:11)

Peter the realist writes much about the suffering and trials of Christians. Read 3:13—4:11 and observe how Peter writes about these attitudes of Christians in suffering:

CHART 112

THE LAMB IN SCRIPTURE

PASSAGE	MAIN TEACHING	SETTING
1. Genesis 4:4-8 (Abel)	necessity of the lamb	for the offerer
2. Genesis 22:7-8 (Abraham and Isaac)	provision of the lamb	for another individual
3. Exodus 12:12-14 (Passover)	slaying and eating of the lamb	a family
4. Leviticus 1:10	character of the lamb	a nation
5. Isaiah 53	the lamb is a person	all elect
6. John 1:29-36	the lamb is **that** person	world
7. Acts 8:32-35	that person is **promised**	whosoever
8. 1 Peter 1:18-21	resurrection of the lamb	all time
9. Revelation 5:12-13	enthronement of the lamb	all the universe
10. Revelation 21-22	glory of the lamb	all eternity

1. attitude of goodness in action (3:13-17)
2. attitude of newness of life (3:18-22)
3. attitude of separation in living (4:1-6)
4. attitude of service in suffering (4:7-11).

In 4:12—5:11 Peter writes more about the trials (e.g., "fiery ordeal" 4:12) of a Christian. Chart 113 shows a breakdown of this passage.

The glory and help of God are two of the triumphant notes with which Peter concludes this section. As an optimist the apostle was confident that the suffering and trials of Christians can reflect the glory of God, and that the Lord is an ever-present help and inspiration in every trial.

VI. THEME, KEY WORDS AND VERSES

The theme of 1 Peter is that of hope in the midst of severe trial. Such hope comes from a firm faith in the "God of all grace" (5:10).

What key words and verses did you observe in your survey study? Compare these with what is shown on Chart 111.

CHART 113

TRIALS OF 1 PETER 4:12-5:11

4:12	5:1	5:5 5:11
Trials of Judgment	Trials of Service	Trials of Submission
—judged by the world (falsely)	—the load of responsibility	—subjection (to one another) (to God)
—judged by God (rightly)	—the demand of integrity	—but resistance (vs. Satan)

VII. APPLICATIONS

Reflect on things you observed in the text of 1 Peter. Apply these in the following areas:
1. gratitude for one's salvation
2. holy Christian living
3. pure fervent love among Christians
4. life of submission to others
5. suffering and trials.

VIII. REVIEW QUESTIONS

1. What is significant about Peter's name?
2. What were the four periods of Peter's life? Recall some of the highlights of each period.
3. What were Peter's three calls by Jesus? What was the significance of each call?
4. What role does Peter play in the book of Acts?
5. Reconstruct a probable biography of Peter after the Jerusalem Council of Acts 15.
6. Describe in your words the character of Peter as of the time of the writing of his epistles.
7. Describe the people to whom Peter wrote this epistle.
8. Where were they living?
9. What was their relationship to Peter?
10. What were their particular spiritual needs at that time?
11. What is the theme of 1 Peter?
12. What are some important subjects reiterated in the epistle?
13. Name the points of one major outline of Chart 111, page 448.
14. How many key words of Chart 111 do you recall?
15. Write down the key verse of Chart 111 from memory.

IX. FURTHER STUDY

1. Investigate the extent of persecution of Christians in the Roman Empire during the last half of the first century.

2. Study the subject of *fear* as it appears in the Bible. Include the attitude that a Christian should have (e.g., 1 Pet. 1:17); and the fear he need not have (e.g., "Perfect love casts out fear" 1 John 4:18).

3. Make a study of the Christian's relation to governmental authority in the first century. The book of Acts furnishes much information on this subject. Study also what Jesus said about this.

4. Study what the letters of Peter reveal about his character.

X. OUTLINE

1 PETER: God's Chosen People

Salutation and Benediction	1:1-2
THEIR SUFFERING AND SALVATION	1:3-12
THEIR PILGRIMAGE	1:13-25
THEIR UNIQUE POSITION	2:1-10
HOW THEY SHOULD LIVE	2:11—3:12
THEIR SUFFERING AND GLORY	3:13—5:11
Greetings and Benediction	5:12-14

XI. SELECTED READING

(Refer to the list at the end of Chapter 22.)

22

2 Peter: True and False Prophecy

About three years after Peter penned his first letter to saints in exile, the Spirit moved him to write again. The second epistle is shorter, but no less important.

I. BACKGROUND

There are not as many personal references in 2 Peter as there are in 1 Peter. Nevertheless, a fairly accurate picture can be composed concerning the epistle's background.

A. AUTHOR

The opening verse of the epistle identifies the author as Simon Peter, an apostle of Christ. This Petrine authorship has been challenged by critics, who have maintained, among other things, that internal evidence points to a date later than Peter's lifetime, and that the style of the second epistle differs from that of the first.

External evidences of the church's *early* acceptance of 2 Peter as one of the inspired books of the New Testament canon are relatively scanty. For example, the epistle is not quoted directly by any of the church fathers before Origen (c. A.D. 250).[1] By the end of the fourth century, however, the book's rightful place in the canon was recognized by the Christian church. The arguments favoring Petrine authorship are strong. Consider these internal evidences:

1. The name of Simon Peter appears in the text (1:1).[2]
2. The writer is identified as an apostle of Jesus Christ in 1:1.

---

1. Merrill C. Tenney in *Zondervan Pictorial Bible Dictionary*, p. 643, gives this reason: "The relative silence of the early Church may be explained by the brevity of the epistle, which could have made it more susceptible to being overlooked or lost."
2. Some of the earliest manuscripts read only the name "Simeon." But this is a reference to the same person. (Cf. Acts 15:14.)

3. The writer refers to an earlier epistle having been written by him to the same readers (3:1).
4. The writer was a close friend of Paul and had read many if not all of Paul's epistles (3:15-16).[3]
5. Autobiographical references in the epistle are about Peter. Read these:
 a. Mount of Transfiguration experience (1:16-18; cf. Mark 9:2-9).
 b. Christ's foretelling Peter's death (1:13-15; cf. John 21:18-19).

B. DATE AND PLACE WRITTEN

  Peter wrote this letter from Rome around A.D. 67, when his death was imminent (1:14; cf. 2 Tim. 4:6, concerning Paul).

C. DESTINATION

  From 3:1 we conclude that the Christian exiles addressed in 1 Peter also received this letter. Others besides them may have been addressed in the second epistle, however.

D. OCCASION AND PURPOSE

  In his first epistle Peter had much to say about opposition to Christians originating outside the group, in the form of persecution. In this epistle he refers mostly to the more serious danger originating inside the group, namely, apostasy and false teaching. Thus his purpose in writing the epistle was to expose the false teachers and instruct the Christians on what they should do to combat the ugly threat of apostasy.

  The following further comparisons of 1 and 2 Peter reveal more of the purposes of this second letter of Peter.[4]

FIRST AND SECOND PETER COMPARED

1 Peter	2 Peter
emphasis: suffering	emphasis: false teaching
suffering of Christ	glory to follow
redemptive title: Christ	title of dominion: Lord
consolation	warning
hope, to face trial	full knowledge, to face error

---

3. Paul was executed by Nero in A.D. 67, probably the same year Peter wrote this second epistle.
4. From Merrill F. Unger, *Unger's Bible Handbook*, p. 809.

II. Survey

A. FIRST READING

1. Scan the book quickly, noting such things as its length, as compared to 1 Peter.

2. Mark paragraph divisions in your Bible beginning at these verses: 1:1, 3, 16; 2:1, 4, 10*b*, 17; 3:1, 11, 14.

3. Read the epistle in one sitting, paragraph by paragraph. What is the atmosphere? What are your first impressions of the letter?

4. What key words and verses stand out as of this first reading?

B. FURTHER READINGS

1. Read the letter again and assign a title to each paragraph.

2. What do you regard as the introduction and the conclusion of the epistle?

3. Do you see any grouping of paragraphs as to similar general content?

4. Observe references to true prophecy and to false prophecy.

5. Be on the constant lookout for key words and phrases. For example, observe how often the word *know* and its cognates appear in the book. Why would the subject of knowledge be emphasized in a book like 2 Peter, considering the dangers threatening the Christians?

6. Observe various exhortations and commands in the epistle.

7. Try making outlines of the epistle.

C. SURVEY CHART

Chart 114 is a simplified diagram of the organization of 2 Peter. Note the following things.

1. The epistle opens and closes with the appeal to give diligence (identify the verses in the text).

2. The main body of the letter (1:16—3:10) is about prophecy. (This is forthtelling as well as foretelling; teaching as well as predicting.)

3. What are the three sections of 1:16—3:10?

4. Study the sequence of four parts in the section *false prophets*.

5. Note the title assigned to the book.

6. Expand on this survey chart with your own outlines.

III. Prominent Subjects

A. THE KNOWLEDGE OF GOD (1:1-15)

Peter was convinced that an intimate knowledge of God was an antidote to false teaching and apostasy, which were threatening the spiritual health of some Christians. So he writes about this in the first part of his letter. Follow this outline as you read the passage:

CHART 114

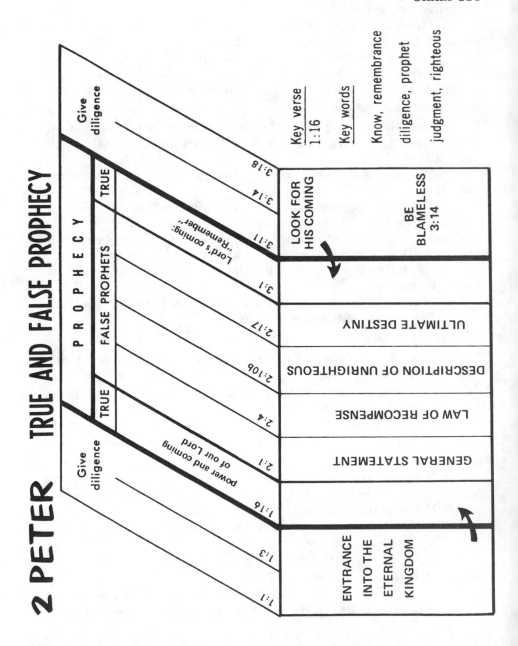

2 PETER — TRUE AND FALSE PROPHECY

PROPHECY

TRUE | FALSE PROPHETS | TRUE

Give diligence — Give diligence

"Power and coming of our Lord" — "Lord's coming:" "Remember."

1:1 — 1:3 — 1:16 — 2:1 — 2:4 — 2:10b — 2:17 — 3:1 — 3:11 — 3:14 — 3:18

ENTRANCE INTO THE ETERNAL KINGDOM — GENERAL STATEMENT — LAW OF RECOMPENSE — DESCRIPTION OF UNRIGHTEOUS — ULTIMATE DESTINY — LOOK FOR HIS COMING — BE BLAMELESS 3:14

Key verse
1:16

Key words
Know, remembrance
diligence, prophet
judgment, righteous

The Man Who Knows God
I. Is Blessed for This Knowledge (1:1-2)
II. Acts on This Knowledge (1:3-11)
III. Should Not Forget What He knows (1:12-15)

B. TRUE AND FALSE PROPHECY (1:16—3:10)

Here Peter seeks to stir up his readers concerning things present and things to come. On the bright side, he reminds his Christian readers of the inspiring prophecy of Christ's return. What are the different references to this return in 1:16-21 and 3:1-10? On the dark side are his descriptions of the shocking state and destiny of false teachers and their followers. Observe how each of the four sections under *false prophets* (Chart 114) leads into the next section. For example:

2:1-3. General Statement. "There will also be false teachers"

2:4-10*a*. Law of Recompense. These unrighteous men will reap judgment (just as the righteous will be rewarded).

2:10*b*-16. Description of the Unrighteous. (The one group of 2:4-10*a* is singled out.)

2:17-22. Destiny of the Unrighteous. (Their destiny is spelled out in more detail.)

C. DISSOLUTION OF THE PHYSICAL WORLD (3:7-10)

Peter's description of the cataclysmic dissolution of the physical world is not a strange picture to this twentieth-century nuclear age. He writes that "the heavens will pass away with a roar and the elements will be destroyed with intense heat, and the earth and its works will be burned up" (3:10).

The prophecy of this cataclysm was brought on by scoffers who challenged the truthfulness of prophecies of Christ's return, "Where is the promise of His coming?" (3:4). Peter answered by citing three supernatural events that originated by decree of God (word of God):

a. *First*. The universe was created (heavens and earth, 3:5).[5]

b. *Later*. The world perished in the Flood (3:6). (The word "whereby" connects the Flood with God's Word. Literally, the Greek is "through which things," i.e., through the Word of God and the flood water.)[6]

---

5. *Today's English Version* interprets 3:5*b* in this way: "Long ago God spoke, and the heavens and earth were created."
6. Cf. Charles F. Pfeiffer and Everett F. Harrison, eds., *The Wycliffe Bible Commentary*, p. 1461.

c. *Yet to come*. Dissolution of the universe "by the same word of God" (3:7). Peter cites the Flood cataclysm to disprove historically the status quo argument of the scoffers. Having done that, Peter clinches his original point by saying that history can and will repeat itself — another cataclysm will take place, at God's command, in the "day of judgment" (3:7).[7] This will be the dissolution of the universe. The day of the Lord *will* come, declares Peter (3:10).

IV. Theme, Key Words and Verses

State the theme of 2 Peter in your own words.

What key words and verses did you observe in the epistle? How do they reflect the theme?

V. Applications

1. Show how the steps of 1:5-7 can be the active experience of a Christian. Do you see a progression in the steps?

2. What does this epistle teach about living the Christian life in light of the imminent return of Christ?

VI. Review Questions

1. Was 2 Peter quickly recognized in the early centuries as an inspired book?

2. Name some arguments supporting the Petrine authorship of 2 Peter.

3. Where and when did Peter write this letter?

4. Who were its original readers?

5. What were Peter's main purposes in writing?

6. Compare 1 and 2 Peter in various ways.

7. How is *know* a key word of the epistle?

8. Compare the opening (1:1-15) and closing (3:11-18) sections of 2 Peter.

9. Where in the epistle do the four paragraphs on *false prophets* appear?

10. What is the subject of the paragraphs on each side of that group of four?

11. Name some key words shown on Chart 114.

12. What title is assigned to 2 Peter on Chart 114?

---

7. The "day of judgment" is also called the "day of the Lord" (3:10) and "day of God" (3:12). This is not a 24-hour day, but an extended period of time, the dawn of which will be Christ's coming to rapture the church.

VII. FURTHER STUDY

1. Study what the Bible teaches about degrees of punishment in hell and degrees of reward in heaven.
2. Make an extensive comparative study of 1 and 2 Peter.

VIII. OUTLINE

2 PETER: True and False Prophecy

SALUTATION AND BENEDICTION	1:1-2
THE MAN WHO KNOWS GOD	1:3-15
TRUE PROPHECY: SURETY OF CHRIST'S SECOND COMING	1:16-21
FALSE PROPHECY	2:1-22
General Statement	2:1-3
Law of Recompense	2:4-10*a*
Description of the Unrighteous	2:10*b*-16
Destiny of the Unrighteous	2:17-22
TRUE PROPHECY: FACT AND DELAY OF CHRIST'S SECOND COMING	3:1-18*a*
DOXOLOGY	3:18*b*

IX. SELECTED READING FOR 1 AND 2 PETER

GENERAL INTRODUCTION

Hiebert, D. Edmond. *The Non-Pauline Epistles*, pp. 105-58.
Tenney, Merrill C. "First and Second Epistle of Peter." In *The Zondervan Pictorial Bible Dictionary*, pp. 642-44.

COMMENTARIES

Clark, Gordon H. *II Peter. A Short Commentary*.
Cramer, George H. *First and Second Peter*.
Lange, John Peter. *Commentary on the Holy Scriptures: I, II Peter*.
Stibbs, A. M. *The First Epistle General of Peter*. The Tyndale New Testament Commentaries.

RELATED SOURCES

Rees, Paul S. *Triumphant in Trouble, Studies in 1 Peter*.
Robertson, A. T. *Word Pictures in the New Testament*.
Thomas, W. H. Griffith. *The Apostle Peter*.
Wuest, Kenneth S. *In These Last Days*.

23

Epistles of John and Jude

1 John: Fellowship with God and His Children
2 John: Truth and the Christian
3 John: Spiritual Health and Prosperity
Jude: Keeping Oneself in the Love of God

About a half century after Christ ascended to heaven, the Spirit moved one man, John the Elder, to write the last five New Testament books (a gospel, three epistles, Revelation). The other twenty-two had been written and distributed from about A.D. 45 to the years just prior to the fall of Jerusalem (A.D. 70).

John's experience as the writer of New Testament books was unique. Besides his dramatic experience in old age of visions on the Island of Patmos (when he authored the book of Revelation), the apostle had the blessed privilege of meditating long on the wonderful truths of Jesus' life. He recorded his reflections under the inspiration of the Holy Spirit in a gospel record and in the three epistles of 1, 2, and 3 John. We have already studied his gospel. Now we turn our attention to his three letters. This will be followed by a survey of Jude, a short letter that appears immediately after John's letters in the New Testament canon.

I. PREPARATION FOR STUDY

Think back over all the books of the New Testament that had been written up to the writing of John's letters and Revelation. Had any major areas of doctrine been overlooked? If not, what might have been God's reasons for adding new books to His collection of Scripture?

II. The Man John

It is very helpful to study biographical notes about this beloved disciple of Jesus. For to be acquainted with the man John is to stand in his shoes and empathize with him as he shares the truths so precious and glorious in his sight. (Chapter 8 discussed some of these notes.)

A. NAME

The name John was a common one in Jesus' day, just as it was in Old Testament days and as it is today. The Greek name is *Ioannes*, derived from the Hebrew *Yohanan*, which means literally, "Jehovah is gracious." Often this name was given to a child as a testimony of the parents' gratitude to God for the initial gift of a baby (cf. 1 Chron. 3:15).

There are five different men in the New Testament bearing the name John:

1. John the Baptist (e.g., Matt. 3:1; Luke 1:57-66)
2. John Mark (e.g., Acts 12:12; 2 Tim. 4:11)
3. Jona, or Jonas, father of Simon Peter (John 1:42; 21:15, 17)
4. John, a relative of Annas the high priest (Acts 4:6)
5. John, son of Zebedee (Matt. 4:21), an apostle of Jesus (Matt. 10:2), who called himself "the elder" in 2 John and 3 John. This John was the author of the epistles.

B. BIRTH

The place of John's birth may have been the city of Bethsaida, at the northern tip of the Sea of Galilee. This was the hometown of Philip, Andrew, and Peter (John 1:44). We do not know the date of his birth, but he may have been at least five years younger than Jesus.

C. FAMILY

John's mother was Salome (see Matt. 27:56, with Mark 15:40; 16:1). If, as suggested by John 19:25, Salome was a sister of Mary, the mother of Jesus, then Jesus and John were cousins. This would partly explain the special place John had in Jesus' "inner circle."

John's father was Zebedee (Matt. 4:21; Mark 1:19), a fisherman on the Sea of Galilee. John had at least one brother, James the apostle (Matt. 4:21), who was executed by Herod Agrippa I around A.D. 44 (Acts 12:1-2). Jesus surnamed both brothers Boanerges, or "sons of thunder," a name indicating perhaps a fiery personality in the young men (see Luke 9:52-56). Before becoming a disciple of Jesus, John was in the fishing trade with his father and brother.

It appears that John's parents were well to do, as suggested by the following:

1. Their household had servants (Mark 1:20).

2. Salome helped with the financial support of Jesus during His public ministry (cf. Mark 15:40-41; Luke 8:3).

3. Salome bought spices for Jesus' body (Mark 16:1).

4. John was a personal acquaintance of the high priest (John 18:15), and usually high priests were of the upper class.

D. EDUCATION

John as a boy and youth very likely had a thorough Jewish religious training at home. Devout Jewish parents, such as Salome was, placed a priority on this. As noted earlier, the reference of Acts 4:13 to Peter's and John's being unschooled men simply tells us that these apostles did not have *formal* training in the rabbinical schools of that day. In present-day parlance, they were well-informed Christian laymen without a theology degree. As a disciple of John the Baptist (see John 1:35), John must have learned much from the forerunner of Jesus.

E. EXPERIENCE

John's life may be divided into two eras: (1) before meeting Jesus, and (2) after meeting Jesus. Of that first era we know practically nothing. The second era was of two periods, which we shall identify as (1) pre-Pentecost period (i.e., up to the event of Acts 2), and (2) post-Pentecost period. Let us now study each of these periods, keeping in mind that the John who, toward the end of his life, wrote the epistles of our study, is the John who was molded and perfected by the experiences of the periods.

1. *Pre-Pentecost period*. The approximately three and one-half years of Jesus' public ministry constituted this pre-Pentecost period. John was with Jesus most of this time. He was the disciple greatly loved by the Master (John 21:7, 20). Of the three disciples of Jesus' "inner circle" (Peter, James, and John), John was the most prominent, while Peter was the most active one. (Read Matthew 17:1; 26:37; Mark 5:37).

a. Stages of discipleship. The part John played in Jesus' public ministry may be broken down according to three stages. (Read all the passages cited.)

    (1) FIRST STAGE (during the first year of Jesus' ministry).

        (a) John meets Jesus, and becomes one of His disciples (John 1:35-39).

        (b) John is with Jesus during most of the first year of Jesus' public ministry.

(c) John returns to the fishing occupation, at least temporarily. (We cannot be sure of this transfer of activity.)

(2) SECOND STAGE (at the beginning of the second year of Jesus' ministry).

(a) Jesus calls disciples (Peter and Andrew; James and John) to become "fishers of men" (Matt. 4:18-22; Mark 1:16-20; Luke 5:1-11).

(b) Jesus continues His training of the disciples to be witnesses for Him.

(3) THIRD STAGE (four months into the second year of Jesus' public ministry).

(a) John with eleven others is ordained to the apostolate (Matt. 10:2-4; Mark 3:13-19; Luke 6:12-19). What three aspects of this ordination are mentioned in Mark 3:14-15?

(b) John remains close to Jesus up to His Gethsemane experience (read Matt. 26:37 ff.); then flees from His presence at His arrest (Matt. 26:56).

(c) John is one of the first ones to view the empty tomb of Jesus (John 20:1-10).

(d) John with the other apostles obeys Jesus' command to wait in Jerusalem for the descent of the Holy Spirit upon them (Acts 1:8, 12-14).

b. Key experiences. There were many key experiences of John as he served his Master during this pre-Pentecost period. Here is a list of the references of most of these (when you read the passages, consider also the surrounding context in each case): Matthew 17:1; 26:37, 56; Mark 5:37; 9:2, 38; 10:35; 13:3; 14:33, 37; Luke 8:51; 9:28, 49, 54; 22:8; John 13:23, 25; 18:15-16; 19:26; 20:2-3; 21:1-7, 20-24.

2. *Post-Pentecost period*. From Galatians 2:9 we learn that Peter (Cephas), James, and John were leaders of the church at Jerusalem during the first years after Pentecost. Read the following passages, which record some of John's activities during that time: Acts 3:1 ff.; 4:1-22; 8:14-15. After chapter 8 of Acts there is no mention of John, though he surely attended the Jerusalem Council of Acts 15 *if* he was in the vicinity at the time. There is no mention of him in Acts 21, when Paul was in Jerusalem, which could mean that by that time John at least had moved to another place.

The latter years of John's life were probably spent around Ephesus, hub city of Asia Minor, where the apostle was teaching, preaching, and writing. The Bible books that he wrote (the gospel, three epistles, Revelation) probably were all written between A.D. 85 and 96. Ephesus was the city where Paul, on his third missionary journey, spent about three years evangelizing the pagan city and teaching the Word of God to many converts (Acts 19:1-20). How strong and spiritually mature the young Ephesian church became is suggested by Acts 19:20 and by the profound depths of Paul's epistle to the Ephesians, which the apostle wrote from prison at Rome. It was among such Ephesian Christians that John ministered during the last years of his life.

While John's home may have been in Ephesus at this time, he was very well acquainted with churches in surrounding cities, such as Smyrna, Pergamos, Thyatira, Sardis, Philadelphia, and Laodicea. (Consult Map V, page 337, for these locations.) These are the churches to whom he sent the scroll of his visions, which were received on the Island of Patmos about A.D. 95 (Rev. 1:9-11).

F. DEATH

John apparently died in Ephesus soon after writing Revelation. His age at death was around 100. Read John 21:23 and note an interesting reference to the apostle made by Jesus. Of this, *Unger's Bible Dictionary* comments:

> If to this [known lot of John, including the Patmos experience] we add that he must have outlived all, or nearly all, of those who had been the friends and companions even of his maturer years; that this lingering age gave strength to an old impression that his Lord had promised him immortality (John 21:23); that, as if remembering the actual words which had been thus perverted, the longing of his soul gathered itself up in the cry, "Even so, come, Lord Jesus" (Rev. 22:20), we have stated all that has any claim to the character of historical truth.[1]

Who would not like to know how soon after writing "Come, Lord Jesus" (Rev. 22:20) John's spirit was ushered into the presence of Christ?

G. CHARACTER

John, like Peter, is an example of a man with an intense, vigorous nature that Christ directed to the glory of God. At times John's intensity was unfortunately the channel for evil words and deeds. Read Matthew 20:20-28; Mark 9:38; 10:35; Luke 9:49, 54; and observe the apostle in the dark moments of intolerance, vindictiveness, undue vehemence, and selfish ambition. For the most part, however, the New Testament's picture of John is an attractive and

---

1. Merrill F. Unger, *Unger's Bible Dictionary*, p. 597.

beautiful one. Charles C. Ryrie says, "In actions, in love for the brethren, in condemnation of heresy, John was the intense apostle."[2]

John is known as the apostle of love. Writes Tenney, "As Christ tamed his ardor and purified it of unrestrained violence, John became the apostle of love whose devotion was not excelled by that of any other writer of the New Testament."[3] His tender concern for other Christians is manifested most clearly in his epistles where he addresses his readers as "my little children" and "beloved." As we study John's epistles we will be learning more of the character of the one so loved of Christ.

III. BACKGROUND OF 1 JOHN

A. AUTHOR

Let us now look at the evidences for John's authorship of his first epistle. Internal evidence and early church tradition give ample support to the view that the apostle John wrote the epistles as well as the fourth gospel.[4] Arguments favoring another author, such as a different John with the designation "John the elder," are not as strong.

Our starting point here is that the same author wrote the gospel of John and 1 John. Identification of the author of the fourth gospel is narrowed down to the one man John the apostle when one considers the following descriptions of the author. (Note: Study this section not only for the identification of authorship, but also to learn more about the person John.)

1. *He was a Palestinian Jew.* This is shown, for example, by his use of the Old Testament (John 6:45; 13:18; 19:37); by his knowledge of Jewish traditions (John 1:19-49; 2:6, 13; 3:25; 4:25; 5:1; 6:14-15; 7:26 ff.; 10:22; 11:55; 12:13; 13:1; 18:28; 19:31, 42); and by his knowledge of Palestine (John 1:44, 46; 2:1; 4:47; 5:2; 9:7; 10:23; 11:54).

2. *He was an eyewitness.* This is shown by the exactness of details in his reporting (e.g., John 1:29, 35, 43; 2:6; 4:40, 43; 5:5; 12:1, 6, 12; 13:26; 19:14, 20, 23, 34, 39; 20:7; 21:6), and by the intimate character descriptions he gives of such men as Andrew, Philip, Thomas, Nathanael, and Nicodemus.

3. *He was one of Jesus' intimate associates, the "beloved disciple."* (See John 13:23; 18:15-16; 19:26-27). Of these associates, James was

---

2. Charles C. Ryrie, "I, II, III John," in *The Wycliffe Bible Commentary*, p. 1463.
3. Merrill C. Tenney, *New Testament Survey*, rev. ed., p. 189.
4. Testimony is by such church Fathers as Polycarp, Irenaeus, Clement of Alexandria, and Tertullian.

killed in the early years of the church's life (Acts 12:2), and Peter, Thomas, and Philip are referred to in the gospel in the third person so frequently that they may be eliminated as possible authors. This leaves John, son of Zebedee, as the most likely author of the gospel.

Now the question is, Did the author of the fourth gospel also write 1 John? Most scholars agree that both books were written by the same man. Internal evidence, based mainly on similarities between the books, answers *Yes* to the question. This evidence includes:

a. similarities in the openings of each book (compare John 1:1-18 and 1 John 1:1-4)

b. common phrases in the two books — for example, "only begotten" (John 1:14, 18; 3:16, 18; 1 John 4:9; cf. 5:1, 18), and "born of God" (e.g., John 1:13; 1 John 3:9; 4:7; 5:1, 4, 18)

c. similar grammatical and stylistic structure

d. common themes prominent in both books — for example, love, light, life, abide, darkness, world, eternal life, new commandment, the Word, beginning, believe (ninety-eight times in the gospel, nine times in the epistle), witness (thirty-three times in the gospel, six times in the epistle).

e. evidence in both books that the author personally knew Jesus (for 1 John, read 1:1-4 and 4:14).

When external evidence (such as testimony of the early church Fathers) is added to this strong internal evidence, the firm conclusion is reached that it was the apostle John who wrote the epistle as well as the gospel.

B. DATE AND PLACE OF WRITING

Although John's epistles do not identify where they were written, it is generally believed that the apostle wrote them from Ephesus. This conclusion is based on the concurrence of two data: (1) the epistles were written in the latter years of John's life; and (2) John spent his latter years in Ephesus.

The date of the writing of 1 John is approximately A.D. 85-90. The time is narrowed down to these years in the following way:

The epistle was written before the persecution of A.D. 95 under Emperor Domitian (otherwise the epistle might have made mention of this).

The epistle was written near the end of the century. Tenney suggests these hints: (1) the church and synagogue had become separate, (2) the controversy over faith versus works had largely died out, (3) philosophical inquiries into the nature of Christ had begun.[5]

_____

5. Merrill C. Tenney, *New Testament Survey*, p. 376.

Of his five books, John wrote Revelation last (c. A.D. 95). The gospel and 1 John were published about the same time. The logical relationship between the gospel and the epistle favors the former being written first.

JOHN'S GOSPEL AND FIRST EPISTLE COMPARED

Gospel	1 John
written to arouse faith (Jn 20:31)	written to establish certainty regarding that faith (1 Jn 5:13)
the good news historically	the good news experientially

Refer to Chart 1, page 20, and observe when John wrote his epistles. How many years had elapsed between the writings of Peter and John? Why do you think God inspired John's books to be written so long after the other New Testament books? What emphases might you expect to see in letters written at this time? Why?

C. ADDRESSEES

The readers of 1 John were probably a congregation or group of congregations of Asia Minor closely associated with the apostle. Read 2:7, 18, 20, 21, 24, 27; 3:11 for suggestions that the readers had been believers for a long time. Various teachers and preachers had ministered to the people living in the vicinity of Ephesus long before John wrote his books. (Among those who ministered were Paul, Acts 18:19; 19:1-20; Aquila and Priscilla, Acts 18:18-19, 24-26; Trophimus, Acts 21:29; the family of Onesiphorus, 2 Tim. 1:16-18; 4:19; and Timothy, 1 Tim. 1:3.) That most of John's readers were converts from heathenism is only intimated by the absence of Old Testament quotations and by the warning regarding idols in the last sentence of the epistle (5:21).

Whoever the readers were, John knew them intimately. Hence the very personal, warm atmosphere of this letter to his "children."

D. OCCASION AND PURPOSE

John wrote this letter to Christians who were falling prey to the deceptive devices of Satan so common in our own day. Christians were fighting each other, and John was frank to declare that "the one who hates his brother is in the darkness . . . and does not know where he is going because the darkness has blinded his eyes" (2:11). Christians were beginning to love the evil things of the world, and John wanted to warn them of the tragic consequences.

And then there were the false teachers — John calls them antichrists — who were trying to seduce the believers by false doctrine to draw them away from Christ. John warned his readers about such false teachers and encouraged them to stand true to the message of the gospel and to abide in Christ.

Also there were those who were doubting their own salvation. So John wrote to instill confidence, that such doubters might *know* that they had eternal life (5:13). In his gospel his purpose was to arouse a saving faith (John 20:31); in 1 John his purpose was to establish certainty regarding that faith.

The false teaching that John was especially trying to combat in his epistle was a form of Gnosticism in its infant stage. The basic tenet of the Gnostics was that matter was evil and spirit was good. One of the heresies that grew from this came to be known as Docetism, which held that Jesus did not have a real body (for then God would be identified with evil matter, or flesh), but that he *seemed* (Greek *dokeo*) to people to have a body. John makes it very clear in this epistle that Jesus, the Son of God, appeared to man in real, human flesh. Read 1:1 and 4:2-3 and observe how unequivocally John declares this truth about Christ.

John's first letter also may have been addressed in part to two other false views: (1) that of the Ebionites, who denied the deity of Christ; and (2) that of the Cerinthians, who denied the eternal union of the divine and human natures of Christ.

Four times in the epistle, John specifically tells why he is writing this epistle. Read these verses and record John's purposes: 1:4; 2:1, 26; 5:13.

E. FORM AND STYLE

1. *Form.* The first epistle of John has a unique combination of form and style qualities. It is classified as an epistle, even though it does not have the usual opening salutation, personal conclusion, references to proper names (except that of Jesus), or specific references to details of the lives of either the readers or the writer. Its many personal references to *writing* (e.g., "My little children, I am writing these things to you that you may not sin," 2:1*a*) are enough justification for considering the book as an epistle. On the basis of its contents one may say that the book is a personal letter of an aged Christian leader to congregations of mature Christians with whom the writer was acquainted.

More will be said about the form, or structure, of the epistle in the Survey section of this chapter.

2. *Style.* In Hebraistic style, John writes short, simple, straightforward, picturesque sentences. The extended opening sentence (1:1-3) is the one exception to the short pattern. Parallelisms and contrasts abound in the book. Concerning the latter, one writer comments, "His colours are black and white; there is no grey."[6] John speaks with a tone of authority and finality based on experience ("we have seen," 1:1). And yet there is a paternal tenderness about the epistle that makes the reader want to pause and meditate over the great truths being declared. Concerning this combination of tenderness and authority, Merrill Tenney writes, "The mellowness of the teaching ... is not to be confused with vagueness of belief or with theological indecision."[7]

F. W. Farrar has written this very accurate appraisal of the epistle's style: "It is a style absolutely unique, supremely original, and full of charm and sweetness. Under the semblance of extreme simplicity, it hides unfathomable depths. It is to a great extent intelligible to the youngest child, to the humblest Christian; yet to enter into its full meaning exceeds the power of the deepest theologian."[8]

IV. SURVEY OF 1 JOHN

A. A FIRST READING

1. Prepare mind and heart to search diligently for all the grand truths that God would have you learn in this study. Humbly ask God to reveal Himself to you in a fresh, vivid way as you examine the Bible text. Maintain an attitude of dependency on the Holy Spirit's enlightenment throughout your survey study of this epistle.

2. Mark new paragraph divisions in your Bible beginning at these verses:

  1:1, 5, 8
  2:1, 3, 7, 12, 15, 18, 20, 22, 24, 26, 28
  3:1, 4, 11, 19
  4:1, 7, 13, 17
  5:1, 4, 6, 9, 13, 14, 18.

3. Keep pencil or pen in hand for marking your Bible and recording observations on paper as you read.

4. Have a sheet of paper available for recording observations.

6. W. Graham Scroggie, *Know Your Bible*, Vol. 2, p. 346.
7. Tenney, *New Testament Survey*, p. 381.
8. F. W. Farrar, *The Early Days of Christianity*, pp. 520-21.

5. Now read the five chapters in one sitting. If possible, read the book aloud. As you read, do not tarry over details. Seek rather to catch the large emphases of the epistle.

6. You may want to underline words and phrases that appear prominent during this first reading.

7. After you have completed this reading, ask yourself these two questions: What is the tone or atmosphere of this epistle? What main point is John trying to get across? If you cannot arrive at an answer for either of these, try reading the epistle in a modern paraphrase such as J. B. Phillips's *The New Testament in Modern English* or *The Living Bible*.

B. FURTHER READINGS

1. Now read the epistle a little more slowly, with paragraph divisions in mind. Choose a word or phrase from each paragraph to represent its contents (paragraph titles).

2. On Chart 115, record the paragraph titles, similar to the ones shown. This simple exercise will give you initial momentum as you begin your study of the text.

CHART 115

PARAGRAPH TITLES FOR 1 JOHN

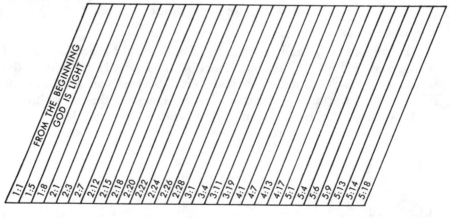

3. After you have recorded the paragraph titles, read the entire group in succession. You may not see a pattern or progression here, because the group of paragraph titles is not intended to show an outline as such; but this is a helpful exercise to review some of the highlights of John's letter.

4. Do you see any groups of paragraphs with similar content?

5. Scan the epistle for every reference to God. Record your

observations on paper. Meditate on how much is known of God from these statements.

6. Read the following verses, which refer to the Father: 1:2, 3; 2:1, 13, 15, 16, 22, 23, 24; 3:1; 4:14; 5:7.

7. Go through the epistle and note the various contrasts that John uses to emphasize his points. (As was mentioned earlier in this chapter, John does not paint with the color gray — the predominant colors are the contrasting black and white.) Compare your observations with this list: light and darkness, truth and error, love and hate, love of the Father and love of the world, children of God and children of the devil, life and death, Christ and antichrist, believers and unbelievers. Why is the Bible written in such bold contrasts?

8. The word *know* and its cognates appear more than thirty times in the epistle. Make a study of the appearances of the phrase "we know," and record what is known in each instance: 2:3, 5, 29 ("you know"); 3:14, 16, 19, 24; 4:13, 16 ("we have come to know"); 5:15, 18, 19, 20.

9. Two of the grandest statements of the epistle are "God is light" (1:5) and "God is love" (4:8, 16). See how these two themes are referred to throughout the book.

10. Observe where and how John refers to false teaching in his epistle.

C. STRUCTURE OF 1 JOHN

1. Compare the opening paragraph (1:1-4) with the concluding one (5:18-21). For example, note in their context such similar terms as "eternal life."

2. Various attempts have been made to outline this epistle.[9] Most students of this book agree that an outline is not too obvious because John's approach is not logical and argumentative but contemplative. Having stated his theme in the opening paragraph (1:1-4), John proceeds to support the theme in various ways, item added to item, until he arrives at the conclusion of his letter (5:13-21).

Although an outline, as such, is difficult to detect in the core of the epistle (1:5—5:12), one cannot help but feel that John reaches a turning point at 3:1, where he wants to pursue the subject of fellow-

---

9. Such variety is evidenced by these possible breakdowns in the structure of the epistle:
      Twofold: 1:5—2:27; 2:28—5:5
      Threefold: 1:1—2:11; 2:12—4:6; 4:7—5:21
      Fourfold: 1:5—2:11; 2:12-28; 2:29—3:22; 3:23—5:17
      Fivefold: 1:5—2:11; 2:12-27; 2:28—3:24*a*; 3:24*b*—4:21; 5:1-21
      (Cf. James Moffatt, *An Introduction to the Literature of the New Testament*, p. 584.)

CHART 116

1 JOHN

FELLOWSHIP WITH GOD AND WITH HIS CHILDREN

"IF WE WALK IN THE LIGHT ..."

WE HAVE FELLOWSHIP ONE WITH ANOTHER*

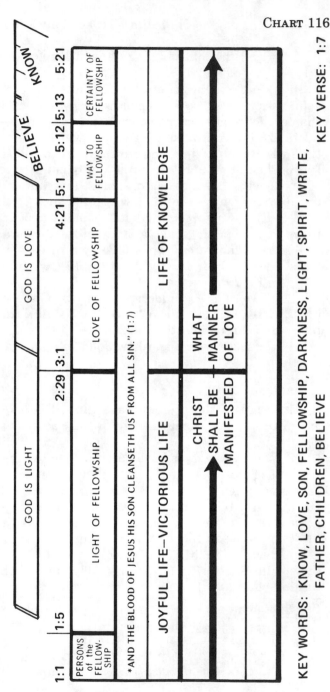

| 1:1 | 1:5 | 2:29 | 3:1 | 4:21 | 5:1 | 5:12 | 5:13 | 5:21 |

GOD IS LIGHT

GOD IS LOVE

BELIEVE   KNOW

| PERSONS of the FELLOWSHIP | LIGHT OF FELLOWSHIP | LOVE OF FELLOWSHIP | WAY TO FELLOWSHIP | CERTAINTY OF FELLOWSHIP |

*AND THE BLOOD OF JESUS HIS SON CLEANSETH US FROM ALL SIN." (1:7)

JOYFUL LIFE—VICTORIOUS LIFE

LIFE OF KNOWLEDGE

CHRIST SHALL BE MANIFESTED

WHAT MANNER OF LOVE

KEY WORDS: KNOW, LOVE, SON, FELLOWSHIP, DARKNESS, LIGHT, SPIRIT, WRITE, FATHER, CHILDREN, BELIEVE

KEY VERSE: 1:7

ship from a slightly different vantage point. Read chapter 2 again, and then read 3:1 ff., to see if there appears to you to be a turning point at 3:1. See Chart 116, which shows the epistle built around this turning point.

3. Note the outline on *fellowship* shown on the chart. This may suggest outlines on other subjects, which you will want to develop in this survey study. For example, try making an outline on the subject, "What the Christian Life Is."[10]

4. Observe near the top of Chart 116 the two statements *God is light* and *God is love.* Locate each in the text of the epistle. Then go through the epistle paragraph by paragraph and see how its two main parts (1:5—2:29 and 3:1—4:21) are represented by those two statements.

5. Study the other parts of Chart 116 if you have not already done so. Read the Bible text to observe how the last two segments (5:1-12 and 5:13-21) focus on the key words "believe" and "know."

6. Note the key words shown at the bottom of Chart 116. Add to the list other words and phrases that you may have observed in your study so far.

V. Prominent Subjects of 1 John

A. FELLOWSHIP (1:1—2:2)

1. *Persons of the fellowship.* The center of John's message is not a theological system or religious creed, but a person — Jesus Christ. He is the one whom John writes about first (1:1 ff.).

John also has much to say in his epistle concerning God the Father, whom he introduces in the opening paragraph (1:2-3). And when the apostle thinks about how Jesus the Son and God the Father are related to believers like himself, the first grand truth that comes to his mind is that of *fellowship.* The Son and the Father are the *persons* of the fellowship.

2. *Conditions for fellowship with God.* In 1:5—2:2 the apostle identifies the conditions or requirements of fellowship with God, so that there will be no question in the minds of his readers regarding how one can enjoy the full blessings that such a fellowship brings. Observe in the passage these three conditions:

a. walk in the light (1:5-7)
b. confess sins (1:8-10)
c. do not sin (2:1-2).

10. Such an outline by one author is: (1) A Joyful Life, (2) A Victorious Life, (3) A Guarded Life, (4) A Life of Knowledge. (From Robert Lee, *The Outlined Bible.*)

B. ANTICHRISTS (2:8-29)

Up to this point in the epistle, John has written much about sin, Satan (the "wicked one"), the world, and darkness. Now he introduces another hostile element — a personal one that he labels antichrist (Greek *antichristos*).[11] The apostle calls the enemies of Christ, as described in this passage, "antichrists." How many were there, as of his time (2:18)? How did they oppose Christ?

Note John's reference to an antichrist in 2:18. Compare this with 4:3-4. In John's day, Christians knew that a personal antichrist would one day appear in this world. The Old Testament, Jesus, and Paul's writings all taught about such a person as the "man of sin." Compare 2 Thessalonians 2:4 with Daniel 11:36-37; Revelation 13:1-8 with Daniel 7:8, 20 ff.; 8:24; 11:28-30. Read also Ezekiel 38-39; Zechariah 12-14; Matthew 24:15, 24; Mark 13:22; 2 Thessalonians 2:1-12; Revelation 17:8.

C. TRUTH AND LOVE (4:1-21)

Chapter 4 is about two main subjects: truth in doctrine (vv. 1-6) and love in action (vv. 7-21). John had briefly mentioned this relationship between truth and love in 3:18: "Love . . . in truth." Now he dwells on the subject in detail. True doctrine is the foundation of life with God; Christian love is the natural expression of life with God.

In what ways does John write about true doctrine in 4:1-6? What does he teach about love in 4:7-21?

D. ASSURANCE OF ETERNAL LIFE (5:13-21)

John's inspiring epistle could not end on a higher, more climactic note than that of assurance and security. The last segment of nine verses is bathed in this atmosphere, with the words "we know" resounding over and over again in a symphony of triumph. In writing his epistle, John wanted to show that those who believe and obey the message of the gospel can and do know with assurance that the prize of eternal life, with all its attendant blessings, is their own present and abiding possession.

Read the passage and record all that it teaches about assurance.

VI. THEME, KEY WORDS AND VERSES FOR 1 JOHN

What key words and verses did you observe in your survey of 1 John? What is the epistle's theme, in your own words?

---

11. The word *antichrist* is used only by John in the New Testament, at these places: 1 John 2:18, 22; 4:3; 2 John 7. The prefix *anti* of the Greek may be translated either "against" or "instead of." *The Zondervan Pictorial Bible Dictionary* says, "The word antichrist may mean either an enemy of Christ or one who usurps Christ's name and rights," p. 47.

VII. Applications from 1 John

1. Recall from the passage about antichrists (2:18-29) what basic truths concerning Christ and God are denied by such men. Is this spirit of denial prevalent in Christendom today? What do modern liberal theologians, who profess to be Christians, deny about Christ? What stand and action do you think born-again Christians ("born of him," 2:29) should take in view of the alarming "antichrist" movement in the world today?

2. Apply the truths of 1 John to everyday living in these areas:
    a. the Christian's hope
    b. the Christian's righteous walk
    c. love among Christians
    d. the Christian's assurances.

VIII. Review Questions on 1 John

1. What does the Hebrew word for John mean, literally?

2. Who are the different Johns of the New Testament? Which one is the biblical author?

3. Describe what is known of this John's family.

4. Reconstruct a probable biography of John's life up to his meeting Jesus for the first time. How did he compare in age with Jesus?

5. Review the three stages of John's ministry in his association with Jesus.

6. Why do you think Jesus chose John to be one of His closest disciples?

7. What was John's ministry after Pentecost while he remained in Jerusalem?

8. What was John's ministry at Ephesus up to the time of his death?

9. What Bible books did John write, and when did he write them?

10. Write a paragraph describing the character of John.

11. What evidence points to John's being the author of the fourth gospel *and* 1 John?

12. Where and when did John write his first epistle? How old was he at the time? Justify your answers.

13. To whom may John have written this epistle? Did he know his readers intimately?

14. What were the needs of John's readers, and how did he attempt to help them in those needs?

15. Describe the epistle concerning its form and style. In these respects compare it with an epistle like Romans.

16. For what specific reasons do you think God included 1 John in the New Testament canon?

17. From your survey study, what would you say is the main theme of 1 John? Cite a key verse to support this.

18. Identify or describe the two main divisions of the letter.

19. Try to recall the outline on *fellowship* beginning with *persons of the fellowship*.

20. What are some of the key words and phrases of the epistle?

21. What is the tone or atmosphere of the book? Does this throw any light on John's purpose in writing?

22. What are two of the grandest statements of the epistle? How much is the world in need of hearing these truths today?

IX. FURTHER STUDY OF 1 JOHN

1. Make a topical study of the word *fellowship* (Greek *koinonia*) as it is used in the New Testament. (It is interesting to note that this word is mainly found in the Pauline writings, 1 John being the exception.) Use an exhaustive concordance to locate the various places where the word is used. Among the passages that you will want to consult are: Acts 2:42; 1 Corinthians 1:9; 2 Corinthians 8:4; Philippians 1:5; 3:10.

2. Study the words *sin*, *know*, and the phrase *eternal life* as these appear in the Bible.

X. OUTLINE

1 JOHN: Fellowship with God and His Children	
PERSONS OF THE FELLOWSHIP	1:1-4
LIGHT OF FELLOWSHIP	1:5—2:29
Conditions for Fellowship with God	1:5—2:2
Abiding in Christ	2:3-17
Antichrists and Christians	2:18-29
LOVE OF FELLOWSHIP	3:1—4:21
Beloved Sons of God	3:1-24
Truth and Love	4:1-21
WAY TO FELLOWSHIP	5:1-12
CERTAINTY OF FELLOWSHIP	5:13-21

XI. BACKGROUND OF 2 JOHN

One very valuable contribution of John's second and third epistles is their picture of typical local churches. These churches were existing a half century after Christ's ascension to heaven. Problems in churches today are not unique to our age. Concerning John's third epistle, Charles Ryrie says, "This brief and very personal letter shatters the notion that the state of things was ideal, or nearly so, in the first century. Contrariwise, it reveals the problems of a vigorously growing faith."[12] When considering this, one begins to see something of God's purpose in including such short letters as 2 and 3 John in His Holy Book.

A. AUTHOR

The writer identifies himself only as "the elder." Internal evidence and tradition point to the apostle John as the author.

B. ADDRESSEES

The epistle was written to "the chosen lady and her children." This designation has two possible interpretations.

1. *Figurative*. By this the "chosen lady" refers to a local church or the church as a whole; and "her children" refers to members of the church.

2. *Literal*. By this "the chosen lady" is an unnamed lady; or her name is Cyria (Greek *eklekta kuria*, translated "elect Cyria"), or Electa (translating the Greek as "the lady Electa"). The lady was a Christian friend of John, mother of children, well known in her community, whose sister's children were probably residents of Ephesus.

The informal, personal style of the epistle favors the literal view.

C. DATE AND PLACE WRITTEN

Written around A.D. 90 from the city of Ephesus.

D. CANONICITY

The second and third epistles of John were not recognized as Holy Scripture by the church as quickly as John's other writings. This is mainly because the letters took longer in becoming part of the churches' public reading programs because of their brevity and their appearance as merely private letters.[13] But the internal and external evidence is strong in favoring canonicity of these letters.

E. OCCASION AND PURPOSE

You will observe these as you survey this short epistle.

---

12. Charles C. Ryrie, "I, II, III John," *The Wycliffe Bible Commentary*, p. 1483.
13. These are the two shortest books of the Bible, 3 John being one line shorter than 2 John in the Greek text.

CHART 117

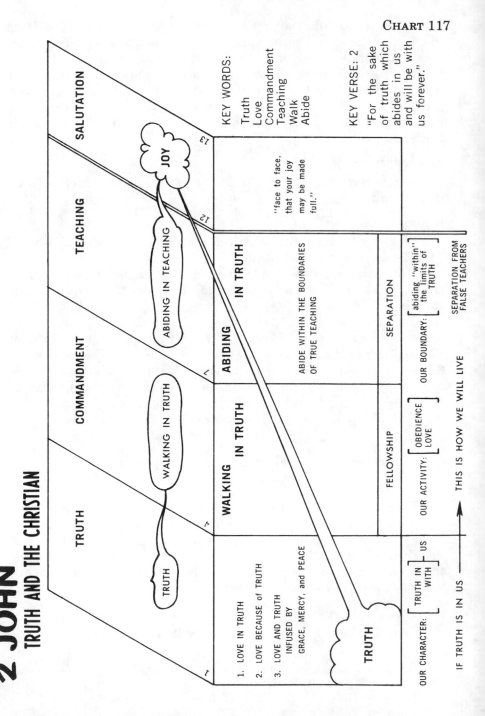

2 JOHN
TRUTH AND THE CHRISTIAN

| TRUTH | COMMANDMENT | TEACHING | SALUTATION |

TRUTH — WALKING IN TRUTH — ABIDING IN TEACHING — JOY

| WALKING IN TRUTH | ABIDING IN TRUTH |

1. LOVE IN TRUTH
2. LOVE BECAUSE of TRUTH
3. LOVE AND TRUTH INFUSED BY GRACE, MERCY, and PEACE

FELLOWSHIP   SEPARATION

"face to face, that your joy may be made full."

OUR CHARACTER: [TRUTH IN / WITH] US

OUR ACTIVITY: [OBEDIENCE / LOVE]

OUR BOUNDARY: [abiding "within" the limits of TRUTH]

IF TRUTH IS IN US ➡ THIS IS HOW WE WILL LIVE

ABIDE WITHIN THE BOUNDARIES OF TRUE TEACHING

abiding "within" the limits of TRUTH

SEPARATION FROM FALSE TEACHERS

KEY WORDS:

Truth
Love
Commandment
Teaching
Walk
Abide

KEY VERSE: 2

"For the sake of truth which abides in us and will be with us forever."

XII. Survey of 2 John

1. Read this short letter a few times, observing key words and phrases. Mark your Bible as you read.

2. According to the text, what were some of the conditions existing at this time that occasioned the writing of the epistle? What were some of John's main purposes in writing the letter?

3. Mark your Bible to show paragraph beginnings at these verses: 1, 4, 7, 12. Read the paragraphs and assign a title for each. What is the main subject of each paragraph? Is there an introduction and conclusion?

4. Compare the paragraphs starting with verses four and seven.

5. Study the subject of *truth* from paragraph to paragraph.

6. Study Chart 117. Compare its outlines and solitary entries with observations you have already made. For new items, refer to the Bible text to justify the entries.

7. Note the title assigned to 2 John.

XIII. Prominent Subjects of 2 John

Study the Bible text and record what John teaches about each of these subjects: truth (1-3); commandment (4-6); teaching (7-11).

XIV. Theme, Key Words and Verses for 2 John

What key words and verses do you observe in 2 John? Compare these with the ones shown on Chart 117.

In your own words, what is the theme of 2 John?

XV. Applications of 2 John

Write a list of applications based on this second letter of John. For example, what does it mean for a Christian to walk in the truth?

XVI. Review Questions on 2 John

1. How is the author identified in the text?

2. To whom was this letter sent?

3. When and where was it written?

4. Why was the early church's recognition of the divine inspiration of 2 and 3 John delayed?

5. What is the main point of each of the four paragraphs?

6. Name some key words, and quote a key verse.

XVII. Further Study of 2 John

Topical studies on each of the three words, *grace*, *mercy*, and *peace* are recommended.

XVIII. Outline

2 JOHN: Truth and the Christian
    SALUTATION   vv. 1-3
    WALKING IN THE TRUTH   4-6
        Report   4
        Appeal   5-6
    ABIDING IN THE TRUTH   7-11
        Warning Against False Teachers   7-9
        Prohibition against Aiding False Teachers   10-11
    GREETINGS   12-13

XIX. Background of 3 John

A. AUTHOR, DATE AND PLACE WRITTEN

The author is John the apostle; date and place are essentially the same as for 2 John: A.D. 90, the city of Ephesus.

B. ADDRESSEE

Third John is addressed to a man, Gaius, whereas 2 John is addressed to a woman. There is no way to identify who this Gaius was. The name itself was one of the most commonly used names of the Roman Empire. Men of the New Testament with this name are:

1. Gaius of Macedonia (Acts 19:29)
2. Gaius of Derbe (Acts 20:4)
3. Gaius of Corinth (Rom. 16:23)
4. Gaius whom Paul baptized, who may be the same as Gaius of Corinth (1 Cor. 1:14).

There is no reference in 3 John to Gaius's being an official in the church. We may regard him as an active lay member, a personal friend of John.

C. OCCASION

An immediate occasion for writing this letter was Diotrephes's rejection of messengers of the gospel whom John had sent to the church, of which Gaius and Diotrephes were members (3 John 9-10).

XX. Survey of 3 John

1. First, compare the length of this letter with that of 2 John.
2. Compare 2 and 3 John concerning:
    a. salutation and conclusion
    b. similar repeated words and phrases

        c. tone

        d. church problems

        e. what is taught about God and Christ (account for the small amount of theological teaching in 3 John).

3. Mark your Bible to show paragraphs beginning at these verses: 1, 2, 3, 5, 9, 13.

4. Read the letter a few times and underline key words, phrases, and verses as you read. What are your impressions of the letter?

5. Assign paragraph titles. What is the subject of each paragraph?

6. What is the epistle mainly about — doctrine, narrative, command, warning, prophecy, personal communication?

7. Where in the epistle does John write about truth? Construct an outline revolving around that concept.

8. What three men are mentioned by name in 3 John?

9. Where in the letter does John write about love?

10. Study Chart 118. Compare the outlines and recorded points with observations you have made in your survey of the epistle.

11. What title is assigned to 3 John on the chart? What is the title derived from, as shown on the chart?

XXI. Prominent Subjects of 3 John

A. THE LOCAL CHURCH

The local church is prominent in the lines of 3 John. As you study the letter, keep before your mind the church of the twentieth century. Observe what the epistle teaches, interpret the meanings, and apply these to the contemporary scene. Of course, because of its brevity, the epistle cannot speak about many of the aspects of church life. But it does single out important items, thereby fulfilling its intended purpose.

B. CHRISTIAN HOSPITALITY

Study the letter, especially verses 5-8, for what it teaches about the important ministry of Christian hospitality for God's people.

C. WARM CHRISTIAN RELATIONSHIPS

John's epistles end on a bright, warm note in the last two words: "by name" (3 John 14). The words are an appropriate reflection of the man who wrote them. A. Plummer writes, "S. John as shepherd of the Churches of Asia would imitate the Good Shepherd and know all his sheep by name."[14]

---

14. A. Plummer, *The Epistles of St. John*, p. 153.

CHART 118

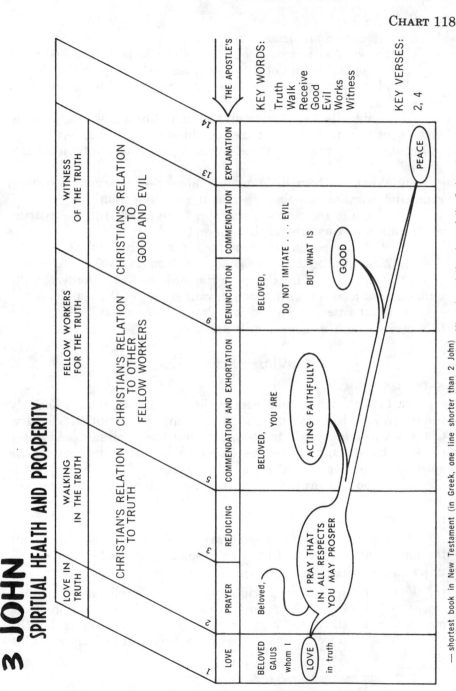

3 JOHN
SPIRITUAL HEALTH AND PROSPERITY

LOVE IN TRUTH	WALKING IN THE TRUTH	FELLOW WORKERS FOR THE TRUTH	WITNESS OF THE TRUTH
CHRISTIAN'S RELATION TO TRUTH		CHRISTIAN'S RELATION TO OTHER FELLOW WORKERS	CHRISTIAN'S RELATION TO GOOD AND EVIL

LOVE	PRAYER	REJOICING	COMMENDATION AND EXHORTATION	DENUNCIATION	COMMENDATION	EXPLANATION
1	2	3	5	9		13	14

THE APOSTLE'S

BELOVED GAIUS whom I LOVE in truth

Beloved, I PRAY THAT IN ALL RESPECTS YOU MAY PROSPER

Beloved, YOU ARE ACTING FAITHFULLY

BELOVED, DO NOT IMITATE . . . EVIL BUT WHAT IS GOOD

PEACE

KEY WORDS:
Truth
Walk
Receive
Good
Evil
Works
Witness

KEY VERSES:
2, 4

— shortest book in New Testament (in Greek, one line shorter than 2 John)
— epistle gives an intimate glimpse into some aspects of church life in Asia Minor toward the close of the first century

XXII. Theme, Key Words and Verses for 3 John

What key words and verses did you observe in your study? Compare them with the list on Chart 118. How would you identify the theme of this personal letter?

XXIII. Applications from 3 John

Make a list of ten practical lessons for today taught by this epistle.

XXIV. Review Questions on 3 John

1. Who is the author of 3 John? To whom did he write the letter?
2. What was one immediate situation that brought on the writing of this letter?
3. What does John write in the introduction (1) and conclusion (13-14) of the letter?
4. What is the main point of these three parts: 2-4; 5-8; 9-12?
5. Name some key words and quote a key verse of 3 John.
6. Describe the tone of this letter.

XXV. Further Study of 3 John

With the help of outside sources, study the three persons mentioned in 3 John: Gaius, Diotrephes, and Demetrius.

XXVI. Outline

3 JOHN: Spiritual Health and Prosperity
Salutation	v. 1
CHRISTIAN'S RELATION TO TRUTH	2-4
CHRISTIAN'S RELATION TO OTHER	
FELLOW WORKERS	5-8
CHRISTIAN'S RELATION TO GOOD	
AND EVIL	9-12
Greetings	13-14

XXVII. Background of Jude

The epistle of Jude is a passionate plea to Christians to beware of spiritual contamination by evil men. Jude had originally intended to write a doctrinal epistle, dwelling on the grand subject of salvation. But the infiltration of false teachers and immoral persons into Christian circles had become so widespread that Jude was constrained by the Spirit to devote most of his letter to warning his fellow believers about that serious threat.

A. AUTHOR AND ADDRESSEES

The author is identified in verse 1 by name: Jude; kinship: brother of James; and relation to Christ: servant (bondslave). There are strong reasons for believing that this James was the half brother of Jesus, which associates Jude to Jesus in the same way. (On James, read Matt. 13:55; Mark 6:3; Acts 12:17; 15:13; 21:18 ff.; Gal. 1:19; 2:9.) If Jude was Jesus' half brother, then he became a believer after Christ's resurrection (see John 7:5 and Acts 1:14). From verse 17 we gather that Jude did not class himself as an apostle.

Those to whom Jude wrote this letter may have been members of Jewish churches of Palestine or Asia Minor, where he probably was ministering at this time.

B. DATE

A suggested date for the writing of the epistle is around A.D. 67-68, shortly before the fall of Jerusalem (A.D. 70).[15]

C. OCCASION AND PURPOSE

Jude clearly states in his epistle what impelled him to write what he did. The leaven of such evils as gross immorality, antinomianism, rejection of the lordship of Christ, and mockery was beginning to spread in the churches through the influences of "certain men" (e.g., v. 4).[16] This stirred Jude to write what Dean Alford has called "an impassioned invective, in the impetuous whirlwind of which the writer is hurried along ... laboring for words and images strong enough to depict the polluted character of the licentious apostates against whom he is warning the Church."[17] It is for this content that S. Maxwell Coder calls the book of Jude "The Acts of the Apostates." Read verses 3, 17, 21, and 22 for Jude's commands to his readers in view of the threatening situation.

D. CANONICITY

Like 2 and 3 John, Jude was not recognized as canonical as early as were the longer books of the New Testament. Its brevity, nonapostolic authorship, polemical character, and apparent use of apocryphal sources delayed the church's acceptance. But the acceptance came, and the epistle deservedly found its place among the other inspired New Testament books.[18]

---

15. See Chart 1, page 20. If verses 17 and 18 refer to things Peter wrote in 2 Peter (e.g., 3:3), then Jude was written after Peter's epistles.
16. The word *antinomianism* comes from *anti-nomos* ("against law"), and represents a libertine spirit that rejects the restrictions of commandments as such.
17. Quoted by J. H. Kerr, *Introduction to the New Testament*, p. 308.
18. See D. Edmond Hiebert, *The Non-Pauline Epistles*, pp. 159-64, for a discussion of the canonicity of Jude.

E. REFERENCES TO OLD TESTAMENT HISTORY

For background to Jude's references to past history, read the passages cited in the accompanying chart.

JUDE'S REFERENCES TO THE OLD TESTAMENT

JUDE PASSAGE	EVENT REFERRED TO
v. 5 (Israelites)	Num. 13-14 (cf. 1 Cor. 10:5-10)
v. 6 (fallen angels)	cf. 2 Pet. 2:4
v. 7 (Sodom and Gomorrah)	Gen. 18-19
v. 11 (Cain)	Gen. 4
v. 11 (Balaam)	Num. 22-24
v. 11 (Korah)	Num. 16
v. 14 (Enoch)	cf. Gen. 5:18-24

XXVIII. SURVEY OF JUDE

A. READINGS

1. First mark paragraph divisions in your Bible beginning at verses 1, 3, 5, 8, 14, 17, 24.

2. Read the epistle once or twice for initial observations. What are your first impressions? Assign a title to each paragraph.

3. What is the general tone of the epistle? What is Jude's main burden?

4. How much Old Testament history does Jude use to support his message?

5. What paragraphs mainly have an Old Testament historical association? What paragraphs diagnose the times of Jude's writing?

6. Observe every appearance of the word "beloved" and the phrase "but you, beloved."

7. Compare the first two and the last two verses.

8. Where is there a main turning point in the epistle?

9. Jude has been called the "vestibule to the book of Revelation." What future events are cited?

10. From the things Jude says, how intimately did he know his readers?

B. SURVEY CHART

1. Study Chart 119 carefully, and compare outlines and observations with those you made in your survey studies.

2. How is the turning point shown on the chart?

3. What paragraphs are mainly *exhortation*?

4. Note the three central paragraphs of *warning*. How is each identified? Refer to the Bible text to justify this outline.

5. What title is given to this epistle?

6. Would you say that the organization of the epistle is very orderly?

XXIX. PROMINENT SUBJECTS OF JUDE

A. JUDGMENTS OF GOD

Jude cites past judgments of God (5-7) to strengthen the prophecies of judgments to come (13b-16). The sins and sinners of judgments are graphically described in verses 8-13.

One of Jude's references to God's judgments is his citing of Enoch's prophecy (read vv. 14-15). Of the apocryphal book of Enoch, Wuest writes:

> This book, known to the Church Fathers of the second century, lost for some centuries with the exception of a few fragments, was found in its entirety in a copy of the Ethiopic Bible in 1773 by Bruce. It consists of revelations purporting to have been given to Enoch and Noah. Its object is to vindicate the ways of divine providence, to set forth the retribution reserved for sinners, and to show that the world is under the immediate government of God.[19]

Bible scholars are not in agreement as to whether Jude is here quoting from the apocryphal book of Enoch, or referring to an unrecorded prophecy of the Enoch of Genesis.[20]

Jude writes to warn his readers about these awful judgments. But he also gives *positive* counsel to guard Christians against the snares of ungodly persons. Two key exhortations are "Contend earnestly for the faith which was once for all delivered to the saints" (v. 3); and "keep yourselves in the love of God" (v. 21).

B. ANGELS

Angels are part of Jude's message. Note the two references.

1. Fallen angels "angels who did not keep their own domain" (v. 6). Peter also teaches the fact of the fall of evil angels (2 Pet. 2:4). Some identify Lucifer, who became Satan, as one of these angels. Such commentators derive their interpretation from Isaiah 14:12-17; Ezekiel 28:12-19; Matthew 25:41; and Revelation 12:4. Others hold

---

19. Kenneth S. Wuest, *In These Last Days*, p. 251.
20. See Charles C. Ryrie, "I, II, III John," *The Wycliffe Bible Commentary*, p. 1489.

CHART 119

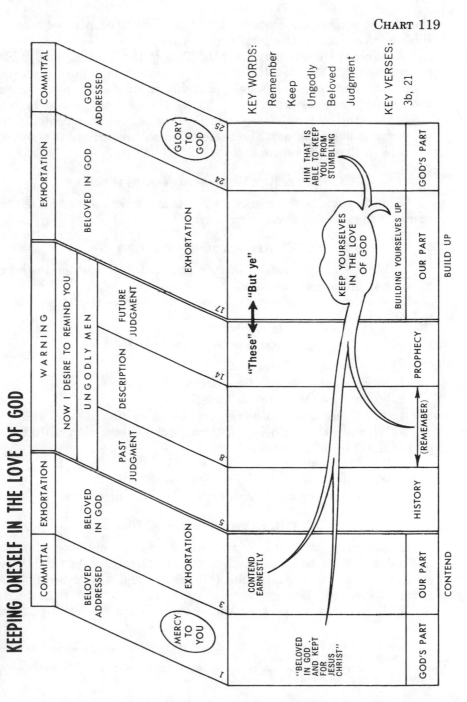

JUDE

KEEPING ONESELF IN THE LOVE OF GOD

| COMMITTAL | EXHORTATION | WARNING | EXHORTATION | COMMITTAL |

| BELOVED ADDRESSED | BELOVED IN GOD | NOW I DESIRE TO REMIND YOU — UNGODLY MEN | BELOVED IN GOD | GOD ADDRESSED |

MERCY TO YOU

GLORY TO GOD

PAST JUDGMENT | FUTURE JUDGMENT | DESCRIPTION

EXHORTATION

"These" — "But ye"

CONTEND EARNESTLY

KEEP YOURSELVES IN THE LOVE OF GOD

HIM THAT IS ABLE TO KEEP YOU FROM STUMBLING

BUILDING YOURSELVES UP

"BELOVED IN GOD AND KEPT FOR JESUS CHRIST"

(REMEMBER)

| GOD'S PART | OUR PART | HISTORY | PROPHECY | OUR PART | GOD'S PART |

CONTEND | BUILD UP

1 3 5 8 14 17 24 25

KEY WORDS:

Remember
Keep
Ungodly
Beloved
Judgment

KEY VERSES:

3b, 21

that Jude 6 refers to Genesis 6:1-4.[21] Many Bible students feel that no Bible account records the details of this event.

2. Michael the archangel (v. 9). This is the only explicit Bible reference to this Michael. His chief responsibility may have been the care of the Jewish people. Jude is probably citing a story given in the apocryphal book, Assumption of Moses. In so doing, Jude is not recognizing the book as having canonical status, but he is recognizing the event as being factual. The same principle applies to his quote of the book of Enoch in verses 14-15.

XXX. THEME, KEY WORDS AND VERSES FOR JUDE

What key words and verses do you identify with Jude? State the theme of the epistle in your own words.

XXXI. APPLICATIONS FROM JUDE

1. What forces threaten Christ's church today, similar to those mentioned in the epistle?

2. In your own words, paraphrase Jude 17-25 as the verses apply to Christians today.

XXXII. REVIEW QUESTIONS ON JUDE

1. Identify the author of Jude.
2. To whom was the epistle written?
3. When did Jude write the letter?
4. What were some of Jude's purposes in writing?
5. Why was there a delay in the church's recognition of Jude as part of the inspired Scriptures?
6. What is the main section of Jude (5-16) mostly about?
7. Where in Jude is there a turning point?
8. Name five key words of Jude, and quote a key verse.

XXXIII. FURTHER STUDY OF JUDE

1. Study the similarities of the epistles of Jude and 2 Peter. With the aid of outside sources, reach a conclusion regarding how these similarities can be accounted for. (For example, did Jude use Peter's letter as a source?)

2. Read what various authors have written concerning these subjects:[22]

---

21. See S. Maxwell Coder, *Jude: The Acts of the Apostates*, pp. 36-43, for a defense of this view.

22. A highly recommended book for supplementary study is S. Maxwell Coder, *Jude: The Acts of the Apostates*.

a. the Bible's full teaching about the evil angels' fall (v. 6)

b. Jude's sources for his references to Michael the archangel (v. 9) and Enoch (vv. 14-15).

XXXIV. OUTLINE

XXXV. SELECTED READING FOR THE EPISTLES OF JOHN AND JUDE

GENERAL INTRODUCTION

Drummond, R. J., and Morris, Leon. "1, 2, 3 John." In *The New Bible Commentary*, pp. 1259-60; 1270-71.

Hiebert, D. Edmond. *An Introduction to the Non-Pauline Epistles.* Pages 159-80 (Jude); pp. 181-228 (1, 2, 3 John).

Ryrie, Charles C. "I, II, III John," In *The Wycliffe Bible Commentary*, pp. 1463-66.

COMMENTARIES

Candlish, R. S. *The First Epistle of John.*

Coder, S. Maxwell. *Jude: the Acts of the Apostates.*

Leaney, A.R.C. *The Letters of Peter and Jude.*

Plummer, A. *The Epistles of St. John.*

OTHER RELATED SOURCES

Findlay, G. C. *Fellowship in the Life Eternal.*

Ironside, H. A. *Addresses on the Epistle of John.*

Thomas, Robert L., ed. *New American Standard Exhaustive Concordance of the Bible.*

Thomas, W. H. Griffith. *Life and Writings of the Apostle John.*

Vincent, Marvin R. *Word Studies in the New Testament*, vol. 2.

Wuest, Kenneth S. *In These Last Days.*

Part 4

THE CLIMAX

Christ Triumphant

The book of Revelation is the climax of God's Book, the last chapter of world history. The opening book of Genesis records the beginnings of the universe and the human race, and this closing book prophetically views the coming eternal new heaven and new earth. In Revelation, Genesis's reporting of man's Fall and consequent curse sees its fulfillment in divine judgments for sin, which reaches into eternity.

Truly a study of the Bible is incomplete without a study of Revelation.

REVELATION

24

Apocalypse: The Revelation of Jesus Christ

The book of Revelation (Apocalypse) is the written record of dramatic, God-sent visions given to one of God's servants. John says he was "in the Spirit on the Lord's day" (1:10) when he heard and saw the things that he was commanded to write down. A study of this last book of the Bible can be one of the most fascinating and awe-inspiring experiences you can have.

I. BACKGROUND

This section of the background of Revelation should be studied carefully as a solid preparation for surveying the Bible text.

A. AUTHOR

Four times the author is identified by name as John (1:1, 4, 9; 22:8). Read the verses and note how John relates himself to others. Both internal and external witness is strong in identifying this John as the beloved apostle, author of the gospel and the three epistles. It is interesting to note that John does not name himself in the gospel or in his epistles, whereas he does so here. This may be because the very nature of prophecy calls for identification and credentials of the author.

B. DATE AND DESTINATION

John probably wrote this book around A.D. 96, at the end of the reign of the Roman emperor Domitian (A.D. 81-96). Domitian banished John to the Island of Patmos (see Map Y) because of his Christian stand (Rev. 1:9). In such trying circumstances the apostle received visions from God, which he recorded on a scroll.

The Geography of Revelation

HISTORICAL SETTING OF REVELATION CHART 120

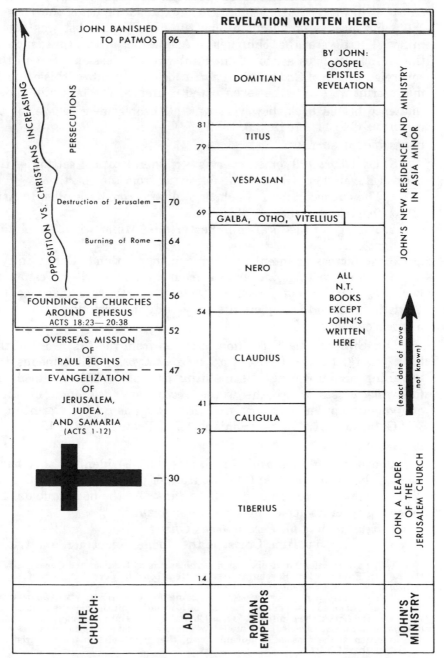

REVELATION WRITTEN HERE

JOHN BANISHED TO PATMOS — 96

BY JOHN:
GOSPEL
EPISTLES
REVELATION

DOMITIAN

81
79
TITUS

VESPASIAN

PERSECUTIONS

OPPOSITION VS. CHRISTIANS INCREASING

Destruction of Jerusalem — 70
69

GALBA, OTHO, VITELLIUS

Burning of Rome — 64

NERO

ALL
N.T.
BOOKS
EXCEPT
JOHN'S
WRITTEN
HERE

FOUNDING OF CHURCHES AROUND EPHESUS
ACTS 18:23— 20:38
56
54
52

OVERSEAS MISSION OF PAUL BEGINS
47

CLAUDIUS

EVANGELIZATION OF JERUSALEM, JUDEA, AND SAMARIA
(ACTS 1-12)
41
37

CALIGULA

— 30

TIBERIUS

14

JOHN'S NEW RESIDENCE AND MINISTRY IN ASIA MINOR

(exact date of move not known)

JOHN A LEADER OF THE JERUSALEM CHURCH

THE CHURCH:

A.D.

ROMAN EMPERORS

JOHN'S MINISTRY

God directed John to send his inspired manuscript to seven churches in western Asia Minor (Turkey). Read the list of churches in 1:11, and observe on the map how the order of the list was determined. There were other churches in Asia Minor at this time, such as the church at Colossae, to whom Paul wrote Colossians. But in the sovereign design of God the *designated* local recipients of this original manuscript were only the seven listed churches. The larger intended audience of the book, however, was all people, everywhere, of all centuries (2:7, 11, 17, 19; 3:6, 13, 22).

C. HISTORICAL SETTING

Study Chart 120 for an overview of the historical setting of the book of Revelation.[1] Observe the following from the chart:

1. The change of area of John's ministry from Jerusalem to Asia Minor (particularly the city of Ephesus).

2. The age of the local churches of Asia Minor when Revelation was written.

3. An increasing intensity of imperial opposition to Christianity.[2]

4. John's writings, separated from the other New Testament books by a period of fifteen to twenty years, were given to the Christian church to complete the body of divine Scripture.

D. TITLE OF THE BOOK

Our English title *Revelation* is taken from the first word of the book (read 1:1). The Greek word is *apokalypsis*, which means the unveiling or uncovering of something previously hidden. Read the following verses where the words *reveal* and *revelation* or their equivalents appear with that meaning: Romans 8:18; 1 Corinthians 1:7; Galatians 1:12; 2 Thessalonians 1:7; 1 Peter 1:7, 13; 4:13; 5:1.

E. THEME

The opening verses of Revelation (1:1-3) identify this basic twofold theme of the book: (1) revelation of the Person, Jesus Christ; (2) revelation of instruction for Christians.[3] As the book unfolds, the following specifics appear over and over again:

1. *Revelation of the Person Jesus Christ.*

    a. About Him. Christ is the Judge, Redeemer, and trium-

---

1. For a very informative discussion of the status of Judaism and Christianity in the Roman Empire when Revelation was written, consult Merrill C. Tenney, *Interpreting Revelation*, pp. 20-27.

2. The worst persecution was yet to come for Christians, when John wrote Revelation. This made the ominous message of Revelation all the more relevant.

3. In the Greek, the genitive "of Jesus Christ" in 1:1 is either an objective genitive (i.e., Jesus is the one revealed) or a subjective genitive (i.e., Jesus is the one revealing). The intention of the passage is probably both, that is, revelation *about* Christ and revelation *from* Christ.

phant King. The book of Revelation is the climax of the Christocentric theme of the Bible. See Chart 41, page 180.

b. From and by Him. This in word (e.g., 1:2; 2:1—3:22), and in deed (e.g., 5:5).

2. *Revelation of instruction for Christians.*

a. Prophecy. Most of the book predicts events future to John's day, especially those of the end of time. And most of that predictive section describes divine judgments of sin; the last few chapters describe the glorious triumphs of Christ culminating in a thousand-year reign (20:1-6) and in an eternal heaven (chaps. 21-22).

b. Historical perspective. Revelation shows world history of the end times as God views it, and it describes His application of justice to both individuals and nations. World history is sovereignly controlled by God and will culminate in the Person of Jesus Christ (read 11:15).

c. Doctrinal instruction. If Revelation were the only book of the Bible, we would still have much light on the vital areas of truth, such as man, sin, angels, Satan, judgment, salvation, church, worship, heaven, hell, and the Trinity.

d. Spiritual application. Exhortation is another aspect of the theme of Revelation, made very prominent in the book. As an example, read 1:3 and note the three words "read," "hear," and "heed."

F. PURPOSES

Revelation is addressed to believers (God's "bond-servants," 1:1), although its message is a loud and clear warning to unbelievers as well. It is a book "for a troubled age ... in which the darkness deepens, fear spreads over all mankind, and monstrous powers, godless and evil, appear on the stage of history."[4]

The book encourages Christians to persevere under the stress of persecution, in hope of justice that must ultimately triumph at the enthronement of Jesus Christ as King of kings and Lord of lords. Christians living in John's day, under the growing threat of imprisonment, and even death, by Emperor Domitian, found comforting refuge in the message of Revelation, even as have persecuted Christians of all the ages since then.

The book of Revelation also warns Christians against the treacherous swamplands of apostasy, and it appeals for a faithful

4. Wilbur M. Smith, "Revelation," in *The Wycliffe Bible Commentary*, p. 1492.

allegiance to Christ. The letters of chapters 2 and 3 especially emphasize such warnings and appeals.

Revelation does not aim to give all the prophetic details of the end times. Nor is the program of church history spelled out. Enough details are recorded to (1) describe the crucial events (such as the great white throne judgment, 20:11-15); (2) portray the large movements and trends of world history; and (3) teach spiritual principles underlying God's sovereign plan.

G. APOCALYPTIC WRITING

Revelation is prophetic in character and apocalyptic in form.[5] Here are some of its major features as apocalyptic literature:[6]

1. mainly eschatological (*eschatos*: last times)
2. written during times of persecution
3. visions abound
4. style generally figurative, with an abundance of symbols.

H. SYMBOLISM OF REVELATION

As noted earlier, Revelation is filled with symbols, such as numbers, colors, animals, stones, persons, groups, places, and actions. Three categories of symbols appear in the book: (1) those interpreted in the text itself (e.g., 1:20); (2) those to be interpreted in the light of Old Testament usage; (3) symbols of no apparent biblical connection. (See Further Study.)

I. SCHOOLS OF INTERPRETATION

Basically, there are four different schools of interpretation of the book of Revelation. These are shown on Chart 121. Observe on the chart where each view places each of the twenty-two chapters of Revelation. This is one of the best ways to see the major differences between the schools. Observe the following descriptions of the different views.

1. The symbolic view interprets Revelation as only a series of pictures teaching spiritual truths. It sees no prophecy of specific historical events in Revelation. The first and last chapters of the book are a clear argument against such a static view.

2. The preterist view sees all of Revelation historically fulfilled in the first century, with eternal destinies taught in the last two chapters. This view suffers much of the anemia of the symbolic view.

---

5. Other apocalyptic books of the Bible are Daniel, Ezekiel, and Zechariah. Because Revelation's apocalyptic form made it so different from the other New Testament books, there was delay in this book's being accepted as canonical by the Eastern church. The Western church, however, early recognized Revelation's divine inspiration.

6. In many ways Revelation differs from noncanonical apocalyptic writings, such as in its overall optimism, moral urgency, and identification of authorship.

3. The continuous-historical view applies Revelation prophetically to all the centuries since the time of Christ. Only chapters 19-22 foretell events after Christ's second coming. Proponents of this view differ widely in identifying historical events prophesied in chapters 4-18. Some typical interpretations are shown on the chart (e.g., the mighty angel of chap. 10 is the Reformation).

4. Of the four schools, the futurist position sees most of Revelation (chaps. 4-22) as prophetical of the *end times*.

5. There are two kinds of futurists: (1) those who hold that the seven churches of chapters 2-3 represent periods of church history up to the rapture (as shown on the chart); and (2) those who hold that chapters 2-3 are intended not to be prophetic, but rather descriptive of the churches in John's day, with chapter 4 beginning the predictive section. This view also sees the seven letters as descriptive of local churches of all ages, up to the end times.

CHART 121

THE FOUR MAIN SCHOOLS OF INTERPRETATION OF REVELATION

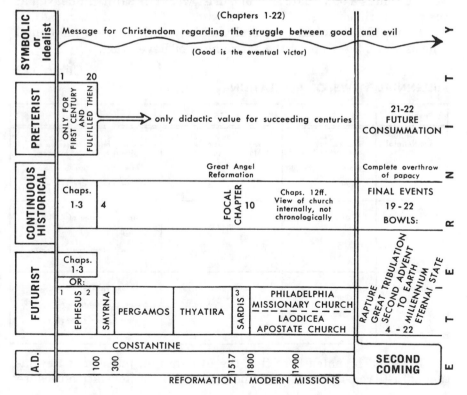

J. MILLENNIAL VIEWS

The Millennium passage of 20:1-6 is the classic passage giving rise to three different viewpoints of the "thousand years." Here are the main tenets of these schools of eschatology:

1. *Premillennialism*. Christ will come to the earth *before* (hence the prefix *pre*) the Millennium begins, to rule the world with His saints, for a literal one thousand years. Satan is bound, as to activity and power, during this time.

2. *Postmillennialism*. The second coming of Christ is at the end of, or after *(post)* the Millennium. This millennium is a period of time (not necessarily a literal thousand years) of blessedness, prosperity, and well-being for God's kingdom in the world. According to this view, we are now living in the Millennium. This school has relatively few adherents today, for the simple reason of the apparent intense current activity of Satan throughout the world.

3. *Amillennialism*. There is no (prefix *a*) literal reign of Christ on this earth for a literal thousand years. A common view is that the Millennium is a spiritual reign of Christ with His saints in heaven at the present time.

Chart 122 shows in a general way how each of these millennial schools views the scope of the entire book of Revelation.

CHART 122

MILLENNIAL VIEWS OF REVELATION

Revelation	1-3	4-18	19-22
Premillennial	First-century churches; (possibly representative of historical stages)	generally same as futurist school	—Christ returns to set up a literal millennial kingdom —great white throne judgment —new heaven and new earth
Postmillennial	First-century churches	generally same as continuous-historical school	—second coming of Christ —last judgments —new heaven and new earth
Amillennial	First-century churches	symbolic, preterist, or continuous-historical school	—second coming of Christ —last judgments —new heaven and new earth

It should be noted here that the Millennium passage of Revelation (20:1-6) constitutes a very small proportion of Revelation because the book does not purpose to give a detailed description of the church and Israel in the end times.

K. RELATION TO OTHER SCRIPTURES

The book of Revelation is the natural climax and conclusion to all the other Scriptures. Genesis is the book of beginnings ("In the beginning," Gen. 1:1); Revelation is the book of consummation ("for ever and ever," Rev. 22:5). And, as Revelation 22:13 boldly asserts, Jesus is the key to all of history, for He is "Alpha and the Omega, the first and the last, the beginning and the end."

1. *Relation to the Old Testament.* Allusions to Old Testament imagery and prophecy appear throughout Revelation, though there are no direct quotations as such. Of its 404 verses, it has been observed that 265 contain lines that embrace approximately 550 Old Testament references. A few examples of allusions to the Old Testament are listed in the accompanying chart. Read the passages involved.

REVELATION'S ALLUSIONS TO THE OLD TESTAMENT

OT	Revelation	OT	Revelation
Jer 51	chap. 18 (Babylon)	Dan 7:13; Zec 12:10, 12	1:7
Dan. 7, 8	chap. 13 (2 beasts)	Dan 7:9, 13; 10:5	1:14
Zec 4	chap. 11 (olive trees and candlesticks)	Dan 10:6; Eze 1:24	1:15
		Is 11:4; 49:2	1:16
Dan 12:7	12:14 (time periods)	Is 44:6; 48:12	1:17
Ex 19:6	1:6	Is 38:10	1:18

2. *Relation to the New Testament as a whole.* Review Chart 41, page 180, which shows some of this relationship. Spend more time thinking about how Revelation is a vital complement to the other New Testament books.

3. *Relation to the Olivet discourse* (Matt. 24:1—25:46; Mark 13:1-37; Luke 21:5-36). This would be a good time for you to reread this prophetic discourse of Jesus, which concerns the end times and His second coming. Keep its prophecies in mind as you study Revela-

tion. Some expositors consider the Olivet discourse to be the key to an understanding of the prophetic calendar of Revelation.[7]

4. *Relation to John's other writings*. John was given the happy privilege of writing about the gospel of *life* in three different kinds of Scripture. These may be compared in this way:

> *The fourth gospel* (biography):
> Eternal *life* for the Christian
> *Three epistles* (letters):
> Divine *life* in Christian living today
> *The Revelation* (visions):
> Victorious *life* now and for eternity

It was not by coincidence that the last three inspired sentences penned by John were on such a victorious note: "'Yes, I [Jesus] am coming quickly.' Amen. Come, Lord Jesus. The grace of the Lord Jesus be with all. Amen" (22:20-21).

II. SURVEY

A. FIRST READINGS

Scan through the entire book of Revelation in one sitting, not reading every word as such, but glancing at its content in a general way. Record your first impressions. For example, how much of the book is action? How much is description?

One effective way of viewing the overall movement of a book is to observe the opening phrases of most of its paragraphs. Do this for the paragraphs of Revelation. What does this scanning reveal concerning the general contents of Revelation?

B. FURTHER READINGS

1. Go through the book again to identify the main subject of each chapter. Record chapter titles on a worksheet.

2. Look for *groups* of chapters according to content. What chapters record the following groups: letters to the churches; judgments of seals; trumpets; bowls? Record those on your work sheet.

3. Songs: Mark in your Bible the songs of Revelation.[8] What is the usual theme of the songs?

4. Time references: The phrases "after this I saw" and "and I saw" appear often, suggesting an orderly *sequence* in the course of the book. Do you see any other patterns?

5. Christ: Christ appears in various forms, such as a lamb.

---

7. See Wilbur M. Smith, *A Treasury of Books for Bible Study*, pp. 235-42, for an extensive comparative study of the two scriptures.
8. The NASB identifies most of the songs by setting them in indented and blocked form (e.g., 4:11).

Merrill Tenney's outline shows the overall ministry of Christ in the book.[9]

CHRIST IN THE BOOK OF REVELATION

1:1	1:9	4:1	17:1	21:9	22:6
Christ Communicating	Christ in the Church: The Living One	Christ in the Cosmos: The Redeemer	Christ in Conquest: The Warrior	Christ In Consummation: The Lamb	Christ Challenging

6. God: Much about God can be learned from Revelation. The name "God the Almighty" appears eight times. Read these verses: 1:8; 4:8; 11:17; 15:3; 16:7, 14; 19:15; 21:22.

7. Other prominent subjects appearing in the book include: angels (seventy-six times in the text), wars, sin, Satan, beasts, thrones, the number seven, church, temple, kingdom, and geographical names. What other subjects have you observed?

8. In your survey reading did you observe the recurrence of certain phrases? Compare your observations with this list: "I was in the Spirit" (1:10; 4:2; 17:3; 21:10); "and I saw" (over forty times); "lightning . . . thunder" (4:5; 8:5; 11:19; 16:18); "It is done" (16:17; 21:6); "Blessed is (are)" (1:3; 14:13; 16:15; 19:9; 20:6; 22:7, 14).

9. How would you compare these three divisions of Revelation, on the basis of your study so far: chapters 1-5; 6-20; 21-22? This is an important exercise in your survey study.

C. SURVEY CHART

One of the clearest ways to show the structure of a book's content is by use of the survey chart. This especially applies to a book like Revelation, in which there are so many parts, movements, and complex relationships. One of the advantages of a survey chart is that one can see the many parts of the book *simultaneously* and make comparisons.

Study carefully Chart 123. Observe the following, comparing the items with your own survey.

1. There are three main divisions of Revelation. What are they? Why is a main division made at chapter 6? Why one at chapter 21? Note also the outline that divides the book into two parts: "things which are"; "things which shall be hereafter." These phrases come

9. Merrill C. Tenney, *Interpreting Revelation*, p. 33. Such an outline is arrived at in the later, more advanced stages of survey study.

CHART 123

REVELATION
THE REVELATION OF JESUS CHRIST

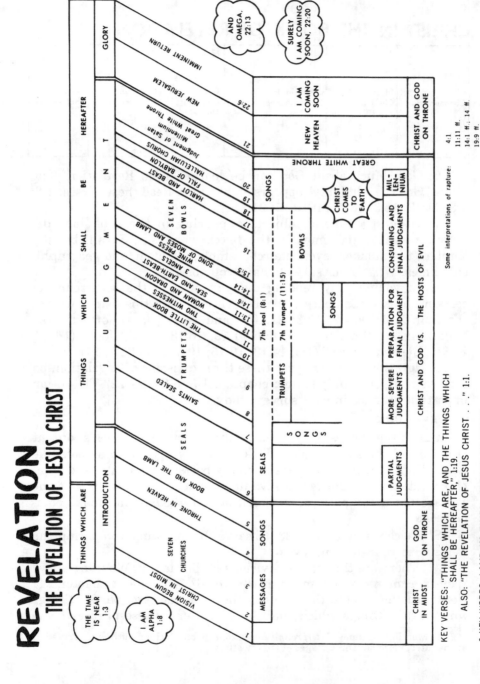

KEY VERSES: "THINGS WHICH ARE, AND THE THINGS WHICH SHALL BE HEREAFTER," 1:19.

ALSO: "THE REVELATION OF JESUS CHRIST . . ." 1:1.

2 KEY WORDS: LAMB (29 TIMES), THRONE (44 TIMES)

Some interpretations of rapture: 4:1
11:11 ff.
14:1 ff.; 14:14 ff.
19:9 ff.

from 1:19, where the time references are brought out clearly: "Write therefore the things which you have seen, and the things which are, and the things which shall take place after these things." Why is the division point for this outline made at chapter 4? As of John's day, what proportion of Revelation was history yet to be fulfilled? Compare also 1:1.

2. Judgments do not appear until chapter 6. How are chapters 1-5 introductory to the judgments?

3. For clarity's sake, a proportionately larger space is devoted on the chart to the three series of judgments than to the other events. This trio *(seals → trumpets → bowls)* is the unifying element of the judgments division (chaps. 6-20).

4. How are the judgment series (seals, trumpets, and bowls) related to each other? Observe, for example, that the seventh seal (8:1) constitutes the whole series of trumpets; and the seventh trumpet (11:15) constitutes the whole series of bowls. Is there a seventh bowl? (See chapter 16.)

5. Note that there is a parenthesis, or interlude, between the seals and trumpets and between the trumpets and bowls. How many chapters are involved in each parenthesis? (See Chart 124.)

CHART 124

THE CONTEXT OF REVELATION 10:1-15:4

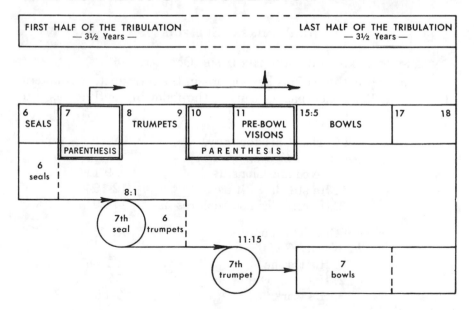

6. Observe the progression on Chart 123: partial judgments —
more severe judgments — consuming and final judgments.

7. The great white throne judgment (chap. 20) is the final
judgment for mankind. Beyond this there are no further judgments
cited in Revelation.

8. Observe on the chart how *songs* appear just before each event
or era of judgment.

9. Quantitatively, most of Revelation is about judgment and
conflict. What does this reveal concerning one of the purposes of
Revelation?

10. How do chapters 21 and 22 differ from the general content of
chapters 6-20?

11. Make a list of the chronological sequence of periods appearing
in Revelation. Include the event of Christ's return to earth. Compare
your list with the following:

      a. The church in the first century and onward (chaps. 1-5)
      b. Judgments of end times   (chaps. 6-20)
      c. Christ's return to earth   (chap. 19)
      d. The Millennium   (20:1-6)
      e. Heaven   (chaps. 21-22)

12. Continue your survey of Revelation until you are satisfied
that you have a grasp of its structure, theme, and emphases, and a
grasp of why God included it in the canon of Scripture.

III. PROMINENT SUBJECTS

A. VISIONS OF CHRIST, GOD, AND THE LAMB (Chapters 1-5)

John reports three of his key visions in the introductory chapters
of the book. Read each passage, using the following outlines as you
read:

Vision of Christ (Christophany)   1:9-20
    Jesus Christ the Son of Man
        1. He commissions us   vv. 9-11
        2. He stands with us   12-16
        3. He consoles and inspires us   17-20

Vision of God (Theophany)   4:1-11
    The Worthy God
        1. His throne   vv. 1-6*a*
        2. His character   6*b*-8
        3. His work   9-11

Vision of the Lamb	5:1-14
The Worthy Lamb	
1. Prevails with power	vv. 1-5
2. Redeems with blood	6-10
3. Merits all praise	11-14

B. LETTERS TO THE SEVEN CHURCHES (2:1—3:22)

Mainly because of the chapters' clear content, this is the section of Revelation most familiar to Christians. The section is mostly descriptive and does not have an abundance of difficult symbols and prophecies. It is like a mirror for the reader, as he sees himself and his local church described in the text.

CHART 125

REVELATION 1-5

MESSAGES AND SONGS

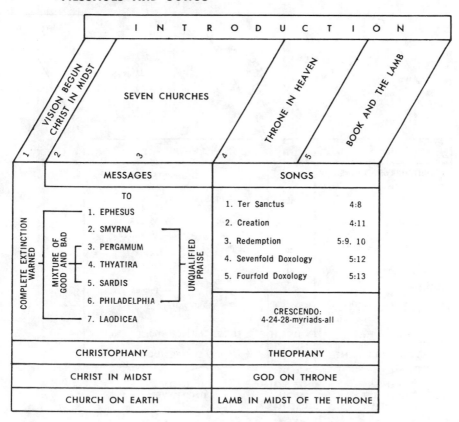

Four different views have been held concerning the purpose of the seven letters of Revelation, 2:1—3:22 (Chart 125):

1. Historical — local churches of John's day are described as examples (good or bad)
2. Representative — the different kinds of local churches also represent other of the same kinds of local churches, which coexist down through the ages
3. Restorative — the particular churches will be literally restored in the end times, as predicted

CHART 126

REVELATION 6-9

SEALS AND TRUMPETS

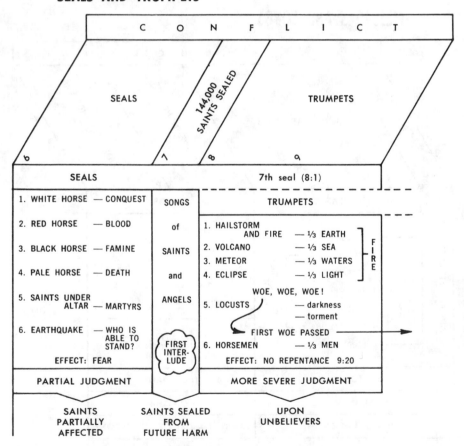

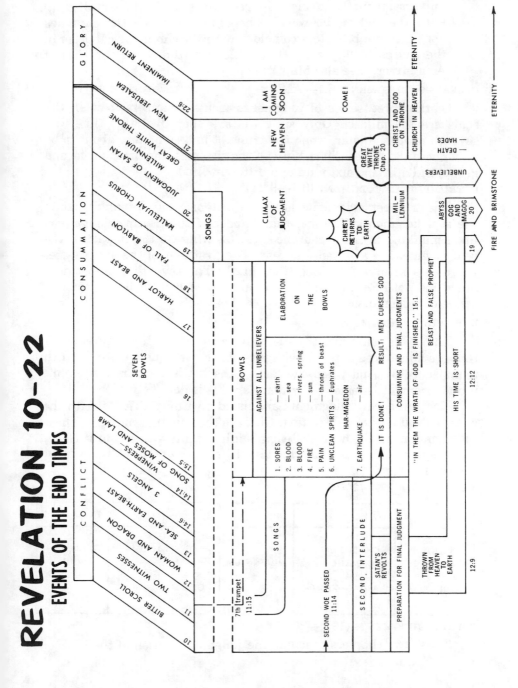

REVELATION 10–22
EVENTS OF THE END TIMES

4. Futuristic — each local church symbolizes the spiritual state of the universal church during a particular era of Christianity, up until the end of the world. The order in which the churches appear in the Bible text coincides with the chronological order of the church history eras. Chart 125 lists the seven churches of Asia Minor. (See also Map Y, page 494.)

C. SEALS OF JUDGMENT (6:1—7:17)

Of the three series of judgments (seals, trumpets, bowls), the seals are the mildest. Only six seals are opened at this time; the seventh is opened later, when the trumpet judgments are about to be announced (8:1). (See Chart 126.) Of the six seals, the first four form a group; the fifth and sixth are of a different kind.

D. TRUMPETS OF JUDGMENT (8:1—9:21)

The trumpet judgments are more intense and destructive than the seal judgments. The spiritual impact of the trumpet judgments upon mankind is "no repentance" (9:20), whereas the impact of the seal judgments was a sense of fear. The first four of the six trumpet judgments involve fire. (See Chart 126.) The seventh trumpet does not sound until Revelation 11:15, in anticipation of the bowls, the last series of judgments.

E. BOWLS OF JUDGMENT (15:1—16:21)

The bowls constitute the final and most awful of the three woes that are announced to the inhabitants of the earth just before the fifth trumpet (8:13). And when the last of the bowls is poured, heaven's pronouncement is terse, yet triumphant "It is done" (16:17).

The seven bowl judgments are listed on Chart 127. Refer to the chart as you read the Bible text. Observe the spiritual impact of these judgments upon the hearts of earth's inhabitants — men curse God.

Note on Chart 127 that chapters 17 and 18 are an elaboration of the bowl judgments.

REVELATION 19:1–20:15

19:1	19:11	20:1	20:7	20:11 20:15
—SONGS —MARRIAGE OF THE LAMB	—CHRIST'S RETURN TO EARTH —WAR: ARMAGEDDON	MILLENNIUM	—SATAN'S LOOSING —WAR: GOG AND MAGOG	GREAT WHITE THRONE JUDGMENT

F. FINAL JUDGMENTS (19:1—20:15)

These two chapters conclude the judgment section of the book of

Revelation (chaps. 6-20). Five units of the passage are identified by subject in the accompanying table.

The two battles and the great white throne judgment are shown on the premillennial timetable of Chart 128. What transpires between the two battles?

CHART 128

THE WORLD'S LAST TWO BATTLES

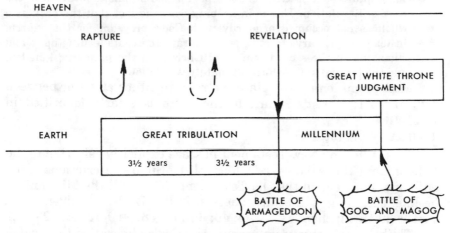

(dotted line shows the view of a midtribulation rapture)

What is the last phrase of judgment in the biblical text? (20:15)

G. THE SECOND COMING OF CHRIST

When John wrote Revelation he recorded Christ's clear words that He would return to this earth. Among those references are: 2:25, "Hold fast until I come"; 3:11, "I am coming quickly"; 22:20 (after the visions end at 22:5), "Yes, I am coming quickly."

There are references in Revelation that show that Christ will be on this earth when the particular vision being recorded is fulfilled. For example, in chapter 19, Christ the "Faithful and True" (v. 11), is shown in combat against the kings of the earth (v. 19).

The premillennialist position sees two phases of Christ's second coming, as shown on Chart 128.[10] The first is the rapture, when Christ comes to the "air" (atmosphere) above the earth to "catch up" deceased and living saints (1 Thess. 4:14-17). The second phase (sometimes known as the revelation) is His coming to earth with the

10. Chart 128 shows the view of a mid-tribulation rapture (dashed line). There is also a posttribulation view that places the rapture at the end of the Tribulation, followed immediately by Christ's return to the earth.

already-raptured saints, to conquer the hosts of Satan at the end of the Great Tribulation and to inaugurate His millennial reign. Normal questions to ask here are, Can two phases of Christ's second coming be seen in Revelation? If so, where?

Although the second coming of Christ is an important teaching of the book of Revelation, some detailed events attending it, such as the rapture, are noticeably absent. On this Walvoord writes,

> The rapture as a doctrine is not a part of the prophetic foreview of the book of Revelation. This is in keeping with the fact that the book as a whole is not occupied primarily with God's program for the church. Instead the primary objective is to portray the events leading up to and climaxing in the second coming of Christ and the prophetic kingdom and the eternal state which ultimately will follow.[11]

Most premillennialists place the rapture either at 4:1 or between 3:22 and 4:1. Christ's return to the earth is clearly identified in 19:11-21.

H. MILLENNIUM (20:1-6)

This is the one New Testament passage explicitly referring to the Millennium ("thousand years"). Most of the Bible's descriptions of the Millennium appear in the Old Testament. What will the Millennium be like, according to these prophecies: Psalm 72; Isaiah 2:2-4; 9:6-7; 11:4-9; 30:15-33; chapters 35, 44, 49; 65:17—66:14; Jeremiah 23:5-6?

The millennial kingdom is primarily God's restoration to Israel of an earthly kingdom in the last days, promised through His Old Testament prophets (see Ezekiel 20:34-38). It will come to an end after one thousand years and will be followed by the new heaven and the new earth (21:1 ff.). (See Chart 129.)

How does the chart show the Millennium to be the dwelling place of both Jewish believers and non-Jewish believers?

I. HEAVEN (21:1—22:21)

The Bible opens with the story of the creation of the heavens and earth, followed by man's sin and the curse it incurred (Gen. 1-3). The Bible closes with the appearance of a new heaven and new earth, followed by a description of the saints' eternal home, where sin and curse will have no part (Rev. 21-22).

This final section of Revelation is the brightest part of the book. Any Christian reading its pages must feel relieved to move from the long, dark catacombs of the judgment chapters (6-20) to the fresh, heavenly air of John's last visions. This glorious message for believers is God's last recorded words.

---

11. John F. Walvoord, *The Revelation of Jesus Christ*, p. 103. Walvoord's reference to "second coming" here is to Christ's return to the *earth* (19:11-21), which is a key event of Revelation.

No earthly words can fully describe heaven. John's vision was of a city — New Jerusalem — a glimpse of heaven. Use the following outline as you read the text:

CHART 129

THE MILLENNIUM IN GOD'S TIMETABLE

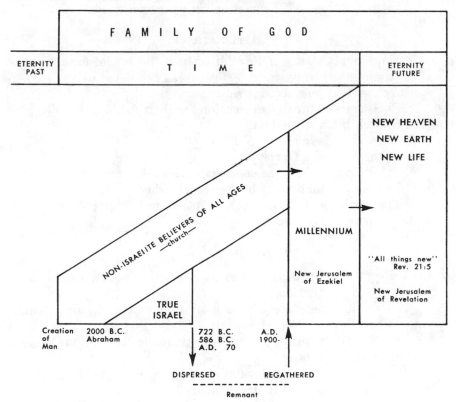

THE NEW JERUSALEM	(21:1—22:5)
1. Its Appearance in the New Universe	21:1-5
2. Its Inhabitants	21:6-8
3. Its Description	21:9-21
a. structure	21:9-14
b. dimensions	21:15-17
c. adornments	21:18-21
4. Its Exclusions	21:22-27
5. Its Life	22:1-5

What does John write about in the last section of Revelation (22:6-21)? Does he refer to heaven?

Compare verses 20 and 21. How do they conclude the Bible?

IV. THEME, KEY WORDS AND VERSES

What key words and verses did you observe in your study of Revelation? Compare these with the entries on Chart 123.

What is the theme of Revelation, in your own words?

V. APPLICATIONS

Various applications of Revelation may be made, for believers and for the nonbelieving world. A few areas are listed below. Add to the list others that you noted in your survey.

1. Christians enduring persecution for their faith.
2. Church life and conduct.
3. Sin and its judgment.
4. Witnessing as a Christian.
5. Satan and his hosts as enemies of the believer.
6. The status and destiny of the world today.
7. The ministry of Christ in redemption and judgment.
8. The hope of heaven.

VI. REVIEW QUESTIONS

1. Recall what you have learned about this book's author, date of writing, and destination.

2. Describe the state of the Christian church in the Roman Empire when Revelation was written.

3. In your own words, identify the theme of Revelation. Make a list of its main subjects.

4. In what ways was Revelation very relevant to the needs of Christians at the turn of the first century?

5. Do you think the original readers understood all the details of Revelation? Do you think John did? Is the book more understandable today in light of what is now history and in light of current events? Explain.

6. What are some of the main characteristics of Revelation as an apocalyptic writing?

7. What are the distinctive contributions of Revelation to the canon of Holy Scripture?

8. What are the three main divisions of the book of Revelation?

9. How much of Revelation is about judgment?

10. Identify, by chapter, where these groups appear: letters to seven churches, seals, trumpets, bowls.

11. Where does the Millennium appear in the text?
12. What will be the last two battles of the world?
13. Name some key words of Revelation.
14. Name and describe the different schools of interpretation of Revelation. According to which view is most of Revelation still future?
15. Compare premillennialism, postmillennialism, and amillennialism concerning their views of the Millennium.

VII. FURTHER STUDY

Because of Revelation's variety of coverage, many subjects for further study appear as one surveys the text. Here are a few:
1. what the Bible teaches about God as Judge
2. eternal judgment
3. Ezekiel and the book of Revelation compared
4. the nation of Israel in last times
5. the world of evil spirits
6. Antichrist
7. the rapture in Revelation
8. the church in Revelation
9. the Millennium
10. heaven
11. symbols in Revelation. (Recommended sources for study of this important subject are J. P. Lange, *Revelation*, pp. 14-41; Merrill C. Tenney, *Interpreting Revelation*, pp. 186-93; and John F. Walvoord, *The Revelation of Jesus Christ*, pp. 25-30.)

VIII. OUTLINE

REVELATION: The Revelation of Jesus Christ

INTRODUCTION	1:1-8
VISIONS, MESSAGES AND SONGS	1:9—5:14
John's Vision of Christ	1:9-20
Letters to the Seven Churches	2:1—3:22
Visions of God and the Lamb	4:1—5:14
JUDGMENTS	6:1—20:15
Seals of Judgment	6:1—7:17
Trumpets of Judgment	8:1—9:21
Little Book, Two Witnesses, and Seventh Trumpet	10:1—11:19
The Woman, Dragon, and Two Beasts	12:1—14:20

Bowls of Judgment	15:1 — 16:21
Fall of Babylon	17:1 — 18:24
Final Judgment	19:1 — 20:15
GLORY	21:1 — 22:20
Eternal Home of the Saints	21:1 — 22:5
"I am Coming Soon"	22:6-20
BENEDICTION	22:21

IX. Selected Reading

GENERAL INTRODUCTION

Smith, Wilbur, M. "Revelation." In *The Wycliffe Bible Commentary*, pp. 1491-1501.

Thiessen, Henry C. *Introduction to the New Testament*, pp. 316-29.

COMMENTARIES

Ladd, George E. *Commentary on the Revelation of John*.

Lange, John Peter. *Revelation*.

Newell, William R. *The Book of Revelation*.

Ryrie, Charles C. *Revelation*. Everyman's Bible Commentary.

Walvoord, John F. *The Revelation of Jesus Christ*.

OTHER RELATED SOURCES

Jensen, Irving L. *Revelation*. A Self-Study Guide.

Payne, J. Barton. *Encyclopedia of Biblical Prophecy*.

Pentecost, J. Dwight. *Prophecy for Today*.

Sauer, Erich. *From Eternity to Eternity*.

Smith, Wilbur M. *The Biblical Doctrine of Heaven*.

Tenney, Merrill C. *Interpreting Revelation*.

Appendix A

The Herodian Family
HEROD THE GREAT*
King of Judea
37–4 B.C.

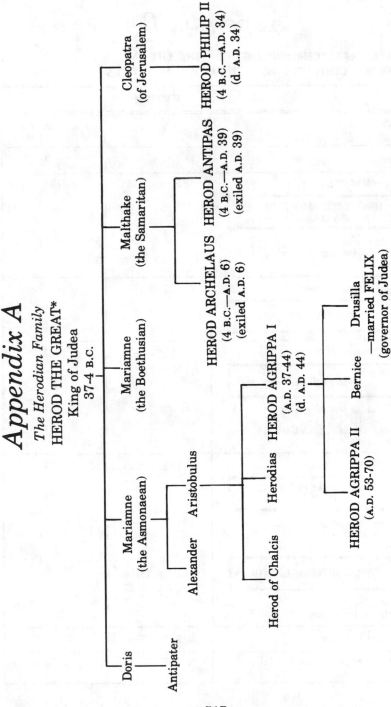

* Names of kings noted in the New Testament are capitalized

517

Appendix B

EVENT	SCRIPTURE	DATE
1. Birth		around the time of Christ's birth
2. Conversion	Ac 9:1-19a	A.D. 33
3. First missionary journey	Ac 13:1—14:28	47-48
TIMOTHY CONVERTED AT DERBE, probably in his late teens		
Galatians written possibly at the end of the mission, from Antioch		
4. At the Jerusalem council	Ac 15:1-35 Ga 2:1	49
TITUS ACCOMPANIES PAUL		
5. Second missionary journey	Ac 15:36—18:22	49-52
TIMOTHY JOINS PAUL		
Included the first mission to Thessalonica 1 and 2 Thessalonians written from Corinth		
6. Third missionary journey	Ac 18:23—21:17	52-56
ABOUT 3 YEARS IN EPHESUS, WITH TIMOTHY		
Included at least two visits to Macedonia (cf. Ac. 20:1-3; 2 Co 2:12-13)		
TITUS MINISTERS IN CORINTH	2 Co 7:6, 13, 14; 8:6, 16, 23	
1 and 2 Corinthians and Romans written on this journey		
7. Arrest at Jerusalem	Ac 21:18—23:30	56
8. Appearances before governors Felix and Festus	Ac 23:31—25:12	56-58

9.	Appearance before King Agrippa	Ac 25:13—26:32	58
10.	Journey to Rome and imprisonment Written from prison: Colossians, Ephesians, Philemon, Philippians	Ac 27:1—28:31	58-61
11.	Release from prison	cf. Phile 22; Phil 1:25	62
12.	Travels after release Eventually reaches Asia Minor **LEAVES TIMOTHY AT EPHESUS** **(1 TI 1:3)** Goes to Macedonia **WRITES TO TIMOTHY** Possibly returns to Ephesus Goes to Crete **LEAVES TITUS AT CRETE** **(TITUS 1:5)** Goes to Corinth **WRITES TO TITUS** Other journeys[1]		62-66 62 66
13.	Burning of Rome; increased persecution of Christians by Nero		64
14.	Second arrest (at Troas?)	cf. 2 Ti 1:16-17: 4:6-18	66 or 67
15.	Second imprisonment at Rome **WRITES SECOND LETTER TO TIMOTHY**		67
16.	Death Executed by Nero		67

1. Paul may have visited Spain either at the beginning or end of this period of freedom. The details of Paul's travels in between the two imprisonments are very sketchy. See D. Edmond Hiebert, *An Introduction to the Pauline Epistles*, pp. 322-23, for a suggested chronology.

Bibliography

BOOKS

Adams, J. McKee. *Biblical Backgrounds*. Rev. ed. Nashville: Broadman, 1965.

Adeney, Walter F. *The Expositor's Bible*. New York: Hodder & Stoughton, n.d.

Aharoni, Yohanan. *The Land of the Bible*. Philadelphia: Westminster, 1967.

Aharoni, Yohanan, and Avi-Yonah, Michael. *The Macmillan Bible Atlas*. New York: Macmillan, 1968.

Alford, Henry. *The Greek Testament*. Chicago: Moody, 1958.

Andrews, Samuel J. *The Life of Our Lord Upon Earth*. Rev. ed. Grand Rapids: Zondervan, 1954.

Archer, Gleason L. *A Survey of Old Testament Introduction*. Chicago: Moody, 1964.

Bailey, Albert Edward. *Daily Life in Bible Times*. New York: Scribner's, 1943.

Ball, Charles Ferguson. *The Life and Journeys of Paul*. Chicago: Moody, 1951.

Baly, Dennis. *The Geography of the Bible*. New York: Harper, 1957.

Baughman, Ray E. *Bible History Visualized*. Chicago: Moody, 1963.

Baxter, J. Sidlow, *Explore the Book*. 6 vols. Grand Rapids: Zondervan, 1960.

———. *The Strategic Grasp of the Bible*. Grand Rapids: Zondervan, 1968.

Bernard, Thomas D. *The Progress of Doctrine in the New Testament*. Grand Rapids: Eerdmans, 1949.

Blaikie, William G. *A Manual of Bible History*. Rev. ed. New York: Ronald, 1940.

Blaiklock, E. M. *The Acts of the Apostles*. The Tyndale New Testament Commentaries. Grand Rapids: Eerdmans, 1959.

———. *Mark: The Man and His Message*. Chicago: Moody, 1967.

Booth, Henry Kendall. *The Background of the Bible*. New York: Scribner's, 1930.

Bouquet, A. C. *Everyday Life in New Testament Times.* New York: Scribner's, 1953.

Broadus, John A. *Commentary on the Gospel of Matthew.* The American Commentary. Philadelphia: American Baptist Publication Soc., 1886.

Bruce, F. F. *The Acts of the Apostles.* Chicago: InterVarsity, 1952.

———. *The Books and the Parchments.* Rev. ed. Westwood, N.J.: Revell, 1963.

———. *Commentary on the Books of the Acts.* The New International Commentary on the New Testament. Grand Rapids: Eerdmans, 1954.

———. *The Epistle of Paul to the Romans.* London: Tyndale, 1963.

———. *The Epistle to the Ephesians.* Westwood, N.J.: Revell, 1961.

———. *The Epistle to the Hebrews.* The New International Commentary on the New Testament. Grand Rapids: Eerdmans, 1964.

———. *The Letters of Paul: An Expanded Paraphrase.* Grand Rapids: Eerdmans, 1965.

———. *Paul: Apostle of the Heart Set Free.* Grand Rapids: Eerdmans, 1977.

Burgon, John W. *The Last Twelve Verses of the Gospel According to S. Mark.* 1871. Reprint. Sovereign Grace Book Club, 1959.

Candlish, R. S. *The First Epistle of John.* Grand Rapids: Zondervan, 1952.

Chafer, L. S. *He That Is Spiritual.* Grand Rapids: Zondervan, 1918.

———. *Systematic Theology.* 8 vols. Dallas: Dallas Seminary, 1947. Vol. 1, *Prolegomena; Bibliology; Theology Proper.*

Chestnut, D. Lee. *The Atom Speaks.* Grand Rapids: Eerdmans, 1951.

Clark, Gordon H. *II Peter, A Short Commentary.* Nutley, N.J.: Presbyterian and Reformed, 1972.

Coder, S. Maxwell. *Jude: The Acts of the Apostates.* Everyman's Bible Commentary. Chicago: Moody, 1958.

Cole, R. A. *The Epistle of Paul to the Galatians.* Grand Rapids: Eerdmans, 1965.

———. *The Gospel According to St. Mark.* The Tyndale New Testament Commentaries. Grand Rapids: Eerdmans, 1961.

Conybeare, W. J., and Howson, J. S. *The Life and Epistles of St. Paul.* Grand Rapids: Eerdmans, 1957.

Corswant, W. A. *A Dictionary of Life in Bible Times.* New York: Oxford, 1960.

Cramer, George H. *First and Second Peter.* Chicago: Moody, 1967.

Culver, Robert D. *Daniel and the Latter Days.* Chicago: Moody, 1954.

———. *The Suffering and the Glory of the Lord's Righteous Servant.* Moline, Ill.: Christian Service, 1958.

Darrow, Karl K. *Atomic Energy.* New York: Wiley, 1948.

Davidson, F., ed. *The New Bible Commentary.* Grand Rapids: Eerdmans, 1963.

Demaray, Donald E. *Bible Study Source-Book.* Grand Rapids: Zondervan, 1972.

Douglas, J. D., ed. *The New Bible Dictionary*. Rev. ed. Grand Rapids: Eerdmans, 1965.

Dunnett, Walter M. *An Outline of New Testament Survey*. Chicago: Moody, 1960.

Earle, Ralph. *Mark: The Gospel of Action*. Everyman's Bible Commentary. Chicago: Moody, 1970.

Eason, J. Lawrence. *The New Bible Survey*. Grand Rapids: Zondervan, 1963.

Edersheim, Alfred. *The Life and Times of Jesus the Messiah*. 2 vols. Rev. ed. Grand Rapids: Eerdmans, 1953.

———. *The Temple: Its Ministry and Services*. Reprint. Grand Rapids: Eerdmans, 1950.

Erdman, Charles R. *The Epistle of Paul to the Romans*. Philadelphia: Westminster, 1942.

———. *The Pastoral Epistles of Paul*. Philadelphia: Westminster, 1923.

Ernst, Karl J. *The Art of Pastoral Counselling. A Study of the Epistle to Philemon*. Grand Rapids: Zondervan, 1941.

Fairbairn, P. *The Typology of Scripture*. Grand Rapids: Zondervan, n.d.

Farrar, F. W. *The Early Days of Christianity*. New York: Funk & Wagnalls, n.d.

———. *The Life and Work of St. Paul*. New York: Dutton, 1893.

Findlay, G. C. *Fellowship in the Life Eternal*. Grand Rapids: Eerdmans, 1955.

Finegan, Jack. *Handbook of Biblical Chronology*. Princeton: Princeton U., 1964.

———. *Light from the Ancient Past*. Princeton: Princeton U., 1959.

Foakes-Jackson, F. J., and Lake, Kirsopp, eds. *The Beginnings of Christianity*. 5 vols. London: Macmillan, 1920-1933.

Frair, Wayne, and Davis, P. William. *The Case for Creation*. Chicago: Moody, 1967.

Frank, Harry Thomas. *Discovering the Biblical World*. Maplewood, N.J.: Hammond, 1975. (Contains very helpful maps.)

Free, Joseph P. *Archaeology and Bible History*. Rev. ed. Wheaton, Ill.: Scripture Press, 1964.

Freeman, James M. *Manners and Customs of the Bible*. Plainfield, N.J.: Logos, 1973.

Gaebelein, Frank. *Philemon: The Gospel of Emancipation*. New York: Loizeaux, 1960.

Gaussen, L. *Theopneustia: The Plenary Inspiration of the Holy Scriptures*. Translated by David Scott. Rev. ed. Chicago: Bible Institute Colportage Assn., n.d.

Geisler, Norman L. *Christ: The Theme of the Bible*. Chicago: Moody, 1968.

Geisler, Norman L., and Nix, William E. *A General Introduction to the Bible*. Chicago: Moody, 1968.

Geldenhuys, Norval. *Commentary on the Gospel of Luke*. The New International Commentary on the New Testament. Grand Rapids: Eerdmans, 1951.

Gettys, Joseph M. *How to Study I Corinthians*. Richmond: John Knox, 1951.

Godet, F. *A Commentary on the Gospel of Luke.* 2 vols. Reprint. Grand Rapids: Zondervan, n.d.

———. *Commentary on the Gospel of John.* 2 vols. Grand Rapids: Zondervan, n.d.

Goodspeed, Edgar J. *An Introduction to the New Testament.* Chicago: U. of Chicago, 1937.

Goodwin, Frank J. *A Harmony of the Life of St. Paul.* 3d ed. Grand Rapids: Baker, 1953.

Gray, James M. *Synthetic Bible Studies.* New York: Revell, 1923.

Griffith-Thomas, W. H. *The Apostle John: His Life and Writing.* Grand Rapids: Eerdmans, 1946.

Grollenberg, L. H. *Atlas of the Bible.* New York: Nelson, 1956.

Gromacki, Robert G. *New Testament Survey.* Grand Rapids: Baker, 1974.

Grosvenor, Gilbert, ed. *Everyday Life in Ancient Times.* Washington, D.C.: National Geographic, 1951.

Gundry, Robert H. *A Survey of the New Testament.* Grand Rapids: Zondervan, 1970.

Guthrie, Donald. *New Testament Introduction.* 3d ed., rev. Downers Grove, Ill.: InterVarsity, 1970.

———. *A Shorter Life of Christ.* Grand Rapids: Zondervan, 1970.

Guthrie, D., and Motyer, J. A., eds. *The New Bible Commentary.* Rev. ed. Grand Rapids: Eerdmans, 1970.

Hallesby, O. *Temperament and the Christian Faith.* Minneapolis: Augsburg, n.d.

Harris, R. Laird, *Man: God's Eternal Creation.* Chicago: Moody, 1971.

Harrison, Everett F. *Introduction to the New Testament.* Grand Rapids: Eerdmans, 1964.

———. *A Short Life of Christ.* Grand Rapids: Eerdmans, 1968.

Heaton, E. W. *Everyday Life in Old Testament Times.* New York: Scribner's, 1956.

Hendriksen, William. *Bible Survey: A Treasury of Bible Information.* 3d ed. Grand Rapids: Baker, 1949.

———. *Exposition of Galatians.* New Testament Commentary. Grand Rapids: Baker, 1968.

———. *Exposition of the Gospel According to John.* New Testament Commentary. Grand Rapids: Baker, 1954.

———. *Exposition of the Gospel According to Mark.* New Testament Commentary. Grand Rapids: Baker, 1953.

Henry, Carl F. H., ed. *Revelation and the Bible.* Grand Rapids: Baker, 1958.

Hiebert, D. Edmond. *First Timothy.* Everyman's Bible Commentary. Chicago: Moody, 1957.

———. *An Introduction to the New Testament.* 3 vols. Chicago: Moody, 1975. Vol. 1, *The Gospels and Acts.*

———. *An Introduction to the New Testament.* 3 vols. Chicago: Moody, 1954. Vol. 2, *The Pauline Epistles.*

————. *An Introduction to the New Testament.* 3 vols. Chicago: Moody, 1962. Vol. 3, *The Non-Pauline Epistles and Revelation.*

————. *An Introduction to the Pauline Epistles.* Chicago: Moody, 1954.

————. *Mark: A Portrait of the Servant.* Chicago: Moody, 1974.

————. *Personalities Around Paul.* Chicago: Moody, 1973.

————. *The Thessalonian Epistles.* Chicago: Moody, 1971.

Hobart, William K. *The Medical Language of St. Luke.* London: Longmans, 1882.

Hodge, Charles. *A Commentary on the Epistle to the Ephesians.* Reprint. Grand Rapids: Eerdmans, 1950.

————. *Commentary on the Epistle to the Romans.* New York: Armstrong, 1890.

————. *An Exposition of the First Epistle to the Corinthians.* Grand Rapids: Eerdmans, n.d.

————. *Systematic Theology.* Grand Rapids: Eerdmans, 1878.

Hogg, C. F., and Vine, W. E. *The Epistle to the Galatians.* London: Pickering & Inglis, 1921.

————. *The Epistles to the Thessalonians.* London: Pickering & Inglis, 1929.

Hoyt, Herman A. *The End Times.* Chicago: Moody, 1969.

Hughes, Phillip Edgcumbe. *Paul's Second Epistle to the Corinthians.* The New International Commentary on the New Testament. Grand Rapids: Eerdmans, 1962.

Hunter, A. M. *The Gospel According to John.* Cambridge: Cambridge U., 1965.

Ironside, H. A. *Addresses on the Epistles of John.* New York: Loizeaux, n.d.

Jensen, Irving L. *Acts: An Independent Study.* Chicago: Moody, 1968.

————. *Enjoy Your Bible.* Chicago: Moody, 1969.

————. *Independent Bible Study.* Chicago: Moody, 1963.

————. *Jensen's Survey of the Old Testament.* Chicago: Moody, 1978.

————. *The Layman's Bible Study Notebook.* Irvine, Calif.: Harvest House, 1978.

————. *The Life of Christ.* Chicago: Moody, 1969.

————. *Revelation.* Chicago: Moody, 1971.

Jeremias, Joachim. *Jerusalem in the Time of Jesus.* Philadelphia: Fortress, 1969.

Join-Sambert, Michel. *Jerusalem.* New York: Putnam, 1958.

Kelso, James L. *An Archaeologist Follows the Apostle Paul.* Waco, Texas: Word, 1970.

Kent, Homer A., Jr. *Jerusalem to Rome: Studies in the Book of Acts.* Grand Rapids: Baker, 1974.

————. *The Pastoral Epistles.* Chicago: Moody, 1958.

Kenyon, Kathleen M. *Jerusalem.* New York: McGraw-Hill, 1967.

Kerr, J. H. *Introduction to the New Testament.* Westwood, N.J.: Revell, 1931.

Knowling, R. J. *The Epistle of St. James.* Westminster Commentaries. London: Methuen, 1904.

Kraeling, Emil G. *Bible Atlas.* New York: Rand-McNally, 1956.

Kubo, Sakae, and Specht, Walter. *So Many Versions?* Grand Rapids: Zondervan, 1975.

Lace, O. Jessie, ed. *Understanding the New Testament*. Cambridge: Cambridge U., 1965.

Ladd, George E. *Commentary on the Revelation of John*. Grand Rapids, Eerdmans, 1972.

Lammerts, Walter E., ed. *Scientific Studies in Special Creation*. Grand Rapids: Baker, 1971.

Lange, John Peter, ed. *Commentary on the Holy Scriptures*. Translated and edited by Philip Schaff. Grand Rapids: Zondervan, n.d.

————. *The Gospel According to Matthew*. 6th ed. New York: Scribner's, 1867.

LaSor, William Sanford. *Daily Life in Bible Times*. Cincinnati: Standard, 1966.

Latourette, Kenneth Scott. *A History of the Expansion of Christianity*. 7 vols. New York: Harper, 1937. Vol. 1, *The First Five Centuries*.

Leaney, A. R. C. *The Letters of Peter and Jude*. Cambridge: Cambridge U., 1967.

Lee, Robert. *The Outlined Bible*. New York: Revell, n.d.

Lenski, R. C. H. *The Interpretation of the Epistle to the Hebrews and of the Epistle of James*. Minneapolis: Augsburg, 1938.

————. *The Interpretation of Mark*. Columbus, Ohio: Wartburg, 1946.

————. *The Interpretation of St. Matthew's Gospel*. Columbus, Ohio: Wartburg, 1943.

————. *The Interpretation of St. Paul's First and Second Epistle to the Corinthians*. Columbus, Ohio: Wartburg, 1946.

Levine, Moshe. *The Tabernacle*. Jerusalem: Soncino, 1969.

Lewis, C. S. *Miracles*. New York: Macmillan, 1947.

Lightfoot, J. B. *The Epistle of Paul to the Galatians*. Grand Rapids: Zondervan, 1957.

Lindsell, Harold, ed. *Harper Study Bible*. New York: Harper & Row, 1964.

Longenecker, Richard. *The Ministry and Message of Paul*. Grand Rapids: Zondervan, 1971.

Lockyer, Herbert. *All the Doctrines of the Bible*. Grand Rapids: Zondervan, 1964.

————. *All the Parables of the Bible*. Grand Rapids: Zondervan, 1963.

Luck, G. Coleman. *James: Faith in Action*. Everyman's Bible Commentary. Chicago: Moody, 1969.

Luther, Martin. *A Commentary on St. Paul's Epistle to the Galatians*. Abridged translation by Theodore Graebner. Grand Rapids: Zondervan, n.d.

Maclaren, Alexander. *The Epistles of Paul to the Colossians and to Philemon*. The Expositor's Bible. New York: Armstrong, 1903.

Manley, G. T., ed. *The New Bible Handbook*. Chicago: InterVarsity, 1947.

Manley, G. T., and Oldham, H. W. *Search the Scriptures*. Chicago: InterVarsity, 1949.

Marsh, Frank Lewis. *Life, Man, and Time*. Escondido, Calif.: Outdoor Pictures, 1967.

————. *Studies in Creationism.* Washington, D. C.: Review & Herald, 1950.

Martin, Ralph P. *The Epistle of Paul to the Philippians.* The Tyndale New Testament Commentaries. Grand Rapids: Eerdmans, 1959.

Martin, W. S., and Marshall, A. *Tabernacle Types and Teachings.* London: Pickering & Inglis, n.d.

Mayor, Joseph B. *The Epistle of James.* Grand Rapids: Zondervan, 1954.

McClain, Alva J. *Daniel's Prophecy of the Seventy Weeks.* Grand Rapids: Zondervan, 1940.

————. *The Greatness of the Kingdom.* Chicago: Moody, 1959.

Mears, Henrietta. *What the Bible Is All About.* Glendale, Calif.: Gospel Light, 1953.

Metzger, Bruce M. *The New Testament: Its Background, Growth, and Content.* New York: Abingdon, 1965.

Miller, H. S. *The Book of Ephesians.* Houghton, N.Y.: Word-Bearer, 1931.

Miller, M. S., and Miller, J. L. *Encyclopedia of Bible Life.* New York: Harper & Row, 1944.

Moe, Olaf. *The Apostle Paul.* Reprint. Grand Rapids: Baker, 1968.

Moffat, James. *An Introduction to the Literature of the New Testament.* 3d rev. ed. Naperville, Ill.: Allenson, 1918.

Moldenke, Harold N., and Moldenke, Alma L. *Plants of the Bible.* New York: Ronald, 1952.

Morgan, G. Campbell. *The Acts of the Apostles.* New York: Revell, 1924.

————. *The Analyzed Bible.* Westwood, N.J.: Revell, 1944.

————. *The Corinthian Letters of Paul.* London: Oliphants, 1947.

————. *The Crises of the Christ.* Westwood, N.J.: Revell, 1936.

————. *The Gospel According to John.* Westwood, N.J.: Revell, n.d.

————. *The Gospel According to Mark.* Westwood, N.J.: Revell, 1927.

————. *The Gospel According to Matthew.* Westwood, N.J.: Revell, 1929.

————. *The Gospel According to St. Luke.* Westwood, N.J.: Revell, 1931.

————. *Living Messages of the Books of the Bible.* Westwood, N.J.: Revell, 1912.

————. *The Parables and Metaphors of Our Lord.* Westwood, N.J.: Revell, 1943.

Morris, Leon. *The Epistles of Paul to the Thessalonians.* The Tyndale New Testament Commentaries. Grand Rapids: Eerdmans, 1957.

————. *The First Epistle of Paul to the Corinthians.* The Tyndale New Testament Commentaries. Grand Rapids: Eerdmans, 1958.

————. *The Gospel According to John.* The New International Commentary on the New Testament. Grand Rapids: Eerdmans, 1971.

————. *The Gospel According to St. Luke.* The Tyndale New Testament Commentaries. Grand Rapids: Eerdmans, 1974.

Moule, H. C. G. *Ephesian Studies.* Westwood, N.J.: Revell, n.d.

————. *Philippian Studies.* London: Pickering & Inglis, n.d.

————. *The Second Epistle to Timothy.* London: Religious Tract Soc., n.d.

Murray, Andrew. *The Holiest of All.* Westwood, N.J.: Revell, n.d.

National Geographic Society. *Everyday Life in Bible Times*. Washington, D.C.: National Geographic Soc., 1951.

Neil, William. *The Letter of Paul to the Galatians*. New English Bible Commentaries, New Testament. Cambridge: Cambridge U., 1967.

Newell, William R. *The Book of Revelation*. Chicago: Moody, 1935.

————. *Hebrews Verse by Verse*. Chicago: Moody, 1947.

————. *Romans Verse by Verse*. Chicago: Moody, 1948.

Nicoll, W. Robertson. *The Expositor's Bible*. London: Hodder & Stoughton, 1887.

Orni, Efrain, and Efrat, Elisha. *Geography of Israel*. 3d rev. ed. Philadelphia: Jewish Pubn. Soc., 1973.

Orr, James, ed. *The International Standard Bible Encyclopedia*. 5 vols. Grand Rapids: Eerdmans, 1946.

Orr, James. *The Resurrection of Jesus*. Cincinnati: Jennings & Graham, 1909.

Pache, René. *The Inspiration and Authority of Scripture*. Chicago: Moody, 1969.

Payne, J. Barton. *Encyclopedia of Biblical Prophecy*. New York: Harper & Row, 1973.

————. *The Theology of the Older Testament*. Grand Rapids: Zondervan, 1962.

Pentecost, J. Dwight. *Israel in Prophecy*. Grand Rapids: Zondervan, 1962.

————. *Prophecy for Today*. Grand Rapids: Zondervan, 1961.

————. *Things to Come*. Grand Rapids: Dunham, 1964.

Pfeiffer, Charles F. *Baker's Bible Atlas*. Grand Rapids: Baker, 1961.

————. *Between the Testaments*. Grand Rapids: Baker, 1959.

Pfeiffer, Charles F., ed. *The Biblical World*. Grand Rapids: Baker, 1966.

Pfeiffer, Charles F., and Harrison, Everett F., eds. *The Wycliffe Bible Commentary*. Chicago: Moody, 1962.

Pfeiffer, Charles F.; Vos, Howard F.; and Rea, John, eds. *Wycliffe Bible Encyclopedia*. 2 vols. Chicago: Moody, 1975.

Pfeiffer, Charles F., and Vos, Howard F. *The Wycliffe Historical Geography of Bible Lands*. Chicago: Moody, 1967.

Pfeiffer, R. H. *History of New Testament Times*. New York: Harper & Row, 1964.

Phillips, John. *Exploring Romans*. Chicago: Moody, 1969.

————. *Exploring the Scriptures*. Chicago: Moody, 1965.

Pinnock, Clark H. *Biblical Revelation*. Chicago: Moody, 1971.

Plummer, A. *The Epistles of St. John*. Cambridge: Cambridge U., 1916.

Plummer, A., and Robertson, A. T. *First Epistle of St. Paul to the Corinthians*. Edinburgh: T. & T. Clark, 1911.

Plummer, Alfred. *Second Epistle of St. Paul to the Corinthians*. The International Critical Commentary. Edinburgh: T. & T. Clark, 1915.

Plumptre, E. H. *The General Epistle of St. James*. Cambridge Bible for Schools and Colleges. Reprint. Cambridge: Cambridge U., 1915.

Price, Walter K. *The Coming Antichrist.* Chicago: Moody, 1974.

Purves, George T. *The Apostolic Age.* New York: Scribner's, 1900.

Rackham, Richard B. *The Acts of the Apostles.* 13th ed. London: Methuen, 1947.

Ramm, Bernard. *Protestant Biblical Interpretation.* Boston: Wilde, 1956.

Ramsey, William. *The Bearing of Recent Discoveries on the Trustworthiness of the New Testament.* 4th ed. London: Hodder & Stoughton, 1920.

————. *The Cities of St. Paul.* Grand Rapids: Baker, 1949.

————. *St. Paul the Traveler.* Grand Rapids: Baker, 1951.

Rees, Paul S. *Triumphant in Trouble. Studies in I Peter.* Westwood, N.J.: Revell, 1962.

Robertson, A. T. *Commentary on the Gospel According to Matthew.* New York: Macmillan, 1911.

————. *Epochs in The Life of Jesus.* New York: Scribner's, 1907.

————. *Epochs in the Life of Paul.* New York: Scribner's, 1909.

————. *A Harmony of the Gospels for Students of the Life of Christ.* Nashville: Broadman, 1922.

————. *Luke the Historian in the Light of Research.* New York: Scribner's, 1923.

————. *Making Good in the Ministry.* Westwood, N.J.: Revell, n.d.

————. *Paul and the Intellectuals.* N.Y.: Doubleday, Doran, 1928.

————. *Paul's Joy in Christ.* Westwood, N.J.: Revell, 1917.

————. *Studies in the Epistle of James.* Rev. ed. Nashville: Broadman, 1959.

————. *Word Pictures in the New Testament.* 4 vols. New York: Harper, 1930.

Russell, D. S. *Between the Testaments.* London: S. C. M., 1960.

Ryrie, Charles C. *First and Second Thessalonians.* Chicago: Moody, 1959.

————. *Revelation.* Everyman's Bible Commentary. Chicago: Moody, 1968.

The Sacred Land. Atlas of Bible Geography. Philadelphia: Holman, n.d.

Salmon, Edward T. *A History of the Roman World from 30 B.C. to A.D. 138.* New York: Macmillan, 1944.

Sauer, Erich. *The Dawn of World Redemption.* Grand Rapids: Eerdmans, 1953.

————. *From Eternity to Eternity.* Grand Rapids: Eerdmans, 1954.

Schaff, Philip. *Apostolic Christianity.* History of the Christian Church. Vol. 1. Grand Rapids: Eerdmans, 1955.

Scroggie, W. Graham. *The Acts of the Apostles.* New York: Harper, n.d.

————. *A Guide to the Gospels.* London: Pickering & Inglis, 1948.

————. *Know Your Bible.* Vol. 2. Westwood, N.J.: Revell, 1965.

————. *St. John: Introduction and Notes.* New York: Harper, 1931. (Contains excellent outlines.)

Smith, Arthur E. *The Temple and Its Teaching.* Chicago: Moody, 1956.

Smith, George Adam. *The Historical Geography of the Holy Land.* London: Hodder & Stoughton, 1931.

Smith, Wilbur M. *The Biblical Doctrine of Heaven.* Chicago: Moody, 1968.

————. *The Incomparable Book.* Minneapolis: Beacon, 1961.

————. *A Treasury of Books for Bible Study.* Natick, Mass.: Wilde, 1960.

Snaith, Norman H. *The Jews from Cyrus to Herod.* New York and Nashville: Abingdon, n.d.

Soltau, Henry W. *The Tabernacle.* Reprint. Fincastle, Va.: Scripture Truth, n.d.

Souter, Alexander. *The Text and Canon of the New Testament.* New York: Scribner's, 1923.

Spink, James F. *Types and Shadows of Christ in the Tabernacle.* New York: Loizeaux, 1946.

Stalker, James. *The Life of Jesus Christ.* Rev. ed. Westwood, N.J.: Revell, 1891.

———. *The Life of St. Paul.* Rev. ed. Westwood, N.J.: Revell, 1912.

Stanton, V. H. "New Testament Canon." In *A Dictionary of the Bible,* edited by James Hastings. Vol. 3. New York: Scribner's, 1902.

Stibbs, A. M. *The First Epistle General of Peter.* The Tyndale New Testament Commentaries. Grand Rapids: Eerdmans, 1959.

Stonehouse, N. B., and Woolley, Paul, eds. *The Infallible Word.* Grand Rapids: Eerdmans, 1953.

Strong, James, ed. *The Exhaustive Concordance of the Bible.* New York: Abingdon, 1890.

Strong, James. *The Tabernacle of Israel.* Reprint. Grand Rapids: Baker, 1952.

Tan, Paul Lee. *The Interpretation of Prophecy.* Winona Lake, Ind.: Brethren Missionary Herald, 1974.

Tasker, R. V. G. *The Gospel According to St. John.* The Tyndale New Testament Commentaries. Grand Rapids: Eerdmans, 1960.

———. *The Gospel According to St. Matthew.* The Tyndale New Testament Commentaries. Grand Rapids: Eerdmans, 1962.

———. *The Second Epistle of Paul to the Corinthians.* The Tyndale New Testament Commentaries. Grand Rapids: Eerdmans, 1958.

Tenney, Merrill C. *Galatians: The Charter of Christian Liberty.* Grand Rapids: Eerdmans, 1950.

———. *Interpreting Revelation.* Grand Rapids: Eerdmans, 1957.

———. *John: The Gospel of Belief.* Grand Rapids: Eerdmans, 1948.

———. *New Testament Survey.* Grand Rapids: Eerdmans, 1953.

———. *New Testament Times.* Grand Rapids: Eerdmans, 1965.

———. *Philippians: The Gospel at Work.* Grand Rapids: Eerdmans, 1956.

Tenney, Merrill C., ed. *The Zondervan Pictorial Bible Dictionary.* Grand Rapids: Zondervan, 1963.

Thiessen, Henry C., *Introduction to the New Testament.* Grand Rapids: Eerdmans, 1952.

———. *Introductory Lectures in Systematic Theology.* Grand Rapids: Eerdmans, 1956.

Thomas, Robert L., ed. *New American Standard Exhaustive Concordance of the Bible.* Nashville: Holman, 1981.

Thomas, Robert L., and Gundry, Stanley N. *A Harmony of the Gospels.* Chicago: Moody, 1978.

Thomas, W. H. Griffith. *The Apostle Peter.* Grand Rapids: Eerdmans, 1946.

———. *Life and Writings of the Apostle John.* Grand Rapids: Eerdmans, 1946.

530   Jensen's Survey of the New Testament

Thompson, J. A. *The Bible and Archaeology.* Grand Rapids: Eerdmans, 1954.

Unger, Merrill F. *Unger's Bible Dictionary.* Chicago: Moody, 1957.

———. *Unger's Bible Handbook.* Chicago: Moody, 1966.

Vincent, Marvin R. *Word Studies in the New Testament.* 4 Vols. Grand Rapids: Eerdmans, 1946.

Vine, W. E. *An Expository Dictionary of New Testament Words.* Westwood, N.J.: Revell, 1961.

Vos, Howard F., ed. *Can I Trust My Bible?* Chicago: Moody, 1963.

Vos, Howard F. *The Life of Our Lord.* Chicago: Moody, 1958.

Walton, Robert C., ed. *A Source Book of the Bible for Teachers.* Camden, N.J.: Nelson, 1970.

Walvoord, John F. *The Blessed Hope and the Tribulation.* Grand Rapids: Zondervan, 1976.

———. *Daniel: Key to Prophetic Revelation.* Chicago: Moody, 1971.

———. *The Holy Spirit.* Wheaton, Ill.: Van Kampen, 1954.

———. *Israel in Prophecy.* Grand Rapids: Zondervan, 1962.

———. *Jesus Christ Our Lord.* Chicago: Moody, 1969.

———. *Matthew.* Chicago: Moody, 1974.

———. *The Millennial Kingdom.* Grand Rapids: Dunham, 1959.

———. *The Nations in Prophecy.* Grand Rapids: Zondervan, 1967.

———. *The Rapture Question.* Grand Rapids: Zondervan, 1970.

———. *The Revelation of Jesus Christ.* Chicago: Moody, 1966.

Walvoord, John F., ed. *Inspiration and Interpretation.* Grand Rapids: Eerdmans, 1957.

Warfield, B. B. *The Inspiration and Authority of the Bible.* Philadelphia: Presbyterian & Reformed, 1948.

Westcott, B. F. *Commentary on John.* Grand Rapids: Eerdmans, 1951.

———. *The Epistle to the Hebrews.* 2d ed. Grand Rapids: Eerdmans, 1950.

———. *Saint Paul's Epistle to the Ephesians.* Grand Rapids: Eerdmans, 1950.

The Westminster Study Edition of the Holy Bible. Philadelphia: Westminster, 1948.

Wight, Fred H. *Manners and Customs of Bible Lands.* Chicago: Moody, 1953.

Wilson, Clifford A. *Exploring Bible Backgrounds.* Melbourne, Australia: Word of Truth, 1966.

Wilson, Walter Lewis. *Wilson's Dictionary of Bible Types.* Grand Rapids: Eerdmans, 1957.

Wuest, Kenneth S. *In These Last Days.* Grand Rapids: Eerdmans, 1954.

———. *Romans in the Greek New Testament.* Grand Rapids: Eerdmans, 1955.

Young, Edward J. *An Introduction to the Old Testament.* Grand Rapids: Eerdmans, 1949.

Young, Robert, ed. *Analytical Concordance to the Bible.* Grand Rapids: Eerdmans, n.d.

Zwemer, Samuel M. *Into All the World.* Grand Rapids: Zondervan, 1943.

CHARTS

Boyer, James L. *New Testament Chronological Chart*. Rev. ed. Chicago: Moody, 1968.

Jensen, Irving L. *Jensen's Bible Study Charts*. Rev. ed. Chicago: Moody, 1981.

New Testament Time Line, Charts 1-3. Copyright 1975, Bill Hovey. (These charts, distributed by Moody Press, Chicago, are now out of print but are available in many schools and libraries.)

General Index

Boldface entries (and italicized page numbers) are subjects also contained in the Further Study sections.